SIGNATURE SERIES

Advanced

MICROSOFT® WORD

2013

Desktop Publishing

B I U ▾ abc X X | A ▾ ab ▾ A ▾

FILE   INSERT   DESIGN   PAGE LAYOUT   RE

Joanne Arford
College of DuPage, Glen Ellyn, Illinois

Audrey Roggenkamp
Pierce College at Puyallup, Puyallup, Washington

Ian Rutkosky
Pierce College at Puyallup, Puyallup, Washington

PARADIGM
EDUCATION SOLUTIONS

St. Paul

Director of Editorial: Christine Hurney
Director of Production: Timothy W. Larson
Developmental Editor: Sarah Kearin
Production Editor: Carla Valadez
Cover Designer: Jaana Bykonich
Text Designer: Valerie King

Senior Design and Production Specialist: Jack Ross
Production Specialists: Sara Schmidt Boldon, Valerie King, and Tammy Norstrem
Copy Editor: Crystal Bullen, DPS Associates, Inc.
Proofreader: Kristin Melendez
Indexer: Ina Gravitz

Care has been taken to verify the accuracy of information presented in this book. However, the authors, editors, and publisher cannot accept responsibility for Web, email, newsgroup, or chat room subject matter or content, or for consequences from the application of the information in this book, and make no warranty, expressed or implied, with respect to its content.

Trademarks: Access, Excel, Internet Explorer, Microsoft, PowerPoint, and Windows are trademarks or registered trademarks of Microsoft Corporation in the United States and/or other countries. Some of the product names and company names included in this book have been used for identification purposes only and may be trademarks or registered trade names of their respective manufacturers and sellers. The authors, editors, and publisher disclaim any affiliation, association, or connection with, or sponsorship or endorsement by, such owners.

Photo Credits: page 4, ©Hector Sanchez/Shutterstock.com, ©Fer Gregory/Shutterstock.com, ©Yulia Nikulyasha Nikitina/Shutterstock.com

Permissions: The following individuals and organizations have generously given permission for use of their materials: Edward Cardiovascular Institute, Naperville, Illinois; Floyd Rogers, Butterfield Gardens, Glen Ellyn, Illinois; Naperville Chamber of Commerce, Naperville, Illinois; Dr. Bradley Kampschroeder and Dr. Michael Halkias, Naper Grove Vision Care, Naperville, Illinois; Barbara Blankenship, Michael Kott, and Terri McCormick, desktop publishing students at the College of DuPage, Glen Ellyn, Illinois; and Jody Bender and Charles McLimans at Loaves & Fishes Community Pantry, Naperville, Illinois.

We have made every effort to trace the ownership of all copyrighted material and to secure permission from copyright holders. In the event of any question arising as to the use of any material, we will be pleased to make the necessary corrections in future printings. Thanks are due to the aforementioned authors, publishers, and agents for permission to use the materials indicated. Paradigm Publishing is independent from Microsoft Corporation, and not affiliated with Microsoft in any manner. While this publication may be used in assisting individuals to prepare for a Microsoft Business Certification exam, Microsoft, its designated program administrator, and Paradigm Publishing do not warrant that use of this publication will ensure passing a Microsoft Business Certification exam.

ISBN 978-0-76385-207-8 (text)
ISBN 978-0-76385-211-5 (text and CD)

Internet Resource Center: www.ParadigmCollege.net/AdvancedWord2013

© 2014 by Paradigm Publishing, Inc.
875 Montreal Way
St. Paul, MN 55102
Email: educate@emcp.com
Website: www.ParadigmCollege.com

Printed in the United States of America

22 21 20 19 18 17 16 15 14 13   1 2 3 4 5 6 7 8 9 10

Brief Contents

Contents

Preface

Signature Series: Advanced Microsoft® Word 2013: Desktop Publishing by Joanne Arford, Audrey Roggenkamp, and Ian Rutkosky focuses on advanced Word 2013 features with an emphasis on desktop publishing concepts and terminology. It also introduces the desktop publishing learner to PowerPoint 2013 and Publisher 2013. These applications allow users to create professional-looking documents with attractive graphics, text effects, and eye-catching design elements. Publishing from the desktop computer greatly reduces production costs, combines the tasks of page design and layout, offers immediate results, and allows control of production from start to finish.

Textbook and Chapter Features

Advanced Microsoft® Word 2013: Desktop Publishing is designed for students who are proficient in word processing. This textbook assumes that students are using Microsoft Word 2013 in a computer lab or home-study setting.

Course Outcomes

Students who successfully complete a course based on this textbook will have mastered the following competencies:

- Using and applying the design concepts of focus, balance, proportion, contrast, directional flow, consistency, and color
- Evaluating documents for the use of basic design concepts
- Using desktop publishing features of Microsoft Word 2013 to integrate basic layout and design concepts in order to enhance the readability of multiple-page, portrait, or landscape documents such as letterheads, postcards, business cards, certificates, flyers, brochures, online forms, and newsletters
- Producing and enhancing business and personal documents with variable page layouts using standardized type and graphic design techniques while incorporating updated Word 2013 features such as watermarks, cover pages, page borders, themes, style sets, shapes, WordArt, SmartArt, quick parts, picture tools, table tools, Microsoft Office templates, and clip art on Office.com
- Managing Word 2013 document files and folders using a Windows 8 operating system
- Publishing Word documents in a variety of formats, including PowerPoint presentations and web pages
- Becoming familiar with the basic features and capabilities of Microsoft Publisher 2013 to produce professional-looking flyers, brochures, and newsletters

What's New in *Advanced Microsoft® Word 2013: Desktop Publishing*

Users familiar with the Advanced Word 2010 book and previous editions will notice the following enhancements to the textbook and software:

- All Word skills have been updated to correspond with Word 2013, including all features, steps, and screen captures.
- All documents have been updated and refreshed.
- Chapter exercises with multiple parts are now clearly labeled with letters and Part *X* of *Y* designations.
- The book now contains 13 chapters broken out into four units, with an additional section of unit performance assessments.
- Unit 1 now focuses on desktop publishing concepts and the basic Word features used to carry out the desktop publishing process.
- Unit 2 eases students into creating personal and business documents, starting with simple projects such as calendars and letterheads, and moving on to more complex documents such as newsletters.
- Unit 3 expands on students' knowledge of creating business documents by having them create promotional documents such as flyers and announcements.
- Unit 4 covers creating web pages and forms in Word and introduces students to Publisher and PowerPoint.

Instructional Design

Most of the key desktop publishing concepts addressed in this textbook are presented in Chapter 1. Subsequent chapters reinforce the concepts through instruction and exercises in which students create commercial-quality documents. Exercises are designed not only to help students build proficiency in the desktop publishing features of Word 2013 but also to develop critical thinking, decision making, and creativity. Many activities reinforce collaborative learning as students work in teams to plan, design, and evaluate business and personal documents for publication. Several exercises incorporate a scenario framework in which basic information for a task is supplied as it might be presented in real-life situations.

Students who wish to build a portfolio of documents for course requirements or job applications should take special note of the exercises identified with a portfolio icon. The final portfolio can be printed and bound in hard copy format, or the documents can be saved in PDF format, organized as a portfolio, and then viewed electronically. Note that, for portfolio exercises with two or more parts, the Portfolio icon only appears with the last part of the exercise.

Emphasis on Visual Learning

Numerous images combined with clearly written instruction offer a highly effective visual learning experience. Screen captures of the entire Word screen highlight ribbon elements and other tools and help students connect concepts with clicks. As students follow the step-by-step practice exercises, they can confirm they are performing the correct actions by comparing their screens with the screen captures displayed. Key steps are labeled on the screen captures to make following the exercise directions as easy as possible. In addition, images of the completed documents are displayed so students can check their work. Sample model answers also are provided for end-of-chapter and end-of-unit assessments.

Chapter Structure

The textbook contains four units with a total of thirteen chapters. Each chapter contains the following elements:

Chapter 3

Inserting and Modifying Page Elements

Performance Objectives

Upon successful completion of Chapter 3, you will be able to:

- Use building blocks
- Insert predesigned cover pages
- Insert headers and footers
- Insert page numbers
- Insert page breaks
- Create watermarks
- Insert and customize images
- Create and insert bullets
- Insert text boxes and shapes
- Insert tables
- Use and customize templates

Desktop Publishing Terms

cell	header	template
footer	placeholder	watermark
hard page break	soft page break	

Word Features Used

breaks	cover page	page numbers	tables
Bring Forward	headers and footers	pictures	templates
building blocks	layout	quick parts	text boxes
bullets	Normal.dotm	Send Backward	watermark
clip art	page breaks	shapes	

Note: Before beginning computer exercises for this chapter, copy to your storage medium the Chapter03 folder from the CD that accompanies this textbook and then make Chapter03 the active folder. Remember to substitute for graphics that may no longer be available.

85

Performance objectives outline learning goals for the chapter.

Lists of **desktop publishing terms** and **Word features** prepare students for the chapter work.

Key terms and definitions in the margins provide quick reference for chapter vocabulary.

Desktop publishing (DTP) pointers reinforce key ideas.

Images of important **Word 2013 buttons** help students navigate the application's interface.

Hands-on exercises with screen captures allow students to practice what they have just learned.

Creating Em and En Dashes

em dash
A dash that indicates a pause in speech; as wide as the typeface's uppercase *M*

en dash
A dash that indicates a continuation; as wide as the typeface's lowercase *n*

An *em dash* (—) is used to indicate a pause in speech and an *en dash* indicates a continuation, such as in the ranges 116–133 and January–March. An em dash is generally the width of a typeface's uppercase *M* and an en dash is the width of a lowercase *n*. Besides inserting em and en dashes using the Special Characters tab of the Symbol dialog box, you may insert an em dash from the keyboard by pressing Alt + Ctrl + Num - (minus key on the numbers pad) or an en dash by pressing Ctrl + Num - . Do not include spaces before or after en dashes and em dashes. Additionally, the AutoCorrect feature includes an option that will automatically create em dashes. To create an em dash, type the word, type two hyphens, type the next word, and then press the spacebar. When you press the spacebar, AutoCorrect automatically converts the two hyphens to an em dash.

Using Smart Quotes

DTP POINTER ▶
Use straight quotation marks to indicate inches or feet.

In typesetting, the *tail* of the punctuation mark extends upward for the open quotation mark (") and downward for the close quotation mark ("). Straight quotes should be used only to indicate inches (") or feet ('). Word's Smart Quotes feature, which is active by default, will automatically choose the quote style that is appropriate.

To turn the Smart Quotes feature on or off, click the FILE tab, click *Options*, click *Proofing* in the left panel, click the AutoCorrect Options button, click the AutoFormat As You Type tab, and then click the "*Straight quotes" with "smart quotes"* check box to insert or remove the check mark. In addition, symbols and special characters may be added to the AutoCorrect feature, which will automatically insert the desired symbol when using a specific keyboard command. For example, if you type (c), AutoCorrect will automatically change the three characters to the © special character. Symbols may also be copied to the Clipboard and pasted when needed.

In Exercise 2.3, you will practice adding special characters to a sales flyer.

Ω Symbol

Exercise 2.3 Formatting a Sales Flyer with Special Characters

1. Open **CCarpet.docx** from your Chapter02 folder and then save the document with the name **C02-E03-CCarpet**.
2. Click in the text box in the upper left corner of the document and then type **Create a comfortable, warm, and inviting home with an Adana area rug.**
3. Insert a registered trademark symbol after *Adana* by completing the following steps:
   a. Position the insertion point after the word *Adana*.
   b. Click the INSERT tab.
   c. Click the Symbol button in the Symbols group and then click *More Symbols* at the drop-down list.
   d. At the Symbol dialog box, click the Special Characters tab.
   e. Double-click the *Registered* option in the *Character* list box.
   f. Click the Close button to close the dialog box.

Chapter Summary reviews important concepts and features.

Commands Review summarizes the main Word features learned in the chapter.

Chapter Assessments give students the opportunity to practice what they have learned in the chapter without screen captures or step-by-step instructions.

Key Points Review questions allow students to assess what they have learned in the chapter.

Model answers and sample solutions for the chapter assessments are provided as necessary.

Chapter Summary

- A letterhead contains a design and layout that conveys specific information, establishes an identity, and projects an image for a business. Designing and producing your own letterhead can be a less costly alternative to having it designed and produced through a professional designer and printer.
- A number of letterhead templates are available for download at Office.com or a template partner.
- Objects can be grouped, ungrouped, and regro... clicking the Group button in the Arrange gro...
- The Selection pane lists each item in a docume... button in the Editing group on the HOME ta...
- Use the Click and Type feature to insert text, gr... document.
- To view the vertical location of your insertion p... right click, and then click the *Vertical Page Posi...*
- A text box is used as a container for text and gr... publishing because text and graphics can be pla... page. They can also serve as placeholders for ite...
- Adjust text box margins with options at the For... icon selected and the TEXT BOX options expa...
- Position a text box precisely on a page using optio...
- A pixel is a single unit of measurement that yo...
- All objects, including text boxes, are automatically...
- Format a text box with buttons and options on...
- Specify how you want text to wrap around, beh... Text button drop-down gallery.
- Word includes predesigned text boxes you can... the Text group on the INSERT tab and then cl...
- Ruled lines act as boundaries to the surrounding... focal point, draw the eye across or down the pa...
- Lines can be created using the Line button in t... straight line, hold down the Shift key as you dr... with buttons and options on the DRAWING T...
- To create lines around a paragraph, click the do... the Paragraph group on the HOME tab and th...
- When creating a design for an envelope, select... link is established in the viewer's mind betwee...
- Create an envelope by clicking the MAILINGS... group, and then clicking the Add to Documen... Envelope Options dialog box. Display this dial... and Labels dialog box with the Envelopes tab s...
- Business cards are another way to establish ide... connection between a business card and a letter... the letterhead.
- Save frequently used text and graphics, such as... Quick Part gallery.

Commands Review

FEATURE	RIBBON TAB, GROUP/OPTION	BUTTON
envelopes	MAILINGS, Create	
group	PAGE LAYOUT, Arrange	
kerning	HOME, Font	
labels	MAILINGS, Create	
Layout dialog box	DRAWING TOOLS FORMAT, Size	
line spacing	HOME, Paragraph	
position	DRAWING TOOLS FORMAT, Arrange	
quick parts	INSERT, Text	
select	HOME, Editing	

Key Points Review

Multiple Choice: Fill in the blanks with the correct term from the choices listed be...

1. By default, a text box has left and right internal margins of ____
   a. 0.05   b. 0.1
   c. 0.5   d. 1.0

2. In typesetting, the thickness of a line is called its weight and is me...
   a. points   b. pixels
   c. inches   d. dots per inch

3. Press the _____ key while drawing a line with the Line Shape to...
   a. Ctrl   b. Shift
   c. spacebar   d. Alt

4. To transform the shape of WordArt text, click this button on the D... FORMAT tab.
   a. Text Outline   b. Text Effects
   c. Text Fill   d. Transform

5. Save frequently used text or graphics as a building block in this gall...
   a. Document Formatting   b. Text
   c. Styles   d. Quick Part

6. Use this feature to distort or modify text to create a variety of shape...
   a. Clip Art   b. Shapes

Creating Letterheads, Envelopes, Business...

Assessment 5.2   Create a Hotel Envelope

Use some of the letterhead elements you created in Assessment 1 to create an envelope for the hotel (as shown in Figure 5.38) with the following specifications:

1. Insert an envelope in a new, blank document.
2. Insert in the envelope **IsarHotel.png** from your Chapter05 folder.
3. Change the height of the image to 0.9 inch.
4. Change the text wrapping to *Tight*.
5. Insert a text box with no fill and no outline. Type the hotel address in the text box, select the text you just typed, and then change the font to 9-point Microsoft JhengHei and apply the Dark Blue font color. Apply bold formatting and change the paragraph alignment of the text to right.
6. Insert a text box with no fill and no outline and then type **ISAR HOTEL MÜNICH.**
7. Select the text you just typed and then apply the Gradient Fill - Blue, Accent 1, Reflection text effect (use the Text Effects and Typography button in the Font group on the HOME tab).
8. With the text still selected, change the font to 11-point Segoe UI Semibold; the font color to Orange, Accent 2, Darker 50%; and expand the spacing of the text by 6 points.
9. Size and position the elements so your envelope is similar to the envelope in Figure 5.38.
10. Save the envelope document with the name **C05-A02-HotelEnvelope.**
11. Print and then close **C05-A02-HotelEnvelope.docx.** (Manual feed of the envelope may be necessary.)

Figure 5.38   Envelope Created in Assessment 5.2

INTEGRATED

GROUP PROJECT

In most chapters, the Chapter Assessments include Integrated assessments and Group Project assessments, which are identified with the icons shown at the left. For Integrated assessments, students incorporate skills learned in the current chapter with techniques and features of other Office programs. The Group Project assessments promote collaborative learning, team building and organization, critical thinking, and individual and group creativity.

At the end of each unit is a Performance Assessments section with problems that evaluate student mastery of both desktop publishing concepts and software skills presented in the unit.

Guidelines for Students on Completing Computer Exercises

Some of the computer exercises in this textbook require students to access and use an existing file (Student Data file). These files are available on the Student Resources CD that accompanies this textbook, as well as on the Internet Resource Center for the book at www.ParadigmCollege.net/AdvancedWord2013. The files are contained in individual folders for each chapter. A CD icon and folder name is displayed on the opening page of each chapter and each set of unit assessments. Students need to copy the chapter folder from the CD before beginning the chapter activities. Instructions on how to copy and delete folders are provided on the inside back cover of the book.

As you work through the desktop publishing information and exercises, keep the following points in mind:

- All default formatting settings (such as fonts, margin settings, line spacing, and justification), templates, and folders used in this textbook are based on the assumption that none of the original program defaults have been customized after installation.

- Instructions for all features and exercises emphasize using the mouse. Where appropriate, keyboard shortcuts are provided as an alternative.

- As you complete the exercises, view the completed figure that follows many of the exercises to see what the document should look like. However, be aware that the final appearance of your printed documents depends on the printer you use to complete the exercises. Your printer driver may be different from the printer driver used for the exercises in this textbook. Consequently, you may have to make some minor adjustments when completing the exercises in this book. For example, if you have to select a font different from the one called for in the instructions, you may need to change the type size to fit the text in the space allotted. You may also need to adjust the spacing between paragraphs or specific blocks of text. If a clip art image or photograph is not available, select a similar image. As a result, your documents may look slightly different from the examples you see in this text. As you will discover in the chapters that follow, creating desktop published documents is a constant process of making small adjustments to fine-tune the layout and design.

Student and Instructor Ancillaries

The following resources are available for students and instructors:

Student Resources CD

Packaged with the textbook is a Student Resources CD that contains files required for completing the exercises in the book. See the inside back cover for instructions on copying the chapter folders to your storage medium.

Internet Resource Center: Student and Instructor Views

The website for *Advanced Microsoft® Word 2013: Desktop Publishing* is located at www.ParadigmCollege.net/AdvancedWord2013. For students, the website contains student files, online quizzes, PowerPoint slides with audio support, and a variety of tips and links. The password-protected instructor resources include course planning materials, teaching tips and exercise hints, PowerPoint presentations with lecture notes, model answers, rubrics, supplemental assessments, and additional tests and quizzes.

eBook

For students who prefer studying with an eBook, *Advanced Microsoft® Word 2013: Desktop Publishing* is available in an electronic form. The web-based, password-protected eBook features dynamic navigation tools, including bookmarking, searching, a linked table of contents, and the ability to jump to a specific page. The eBook format also supports helpful study tools such as highlighting and note taking.

Printed Instructor's Guide and Instructor's CD

The Instructor's Guide includes course planning resources, such as teaching hints and a sample course syllabus; PowerPoint presentations for each chapter with lecture notes (on the Instructor Resources CD); and assessment resources, including model answers and grading rubrics for end-of-chapter and end-of-unit assessments, a grading sheet, and supplemental assessments.

Computerized Test Generator

Instructors can use the ExamView® Assessment Suite and test banks of multiple-choice items to create customized web-based or print tests. The ExamView® Assessment Suite and test banks are provided on the Instructor Resources CD.

Blackboard Cartridge

This set of files allows instructors to create a personalized Blackboard website for their course and provides supplementary content, communication via e-discussions and online group conferences, and testing resources. Content items include a syllabus, assignments, quizzes, exams, and additional course links and study aids.

System Requirements

This interactive text is designed for the student to complete chapter and unit work on a computer running a standard installation of Microsoft Office 2013, Standard or Professional, and the Microsoft Windows 8 operating system. To effectively run this suite and operating system, your computer should be outfitted with the following:

- 1 gigahertz (GHz) processor or higher; 1 gigabyte (GB) of RAM (32 bit) or 2 GB of RAM (64 bit)
- DVD drive
- 3 GB of available hard-disk space
- .NET version 3.5, 4.0, or 4.5
- DirectX 10 graphics card
- Minimum 1024 x 576 screen resolution monitor
- Computer mouse, multi-touch device, or other compatible pointing device

Microsoft Office 2013 will also operate on computers running Windows 7, the Windows XP Service Pack 3, or the Windows Vista operating system.

Screen captures in this book were created using a screen resolution display setting of 1600 × 900. Choose the resolution that best matches your computer; however, be aware that using a resolution other than 1600 × 900 means that your screens may not exactly match the illustrations in this book.

About the Authors

Joanne (Marschke) Arford is originally from Berrien Springs, Michigan, lived in South Bend, Indiana, for several years, and has been residing in Naperville, Illinois, for the past 20 years. She and her husband, Frank, are the parents of three grown daughters, Rachel, Lisa, and Kaitlin. Joanne graduated from Western Michigan University in Kalamazoo, where she received her Bachelor's and Master's degrees in Business Education. Joanne is currently an adjunct faculty member at the College of DuPage in Glen Ellyn, Illinois. Her first desktop publishing textbook was co-authored with Nita Rutkosky and Judy Burnside. Since then she has written several editions of the Advanced Word Desktop Publishing textbook. Joanne is a member of the College of DuPage Adjuncts Association (CODAA) and has received the Illinois Business Education Association Writer's Hall of Fame awards for all of her textbooks.

Joanne enjoys reading, walking, and traveling. She has visited China, South Africa, Europe, and other destinations with her husband. Joanne also enjoys volunteering at the Loaves and Fishes Community Pantry in Naperville.

Audrey Roggenkamp has been teaching courses in the Business Information Technology department at Pierce College in Puyallup since 2005. Her courses have included keyboarding, skill building, and Microsoft Office program training. In addition to this title, she has coauthored *Benchmark Series: Microsoft® Office 2013, 2010, and 2007*; *Marquee Series: Microsoft® Office 2013, 2010, and 2007*; *Using Computers in the Medical Office: Microsoft® Word, Excel, and PowerPoint 2013, 2010, 2007, and 2003*; *Signature Series: Microsoft Word 2013, 2010, and 2007*; *Paradigm Keyboarding and Applications I: Using Microsoft® Word 2013, Sixth Edition, Sessions 1–60* and *Sessions 61–120*; and *Computer and Internet Essentials: Preparing for IC³*, all for Paradigm Education Solutions.

Ian Rutkosky teaches business technology courses at Pierce College in Puyallup, Washington. In addition to this title, he has coauthored *Computer and Internet Essentials: Preparing for IC³*; *Benchmark Series: Microsoft® Office 2013*; *Marquee Series: Microsoft® Office 2013*; and *Using Computers in the Medical Office: Microsoft® Word, Excel, and PowerPoint 2010*. He is also a coauthor and consultant for Paradigm's SNAP training and assessment software.

Acknowledgments

The authors and editors would like to extend a tremendous thank you to Nita Rutkosky for all of her hard work, dedication, commitment, and valuable feedback on this revision. Words cannot express our gratitude to Nita for her professional expertise and assistance in enhancing this textbook.

We would also like to thank Brienna McWade for her thorough and valuable contributions to the testing of exercises and assessments and her assistance in preparing images, publications, and supplemental materials; Cheryl Drivdahl and Traci Post for their important input as testers of exercises and assessments; and Ann Mills of Ivy Tech Community College in Evansville, Indiana, Traci Post, and Janet Blum of Fanshawe College in London, Ontario, for their work in helping to prepare supplemental materials.

UNIT 1

Understanding and Applying Desktop Publishing Concepts

Chapter 1

Understanding the Desktop Publishing Process

Performance Objectives

Upon successful completion of Chapter 1, you will be able to:

- Define desktop publishing
- Plan, design, and evaluate documents
- Create focus, balance, and proportion in documents
- Achieve contrast, consistency, and directional flow in documents
- Apply guidelines for color
- Identify Word 2013 features that can be used to enhance the desktop publishing process
- Create documents with templates from Office.com
- Use the Microsoft Snipping Tool application

Desktop Publishing Terms

⅓–⅔ rule	desktop publishing	readability	thumbnail sketch
alignment	directional flow	resolution	white space
asymmetrical design	focus	reversed text	Z pattern
balance	harmony	rule of thirds	
consistency	legibility	spread	
contrast	proportion	symmetrical design	

Word Features Used

clip art	themes	SmartArt	templates
cover page	pictures	styles	WordArt
crop	shapes	style sets	

Note: Before beginning computer exercises for this chapter, copy to your storage medium the Chapter01 folder from the CD that accompanies this textbook and then make Chapter01 the active folder. Substitute similar graphics for any graphics that may no longer be available.

Defining Desktop Publishing

Since the 1970s, computers have been an integral part of the business environment. For many years, the three most popular types of software purchased for computers were word processing, spreadsheet, and database programs. The introduction of laser and inkjet printers, with their ability to produce high-quality documents in black and white as well as in color, led to the growing popularity of another category of programs called desktop publishing software.

Desktop publishing software allows the user to produce professional-looking documents for both office and home use. The phrase ***desktop publishing***, coined by Aldus Corporation president Paul Brainard in 1984, means that publishing can literally take place at your desk.

Desktop publishing may involve using dedicated software, such as Adobe InDesign, or an advanced word processing program with desktop publishing capabilities, such as Microsoft Word. For simpler desktop publishing projects, Word is a good choice; for more complex documents, high-end desktop publishing software may be more appropriate. Microsoft Publisher is a mid-range desktop publishing program that comes with many professional-looking document templates. Adobe Illustrator and PhotoShop are programs that may be used to supplement the desktop publishing process.

Until the mid-1980s, graphic design depended almost exclusively on design professionals. However, desktop publishing software changed that. Faster micro-processors; larger storage capacity; improved printer capabilities; an increased supply of clip art images and photos; and the advent of CDs and DVDs, flash drives, and memory card readers; along with access to the Internet, have further expanded the role of desktop publishing. As illustrated in Figure 1.1, the past 50 years have seen an evolution from electric typewriters to personal computers to laptop computers as the most common desktop publishing tool. What will be next?

In traditional publishing, several people may have been involved in completing a publication project, which naturally involved greater costs and time compared with today's desktop publishing. Using desktop publishing software, one person may be able to perform all of the tasks necessary to complete a project, which greatly reduces the costs of publishing documents. The two approaches, however, do have a great deal in common. Both processes involve planning the project, organizing content, analyzing the layout and design, arranging design elements, typesetting, printing, and distributing the project.

Desktop publishing can be used as the sole method for creating a publication, or it can be used in combination with traditional publishing. When carried out from start to finish by an individual or group of people, desktop publishing produces results quickly and provides the ability to control the production from the initial layout and design to the final printing and distribution. However, desktop publishing and traditional

desktop publishing
Using specific desktop publishing software or high-end word processing software to produce professional-looking documents containing text and/or graphics

Figure 1.1 Producing Documents with a Typewriter, a Personal Computer, and a Laptop Computer

The desktop publishing process progressed through using a typewriter, then a personal computer, and now a laptop computer. What will be next?

publishing work well together. A project may begin on a desktop, where the document is designed and created, but an illustrator may be commissioned to create some artwork, and the piece may be sent to a commercial printer for printing and binding.

Using the results-oriented interface of Microsoft Office 2013, along with the enhanced desktop features found in Word 2013 and Publisher 2013 with the integration of PowerPoint 2013, Excel 2013, and Access 2013, you will find it easier to create, contribute to, manage, review, edit, customize, print, and publish professional-looking publications. The availability of OpenType fonts in Office 2013 also promotes cross-platform sharing between Apple computers and PCs.

When using desktop applications with publishing and data merge capabilities, you will be able to control and complete in-house those projects that used to be outsourced. Word 2013 and Publisher 2013, along with application-independent file formats (such as PDF, XML, and XPS), allow you to share documents regardless of the type of computer and applications your audience is using. In addition, you will be able to prepare and send publications more efficiently to professional printers accustomed to working with PDF and XML file formats. Shared document technology, the Internet, and email provide opportunities for you to collaborate with others outside your home and office, even as you travel.

Note: Comments on how to use this textbook or hints on the exercises will appear in italicized bold type. This book is designed to help those with an advanced skill level in Microsoft Word but little or no design experience. In addition to creating documents from scratch, you will learn how to access professionally prepared online Office templates, customize them to fit your individual or corporate needs, save them in PDF format, and print them on a personal printer or send them electronically to a professional printer.

Initiating the Desktop Publishing Process

The process of creating a publication begins with two steps—planning the publication and creating the content. During the planning process, the desktop publisher must decide on the purpose of the publication and identify the intended audience. When creating the content, the desktop publisher must make sure that the reader understands the intended message of the publication.

Planning the Publication

Initial planning is one of the most important steps in the desktop publishing process. During this stage, complete the following steps:

- Clearly identify the purpose of your communication. Are you trying to provide information? Are you trying to sell a product? Are you announcing an event? Distinctly defining your goal will make it easier for you to organize your material in a way that helps you achieve that goal.

- Assess your target audience. Who will read your publication? Are they employees, coworkers, clients, friends, or family? What will your target audience expect from your publication? Will they expect a serious, more conservative approach, or an informal, humorous approach? Make sure you keep their needs and desires in mind as you create your content.

- Determine in what form your intended audience will be exposed to your message. Will your message be in a brochure as part of a packet of presentation materials for a company seminar? Or will your message take the form of a

◀DTP POINTER
Consider the demographics of your target audience.

newspaper advertisement, surrounded by other advertisements? Will your message be in the form of a business card distributed when making sales calls? Or will your message be tacked on to a bulletin board? Understanding the method of delivery will help to refine the content of your publication.

- Decide what you want your readers to do after reading your message. Do you want them to ask for more information? Do you want them to respond in some way? Do you want them to be able to contact you in person, by telephone, or via email? Remember to include any necessary contact information based on your response to this step.

- Determine the budget for the entire project. Costs may include paper expenses based on quality, weight, and size; trimming, folding, and binding expenses; number of copies needed; delivery method used; and printing method used (color or black and white).

DTP POINTER

Pick up design ideas from the works of others.

- Collect examples of effective designs. Keep a design idea folder. Put copies of designs that impress you into this folder. These designs may include flyers, promotional documents, newsletters, graphic images, interesting type arrangements, and the like. Look through your idea folder every time you begin a new project. Let favorite designs serve as a catalyst for developing your own ideas.

Creating the Content

The most important goal in desktop publishing is to communicate the message. Design is important because it increases the visual appeal of your document, but content is still the most important element. Create a document that clearly conveys your intended message to your intended audience.

To determine your message, identify your purpose and start organizing your material. Establish a hierarchy of importance among the items in your communication. Consider what items will be the most important to the reader, what will attract the reader's attention, and what will spark enough interest to retain the reader's focus. Think about the format or layout you want to follow. (Check your idea folder!) Clear and organized content combined with an attractive layout and design create an effective message.

Designing the Document

If the message is the most significant part of a communication, it may seem like a waste of time to worry about design. However, a well-planned and relevant design sets your work apart from others and can help to focus readers' attention on the message. Just as people may be judged by their appearance, a publication may be judged by its design. Whether you are creating a business flyer, letterhead, or newsletter, anything you create will look more attractive, more professional, and more convincing if you take a little extra time to design it. As with planning the content of your publication, when planning the design, consider the purpose of the document, the target audience, and the method of distribution. In addition, think about the following factors:

DTP POINTER

Take the time to design!

- What feeling should the document elicit?
- What is the most important information, and how can it be emphasized so that the reader can easily identify the purpose of the document?
- What different types of information will be presented, and how can these elements be distinguished, yet kept internally consistent?
- How much space is available?

An important first step in planning your design and layout is to prepare a thumbnail sketch. A ***thumbnail sketch*** is a miniature draft of the document you are attempting to create, and is also known as *thinking on paper*. As you can see in Figure 1.2, thumbnail sketches let you experiment with alternative locations for such elements as graphic images, rules (horizontal or vertical lines), columns, and borders.

A good designer continually asks questions, pays attention to details, and makes thoughtful decisions that enhance the content of the publication. Consider examples A and B in Figure 1.3 on page 8. Which document attracts your attention, entices you to read on, looks convincing, and encourages you to take action?

Overdesigning is one of the most common tendencies of beginning desktop publishers. The temptation to use as many of the desktop publishing features as possible in one document is often difficult to resist. However, you should use design elements to communicate, not to decorate. To create a visually appealing publication, start with the same classic design concepts used by professional designers. These concepts include focus, balance, proportion, contrast, directional flow, consistency, and color.

Creating Focus

The ***focus***, or focal point, on a page is an element that draws the reader's attention. Elements that tend to draw focus are large, dense, unusual, and/or surrounded by white space.

Two ways to create focus in a document are to use:

- text created in larger, bolder, contrasting typefaces
- graphic elements, such as lines, clip art images, photographs, illustrations, watermarks, and logos

Whether focus is created through text or through graphics, you will recognize it instantly.

Creating Focus with Text

In Word, OpenType fonts and TrueType fonts are available for text formatting. OpenType fonts were created jointly by Microsoft and Adobe in an effort to promote cross-platform compatibility between Macintosh and Windows. In some cases, a document created on a Macintosh computer might not print in the same way on a Windows-based computer.

thumbnail sketch
A rough sketch used in planning a layout and design

◀**DTP POINTER**
Use design elements to communicate, not decorate.

focus
An element used to attract the reader's attention

Figure 1.2 **Preparing Thumbnail Sketches: Thinking on Paper**

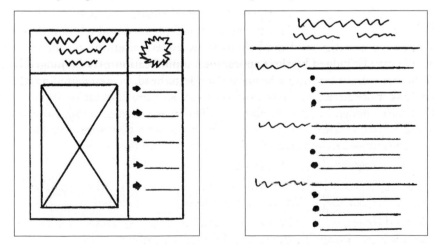

Figure 1.3 Using Design to Enhance Content

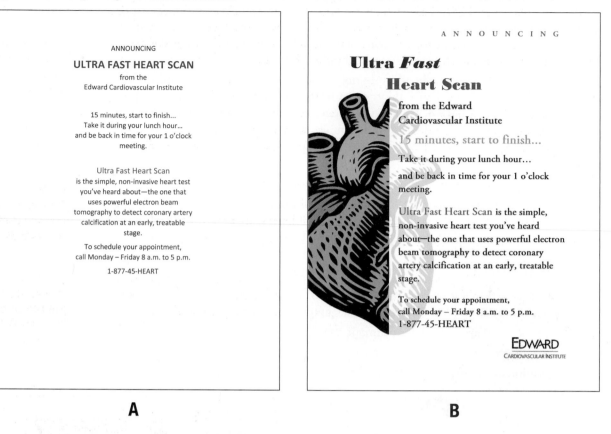

However, as OpenType fonts become more common, this difficulty may become less prevalent. OpenType fonts include exaggerated serifs and special ligatures for advanced users working with fine typographic controls (see Chapter 2 for more details). In addition, OpenType fonts can make it easier to set blocks of text that contain more than one language because they include multiple language character sets in each font.

In Word, the majority of fonts are OpenType fonts; however, you will see a few TrueType fonts still available as well. TrueType fonts were developed by Apple and Microsoft to replace the PostScript fonts that were used in earlier versions of Windows, but they are now being replaced with OpenType fonts.

white space

Background space with no text or graphics

⅓ – ⅔ rule

If two-thirds of a page contains text, graphics, and other content, at least one-third should be white space

Changing the weight, size, style, or letter spacing (tracking) of text, as well as applying text effects (glow, shadow, reflection, or outline), color, rotation, shapes (WordArt), or even drop caps can effectively draw the reader's attention. Grouping blocks of similar text, using a consistent alignment, and providing generous amounts of white space help to create focus using text. **White space** is the background where no text or graphics are located (although it may not always be white). The amount of white space around a focal element can enhance its appearance and help to balance other design elements on the page. Use white space to emphasize the main message and give the reader's eyes a break from too much text. Consider using a guideline called the **⅓ – ⅔ rule**, which says that at least one-third of your page should consist of white space if the remaining two-thirds contains text and other design elements.

Notice the use of text as a focal point in Figure 1.4B. The title "Kids at College" is formatted in Whimsy ICG Heavy, which is a youthful, energetic font. This formatting, along with a generous amount of white space, is much more effective at creating focus than the unformatted text in Figure 1.4A. Also, notice the impact the **reversed text** (white type on a black background) has on creating focus for the school name.

Creating Focus with Titles, Headlines, and Subheadings

When creating titles, headlines, and subheadings in reports, procedure manuals, newsletters, term papers, or tables of contents, use large or bold type surrounded by enough white space to contrast with the main text. In addition, keep the following points in mind:

- State your title or headline using precise, easily understood language.

- Select easy-to-read typefaces. **Legibility** is of utmost importance. Readers must be able to clearly see and read the individual letters in the title or headline.

- Size your title or headline in proportion to its importance relative to the surrounding text.

- Keep the line length of your headline fairly short, set it in a larger point size than the body type, and include enough white space around it so that it is clearly visible to your reader. This helps to improve **readability**, or the ease with which the reader's eyes move throughout your text.

Figure 1.4 Creating Focus with Text

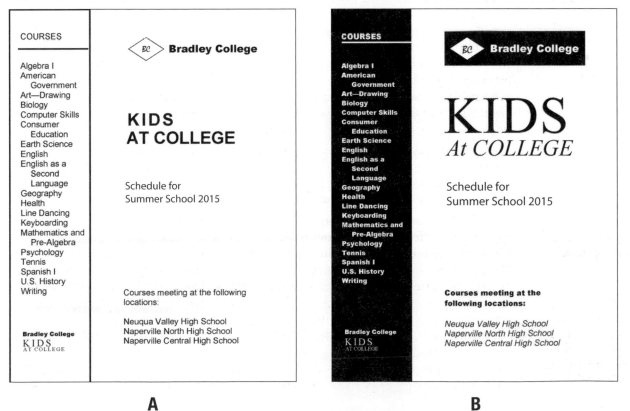

A

B

DTP POINTER

Subheads provide order to your text and give the reader further clues about the content of your publication.

In any type of communication—semiannual report, office procedures manual, company newsletter, advertising flyer, or brochure—subheads may provide a secondary focal element. While headlines attract the reader's attention, the subheads may be the key to maintaining it. Subheads provide order to your text and give the reader further clues about the content of your publication. Make sure subheads are set in legible fonts, with appropriate line length, line spacing, and alignment.

Look at document A in Figure 1.5. Does any particular location on the page attract your attention? You might say the title attracts your attention slightly. Now look at document B in the same figure. Do you agree that the bolded text attracts your attention? Now look at document C. Do the title and headings attract your attention more so than in documents A and B? In document C, the title is the primary focus and the headings, set in white text with a shaded background, provide secondary focal points on the page. Notice how the consistent font selection in all of the headings makes the document organization readily apparent to the reader. Also, notice that more white space appears before the headings than after them. This spacing connects the headings to the text that follows. Consistent formatting and font colors and sizes were created by applying styles, a style set, and a theme. These features will be discussed later in the chapter.

Creating Focus with Graphic Elements

Graphic elements can be used to create focus on a page and can enhance the overall appearance of a publication. Many Word features may be used to add visual elements to your publications, as shown in Figures 1.6 through 1.9.

A SmartArt graphic is a visual representation of information that you can quickly and easily create, choosing from many different layouts, to effectively communicate your message or ideas. SmartArt, which can be inserted using the SmartArt button in the Illustrations group on the INSERT tab and edited using the SMARTART TOOLS contextual tabs, uses text, shape, and color to create a focal point in a document, as shown in Figure 1.6. WordArt, photos, clip art, watermarks, shapes, lines, and text boxes with fill effects are other graphical Word features and are shown in Figures 1.7, 1.8, and 1.9. As you look at each document in the figures, ask yourself where the focal point is. Which design elements draw you into the document?

Figure 1.5 Creating Focus with Titles and Subheadings

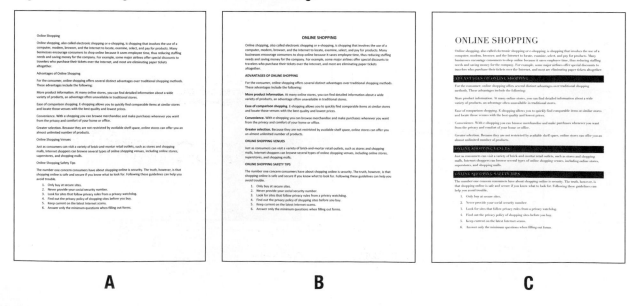

A　　　　　　　　　　B　　　　　　　　　　C

Figure 1.6 Using a SmartArt Graphic for Focus

Figure 1.7 Using Photos for Focus

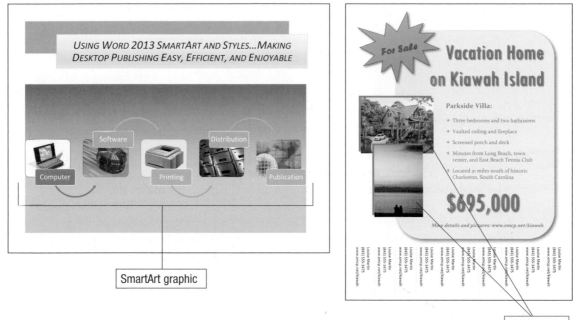

SmartArt graphic

photographs

Figure 1.8 Using a Clip Art Image for Focus

Figure 1.9 Using a Watermark for Focus

clip art image

watermark

When considering a graphic element as a focal point, remember the following points:

- Legibility is just as important with graphic elements as it is with titles and subheads. Graphic elements should support the message in your text and not interfere with the message's readability in any way.

DTP POINTER

Graphic images should be relevant to your intended message.

- Communicate rather than decorate. Let your message dictate the use of graphic elements. Does the graphic element enhance your message, or does it overshadow your message? Is it relevant, meaningful, and appropriate? If not, it is probably best to leave out the graphic.

DTP POINTER

Keep your design simple.

- Less is best; keep it simple. One larger, well-chosen graphic image provides more impact than using several smaller images. Too many images create visual confusion for the reader.

- Crop an image if necessary to increase impact. Crop to eliminate unnecessary elements and zoom in on the key parts of an image, or crop in unexpected ways to draw attention to the image. See Figure 1.10 for cropping examples. You will learn more about cropping in Chapter 4.

DTP POINTER

Graphics should face the text.

- Position the graphic to face the text. Graphics or photographs facing away from the text draw the reader's eyes away from the most important part of the document—the content. Compare documents A and B in Figure 1.11. The graphic in document B creates a focal point that leads the reader's eye toward the text rather than away from it (as in document A).

If all other factors are equal, publications containing graphic elements are noticed and perused before text-only publications. In Figure 1.12, announcement A is not as effective as announcement B. The sun graphic/watermark in announcement B creates a major focal point that draws in the reader. "Good Morning Naperville" is also easier to read in announcement B, immediately giving the reader an idea of the content he or she can expect to find in the document. Varying the type size and type style helps to organize the remaining information and provide minor focal points on the page.

Figure 1.10 Cropping an Image to Increase Impact

A
Original Image

B
Cropping Using Aspect Ratio in Portrait at 4:5

C
Cropping Using the Crop Tool

D
Cropping to a Shape

Figure 1.11 Positioning Graphics to Face the Text

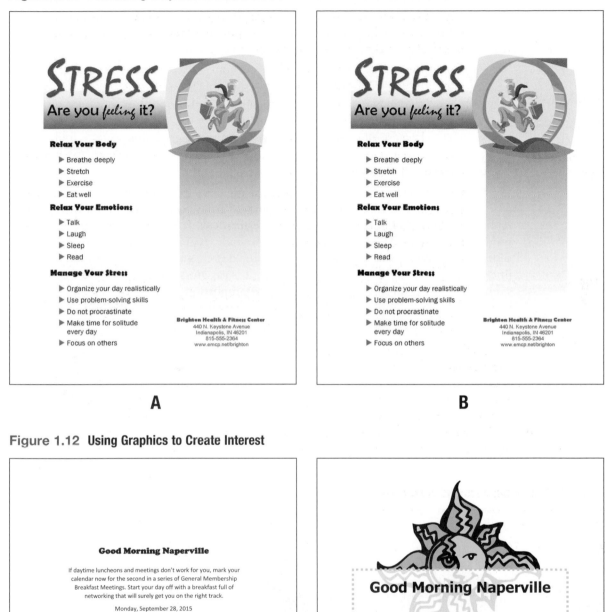

A

B

Figure 1.12 Using Graphics to Create Interest

A

B

Creating Balance

balance

The equal distribution of design elements on a page

Attain **balance** by equally distributing the visual weight of various elements such as blocks of text, graphic images, headings, ruled lines, and white space on the page. Balance is either symmetrical or asymmetrical.

Creating Symmetrical Balance

symmetrical design

Balancing similar elements equally on either side of a page

A **symmetrical design** contains similar elements of equal proportion or weight on the left and right sides and the top and bottom of the page. Symmetrical balance is easy to achieve because all elements are centered on the page. If you were to fold a symmetrically designed document in half vertically (in other words, along its vertical line of symmetry), you would see that both halves of the document contain the same elements.

To better visualize the concept of symmetrical balance, look at the shapes in the top half of Figure 1.13. The squares, representing identical graphic elements, are positioned on the left and right sides of the page. The rectangle, representing a block of text, is centered in between the two squares. Notice the dotted line, representing the vertical line of symmetry, splitting the design in half. It is easy to see that the elements on either side of the dotted line are equal in weight and proportion because they are the same. Now look at the example of a symmetrically designed letterhead in the bottom half of Figure 1.13. If you were to extend that same line of symmetry down through the sample letterhead, you would see equally distributed design elements on both sides of the page.

Creating Asymmetrical Balance

asymmetrical design

Balancing contrasting elements on a page

Symmetrical balance is easy to identify and to create. However, contemporary design favors asymmetrical balance. An **asymmetrical design** uses different design elements of varying weights and/or proportions to achieve balance on a page. Asymmetrical design is more flexible and visually stimulating than symmetrical design. Look at the shapes in the top half of Figure 1.14. Notice the dotted line (the line of vertical symmetry) that divides the page in half. Even without the dotted line, you can see that the two sides do not match. Therefore, you know immediately that this is not a symmetrical design. However, just because the design is not symmetrical does not automatically mean that it is asymmetrically balanced.

Remember, the key to an effective asymmetrical design is achieving a visual balance on the page by using dissimilar or contrasting elements. Look again at the shapes and the white space in Figure 1.14. Even though they are not the same and are not centered, would you agree that a visual balance is achieved on the page? The darker, denser square and its surrounding white space on the left half of the page are balanced by the longer, less dense rectangle and its surrounding white space on the right half of the page. Now look at how those same shapes are converted into the design elements used in the sample letterhead in the bottom half of Figure 1.14. The dissimilar design elements balance each other, resulting in an effective asymmetrical design.

spread

Set of pages facing each other

Multiple-page documents add another dimension to the challenge of achieving balance. In the case of a multiple-page publication, it is essential that you evaluate the balance of type and graphics in terms of each two-page unit, or **spread**, which is a set of pages facing each other, as shown in document B in Figure 1.15 on page 16. Notice that the layout of document A is symmetrical, and the layout of document B is asymmetrical.

Figure 1.13 Creating Symmetrical Balance

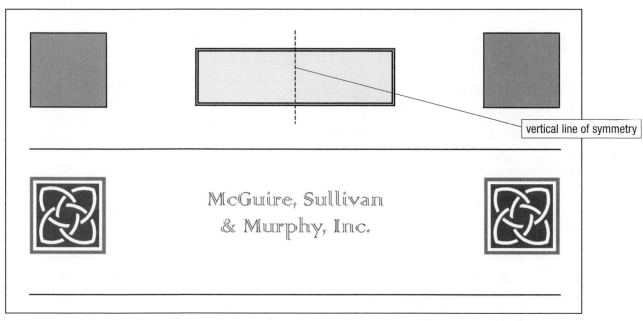

Figure 1.14 Creating Asymmetrical Balance

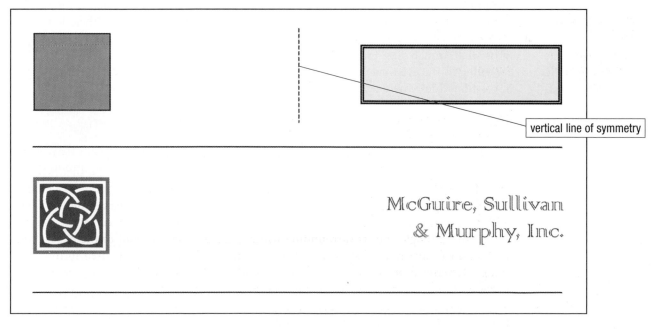

Figure 1.15 Comparing Symmetrical and Asymmetrical Newsletters

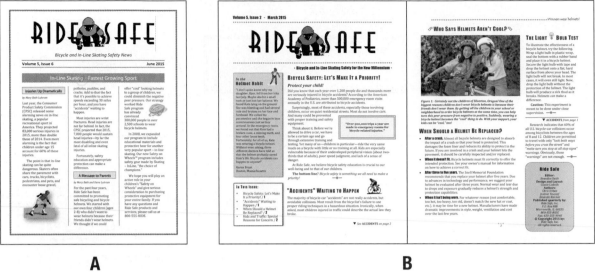

A

Symmetrical Balance

B

Asymmetrical Balance
(Two-Page Spread)

Using the Rule of Thirds

harmony

Achieved when all elements on the page work together

However you choose to balance your design, strive to maintain **harmony** on each page or spread. This means that all the elements work together to create a page that is interesting to look at and easy to read. One way to promote design harmony is to apply a design guideline called the **rule of thirds**. This rule states that pages should be arranged in thirds rather than in halves or fourths. Studies indicate that this division of sections is more appealing to the eye than any other design. Figure 1.16 illustrates a document that is not in harmony (document A) and one that is in harmony (document B).

rule of thirds

Design guideline that states that a page or image designed in thirds is more appealing to the eye

Creating Proportion

When designing a communication, think about all of the individual parts as they relate to the document as a whole. Readers tend to view larger elements as more important. Readers also are more likely to read a page where all of the elements are in **proportion** to one another. When incorporating the concept of proportion into your documents, consider the following points:

proportion

Sizing elements according to their relative importance

- Size design elements, whether text or graphics, according to their relative importance to the message.

- Strive for variety. Try not to make all design elements the same size.

- Text, graphics, and other design elements should take up two-thirds of the document and at least one-third of the document should be left for white space.

Figure 1.16 Applying the Rule of Thirds to Create Harmony in a Document

A

Without Harmony

B

With Harmony

Decide which elements in your document are the most important in conveying your message. Next, decide which elements are the second most important, and so on. Once you have created this hierarchy, proportionally size the visual elements in your publication according to their priority. This way you can make sure your readers see the most important information first. The typefaces and type sizes you choose for headlines, subheads, and body text can set the proportional standards for a document.

◀**DTP POINTER**
Proportionally size visual elements according to their priority.

Evaluating Proportion

When viewing the documents in Figure 1.17 on page 18, look at the headline size in proportion to the body text. Think about this relationship when selecting the type size for the title or headline and the body text. When selecting the type size for subheads, consider how the subhead relates proportionally to the headline and to the body text.

Sizing Graphic Elements to Achieve Proportion

Sizing of graphic elements is also important in maintaining proportion among all of the design elements on a page. For instance, look at Figure 1.18A on page 19. The size of the image visually tells the reader that it is the most important item on the page. But should it be? As discussed earlier in this chapter, the message that you want to get across to the reader always takes top priority. The image in document A may be relevant, but it is overpowering the message rather than supporting it. The image is out of proportion to its relative importance in the message.

Now look at Figure 1.18B. The musical image is too small to be effective. Looking at the document as a whole, the image is out of proportion to the surrounding elements. What is your reaction to Figure 1.18C? Look at the individual elements as they relate to the whole document. All of the design elements appear to be in proportion to each other and to their ranking of importance in the intended message.

Figure 1.17 Evaluating Headline Proportions

A

Headline Too Large

B

Headline Too Small

C

Headline Just Right

Figure 1.18 Sizing Graphics in Appropriate Proportion

A	B	C
Image Too Large	Image Too Small	Image Just Right

Using White Space

White space must also be considered when evaluating proportion in a document. Keep the following pointers in mind:

- Narrow margins can make lines too long to read easily.
- Too much white space between columns makes the line length look choppy.
- Too little space between columns makes the text squished and harder to read.
- Excess white space between lines of text creates gaps that look out of proportion to the type size.
- Too little white space between lines of text reduces legibility.

Apply proportion consistently throughout your entire project. An integrated, unified look is established when elements are in proportion to one another.

Creating Contrast

Contrast is the difference between degrees of lightness and darkness on the page. Text with a low level of contrast gives an overall appearance of gray. Consider using strong contrast to achieve some emphasis or focus on your page. A high level of contrast is more visually stimulating and helps to draw your audience into the document. Use contrast as an organizational aid to help your reader move through the document and follow the flow of information. Headlines and subheads set in larger and denser type help to create contrast on an otherwise gray page, as shown in Figure 1.19 on page 20.

As shown in Figure 1.20 on page 20, the contrast achieved by using a larger type size for the word *London*, as well as reversed, bold text, helps to grab your attention. A black image against a solid white background produces a sharp contrast, as illustrated by the English guard graphic in Figure 1.20A. In addition, look at the program cover in Figure 1.20B. A sharp contrast exists between the black background and the white text and piano image, and a less sharp contrast exists between the light gray text and the watermark of musical notes in the background of the cover.

contrast
Difference in degrees of lightness and darkness

◀DTP POINTER
Add contrast by setting headings and subheads in larger, denser type.

◀DTP POINTER
Make contrasting elements strong enough to be noticed.

Figure 1.19 Using Contrast in Headlines and Text

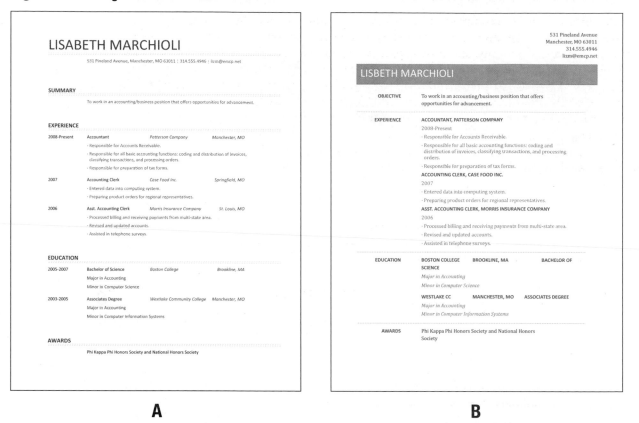

A

Resume with No Visual Contrast

B

Resume with Visual Contrast

Figure 1.20 Creating Contrast with Black-and-White Graphics and Text

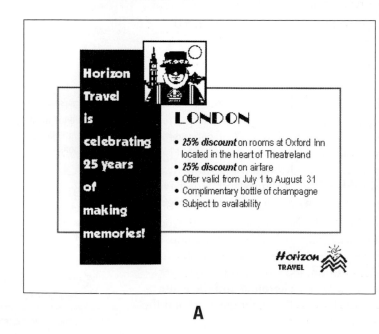

A

B

Achieving Contrast with Text

Text contrast can be accomplished by changing text direction and by mixing serif and sans serif fonts, larger and smaller font sizes, uppercase and lowercase, roman and italics, thick fonts and thin fonts, and drop caps and normal text. See Figure 1.21 for examples. Avoid pairing fonts that are only slightly different from one another, such as Times New Roman and Bell MT. Instead, choose fonts with obvious differences, such as Arial Black (sans serif) and Invitation (serif). Word 2013 theme fonts take some of the guesswork out of choosing contrasting yet complementary fonts. The drop-down gallery shown in Figure 1.22 shows the theme fonts name, such as *Office*, followed by the heading font, such as *Calibri Light*, and the body font, such as *Calibri*. These theme fonts are determined by the theme applied to the document. You will learn more about themes later in this chapter.

Figure 1.21 Illustrating Contrasting Font Pairs

Figure 1.22 Selecting Fonts at the Theme Fonts Button Drop-down Gallery

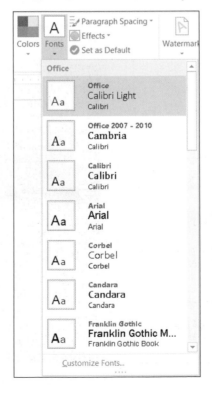

In addition to predesigned theme fonts, you have an option to create your own font pairs. Do this by clicking the DESIGN tab, clicking the Theme Fonts button in the Document Formatting group, clicking *Customize Fonts* at the drop-down gallery, and then saving your font pairs with a name of your choosing.

Special characters used as bullets to define a list of important points, such as 👪, ⚓, 👁, 🖼, ☎, 🍴, 🚗, and ✋, not only serve as organizational tools but also contribute visual contrast to your page. Placing these special characters in a bolder and larger type size provides a higher level of contrast. Notice the family symbol and the pen bullets used in Figure 1.23A. You will learn more about inserting bullets in Chapter 3.

DTP POINTER

Use bullets to organize information and add visual contrast.

Achieving Contrast with White Space

White space is an important tool in achieving contrast. Use more white space on a page to project a more open, lighter feeling. When white space is limited, a more closed, darker feeling is projected. Think of white space as the floor space in a room. The more furniture and accessories in the room, the more crowded the room becomes. Rearranging or removing some of the furniture can provide more floor space, which produces an open, lighter feeling. Your page design, like a room, may need to be rearranged or pared down to create some contrasting white space. Too many design elements are crowding the page in Figure 1.23A. Notice how eliminating and rearranging some of the design elements to create more white space makes for a more open and lighter design in Figure 1.23B.

DTP POINTER

Use plenty of white space to convey an open, lighter feeling.

Figure 1.23 Adding White Space

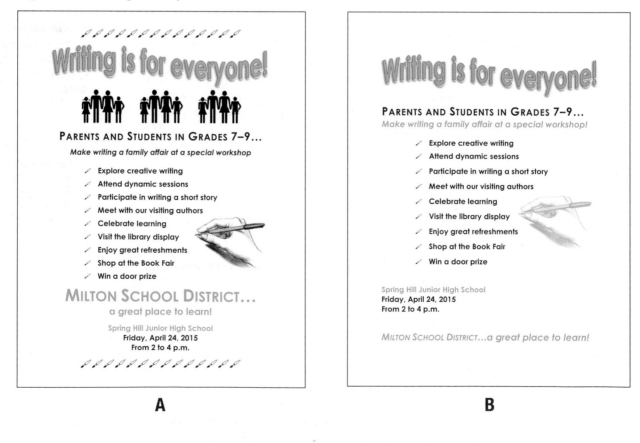

A   B

Figure 1.24 Using Contrast to Improve Legibility

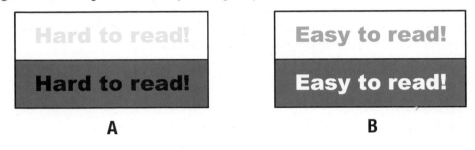

Achieving Contrast with Color

The use of color in a heading, a logo, a graphic image, a ruled line, or as a background can also create contrast on a page. When using more than one color, select colors that provide a pleasing sense of variety, not colors that create an unpleasant conflict. In addition, consider whether the color(s) used increases or decreases the legibility of your document. Color may look nice, but it will confuse the reader if there is not enough contrast in the text. Look at the examples in Figure 1.24. In illustration A, the color of the text and the color of the background are too similar, making the text barely legible. As you can see in Figure 1.24B, the stark contrast between the color of the text and the color of the background makes the text easy to read. Use high contrast to maximize legibility.

Creating Directional Flow

Establish smooth *directional flow* in a document by organizing and positioning elements in such a way that the reader's eyes scan through the text and find particular words or images that you wish to emphasize. Graphics and display type (larger than 14 points) act as focal elements that attract the eye as it scans a page. Focal elements may include a well-designed headline, subheads, logo, graphic images, ruled lines, boxes with text inside, charts, reversed text, or a shaded background. When establishing the directional flow of your document, you must:

- organize your information into groups of closely related items and then rank the groups in order of importance
- decide how to emphasize the most important information
- place related items close to each other on the page
- use left or right alignment to establish a stronger visual connection between all of the elements on your page
- position elements so that the reader is drawn into the document and then directed through the document

Organizing Your Information Visually

Organize your information by grouping related items. Place the related items close to each other so the reader views them as one unit rather than as separate pieces. For example, a subheading should be close to the paragraph that follows it so that the reader recognizes the relationship between the two. Dates, times, and locations are also frequently grouped close together because they provide related information.

What happens when there is little or no organization to the information in a document? Look at Figure 1.25A on page 24. Aside from being boring and uninviting to read, it is difficult to tell what the document is really about. Now look at Figure 1.25B. What has changed to make it so much more appealing? The arrow

directional flow
Positioning elements to draw the reader's eyes through the document

◀ DTP POINTER
Rank information according to its importance in conveying the intended message.

◀ DTP POINTER
Position related items close to each other on the page.

Figure 1.25 Grouping Related Items and Creating Strong Directional Flow

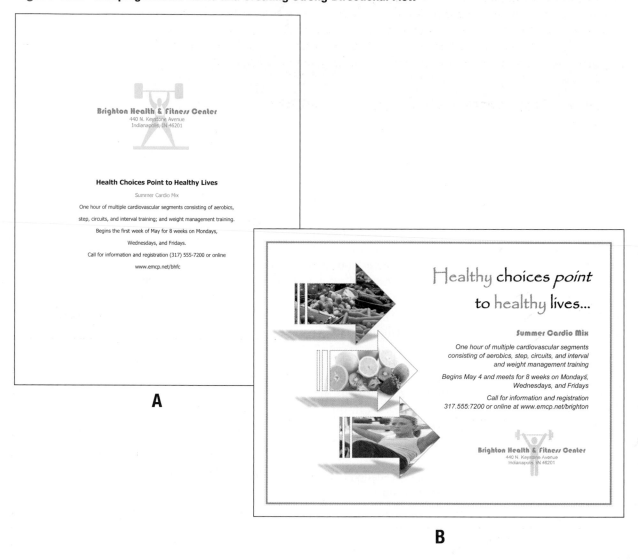

A

B

shapes filled with relevant graphics point toward the document content. Therefore, the directional flow directs the reader's eyes from the left side (focal point) to the right side where the content is grouped in a logical, easy-to-read manner. The italicized word *point* reinforces the right-pointing arrow shapes, and the slant of the text gives a feeling of movement.

You can also use color to organize a document, but remember that the colors you choose should reflect the nature of the business you represent. Someone in an artistic line of work may use bolder, splashier colors than someone creating documents for a financial institution.

Headers and footers—text that appears repetitively at the top or bottom of each page—also contribute to directional flow and visual organization in a publication. Chapter name, chapter number, report title, and page number are common items included in headers or footers. These page identifiers direct the reader to specific locations in a document. You will learn more about inserting headers and footers in Chapter 3.

One of the easiest and most effective ways to visually organize your document is to apply a unified, preformatted design theme. When you apply a design theme to a document, you can insert specific elements in your document with the design theme applied. For example, if you apply the Facet theme to a document, you can insert a cover page along with coordinating headers and footers, as shown in Figure 1.26.

Figure 1.26 Using a Coordinated Cover Page, Header, and Footer

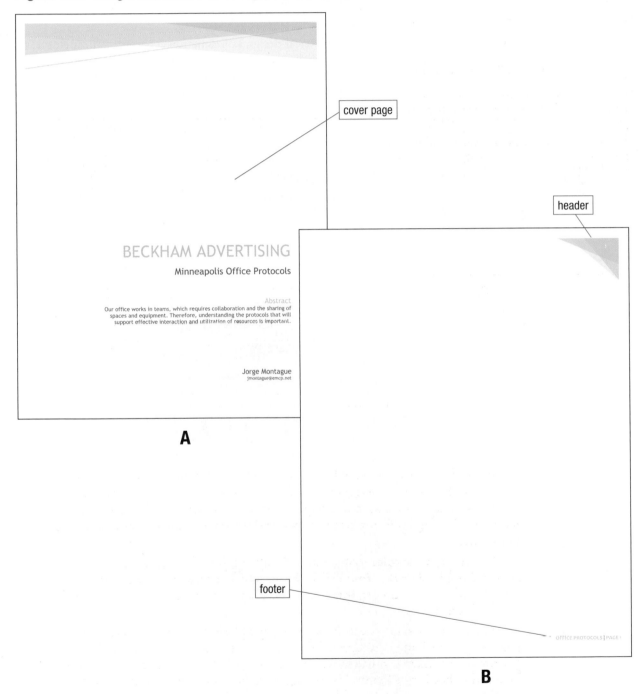

Ranking Elements

After you have organized your information into groups of related items, decide which information plays the most important role in conveying your message and then emphasize that information. For example, the purpose of the flyer in Figure 1.27 is to inform readers of the class schedules for the Kids at College program. The courses and locations offered are important facts. Reverse text and larger font sizes emphasize these facts. The gradient fill adds to the overall appeal of the flyer.

Recognizing the Z Pattern

Z pattern

When scanning a page, the eyes tend to move in a Z pattern—upper left corner to bottom right corner

Directional flow in a strictly symmetrical design (all elements centered) is limited to movement down the visual center of the page, producing a static design. Conversely, an asymmetrical design creates a dynamic directional flow. When scanning a page, the eyes tend to move in a **Z pattern**: they begin at the upper left corner of the page, move to the right corner, then drop down to the lower left corner, and finally end up in the lower right corner of the page. In text-intensive publications such as magazines, newspapers, and books, visual landmarks are frequently set in these positions so that the reader will notice them. In an advertisement, the company name, address, and phone number often appear in the lower right corner.

Figure 1.28 helps you visualize the Z pattern in a document. Remember that placing content according to the Z pattern is only a guideline. Some designs may use modified versions of the Z pattern, or they may not use it at all. However, when you are first getting started designing, it is often easier to follow certain rules rather than trying to figure it all out on your own.

Figure 1.27 Emphasizing Important Information

Figure 1.28 Recognizing Z-Pattern Directional Flow

Choosing Alignment

The way you choose to position text and graphics on a page greatly influences the directional flow in a document. One of the keys to creating dynamic directional flow and producing professional-looking documents is *alignment*, or the linear arrangement of items on a page. Center alignment is fine when you are trying to achieve a more formal look, as in a wedding invitation, but tends to be dull and boring in other types of documents. Break away from the center alignment habit! Experiment with using a strong left or right alignment to connect different elements on your page.

In Figure 1.29A, the varied alignment of all the elements causes them to appear disconnected, and the reader's eyes tend to jump from one corner to another. The business card in Figure 1.29B uses strong right alignment, grouped text, and bold formatting to lead the eyes from the top to the bottom.

alignment
Linear arrangement of objects on a page

◀ **DTP POINTER**
Save center alignment for formal, conservative documents.

◀ **DTP POINTER**
Use a strong left or right alignment to visually connect elements on a page.

Figure 1.29 Analyzing the Importance of Visual Alignment

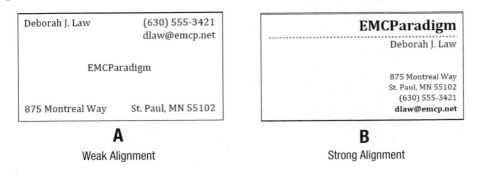

A
Weak Alignment

B
Strong Alignment

Establishing Consistency

Uniformity among specific design elements establishes a pattern of **consistency** in your document. Inconsistency can confuse and frustrate the reader and can lead to a reduction in your readership. To avoid this, design elements such as margins, columns, typefaces, type sizes, spacing, alignment, and color should remain consistent throughout a document. In any document, whether single-page or multiple-page, consistent elements help to integrate all of the individual parts into a whole unit. Repetitive, consistent elements can lend identity to your documents and provide the reader with a sense of familiarity.

Consistent elements are evident in many of the figures in this chapter. Consider, for example, the flyer in Figure 1.28 on page 27. Consistency is achieved by using the same color blue in the heading, the bullets, the sky in the sailboat clip art, the title of the event, and the phone number. Additional consistent elements in the flyer include the left alignment, the flag bullets, the spacing between the bullets, the typeface used for the text, and the margins.

Use consistent elements when designing separate business documents for the same company or person. These documents may include business cards, a letterhead, and envelopes. In Figure 1.30, the consistent elements (the company name, logo, and colors) included in each document are obvious. You know immediately that all three documents are associated with the same company, which serves to reinforce the brand and identity of that organization.

Evaluating Consistency

Consistency establishes unity not only *within* a section or chapter (or newsletter or advertisement) but also *among* the sections or chapters (or a series of newsletters or advertisements). Notice how the consistent elements used in the pages in Figure 1.31 contribute to the unified appearance of the document. The blue color scheme is carried throughout the pages of the manual, including the cover page. The same typeface appears on the cover and in the headers, section headings, and subheadings. A different typeface displays in the body text and remains consistent throughout the document. Additionally, a thin horizontal line appears in the header on every page except the cover.

Figure 1.30 Creating Consistency among Documents

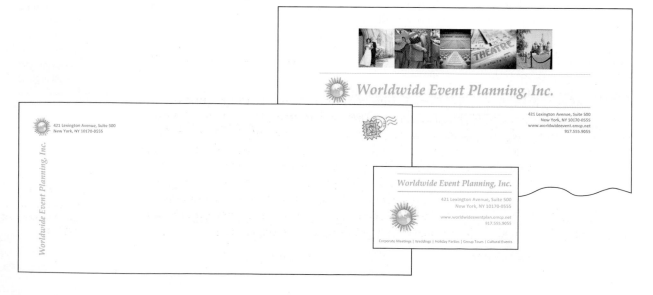

Figure 1.31 Applying Consistent Formatting and Color

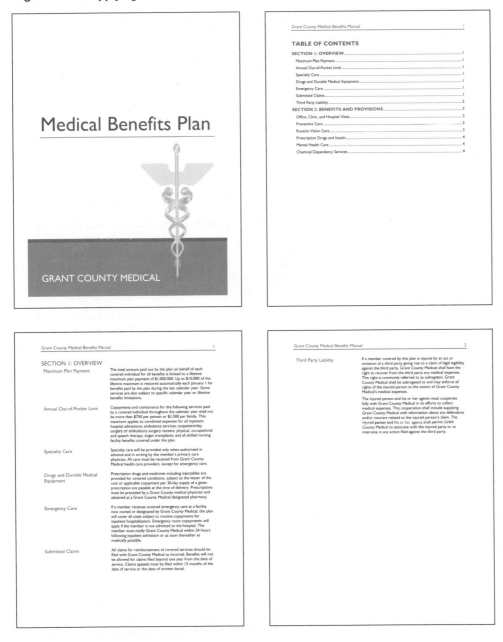

If you plan to insert a graphic image into your document, use the graphic to provide you with some ideas for creating consistency. For example, in Figure 1.32 on page 30, the globe/plane/mailbox graphic in the postcard provided the basis for the color scheme. The arrow pointing to the mailbox slot inspired the use of a dotted line and arrow pointing to the new address. The arrow was then repeated in the return address box and in the delivery address section. Three rectangles were also arranged to resemble a mailbox in the return address section of the postcard. When designing your work, remember that because consistent elements are repetitive elements, you should keep it simple and distinct. Too much of a good thing can be distracting.

◀ DTP POINTER
Do not distract the reader by overusing graphics.

Figure 1.32 Using a Graphic to Create Consistency

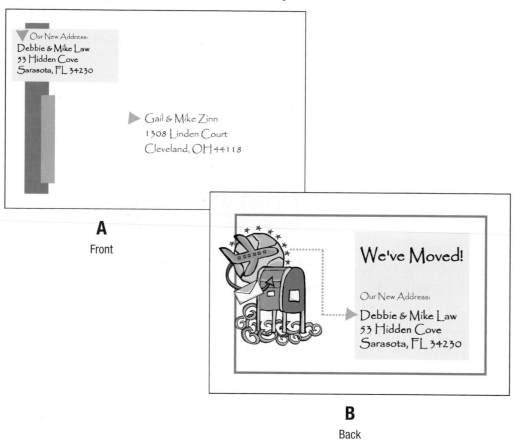

A

Front

B

Back

Applying Styles for Consistency within a Document

One way to ensure consistent formatting throughout a document is to apply styles. Word 2013 provides a gallery of professionally designed styles for titles, headings, subheadings, and body text, among others. These styles include preselected combinations of fonts, font sizes, colors, and spacing. Apply a style by clicking in the text you wish to format and then clicking a style thumbnail in the Styles group on the HOME tab. The formatting applied by a style will vary depending on the style set. Style sets, such as Basic (Stylish), Casual, Centered, Lines (Simple), and Shaded, can be applied by clicking one of the thumbnails in the Document Formatting group on the DESIGN tab. Using styles and style sets greatly simplifies the process of applying and adjusting formatting in your document.

Applying Themes for Consistency among Documents

Just as styles reinforce consistency within a document, themes help to promote consistency among different files created in Word, Excel, Access, and/or PowerPoint. Because the same themes are available in each of the programs in the Office 2013 suite, you can quickly and easily format a group of related documents to give them a cohesive and professional look. Each theme contains a set of formatting choices that includes theme colors, theme fonts (including heading and body text fonts), and theme effects (including lines and fill effects). Look at the examples in Figure 1.33, which have all been formatted using the Quotable theme. Although they are different types of documents, they still convey a united appearance, making it clear that they are related. Apply a theme by clicking the DESIGN tab, clicking the Themes button, and then clicking one of the options at the drop-down gallery.

DTP POINTER The formatting applied by each style depends on the active style set in the document.

DTP POINTER A theme is a set of formatting characteristics that includes theme colors, fonts, and effects.

Themes

Figure 1.33 Using the Quotable Theme in Word, PowerPoint, and Excel

A
Word Document

B
PowerPoint Slide

C
Excel Worksheet

Using Color

As discussed earlier, color can help to create focus. In addition, it is a powerful tool in communicating a message and portraying an image. The colors you choose should reflect the nature of the message you want to convey and/or the business you represent. Always identify your target audience in planning your documents, and think about the impact color will have on your audience. Someone who is trying to attract the attention of a youthful audience may use bolder, splashier colors than someone creating documents for an accounting business. In addition, men and women often respond differently to the same color. Color can even elicit an emotional response from the reader; keep in mind cultural differences and how other cultures interpret the use of color.

The colors in the fall leaves in Figure 1.34 reinforce the subject of the text, which is a list of courses offered during the fall semester at a college. Color can help organize ideas and highlight important facts. When used appropriately, color can enhance the professional look of a document.

◀ DTP POINTER
Use color to create focus, organize ideas, and emphasize important elements.

Figure 1.34 Using Color to Communicate

Applying Guidelines for Using Color

The following are a few guidelines to follow when using color in documents:

DTP POINTER
Use color sparingly.

- Use color sparingly—less is best! Limit your use of colors to two or three, including the color of the paper.

- Use color to identify a consistently recurring element.

- Do not let color overpower content. Color can add emphasis and style, but the message is most important!

- Remember the importance of contrast. If the background of your document is white or light-colored, do not set text in light colors—it is too difficult to read. Black text is still the easiest to read. Conversely, do not set text in black if the background of your document is dark.

- Avoid changing all text to one color, such as red. It is harder to read and defeats the purpose of using color to create focus and emphasis.

- Use light colors for shaded backgrounds or watermarks.

Using Color in Graphics and Text Elements

Word provides many ways of inserting color into your documents. You may use pre-designed graphic pictures, borders, page colors, bullets, and lines. You may also create your own colored shapes, lines, borders, text boxes, and text. For instance, the event invitation in Figure 1.35 uses WordArt to emphasize the event name and an attention-getting zebra border to reinforce the safari theme. The zebra facing the grouped text also reinforces the invitation theme, and the green gradient fill in the text boxes on the front and back side of the invitation make you feel like you are with the animals on a green savanna in Africa.

Using Colored Paper

If a color printer is not available, consider using colored paper to add interest to your publication. Colored paper can match the tone or mood you are creating in your document. Orange paper used for a Halloween flyer, as shown in Figure 1.36B on page 34, is an inexpensive alternative to color graphics and text like the ones shown in Figure 1.36A. Your audience will recognize the theme of the flyer by associating the paper color with the event. The colored paper provides contrast and adds vitality and life to the publication.

Using Preprinted Stationery

You may also turn plain white documents into colorful, attention-grabbing documents by purchasing preprinted stationery, envelopes, brochures, or presentation packets from paper supply companies or your local office supply store. Achieve color, emphasis, and contrast through an assortment of colorful page borders, patterned and solid-colored papers, as well as gradient, marbleized, and speckled papers. Many paper suppliers provide free catalogs and offer inexpensive sample paper packets.

DTP POINTER
Find information on providers of specialty papers in your area by conducting an Internet search.

Figure 1.37A on page 34 shows a certificate created in Word, and Figure 1.37B illustrates that same certificate printed on paper with a preexisting star design. The gray fill and blue border applied in Word reinforce the colors in the paper. When printing on predesigned paper, make sure to place the elements in your document appropriately so that they will print in the right location. (Experiment with plain paper first!)

Figure 1.35 Using Color Graphics and WordArt

A
Front

B
Back

Printing Options

Even though laser printers have become more affordable, color laser printers (and color laser printer cartridges) remain rather expensive. A less expensive, but still good, alternative is the inkjet color printer. An inkjet printer uses color ink cartridges to produce color. (The paper may be slightly damp when first removed from the printer.) Improve the ***resolution*** of the printed document by using specially designed inkjet paper. Some inkjet printers are capable of achieving near-photographic quality with a resolution of 5760 × 1440 or higher. Learn more about your printer settings by accessing the Print backstage area and clicking the <u>Printer Properties</u> link.

Another option for printing documents in color is to send your formatted copy to a commercial printer. You can get almost any color you want from a commercial printer, but it can add significantly to the cost of your project. Always check prices and your budget first.

resolution

The fineness of detail in an image or text produced by a monitor or printer

Figure 1.36 Comparing Color Graphics and Colored Paper

Figure 1.37 Using Preprinted Paper

A

Layout and Text Created in Word

B

Printed on a Paper Style Called *Star Gala* by Paper Direct

Evaluating Documents Using the Document Analysis Guide

Up to this point, you have learned the importance of carefully planning and designing your publication according to the desktop publishing concepts of focus, balance, proportion, contrast, directional flow, consistency, and color. In Exercise 1.1, you will evaluate a document using a Document Analysis Guide, which can be printed from the Chapter01 folder on the CD that accompanies this textbook. The Document Analysis Guide is a tool used to evaluate design concepts in selected documents.

A Document Evaluation Checklist may also be printed from the Chapter01 folder on the CD that accompanies this textbook. This tool serves as a way for you to evaluate your progress during the planning and creation stages of your document and is directed toward the finished product. The Document Evaluation Checklist will be used in Units 2, 3, and 4 in this book. Both forms will be used to analyze your own documents, existing commercial publications, and/or other students' desktop publications.

Creating desktop published documents involves many steps and, often, a lot of experimentation. Frequently save your documents so you always have a recent version to fall back on and to avoid losing your work if a power or system failure occurs. Word automatically saves a document recovery file every 10 minutes. You can change this setting at the Word Options dialog box with *Save* selected in the left panel. Display the Word Options dialog box by clicking the FILE tab and then clicking *Options*.

◀ **DTP POINTER**
Save your documents often.

Note: In several exercises in each chapter, you will open documents from the CD that accompanies this textbook. The files you need for each chapter and for each set of unit assessments are saved in individual folders. Before beginning a chapter, copy the necessary folder from the CD to your storage medium (e.g., a flash drive or SkyDrive account). Steps to create a folder, make a folder active, and delete a folder are presented in the textbook Preface and on the inside of the back cover.

Exercise 1.1 Evaluating a Document

Evaluate the flyer illustrated in Figure 1.38 on page 36 by completing the following steps:

1. Open **DocumentAnalysisGuide.docx** from your Chapter01 folder on the student data CD.
2. Save the document with the name **C01-E01-Evaluate**.
3. Turn to page 36 to view Figure 1.38.
4. Complete an analysis of the flyer in Figure 1.38 by typing short answers to the questions in the Document Analysis Guide.
5. Save, print, and then close **C01-E01-Evaluate.docx**.

Figure 1.38 Flyer to Be Evaluated in Exercise 1.1

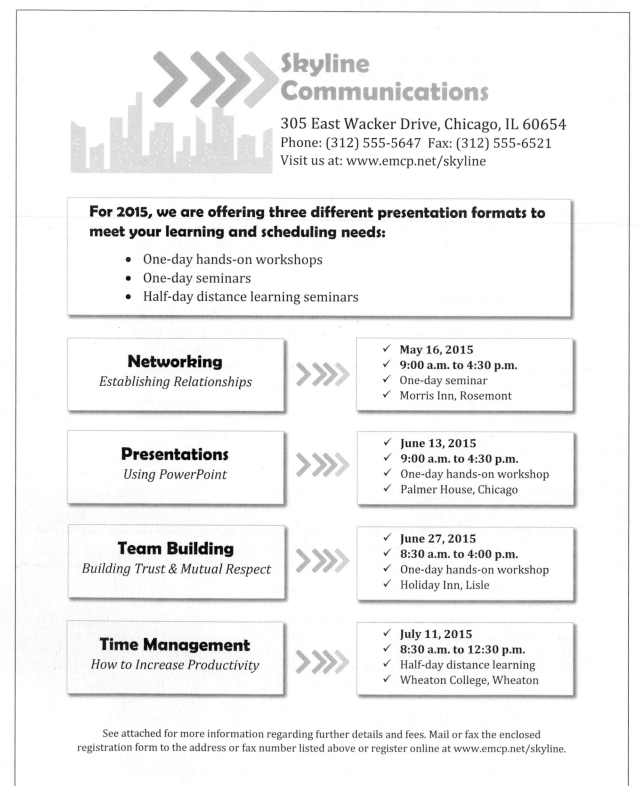

Using Word 2013 in Desktop Publishing

Microsoft Word 2013 is a visual word processing program that provides an efficient means of editing and manipulating text and graphics to produce professional-looking documents. Word is linear in nature, in that every character, picture, and object is part of a line of text. However, Word also contains many features and options that allow you to change linear objects to floating objects that can be moved easily around the document screen.

Familiarize yourself with design principles by studying well-designed publications and by experimenting. Analyze what makes a specific design and layout visually appealing and unique, and try using the same principles or variations in your publications. Take advantage of the special design and layout features that Word 2013 has to offer. Make sure to allow time for trial and error. Creating a quality publication requires a lengthy process of revising, refining, and making adjustments. Above all else, experiment! View each document in terms of focus, balance, proportion, contrast, directional flow, consistency, and use of color. Ask the opinion of your peers, fellow workers, and advisors, and listen to their feedback. The final judge is the reader, so always try to look at your document from the reader's perspective.

◀ DTP POINTER
Experiment with different layouts and designs.

The remaining chapters in this book will take you through the steps for creating specific personal and business desktop publishing products, such as letterheads, business cards, newsletters, flyers, brochures, postcards, online and hard-copy forms, and presentations. In addition to step-by-step directions for completing the products using Word 2013, each project will introduce guidelines relevant to that document type as well as reinforce the design concepts introduced in this chapter. Remember:

- Take the time to design!
- Communicate, rather than decorate!
- Less is always best!
- Readability is the key!

In Exercise 1.2, you will learn about creating a portfolio to showcase the documents you create during this course.

Exercise 1.2 Creating a Portfolio

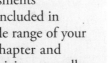
PORTFOLIO

Begin a job-hunting portfolio of the documents you will create in the exercises and assessments throughout this book. Exercises marked with the portfolio icon shown above should be included in your portfolio. These documents have been chosen to show a prospective employer a wide range of your desktop publishing skills. You may also include any additional documents from the chapter and unit assessments. Because the assessments are less structured than the exercises, your creativity can really shine. Your instructor will determine a due date and any other specific requirements for your portfolio. If possible, purchase plastic sheet protectors for your documents and a binder to hold them. You may also want to create a title page and/or a table of contents for your portfolio. See Figure 1.39 on page 38 for sample portfolios. Open **PortfolioRequirements.docx** located in the Chapter01 folder and then print a copy of the document.

As an alternative, your instructor may request that you prepare an electronic version of your portfolio by saving your cover, divider pages, and a select number of publications in PDF format and then sending them to him or her as an email attachment. These pages may also be posted to your blog, if you have one, or uploaded to SkyDrive. You might also consider preparing your portfolio as a PowerPoint presentation and sending it to your instructor electronically.

Figure 1.39 Comparing Photos of Sample Portfolios

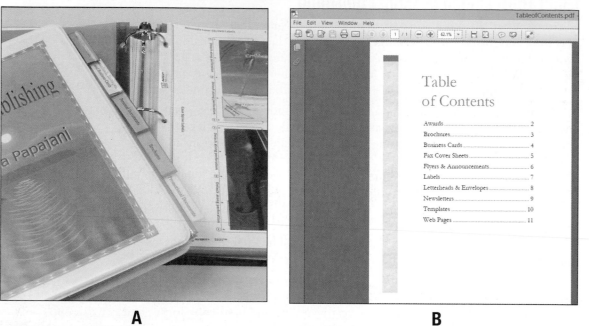

A
Hard Copy Portfolio

B
Electronic Portfolio

Using Online Resources

The Internet can provide you with a wealth of information on desktop publishing as well as resources such as templates and images that can be downloaded from websites. In your preferred browser or search engine, type *desktop publishing* in the search box. The search results will provide access to websites on various aspects of the desktop publishing field, which may include reviews on the newest books; definitions for common terms; discussions on graphics, layout, and design; and facts on career opportunities. You can also find links to free clip art, fonts, photos, and templates. You may also try searching using other keywords such as *clip art*, *free clip art*, *fonts*, *graphics*, *graphic designers*, *Microsoft Word*, *word processing*, *Web design*, *logos*, *digital cameras*, and *scanning* to learn about different techniques and approaches to producing professional-looking documents.

Search engines that provide image results include Google, Bing, and Yahoo. Be sure that you read the copyright information associated with each collection. Many images are free to use privately, but permission may be needed if the images are used for profit-making endeavors.

You can download most graphics you see on the Web by right-clicking an image and then clicking the *Save picture as* option at the shortcut menu that displays. A regular Save As dialog box displays where you may choose to name the file and save it to your hard drive or any other location. Again, be careful to make sure you have the rights to use the images you select. Most images are copyrighted!

Using Office.com Templates

If you have previously used Microsoft Word 2013, you may be familiar with the hundreds of Office templates that are available through Office.com. Access these templates by clicking the FILE tab and then clicking the *New* option. Microsoft has collaborated with various content experts to provide hundreds of professionally designed templates for Word, Excel, Access, Publisher, PowerPoint, Visio, and OneNote. You may initiate a search to find a template and then double-click the template thumbnail to open a document based on the template. You can tailor the document based on the template to your exact needs. Many of the templates reinforce integration of the Office programs by using a common theme.

Occasionally, the words *Compatibility Mode* will display in the Title bar next to the document name. *Compatibility Mode* displays to indicate that some new features are disabled to prevent problems when working with previous versions of Office. Converting the file to the newer version will enable these features but may result in layout changes. To convert the document to Word 2013 format, click the FILE tab and then click the Convert button at the Info backstage area.

In Exercise 1.3A, you will begin creating an invitation from an Office.com template.

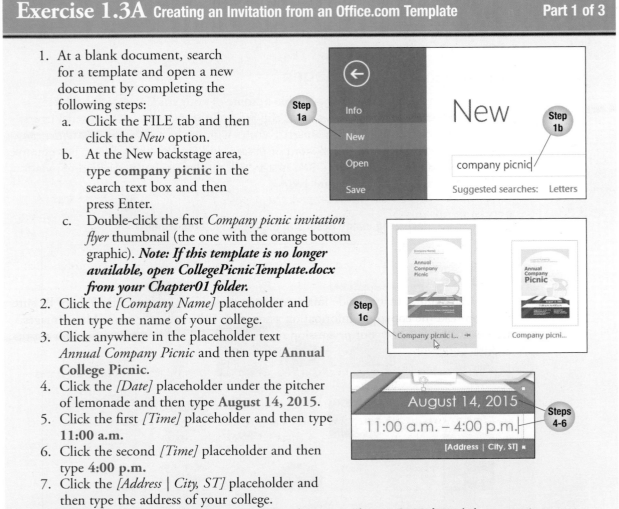

Exercise 1.3A Creating an Invitation from an Office.com Template — **Part 1 of 3**

1. At a blank document, search for a template and open a new document by completing the following steps:
   a. Click the FILE tab and then click the *New* option.
   b. At the New backstage area, type **company picnic** in the search text box and then press Enter.
   c. Double-click the first *Company picnic invitation flyer* thumbnail (the one with the orange bottom graphic). ***Note: If this template is no longer available, open CollegePicnicTemplate.docx from your Chapter01 folder.***
2. Click the *[Company Name]* placeholder and then type the name of your college.
3. Click anywhere in the placeholder text *Annual Company Picnic* and then type **Annual College Picnic**.
4. Click the *[Date]* placeholder under the pitcher of lemonade and then type **August 14, 2015**.
5. Click the first *[Time]* placeholder and then type **11:00 a.m.**
6. Click the second *[Time]* placeholder and then type **4:00 p.m.**
7. Click the *[Address | City, ST]* placeholder and then type the address of your college.
8. Click the *[Date]* placeholder at the right of the text *Please R.S.V.P. by* and then type **August 1.**

9. Click the *[Name]* placeholder and then type **Stephanie Bourne**.
10. Click the *[Email]* placeholder and then type **bourne@emcp.net**.
11. Click the *[Phone]* placeholder and then type **(242) 555-0177**.
12. Save the document by completing the following steps:
    a. Click the FILE tab and then click the *Save As* option.
    b. At the Save As backstage area, click the Browse button.
    c. Navigate to your Chapter01 folder and double-click the folder to open it.
    d. Type **C01-E03-CollegeInvitation** in the *File name* text box.
    e. Click the Save button.

13. Leave the file open for the next exercise.

Using Office.com Images

Besides the included image files available in some of your student data file folders, you can access more image files such as clip art and photographs at the Insert Pictures window. Search for images at the Insert Pictures window by clicking in the *Office.com Clip Art* text box, typing a search word or phrase, and then pressing Enter. For example, search for images related to "sun" and images will display in the Insert Pictures window similar to what is shown in Figure 1.40.

Figure 1.40 Reviewing Image Results at the Insert Pictures Window

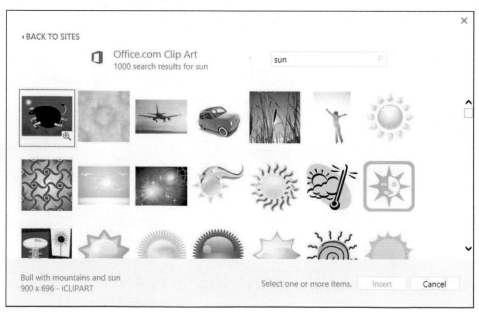

In Exercise 1.3B, you will search for and insert clip art from Office.com into your invitation document. You will then format the clip art to make it fit within the document.

Print

Exercise 1.3B Inserting Clip Art from Office.com   Part 2 of 3   PORTFOLIO

1. With **C01-E03-CollegeInvitation.docx** open, add a sun clip art image by completing the following steps:
   a. Press Ctrl + Home to move the insertion point to the beginning of the document.
   b. Click the INSERT tab and then click the Online Pictures button in the Illustrations group.

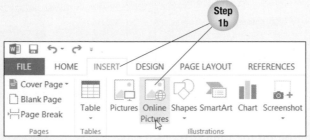

   c. At the Insert Pictures window, click in the *Office.com Clip Art* text box, type **sun**, and then press Enter.
   d. Double-click the sun clip art image shown below.

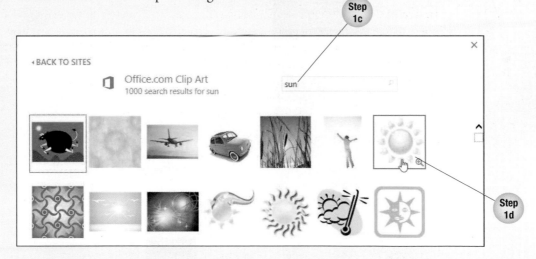

2. With the clip art image still selected, format the image by completing the following steps:

a. Decrease the size of the image by clicking in the *Shape Height* measurement box in the Size group on the PICTURE TOOLS FORMAT tab, typing **2**, and then pressing Enter.

Step 2a

b. Change the text wrapping by clicking the Wrap Text button in the Arrange group and then clicking *Behind Text* at the drop-down list.

c. Drag the selected image to the location indicated in the image below (see also Figure 1.41).

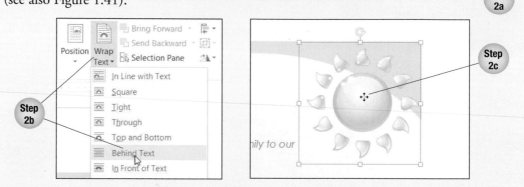

Step 2b

Step 2c

3. Click the Save button on the Quick Access toolbar.

4. Print the document by clicking the FILE tab, clicking the *Print* option, and then clicking the Print button. (Leave the document open for the next exercise.)

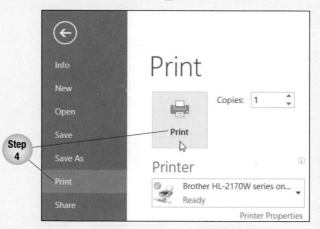

Step 4

Figure 1.41 **Invitation Created in Exercises 1.3A and 1.3B**

Figure 1.42 **Using the Snipping Tool**

Using the Windows 8 Snipping Tool

In addition to all of the Office 2013 components, most editions of Microsoft Windows include an assortment of office tools. One of the tools with which you may want to become familiar is the Snipping Tool. You can use the Snipping Tool to capture a screenshot, or a snip, of any object on your screen and then annotate, save, or share the image. After the image is saved, it may be inserted into a document. Figure 1.42 illustrates the Snipping Tool window next to a logo that can be captured and reused in a variety of documents.

In Exercise 1.3C, you will practice opening the Snipping Tool and creating a snip. This will help to ensure that you will be familiar with the tool when you need to use it.

Exercise 1.3C Using the Windows 8 Snipping Tool   Part 3 of 3

1. With **C01-E03-CollegeInvitation.docx** open, scroll down the document to display the lemonade glass and pitcher image.
2. Display the Windows 8 Charms bar by positioning the mouse pointer in the upper right corner of your computer screen.
3. Click the Search button on the Charms bar.
4. At the Start screen, with the insertion point positioned in the search text box, type **snip**.
5. Click the Snipping Tool tile that displays in the results window.
6. At the Snipping Tool dialog box, click the down-pointing arrow at the right of the New button and then click *Free-form Snip* at the drop-down list.
7. With the scissors tool, draw a free-form shape around the lemonade glass and the image.
8. Click the Save Snip button and then save the picture as **C01Lemonade.png** in your Chapter01 folder. *Hint: This image has now been saved in a graphic format and may later be inserted into a document.*
9. Close the Snipping Tool window.
10. Save and then close **C01-E03-CollegeInvitation.docx**.

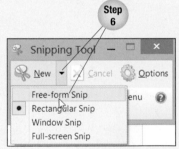

Step 6

Step 7

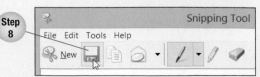

Step 8

Chapter Summary

➤ Use desktop publishing software to produce professional-looking documents for office and home use. For simple desktop publishing projects, use Microsoft Word; for more complex projects use a high-end desktop publishing application.

➤ When creating a publication, clearly define your purpose, assess your target audience, decide the format in which your audience will see your message, and decide what outcome you are expecting.

➤ Effective design involves planning and organizing content. Decide what items are most important to the reader. Design concepts such as focus, balance, proportion, contrast, directional flow, consistency, and the use of color are essential to creating a visually attractive publication that presents information in a logical, organized manner.

➤ Focus can be created by using large and/or bold type, such as for titles and subheads; by using graphic elements, such as ruled lines, clip art, and photographs; and by using color for emphasis.

➤ White space is the background where no text or graphics are located. Use white space to emphasize the main message and give the reader's eyes a break from too much text.

➤ At least one-third of your publication should consist of white space if the remaining two-thirds contain text and other design elements.

➤ Balance on a page is created by equally distributing the weight of elements on a page in either a symmetrical or asymmetrical manner. Symmetrical design (all elements centered) balances similar elements of equal weight and proportion on the left and right sides and the top and bottom of the page. Asymmetrical design balances contrasting elements of unequal proportion and weight on the page.

➤ Design harmony may be accomplished by applying a design guideline called the rule of thirds. This rule states that pages should be arranged in thirds rather than in halves or fourths. Studies indicate that this basic grid is more appealing to the eye than any other design.

➤ In establishing a proportional relationship among the elements on a page, think about all of the parts as they relate to the total appearance. Proportionally size the visual elements in your publication according to their relative importance to the intended message.

➤ Contrast is the difference between varying degrees of lightness and darkness on the page. A high level of contrast is more visually stimulating and helps to draw your target audience into the document. Contrast is also used as an organizational aid so that the reader can distinctly identify the organization of the document and easily follow the logical flow of information.

➤ Directional flow can be produced by grouping related elements and placing them close to each other on the page, by using a consistent alignment to establish a visual connection between the elements on a page, and by positioning elements in such a way that the reader's eyes are drawn through the text and to particular words or images that the designer wishes to emphasize.

➤ Consistent elements in a document such as margins, columns, typefaces, type sizes, spacing, alignment, and color help to provide a sense of unity within a document or among a series of documents. Repetitive, consistent elements can also lend identity to your documents.

➤ Style sets and document themes in Word help to make formatting efficient and consistent for any publication or group of similarly designed publications.

➤ A document theme is a set of formatting choices that include a set of theme colors, a set of theme fonts (including heading and body text fonts), and a set of theme effects (including lines and fill effects).

➤ Apply a theme to a document and insert specific elements in the document with the theme applied.

➤ You can modify fonts, colors, margins, table formatting, and other elements by choosing different style formats from the Styles group on the HOME tab. You can also change the look of the styles by applying different style sets with options in the Document Formatting group on the DESIGN tab.

➤ Use color on a page to help organize ideas; emphasize important information; provide focus, contrast, directional flow, and consistency; and establish or reinforce an identity.

➤ Use the Internet for free clip art, photographs, templates, and helpful newsletters.

➤ Access the Microsoft Office.com templates by clicking the FILE tab and then clicking *New*. At the New backstage area, search for a template from Office.com by entering a search phrase and then pressing Enter.

➤ You can use the Snipping Tool to capture a screen shot, or snip, of any object on your screen, and then annotate, save, or share the image.

Commands *Review*

FEATURE	RIBBON TAB, GROUP/OPTION	BUTTON	KEYBOARD SHORTCUT
blank document	FILE, *New, Blank document*		Ctrl + N
clip art	INSERT, Illustrations		
pictures	INSERT, Illustrations		
Print backstage area	FILE, *Print*		Ctrl + P
save	FILE, *Save*		Ctrl + S
Save As backstage area	FILE, *Save As*		F12
Snipping Tool	Windows 8 Start screen		
styles	HOME, Styles		
templates	FILE, *New*		
themes	DESIGN, Document Formatting		

Key Points Review

A. proportion
B. asymmetrical
C. directional flow
D. consistency
E. SmartArt
F. color

G. balance
H. theme
I. crop
J. alignment
K. style sets
L. contrast

M. white space
N. focus
O. thumbnail sketch
P. symmetrical
Q. readability

Matching: In the space at the left, provide the correct letter or letters from the above list that match each definition.

_____M_____ 1. Areas in a document where no text or graphics appear

_____P_____ 2. Type of balance achieved by evenly distributing similar elements of equal weight on a page

_____G_____ 3. Attain this by equally distributing the visual weight of various elements such as blocks of text, graphic images, headings, ruled lines, and white space on the page

_____A_____ 4. Design technique used to help organize ideas, highlight important information, provide focus and consistency, and reinforce the identity of an organization

_____C_____ 5. Positioning elements in such a way that the reader's eyes are drawn through the text and to particular words or images that the designer wishes to emphasize

_____N_____ 6. An element that draws the reader's eye to a particular location in a document

_____O_____ 7. A preliminary rough draft of the layout and design of a document

_____D_____ 8. Uniformity among specific design elements in a publication

_____A_____ 9. The sizing of various elements so that all parts relate to the whole

_____I_____ 10. To remove unnecessary parts of a graphic

_____B_____ 11. Contemporary design in which contrasting elements of unequal weight and proportion are positioned on a page to achieve balance

_____K_____ 12. A graphical representation of information—graphical lists, organizational charts, and process diagrams

_____L_____ 13. The difference between varying degrees of lightness and darkness on the page

_____H_____ 14. Word feature that includes sets of unified formatting choices that affect color, fonts, and effects

_____E_____ 15. A visual representation of your information that you can quickly and easily create, choosing from among many different layouts, to effectively communicate your message or ideas

Chapter Assessments

Assessment 1.1   Create a Presentation

The purpose of this assignment is to provide you with experience in planning, organizing, creating, and making a class presentation using Microsoft Word or PowerPoint. Specific instructions are provided for you in the document named **Presentation.docx**. To print this document, complete the following steps:

1. Open **Presentation.docx** from your Chapter01 folder.
2. Print one copy and then close **Presentation.docx**.

Begin researching a topic for your presentation. You may compose and create a presentation on a desktop publishing or Web publishing article or concept, a Word or PowerPoint desktop publishing or Web publishing feature(s) or process used to create a specific document, or an instructor-approved topic that you would like to share with your class. You may consider using any of the topics presented in this textbook. Include any Word or PowerPoint tips or techniques you may have discovered while creating your presentation. Use any one of the many desktop publishing, Word, and PowerPoint resources available online or at your local library or bookstore. Your instructor will notify you of a scheduled date for your presentation, which you will give after completing Chapter 13.

Assessment 1.2   Evaluate Documents

The Internet contains many well-designed and poorly designed documents. Looking critically at as many publications as possible will give you a sense of what works and what does not. In this skill assessment, find two different examples of documents—flyers, newsletters, resumes, brochures, business cards, announcements, certificates, and so on—and print a hard copy of the documents. Evaluate these documents according to the desktop publishing concepts discussed in this chapter using **DocumentAnalysisGuide.docx**. To do this, complete the following steps:

1. Open **DocumentAnalysisGuide.docx** from your Chapter01 folder and then save the document with the name **C01-A02-Analysis01**.
2. Complete the document analysis guide for the first example document (type **Assessment 1.2A** on the *Exercise #* line) and then save and print **C01-A02-Analysis01.docx**. Attach the printed evaluation guide to the front of the printed example document. Close **C01-A02-Analysis01 .docx**.
3. Open **DocumentAnalysisGuide.docx** and then save the document and name it **C01-A02-Analysis02**.
4. Complete the document analysis guide for the second example document (type **Assessment 1.2B** on the *Exercise #* line) and then save and print **C01-A02-Analysis02.docx**. Attach the printed evaluation guide to the front of the other printed example document. Close **C01-A02-Analysis02.docx**.

Assessment 1.3 Arrange Design Elements in a Flyer

1. Open **HappySummerFlyer.docx** from your Chapter01 folder and then save the document with the name **C01-A03-HappySummer**.
2. Apply the design principles discussed in Chapter 1 to create a professional-looking advertisement for the Happy Summer Nursery. Eight design elements have been created and placed randomly on the page. Rearrange the text boxes and graphics displayed on the page to create a harmonious design that attracts attention and reinforces the message. Make the following changes:
   a. Click and drag each design element to create a layout with good directional flow.
   b. Apply a different theme.
   c. Make sure all of the fonts are consistently used and that the text is appropriately sized.
3. Save, print, and then close **C01-A03-HappySummer.docx**.

Assessment 1.4 Use the Internet to Research Elements of Professional Design

1. Access your favorite search engine and then search for at least ten elements that comprise a professional-looking flyer, brochure, or newsletter.
2. Working with a group of two or three students, combine your notes into a fact sheet using a table to help organize your findings.
3. Use any Word 2013 features that you are familiar with to enhance the design and layout of your fact sheet. Refer to Figure 1.43 on page 50 as a guide to the type of information you may want to include in your document.
4. Below the table, include your resources. If necessary, review a current reference manual or the Internet to find the appropriate format for typing your resources.
5. Save the completed fact sheet and name it **C01-A04-ElementsFacts**.
6. Print a copy for each member of your class and then close the document.

Assessment 1.5 Draw a Thumbnail Sketch to Plan a Document

Create a flyer for one of the situations described below. Start by drawing a thumbnail sketch using lines, boxes, and rough illustrations to plan the placement of text and graphics on the page. Your group should discuss how to include focus, balance, proportion, contrast, white space, directional flow, and consistency in your flyer. Be sure to consider the purpose and target audience for the situation. Designate areas in your sketch for such items as time, date, location, and response information. Label your sketch as **C01-A05-Sketch**. Next, create the final flyer in Word and name it **C01-A05-Flyer**. Elect one person on your team to act as a spokesperson for your group to explain how your team used the design elements discussed in Chapter 1 in the creation of your flyer.

Situation 1: Volunteer project

Situation 2: Software training seminar

Assessment 1.6 Evaluate a Promotional Document

In this assessment, you will evaluate a poorly designed flyer according to the items listed on the **DocumentAnalysistGuide.docx** located in your Chapter01 folder.

1. Open **DocumentAnalysisGuide.docx** from your Chapter01 folder and then save the document with the name **C01-A06-Analysis**.
2. Open **CleaningFlyer.docx** from your Chapter01 folder.
3. Print one copy and then close **CleaningFlyer.docx**.
4. Complete the document analysis guide. At the end of the document, list three suggestions for improving the document.
5. Print and then close **C01-A06-Analysis.docx**.

Figure 1.43 Sample Solution for Assessment 1.4

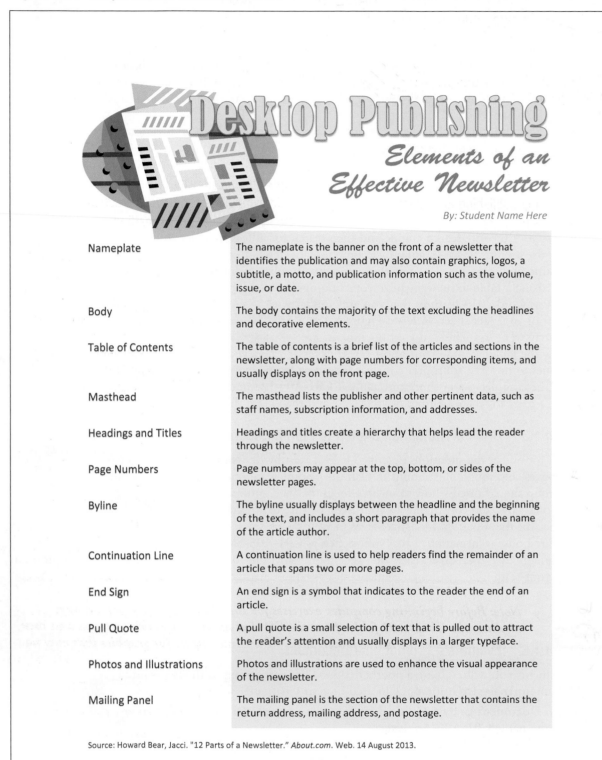

Desktop Publishing
Elements of an Effective Newsletter

By: Student Name Here

Nameplate	The nameplate is the banner on the front of a newsletter that identifies the publication and may also contain graphics, logos, a subtitle, a motto, and publication information such as the volume, issue, or date.
Body	The body contains the majority of the text excluding the headlines and decorative elements.
Table of Contents	The table of contents is a brief list of the articles and sections in the newsletter, along with page numbers for corresponding items, and usually displays on the front page.
Masthead	The masthead lists the publisher and other pertinent data, such as staff names, subscription information, and addresses.
Headings and Titles	Headings and titles create a hierarchy that helps lead the reader through the newsletter.
Page Numbers	Page numbers may appear at the top, bottom, or sides of the newsletter pages.
Byline	The byline usually displays between the headline and the beginning of the text, and includes a short paragraph that provides the name of the article author.
Continuation Line	A continuation line is used to help readers find the remainder of an article that spans two or more pages.
End Sign	An end sign is a symbol that indicates to the reader the end of an article.
Pull Quote	A pull quote is a small selection of text that is pulled out to attract the reader's attention and usually displays in a larger typeface.
Photos and Illustrations	Photos and illustrations are used to enhance the visual appearance of the newsletter.
Mailing Panel	The mailing panel is the section of the newsletter that contains the return address, mailing address, and postage.

Source: Howard Bear, Jacci. "12 Parts of a Newsletter." *About.com*. Web. 14 August 2013.

Chapter 2

Applying and Modifying Fonts

Performance Objectives

Upon successful completion of Chapter 2, you will be able to:

- Understand basic typography
- Apply desktop publishing guidelines when choosing fonts
- Apply themes, styles, and style sets
- Add symbols and special characters
- Apply advanced font formatting

Desktop Publishing Terms

ascenders	font	pitch	serif
baseline	hue	point size	swash
cap height	kerning	proportional	typeface
descenders	ligatures	sans serif	typestyle
em dash	luminescence	saturation	x-height
en dash	monospaced		

Word Features Used

font color	live preview	styles	text effects
font size	special characters	symbols	themes
Format Painter			

Note: Before beginning computer exercises for this chapter, copy to your storage medium the Chapter02 folder from the CD that accompanies this textbook and then make Chapter02 the active folder. Remember to substitute for graphics that may no longer be available.

Understanding Basic Typography

An important element in the creation of any type of document is the font used to format the text. To choose a font for a document, you need to understand basic typography and the terms that apply. As you learned in Chapter 1, when planning a document, consider the intent of the document, the audience, the feeling the document is to elicit, and how you plan to emphasize the most important information. Make sure the headlines, graphics, and typography work together to support the desired message.

In this chapter, you will be introduced to important desktop publishing terms and guidelines related to applying and modifying fonts. You will then practice applying these concepts by creating documents such as a conference sign, a medical plan, a sales flyer, and a corporate invitation.

Defining Typefaces

One of the most important considerations in establishing a particular mood or feeling in a document is choosing the right typeface. A *typeface* is a set of characters with a common design and shape (Word refers to typeface as *font*). For example, you might choose a decorative typeface for invitations or menus, but use a simple block-style typeface for headlines or reports. Choose a typeface that reflects the content, the expectations of your audience, and the image you want to project.

Certain elements distinguish one typeface from another. The characters in a line of text rest on an imaginary horizontal line called the *baseline*. Parts of certain characters may extend above and below this baseline. Figure 2.1 illustrates the various parts of type.

The *x-height* is the height of the main body of the lowercase characters in the typeface and is equivalent to the height of the lowercase *x*. The *cap height* is the distance between the baseline and the top of capital letters. *Ascenders* are the parts of lowercase characters that rise above the x-height, (for example, the upper part of a lowercase *h*) and *descenders* are parts of characters that extend below the baseline (for example, the swoop of a lowercase *j*). *Serifs* are the small strokes at the ends of characters.

Typefaces are either *monospaced* or *proportional*. A monospaced typeface allots the same amount of horizontal space for each character; professional publications rarely use this typeface. Courier is an example of a monospaced typeface. Proportional typefaces allow a varying amount of space for each character. For example, the lowercase letter *i* takes up less space than an uppercase *M*. In addition, different proportional typefaces take up different amounts of horizontal space. For example, the same sentence takes up far more horizontal space when set in Century Gothic than it does in Times New Roman.

Figure 2.1 Identifying the Parts of Type

<div class="sidebar">

typeface or font

A set of characters with a common design and shape

baseline

An imaginary horizontal line upon which characters rest

x-height

Height of the lowercase x of a font

cap height

The distance between the baseline and the top of capital letters

ascenders

The parts of a lowercase character that rise above the x-height

descenders

The parts of a lowercase character that extend below the baseline

serif

A small stroke at the end of a character

monospaced

Same amount of character spacing for each character in a typeface

proportional

Varying amount of space for each character in a typeface

</div>

Proportional typefaces fall into two main categories: serif and sans serif. Traditionally, serif typefaces are easier to read and are used with text-intensive documents, such as business letters, manuals, and reports. Serifs help move the reader's eyes across the page.

The characters in a **sans serif** typeface do not have serifs (*sans* is French for *without*). Sans serif typefaces are generally more legible (characters are easier to recognize) and are often used for headlines and advertisements. In modern designs, sans serif typefaces may also be used for body text, but in doing so, you should avoid using more than seven or eight words per line; using bold, italics, outlining, or shadowing; or using a long line length. Figure 2.2 shows examples of serif, sans serif, and monospaced typefaces.

When using a proportional typeface, press the spacebar once after end-of-sentence punctuation and after colons. Proportional typeface is set close together, so extra white space is not needed at the end of a sentence or after a colon. Additionally, since proportional fonts take up varying amounts of horizontal space, you should never attempt to use the spacebar to align text or objects.

Microsoft Office 2013 includes many typefaces designed for clear, extended on-screen reading, and they are integrated into the new templates offered as part of Microsoft Office. These typefaces include the default—Calibri—as well as Cambria, Candara, Consolas, Constantia, and Corbel. Calibri, Candara, and Corbel are sans serif typefaces; Cambria and Constantia are serif typefaces; and Consolas is monospaced.

Defining Type Sizes

Type size (font size) is defined by two categories: pitch and point size. **Pitch** is a measurement used for monospaced typefaces; it reflects the number of characters that can be printed in 1 horizontal inch. For some printers, the pitch is referred to as cpi, or characters per inch. For example, the font Courier 10 cpi is the same as 10-pitch Courier.

Point size is a vertical character measurement. The characters in a proportional typeface are measured in units called *points* (measured vertically from the top of the ascenders to the bottom of the descenders). A point is approximately 1/72 of an inch. The higher the point size, the larger the characters. Figure 2.3 on page 54 shows Wide Latin and Arial typefaces in a variety of point sizes. For each point size, the two typefaces vary greatly in width, but their heights are identical.

Figure 2.2 Comparing Serif, Sans Serif, and Monospaced Typefaces

SERIF TYPEFACES	SANS SERIF TYPEFACES	MONOSPACED
Cambria	Calibri	Consolas
Constantia	Candara	Lucida Console
Times New Roman	Corbel	OCR A Extended
Bell MT	Agency FB	Courier New
Harrington	Arial	
Bookman Old Style	Tahoma	
Book Antiqua	Impact	

◄DTP POINTER

Use a serif font for text-intensive documents.

sans serif

Describes a typeface whose characters do not have a small stroke at the end

◄DTP POINTER

Use a sans serif font for headings.

◄DTP POINTER

Use the Find and Replace feature in Word to find end punctuation followed by two spaces and replace them with one.

◄DTP POINTER

To view a list of the fonts that are installed with Office 2013, go to http://support .microsoft.com /kb/2800393.

pitch

The number of characters that can be printed in 1 horizontal inch

point size

A vertical character measurement; approximately equal to 1/72 of an inch

◄DTP POINTER

Sans serif faces are more readable than serif faces when set in very small point sizes.

Figure 2.3 Comparing Point Sizes in Wide Latin and Arial Fonts

8-point Wide Latin   8-point Arial

12-point Wide Latin   12-point Arial

18-point Wide Latin   18-point Arial

24-point Wide Latin 24-point Arial

Defining Typestyles

typestyle

Variations within a typeface, including regular or normal, bold, italic, and bold italic

A **typestyle** is a variation of a font that causes the text to display thicker (bold) and/or slanted (italic). Within a typeface, characters may have various typestyles. There are four main categories of typestyles: normal (also known as light, black, regular, or roman), bold, italic, and bold italic. Apply a typestyle to your text by clicking the Bold button and/or the Italic button in the Font group on the HOME tab. Alternatively, click the Font group dialog box launcher to access the Font dialog box, where you may select a typestyle to apply regular, italic, bold, or bold italic formatting to a desired font.

Applying Desktop Publishing Guidelines

Desktop publishing includes general guidelines, or conventions, that provide a starting point for designing documents. Use moderation in choosing typefaces and type sizes—two fonts and three different font sizes are usually adequate for most publications. Too many typefaces give the document a disorderly appearance, confuse the reader, and take away from the content of the document. Remember that serif fonts are more formal and are the standard for long blocks of text. Sans serif typefaces are cleaner and more contemporary in form and thus are favored for large text or headlines. Line length and line spacing are also factors to consider in choosing appropriate typefaces.

Using OpenType Fonts

OpenType is a font format that was developed jointly by Microsoft and Adobe. OpenType fonts can potentially contain many thousands of characters. This means that an OpenType font may contain multiple alphabets (such as Latin, Greek, Japanese, and more). This font format provides several advantages over older font technologies such as TrueType. OpenType fonts have better support for international character sets, cross-platform support between Windows and Macintosh computers, support for Postscript and TrueType fonts, and support for advanced typographic features, which include special ligatures (combined characters, which will be discussed in more detail later in the chapter) and **swashes** (exaggerated serifs).

swash

An exaggerated serif

DTP POINTER

To read an overview on topics related to typography and free fonts, go to www.microsoft.com/typography.

Using Fonts that Save Ink

In addition to reinforcing the message of your document, choosing the right font can also help save money on printing. The amount of ink used in printing is determined by the thickness of the font. Choosing a font with *narrow* or *light* in its name is usually more ink-efficient than using a font with *bold* or *black* in its name. Also, serif fonts tend to use less ink than sans serif fonts.

The following fonts are listed in order from most to least ink-efficient: Century Gothic, Times New Roman, Calibri, Verdana, Arial, Trebuchet, Tahoma, and Franklin Gothic Medium. However, note that Century Gothic is a wider font and may extend the text to an additional page—which means that it could be less paper-efficient.

◀ DTP POINTER
Choose ink-efficient fonts to reduce printing costs.

Using Fonts to Enhance Design

The fonts you choose for your document can greatly affect the feeling the document elicits in the reader, thus contributing to or detracting from its effectiveness. The combination of fonts may create a harmonious, contrasting, or conflicting design, as shown in Figure 2.4. The harmonious and contrasting designs shown in documents A and B are desirable, whereas the conflicting design shown in document C is not.

A harmonious design is calm and comfortable, although not particularly exciting. This makes it well-suited for more traditional documents, such as formal invitations. A harmonious design is created using one font with different effects applied to it. Other design elements (borders, graphics, and symbols) with the same qualities as the chosen font may also be used to enhance the design.

Figure 2.4 Comparing Harmonious, Conflicting, and Contrasting Font Designs

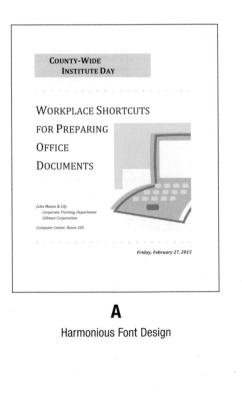

A

Harmonious Font Design

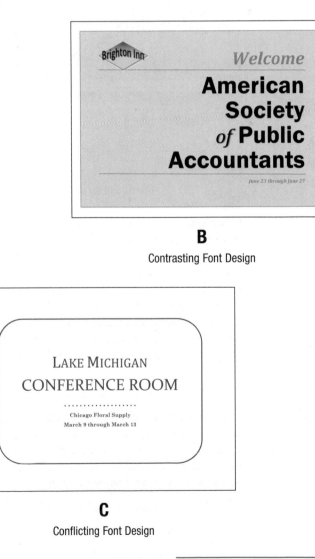

B

Contrasting Font Design

C

Conflicting Font Design

Contrasting design is created by using fonts that are very different from one another but still complementary. Achieve contrasting design by using font pairs that are thick and thin, dark and light, sans serif and serif, plain and ornate, or set in two different colors or sizes, as shown in Figure 2.5. Using a contrasting design helps to create a bold, interesting look that draws the reader in and holds his or her interest.

Conflicting design is created when you choose two or more fonts that look too similar. The fonts are different, but not different enough to easily tell them apart. Avoid using conflicting fonts in your documents.

Additionally, remember to use fonts that complement the message of your document. Figure 2.6 displays examples of unique fonts that may be well suited to particular applications.

Figure 2.5 Creating Interesting Designs with Fonts

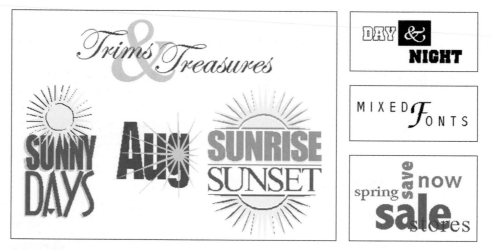

Figure 2.6 Matching Fonts to Your Message

Sample	Font Name
Alleycat Seafood Restaurant	Alleycat
CARIBBEAN CRUISE	BERMUDA SOLID
South of the Border	Chilada ICG Uno
Wedding Invitation	Calligrapher
Casper the Ghost	Chiller
Kids on Campus	Curlz MT
Certificate of Completion	Diploma
COMPUTER SEMINAR	NEWTRON ICG
LINE DANCING CLASS	COTTONWOOD
RED PAPERCLIPS	PAPERCLIP
Camp Sandy Feet	KidTYPEPaint
Four Corners Art Gallery	Matura MT Script Capitals

Using Fonts in Windows 8

When software is loaded on your computer, any fonts associated with that software are loaded into Windows 8. You can view all the fonts that have been loaded into your computer by displaying the Control Panel, clicking the *Appearance and Personalization* category, and then clicking the *Fonts* option.

If your printer does not support a font or font size you are using to format your text, Word may substitute the closest possible font and font size. You can view the substitution fonts in the Font Substitution dialog box (shown in Figure 2.7) by displaying the Word Options dialog box, clicking the *Advanced* option in the left panel, and then clicking the Font Substitution button in the *Show document content* section. *Note: If an exercise in this textbook calls for a particular font that is not available on your computer, simply substitute another font.*

◀ DTP POINTER

Substitute a different font if a particular font is not available.

Embedding Fonts in Word

Embedding fonts in your Word documents is a good way to make sure that they will look the same when viewed on other computers. Embedding a font attaches the associated font file to the document so that the font will display on computers that do not contain that particular font file. To embed fonts in Word, display the Word Options dialog box, click the *Save* option in the left panel, and then insert a check mark next to the desired embedding option, as shown in Figure 2.8. Note that embedding fonts can increase your document's file size and may not work for some commercially restricted fonts.

Figure 2.7 Viewing the Font Substitution Dialog Box

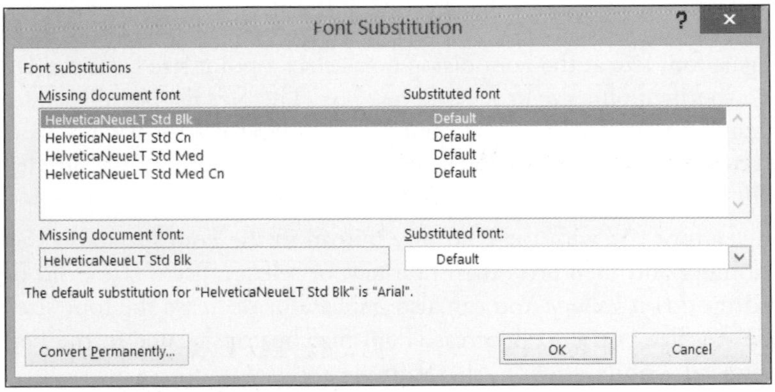

Figure 2.8 Embedding Fonts in Word Documents

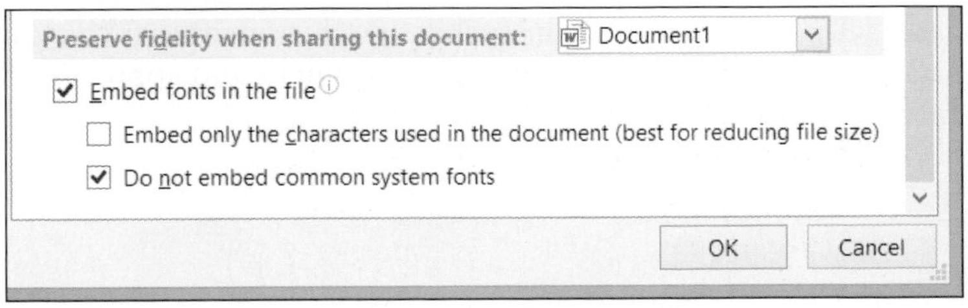

Changing Default Font Formatting

Word documents are based on a template that applies default formatting. For Word 2013, this default formatting includes 11-point Calibri font, 1.08 line spacing, and 8 points of spacing after paragraphs (a press of the Enter key).

To change the default font, click the Font group dialog box launcher to display the Font dialog box. At the Font dialog box, select the font you want to use as the default and then click the Set As Default button located in the bottom left corner of the dialog box. At the dialog box that displays, determine whether you want to set the new default font for just the current document or for all documents created based on the Normal.dotm template and then click OK. Font selections made within a document through the Font dialog box will override the default font settings for the current document only.

Modifying Font Elements

You can modify text formatted in the default font by changing the font, font size, font style, and text effects; applying a theme; changing theme fonts, theme colors, and theme effects; using styles or style sets; inserting WordArt; and adjusting character spacing and kerning characters.

Changing Fonts, Font Styles, and Font Sizes

You can select fonts at the Font button drop-down gallery in the Font group on the HOME tab, at the Font dialog box, or at the Mini toolbar that displays when you select or right-click any text in a document. As you scroll through the list of fonts in the Font button drop-down gallery, the live preview feature displays the selected text with the font applied.

Font

To change a font size at the Font dialog box, select a point size from the *Size* list box, or type a specific point size in the *Size* text box. The *Size* list box displays common increments ranging from 8 to 72 points, but you may type a point size not listed. For instance, to change the font size to 250 points, select the number in the *Size* text box and then type *250*.

Font Size

To change a font size with the Font Size button in the Font group on the HOME tab, type a number and then press the Enter key, or select a point size from the Font Size button drop-down gallery. You can also increase or decrease the font size by clicking the Increase Font Size button or Decrease Font Size button located in the Font group, or by pressing Ctrl + Shift + > or Ctrl + Shift + <.

Increase Font Size

To change the typestyle at the Font dialog box, select a font style in the *Font style* list box. As you select different typefaces, the list of available typestyles in the *Font style* list box changes.

Decrease Font Size

In Exercise 2.1A, you will open a conference sign document that contains some existing formatting. You will then add text to the document and apply font formatting to enhance the appearance of the document.

1. Open **Sign.docx** from your Chapter02 folder. (The document has been formatted with a text box, a line shape, and a logo. The line spacing has been changed to single, and the 8 points of spacing after paragraphs has been removed.)
2. Save the document with the name **C02-E01-Sign**.
3. Click the Show/Hide ¶ button in the Paragraph group on the HOME tab to turn on the display of nonprinting characters.
4. Insert a right tab on the horizontal ruler by completing the following steps:
   a. Click immediately to the left of the paragraph symbol inside the text box to position the insertion point.
   b. Make sure the horizontal ruler is visible. (If it is not visible, click the VIEW tab and then click the *Ruler* check box in the Show group to insert a check mark.)
   c. Click the Alignment button at the left side of the ruler until the right tab symbol displays.
   d. Position the arrow pointer on the 8.25-inch mark on the horizontal ruler and then click the left mouse button.

5. Type text in the text box (refer to Figure 2.9 on page 60) by completing the following steps:
   a. Press the Enter key three times.
   b. Press the Tab key, type **Welcome**, and then press the Enter key twice.
   c. Press the Tab key, type **American**, and then press the Enter key once.
   d. Press the Tab key, type **Society**, and then press the Enter key once.
   e. Press the Tab key, type **of Public**, and then press the Enter key once. (You may need to change the *o* in *of* back to lowercase.)
   f. Press the Tab key, type **Accountants**, and then press the Enter key twice.
   g. Press the Tab key, type **June 23 through June 27**, and then press the Enter key twice.

6. Apply font formatting to text by completing the following steps:
   a. Select the word *Welcome*. (Do not select the paragraph symbol.)
   b. Change the font to 48-point Cambria and then apply bold and italic formatting.
   c. Select the text *June 23 through June 27*.
   d. Change the font to 14-point Cambria and apply bold and italic formatting.
   e. Select the text *American Society of Public Accountants*.
   f. Change the font to 66-point Franklin Gothic Demi. ***Hint: Type the value in the Font Size button text box.***
7. With the text *American Society of Public Accountants* still selected, change the line spacing by completing the following steps:
   a. Click the Paragraph group dialog box launcher.

b. At the Paragraph dialog box, click the down-pointing arrow at the right side of the *Line spacing* option box and then click *Exactly* at the drop-down list.

c. Select the current measurement in the *At* measurement box and then type **66**.

d. Click OK.

8. Copy the red horizontal line by completing the following steps:

a. Select the red horizontal line below *Welcome*.

b. Press Ctrl + C to create a copy of the line.

c. Press Ctrl + V to paste the copy of the line.

d. With the new copy of the line selected, drag the line so it is positioned below *Accountants*, as shown in Figure 2.9. You will make further formatting changes to this file in Exercise 2.1B.

9. Click the Show/Hide ¶ button in the Paragraph group on the HOME tab to turn off the display of nonprinting characters.

10. Save **C02-E01-Sign.docx**.

Figure 2.9 **Conference Sign Created in Exercises 2.1A and 2.1B**

Changing Font Color

Another way to modify fonts is by applying color. You may apply font colors to text by clicking the Font Color button in the Font group on the HOME tab. While the Font Color button drop-down gallery displays two groups of colors (*Theme Colors* and *Standard Colors*, as shown in Figure 2.10), you can access a wider variety of colors by clicking the *More Colors* option to open the Colors dialog box. At the Colors dialog box, click the Standard tab to display 124 colors and 15 shades of gray, as shown in Figure 2.11. ***Hint: If you choose* Automatic *at the Font Color button drop-down gallery and then change the background of the document to black, the text color changes automatically to white.***

At the Colors dialog box with the Custom tab selected, you may customize your font in any of 16 million different colors. You may create your own custom colors by either choosing the RGB or HSL color models, as shown in Figure 2.12 on page 62. To create a custom color using the RGB model, adjust the values in the *Red*, *Green*, and *Blue* measurement boxes by entering values between 0 and 255 or by using the up- or down-pointing arrows at the right of the measurement boxes. Colors in the HSL model are adjusted using three factors: the ***luminescence***, which is the brightness of the color; the ***hue***, which is the color itself; and the ***saturation***, which is the color's intensity. Adjust the values in the same way you would adjust the values in the RGB model. If the document you are working in contains an object or text with a color you want to use, copy the color from one object to another using the Format Painter.

Applying Underlining

To apply underlining to text, use the Underline button in the Font group on the HOME tab. To change the underline style, click the Underline button arrow and then click an option at the drop-down gallery. To apply or change underlining at the Font dialog box, click the down-pointing arrow at the right side of the *Underline Style* option box arrow and then click an option. Note that underlining is considered to be a somewhat dated method of emphasizing text in desktop publications. Try enhancing your text with italics, bold, all caps, small caps, or a different font size or color instead.

Font Color

luminescence
The brightness of a color

hue
The color itself

saturation
The intensity of a color

Format Painter

Underline

Figure 2.10 Using the Font Color Drop-down Gallery

Figure 2.11 Using the Standard Tab at the Colors Dialog Box

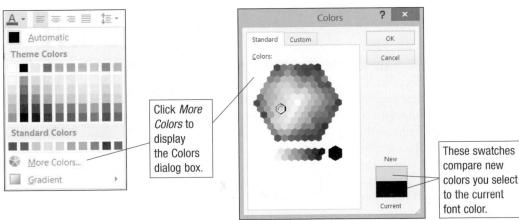

Figure 2.12 Customizing Colors Using Color Models

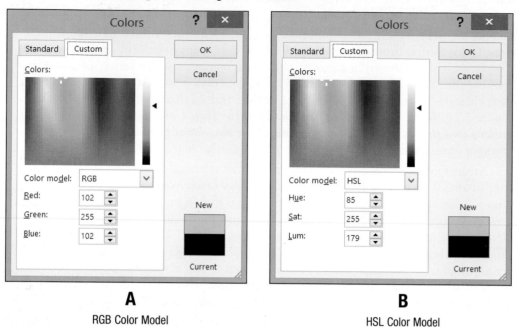

A

RGB Color Model

B

HSL Color Model

Applying Font Effects

DTP POINTER

Use italics or small caps to emphasize text instead of all caps or underline.

The *Effects* section of the Font dialog box contains a variety of formatting options, including *Strikethrough*, *Double strikethrough*, *Superscript*, *Subscript*, *Small caps*, *All caps*, and *Hidden*. To choose an effect, click the check box to insert a check mark. The text in the *Preview* section of the dialog box will illustrate the change. If the text you want to format already exists, select the text before applying these formatting options.

Click the Text Effects button at the bottom of the Font dialog box to open the Format Text Effects dialog box as shown in Figure 2.13. This dialog box provides more options for applying text effects.

Consider using keyboard shortcuts to apply font formatting. For instance, press Ctrl + Shift + A for all caps; press Ctrl + Shift + K for small caps; or press Shift + F3 to toggle capitalization. To access a detailed list of keyboard shortcuts, click the Microsoft Word Help button (the question mark symbol in the upper right corner above the ribbon) and then enter *keyboard shortcuts for Word* in the search text box. Display the article that contains a list of shortcuts and then print it for easy access.

Text Effects and Typography

Clear All Formatting

You can modify the look of your text by changing its fill, by changing its outline, or by adding effects such as shadows, reflections, or glows. To add an effect to text, select the text that you want to enhance, and then click the Text Effects and Typography button in the Font group on the HOME tab. At the drop-down gallery, click one of the preformatted effects at the top, or point to a category to open a side menu where you can apply or adjust a specific effect or aspect of the text, as shown in Figure 2.14. The font colors and effects vary with the theme selected. If you want to remove an effect from text, select the text and then click the Clear All Formatting button in the Font group on the HOME tab.

In Exercise 2.1B, you will continue to enhance the conference sign you started in Exercise 2.1A by applying font colors, adjusting font sizes, and applying font effects.

Figure 2.13 Using the Format Text Effects Dialog Box

Figure 2.14 Using the Text Effects and Typography Drop-down Gallery

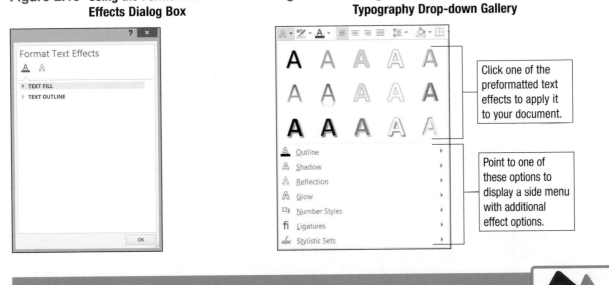

Click one of the preformatted text effects to apply it to your document.

Point to one of these options to display a side menu with additional effect options.

Exercise 2.1B Applying Font Colors and Effects to a Conference Sign

Part 2 of 2

1. With **C02-E01-Sign.docx** open, change font color by completing the following steps:
   a. Select the text *Welcome*.
   b. Click the Font Color button arrow.
   c. Click the *White, Background 1, Darker 50%* color (first column, last row in the *Theme Colors* section).
   d. With the text selected, click the Format Painter button in the Clipboard group on the HOME tab.
   e. Select the text *June 23 through June 27*. (This applies the same gray color you applied to *Welcome*.)

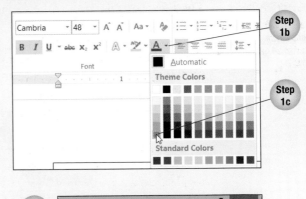

2. Change font color at the Colors dialog box by completing the following steps:
   a. Select the text *American Society of Public Accountants*.
   b. Click the Font Color button arrow.
   c. Click *More Colors* at the drop-down gallery.
   d. At the Colors dialog box, click the Custom tab.
   e. Select the current number in the *Red* measurement box and then type **30**.
   f. Press the Tab key (this selects the current measurement in the *Green* measurement box) and then type **90**.
   g. Press the Tab key (this selects the current measurement in the *Blue* measurement box) and then type **160**.
   h. Click OK.

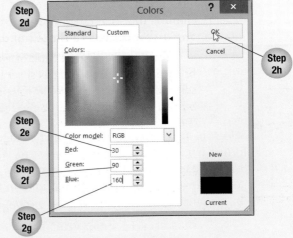

3. Apply text effects and change font color by completing the following steps:

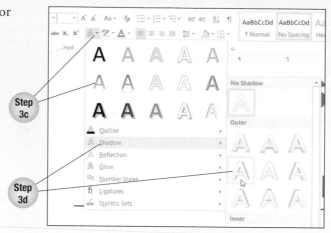

a. Select the word *of*.
b. Change the font to 54-point Cambria and then apply italic formatting.
c. Click the Text Effects and Typography button in the Font group on the HOME tab and then click the *Gradient Fill - Gray* option (first column, second row).
d. Click the Text Effects and Typography button, point to *Shadow* at the drop-down gallery, and then click the *Offset Right* option (first column, second row in the *Outer* section).
e. Click the Font Color button arrow and then click *More Colors* at the drop-down gallery.
f. At the Colors dialog box, click the Standard tab.
g. Click the third red color from the right in the bottom row of the honeycomb.
h. Click OK.

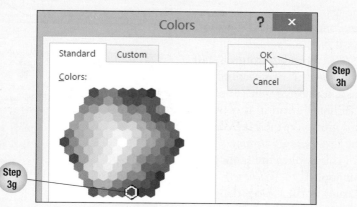

4. Click the Show/Hide ¶ button to turn on the display of nonprinting characters, position the insertion point immediately to the left of the second paragraph mark under the text *June 23 through June 27*, and then complete the following steps:
a. Set a left tab at the 0.5-inch mark on the horizontal ruler.
b. Press the Tab key, type **Sponsored by**, and then press the Enter key.
c. Press the Tab key and then type **Banks&Wells**. (Do not add a space before or after the & symbol.)
5. Select the text *Sponsored by* and then change the font to 12-point Cambria, apply bold italic formatting, and change the font color to *White, Background 1, Darker 50%*.
6. Select the text *Banks&Wells* and then make the following changes:
a. Change the font to 12-point Franklin Gothic Demi.
b. Change the font color to *Blue, Accent 1, Darker 50%* (fifth column, bottom row in the *Theme Colors* section).

7. Select the *&* symbol in the text *Banks&Wells* and then make the following changes:

   a. Click the Shading button arrow in the Paragraph group on the HOME tab and then click the *Blue, Accent 1, Darker 50%* option at the drop-down gallery (fifth column, bottom row in the *Theme Colors* section).

   b. Click the Font Color button arrow and then click the *White, Background 1* color (first column, first row in the *Theme Colors* section).

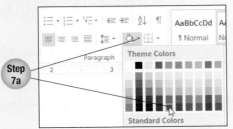

8. Apply a red border and a texture to the text box by completing the following steps:

   a. Click the border of the text box to select the text box (the border will turn to a solid line when it has been selected).

   b. Click the DRAWING TOOLS FORMAT tab.

   c. Click the Shape Outline button arrow in the Shape Styles group and then click the *Dark Red* color (first option in the *Standard Colors* section).

   d. Click the Shape Outline button arrow, point to *Weight*, and then click *1½ pt* at the drop-down gallery.

   e. Click the Shape Fill button arrow, point to *Texture*, and then click the *Recycled paper* option (second column, fourth row).

   f. Click the Show/Hide ¶ button to turn off the display of nonprinting characters.

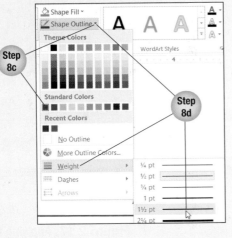

9. Compare your document to the document shown in Figure 2.9 on page 60 and make any necessary changes.

10. Save, print, and then close **C02-E01-Sign.docx**.

Changing Fonts Using Themes

As you have learned, Word 2013 makes it easy to apply font formatting to a portion of selected text. The Themes button in the Document Formatting group on the DESIGN tab makes it just as easy to apply a full set of formatting options, including font formatting, to an entire document. The Themes button drop-down gallery is shown in Figure 2.15 on page 66. The default theme in Word 2013 is the Office theme.

As you learned in Chapter 1, a theme can include a color scheme (a set of colors) as shown in Figure 2.16 on page 66, a font scheme (a set of heading and body text fonts) as shown in Figure 2.17, and an effects scheme (a set of lines and fill effects) as shown in Figure 2.18. The theme defines the major and secondary fonts used in the document, the color palette for the document, and the effects used for shapes, charts, and graphics inserted into the document. By basing the content of a document on the same theme, you can help ensure a consistent look and easily make changes to the content without having to spend time reformatting. Keep in mind that you can customize each of the themes by selecting different color combinations, font combinations, and effects.

Theme Colors

Theme Effects

Theme Fonts

If the Themes button is dimmed and not accessible, you may need to convert the document from compatibility mode to the newest format by clicking the FILE tab, clicking the Convert button, and then clicking OK at the prompt that displays.

Figure 2.15 Accessing the Themes Gallery

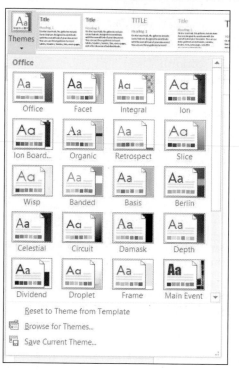

Figure 2.16 Applying Color Schemes

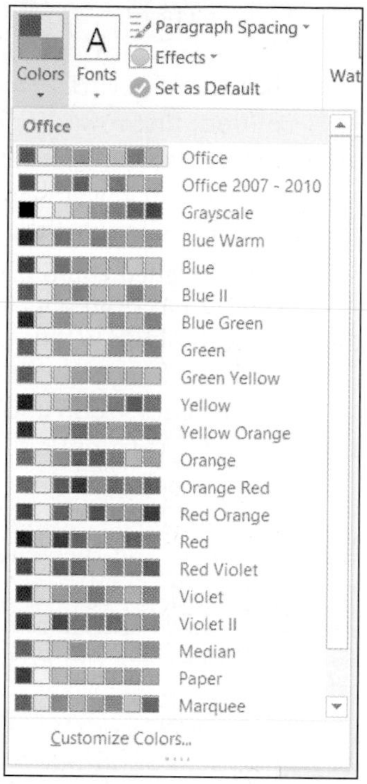

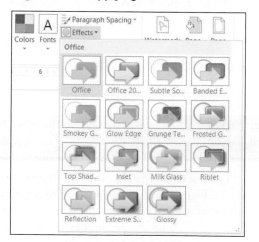

Figure 2.17 Applying Font Schemes

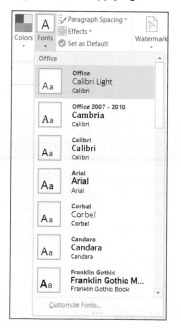

Figure 2.18 Applying Effects Schemes

Applying Styles and Style Sets

As you learned in Chapter 1, styles are another way to ensure consistent formatting throughout a document. At the Styles gallery, you can choose styles for titles, headings, subheadings, and body text, among other text elements. To apply a style from the Styles gallery, select the text to which you want to apply the style and then click the desired style in the Styles gallery on the HOME tab. When you click the More button in the lower right corner of the gallery, it will expand to display more style options, as shown in Figure 2.19. Additionally, you may display the Styles task pane by clicking the Styles task pane launcher in the bottom right corner of the Styles group or by pressing Alt + Ctrl + Shift + S.

If the style that you want does not appear in the Styles gallery, press Ctrl + Shift + S to open the Apply Styles window. Click the down-pointing arrow at the right of the *Style Name* option box and then click the desired style at the drop-down list.

Style sets are predesigned combinations of styles, colors, and fonts. To apply a style set, click the DESIGN tab and then click a style set in the style set gallery, which displays in the Document Formatting group. To expand the style set gallery, click the More button in the lower right corner of the gallery. Live preview enables you to view how each style set would look if applied to the document.

In Exercise 2.2, you will apply consistent, uniform formatting to a medical plan document by using styles, style sets, and themes. You will then adjust the theme colors and theme fonts to best fit the document.

Figure 2.19 Applying Styles at the Styles Gallery on the HOME tab

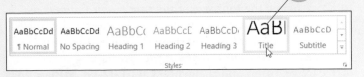

Exercise 2.2 Applying Styles, Style Sets, and Themes to a Medical Plan Document

1. Open **GCMPlan.docx** from your Chapter02 folder and then save the document with the name **C02-E02-GCMPlan**.
2. With the insertion point positioned at the beginning of the title *Grant County Medical Plan*, click the *Title* style option in the Styles group on the HOME tab.
3. Click anywhere in the heading *SECTION 1: OVERVIEW* and then click the *Heading 1* style option in the Styles group. (The remaining headings and subheadings in the document already have styles applied.)

4. Apply a style set by completing the following steps:
    a. Click the DESIGN tab.
    b. Click the *Centered* style set in the Document Formatting group. ***Hint: Hover the mouse over each thumbnail to see the name of the style set.***

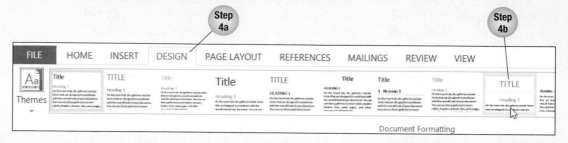

5. Change the theme colors by clicking the Theme Colors button in the Document Formatting group on the DESIGN tab and then clicking the *Green* option at the drop-down gallery.

6. Change the style set by clicking the *Lines (Simple)* style set option in the Document Formatting group. ***Hint: You may need to click the More button in the Document Formatting group to display the* Lines (Simple) *option.***

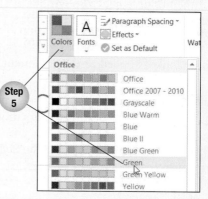

7. Change the theme fonts so that headings are set in a sans serif typeface and body text appears in a serif typeface by completing the following steps:
    a. Click the Theme Fonts button in the Document Formatting group.
    b. Scroll down the drop-down gallery and then click the *Century Gothic-Palatino Linotype* option.
    c. Select the title *Grant County Medical Plan* and then change the font size to 28 points.

8. Save and then print **C02-E02-GCMPlan.docx**.

9. Change the theme by clicking the Themes button in the Document Formatting group on the DESIGN tab and then clicking the *Dividend* option at the drop-down gallery.

10. Change the theme colors by clicking the Theme Colors button in the Document Formatting group and then clicking the *Blue II* option at the drop-down gallery.

11. Change the theme fonts by clicking the Theme Fonts button in the Document Formatting group, scrolling down the drop-down gallery, and then clicking the *Calibri-Cambria* option.

12. Change the font size of the title *Grant County Medical Plan* to 36 points and then apply the small caps effect. ***Hint: Apply small caps at the Font dialog box with the Font tab selected.***

13. Save, print, and then close **C02-E02-GCMPlan.docx**.

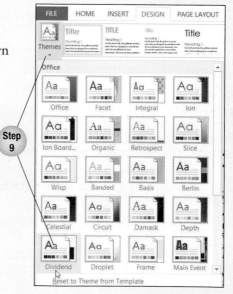

Adding Symbols and Special Characters to a Document

Symbols and special characters add interest and originality to documents. Sometimes, it is the small touches that make a difference, such as adding a symbol (❖) at the end of an article in a newsletter, enlarging a symbol (ϓ) and using it as a graphic element on a page, or adding a special character (©) to clarify text. Interesting symbols are found in such fonts as (normal text), Wingdings, Wingdings 2, Wingdings 3, and Webdings. Examples of special characters include an em dash (—), en dash (–), copyright symbol (©), registered trademark symbol (®), ellipses (. . .), and nonbreaking hyphens.

To insert a symbol, click the Symbol button in the Symbols group on the INSERT tab and then select one of the symbols displayed in the drop-down list or click *More Symbols* at the bottom of the drop-down list to display the Symbol dialog box. At the Symbol dialog box, shown in Figure 2.20, select the Symbols tab, select the desired font, and then double-click the symbol or click the symbol once, click the Insert button, and then click the Close button (or press Esc). To insert a special character from the Symbol dialog box, click the Special Characters tab and then insert the desired character in the document using one of the methods described above.

Recently used symbols display toward the bottom of the Symbol dialog box for easy access. Another way to quickly access a symbol you use frequently is to write down the character code for that symbol and then enter that number in the *Character code* text box near the bottom of the Symbols tab in the Symbol dialog box when you need to insert it.

◀ DTP POINTER

Special characters add visual interest to a document.

Ω

Symbol

Figure 2.20 **Inserting a Symbol**

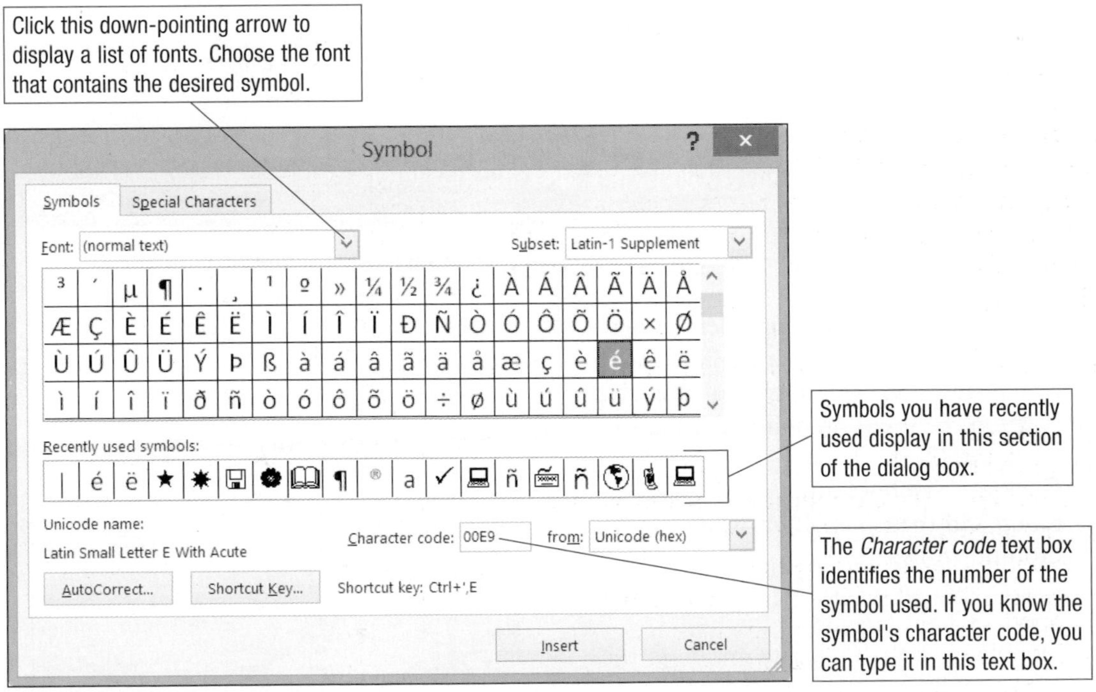

Click this down-pointing arrow to display a list of fonts. Choose the font that contains the desired symbol.

Symbols you have recently used display in this section of the dialog box.

The *Character code* text box identifies the number of the symbol used. If you know the symbol's character code, you can type it in this text box.

Creating Em and En Dashes

An ***em dash*** (—) is used to indicate a pause in speech and an ***en dash*** indicates a continuation, such as in the ranges 116–133 and January–March. An em dash is generally the width of a typeface's uppercase *M* and an en dash is the width of a lowercase *n*. Besides inserting em and en dashes using the Special Characters tab of the Symbol dialog box, you may insert an em dash from the keyboard by pressing Alt + Ctrl + Num - (minus key on the numbers pad) or an en dash by pressing Ctrl + Num - . Do not include spaces before or after en dashes and em dashes. Additionally, the AutoCorrect feature includes an option that will automatically create em dashes. To create an em dash, type the word, type two hyphens, type the next word, and then press the spacebar. When you press the spacebar, AutoCorrect automatically converts the two hyphens to an em dash.

Using Smart Quotes

DTP POINTER

Use straight quotation marks to indicate inches or feet.

In typesetting, the *tail* of the punctuation mark extends upward for the open quotation mark (") and downward for the close quotation mark ("). Straight quotes should be used only to indicate inches (") or feet ('). Word's Smart Quotes feature, which is active by default, will automatically choose the quote style that is appropriate.

To turn the Smart Quotes feature on or off, click the FILE tab, click *Options*, click *Proofing* in the left panel, click the AutoCorrect Options button, click the AutoFormat As You Type tab, and then click the *"Straight quotes" with "smart quotes"* check box to insert or remove the check mark. In addition, symbols and special characters may be added to the AutoCorrect feature, which will automatically insert the desired symbol when using a specific keyboard command. For example, if you type *(c)*, AutoCorrect will automatically change the three characters to the © special character. Symbols may also be copied to the Clipboard and pasted when needed.

In Exercise 2.3, you will practice adding special characters to a sales flyer.

Exercise 2.3 Formatting a Sales Flyer with Special Characters

1. Open **CCarpet.docx** from your Chapter02 folder and then save the document with the name **C02-E03-CCarpet**.
2. Click in the text box in the upper left corner of the document and then type **Create a comfortable, warm, and inviting home with an Adana area rug.**
3. Insert a registered trademark symbol after *Adana* by completing the following steps:
   a. Position the insertion point after the word *Adana*.
   b. Click the INSERT tab.
   c. Click the Symbol button in the Symbols group and then click *More Symbols* at the drop-down list.
   d. At the Symbol dialog box, click the Special Characters tab.
   e. Double-click the *Registered* option in the *Character* list box.
   f. Click the Close button to close the dialog box.

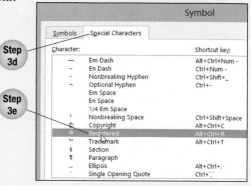

---

4. Delete the *o* in *Camino* and then insert the *ó* symbol (the letter *o* with an acute accent) by completing the following steps:
   a. Select the *o* in *Camino* in the text box at the bottom of the document and then press the Delete key.
   b. Click the Symbol button in the Symbols group and then click *More Symbols* at the drop-down list.
   c. At the Symbol dialog box, make sure that *(normal text)* is selected in the *Font* option box. If *(normal text)* does not display, click the down-pointing arrow at the right of the *Font* option box and then click *(normal text)* at the drop-down list.
   d. Scroll down to approximately the tenth row in the symbol list box and then double-click the *ó* symbol (Character code 00F3).
   e. Click the Close button.

5. Turn off smart quotes by completing the following steps:
   a. Click the FILE tab and then click *Options*.
   b. At the Word Options dialog box, click *Proofing* in the left panel.
   c. Click the AutoCorrect Options button.
   d. At the AutoCorrect dialog box, click the AutoFormat As You Type tab.
   e. Click the *"Straight quotes"* with *"smart quotes"* check box to remove the check mark.
   f. Click OK.
   g. Click OK to close the Word Options dialog box.

6. Click to the right of the first bullet below the *Rectangle sizes:* heading and then type **4' x 6'**.

7. Click to the right of the second bullet below the *Rectangle sizes:* heading and then type **6' x 8'6"**.

8. Click to the right of the third bullet below the *Rectangle sizes:* heading and then type **8' x 9'6"**.

9. Replace the hyphen between *10 a.m.* and *5 p.m.* with an en dash by completing the following steps:
   a. Select the hyphen between *10 a.m.* and *5 p.m.* below the *Store hours:* heading.
   b. Click the Symbol button in the Symbols group on the INSERT tab and then click *More Symbols* at the drop-down list.
   c. At the Symbol dialog box, click the Special Characters tab.
   d. Double-click the *En Dash* option in the *Character* list box.
   e. Click the Close button.

10. Select the hyphen between *9 a.m.* and *6 p.m.* and then replace it with an en dash.

11. Select the hyphen between *Mon.* and *Fri.* and then replace it with an en dash.

12. Turn Smart Quotes back on by completing Steps 5a to 5d, inserting a check mark in the *"Straight quotes"* with *"smart quotes"* check box at the AutoCorrect dialog box, and then clicking OK twice.

13. Save, print, and then close **C02-E03-CCarpet.docx**.

Applying Advanced Font Formatting

Word 2013 offers advanced font formatting features that can improve the appearance of text. Access advanced font formatting options at the Font dialog box with the Advanced tab selected. At this dialog box, you can specify character spacing for text, apply OpenType features, and apply text effects to selected text.

Adjusting Character Spacing

Each typeface is designed with a specific amount of space between characters. This character spacing may be changed with options at the Font dialog box with the Advanced tab selected, as shown in Figure 2.21. Use the *Scale* option to stretch or compress text horizontally as a percentage of the current size (from 1 to 600). Expand or condense the spacing between characters with the *Spacing* option. Choose either the *Expanded* or *Condensed* option and then enter the desired point amount in the *By* measurement box. Raise or lower selected text in relation to the baseline with the *Position* option. Choose either the *Raised* or *Lowered* option and then enter the point amount in the *By* measurement box.

kerning

Decreasing or increasing the horizontal space between specific character pairs

You can adjust the spacing between certain character pairs (referred to as **kerning**) by selecting your text and then inserting a check mark in the *Kerning* check box. Kerning positions certain character combinations closer together to improve readability and help the eye move along the text. Character pairs that are commonly kerned by automatic kerning include AV, TA, Ty, Vi, and WA.

Applying OpenType Features

Word 2013 offers advanced OpenType features at the Font dialog box with the Advanced tab selected (see Figure 2.22) that you can use to enhance the visual appeal of your text. Available OpenType features include ligatures, number spacing, number forms, and stylistic sets.

Applying Ligatures

ligatures

Letters that have been attached to create a single character

A *ligature* is a combination of characters tied together into a single letter. OpenType fonts support four ligature options:

- Standard Only: Standard ligatures are designed to enhance readability. For example, if you use the Candara font, the standard ligatures *fi*, *ff*, and *fl* appear, as shown in the first image in Figure 2.23.
- Standard and Contextual: These ligatures are designed to enhance readability by providing better joining behavior between the characters that make up the ligature, as shown in the middle image in Figure 2.23.

Figure 2.21 Adjusting Character Spacing on the Advanced Tab of the Font Dialog Box

Use the *Scale* option box to stretch or compress text horizontally as a percentage of the current size.

Use the *Position* option box to raise or lower selected text in relation to the baseline.

Turn on *Kerning* to adjust the spacing between character pairs.

Use the *Spacing* option box to expand or condense spacing between characters.

Figure 2.22 Applying OpenType Features at the Advanced Tab of the Font Dialog Box

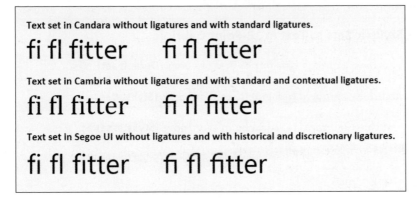

Applies the ligatures most typographers use for that font such as the letter *f*

Applies a combination of standard and contextual ligatures commonly used for that font

Provides fine-tuning of letters based on the surrounding characters

Applies ligatures to create a "period" effect

Applies all ligatures for a font

OpenType Features

Ligatures: None

None
Standard Only
Standard and Contextual
Historical and Discretionary
All

Number spacing:

Number forms:

Stylistic sets:

☐ Use Contextual Alternates

Preview

Palatino Linotype

This is a TrueType font. This font will be used on both printer and screen.

Set As Default   Text Effects...   OK   Cancel

Figure 2.23 Comparing Text with and without Ligatures

Text set in Candara without ligatures and with standard ligatures.

fi fl fitter   fi fl fitter

Text set in Cambria without ligatures and with standard and contextual ligatures.

fi fl fitter   fi fl fitter

Text set in Segoe UI without ligatures and with historical and discretionary ligatures.

fi fl fitter   fi fl fitter

- Historical and Discretionary: These ligatures are designed to be ornamental and are not meant to improve readability. Historical and discretionary ligatures are not commonly used but are available to create a historical or "period" effect, as shown in the bottom image in Figure 2.23.
- All: All ligature combinations will be applied to the selected text.

Adjusting Number Spacing

The *Number spacing* option in the *OpenType Features* section of the Font dialog box with the Advanced tab selected is set at *Default*, which means that spacing between numbers is determined by the font designer. Choosing the *Proportional* option allows a different amount of space for each number; for example, *1* is narrower than *5*, as shown in Figure 2.24A on page 74. Three Microsoft fonts—Candara, Constantia, and Corbel—use proportional number spacing by default. Use the *Tabular* option if you want each number to be allotted the same amount of space, as shown in Figure 2.24B. This is recommended when you want numbers in columns to align vertically. The Cambria, Calibri, and Consolas fonts use tabular spacing by default.

Adjusting Number Forms

The *Number forms* option is also set at *Default*. Change this to *Lining* if you want all numbers to be the same height and not extend below the baseline, as shown in Figure 2.24C. This is recommended for numbers in tables and forms. The Cambria, Calibri, and Consolas fonts use the *Lining* option by default. Choose the *Old-style*

Figure 2.24 Using Number Spacing Options

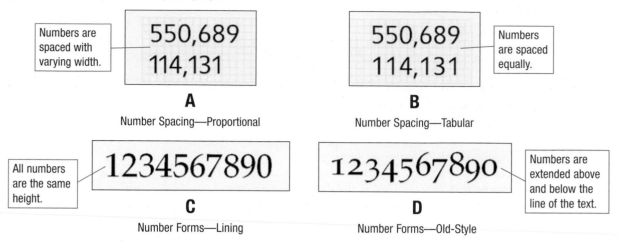

A
Number Spacing—Proportional

Numbers are spaced with varying width.

B
Number Spacing—Tabular

Numbers are spaced equally.

C
Number Forms—Lining

All numbers are the same height.

D
Number Forms—Old-Style

Numbers are extended above and below the line of the text.

Figure 2.25 Applying Stylistic Sets and Contextual Alternates to Text

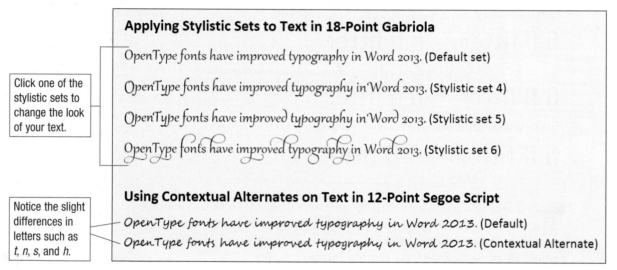

Click one of the stylistic sets to change the look of your text.

Notice the slight differences in letters such as *t*, *n*, *s*, and *h*.

Applying Stylistic Sets to Text in 18-Point Gabriola

OpenType fonts have improved typography in Word 2013. (Default set)

OpenType fonts have improved typography in Word 2013. (Stylistic set 4)

OpenType fonts have improved typography in Word 2013. (Stylistic set 5)

OpenType fonts have improved typography in Word 2013. (Stylistic set 6)

Using Contextual Alternates on Text in 12-Point Segoe Script

OpenType fonts have improved typography in Word 2013. (Default)

OpenType fonts have improved typography in Word 2013. (Contextual Alternate)

option when you want the numbers to extend above and below the baseline, as shown in Figure 2.24D. Three fonts that use the *Old-style* option are Candara, Constantia, and Corbel.

Applying Stylistic Sets

In addition to the previously mentioned OpenType features, you can also apply additional formatting using stylistic sets. Apply a stylistic set to change the appearance of text with a font applied, as shown at the top of Figure 2.25. Use the Text Effects and Typography button drop-down gallery or the Font dialog box with the Advanced tab selected to change the stylistic set.

Another adjustment that may be applied to fine-tune text is the *Use Contextual Alternates* option. Use this feature to give your script font a more natural and flowing appearance, as shown at the bottom of Figure 2.25. Notice the slight differences in letters such as *t*, *n*, *s*, and *h*.

Keep in mind that not all fonts contain ligature combinations, number spacing and forms, stylistic sets, or contextual alternates. You will need to experiment with fonts to find the ones that provide these features.

In Exercise 2.4, you will format a corporate event invitation by applying advanced font formatting features.

Exercise 2.4 Formatting a Corporate Event Invitation

1. Open **ORInvitation.docx** from your Chapter02 folder and then save the document with the name **C02-E04-ORInvitation**.
2. Change the theme colors by completing the following steps:
   a. Click the DESIGN tab.
   b. Click the Theme Colors button in the Document Formatting group.
   c. Click the *Red Violet* option at the drop-down gallery.
3. Select the first two lines of text (*Europe, Middle East*, and *Africa Regional Dinner*) and then make the following changes:
   a. Click the Font group dialog box launcher in the Font group on the HOME tab.
   b. At the Font dialog box with the Font tab selected, scroll down the *Font* list box and then click *Gabriola*. (You can also select the +*Body* text that displays in the option box at the top of the list box, type the letter **g** to display fonts that begin with *g*, and then click *Gabriola* in the list box.)
   c. Select the current measurement in the *Size* option box and then type **42**.
   d. Click the Advanced tab.
   e. Click the down-pointing arrow at the right side of the *Scale* option box and then click *90%* at the drop-down list.
   f. Click the down-pointing arrow at the right side of the *Spacing* option box and then click *Condensed* at the drop-down list.
   g. Click in the *Kerning for fonts* check box to insert a check mark.
   h. Select the current measurement in the measurement box that displays to the right of the *Kerning for fonts* option and then type **14**.
   i. Click the down-pointing arrow at the right side of the *Stylistic sets* option box, scroll down the drop-down list that displays, and then click *6*.
   j. Click OK to close the dialog box.
   k. With the two lines of text still selected, click the Text Effects and Typography button in the Font group on the HOME tab.
   l. Click the *Fill - Pink, Accent 1, Shadow* option at the drop-down gallery (second column, first row).

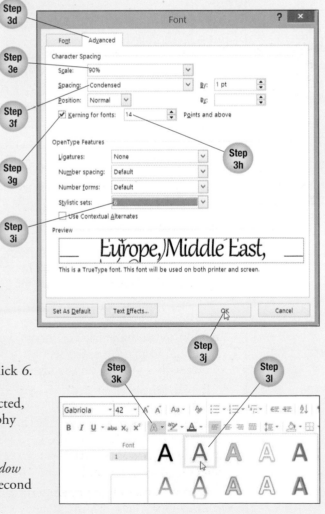

4. Select all of the text except for the last two lines (the text from *Europe, Middle East* through *Sea of Marmara before dinner.*), and then click the Center button in the Paragraph group on the HOME tab.
5. Select the last two lines of text (*Elvan Basaran* and *Managing Partner*) and then click the Align Right button in the Paragraph group.
6. Select the lines of text beginning with *You are invited to join* through *Managing Partner* and then change the font to 16-point Papyrus.
7. Compare your document to the document shown in Figure 2.26.
8. Save, print, and then close **C02-E04-ORInvitation.docx**.

Figure 2.26 Invitation Created in Exercise 2.4

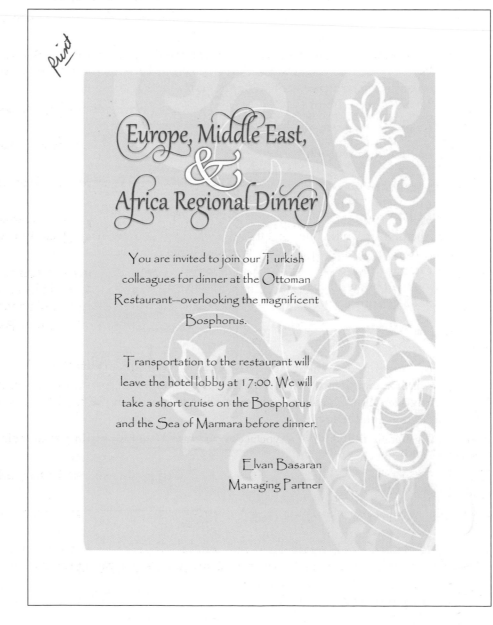

Chapter *Summary*

- The term *typeface* refers to the general design and shape of a set of characters.

- The typeface used in a document helps to establish a particular mood or feeling.

- Characteristics that distinguish one typeface from another include x-height, cap height, height of ascenders, depth of descenders, and serifs.

- A serif is a small stroke on the end of a character. A sans serif typeface does not have serifs.

- Typefaces are either monospaced or proportional. Monospaced typefaces allot the same amount of horizontal space to each character, while proportional typefaces allot a varying amount to each character.

- For text set in a proportional typeface, space once after end-of-sentence punctuation.

- Point size is a vertical measurement and is approximately $1/72$ of an inch. The larger the chosen point size, the larger the characters.

- OpenType fonts support international character sets, cross-platform support between Windows and Macintosh computers, and include advanced typographic features, such as special ligatures (combined characters) and swashes (exaggerated serifs).

- Change the default font of a document by making desired changes at the Font dialog box, clicking the Set As Default button, and then clicking OK at the message that displays.

- Modify fonts in a document with options at the Font button drop-down gallery, the Font dialog box, or the Mini toolbar.

- The Colors dialog box with the Standard tab selected includes 124 colors, as well as 15 shades of gray, and an option to mix your own colors with the Custom tab selected.

- At the Colors dialog box with the Custom tab selected, you can change the *luminescence*, which is the brightness of the color; the *hue*, which is the color itself; and the *saturation*, which is the color intensity. You can also change the values of Red, Green, and Blue.

- Use options in the *Effects* section of the Font dialog box to apply different character formatting such as strikethrough, double strikethrough, superscript, subscript, small caps, all caps, and hidden. You can also click the Text Effects button at the Font dialog box to display additional formatting options.

- Apply a theme and change theme colors, fonts, and effects with buttons in the Document Formatting group on the DESIGN tab.

- Style sets are predesigned combinations of styles, colors, and fonts used in a document.

- Insert special symbols in a document by clicking the Symbol button in the Symbols group on the INSERT tab, clicking *More Symbols*, and then choosing the Symbols tab or the Special Characters tab at the Symbol dialog box.

- An em dash (—) is generally the width of a typeface's uppercase *M* and is used in text to indicate a pause in speech.

- An en dash (–) indicates a continuation, such as 116–133 or January–March, and is the width of a typeface's lowercase *n*.

- In typesetting, the open quotation mark is curved upward (") and the close quotation mark is curved downward ("). In typesetting, straight quotes are used to indicate inches (") or feet (').

- The *OpenType Features* section of the Font dialog box with the Advanced tab selected includes options for choosing a ligature style, specifying number spacing and form, and applying stylistic sets.

Commands Review

FEATURE	RIBBON TAB, GROUP	BUTTON	KEYBOARD SHORTCUT
clear all formatting	HOME, Font		
decrease font size	HOME, Font		Ctrl + <
font	HOME, Font	Calibri (Body)	Ctrl + Shift + F
font color	HOME, Font		
Font dialog box	HOME, Font		Ctrl + D
font size	HOME, Font	11	
Format Painter	HOME, Clipboard		Ctrl + Shift + C
increase font size	HOME, Font		Ctrl + >
styles	HOME, Styles		
symbol	INSERT, Symbols	Ω	
text effects and typography	HOME, Font		
theme colors	DESIGN, Document Formatting		
theme effects	DESIGN, Document Formatting		
theme fonts	DESIGN, Document Formatting	A	
themes	DESIGN, Document Formatting		

Key Points *Review*

A. baseline
B. pitch
C. serif
D. descenders
E. saturation
F. point size
G. TrueType
H. monospaced

I. proportional
J. ligatures
K. typestyle
L. sans serif
M. typeface
N. cap height
O. ascenders
P. em dash

Q. luminescence
R. hue
S. theme
T. OpenType
U. x-height
V. kerning
W. en dash

Matching: In the space at the left, provide the correct letter or letters from the above list that match each definition.

___M___ 1. A set of characters with a common design and shape

___A___ 2. Imaginary horizontal line on which text rests

___B___ 3. The number of characters that can be printed in 1 horizontal inch

___S___ 4. A set of colors, fonts, and other formatting details that work together to give your documents a stylish, professional design

___O___ 5. Parts of lowercase characters that rise above the x-height

___W___ 6. A special character that is used in durations of time or continuation

___C___ 7. A small stroke at the end of characters

___D___ 8. Parts of characters that extend below the baseline

___L___ 9. A typeface that does not contain serifs

___F___ 10. Approximately ½ of an inch

___P___ 11. A special symbol that is used to indicate a pause in speech

___E___ 12. The intensity of color

___T___ 13. Fonts that were created jointly by Adobe and Microsoft to support cross-platform applications, ligatures, and foreign characters

___J___ 14. Letters that have been attached to create a single character

___Q___ 15. The brightness of a color

Chapter Assessments

Assessment 2.1 Format a Training Flyer

1. Open **CWFlyer.docx** from your Chapter02 folder and then save the document with the name **C02-A01-CWFlyer**.
2. Select the text in the text box at the top of the flyer, change the font to 26-point Cambria, and then apply bold formatting and the small caps effect.
3. Select the text *Workplace Shortcuts for Preparing Office Documents* and then change the font to 36-point Cambria and apply the small caps effect.
4. Select the text beginning with *Jules Mason* and ending with *Room 205* and then change the font to 12-point Cambria and apply italic formatting.
5. Select the date in the lower right corner of the document and then change the font to 14-point Cambria and apply bold and italic formatting. (Your document should appear similar to the document shown in Figure 2.4A on page 55.)
6. Save, print, and then close **C02-A01-CWFlyer.docx**.

Assessment 2.2 Format a Meeting Agenda

1. Open **DominicanAgenda.docx** from your Chapter02 folder and then save the document with the name **C02-A02-DominicanAgenda**.
2. Apply the Quotable theme and the Blue Green theme colors.
3. Type text in the document as shown in Figure 2.27 with the following specifications:
   a. Type the first three lines of text (press the Down Arrow key rather than the Enter key to move to the next line). Make sure the text is set in 26-point Century Gothic, and then change the font color to *Blue, Accent 6, Darker 25%*.
   b. Type the text **Delegates' Program** in the fourth line of the document, set it in 20-point Century Gothic, and then apply bold and italic formatting and the Fill - Aqua, Accent 2, Outline - Accent 2 text effect.
   c. Type the times in the first column of the table as shown in Figure 2.27. Insert an en dash between the times in each time period (e.g., 07:00–08:15).
   d. Insert the ® (registered symbol) immediately to the right of the company name *Leading Edge Consultants* that displays about halfway down in the second column of the table. Be sure the symbol displays as a superscript character.
   e. Select the space between the words *address* and *Ambassador* (located in the second column in the second row from the bottom of the page) and then insert an em dash.
4. Make sure the entire document fits on one page. If necessary, delete blank lines or decrease spacing before or after paragraphs to ensure the text fits on one page.
5. Save, print, and then close **C02-A02-DominicanAgenda.docx**.

Figure 2.27 Meeting Agenda Formatted in Assessment 2.2

2015 Annual Meeting
Casa de Campo
Dominican Republic

Delegates' Program

Saturday, November 7	
12:30–16:00	Business meetings (starting with lunch)
17:00–18:15	First-time attendees meeting and reception
18:30	Transportation of participants to Las Minitas Beach
Sunday, November 8	
07:00–08:15	Breakfast
08:30–09:00	Opening ceremony
09:15–10:45	*"A Time for Change"* presentation by Dr. Carl Wilhelm, President, Leading Edge Consultants®
10:45–11:15	Break
11:15–12:15	*"An International Perspective"* presentation by Samuel Reed, President and CEO, Global Management, LLP
12:30–13:30	Summary of report on regional specialties Lunch
13:45–15:30	Breakout sessions on specialties Remainder of afternoon free for networking
Evening	Regional dinners
Monday, November 9	
09:00–10:00	*"Business Opportunities in Emerging Markets"* presentation by Julia Reyes, President, Reyes Associates
10:00–10:30	Break
10:30–11:30	Keynote address—Ambassador Author Smith
11:30	Adjournment

Assessment 2.3   Format a Fundraiser Invitation

1. Open **MardiGrasInvitation.docx** from your Chapter02 folder and then save the document with the name **C02-A03-MardiGrasInvitation**.
2. Format the document so it appears as shown in Figure 2.28 with the following specifications:
   a. Change the theme colors to *Violet II*.
   b. Change the paragraph alignment to right for the body of the invitation, as shown in Figure 2.28.
   c. Set the first line of text and the last two lines of text in the document in 14-point Calibri and apply italic formatting.
   d. Set the two lines of text *Mardi Gras Fundraiser for Loaves & Fishes* in 42-point Gabriola and then apply the Gradient Fill - Purple, Accent 4, Outline - Accent 4 text effect. Display the Font dialog box with the Advanced tab selected, change the *Scale* option to *90%*, turn on kerning at 14 points and above, apply stylistic set 7, and then close the dialog box.
   e. Change the font of the right-aligned text to 16-point Harrington.
   f. Replace the hyphen between 5:30 and 9:30 p.m. with an en dash.
   g. Move and size the two horizontal lines as shown in Figure 2.28.
3. Save, print, and then close **C02-A03-MardiGrasInvitation.docx**.

Figure 2.28 Invitation Formatted in Assessment 2.3

Assessment 2.4   Research and Develop a Workstation Ergonomics Fact Sheet

You work for Horizon Cardiologists. You have been asked to research information on laptop ergonomics and then include your findings in the document titled **HorizonCardiologists.docx**. You have also been asked to apply formatting to the document to improve its appearance. Figure 2.29 shows a sample solution for formatting the document.

1. Open **HorizonCardiologists.docx** from your Chapter02 folder and then save the document with the name **C02-A04-HorizonCardiologists**.
2. Use an Internet search engine to research information on laptop ergonomics and then include information you find as bulleted text below the new heading *Laptop Ergonomics*. Add the source information for the website you used to create the bulleted list, typing the new source below the current source in the document.
3. Apply at least the following formatting to the document:
    a. Apply styles to the heading and subheadings.
    b. Apply a style set.
    c. Apply a theme.
    d. Change the theme colors.
    e. Include a symbol in the clinic address and insert an em dash in place of the two hyphens in the text "Healthy heart--healthy life".
    f. Apply any additional formatting to improve the visual appearance of the document.
4. Save, print, and then close **C02-A04-HorizonCardiologists.docx**.

Figure 2.29 Sample Solution for Assessment 2.4

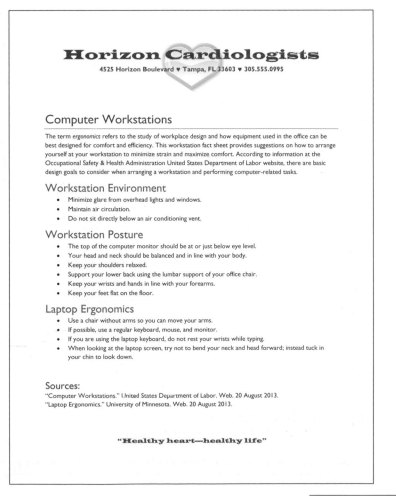

Chapter 3

Inserting and Modifying Page Elements

Performance Objectives

Upon successful completion of Chapter 3, you will be able to:

- Use building blocks
- Insert predesigned cover pages
- Insert headers and footers
- Insert page numbers
- Insert page breaks
- Create watermarks

- Insert and customize images
- Create and insert bullets
- Insert text boxes and shapes
- Insert tables
- Use and customize templates

Desktop Publishing Terms

cell	header	template
footer	placeholder	watermark
hard page break	soft page break	

Word Features Used

breaks	cover page	page numbers	tables
Bring Forward	headers and footers	pictures	templates
building blocks	layout	quick parts	text boxes
bullets	Normal.dotm	Send Backward	watermark
clip art	page breaks	shapes	

Note: Before beginning computer exercises for this chapter, copy to your storage medium the Chapter03 folder from the CD that accompanies this textbook and then make Chapter03 the active folder. Remember to substitute for graphics that may no longer be available.

Inserting Document Elements

Quick Parts

There are a variety of ways to insert the reusable document elements known as building blocks. Building blocks include cover pages, headers and footers, page numbers, and text boxes, among others. To access these document elements, click the Quick Parts button in the Text group on the INSERT tab and then click the *Building Blocks Organizer* option at the drop-down list. A complete list of reusable pieces of content is available at the Building Blocks Organizer dialog box, as shown in Figure 3.1. If you have a logo, letterhead, signature line, or mission statement that you want to reuse often, you can save these items as building blocks by selecting the item, clicking the Quick Parts button, and then clicking *Save Selection to Quick Parts Gallery* at the drop-down list.

Inserting a Cover Page

DTP POINTER ▶

Adding a cover page to a document gives it a professional appearance.

Cover Page

Insert a cover page in a document to give it a formal, professional appearance. Reports and manuals are examples of documents that often require cover pages. Sixteen predesigned cover pages are available, and they can be accessed by two different methods. To insert a cover page using the Building Blocks Organizer dialog box, click the Quick Parts button in the Text group on the INSERT tab and then click *Building Blocks Organizer*. At the Building Blocks Organizer dialog box, click the desired option from the cover pages gallery, click the Insert button, and then close the dialog box, as shown in Figure 3.1. Alternatively, click the Cover Page button in the Pages group on the INSERT tab and then click a predesigned cover page at the drop-down list, as shown in Figure 3.2. After inserting a cover page, you can remove it by clicking the Cover Page button and then clicking the *Remove Current Cover Page* option at the drop-down list.

Figure 3.1 Using the Building Blocks Organizer Dialog Box

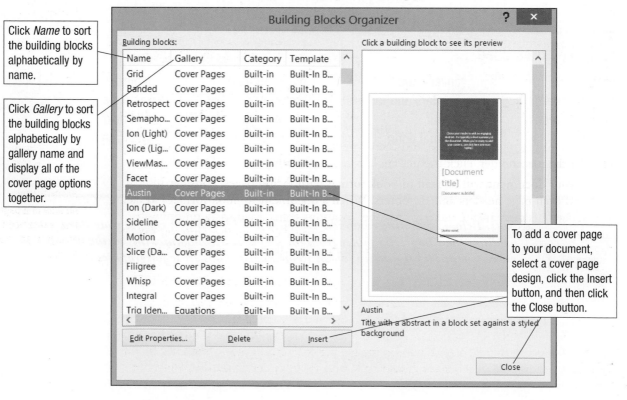

Click *Name* to sort the building blocks alphabetically by name.

Click *Gallery* to sort the building blocks alphabetically by gallery name and display all of the cover page options together.

To add a cover page to your document, select a cover page design, click the Insert button, and then click the Close button.

Figure 3.2 Inserting Predesigned Cover Pages

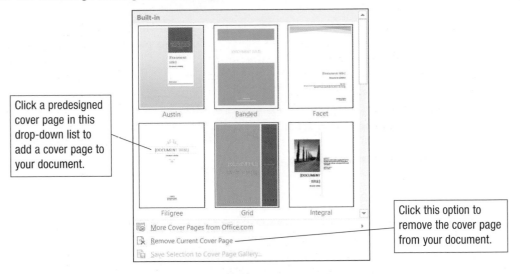

Click a predesigned cover page in this drop-down list to add a cover page to your document.

Click this option to remove the cover page from your document.

You can customize a cover page by adding your business logo, inserting a photo, or changing the color scheme and font style to match your business brand.

Inserting Headers and Footers

Text that appears at the top of every page is called a *header* and text that appears at the bottom of every page is referred to as a *footer* (see Figure 3.3 on page 88). Headers and footers are common components of manuscripts, textbooks, reports, and other publications. Insert a predesigned header or footer in a document by clicking the INSERT tab and then clicking the Header button or the Footer button in the Header & Footer group. At the drop-down list that displays, click a predesigned header or footer or click the *Edit Header* or *Edit Footer* option to create your own header or footer. Alternatively, you can insert a header or footer at the Building Blocks Organizer dialog box. Headers and footers are visible only in Print Layout view.

A predesigned header or footer may contain placeholders for entering specific information. A *placeholder* is an area of a page that is reserved for an object, an image, or text. For example, a header might contain the placeholder *[Document title]*. Click anywhere in the placeholder text and then type the desired text. To delete a placeholder, click in the placeholder, click the placeholder tab, and then press the Delete key.

If your document will be read in book format with facing pages, consider inserting odd and even page headers and/or footers. When a document in book format has facing pages, the outside margins and page number locations generally display on opposite margins. Create an odd and even header and/or footer by clicking the *Different Odd & Even Pages* check box in the Options group on the HEADER & FOOTER TOOLS DESIGN tab. You can navigate among the different headers and/or footers by using the buttons in the Navigation group on the HEADER & FOOTER TOOLS DESIGN tab.

To return to your document after inserting a header or footer, double-click in the document or click the Close Header and Footer button in the Close group on the HEADER & FOOTER TOOLS DESIGN tab. Remove a header or footer from a document by clicking the Header button or the Footer button in the Header & Footer group on the INSERT tab and then clicking either the *Remove Header* or *Remove Footer* option at the drop-down list.

header
Text repeated at the top of every page

footer
Text repeated at the bottom of every page

Header

Footer

placeholder
An area of a page that is reserved for an object, an image, or text

Figure 3.3 **Inserting Headers and Footers**

Inserting Page Numbers

Page Number

Word, by default, does not print page numbers on document pages. If you want to insert page numbers in a document, use the Page Number button in the Header & Footer group on the INSERT tab. When you click the Page Number button, a drop-down list displays with options for specifying where on the page you want to insert the page number. Point to an option in this list to display a side menu with predesigned page number formats, as shown in Figure 3.4. Scroll through the options in the drop-down list and then click the desired option. You can remove page numbering from a document by clicking the Page Number button and then clicking *Remove Page Numbers* at the drop-down list.

To prevent an automatic page number from displaying on the first page of a document, display the HEADER & FOOTER TOOLS DESIGN tab, and then click the *Different First Page* check box in the Options group to insert a check mark.

Inserting Page Breaks

Page Break

soft page break

A page break inserted automatically in an electronic document

At the default standard page size, Word inserts a page break at approximately the 10-inch mark on the page. A page break inserted by Word is called a ***soft page break***. Insert your own page break in a document by pressing Ctrl + Enter or by clicking the INSERT tab and then clicking the Page Break button in the Pages group.

Figure 3.4 Inserting Page Numbers from the Page Number Button Drop-down List

| INSERT | DESIGN | PAGE LAYOUT | REFERENCES | MAILINGS | REVIEW | VIEW |

Table Pictures Online Pictures Shapes SmartArt Chart Screenshot Apps for Office Online Video Comment Header Footer Page Number Text Box Quick Parts WordArt

Tables   Illustrations   Apps   Media   Links   Comments   Header & F

Simple

Plain Number 1

Plain Number 2

- # Top of Page
- Bottom of Page
- Page Margins
- Current Position
- Format Page Numbers...
- Remove Page Numbers

Click the Page Number button to display a drop-down list of numbering positions.

Point to a position option to display a side menu of number formats. Click a format to insert page numbers in your document.

A page break that you manually insert is called a ***hard page break***. A soft page break adjusts automatically when you add or delete text in a document. A hard page does not adjust automatically.

Other types of breaks can be added to your document by clicking the Breaks button in the Page Setup group on the PAGE LAYOUT tab. The Pages group on the INSERT tab includes a Blank Page button, which you can click to add a blank page to a document. You will use these options in later chapters in this book.

In Exercise 3.1A, you will create a protocol manual for an advertising firm. You will insert a predesigned cover page and use styles and themes to format the document. You will also use placeholders and insert headers, footers, page numbers, and page breaks.

hard page break

A page break inserted manually in an electronic document

Breaks

Blank Page

Exercise 3.1A Creating a Protocol Manual   Part 1 of 3

1. Open **Protocol.docx** from your Chapter03 folder and then save the document with the name **C03-E01-Protocol**.
2. Apply the Lines (Stylish) style set to the document.
3. Apply the Facet theme to the document.
4. Change the theme fonts to *Candara*.
5. Insert the Facet predesigned cover page by completing the following steps:
    a. With the insertion point positioned at the beginning of the document, click the INSERT tab and then click the Cover Page button in the Pages group.
    b. Click the *Facet* cover page option at the drop-down list.

Step 5a

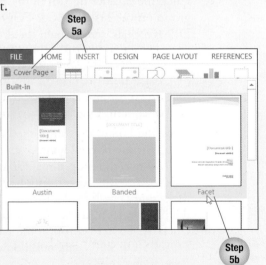

Step 5b

c. Click in the *[Document title]* placeholder in the new cover page and then type **Beckam Advertising**.

d. Click in the *[Document subtitle]* placeholder and then type **Minneapolis Office Protocol**.

e. Click in the placeholder below the text *Abstract* and then type **Our office works in teams, which requires collaboration and the sharing of spaces and equipment. Therefore, understanding the protocols that will support effective interaction and utilization of our resources is important.**

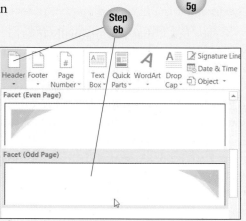

Step 5c

f. Click in the *[Author name]* placeholder that displays above the *[Email address]* placeholder. (You may see a name instead of the placeholder; if you do, select the name.) With the placeholder (or name) selected, type **Jorge Montague**.

Step 5g

g. Click in the *[Email address]* placeholder and then type **jmontague@emcp.net**.

6. Insert an odd-page header and an even-page header by completing the following steps:

a. Scroll to the top of the first page in the document (the page that follows the cover page) and position the insertion point anywhere in the first line of text (*What Are Protocols?*). Make sure the INSERT tab is active.

Step 6b

b. Click the Header button in the Header & Footer group, scroll down the drop-down list, and then click the *Facet (Odd Page)* header option.

c. Click the *Different Odd & Even Pages* check box in the Options group on the HEADER & FOOTER TOOLS DESIGN tab to insert a check mark.

Step 6c

d. Click the Next button in the Navigation group to make the Even Page Header pane active.

Step 6d

e. Click the Header button in the Header & Footer group on the HEADER & FOOTER TOOLS DESIGN tab, scroll down the drop-down list, and then click the *Facet (Even Page)* header option.

f. Click the Close Header and Footer button in the Close group.

7. Insert an odd-page footer and an even-page footer by completing the following steps:

Step 6f

a. Click the Footer button in the Header & Footer group on the INSERT tab.

b. Scroll down the drop-down list and then click the *Facet (Odd Page)* footer option.

c. Make sure a check mark displays in the *Different Odd & Even Pages* check box and then click the Next button in the Navigation group.

d. Click the Footer button in the Header & Footer group on the HEADER & FOOTER TOOLS DESIGN tab, scroll down the drop-down list, and then click the *Facet (Even Page)* footer option.

e. Make sure the name *Jorge Montague* displays at the left side of the even-page footer. If not, click in the name that displays (this selects the *Author* placeholder) and then type **Jorge Montague**.

f. Delete the *[SCHOOL]* placeholder from the even-page footer by clicking in the placeholder, clicking the placeholder tab, and then pressing the Delete key.

g. Click the Close Header and Footer button in the Close group.

8. Move the insertion point to the beginning of the text *General Protocol* and then insert a page break by pressing Ctrl + Enter.

9. Save **C03-E01-Protocol.docx**.

Inserting Watermarks

A ***watermark*** is a lightened graphic or block of text that displays behind existing document content. Watermarks can be used to identify the document status, such as marking a document with the text *SAMPLE*, as shown in Figure 3.5A, or to add graphical interest, as shown in Figure 3.5B. Typically, watermarks are intended for printed documents, but they may also be used to identify a protected document posted on a website—similar to a photographer's picture stamped with *Proof*. Watermarks can be viewed only in Print Layout view and on the printed page.

Insert a watermark in a document by clicking the Watermark button in the Page Background group on the DESIGN tab, as shown in Figure 3.6 on page 92. Clicking this button displays a drop-down list of predesigned watermarks, along with options for creating custom watermarks and removing a watermark.

watermark
A lightened graphic or block of text displayed behind content on a page

Watermark

Figure 3.5 Using Text and Graphics to Create Watermarks

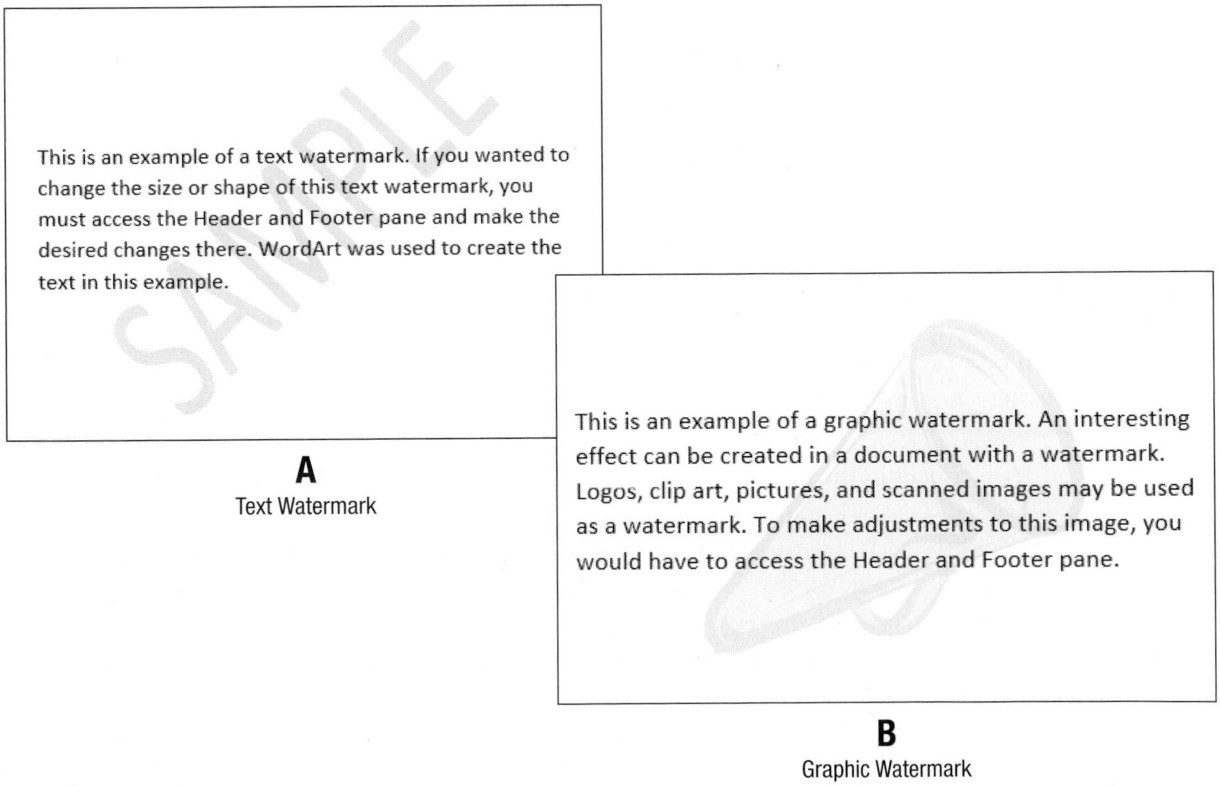

This is an example of a text watermark. If you wanted to change the size or shape of this text watermark, you must access the Header and Footer pane and make the desired changes there. WordArt was used to create the text in this example.

A
Text Watermark

This is an example of a graphic watermark. An interesting effect can be created in a document with a watermark. Logos, clip art, pictures, and scanned images may be used as a watermark. To make adjustments to this image, you would have to access the Header and Footer pane.

B
Graphic Watermark

Figure 3.6 Inserting a Watermark from the Watermark Button Drop-down List

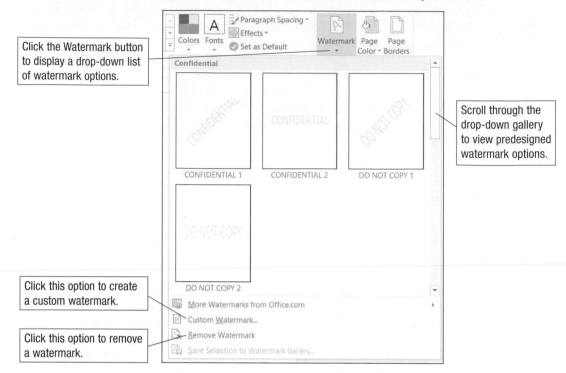

Click the Watermark button to display a drop-down list of watermark options.

Scroll through the drop-down gallery to view predesigned watermark options.

Click this option to create a custom watermark.

Click this option to remove a watermark.

Creating a Custom Watermark and Removing a Watermark

Create a custom watermark by clicking the *Custom Watermark* option at the Watermark button drop-down list. Clicking this option opens the Printed Watermark dialog box, shown in Figure 3.7. To create a custom text watermark, click the *Text watermark* option to select it, and then select the text that appears in the *Text* text box and type the desired text. Change the font, size, color, and layout of your custom watermark as desired, and then click the Apply button.

To create a custom picture watermark using an image from your computer or other storage medium, click the *Picture watermark* option at the Printed Watermark dialog box to select it, and then click the Select Picture button. At the Insert Pictures window, click the Browse button that displays at the right side of the *From a file* option. At the Insert Picture dialog box, locate the folder where your desired image is stored, select the image, and then click the Insert button. If you want to insert a watermark using an image from Office.com, type a search word or phrase in the *Office.com Clip Art* text box at the Insert Pictures window and then press the Enter key. Select the desired image and then click the Insert button. Once you have selected the picture, you can adjust its scale using the *Scale* option box at the Printed Watermark dialog box. Click the Apply button to insert the watermark in the document, and click the Close button to close the dialog box.

Remove a watermark from a document by clicking the *No watermark* option at the Printed Watermark dialog box or by clicking *Remove Watermark* at the Watermark button drop-down list.

Figure 3.7 Using the Printed Watermark Dialog Box

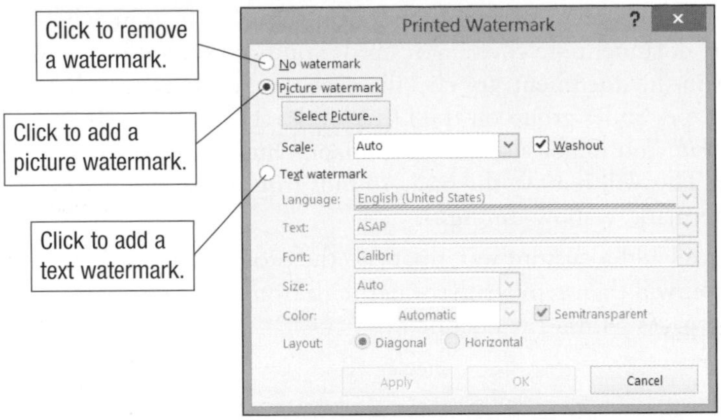

Editing a Watermark

Word inserts a watermark in the Header pane, as shown in Figure 3.8, which causes the watermark to appear on every page of the document by default. You can remove a watermark from a particular page by selecting the *Different First Page* or *Different Odd & Even Pages* options in the Options group on the HEADER & FOOTER TOOLS DESIGN tab. You may need to deselect the Link to Previous button in the Navigation group first. To edit a watermark, click the Header button in the Header & Footer group on the INSERT tab and then click *Edit Header* at the drop-down list.

Figure 3.8 Editing a Watermark Using the HEADER & FOOTER TOOLS DESIGN Tab

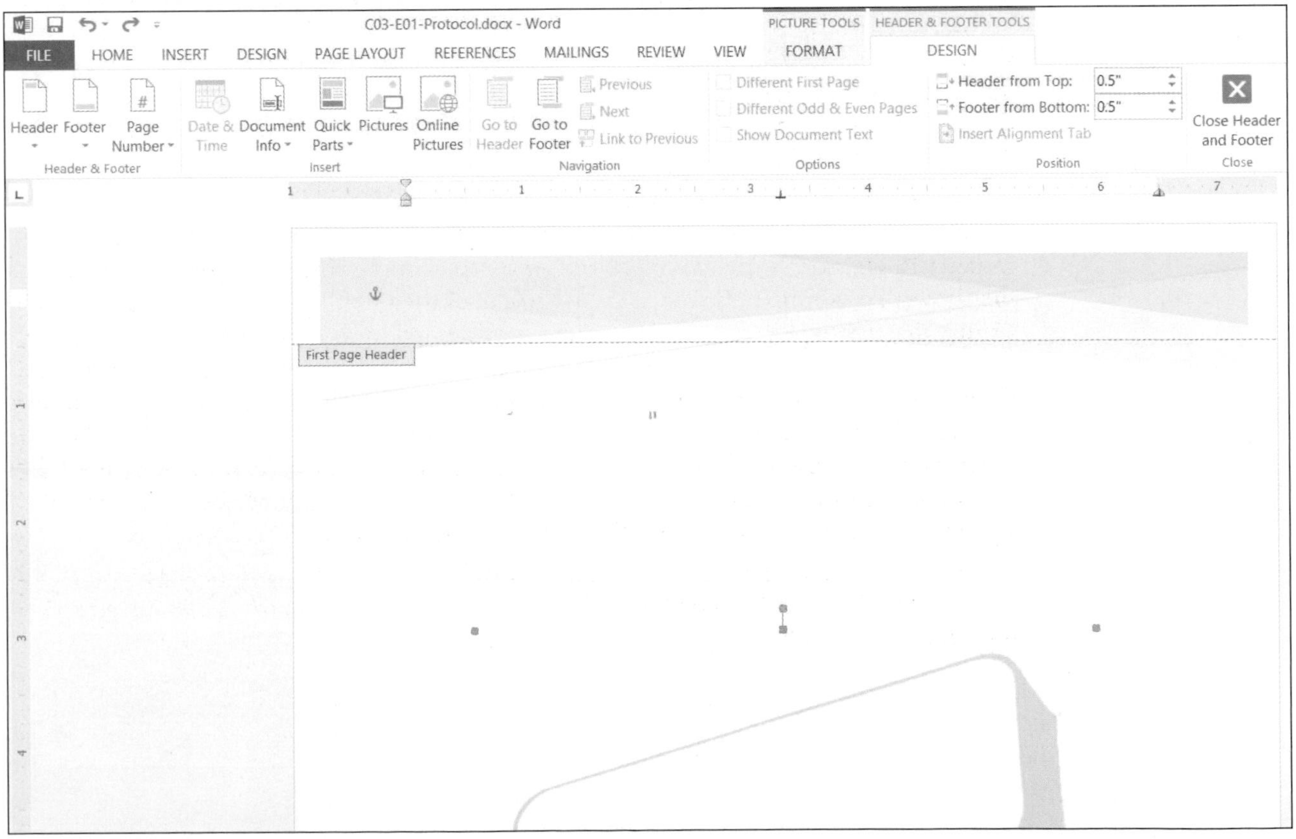

Troubleshooting Watermarks

Shape Fill

Shape Outline

If you insert a watermark in a document but are having trouble seeing it, it may be because other shapes in the document are covering it up. If you have several text boxes, rectangles, or other shapes in the document, try clicking each one, clicking the Shape Fill button arrow in the Shapes Styles group on the DRAWING TOOLS DESIGN tab, and then clicking *No Fill*. You might also click the Shape Outline button arrow and then click *No Outline*. This will remove the backgrounds from those text boxes or shapes and allow your watermark to show through.

In Exercise 3.1B, you will add a custom watermark to the protocol manual you started in Exercise 3.1A. You will then remove the watermark from the cover page so that it only displays on the pages within the document.

Exercise 3.1B   Inserting a Custom Watermark   Part 2 of 3

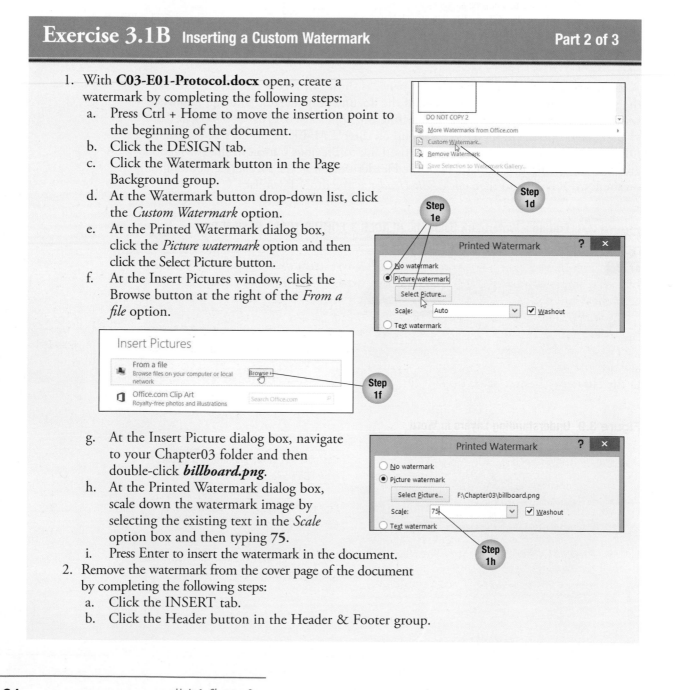

1. With **C03-E01-Protocol.docx** open, create a watermark by completing the following steps:
   a. Press Ctrl + Home to move the insertion point to the beginning of the document.
   b. Click the DESIGN tab.
   c. Click the Watermark button in the Page Background group.
   d. At the Watermark button drop-down list, click the *Custom Watermark* option.
   e. At the Printed Watermark dialog box, click the *Picture watermark* option and then click the Select Picture button.
   f. At the Insert Pictures window, click the Browse button at the right of the *From a file* option.
   g. At the Insert Picture dialog box, navigate to your Chapter03 folder and then double-click *billboard.png*.
   h. At the Printed Watermark dialog box, scale down the watermark image by selecting the existing text in the *Scale* option box and then typing **75**.
   i. Press Enter to insert the watermark in the document.
2. Remove the watermark from the cover page of the document by completing the following steps:
   a. Click the INSERT tab.
   b. Click the Header button in the Header & Footer group.

c. At the Header button drop-down list, click the *Edit Header* option.

d. With the First Page Header pane open, click the watermark image to select it. The PICTURES TOOLS FORMAT tab will appear on the ribbon. ***Hint: To make sure you have selected the watermark image, click the Show/Hide ¶ button to turn on the display of nonprinting characters. This will display the sizing handles around the watermark image.***

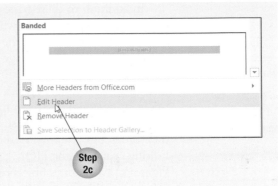

e. Press the Delete key.

f. Click the Close Header and Footer button in the Close group on the HEADER & FOOTER TOOLS DESIGN tab.

3. Scroll down to check that the watermark only displays on the two pages following the cover page.

4. Save **C03-E01-Protocol.docx**.

Using Layers in Documents

Instead of inserting a watermark in the Header pane, you can insert an image or text at the document screen, alter the color of the object, and then send the object to the back of the document so that it appears behind the text. The layers feature makes it possible to do this.

A Word document contains three layers—the foreground layer (or drawing layer), the text layer, and the background layer—as illustrated in Figure 3.9. The text layer is the one you may be the most accustomed to working with if you mainly use Word for word processing. Even when you insert graphics, their Wrap Text setting defaults to *In Line With Text* and they anchor to paragraphs in the text layer. At times, you may find it helpful to change this setting so that you can move the image freely about the screen. This is accomplished by clicking the Wrap Text button on the PICTURE TOOLS FORMAT tab and then clicking one of the following options: *Square, Tight, Behind Text, In Front of Text, Top or Bottom,* or *Through.* By default, shapes, such as lines, ovals, and arrows, display in the foreground layer above the text layer. Text or graphics created in the Header or Footer panes display in the background layer, below the text layer.

Wrap Text

Figure 3.9 **Understanding Layers in Word**

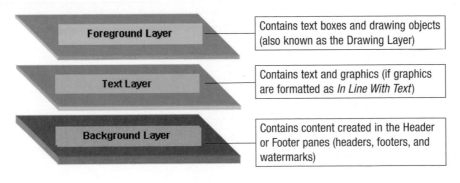

In addition to these basic layers, Word stacks drawing objects in individual layers in the foreground layer, as shown in Figure 3.10. Every time you add another object, it is drawn in a layer on top of the previous layer. The stacked objects are similar to a hand of playing cards. You can change the order of the drawing objects with the Bring Forward and Send Backward buttons in the Arrange group on the PICTURE TOOLS FORMAT tab, the DRAWING TOOLS FORMAT tab, or the PAGE LAYOUT tab just as you might bring certain cards to the front of your hand and move others to the back during a card game. You can also use the Selection pane to select individual objects and change their order and visibility. Display the Selection pane by clicking the Select button in the Editing group on the HOME tab and then clicking *Selection Pane* at the drop-down list. Figure 3.11 illustrates objects and text in the various layers in a document.

Bring Forward

Send Backward

Figure 3.10 Understanding Stacked Drawing Objects in Word

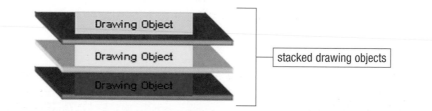

stacked drawing objects

Figure 3.11 Understanding the Contents of the Layers in a Document

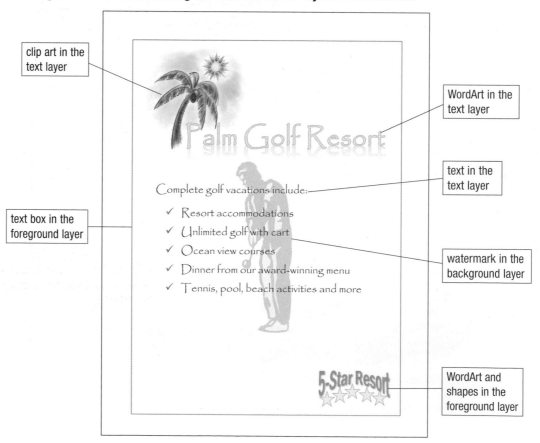

clip art in the text layer

WordArt in the text layer

text in the text layer

text box in the foreground layer

watermark in the background layer

WordArt and shapes in the foreground layer

Inserting Images

Images such as clip art and photographs can be inserted in a document with the Pictures button and the Online Pictures button in the Illustrations group on the INSERT tab. Click the Pictures button to insert an image from a folder on your computer's hard drive or click the Online Pictures button to insert an image from Office.com. When you click the Online Pictures button, the Insert Pictures window displays, as shown in Figure 3.12. Type a search word or phrase into the *Office.com Clip Art* text box and then press the Enter key. The search results will display inside the Insert Pictures window.

Pictures

Online Pictures

In this textbook, you will often be instructed to insert a specific image from Office.com (usually illustrated in an example document in a figure at the end of the exercise). However, if the image is not available, you should replace the image with another similar one. You can use the *Office.com Clip Art* text box at the Insert Pictures window to type a name for a category, such as *beach*, and then press Enter. Choose an available image that is similar to the original image in both content and size, if possible.

Sizing and Moving Images

After an image is inserted into a document, you can adjust its size. One way to do this is by using the sizing handles that display around the image when it is selected. Position the mouse pointer on a sizing handle until the pointer turns into a double-headed arrow, as shown in Figure 3.13A on page 98. Hold down the left mouse button, drag the sizing handle in or out to decrease or increase the size of the image, and then release the mouse button. Use the sizing handles in the corners to change the height and width at the same time and maintain the original proportions of the image.

Figure 3.12 **Searching for Images at the Insert Pictures Window**

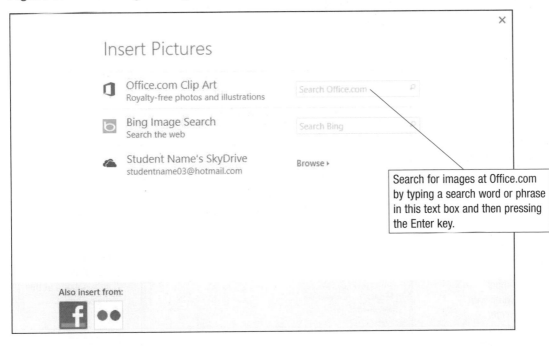

Figure 3.13 Sizing, Rotating, and Moving Images

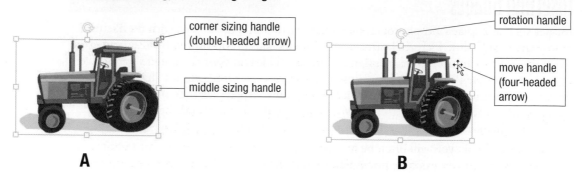

corner sizing handle
(double-headed arrow)

middle sizing handle

rotation handle

move handle
(four-headed
arrow)

A

B

To move an image, you must first select the image and change the text wrapping from the default setting of *In Line with Text*. To do this, click the Wrap Text button in the Arrange group on the PICTURE TOOLS FORMAT tab or the PAGE LAYOUT tab and then choose an option such as *Square, Tight, Through, Top or Bottom, Behind Text,* or *In Front of Text* at the drop-down list. Once a text wrapping option has been applied, position the mouse pointer inside the image until the pointer turns into a four-headed arrow, as shown in Figure 3.13B. Click and hold the left mouse button, drag the image to the desired position, and then release the mouse button. Use the rotation handle that appears at the top of the image to adjust the image's orientation.

Move an image to a specific location on the page with options from the Position button drop-down gallery. The Position button is located in the Arrange group on the PICTURES TOOLS FORMAT tab and the PAGE LAYOUT tab. When you choose an option from the Position button drop-down gallery, the image is moved to the specific location on the page and the text wraps around the image.

You can also size an image using the *Shape Height* and *Shape Width* measurement boxes in the Size group on the PICTURE TOOLS FORMAT tab, as shown in Figure 3.14A. Yet another way is to click the Size group dialog box launcher and then make adjustments at the Layout dialog box with the Size tab selected, as shown in Figure 3.14B.

Position

Figure 3.14 Adjusting the Size of a Picture in the Size Group on the PICTURE TOOLS FORMAT Tab and at the Layout Dialog Box

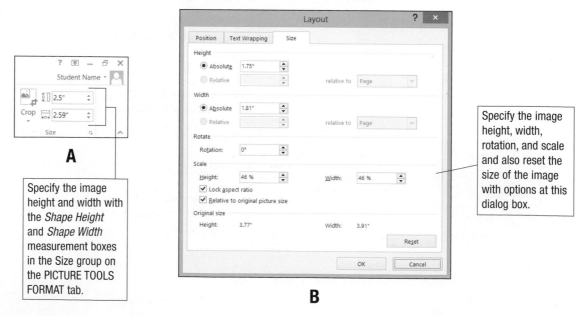

Specify the image height and width with the *Shape Height* and *Shape Width* measurement boxes in the Size group on the PICTURE TOOLS FORMAT tab.

A

Specify the image height, width, rotation, and scale and also reset the size of the image with options at this dialog box.

B

Inserting Bullets

Bullets

Bullets can be inserted in a document by clicking the Bullets button arrow in the Paragraph group on the HOME tab. At the Bullets button drop-down gallery, shown in Figure 3.15, select one of the bullet options displayed or click the *Define New Bullet* option. At the Define New Bullet dialog box, shown in Figure 3.16, select either a symbol, a picture, or a font, and change the alignment if desired.

You can create a bullet from an Office.com clip art image. To do this, click *Define New Bullet* at the Bullets button drop-down gallery and then click the Picture button at the Define New Bullet dialog box, as shown in Figure 3.16. At the Insert Pictures window, enter a search word or phrase in the *Office.com Clip Art* text box and then select and insert an image from the results. Consider using a clip art image that reinforces the topic of the text in the document.

Figure 3.15 Displaying Bullet Options at the Bullet Button Drop-down Gallery

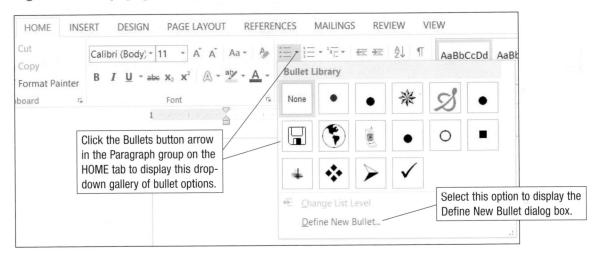

Figure 3.16 Customizing Bullets at the Define New Bullet Dialog Box

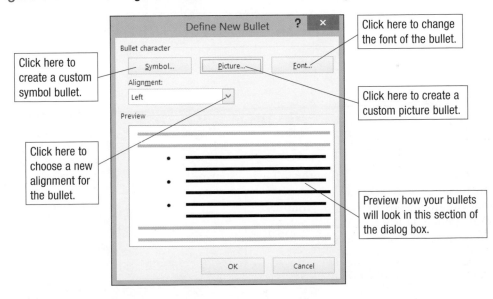

When you apply bullets to existing text, the line spacing between the lines in the bulleted or numbered list is reduced. If you want to increase or decrease the line spacing in a specific list, select the list and then use options in the Paragraph dialog box. If you want to increase or decrease the line spacing for all bulleted lists in a document, modify the List Paragraph style. This is the style that is automatically applied to bulleted lists. Complete the following steps to increase the line spacing in the List Paragraph style:

1. Click the More button in the Styles group on the HOME tab and then right-click the List Paragraph style.
2. Click *Modify* at the shortcut menu.
3. At the Modify Style dialog box, click the Format button that displays in the lower left corner of the dialog box and then click the *Paragraph* option at the pop-up menu.
4. Click the *Don't add space between paragraphs of the same style* check box to remove the check mark and then click OK twice to close both dialog boxes.

In Exercise 3.1C, you will insert an image into the protocol manual you started in Exercises 3.1A and 3.1B and then apply an effect and change the text wrapping to make it part of the watermark. You will also insert custom picture bullets.

Exercise 3.1C Inserting Images and Custom Picture Bullets Part 3 of 3 PORTFOLIO

1. With **C03-E01-Protocol.docx** open, insert the key clip art image on the second page of the document, as shown in Figure 3.17 on page 103, by completing the following steps:
   a. Position the insertion point immediately to the left of the text *What Are Protocols?* on the second page of the document (the page immediately following the cover page).
   b. If necessary, click the INSERT tab.
   c. Click the Online Pictures button in the Illustrations group.
   d. At the Insert Pictures window, type **security key** in the *Office.com Clip Art* text box and then press the Enter key.
   e. Scroll down the search results and then double-click the image shown below.

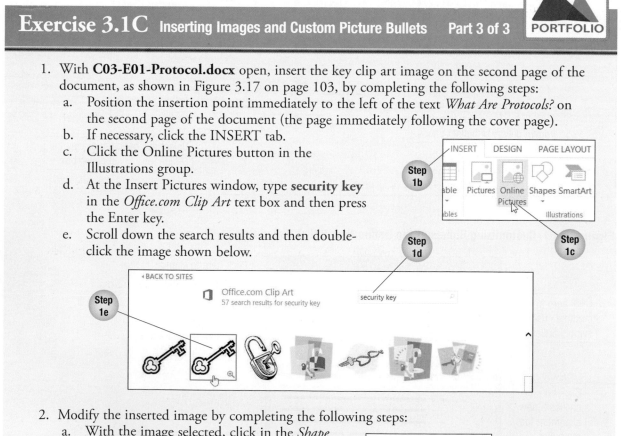

2. Modify the inserted image by completing the following steps:
   a. With the image selected, click in the *Shape Height* measurement box in the Size group on the PICTURE TOOLS FORMAT tab, type **1.1**, and then press the Enter key.

b. Click the Color button in the Adjust group and then click the *Washout* option at the drop-down gallery (fourth column, first row in the *Recolor* section).

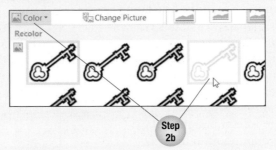

c. Click the Wrap Text button in the Arrange group and then click *Behind Text* at the drop-down list.

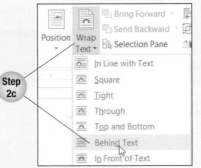

d. Using the mouse, move the image so it is positioned in the middle of the billboard watermark on the second page.

3. Insert the office workers clip art image on the third page of the document, as shown in Figure 3.17, by completing the following steps:

a. Position the insertion point immediately to the left of the text *General Protocol* on the third page.

b. Click the INSERT tab.

c. Click the Online Pictures button in the Illustrations group.

d. At the Insert Pictures window, type **office workers** in the *Office.com Clip Art* text box and then press the Enter key.

e. Scroll down the search results and then double-click the image shown below.

4. Modify the inserted image by completing the following steps:
   a. With the image selected, click in the *Shape Height* measurement box in the Size group on the PICTURE TOOLS FORMAT tab, type **1.1**, and then press the Enter key.
   b. Click the Color button in the Adjust group and then click the *Washout* option at the drop-down gallery (fourth column, first row in the *Recolor* section).
   c. Click the Picture Effects button in the Picture Styles group, point to the *3-D Rotation* option, and then click the *Perspective Contrasting Right* option at the side menu (first column, bottom row in the *Perspective* section).
   d. Click the Wrap Text button in the Arrange group and then click *Behind Text* at the drop-down list.

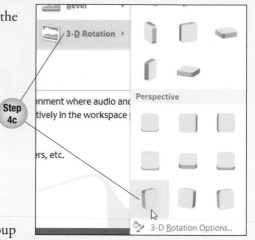

5. Position the image of the office workers on the third page by completing the following steps:
   a. With the image still selected, click the Size group dialog box launcher.
   b. At the Layout dialog box, click the Position tab.
   c. Change the value in the *Absolute position* measurement box in the *Horizontal* section to *2.4"*.
   d. Change the value in the *Absolute position* measurement box in the *Vertical* section to *4.4"*.
   e. Click the *Move object with text* check box to remove the check mark.
   f. Click OK.

6. Create and apply customized bullets by completing the following steps:
   a. Click the HOME tab.
   b. Select the first four paragraphs of text below the *Protocol* subheading in the *Security/Check-In Policy* section on the second page of the document.
   c. Click the Bullets button arrow in the Paragraph group and then click the *Define New Bullet* option at the drop-down gallery.
   d. At the Define New Bullet dialog box, click the Picture button.
   e. At the Insert Pictures window, type **check mark on clipboard** in the *Office.com Clip Art* text box and then press the Enter key.
   f. Double-click the image shown at the right.
   g. Click OK to close the Define New Bullet dialog box.

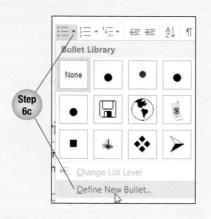

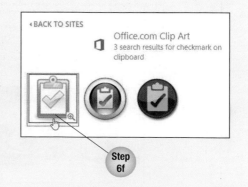

7. Select the nine paragraphs of text below the *Protocol* subheading in the *General Protocol* section on the third page in the document and then click the Bullets button in the Paragraph group to apply the custom picture bullet you created in Step 6.
8. Save, print, and then close **C03-E01-Protocol.docx**.

Figure 3.17 Protocol Manual Created in Exercises 3.1A–3.1C

BECKAM ADVERTISING

Minneapolis Office Protocol

Abstract
Our office works in teams, which requires collaboration and the sharing of spaces and equipment. Therefore, understanding the protocols that will support effective interaction and utilization of our resources is important.

Jorge Montague
jmontague@emcp.net

What Are Protocols?

Protocols are simply the forms of etiquette observed by members of an organization.

Why Are Protocols Necessary?

Our office works in teams, which requires collaboration and the sharing of spaces and equipment. Therefore, it is important for everyone to understand the protocols that will support effective interaction and utilization of our resources. If you have any questions regarding these protocols, please contact Birgit Kaczmarek at Ext. 4438.

Security/Check-In Policy

This is intended to provide a safe and secure workplace for normal working conditions and also in the event of an emergency.

Protocol

- Everyone is required to check in at the front office receptionist desk.
- Photo ID badges must be worn at all times. If you lose your ID badge, please notify office operations staff immediately at x1000.
- Elevators and stairs leading up to the second floor will require card key access with free access between the second and third floors.
- First floor doors and corridors will require card key access (with the exception of the front door unless after hours).

Visitors, whether external or internal, must be met in the first floor office receptionist/lobby area by a CC individual and then taken to the appropriate meeting/office area. Internal visitors may be given access by the office receptionist to the appropriate floor via elevator and then met by staff person.

The security guard will be available to make sure you get to your car safely if leaving the building after dark. If the guard is not present when leaving, please wait until one returns from rounds or call him or her on their pager.

BECKAM ADVERTISING | Minneapolis Office Protocol

General Protocol

To create a level of conscious behavior that promotes a work environment where audio and visual distraction is minimized and that promotes the ability to work effectively in the workspace provided.

Protocol
- Headphones are recommended for use with radios, i-pods, CD-players, etc.
- Cell phones and beepers should be set to "vibrate."
- Phone ringers should be set to low, including cell phones.
- Speakerphones should not be used at workstations.
- Conference calls should be held in enclaves or conference rooms so that others around you won't be disrupted.
- Overhead paging will be available. Call the office receptionist to request a page. Overhead paging is intended for urgent requests only. Individual pagers should be tried first before requesting an overhead page.
- Be conscious of noise and other disruptions to adjacent workstation areas. Individuals being disturbed should not hesitate to discuss these distractions with individuals.
- Children in the office must be accompanied by their parent or adult at all times. If at the office for an extended period, they must be in a designated enclave or small conference room that has been reserved for this purpose.
- Please refer to HR Online for protocols on E-mail, voice mail, flex time and casual business attire.

Jorge Montague |

Inserting Text Boxes

Text Box

If you want to precisely position text in a document, consider using a text box. Text boxes are objects containing text that can be formatted and positioned on the page to meet your requirements. Text boxes are ideal for captions, labels, headlines, and other smaller document components. Text boxes are commonly used in desktop-published documents because they can be formatted using options such as color, borders, and effects.

Word 2013 provides a number of predesigned text boxes that can be inserted into a document. Insert a predesigned text box into a document by clicking the Text Box button in the Text group on the INSERT tab and then clicking an option at the drop-down list, as shown in Figure 3.18. In addition to inserting predesigned text boxes, you can draw a text box and then apply custom formatting to it. Draw a text box by clicking the Text Box button and then clicking the *Draw Text Box* option. This turns the mouse pointer into crosshairs, which looks like a plus sign. Click in the document to insert a text box that will expand as you type, or click and then drag in the document to draw a text box of the desired height and width.

Once a text box has been inserted into a document, you can customize it by using buttons and options on the DRAWING TOOLS FORMAT tab. For example, you can add a shape fill, a shape outline, and a shape effect. Alternatively, you can apply a predesigned shape style to a text box by clicking the More button in the Shape Styles group and then clicking an option at the drop-down gallery. You can also use buttons and options on the DRAWING TOOLS FORMAT tab to size and/or position a text box in a manner similar to sizing and/or positioning an image.

Figure 3.18 Inserting a Text Box with the Text Box Button Drop-down List

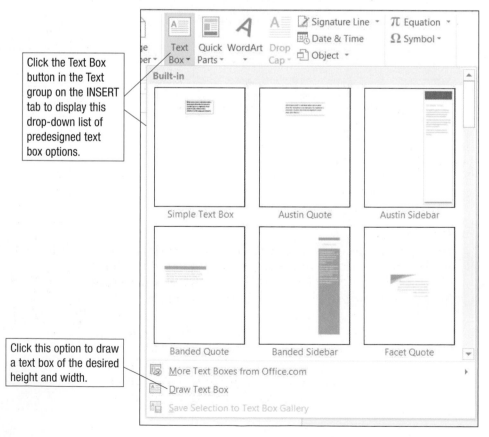

Click the Text Box button in the Text group on the INSERT tab to display this drop-down list of predesigned text box options.

Click this option to draw a text box of the desired height and width.

Inserting Shapes

Click the Shapes button in the Illustrations group on the INSERT tab to display a drop-down list with a variety of shapes. Click a shape in the drop-down list and the mouse pointer displays as crosshairs. Click or drag in the document to insert the shape. Customize the shape with the buttons and options on the DRAWING TOOLS FORMAT tab. You can also use buttons and options on the DRAWING TOOLS FORMAT tab to size and/or position a shape in a manner similar to sizing and/or positioning an image.

Shapes

You will practice inserting, formatting, and positioning text boxes and shapes in Exercise 3.2A.

Exercise 3.2A Inserting, Formatting, and Positioning a Text Box and a Shape   **Part 1 of 3**

1. Open **VMAgenda.docx** from your Chapter03 folder and then save the document with the name **C03-E02-VMAgenda**.
2. Insert, format, and position a text box containing the initials *VM* as shown in Figure 3.19 on page 107 by completing the following steps:

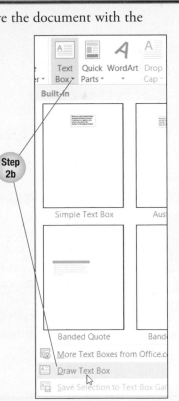

a. Click the INSERT tab.
b. Click the Text Box button and then click *Draw Text Box* at the drop-down list.
c. Click in the upper left corner of the document to insert a text box.
d. Click in the *Shape Height* measurement box in the Size group on the DRAWING TOOLS FORMAT tab and then type **1.4**.
e. Click in the *Shape Width* measurement box, type **2.1**, and then press Enter.

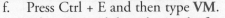

f. Press Ctrl + E and then type **VM**.
g. Select *VM* and then change the font to 72-point Algerian. (Use the Font button and the Font Size button on the HOME tab.)
h. Click the DRAWING TOOLS FORMAT tab, click the Shape Fill button arrow in the Shape Styles group, and then click *No Fill* at the drop-down list.
i. Click the Shape Outline button arrow in the Shape Styles group and then click *No Outline* at the drop-down list.
j. Click the Text Fill button arrow in the WordArt Styles group and then click the *Gold, Accent 4, Lighter 40%* color option (eighth column, fourth row in the *Theme Colors* section).

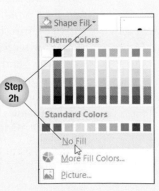

---

k. Click the Text Outline button arrow in the WordArt Styles group and then click the *Gold, Accent 4, Darker 50%* color option (eighth column, bottom row in the *Theme Colors* section).

l. Click the Position button in the Arrange group and then click the *Position in Top Left with Square Text Wrapping* option (first column, first row in the *With Text Wrapping* section).

m. Click outside the text box to deselect it.

3. Insert, format, and position the four-headed arrow shape shown in Figure 3.19 by completing the following steps:

a. Click the INSERT tab.

b. Click the Shapes button in the Illustrations group.

c. Click the *Quad Arrow Callout* shape (second column, third row in the *Block Arrows* section).

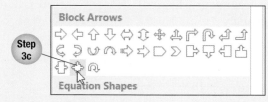

d. Click in the document to insert the shape.

e. With the shape selected, click in the *Shape Height* measurement box in the Size group on the DRAWING TOOLS FORMAT tab and then type **1.45**.

f. Click in the *Shape Width* measurement box, type **2.1**, and then press Enter.

g. Click the More button at the right side of the shape style thumbnails in the Shape Styles group and then click the *Subtle Effect - Gray-50%, Accent 3* shape style option (fourth column, fourth row).

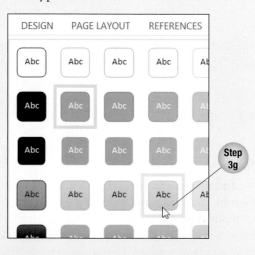

h. Click the Shape Effects button arrow in the Shape Styles group, point to *Bevel* at the drop-down list, and then click the *Circle* option at the side menu (first column, first row in the *Bevel* section).

i. Click the Position button in the Arrange group and then click the *Position in Top Left with Square Text Wrapping* option (first column, first row in the *With Text Wrapping* section).

j. Click the Send Backward button in the Arrange group to send the shape behind the text box.

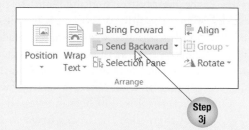

k. Click outside the shape to deselect it.

4. Save **C03-E02-VMAgenda.docx**.

Figure 3.19 Logo Created in Exercise 3.2A

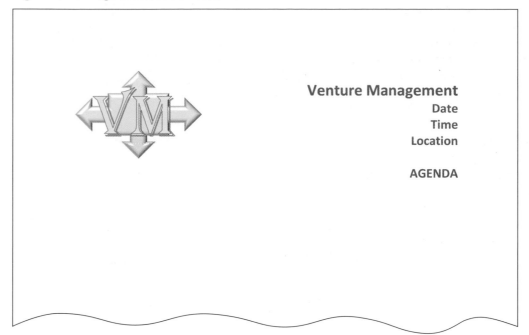

Venture Management
Date
Time
Location

AGENDA

Inserting Tables

Arranging document text in the rows and columns of a table allows you to present complex information in a clear and easy-to-understand manner, which increases your document's readability. Word makes it easy to quickly create organized, attractive tables.

In Word 2013, insert a table by using the Table button in the Tables group on the INSERT tab. At the Table button drop-down list, you can insert a table using the grid in the *Insert Table* section or by clicking the *Insert Table* option, as shown in Figure 3.20 on page 108. To insert a table using the grid, highlight the desired amount of columns and rows and then click the left mouse button. Clicking the *Insert Table* option displays the Insert Table dialog box, as shown in Figure 3.21 on page 108. At the Insert Table dialog box, enter the desired number of columns and rows in the measurement boxes and then click OK.

Information is entered into a table's cells. A *cell* is the intersection of a row and a column. With the insertion point positioned in a cell, type or edit text as you would normally. Use the mouse to move the insertion point to other cells by positioning the arrow pointer in the desired cell and then clicking the left mouse button. If you are using the keyboard, press the Tab key to move the insertion point to the next cell, or press Shift + Tab to move the insertion point to the previous cell. If you want to move the insertion point to a tab stop within a cell, press Ctrl + Tab. If the insertion point is located in the last cell of the table and you press the Tab key, Word automatically adds another row to the table. When all of the information has been entered into the cells, move the insertion point below the table and if necessary, continue typing the document or save the document in the normal manner.

Table

cell

The intersection of a row and a column in a table

◀ **DTP POINTER**

To view table gridlines, click anywhere in a table, and then click the View Gridlines button in the Table group on the TABLE TOOLS LAYOUT tab.

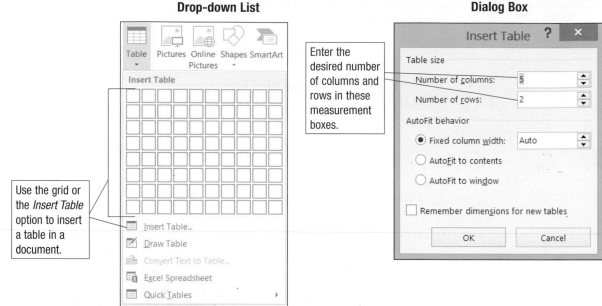

Use the grid or the *Insert Table* option to insert a table in a document.

Enter the desired number of columns and rows in these measurement boxes.

In Exercise 3.2B, you will insert a table into the agenda document you started in Exercise 3.2A. You will add the number of columns and rows, apply a table style, adjust the cell alignment and column width, and practice merging cells.

Exercise 3.2B Inserting and Formatting a Table   Part 2 of 3

1. With **C03-E02-VMAgenda.docx** open, insert a table by completing the following steps (refer to Figure 3.22 on page 112):
   a. Press Ctrl + End to move the insertion point to the end of the document.
   b. Click the INSERT tab.
   c. Click the Table button in the Tables group and then click *Insert Table* at the drop-down list.
   d. At the Insert Table dialog box, type **2** in the *Number of columns* measurement box.
   e. Press the Tab key, type **10** in the *Number of rows* measurement box, and then press Enter.

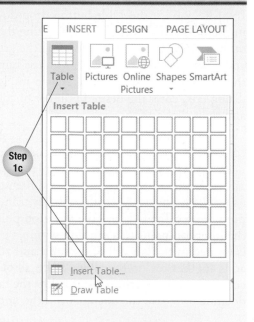

Step 1c

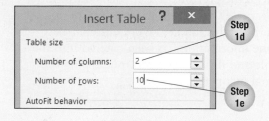

Step 1d

Step 1e

2. Select the entire table by clicking the table move handle that displays outside the upper left corner of the table.

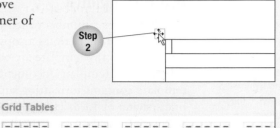

3. With the table selected, apply the following formatting:
   a. Click the More button in the Table Styles group and then click the *Grid Table 2 - Accent 3* table style option (fourth column, second row in the *Grid Tables* section).
   b. Click the TABLE TOOLS LAYOUT tab.
   c. Click in the *Table Row Height* measurement box in the Cell Size group, type **0.4**, and then press Enter.

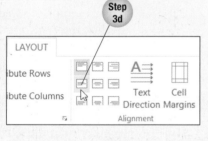

   d. Click the Align Center Left button in the Alignment group.
   e. Change the text color by clicking the HOME tab, clicking the Font Color button arrow, and then clicking the *Blue, Accent 1, Darker 50%* color option (fifth column, bottom row in the *Theme Colors* section).

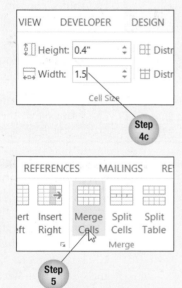

4. Change the widths of the columns by completing the following steps:
   a. Click in the first cell in the first column in the table.
   b. Click the TABLE TOOLS LAYOUT tab.
   c. Click in the *Table Column Width* measurement box in the Cell Size group, type **1.5**, and then press Enter.
   d. Click in the first cell in the second column in the table.
   e. Click in the *Table Column Width* measurement box, type **5**, and then press Enter.
5. Merge the cells in the first row by selecting the two cells in the first row and then clicking the Merge Cells button in the Merge group on the TABLE TOOLS LAYOUT tab.
6. With the merged cells selected, change the alignment and font size by completing the following steps:
   a. Click the Align Center button in the Alignment group on the TABLE TOOLS LAYOUT tab.
   b. Click the HOME tab.
   c. Click the Font Size button arrow in the Font group and then click *14* at the drop-down gallery.
7. Save **C03-E02-VMAgenda.docx**.

Using Templates

Word includes a number of template documents formatted for specific uses. A ***template*** is a document that creates a copy of itself when you open it so that all text and formatting in the template are transferred to the new document. Each Word document is based on a template document, with Normal.dotm as the default. This default template contains formatting such as 11-point Calibri font, left paragraph alignment, line spacing of 1.08, and eight points of spacing after paragraphs. You can create a document based on the default template, create your own template and use that as a basis for a document, or create a document based on a template from Office.com.

Saving a Document as a Template

If a document you create contains features and formatting that you will want to use in future documents, consider saving the document as a template. To save a document as a template, display the Save As dialog box, change the *Save as type* option to *Word Template (*.dotx)*, type a name for the template in the *File name* text box, and then click the Save button.

By default, Word saves template documents in the Custom Office Templates folder on your computer's hard drive. The templates saved at this location will display at the New backstage area when you click the *PERSONAL* option. To open a document based on a template saved in the Custom Office Templates folder, click the FILE tab and then click the *New* option. At the New backstage area, click the *PERSONAL* option, and then double-click the desired template thumbnail.

In some instances, such as in a company or in a classroom, a template might be saved in a different location other than the Custom Office Templates folder. For example, in the next exercise, you will create a template and then save it in your Chapter03 folder. To create a new document based on a template saved in a location other than the Custom Office Templates folder, open File Explorer, navigate to the folder containing the template, and then double-click the template file in the Content pane. This will open a new Word document based on that template.

In Exercise 3.2C, you will save the agenda document you created as a template for future use. You will then open and complete a document based on the template.

Exercise 3.2C	Creating and Using a Template	Part 3 of 3

1. With **C03-E02-VMAgenda.docx** open, save the document as a template in your Chapter03 folder by completing the following steps:
   a. Press F12 to display the Save As dialog box.
   b. At the Save As dialog box, type **Template** at the end of the file name in the *File name* text box.
   c. Click the *Save as type* option box and then click *Word Template (*.dotx)* at the drop-down list.
   d. Navigate to your Chapter03 folder.
   e. Click the Save button.

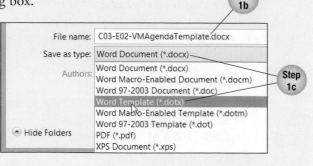

Step 1b

Step 1c

2. Close Word.
3. Open a new document based on **C03-E02-VMAgendaTemplate.dotx** by completing the following steps:
   a. Open a File Explorer window by clicking the File Explorer icon on the Taskbar.
   b. At the File Explorer window, navigate to your Chapter03 folder.
   c. Double-click *C03-E02-VMAgendaTemplate.dotx*.

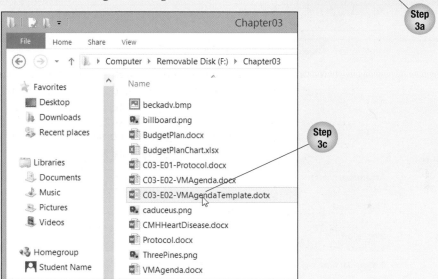

4. At the new Word document based on the template you previously created, enter the information in Figure 3.22 on page 112 by completing the following steps:
   a. Select the text *Date* in the upper right corner of the document and then type **Thursday, July 23, 2015**.
   b. Select the text *Time* below the date and then type **9 a.m.–5 p.m.** *Hint: Make sure you insert an en dash between the times.*
   c. Select the text *Location* below the date and time and then type **Rainier Room**.

   d. Type the information in the table as shown in Figure 3.22. *Hint: Make sure you insert an en dash between the times.*
5. Save the document with the name **C03-E02-VMAgenda-072315**.
6. Print and then close **C03-E02-VMAgenda-072315.docx**.

Figure 3.22 **Agenda Created from a Template in Exercise 3.2C**

Venture Management
Thursday, July 23, 2015
9 a.m.–5 p.m.
Rainier Room

AGENDA

Venture Management Committee
Meeting called by Amy Marsh

Attendees:	Amy Marsh, Kyle Weber, Nick Bjorn, Lisa Hartford, Rachel Smythe, James Westerman, David Hoffman, Julia Ma, Chase Moore
Please read:	*Reengineering the Corporation* by M. Hamilton and J. Vasquez *The Fifth Discipline* by P. M. Sange
Please bring:	Laptop or tablet
9 a.m.–10 a.m.	Introduction, Amy Marsh Review of financial results, Kyle Weber
10 a.m.–Noon	Budget discussion for fiscal year 2016 Kyle Weber and Julia Ma
Noon–1 p.m.	Lunch break, Centre Pointe Café
1 p.m.–2 p.m.	Revenue growth initiative, James Westerman Review of annual meeting, Kyle Weber Breakout feedback, Nick Bjorn and Lisa Hartford Review of growth plan, Chase Moore
2 p.m.–4 p.m.	Formulation of geographic expansion plan, Chase Moore and Rachel Smythe
4 p.m.–5 p.m.	Miscellaneous Adjournment

Creating Documents with Office.com Templates

Word includes a number of template documents formatted for specific uses. These templates are available online at Office.com. To access templates from Office.com, click the FILE tab, and then click the *New* option. At the New backstage area (shown in Figure 3.23), click in the search text box, type a search word or phrase, and then press the Enter key. Word searches Office.com and displays template thumbnails that match the search word or phrase. Double-click a template to open a document based on the template.

In addition to using templates from Office.com or templates you previously created, you can find templates in various places on the Internet. Open your favorite search engine in a web browser and then search using a search phrase and the .dotx file extension. Before using a template you find on the Internet, make sure you have permission to use the template and then credit the source of the template.

◀DTP POINTER

When you search for a template from Office.com and then double-click the template, it is downloaded to your computer and available for future use.

Customizing Templates

When customizing a template to meet your specific needs, remember to apply the basic design concepts discussed in Chapter 1. Always begin with the end result in mind. Plan your text carefully to achieve your desired results without unnecessary wording or formatting. If you replace the existing fonts in a template, be sure the new fonts support the readability of the text.

Templates can help you create professional, attractive documents. However, if it is important to you that your documents look unique, consider the following suggestions for customizing existing templates:

- Change fonts, font styles, font sizes, font colors, and font effects.
- Use expanded, condensed, lowered, or raised character spacing.
- Use reverse text and/or rotated text.
- Add more or less line spacing between lines.
- Add fill color and fill effects (gradient, texture, pattern, or picture).

◀DTP POINTER

Avoid "one size fits all" formatting by customizing a template to fit your needs.

Figure 3.23 Searching in the New Backstage Area

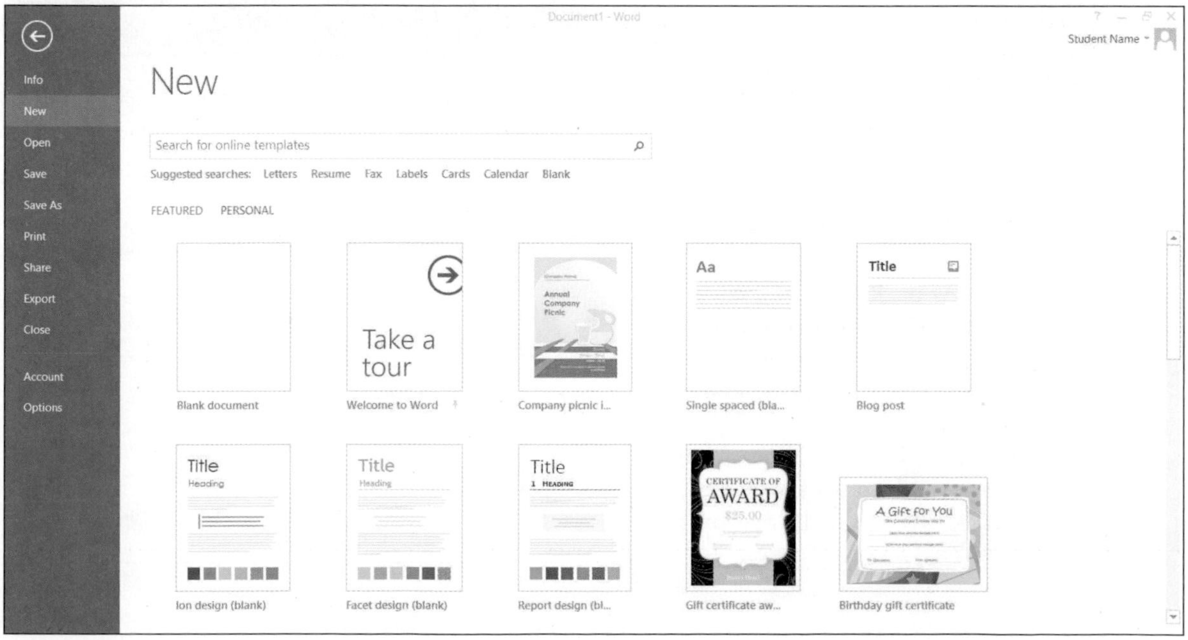

- Add text box shading, shapes, effects, or 3-D effects.
- Apply styles, text box styles, themes, style sets, SmartArt, pictures, clip art, scanned images, shapes, charts, WordArt, building blocks, or any of the graphical design enhancement features available in Word 2013.
- Insert special characters and symbols.
- Create unique bullets.
- Add borders and shading.
- Add drop caps.
- Add a company logo.
- Adjust the alignment.
- Create a watermark.
- Use unique column layout and specialized tables.
- Include links to other documents.

Understanding Placeholders in Templates

In Exercise 3.1A, you added a cover page to a report. The cover page template contained several text placeholders that you customized with your own content. You may have noticed that the Author placeholder already contained a name. Placeholders such as this one are synchronized with the document's properties and therefore populate automatically. You can find the author's name for a document in the *Properties* section of the Info backstage area.

When you moved the mouse pointer over the date placeholder, did you see a calendar (date picker) appear automatically? This is an example of a content control. Content controls are somewhat different from placeholders, but both are often found in Office templates. Content controls can be added to your document with options on the DEVELOPER tab. You will learn more about adding content controls to your documents in later chapters.

In Exercise 3.3, you will download a template from Office.com and then customize it as directed.

Exercise 3.3 Downloading and Customizing a Template

1. Make sure you are connected to the Internet and then open a document based on an Office.com agenda template by completing the following steps:
   a. Click the FILE tab and then click the *New* option.
   b. At the New backstage area, click in the search text box, type **formal agenda**, and then press the Enter key.
   c. Double-click the *Formal meeting agenda* template thumbnail.
   d. Click the FILE tab, click the Convert button at the Info backstage area, and then click OK at the dialog box.

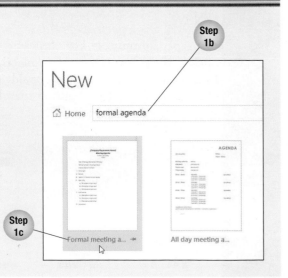

Step 1b

New

⌂ Home   formal agenda

AGENDA

Step 1c

Formal meeting a...   All day meeting a...

---

2. Customize the document by completing the following steps:
   a. Select the entire document and then change the font to Cambria.
   b. Change the top margin to 0.75 inch.
   c. Deselect the text and then insert the image **ThreePines.png** from your Chapter03 folder. *Hint: Do this with the Pictures button in the Illustrations group on the INSERT tab.*
   d. Change the position of the image by clicking the Position button in the Arrange group on the PICTURE TOOLS FORMAT tab and then clicking *Position in Top Center with Square Text Wrapping* at the drop-down gallery.
3. Save the document as a template in your Chapter03 folder by completing the following steps:
   a. Press F12 to display the Save As dialog box.
   b. At the Save As dialog box, click the down-pointing arrow at the right side of the *Save as type* option box and then click *Word Template (*.dotx)* at the drop-down list.
   c. Click in the *File name* text box and then type **C03-E03-TPCCAgendaTemplate**.
   d. Navigate to your Chapter03 folder.
   e. Click the Save button.

4. Close **C03-E03-TPCCAgendaTemplate.dotx**.
5. Open a document based on the template you just saved by completing the following steps:
   a. Click the File Explorer icon on the Taskbar.
   b. At the File Explorer window, navigate to your Chapter03 folder.
   c. Double-click **C03-E03-TPCCAgendaTemplate.dotx**.
6. Click in the *[Company/Department Name]* placeholder and then type **Community Development Committee**.
7. Click in the *[Click to select date]* placeholder, click the down-pointing arrow at the right side of the placeholder, and then click the Today button that displays at the bottom of the drop-down calendar.
8. Click in the *[Time]* placeholder and then type **3:30 p.m.**
9. Click in each of the remaining placeholders and type the text as shown in Figure 3.24 on page 116.
10. Save the completed agenda document in your Chapter03 folder and name it **C03-E03-TPCCMeetingAgenda**.
11. Print and then close **C03-E03-TPCCMeetingAgenda.docx**.

Figure 3.24 Agenda Created from a Template in Exercise 3.3

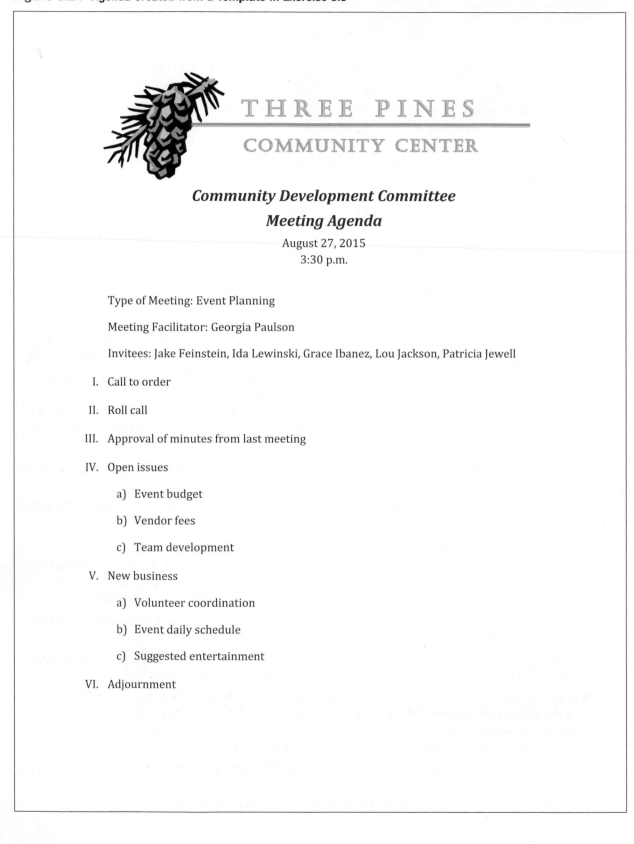

THREE PINES
COMMUNITY CENTER

Community Development Committee
Meeting Agenda

August 27, 2015
3:30 p.m.

Type of Meeting: Event Planning

Meeting Facilitator: Georgia Paulson

Invitees: Jake Feinstein, Ida Lewinski, Grace Ibanez, Lou Jackson, Patricia Jewell

   I. Call to order

  II. Roll call

 III. Approval of minutes from last meeting

 IV. Open issues

    a) Event budget

    b) Vendor fees

    c) Team development

  V. New business

    a) Volunteer coordination

    b) Event daily schedule

    c) Suggested entertainment

 VI. Adjournment

Chapter Summary

➤ Insert document elements using building blocks. Display the Building Blocks Organizer dialog box to view a complete list of predesigned building blocks.

➤ Insert a cover page into longer documents to provide a professional-looking title page. Insert a cover page at the Building Blocks Organizer dialog box or with the Cover Page button in the Pages group on the INSERT tab.

➤ Text that appears at the top of each page is referred to as a header, and text that appears at the bottom of each page is referred to as a footer.

➤ Insert and/or edit a header or footer using the Header pane or Footer pane. You can also insert predesigned headers or footers using the Header button or Footer button on the INSERT tab.

➤ Insert page numbers into the Header pane or Footer pane to provide users sequential page references in longer documents. To insert page numbers, click the Page Number button in the Header & Footer group on the INSERT tab.

➤ A page break moves any text below the break to the next page. A soft page break is automatically inserted, and a hard page break is manually inserted. Insert a hard page break by clicking the Page Break button in the Pages group on the INSERT tab or by pressing Ctrl + Enter.

➤ A watermark is a lightened image or text that displays behind existing document content. Create a watermark by clicking the Watermark button in the Page Background group on the DESIGN tab.

➤ Text and images in Word are arranged in layers. Each document includes a foreground layer, a text layer, and a background layer.

➤ Use the Bring Forward button or the Send Backward button in the Arrange group on the PICTURE TOOLS FORMAT tab, the DRAWING TOOLS FORMAT tab, or the PAGE LAYOUT tab to adjust the layering of objects within a document.

➤ Insert images from Office.com by clicking the Online Pictures button in the Illustrations group on the INSERT tab.

➤ Insert images from the computer's hard drive by clicking the Pictures button in the Illustrations group on the INSERT tab.

➤ Use the sizing handles around a selected image to adjust its size.

➤ Move an image by selecting the image and then using the mouse to drag the image to the desired position.

➤ Use the Wrap Text button in the Arrange group on the PICTURE TOOLS FORMAT tab or the PAGE LAYOUT tab to change the text wrapping for a selected image.

➤ Insert bullets into a document by clicking the Bullets button in the Paragraph group on the HOME tab. Customize bullets at the Define New Bullet dialog box.

➤ Text boxes are useful because they make it easy to move and position different blocks of text. Customize text boxes with buttons and options on the DRAWING TOOLS FORMAT tab.

➤ Insert shapes into a document by clicking the Shapes button in the Illustrations group on the INSERT tab. Customize shapes with buttons and options on the DRAWING TOOLS FORMAT tab.

➤ Tables can be used to present complex information in an easy-to-understand manner. Insert a table by clicking the Table button in the Tables group on the INSERT tab.

➤ Word provides a number of templates that can be used to produce a variety of documents. The default template is Normal.dotm.

➤ Search for and download templates from Office.com at the New backstage area.

- A document you save as a template is saved to the Custom Office Templates folder on your computer's hard drive. Open a document based on a template that has been saved to the Custom Office Templates folder by displaying the New backstage area, clicking the *PERSONAL* option, and then clicking the desired template thumbnail.
- You can save a template in a folder other than the Custom Office Templates folder. Use the File Explorer window to open a document based on a template that has been saved to a folder other than the Custom Office Templates folder.

Commands Review

FEATURE	RIBBON TAB, GROUP	BUTTON	KEYBOARD SHORTCUT
bring forward	PICTURE TOOLS FORMAT, Arrange DRAWING TOOLS FORMAT, Arrange PAGE LAYOUT, Arrange		
bullets	HOME, Paragraph		
cover page	INSERT, Pages		
footer	INSERT, Header & Footer		
header	INSERT, Header & Footer		
Insert Pictures window	INSERT, Illustrations		
page break	INSERT, Pages		Ctrl + Enter
page number	INSERT, Header & Footer		
Insert Picture dialog box	INSERT, Illustrations		
quick parts	INSERT, Quick Parts		
send backward	PICTURE TOOLS FORMAT, Arrange DRAWING TOOLS FORMAT, Arrange PAGE LAYOUT, Arrange		
shape fill	DRAWING TOOLS FORMAT, Shape Styles		
shape outline	DRAWING TOOLS FORMAT, Shape Styles		
shapes	INSERT, Illustrations		
table	INSERT, Tables		
text box	INSERT, Text		

FEATURE	RIBBON TAB, GROUP	BUTTON	KEYBOARD SHORTCUT
view gridlines	TABLE TOOLS LAYOUT, Table		
watermark	DESIGN, Page Background		
wrap text	PICTURE TOOLS FORMAT, Arrange DRAWING TOOLS FORMAT, Arrange PAGE LAYOUT, Arrange		

Key Points *Review*

A.	table	F.	wrap text	K.	cover page
B.	watermark	G.	Info	L.	New
C.	Header & Footer	H.	text box	M.	cell
D.	page break	I.	header	N.	Text
E.	footer	J.	tab		

Matching: In the space at the left, provide the correct letter from the above list that matches each definition.

<u>K</u>   1. A title page that displays at the beginning of a document

<u>I</u>   2. Text that appears at the top of every page in a document

<u>C</u>   3. The group on the INSERT tab containing the Page Number button

<u>D</u>   4. Moves text after the insertion point to the next page

<u>B</u>   5. A lightened graphic or text that displays behind text in a document

<u>A</u>   6. Feature that can be used to change how text is positioned around, in front, or behind an object

<u>H</u>   7. An object that can be used to precisely position text in a document

<u>A</u>   8. Feature that can be used to format text in rows and columns

<u>M</u>   9. Intersection of a row and a column

<u>L</u>   10. The backstage area used to find and open templates

Chapter Assessments

Assessment 3.1   Format a Heart Disease Fact Sheet

1. Open **CMHHeartDisease.docx** from your Chapter03 folder and then save the document with the name **C03-A01-CMHHeartDisease**.
2. Apply the following formatting to the document:
   a. Apply the Lines (Simple) style set.
   b. Apply the View theme.
   c. Change the theme colors to *Blue Warm*.
   d. Insert the Banded cover page. Type **HEART DISEASE FACT SHEET** as the document title, insert your name in place of the name that displays above the [COMPANY NAME] placeholder, type **CHICAGO MERCY HOSPITAL** as the company name, and type **500 State Street, Chicago, IL 60602** as the company address.
   e. Insert the Banded header and the Banded footer.
   f. Insert the **caduceus.png** file (located in your Chapter03 folder) as a picture watermark.
   g. Select the first seven paragraphs of text below the *Heart Disease Facts* heading and then apply custom bullets by creating and inserting a heart symbol bullet (use the Symbol button at the Define New Bullet dialog box and type character code **169** in the *Character code* text box).
   h. Insert a page break at the beginning of the *Heart Disease Facts* heading.
3. Save, print, and then close **C03-A01-CMHHeartDisease.docx**.

Assessment 3.2   Create an Events Document and Template

1. Open a blank document and then create the banquet room events document shown in Figure 3.25 with the following specifications:
   a. Click the No Spacing style in the Styles group on the HOME tab.
   b. Change the font to 18-point Calibri and the font color to *Orange, Accent 2, Darker 50%* (sixth column, bottom row in the *Theme Colors* section).
   c. Press the Enter key seven times.
   d. Insert the maple leaf clip art image from Office.com. Use *maple leaf* as the search text and select the image that most closely matches the one in Figure 3.25. Change the text wrapping to *Through*, change the image height to *1.9"*, and then change the color to *Washout* (fourth column, first row in the *Recolor* section). Position the image as shown in the figure.
   e. Insert the text *Maple Leaf Spa and Resort* in a text box. Select the text, change the font to 26-point Brush Script Std and the font color to *Orange, Accent 2, Darker 50%*. Remove the text box shape fill and shape outline and then move the text box over the leaf image as shown in the figure.
   f. Move the insertion point to the end of the document, type **Banquet Room Events** and then press the Enter key. Type **Week of**, press the spacebar, and then press the Enter key. Apply bold formatting to the two lines of text you just typed.
   g. Press Ctrl + End and then insert a table with 3 columns and 14 rows.
   h. Select the entire table, apply the Grid Table 2 - Accent 4 table style to the table, change the row height to 0.4 inch, and change the alignment to *Align Center Left*.
   i. Type text in the table as shown in Figure 3.25. Make sure the days of the week in column 1 and the headings in row 1 display with bold formatting.
2. Save the document with the name **C03-A02-MLSREvents**.
3. Save the document as a template in your Chapter03 folder with the name **C03-A02-MLSREventsTemplate**.
4. Print and then close **C03-A02-MLSREventsTemplate.dotx**.

Figure 3.25 Document Created in Assessment 3.2

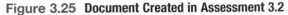

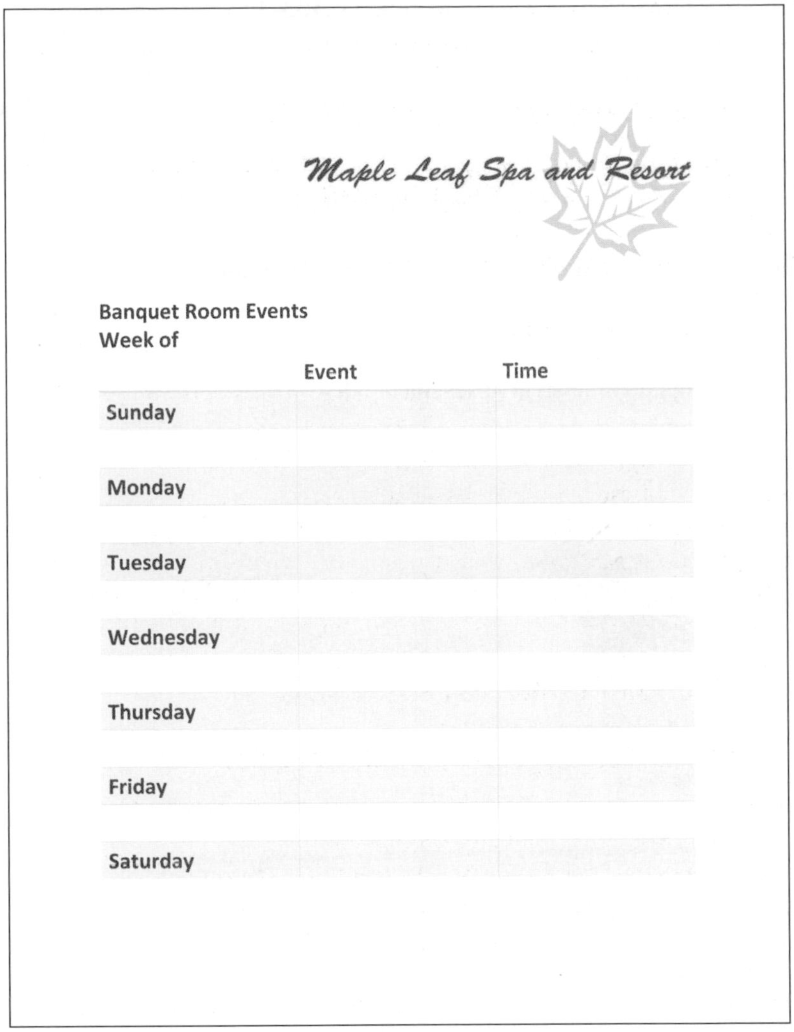

Maple Leaf Spa and Resort

Banquet Room Events
Week of

	Event	Time
Sunday		
Monday		
Tuesday		
Wednesday		
Thursday		
Friday		
Saturday		

Assessment 3.3   Download, Customize, and Save a Template

1. Display the New backstage area, search for templates at Office.com using the search words *time sheet*, and then download the time sheet template that most closely matches what you see in Figure 3.26 on page 122.
2. Make the following modifications to the template:
   a. Change the theme colors to *Green*.
   b. Select the entire document, change the font to Candara, and change the font color to *Green, Accent 1, Darker 25%* (fifth column, fifth row in the *Theme Colors* section).
   c. Press Ctrl + Home, press the Enter key, and then insert **ThreePines.png** from your Chapter03 folder. Change the position of the image to *Position in Top Center with Square Text Wrapping*.
   d. Insert the CONFIDENTIAL 1 watermark.
   e. Click in the *[Company Name]* placeholder and type **Three Pines Community Center**.
   f. Click in the *[Street address]* placeholder and then type **350 Chelan Boulevard**.
   g. Click in the *[City, ST ZIP Code]* placeholder and then type **Wenatchee, WA 98801**.
   h. Click in the *[phone]* placeholder and then type **(509) 555-3500**.
   i. Click in the *[fax]* placeholder and then type **(509) 555-3555**.

3. Save the document as a template (choose *Word Template (*.dotx)* at the *Save as type* option box) in your Chapter03 folder. Name the template **C03-A03-TPCCTimeSheet.**
4. If necessary, click OK at the file conversion dialog box.
5. Close **C03-A03-TPCCTimeSheet.dotx.**
6. Using File Explorer, open a document based on **C03-A03-TPCCTimeSheet.dotx.**
7. Type text in the time sheet with hours for Monday through Friday of the next week (you determine the start and end times) providing for eight hours each day. Include two hours of overtime for at least one day of the week. You determine the data to enter in the other appropriate locations in the time sheet.
8. Save the completed document with the name **C03-A03-TimeSheet.**
9. Print and then close **C03-A03-TimeSheet.docx.**

Figure 3.26 Time Sheet Template Created in Assessment 3.3

THREE PINES
COMMUNITY CENTER

Three Pines Community Center
350 Chelan Boulevard
Wenatchee, WA 98801
Phone (509) 555-3500 Fax (509) 555-3555

TIME SHEET

CONFIDENTIAL

Employee Name: ____________ Title: ____________
Employee Number: ____________ Status: ____________
Department: ____________ Supervisor: ____________

Date	Start Time	End Time	Regular Hrs.	Overtime Hrs.	Total Hrs.
		Weekly Totals			

Employee signature: ____________ Date: ____________
Supervisor signature: ____________ Date: ____________

Assessment 3.4   Create a Memo and Insert an Excel Chart

INTEGRATED

In this assessment, you will customize a Word memo template and then copy and paste a chart from an Excel worksheet into the memo. In addition, you will determine the average monthly cost of propane by inserting a formula into the Excel worksheet and record the amount in the memo. Refer to Figure 3.27 as you work through the assessment. To create the memo, complete the following steps:

1. Download the Memo (Professional design) template from Office.com. (If this memo template is not available, choose a similar template.)
2. Type the following text in the specified placeholders:
   [Company Name]: **Superior Propane**
   [Recipient Name]: **Susan Howard**
   [Your Name]: **Jake Kuo**
   [Name]: **Raymond Cirrus**
   [Click to select date]: (insert today's date)
   [Subject]: **Proposed Letter to Customers**

Figure 3.27   Memo Created in Assessment 3.4

Superior Propane

Memo

To:	Susan Howard
From:	Jake Kuo
cc:	Raymond Cirrus
Date:	Current Date
Re:	Proposed Letter to Customers

We would like to provide our customers with specific information on their monthly propane usage by sending a letter to each customer with information on their propane usage and a chart showing their monthly costs for the previous year. In the letter, we would include information letting our customers know about the Superior Budget Plan that will take the surprise out of monthly bills. The plan allows customers to spread their payments over a 12-month period. The letter would include the customer's yearly propane costs in a chart similar to the one shown below. Also included in the letter will be the average monthly cost; for the sample budget, the monthly average would be [insert average cost here].

We will be finalizing the letter soon so please let me know if you have any feedback on the letter content or chart.

Yearly Propane Costs

C03-A04-SPBudgetPlan.docx

3. Click in the *[Type memo here]* placeholder and then insert **BudgetPlan.docx** from your Chapter03 folder. (Do this with the *Text from File* option at the Object button drop-down list in the Text group on the INSERT tab.)

4. Open Excel, open **BudgetPlanChart.xlsx** from your Chapter03 folder, and then save it with the name **C03-A04-BudgetPlanChart**.

5. Position the insertion point in cell B14 and then type the following formula to compute the average of the monthly bills: **=Average(B2:B13)**. After typing the formula, press the Enter key.

6. Select the chart (make sure you select the chart and not a specific element in the chart) and then click the Copy button in the Clipboard group on the HOME tab.

7. Make the Word memo the active document.

8. Position the insertion point a double-space below the body of the memo (a double-space above the file name) and then insert the Excel chart by completing the following steps:

   a. Click the Paste button arrow in the Clipboard group on the HOME tab and then click *Paste Special* at the drop-down list.

   b. At the Paste Special dialog box, make sure the *Paste* option is selected, click *Microsoft Excel Chart Object* in the *As* list box, and then click OK.

9. Type the average amount that you computed in Excel in place of the text *(insert average cost here)*. **Hint: Do not italicize the average amount.**

10. Adjust margins or resize the chart, if necessary, to make the memo fit on one page.

11. Save the memo document and name it **C03-A04-SPBudgetPlan**.

12. If necessary, click OK at the file conversion dialog box.

13. Print and then close **C03-A04-SPBudgetPlan.docx**.

14. Make Excel the active program, close **C03-A04-BudgetPlanChart.xlsx**, and then close Excel.

Assessment 3.5   Create an International Tipping and Etiquette Fact Sheet

GROUP PROJECT

In some countries tipping is considered offensive, in other countries tipping is automatically included in the final cost of the services provided, and in other countries standard tipping should be added to the total bill as a percentage that varies depending on where you are. Your company is participating in an international conference being held in a foreign country, and in an effort to prepare your conference attendees for cultural differences, you have been asked to create a fact sheet summarizing customary tipping and etiquette guidelines. Figure 3.28 shows a sample solution with formatting, including a rotated text box with no fill and no outline, a shape with inserted text, and a logo created with a clip art image and text box containing text. Your solution should not match the sample exactly but should be your own unique interpretation of the following guidelines:

1. Use an Internet search engine to research the general tipping and etiquette guidelines for a country of your own choosing.

2. Include tipping practices for restaurants, tour guides, hotel personnel, and taxi drivers.

3. Use graphics to add visual appeal and font effects to enhance the text.

4. Include the source of your information.

5. Save the completed fact sheet with the name **C03-A05-TippingFactSheet**.

6. Print and then close **C03-A05-TippingFactSheet.docx**.

Figure 3.28 **Sample Solution for Assessment 3.5**

Tipping in Hong Kong

Cross International
Hong Kong
2015 Annual Meeting

Different countries have different practices in regard to tipping, and here are general guidelines for tipping in Hong Kong.

Even though most restaurants and bars automatically add 10 percent to the bill as a service charge, you are still expected to leave small change for the waiter. A general rule of thumb is to leave 5 percent, unless you are dissatisfied with the level of service. In fine restaurants, you should leave around 10 percent. Yet in some Chinese restaurants where meals are relatively inexpensive, it is acceptable to leave change if paying by cash and round up to the next HK$10 if paying by credit card.

You are also expected to tip cab drivers, bellboys, hairdressers, and beauticians.

For taxi cab drivers, simply round up your bill to the nearest HK$10. For hairdressers and beauticians, the norm is to tip 5 or 10 percent. For bellboys, HK$20 is common, depending on the number of bags. If you use a public restroom with an attendant, you may be expected to leave a small gratuity—HK$5.

In addition, chambermaids and room attendants are usually given about HK$20 to HK$50, depending on the level of service.

Source: http://www.discoverhongkong.com/eng/index.jsp

Understanding and Applying Desktop Publishing Concepts

ASSESSING PROFICIENCIES

In this unit, you have learned about important desktop publishing concepts, as well as how to plan and design documents based on design principles that include focus, balance, proportion, contrast, color, directional flow, and consistency.

Note: Before beginning computer exercises for this section, copy to your storage medium the Unit01 folder from the CD that accompanies this textbook and then make Unit01 the active folder. Remember to substitute for graphics that may no longer be available.

Assessment U1.1   Create an Invitation

1. Open **SpringGala.docx** from your Unit01 folder and then save the document with the name **U1-PA01-SpringGala**.
2. Create a text box for the text you see in Figure U1.1 on page 128. Remove the shape fill and the shape outline from the text box.
3. Type the text shown in the text box in Figure U1.1 (except for the ampersand [&] between *Spring Gala* and *Charity Ball*).
4. Select *Spring Gala* and *Charity Ball* and then make the following changes:
   a. Change the font to 60-point Gabriola.
   b. Apply the Fill - Black, Text 1, Outline - Background 1, Hard Shadow - Accent 1 text effect (second column, bottom row).
   c. Change the text fill to *Blue, Accent 1, Darker 50%* (fifth column, bottom row in the *Theme Colors* section).
   d. Display the Font dialog box with the Advanced tab selected, expand the spacing by 1 point, apply stylistic set 6, and then close the dialog box.
   e. Change the spacing after paragraphs to 12 points.
5. Select the remaining text, change the font to 16-point Harrington, change the font color to *Blue, Accent 1, Darker 50%*, apply bold formatting, and then expand the spacing by 1 point.
6. Create a second text box and then remove the shape fill and shape outline.
7. Type an ampersand *&* inside the text box, select the ampersand, and then make the following changes:
   a. Change the font to 72-point Vivaldi.
   b. Apply the Fill - White, Outline - Accent 1, Shadow text effect (fourth column, first row).
   c. Apply the Green, Accent 6, Lighter 60% text fill (last column, third row in the *Theme Colors* section).
   d. Position the ampersand as shown in Figure U1.1.
8. Make any other necessary changes so that your document appears similar to the document in Figure U1.1.
9. Save, print, and then close **U1-PA01-SpringGala.docx**.

Figure U1.1 Invitation Created in Performance Assessment U1.1

Assessment U1.2   Format a Memo

1. Open **CMHMemo.docx** from your Unit01 folder and then save the document with the name **U1-PA02-CMHMemo**.
2. Format the memo so it appears as shown in Figure U1.2 with the following specifications:
   a. With the insertion point positioned at the beginning of the document, insert **CMHLogo.png** from your Unit01 folder. Change text wrapping to *Behind Text*.
   b. Change the *e* in the name *Medard* to *é* using a symbol from the Symbol dialog box with the (normal text) font selected.
   c. Select the text *(Current Date)* and then type the current date.
   d. Insert the word *Surgery* as a text watermark.
   e. Create the marked check box custom bullets (use the symbol with the Wingding character code 254) and then apply bullet formatting to the paragraphs as shown in the figure.

f. Select the two hyphens between the words *signed* and *admissions* in the first bulleted paragraph and then insert an em dash.

g. Insert the text box containing the word *CONFIDENTIAL.* Change the height of the text box to 0.5 inch and the width to 2 inches and then apply the Blue, Accent 5, Darker 25% shape fill (ninth column, fifth row in the *Theme Colors* section).

h. Change the font for the word *CONFIDENTIAL* in the text box to 14-point Arial Black and then apply the White, Background 1 font color. Remove spacing after paragraphs and change the line spacing to single. Center the text horizontally and vertically in the text box. ***Hint: Use the Align Text button in the Text group on the DRAWING TOOLS FORMAT tab to vertically center the text.***

i. Change the position of the text box to *Position in Bottom Right with Square Text Wrapping.*

3. Save, print, and then close **U1-PA02-CMHMemo.docx**.

Figure U1.2 Memo Formatted in Performance Assessment U1.2

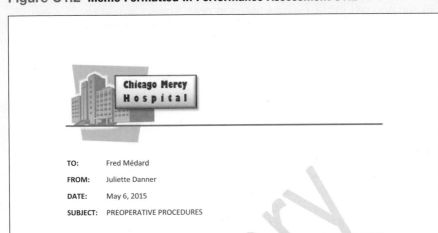

Assessment U1.3 Create and Save an Agenda as a Template

1. Open **CMHAgenda.docx** from your Unit01 folder and then save the document with the name **U1-PA03-CMHAgenda**.
2. Insert in the document **CMHLogo.png** from your Unit01 folder. Change the height of the image to 1.9 inches and change the position to *Position in Top Left with Square Text Wrapping*.
3. Move the insertion point to the end of the document and then create a table with three columns and seven rows.
4. Select the entire table and then apply the following formatting:
   a. Apply the List Table 6 Colorful - Accent 5 table style (sixth column, sixth row in the *List Tables* section).
   b. Change the font to 11-point Arial and then apply the Blue, Accent 1, Darker 50% font color (fifth column, bottom row in the *Theme Colors* section).
   c. Change the row height to 0.7 inch.
   d. Apply center left alignment to the cells.
5. Select the first row of the table and then apply center alignment to the cells.
6. Click in the first cell in the first column and type **Time**, click in the first cell of the second column and type **Topic**, and then click in the first cell of the third column and type **Discussion Leaders**.
7. Select the text you just typed in the first row, change the font size to 14 points, and then apply the small caps effect.
8. Save **U1-PA03-CMHAgenda.docx**.
9. Save the document as a template (in the .dotx file format) in your Unit01 folder and name the template **U1-PA03-CMHAgendaTemplate**.
10. Close **U1-PA03-CMHAgendaTemplate.dotx**.
11. Using File Explorer, open a document based on **U1-PA03-CMHAgendaTemplate.dotx**.
12. Type text in the document as shown in Figure U1.3. (Insert en dashes between the times in the first column and insert the *ë* in the name *Zoë* using the Symbol dialog box.)
13. Save the completed agenda document and name it **U1-PA03-QCProjectsAgenda**.
14. Print and then close **U1-PA03-QCProjectsAgenda.docx**.

Assessment U1.4 ˙ Format a Policies and Procedures Manual

1. Open **Manual.docx** from your Unit01 folder and then save the document with the name **U1-PA04-Manual**.
2. Position the insertion point at the beginning of the document and then insert a cover page of your choosing. If the cover page contains a graphic, consider replacing it with a college-themed photograph or graphic.
3. Click in the title placeholder on the cover and type **Policies and Procedures Manual**.
4. Click in the subtitle placeholder and then type **For Instructors at Midwest Community College**.
5. Click in the abstract placeholder and then type **To familiarize instructors with policies and procedures for successful employment at Midwest Community College**.

Figure U1.3 Agenda Created in Performance Assessment U1.3

Chicago Mercy Hospital
Hospital

Chicago Mercy Hospital
Quality Care Projects
November 5
9:00 a.m. to Noon
Conference Room 8

AGENDA

TIME	TOPIC	DISCUSSION LEADERS
9:00 a.m.–9:30 a.m.	Call to order and introduction of new project members	Becky Peterson, Chair
9:30 a.m.–10:00 a.m.	Presentation of project mission statement	Charles Visconti
10:00 a.m.–11:00 a.m.	Determination of project goals and timelines	Katrina O'Dell, Zoë Benn, and Wendy Mitaki
11:00 a.m.–11:45 a.m.	Brainstorming on public relations activities	Becky Peterson, Chair
11:45 a.m.–Noon	Scheduling of next project meeting	Becky Peterson, Chair
Noon	Adjournment	Becky Peterson, Chair

6. Type your name and the current date in the cover page and apply a text effect of your own choosing to these elements.
7. Apply a style set of your own choosing to the document.
8. Apply the Heading 1 style to the title on the first page (not the cover page).
9. Apply the Heading 2 style to all of the paragraph headings in the text.
10. Apply a theme and then change the theme colors and theme fonts as desired.
11. If necessary, adjust the line spacing.
12. Click the Page Number button in the Header & Footer group on the INSERT tab and then choose a page number style that complements the design of the manual. *Hint: Make sure the* **Different First Page** *check box on the HEADER & FOOTER TOOLS DESIGN tab contains a check mark.*
13. Select the paragraphs of names and telephone numbers located on the last page, click the Table button on the INSERT tab, and then click *Convert Text to Table* at the drop-down list. Apply an appropriate table style and then resize and position the table as desired.
14. Save, print, and then close **U1-PA04-Manual.docx**.

Assessment U1.5   Insert a PowerPoint Slide into a Document

INTEGRATED

1. Create the memo shown in Figure U1.4 with the following specifications:
   a. Download the Memo (Professional design) template from Office.com. (If this template is not available, choose a similar template.)
   b. Insert the text in the memo as shown in Figure U1.4.
   c. Insert the PowerPoint slide in the memo by opening PowerPoint and then opening the presentation named **Presentation.pptx** located in your Unit01 folder. Click the slide in the slide thumbnails pane, copy the slide, make Word the active program, and then paste the slide into the memo document. Size and position the slide in the memo document as shown in the figure.
   d. Make any other necessary changes so your document appears similar to Figure U1.4.
2. Save the document with the name **U1-PA04-PresentationMemo**.
3. Print and then close **U1-PA04-PresentationMemo.docx**.
4. Make PowerPoint active, close **Presentation.pptx**, and then close PowerPoint.

DTP CHALLENGE

Take your skills to the next level by completing this more challenging assessment.

Assessment U1.6   Research and Create a Travel Itinerary

1. Create an itinerary for an imaginary upcoming vacation. Decide on a destination and then use the Internet to find potential flights, a hotel or condo where you would like to stay, taxi or limousine reservations and/or a rental car, and one tourist attraction you would like to visit.
2. Refer to a current style reference manual for information on how to format an itinerary, and consider arranging the information in a table. Organize your itinerary by dates and activities. Include all pertinent times, addresses, and telephone numbers. Include the following information:
   a. Flight information—airline name, flight number, departure time, arrival time, departure and arrival terminals, and seat number
   b. Hotel information—hotel name, confirmation number, phone number, fax number, check-in date and time, and check-out date and time
   c. Transportation information—rental car, taxi, or limousine name, telephone number, confirmation number, pick-up date and time, and return pick-up date and time
   d. Tour information, if relevant—tour company name, destination, pick-up date and time, and telephone number
3. Add any other pertinent information for your trip.
4. Save the document with the name **U01-CA06-ItineraryChallenge**.
5. Print and then close **U01-CA06-ItineraryChallenge.docx**.

Leading Edge Consultants, Inc.

Memo

To:	Dr. Carl Wilhelm
From:	Tasha Slavinski
cc:	Yasmin Rohan
Date:	April 1, 2015
Re:	PowerPoint Presentation

I have prepared the title slide for your presentation at the 2015 annual meeting at Casa De Campo in the Dominican Republic. Please review the PowerPoint slide shown below and let me know if you approve of the design. After you have approved the design, I will complete the remainder of the presentation and have it available for you by tomorrow.

U1-PA05-PresentationMemo.docx

UNIT 2

Preparing Personal and Business Documents

Chapter 4

Creating Personal Documents

Performance Objectives

Upon successful completion of Chapter 4, you will be able to:

- Create a CD/DVD insert and label using templates
- Resize, crop, and compress images
- Create a calendar using a template
- Insert calendar building blocks
- Add a shape to a calendar
- Move and align objects
- Use a drawing canvas
- Stack, group, rotate, and flip objects
- Create personal return address labels
- Create, save, and insert items from the Quick Part gallery
- Add borders to paragraphs, tables, and pages
- Create a form template
- Insert content controls
- Create a certificate using a template
- Create a resume using a template

Desktop Publishing Terms

crop	nonprinting area	stacking
grouping	nudging	

Word Features Used

Bring Forward	DRAWING TOOLS	quick parts	tables
clip art	FORMAT tab	rotate	templates
content controls	forms	Send Backward	text wrapping
crop	form fields	shape fill	themes
Design mode	group	shape outline	ungroup
DEVELOPER tab	page borders	shapes	
drawing canvas	pictures	shape styles	

Note: Before beginning computer exercises for this chapter, copy to your storage medium the Chapter04 folder from the CD that accompanies this textbook and then make Chapter04 the active folder. Remember to substitute for graphics that may no longer be available.

Using Word to Create Personal Documents

In this chapter, you will produce personal documents using Word templates. You will use other Word features such as tables, text boxes, and labels to produce compact disc inserts and labels, calendars, address labels, certificates, resumes, change-of-address postcards, and hanging name tags. You will also apply basic desktop publishing concepts such as planning and designing document content, maintaining consistency, and achieving balance.

While you are creating the documents in this chapter, consider how you can apply what you have learned to create other personal documents. Several examples of personal documents are shown in Figure 4.1.

Figure 4.1 Creating Personal Documents

CD Face Label

CD Case Insert

Graduation Invitation

Nutrition Log

Personalized Calendar

Bookplate

Recipe Card

Gift Tags

Personal Note Cards

Place Cards

Change-of-Address Card

Birthday Party Invitation

Creating CD/DVD Jewel Case Inserts and Labels

Because most CDs and DVDs look very similar to each other, labeling them with their contents is a good idea. While you could simply scribble notes with a marker to indicate what you have saved on a disc, you can create professional-quality jewel case inserts and face labels quickly and easily using Word 2013.

A variety of CD and DVD label vendors and specific product numbers are provided in Word 2013. Some of the vendors include Microsoft, Compulabel, Ace Label, A-ONE, Formtec, and Office Depot. A list of vendors is available by clicking the down-pointing arrow at the right of the *Label vendors* option in the *Label information* section of the Label Options dialog box.

CD-ROM and rewritable CD-RW discs measure approximately 4.63 inches in diameter and may be identified using a cover insert on the disc case. The most common type of CD case is a jewel case, which is a plastic container with a front and back panel. Standard jewel cases also have a spine, but slim-line jewel cases do not. Word provides several jewel case insert options at the Label Options dialog box, including Avery US Letter CD Labels, product number 8691, and Avery US Letter CD/DVD Labeling System—Slim Line Jewel Case, product number 8965, both of which measure 4.63 by 4.63 inches. In addition to those available at the Label Options dialog box, predesigned jewel case inserts can be downloaded from Office.com. Figure 4.2 illustrates a CD jewel case insert template available at Office.com.

Figure 4.2 Using CD/DVD Jewel Case Insert from Office.com

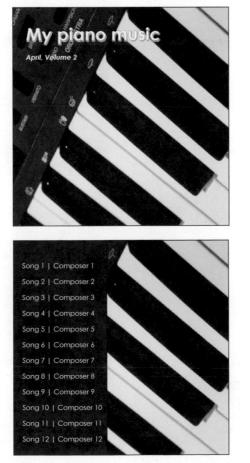

Working with Placeholders in Label Templates

Recall from Chapter 3 that a placeholder is a reserved area on a page where an object, image, or text can be entered. Templates contain various placeholders in the form of text boxes containing formatted sample text or pictures; drawing objects in specific sizes, shapes, and colors; and sample images. The placeholder text or objects may be replaced with other text, objects, pictures, and formatting that you choose to use to customize your document. Generally, you should not delete the placeholder text, but instead select it and replace it with your text or object, keeping the formatting in place. Placeholders save time because they are already sized and formatted to fit properly in the template. Many times, the placeholder text will give you tips on what to insert into the placeholder.

Cropping an Image

crop

To trim the horizontal and vertical edges of an image

At times you may need to resize and/or **crop** an image to fit in a placeholder. While resizing means dragging the sizing handles that display around an image to make the entire image bigger or smaller, cropping involves trimming off the edges of an image. For example, Figure 4.3 depicts a rectangular image that needs to fit in a larger square placeholder. To adjust the image to fit the placeholder, drag the corner sizing handles to resize the image to fit the width of the placeholder (see images B and C) and then crop off the top of the image to make it a square (see images D and E).

Figure 4.3 Resizing and Cropping an Image

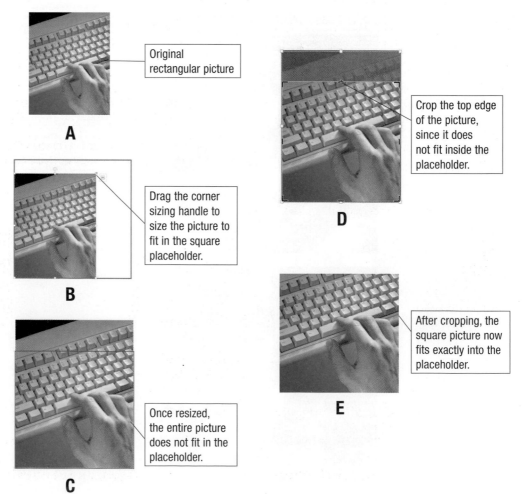

Note that this is just one method of resizing and cropping an image to fit in a placeholder. In addition to adjusting images to fit in placeholders, cropping is also used to create focus on a part of an image and to remove unnecessary parts of an image.

◀DTP POINTER
Crop to maximize the impact of an image.

Using Cropping Options

To access the cropping options displayed in Figure 4.4, select the image, click the Crop button arrow in the Size group on the PICTURE TOOLS FORMAT tab, and then click the desired option at the drop-down list. Some cropping suggestions include:

Crop

- Crop one side by dragging the center cropping handle on the desired side inward.
- Crop equally on two sides at the same time by pressing and holding the Ctrl key while dragging the center cropping handle on either side inward.
- Crop equally on all four sides at the same time by pressing and holding the Ctrl key while dragging a corner cropping handle inward.
- Crop an image to exact dimensions by right-clicking the image and then, at the shortcut menu that displays, clicking *Format Picture*. At the Format Picture task pane, click the Picture icon, click *CROP*, and then adjust the values in the *Width* and *Height* measurement boxes in the *Crop position* section.

Figure 4.5 illustrates the results of applying various cropping options. Experiment with the available options to learn how they can be used to emphasize certain parts of your image.

Figure 4.4 Using Enhanced Cropping Options

Click the Crop button arrow to display a drop-down list of cropping options.

Click this option to crop to change the height and width ratio of the image (see Figure 4.5C).

Click this option to insert the image within a specified area while maintaining the image proportions (see Figure 4.5E).

Click this option to turn on the cropping feature. After you have cropped the edges of the image, click this option again to remove the unwanted areas (see Figure 4.5A).

Click to display a list of shapes to which you can crop your image (see Figure 4.5B).

Click this option to resize the image so that the entire image area is filled (see Figure 4.5D).

Figure 4.5 Applying Cropping Options to a Picture

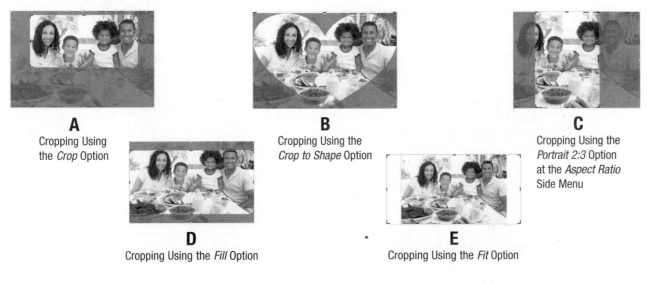

A
Cropping Using the *Crop* Option

B
Cropping Using the *Crop to Shape* Option

C
Cropping Using the *Portrait 2:3* Option at the *Aspect Ratio* Side Menu

D
Cropping Using the *Fill* Option

E
Cropping Using the *Fit* Option

Deleting Cropped Areas of an Image

After you crop an image, the cropped portions remain as part of the image file. You can reduce the file size by removing the cropped portions from the file. ***Note: Deleting the cropped portions of an image cannot be undone. Therefore, you should only do this after you are sure do not want to make any more changes.***

To delete cropped areas from an image, complete the following steps:

Compress Pictures

1. Click the image from which you want to discard cropped portions.
2. Click the Compress Pictures button in the Adjust group on the PICTURE TOOLS FORMAT tab.
3. Click the *Delete cropped areas of pictures* check box in the *Compression options* section to insert a check mark, as shown in Figure 4.6, and make sure a check mark also displays in the *Apply only to this picture* check box.
4. Click OK to close the Compress Pictures dialog box.

In Exercise 4.1, you will create an Avery brand CD/DVD jewel case insert. The insert is formatted in a table, with the first cell used for the cover, the second cell for the spine, and the third cell for the back side of the cover. After you print it, separate the different parts using the perforations (if available) or by trimming along the borders of the cells.

Figure 4.6 Using the Compress Pictures Dialog Box

Insert check marks in these two check boxes to delete the cropped areas of an image.

Exercise 4.1 Creating a CD/DVD Jewel Case Insert

1. Create the CD/DVD jewel case insert shown in Figure 4.7 on page 145 by completing the following steps:
   a. At a blank document, click the MAILINGS tab and then click the Labels button in the Create group.
   b. Click the Options button at the Envelopes and Labels dialog box with the Labels tab selected.
   c. At the Label Options dialog box, click the down-pointing arrow at the right of the *Label vendors* option box in the *Label information* section and then, if necessary, click *Avery US Letter* at the drop-down list.
   d. Scroll down the *Product number* list box and then click *8693 Jewel Case Inserts*.
   e. Click OK.
   f. Click the New Document button at the Envelopes and Labels dialog box.

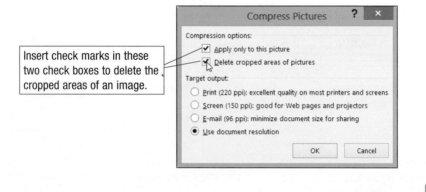

2. Adjust the margins on the front of the jewel case insert and add an image to the front of the insert by completing the following steps:

   a. With the insertion point positioned in the first label (first cell of the table in the template), click the TABLE TOOLS LAYOUT tab.

   b. Click the Cell Margins button in the Alignment group.

   c. At the Table Options dialog box, select the current measurement in the *Left* measurement box and then type **0**.

   d. Select the current measurement in the *Right* measurement box and then type **0**.

   e. Click OK to close the dialog box.

   f. Click the INSERT tab and then click the Online Pictures button in the Illustrations group.

   g. Type **computer woman** in the *Office.com Clip Art* text box and then press Enter.

   h. Double-click the image shown above and to the right or select a similar image if this image is not available.

3. Notice that the image does not fill the label (cell). Crop the image to fit the cell properly by completing the following steps:

   a. Drag the bottom right corner sizing handle outward to the bottom dashed border of the cell.

   b. When you release the mouse, only part of the woman will display. With the image selected, click the Crop button arrow in the Size group on the PICTURE TOOLS FORMAT tab.

   c. At the Crop button drop-down list, point to the *Aspect Ratio* option and then click *1:1* in the *Square* section.

   d. With the image selected (gray areas should display to the left and right of the image), click the Compress Pictures button in the Adjust group.

   e. At the Compress Pictures dialog box, make sure a check mark displays in the *Apply only to this picture* check box and the *Delete cropped areas of pictures* check box and then click OK.

   f. With the image still selected, click the Wrap Text button in the Arrange group and then click *Square* at the drop-down list.

4. Insert an image on the back of the jewel case insert by completing the following steps:

   a. With the image on the front of the jewel case selected, click the HOME tab and then click the Copy button in the Clipboard group.

   b. Position the insertion point inside the bottom label (cell) and then click the Paste button.

   c. Drag the image up so the top border of the image aligns with the top of the table cell.

5. Change the document theme to *Depth* and the theme colors to *Red Violet*.

6. Add text to the front of the jewel case insert by completing the following steps:
   a. Draw a text box in the first cell with a height of 3.75 inches and a width of 2.5 inches.
   b. Remove the text box shape fill and the shape outline.
   c. With the insertion point positioned inside the text box, remove the 8 points of spacing after paragraphs, and then type the following, pressing Enter once at the end of each line unless otherwise directed:

   > **OFTI 1218** (or your course name and #)
   > **Advanced Word 2013 DTP**
   > **Data Files & Exercises**
   > **Fall 2015** (Press Enter twice.)
   > *[Type your name.]*
   > *[Type your email address.]* (Press Enter twice.)
   > *[Type your college name.]*
   > *[Type your college street address.]*
   > *[Type your college city, state, and ZIP.]*

   d. Select *OFTI 1218* and apply the Heading 1 style.
   e. Select *Advanced Word 2013 DTP* through *Fall 2015* and apply the Intense Emphasis style.
   f. Select your name through your college's city, state, and ZIP code and then apply the Subtle Emphasis style.
   g. Select all of the text in the text box and then click once on the Increase Font Size button in the Font group on the HOME tab.
   h. Position the text box as shown in Figure 4.7.

7. Add text to the back of the jewel case insert by completing the following steps:
   a. Create another text box, as described in Steps 6a and 6b, in the bottom cell of the template as shown in Figure 4.7.
   b. With the insertion point positioned inside the text box, remove the 8 points of spacing after paragraphs and then type the following text:

   > **Documents created:** (Press the Enter key and then change the font size to 9 points.)
   > **Signs** (Press the Enter key after each of the following entries.)
   > **Report covers**
   > **Procedures manuals**
   > **Fax covers**
   > **Agendas**
   > **Letterheads & envelopes**
   > **Business cards**
   > **CD/DVD case covers**
   > **Calendars**
   > **Merged postcards**
   > **Certificates**
   > **Flyers & announcements**
   > **Brochures & booklets**
   > **Cards**
   > **Forms**
   > **PowerPoint presentations**
   > **Newsletters**

   c. Select *Documents created:* and then apply the Heading 2 style.
   d. Position the text box as shown in Figure 4.7.

8. Create a spine for the jewel case insert by completing the following steps:
   a. Position the insertion point inside the cell separating the top and bottom cells in the template, change the paragraph alignment to center, and then type **OFTI 1218: Advanced Word 2013 DTP** (or the name and number of your own course) as shown

in Figure 4.7. This row may be cut after the document is printed and used in the spine of the CD/DVD jewel case.

b. With the insertion point positioned in the middle cell, add a black fill to the cell by clicking the Shading button in the Table Styles group on the TABLE TOOLS DESIGN tab and then clicking the *Black, Text 1* color (second column, first row in the *Theme Colors* section). ***Hint: The text color will automatically convert to white.***

c. With the insertion point still positioned in the middle cell, click the TABLE TOOLS LAYOUT tab and then click the Align Center button in the Alignment group.

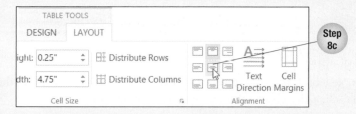

d. Select the text you typed in Step 8a and then apply bold formatting.

9. Save the document with the name **C04-E01-CDCaseInsert**.

10. Print and then close **C04-E01-CDCaseInsert.docx**. ***Hint: Print the cover and back text on a sheet of Avery labels, product number 8693, or on 50# paper.***

Figure 4.7 CD/DVD Jewel Case Insert Created in Exercise 4.1

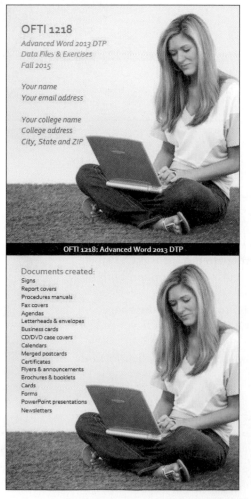

Creating a CD Face Label Using a Template

In Exercise 4.2, you will create a CD face label from an Office.com template located at the New backstage area. When you purchase labels, make sure that you select a label to match the product number of your CD and then select the appropriate Word template for those labels. Print your disc label on regular paper before printing on an actual sticky-backed label, and hold the sample up to your disc to evaluate the fit.

Exercise 4.2 Creating a CD Face Label

PORTFOLIO

1. At a blank document, create a CD face label by completing the following steps:
   a. Click the FILE tab and then click the *New* option.
   b. At the New backstage area, type **CD label** in the search text box and then press the Enter key.
   c. Double-click the CD face label template shown below.

   d. If necessary, click OK at the prompt to convert to the newest format.
2. Use the Insert Pictures window to find a travel photo to use on the label by completing the following steps:

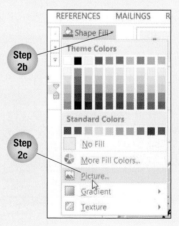

   a. Click twice on the outside edge of the top CD label to select the top CD label and display the DRAWING TOOLS FORMAT tab. (Make sure that only the top CD label is selected. You should see a solid square border around the top CD label, inside a dashed rectangular border around both of the CD labels.)
   b. Click the Shape Fill button arrow in the Shape Styles group on the DRAWING TOOLS FORMAT tab.
   c. At the Shape Fill drop-down gallery, click *Picture*.

d. At the Insert Pictures window, type **Africa** in the *Office.com Clip Art* text box, and then press the Enter key.
e. Double-click the picture of the tree shown in the image below, or a similar picture if this one is not available.

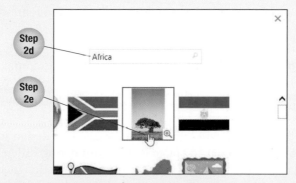

3. Format the text on the label as shown in Figure 4.8A by completing the following steps:
   a. Click the *[CD Title]* placeholder, type **Photos of our safari,** press the Enter key, and then type **South Africa, Fall 2015**.
   b. Select both lines of text, change the font size to 14 points, and then click the Bold button in the Font group on the HOME tab twice.
   c. Delete the *[Date]* placeholder, the text *This CD contains:* and the *[CD contents]* placeholder.
4. Format the blank CD label below the label created in this exercise with text and an image of your choosing. The sample label shown in Figure 4.8B was created for a yoga music CD.
5. Save the document and name it **C04-E02-CDLabels**.
6. Print and then close **C04-E02-CDLabels.docx**. *Note: Check with your instructor before printing.*

Figure 4.8 CD Face Labels Created in Exercise 4.2

Creating a Personal Calendar

A calendar can be one of the most basic tools of organization in your everyday life. Although electronic calendars are becoming increasingly prevalent both at work and at home, many people still prefer the at-a-glance convenience of using a printed calendar to schedule appointments, plan activities, and serve as a reminder of important dates and events.

In addition to its personal applications, a calendar may also be used as a marketing tool in promoting a service, product, or program. For example, a schedule of upcoming events may be typed on a calendar as a reminder to all of the volunteers working for a charitable organization, or the calendar may be sent to prospective donors as a daily reminder of the organization.

In Exercise 4.3, you will create your own calendar design using photos, borders, text boxes, and a 2015 calendar template. When considering different ways to customize your calendar, you may want to view the numerous predesigned templates available in Office 2013. In addition to Word, you will notice that Publisher, PowerPoint, and Excel also include professionally prepared calendar designs, as shown in Figure 4.9.

Figure 4.9 Illustrating Sample Calendar Templates from Office.com

| **A** | **B** |
| Word Calendar Template | Publisher Calendar Template |

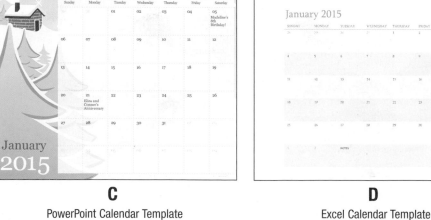

| **C** | **D** |
| PowerPoint Calendar Template | Excel Calendar Template |

Inserting Calendar Building Blocks

As you learned in Chapter 3, building blocks are reusable pieces of content or other document parts that are stored in galleries. You can access and reuse these building blocks at any time. *Calendar 1*, in the Building Blocks Organizer dialog box shown in Figure 4.10, is an example of a calendar building block. Click the building block name and then click the Insert button to insert it into your document.

Predesigned calendar building blocks can also be inserted into a Word document by clicking the Table button in the Illustrations group on the INSERT tab, pointing to *Quick Tables*, and then clicking the desired calendar from the *Built-In* section at the side menu, as shown in Figure 4.11 on page 150. Consider inserting a calendar building block into a newsletter, travel itinerary, flyer, pamphlet, or other business or personal document.

Table

Editing an Image in a Calendar

Many calendar templates include an image placeholder. You may delete the picture placeholder or replace the image by clicking the Pictures button or the Online Pictures button in the Illustrations group on the INSERT tab.

You may also choose to edit an image you insert into a calendar. For example, if you want to make your image into a watermark, click the Color button in the Adjust group on the PICTURE TOOLS FORMAT tab and then click *Washout* in the *Recolor* section (see Figure 4.12 on page 150). Next, click the Wrap Text button in the Arrange group and then click *Behind Text* at the drop-down gallery.

Figure 4.10 Using Calendar Building Blocks

Click *Name* to sort the building blocks alphabetically by name. This will display all of the calendar options together.

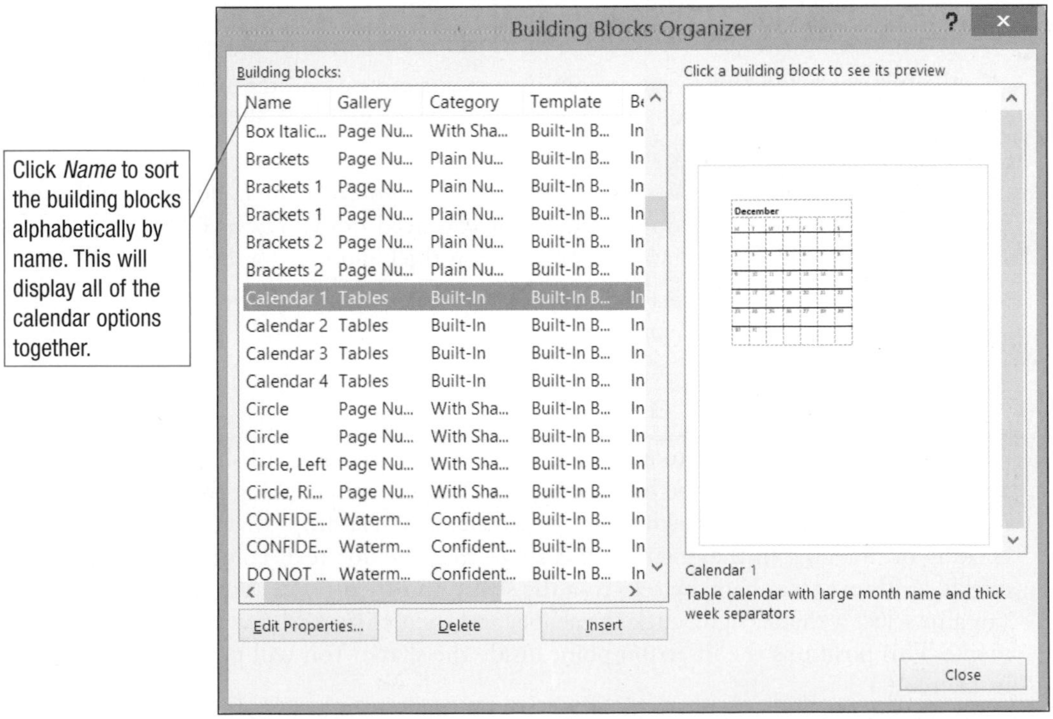

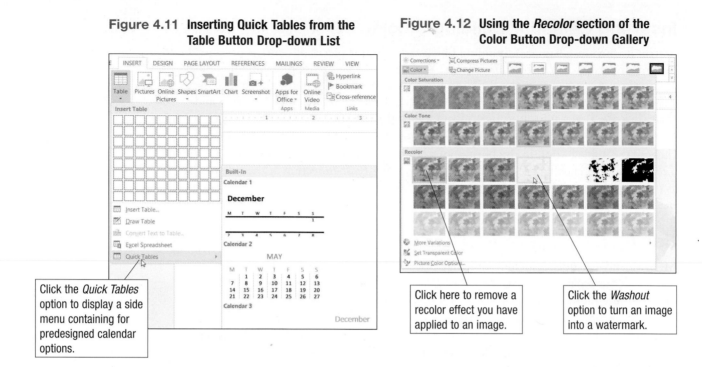

Figure 4.11 Inserting Quick Tables from the Table Button Drop-down List

Figure 4.12 Using the *Recolor* section of the Color Button Drop-down Gallery

Click the *Quick Tables* option to display a side menu containing for predesigned calendar options.

Click here to remove a recolor effect you have applied to an image.

Click the *Washout* option to turn an image into a watermark.

The Color button in in the Adjust group on the PICTURE TOOLS FORMAT tab offers you many opportunities for design creativity. You will learn more about the different options available at the Color button drop-down gallery in Chapter 8, but in Exercise 4.3, you will use the *Recolor* section of the Color button drop-down gallery to edit an image used in the calendar.

The following are some helpful tips for working with recoloring options:

- Before clicking an effect option, hover your mouse pointer over it. The live preview feature will show you what your image will look like with that effect applied.

- Access additional colors by clicking *More Variations* at the Color button drop-down gallery. If you do not find what you need in the *Theme Colors* or *Standard Colors* sections, click *More Colors* to open the Colors dialog box.

- Remove a recolor effect but keep any other changes you have made to an image by clicking the *No Recolor* option (first option in the *Recolor* section).

Adding a Shape to a Calendar

Another way to add interest to a calendar is to insert a predesigned shape as an attention-getter. Insert a shape by clicking the INSERT tab, clicking the Shapes button in the Illustrations group, clicking the desired shape at the drop-down list, and then clicking or dragging in the document. A shape may include text, color, and other special effects. Add text to a shape by selecting the shape and then typing the desired text. You can also select a shape, right-click the shape, and then click *Add Text* at the shortcut menu. This positions the insertion point inside the shape. You will practice doing this in Exercise 4.3.

Exercise 4.3 Creating a Calendar

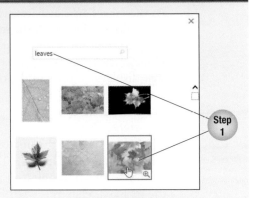

1. At a blank document, click the INSERT tab, click the Online Pictures button, type **leaves** in the *Office.com Clip Art* text box, press the Enter key, and then double-click the image shown at the right. Choose a similar image if this image is not available.

2. With the picture selected, click the Size group dialog box launcher on the PICTURE TOOLS FORMAT tab.

3. At the Layout dialog box with the Size tab selected, remove the check mark from the *Lock aspect ratio* check box, type **9.25** in the *Absolute* measurement box in the *Height* section, type 7 in the *Absolute* measurement box in the *Width* section, and then click OK.

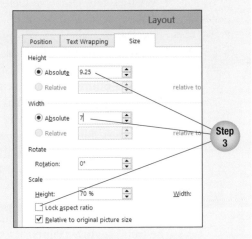

4. With the image still selected, customize the image by completing the following steps:
   a. Click the Color button in the Adjust group and then click the *Washout* option in the *Recolor* section.

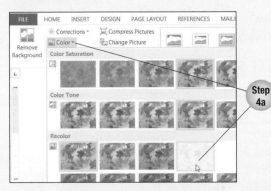

   b. Cick the Position button in the Arrange group and then click the *Position in Middle Center with Square Text Wrapping* option.

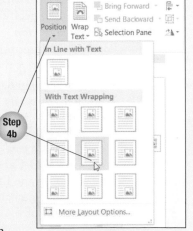

5. Insert and customize the image of the school bus as shown in Figure 4.13 on page 154 by completing the following steps:
   a. Click the INSERT tab, click the Online Pictures button, search for the school bus image shown in the figure, and then double-click the image. Part of the school bus image will display below the leaves image.
   b. With the school bus image selected, click the Wrap Text button in the Arrange group on the PICTURE TOOLS FORMAT tab and then click the *In Front of Text* option.
   c. Change the width of the school bus image to 6.2 inches.
   d. Drag the image so it is positioned as shown in Figure 4.13.

6. Save the document with the name **C04-E03-Calendar**. Keep the document open.

7. Insert a predesigned calendar below the school bus image by completing the following steps:
   a. Click the FILE tab and then click the *New* option.
   b. At the New backstage area, type **September calendar** in the search text box and then press the Enter key.
   c. Double-click the calendar template that displays (similar to the one shown at the right).

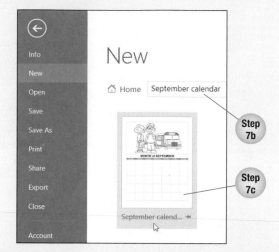

Step 7b

Step 7c

8. Format the calendar by completing the following steps:
   a. Click the image in the first cell of the calendar and then press the Delete key.
   b. With the insertion point positioned in the first cell, click the TABLE TOOLS LAYOUT tab, click the Delete button in the Rows & Columns group, and then click *Delete Rows* at the drop-down list.
   c. Select the entire calendar (table). On the TABLE TOOLS LAYOUT tab, click the Properties button in the Table group. At the Table Properties dialog box, click the Table tab, if necessary, to make it active, change the value in the *Preferred width* measurement box to *6"*, and then click OK. ***Hint: Insert a check mark in the* Preferred width *check box in the* Size *section.***
   d. Select the second row and then change the font size to 9 points.
   e. Select rows 3 through 7, display the Table Properties dialog box, click the Row tab, change the value in the *Specify height* measurement box to *0.7"*, and then click OK. ***Hint: Insert a check mark in the* Specify height *check box in the* Size *section.***

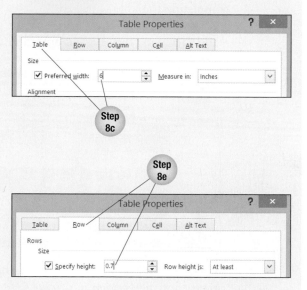

Step 8c

Step 8e

   f. Position the insertion point in cell C3 (below the cell containing the word *Tuesday*) and then type **1**. Press the Tab key and then continue filling in the remaining dates for the month of September 2015. (The last day will display *30* in cell D7.)
   g. Select the entire calendar (table) and then click the Copy button in the Clipboard group on the HOME tab.
   h. Make **C04-E03-Calendar.docx** the active document.
9. Create and format a text box for the calendar table by completing the following steps:
   a. With **C04-E03-Calendar.docx** the active document, click the Text Box button in the Text group on the INSERT tab and then click *Draw Text Box* at the drop-down list. Position the crosshairs below the school bus photo and then drag to create a text box with a height of 4.4 inches and a width of 6.2 inches. (Use the *Shape Height* and *Shape Width* measurement boxes in the Size group on the DRAWING TOOLS FORMAT tab to size the text box.)

b. With the text box selected, click the Shape Fill button arrow in the Shape Styles group and then click the *Gold, Accent 4, Lighter 60%* color (eighth column, third row in the *Theme Colors* section).

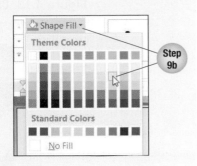

c. Click the Shape Outline button in the Shape Styles group and then click *No Outline* at the drop-down gallery.

d. With the insertion point positioned inside the text box, click the Paste button in the Clipboard group on the HOME tab to paste the calendar.

e. Position the school bus image and the calendar as shown in Figure 4.13.

10. Add the text to the dates shown in Figure 4.13. ***Hint: Reduce the font size of the text you type in this step to 8 points.***

11. Add the starburst shape to the calendar as shown in Figure 4.13 by completing the following steps:

a. Click the INSERT tab, click the Shapes button in the Illustrations group, and then click the *Explosion 1* option in the *Stars and Banners* section.

b. In the top right corner of the school bus picture, draw a star that is approximately 2 inches high and 1.5 inches wide.

c. With the star shape selected, click the More button in the Shape Styles group and then click the *Intense Effect - Gold, Accent 4* option (fifth column, sixth row).

d. Right-click the star shape, click *Add Text* at the shortcut menu, change the font to 12-point Berlin Sans FB, change the font color to *Black, Text 1*, and then type **Welcome back to school!** Resize and position the star if necessary.

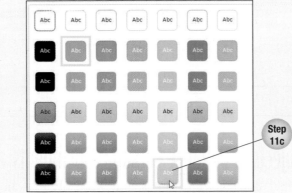

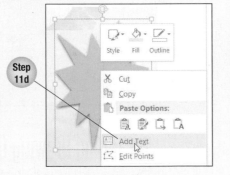

12. Save, print, and then close **C04-E03-Calendar.docx**.

13. Close the calendar template document without saving changes.

Figure 4.13 **Calendar Created in Exercise 4.3**

Arranging Drawing Objects to Enhance Personal Documents

Drawing objects include shapes, diagrams, flow charts, and WordArt. You can enhance these objects with colors, patterns, text borders, and other effects.

Recall from Chapter 3 that drawing objects are inserted in the foreground layer, also known as the drawing layer. This means that their default wrap text setting is *In Front of Text*, so you do not have to change the wrap text settings for drawing objects in order to be able to move or adjust them. When modifying drawing objects, you will use the buttons and options on the DRAWING TOOLS FORMAT tab.

Moving and Positioning Objects Precisely

To move a drawing object, start by selecting the object that you want to move. To move multiple drawing objects at once, select the first object and then press and hold the Shift key while you click the additional objects you want to select. Next, drag the drawing object(s) to the new location.

You can also move a selected drawing object in small increments by pressing the Up Arrow, Down Arrow, Right Arrow, or Left Arrow keys to move the object in the direction you want. This is called *nudging*, and it allows you to position an object more precisely than you could by dragging it. To nudge an object, make sure the text wrapping for the object has been changed to any setting other than *In Line with Text*.

Another way to align a drawing object or group of objects is to select the object or objects, click the Align button on the DRAWING TOOLS FORMAT tab, and then click the desired option to position the object or group of objects precisely on the page or to position the objects in the selected group precisely in relation to each other. The options available at the Align button drop-down list are shown in Figure 4.14.

Using a Drawing Canvas to Align Drawing Objects

When you insert a drawing object in a Word document, you can place it in a drawing canvas. A drawing canvas helps you arrange a drawing in your document and provides a frame-like boundary between your drawing and the rest of your document. By default, the canvas has no border or background, but you can apply formatting to the drawing canvas as you would to any drawing object. This feature also helps you keep parts of your drawing together, which is especially helpful if your drawing consists of several different objects. The best practice is to insert a drawing canvas if you plan to include more than one shape in a drawing. For example, if you want to create a flow chart, start by inserting a drawing canvas and then add the shapes and lines for your chart.

To insert a drawing canvas, click in your document where you want to create the drawing, click the INSERT tab, click the Shapes button in the Illustrations group, and then click *New Drawing Canvas* at the bottom of the drop-down list. A drawing canvas is inserted into your document in which you can draw shapes.

After you have inserted the desired shapes into the drawing canvas, right-click anywhere on the drawing canvas border and then click *Fit, Expand,* or *Scale Drawing* at the shortcut menu. Click the *Fit* option to reduce the area around the drawing objects, as shown in Figure 4.15 on page 156. Notice that the drawing canvas adjusts to fit all three objects into one tight area. If you change the wrapping style of the drawing canvas to *In Front of Text* and then drag the canvas, all three items will move with it.

nudging
Using the arrow keys to move an object in small increments across the document screen

Align

◀**DTP POINTER**
Using the drawing canvas helps keep the different objects in a drawing together.

◀**DTP POINTER**
You can duplicate an object and align the original and duplicate objects at the same time by holding down the Shift key and the Ctrl key and dragging and dropping the image.

Figure 4.14 Viewing Alignment Options at the Align Button Drop-down List

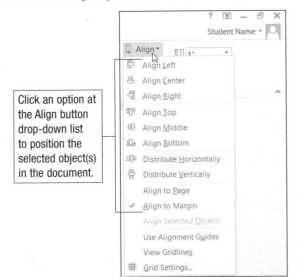

Click an option at the Align button drop-down list to position the selected object(s) in the document.

Figure 4.15 **Adjusting the Drawing Canvas to Fit the Contents**

drawing canvas
fit to the shapes

Stacking Objects

Drawing one object on top of another is known as ***stacking***. Objects automatically stack in individual layers as you add them to a document. You see the stacking order when objects overlap. The top object covers a portion of objects beneath it, as discussed in Chapter 3.

You may stack as many drawing objects as you want and then rearrange them by selecting an object, clicking the Bring Forward button arrow in the Arrange group on the DRAWING TOOLS FORMAT tab, and then clicking *Bring Forward, Bring to Front,* or *Bring in Front of Text*, as shown in Figure 4.16. Alternatively, you can send the object backward by clicking the Send Backward button arrow in the Arrange group and then clicking *Send Backward, Send to Back,* or *Send Behind Text*, as shown in Figure 4.17.

Figure 4.16 **Rearranging Objects with the Bring Forward Button on the DRAWING TOOLS FORMAT Tab**

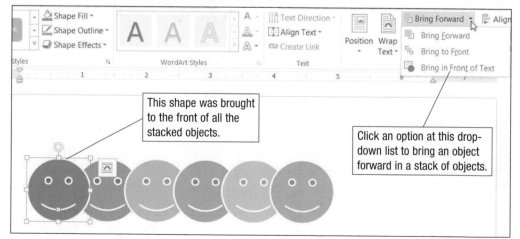

This shape was brought
to the front of all the
stacked objects.

Click an option at this drop-
down list to bring an object
forward in a stack of objects.

Figure 4.17 Rearranging Objects with the Send Backward Button on the DRAWING TOOLS FORMAT Tab

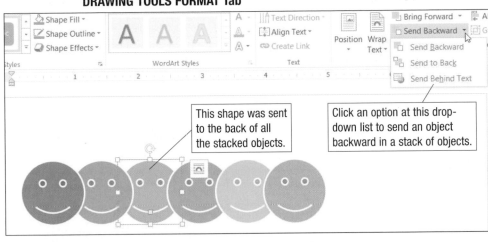

This shape was sent to the back of all the stacked objects.

Click an option at this drop-down list to send an object backward in a stack of objects.

Grouping Objects

Grouping objects combines multiple drawing objects as a single unit. To group drawing objects, hold down the Shift key as you select each object, click the Group button arrow in the Arrange group on the DRAWING TOOLS FORMAT tab, and then click *Group* at the drop-down list, as shown in Figure 4.18. When objects have been grouped, sizing handles should appear around the new unit rather than each individual object, but you can still select individual objects within a group. If you lose an object in a stack that has been grouped together, select the group and then press the Tab key to cycle forward or press Shift + Tab to cycle backward through the objects until the desired object is selected. Ungroup drawing objects by selecting the grouped object, clicking the Group button in the Arrange group, and then clicking *Ungroup* at the drop-down list.

Rotating and Flipping Objects

To rotate or flip objects, select the object or group of objects, click the Rotate button arrow in the Arrange group on the DRAWING TOOLS FORMAT tab, and then click the option that corresponds with the direction you want to turn the object, as shown in Figure 4.19 on page 158. Click the *More Rotation Options* option at the bottom of the

Figure 4.18 Grouping Objects

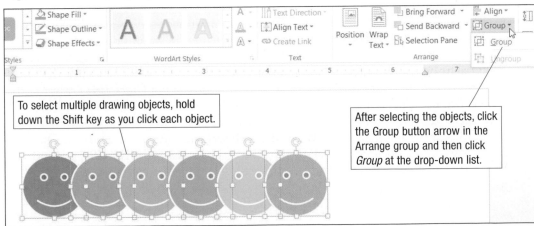

To select multiple drawing objects, hold down the Shift key as you click each object.

After selecting the objects, click the Group button arrow in the Arrange group and then click *Group* at the drop-down list.

grouping
Combining objects as a single unit

Group

Rotate

◄DTP POINTER
Generally, position your graphics facing the document text.

◄DTP POINTER
If the Group feature does not work properly, you may have to change the text wrapping option for the object or use the drawing canvas to group the objects together as one unit.

Figure 4.19 Rotating an Object with the Rotate Button

Figure 4.20 Rotating an Object Using the Rotation Handle

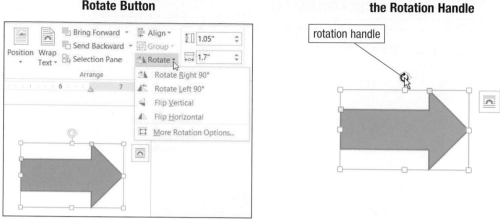

Rotate button drop-down gallery to open the Layout dialog box with the Size tab selected. The measurement box in the *Rotation* section will allow you to rotate an object in more precise increments. You can also use the rotation handle on the selected object, as shown in Figure 4.20.

Creating Personal Return Address Labels

Preprinted return address labels are convenient and cost-effective to use at home and at the office. Whether you are paying bills, addressing holiday cards, or mailing a large number of PTA newsletters, the convenience of having preprinted return address labels is worth the time it takes to create them. Create your own labels using the labels feature in Word. Word includes a variety of predefined label formats that coordinate with labels that can be purchased at office supply stores.

When purchasing labels, be careful to select the appropriate labels for your specific printer. Labels are available in sheets for laser and inkjet printers. Carefully follow your printer's directions and any directions on the label packaging to be sure you insert the sheets properly into the printer.

DTP POINTER

View information on how to use labels and access additional templates at www .averylabels.com.

In Exercise 4.4, you will use the labels feature to create Avery 5160 labels that include a picture. These labels measure 1 inch by 2.63 inches. You may choose to use smaller labels for your own personal return address labels, such as Avery 8167 labels, which measure 0.5 inch by 1.75 inches.

You will also save the personal address label design that you create in Exercise 4.4 to the Quick Part gallery so that you can use it again, if necessary. Recall that the Quick Part gallery contains pieces of content that can be reused in various documents. As you learned in Chapter 3, to save content you have created to the Quick Part gallery, select the content (which can include text and objects), click the INSERT tab, click the Quick Parts button in the Text group, and then click *Save Selection to Quick Part Gallery* at the drop-down list. This displays the Create New Building Block dialog box with *Quick Parts* specified in the *Gallery* option box. Type a name for the building block, type a description (if desired), and then click OK. To insert content you saved to the Quick Part gallery into a document, click the Quick Parts button on the INSERT tab and then click the quick part at the drop-down list.

1. At a blank document, click the MAILINGS tab and then click the Labels button in the Create group.
2. At the Envelopes and Labels dialog box with the Labels tab selected, click the Options button.
3. At the Label Options dialog box, if necessary, change the *Label vendors* option to *Avery US Letter*, click *5160 Easy Peel Address Labels* in the *Product number* list box, and then click OK.
4. At the Envelopes and Labels dialog box, click the New Document button.
5. If the gridlines of the labels (cells) do not display, click the TABLE TOOLS LAYOUT tab and then click the View Gridlines button in the Table group.
6. With the insertion point positioned in the first cell, click the Online Pictures button in the Illustrations group on the INSERT tab. At the Insert Pictures window, type **palm tree island sun** in the *Office.com Clip Art* text box and then press Enter.
7. Double-click the image shown at the right. ***Note: You may insert a clip art image of your own choosing and insert your own name and address instead of the name and address given in the following steps.***
8. With the image selected, click the Rotate button in the Arrange group on the PICTURE TOOLS FORMAT tab and then click *Flip Horizontal* at the drop-down list.
9. Apply Square text wrapping to the image and then position it at the left edge of the first cell.
10. Draw a text box that measures 0.7 inches in height and 1.7 inches in width and then position it at the right of the clip art image. Verify the sizes in the *Shape Height* and *Shape Width* measurement boxes in the Size group on the DRAWING TOOLS FORMAT tab.
11. With the text box selected, click the Shape Styles group task pane launcher.
12. At the Format Shape task pane, make sure *SHAPE OPTIONS* is selected, click the Layout & Properties icon, click *TEXT BOX*, change all margins to 0 inches, and then close the task pane.
13. Remove the text box shape fill and shape outline.
14. Position the insertion point inside the text box and then click the Align Right button in the Paragraph group on the HOME tab.
15. Change the font to 11-point Constantia and then type the following (you may substitute your own name and address):

> **Joan & John Kane** (Press Shift + Enter.)
> **55 Pine Island Road** (Press Shift + Enter.)
> **Myrtle Beach, SC 29472**

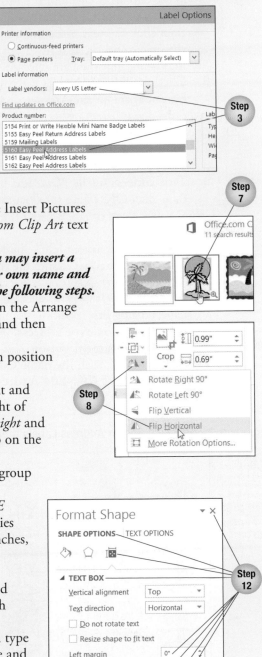

16. Select *Joan & John Kane*, click the Text Effects and Typography button in the Font group on the HOME tab and then click the *Fill - Orange, Accent 2, Outline - Accent 2* option (third column, first row). With the text still selected, change the font size to 13 points.
17. Select the text box containing the name and address and then apply Square text wrapping.
18. If necessary, adjust the text box so it is positioned as shown in Figure 4.21.
19. Group the clip art image and the text box by completing the following steps:
    a. Click the palm tree island sun image, hold down the Shift key, and then click the text box containing the name and address. Make sure the image and the text box both have a solid border around them, indicating that they are selected.
    b. Click the DRAWING TOOLS FORMAT tab, click the Group button arrow in the Arrange group, and then click *Group* at the drop-down list.

20. Save the contents of the label to the Quick Part gallery by completing the following steps:
    a. With the grouped object selected in the first label, click the Quick Parts button in the Text group on the INSERT tab, and then click *Save Selection to Quick Part Gallery*.
    b. Type **address** in the *Name* text box at the Create New Building Block dialog box and then click OK. Close the document without saving changes.
21. Create a new sheet of labels using the quick part you created in Step 20 by completing the following steps:
    a. At a blank document, click the MAILINGS tab, click the Labels button in the Create group, and then make sure the product listed in the *Label* section on the Labels tab is *Avery US Letter, 5160 Easy Peel Address Labels*.
    b. With the Labels tab still selected in the Envelopes and Labels dialog box, position the insertion point in the *Address* text box, type **address**, press F3, and then click the New Document button.
22. Save the document with the name **C04-E04-Address**.
23. Print and then close **C04-E04-Address.docx**.

Figure 4.21 **Personal Return Address Labels Created in Exercise 4.4**

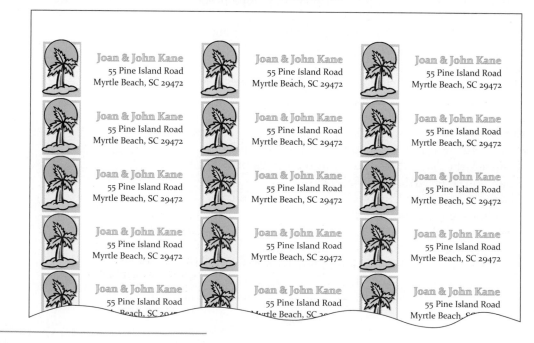

Adding Borders

Borders can add interest and emphasis to various parts of your document. Borders can be added to pages, text, tables, table cells, graphic objects, and and images. You can add borders in many line styles and colors, as well as a variety of graphical borders.

Adding Borders to Tables

To apply a border to specific table cells, select the cells, click the TABLE TOOLS DESIGN tab and then select a predesigned table style with professionally designed borders and shading from the Table Styles gallery, or click the Borders button arrow in the Borders group and then click a desired border at the drop-down gallery. Customize the border by changing the style, color, and width at the Borders and Shading dialog box, which can be displayed by clicking the Borders button arrow in the Borders group and then clicking *Borders and Shading* at the bottom of the drop-down gallery, as shown in Figure 4.22.

Borders

Adding Borders to Pages

Add borders to pages by clicking the Page Borders button in the Page Background group on the DESIGN tab. When you click the Page Borders button, the Borders and Shading dialog box displays with the Page Border tab selected. At the dialog box, click one of the border options in the *Setting* section and then select the style, color, and width of the border in the middle panel. To specify a graphical border, select an option in the *Art* option box, as shown in Figure 4.23 on page 162.

Page Borders

To place borders only on particular sides of the selected area, click *Custom* in the *Setting* section. In the *Preview* section, click the diagram sides or click the buttons to apply and remove borders. To specify a particular page or section in which you want the border to appear, click the desired option in the *Apply to* option box.

To remove a border from a page, click the DESIGN tab, click the Page Borders button in the Page Background group, click *None* in the *Setting* section on the Page Border tab of the Borders and Shading dialog box, and then click OK.

Figure 4.22 Viewing Options at the Borders Button Drop-down Gallery

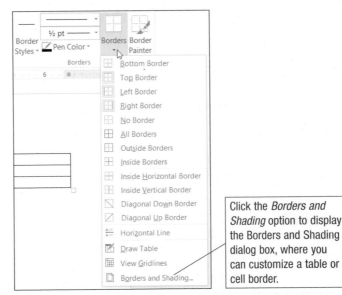

Figure 4.23 Selecting an Artistic Page Border at the Borders and Shading Dialog Box

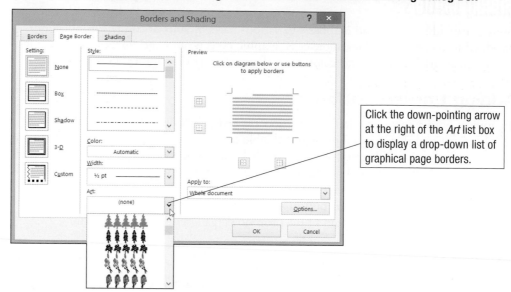

Click the down-pointing arrow at the right of the *Art* list box to display a drop-down list of graphical page borders.

Changing Page Border Margins

By default, a page border displays and prints 24 points from the top, left, right, and bottom edges of the page. Some printers, particularly inkjet printers, have a **nonprinting area** around the outside edges of the page that can interfere with the printing of a page border. One way to compensate for the nonprinting area is to move the page border into the document by increasing the measurements in the *Top, Left, Bottom,* and/or *Right* measurement boxes at the Border and Shading Options dialog box, as shown in Figure 4.24. Display this dialog box by clicking the Options button at the Borders and Shading dialog box with the Page Border tab selected. Click the down-pointing arrow at the right of the *Measure from* option box to position the page border relative to the page margins (*Text*) or the edge of the paper (*Edge of page*). Also experiment with changing your document margins.

nonprinting area
An area where text will not print

DTP POINTER ❯
Inkjet printers usually can print up to 0.5 inch from the edge of the paper, while laser printers can print as close as 0.25 inch, depending on the model.

Adding Borders to Paragraphs

To specify the exact position of a paragraph border relative to the text, select the desired text, display the Borders and Shading dialog box with the Borders tab selected, change the *Apply to* option to *Paragraph*, click the Options button, and then select the desired border options. To specify a cell or table in which you want the border to appear, click the option that applies to that selection in the *Apply to* option box.

Creating a Template and Inserting Content Controls

Whether you are creating a client survey form for the marketing and research department of your company or creating an award certificate for volunteers at your local hospital, using a template that contains content controls saves time and effort.

Figure 4.24 Adjusting Borders at the Border and Shading Options Dialog Box

Click *Text* to position the inside edge of the page border relative to the page margin.

Click *Edge of page* to position the outside edge of the page border relative to the edge of the paper.

Border and Shading Options

Margin
Top: 24 pt   Left: 24 pt
Bottom: 24 pt   Right: 24 pt

Measure from:
Edge of page
Text
Edge of page

☐ Align paragraph borders and table edges with page border
☑ Always display in front
☑ Surround header
☑ Surround footer

Preview

OK   Cancel

Adjust the position of the page border relative to the text or the edge of the page using these measurement boxes.

Creating a Form Template

In Word, a form is a protected document that includes fields where information is entered. A form document contains content controls that you can add and customize. For example, many online forms are designed with a drop-down list content control that provides a restricted set of choices. Content controls can provide instructional text for users and can be set to disappear when users type in their own text, which you will do in Exercise 4.5. Content controls can be found on the DEVELOPER tab, as shown in Figure 4.25.

Complete the following steps to add the DEVELOPER tab to the ribbon:
1. Click the FILE tab and then click *Options*.
2. At the Word Options dialog box, click *Customize Ribbon* in the left panel.
3. In the *Customize the Ribbon* section, click the *Developer* check box to insert a check mark and then click OK.

◀DTP POINTER

If content controls are not available on the DEVELOPER tab, you may have opened a document created in an older version of Word. Convert the file by clicking the FILE tab, clicking the Convert button, and then clicking OK.

Figure 4.25 Using the DEVELOPER Tab

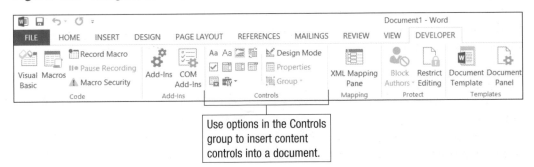

Use options in the Controls group to insert content controls into a document.

Complete the following steps to create a form template:

1. Design the form by sketching a layout, or use an existing form as a guide and then enter the text into a document that will appear in your form template.
2. At the document containing your form text, add content controls and instructional text prompting the user to insert information at the keyboard.
3. Save the document as a protected template.

Inserting a Date Picker Content Control

Date Picker
Content Control

The certificate in Exercise 4.5 will be saved as a template to be used over and over. A date picker content control will be added to the document so that the user can enter the date. A date picker content control contains a pop-up calendar that appears when the user clicks the down-pointing arrow at the right side of the content control. Using a date picker content control helps prevent users from making errors when entering the date. Insert a date picker content control into a document by positioning the insertion point at the desired location in the document and then clicking the Date Picker Content Control button in the Controls group on the DEVELOPER tab.

Adding Instructional Text to a Content Control

Design Mode

Sometimes it is helpful to add placeholder text instructing the user how to fill in a particular content control that you have added to a template. The instructions are replaced by content when the user fills in the template.

To add instructional text to a content control, complete the following steps:

1. Click the Design Mode button in the Controls group on the DEVELOPER tab.
2. With the content control selected, click the Properties button in the Controls group, type the desired instructional text in the *Title* text box in the *General* section of the Content Control Properties dialog box, and then click OK.
3. Click the Design Mode button to exit Design Mode.

Creating a Certificate Using a Template

Certificates are usually created to recognize or commemorate an award or achievement. Example of these types of documents include diplomas, volunteer recognition awards, and program completion certificates. Some other uses for certificates include coupons, warranties, and special-offer documents. Because it is often necessary to create many versions of the same certificate, templates can be great time savers when creating these types of documents.

Office.com provides several certificate templates created in both Word and PowerPoint. These templates are available at http://office.microsoft.com/en-us/templates/default.aspx. You can also create your own custom certificate template, which is what you will do in Exercise 4.5. You will insert content controls in your certificate template to simplify the process of completing it.

When printing a certificate, consider using high-quality uncoated bond stock or parchment paper in conservative colors such as natural, cream, off-white, light gray, or any light marbleized color. In addition, consider using preprinted borders, ribbons, seals, and jackets, which are generally available through many mail order catalogs and office supply stores.

1. At a blank document, begin creating a template for the certificate shown in Figure 4.26 on page 168 by completing the following steps:

   a. Click the FILE tab and then click the *Export* option.

   b. At the Export backstage area, click *Change File Type* in the middle panel, click *Template (*.dotx)* in the *Document File Types* section, and then click the Save As button in the *Change File Type* section.

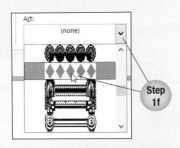

   c. At the Save As dialog box, navigate to your Chapter04 folder, type **C04-E05-AwardTemplate** in the *File name* text box, verify that *Word Template (*.dotx)* displays in the *Save as type* option box, and then click the Save button.

Step 1f

   d. Change the orientation to landscape.

   e. Change the top, bottom, left, and right document margins to 0.75 inch.

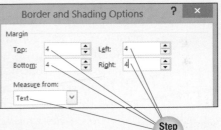

   f. Click the DESIGN tab, click the Page Borders button in the Page Background group, click the down-pointing arrow at the right side of the *Art* option box at the Borders and Shading dialog box with the Page Border tab selected, scroll down, and then click the diamond shape border (as shown above and to the right) at the drop-down list.

Step 1h

   g. Click the Options button at the Borders and Shading dialog box.

   h. At the Border and Shading Options dialog box, click the down-pointing arrow at the right of the *Measure from* option box and then click *Text*. Type 4 in each of the four margin measurement boxes and then click OK twice.

Step 1j

   i. Create a text box inside the border in a position similar to that shown in Figure 4.26 that measures 6.67 inches in height and 5.86 inches in width.

   j. With the text box selected, click the More button in the Shape Styles group on the DRAWING TOOLS FORMAT tab and then click the *Subtle Effect - Blue, Accent 1* option (second column, fourth row).

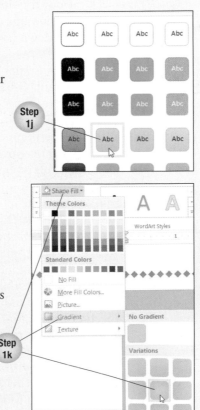

   k. With the text box still selected, click the Shape Fill button arrow in the Shape Styles group, point to *Gradient*, and then click the *From Center* option (second column, second row in the *Variations* section).

   l. Click the Shape Outline button arrow in the Shape Styles group and then the click *Blue, Accent 1, Lighter 60%* color (fifth column, third row in the *Theme Colors* section).

Step 1k

   m. With the insertion point positioned inside the text box, click the Object button arrow in the Text group on the INSERT tab, click *Text from File* at the drop-down list, navigate to your Chapter04 folder, and then double-click *Award.docx* .

2. Display the DEVELOPER tab on the ribbon by completing the following steps (skip to Step 3 if the DEVELOPER tab is already available on the ribbon):
   a. Click the FILE tab and then click *Options*.
   b. At the Word Options dialog box, click *Customize Ribbon* in the left panel.
   c. In the *Customize the Ribbon* section of the Word Options dialog box, click the *Developer* check box to insert a check mark and then click OK.

3. Insert and modify content controls in the template by completing the following steps:
   a. Click the Show/Hide ¶ button in the Paragraph group on the HOME tab to turn on the display of nonprinting characters.
   b. Position the insertion point at the third paragraph symbol below *Awarded to* and then click the DEVELOPER tab.

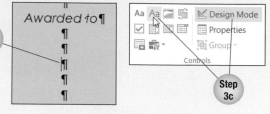

   c. Click the Design Mode button in the Controls group (this toggles the feature on) and then click the Plain Text Content Control button in the Controls group.
   d. With the insertion point positioned in the plain text content control, click the Properties button in the Controls group.
   e. At the Content Control Properties dialog box, type **Insert recipient's name** in the *Title* text box and then click the check box at the left of the *Use a style to format text typed into the empty control* option to insert a check mark. Click the down-pointing arrow at the right of the *Style* option box and then click *Heading 1* at the drop-down list. Click OK to close the dialog box.

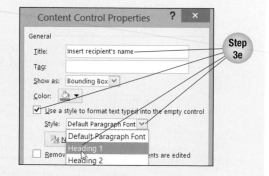

   f. Position the insertion point on the blank line (to the left of the tab symbol) below *Ameeta Singh, M.D.*, and then click the Date Picker Content Control button in the Controls group on the DEVELOPER tab.

   g. With the insertion point positioned in the date picker content control, click the Properties button in the Controls group.
   h. At the Content Control Properties dialog box, type **Select award date** in the *Title* text box, click the third date format in the *Display the date like this* list box in the *Date Picker Properties* section, and then click OK.
   i. To insert a date content control below *Diane Gohlke, R.N.,* position the insertion point in front of the paragraph symbol at the end of the line below the name, and then repeat steps 3f through 3h. ***Alternative: You can drag and drop a copy of the date picker control by clicking the control, holding down the Ctrl key, dragging the pointer to the desired position, and then releasing the mouse and the Ctrl key.***

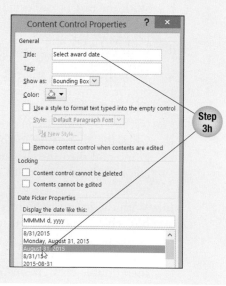

   j. Click the Design Mode button to turn off the feature.

   k. Select the text *Community Service Award* and then change the font to 32-point Broadway.

   l. With the text still selected, click the
Text Effects and Typography button,
point to *Shadow* at the drop-down list,
scroll down the side menu, and then
click the *Perspective Diagonal Upper Left*
option (first column, first row in the
Perspective section).

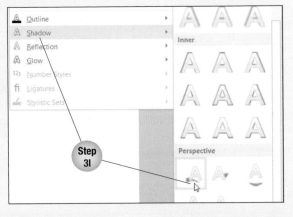

   m. Click the Show/Hide ¶ button to turn
off the display of nonprinting characters.

4. Draw the signature lines in the award by
completing the following steps:

   a. Click the INSERT tab.

   b. Click the Shapes button in the
Illustrations group and then click the
Line option in the *Lines* section.

   c. Hold down the Shift key as you drag the crosshairs to draw a
line above *Ameeta Singh, M.D.* The line should be 2.5 inches
wide. ***Hint: Select the line and then verify the correct width
at the* Shape Width *measurement box in the Size group on
the DRAWING TOOLS FORMAT tab.***

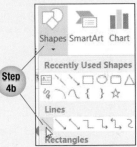

   d. With the line selected, click the DRAWING TOOLS FORMAT
tab, click the Shape Outline button arrow in the Shape Styles
group, and then click the *Black, Text 1* color (second column,
first row in the *Theme Colors* section).

   e. With the line still selected, hold down the Ctrl key as you drag and drop a copy of the line
above *Diane Gohlke, R.N.*, as shown in Figure 4.26.

5. Insert a picture and a logo by completing the following steps:

   a. Position the insertion point in the upper left corner of the document, near the gray
diamond border. Click the INSERT tab and then click the Online Pictures button in
the Illustrations group.

   b. At the Insert Pictures window, type **healthcare
professionals** in the *Office.com Clip Art* text
box and then press Enter.

   c. Double-click the image shown at the right (or
a similar image if this one is not available).

   d. With the image selected, click the Wrap
Text button in the Arrange group on the
PICTURE TOOLS FORMAT tab and then
click *In Front of Text* at the drop-down list.

   e. Change the height and width of the image to 3.5 inches.

   f. Position the image as shown in Figure 4.26.

   g. Insert the logo by clicking the INSERT tab, clicking the Pictures button in the
Illustrations group, navigating to your Chapter04 folder, and then double-clicking
EdwardCardio.png.

   h. With the logo selected, click the Wrap Text button and then click *In Front of Text* at the
drop-down list.

   i. Size and position the image as shown in Figure 4.26.

6. Save and then close **C04-E05-AwardTemplate.dotx**.

7. Open the award template and then create a document based on the template by completing the following steps:
   a. Open File Explorer.
   b. Navigate to your Chapter 04 folder.
   c. Double-click **C04-E05-AwardTemplate.dotx**.
8. Click the placeholder text *Click here to enter text.* and then type **Kathleen Sinnamon**. Press the Tab key, click the down-pointing arrow on the date picker content control, and then click the current date. Press the Tab key and then click the current date again.
9. Save the document with the name **C04-E05-CompletedAward**.
10. Print and then close **C04-E05-CompletedAward.docx**.

Figure 4.26 Certificate Created in Exercise 4.5

Creating a Resume Using a Template

A resume is a document that provides a person's educational background, work history, volunteer experience, and awards and/or certificates. A resume is generally submitted to potential employers when applying for a job. A resume should remain short (one to three pages), be visually appealing to the reader, contain keywords that employers look for in an applicant's information, and be updated on a regular basis.

The three common resume formats include: chronological, which lists a candidate's work experience in chronological order, usually beginning with the most current job; functional, which emphasizes the skills of the candidate and his or her achievements; and hybrid, which is a combination of the chronological and functional resumes.

Word includes several resume templates at the New backstage area. You can enter *resume* in the search text box or click the *Resume* option at the New backstage area to display all available resume templates. In Exercise 4.6, you will create a resume based on a Word resume template.

Exercise 4.6 Creating a Resume

1. At a blank document, create the resume shown in Figure 4.27 on page 170 by completing the following steps:
   a. Click the FILE tab and then click the *New* option.
   b. At the New backstage area, click in the search text box, type **resume**, and then press Enter.
   c. Double-click the first resume option, *Resume*, as shown at the right.
2. Select the current name that displays in the author placeholder at the beginning of the document and then type **Erik Karlsen**.
3. Click in the *[Address, City, ST ZIP Code]* placeholder and then type **4431 Alder Avenue, Salem, OR 97304**.
4. Click in the *[Telephone]* placeholder and then type **(971) 555-2815**.
5. Click in the *[Email]* placeholder and then type **ekarlsen@emcp.net**.

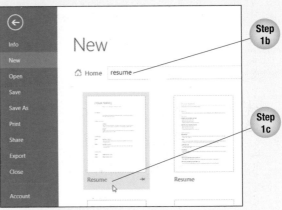

6. Continue filling in all the placeholders as shown in Figure 4.27. Delete the extra table row in the *COMPUTER SKILLS* section.
7. Select the entire document and then change the font color to *Black, Text 1*.
8. Save the document with the name **C04-E06-Resume**.
9. Print and then close **C04-E06-Resume.docx**.

Figure 4.27 Resume Created in Exercise 4.6

Chapter *Summary*

➤ Use Word templates to create personal documents such as disc inserts and labels, calendars, address labels, certificates, resumes, change-of-address postcards, and hanging name tags.

➤ Templates contain various placeholders in the form of text boxes containing formatted sample text or pictures; drawing objects in specific sizes, shapes, and colors; and sample images.

➤ Crop to trim horizontal and vertical edges off an image. Cropping can help to maximize the impact of an image.

➤ Select a predefined label at the Envelopes and Labels dialog box to create personal return labels, shipping labels, address labels, CD labels, place cards, tent cards, and many more useful labels.

➤ A calendar is a basic organizational tool that can also be used as a marketing tool to promote a service, product, or program. Create your own calendar, insert a predesigned calendar building block, or use a predesigned template from Office.com to create a calendar.

➤ Add interest to a document by inserting a shape. Customize a shape with buttons and options on the DRAWING TOOLS FORMAT tab.

➤ Move multiple drawing objects at once by selecting the first object, holding down the Shift key, clicking any additional objects, and then dragging the drawing objects to the desired location.

➤ Move objects in small increments, called *nudging*, by pressing the Up Arrow, Down Arrow, Right Arrow, or Left Arrow keys on the keyboard.

➤ A drawing canvas helps you arrange a drawing in a document. To display the drawing canvas, click the Shapes button in the Illustrations group on the INSERT tab and then click *New Drawing Canvas* at the bottom of the drop-down list.

➤ Align a drawing object or group of objects with options at the Align button drop-down list.

➤ Objects automatically stack in individual layers as you add them to a document. You see the stacking order when objects overlap—the top object covers a portion of the objects beneath it. Rearrange stacked drawing objects by selecting an object and then clicking the Bring Forward button or the Send Backward button in the Arrange group on the DRAWING TOOLS FORMAT tab.

➤ Grouping objects combines the objects into a single unit. Group selected objects with the Group button in the Arrange group on the DRAWING TOOLS FORMAT tab.

➤ Objects can be flipped or rotated with options at the Rotate button drop-down gallery. The Rotate button is located in the Arrange group on the DRAWING TOOLS FORMAT tab.

➤ Return labels may be duplicated on a sheet of labels by saving a formatted label as a building block to the Quick Part gallery where it can be named, saved, and reused.

➤ Add a border to a page, text, table, table cell, graphic object, or image to add interest and emphasis to various parts of a document.

➤ The nonprinting area is an area where text will not print, and this area varies with each printer. Adjustments may be necessary in the size and position of document elements to compensate for the nonprinting area of a particular printer.

➤ Create a form, which is a protected document that includes fields where information is entered, to save the time of recreating the same document.

➤ Content controls are added to documents or templates to allow the user to efficiently insert data into templates, forms, and documents.

➤ A date picker content control can be added to the document so that the user can select a date from a pop-up calendar.

> A resume is a document that lists a job applicant's work experience, educational background, volunteer work, and certificates and/or awards. The three most common resume formats are chronological, functional, and hybrid.

> Resume templates are available at the New backstage area.

Commands *Review*

FEATURE	RIBBON TAB, GROUP	BUTTON
align	PAGE LAYOUT, Arrange	
bring forward	PAGE LAYOUT, Arrange	
compress pictures	PICTURE TOOLS FORMAT, Adjust	
date picker content control	DEVELOPER, Controls	
group	DRAWING TOOLS FORMAT, Arrange	
labels	MAILINGS, Create	
orientation	PAGE LAYOUT, Page Setup	
page borders	DESIGN, Page Background	
pictures	INSERT, Illustrations	
quick parts	INSERT, Text	
recolor	PICTURE TOOLS FORMAT, Adjust	
rotate	PICTURE TOOLS FORMAT, Arrange	
send backward	PAGE LAYOUT, Arrange	
shapes	INSERT, Illustrations	
text box	INSERT, Text	
text content control	DEVELOPER, Controls	Aa
view gridlines	TABLE TOOLS LAYOUT, Table	

Key Points Review

True or False: Select the correct answer by circling T or F.

1. Content controls provide instructional text for users and can be set to disappear when users type in their own text.   T   F

2. To remove areas of a picture that you have cropped, click the Compress Pictures button.   T   F

3. Locate an object in a stack by selecting the group and then pressing Shift ı Tab to cycle forward through the objects until the desired object is selected.   T   F

4. You can nudge a selected object in a document by pressing the plus and minus keys on the keyboard.   T   F

5. Return address labels can be duplicated on a sheet of labels using quick parts, copying and pasting, or pressing the F5 key to repeat the last command as many times as necessary to fill a sheet.   T   F

6. Grouping objects combines all the objects into a single unit with its own set of sizing handles.   T   F

7. The Crop button is located on the PAGE LAYOUT tab.   T   F

8. A date picker content control is added to the document so that the user can select a date from the calendar control.   T   F

9. Hold down the Enter key as you select each object you want to group.   T   F

10. Content controls can be found on the INSERT tab.   T   F

11. The outside edges of a page that do not print are referred to as the nonprinting area.   T   F

12. A page border can be added to any or all sides of a page.   T   F

13. You must use a drawing canvas to stack objects in a document.   T   F

14. A text box is not a shape.   T   F

15. You can search for resume templates at the Open backstage area.   T   F

Chapter Assessments

Assessment 4.1   Create a Change-of-Address Postcard

Create the change-of-address postcard shown in Figure 4.28 with the following specifications:

1. At a blank document, display the Label Options dialog box and then choose the *Avery US Letter 8386 Postcards* option, which contains labels that measure 4 inches by 6 inches.
2. Follow the instructions in the callouts in Figure 4.28 to create the postcards; however, use your name and address and address the postcard as if you were sending it to a friend.
3. Insert a clip art image that is similar to the island stamp image shown in Figure 4.28. Find the clip art by typing the keyword **stamps** or **postage** in the *Office.com Clip Art* text box at the Insert Pictures window. When inserting the image on the back of the card (in the bottom table cell), make sure the insertion point is positioned in the upper left corner of the bottom table cell and not inside the text box containing the blue border. ***Hint: If the image in the sample document is no longer available, select a different image and change the text box fill colors to complement the image.***
4. Use the Papyrus font, or a similar font if Papyrus is not available.
5. The triangle shape on the front of the postcard is located in the Shapes button drop-down list.
6. Apply outside borders to both the front and back of the postcard.
7. Group any related objects.
8. Save the document with the name **C04-A01-AddressChange**.
9. Print and then close **C04-A01-AddressChange.docx**.

Assessment 4.2   Create an Event Invitation

As a volunteer for a community food pantry, you are responsible for creating an invitation that will be sent to the donors of the organization. Figure 4.29 on page 176 shows one formatted invitation. You have been asked to use the same text but create the invitation with different formatting. Because the food and personal items are sorted and packaged in brown paper grocery bags for distribution, you will maintain this theme by using a brown paper bag as the envelope for your invitation. You will size the invitation to fit into a brown lunch bag that measures approximately 5.5 inches by 10.5 inches. Complete the following steps to create the invitation:

1. At a blank document, change the size of the invitation by clicking the PAGE LAYOUT tab, clicking the Size button, and then clicking *More Paper Sizes* at the drop-down list. At the Page Setup dialog box with the Paper tab selected, type **5** in the *Width* measurement box, type **10** in the *Height* measurement box, and then click OK.
2. Refer to Figure 4.29 for the text of the invitation, but create your invitation with different formatting than that shown in Figure 4.29.
3. Insert the **Loaves&FishesBW.png** logo located in your Chapter04 folder.
4. Save the document with the name **C04-A02-Volunteer**.
5. Print the invitation and trim the excess paper.
6. Close **C04-A02-Volunteer.docx**.
7. ***Optional:*** Insert the invitation into a brown paper lunch bag and then create a label to attach to the front of the bag using design elements similar to the ones you used for the invitation. Use the Avery US Label, product number 6572 label. The label should include the text *You're invited! Look inside…* and include the **grocerybag.png** graphic located in your Chapter04 folder.

Figure 4.28 Change-of-Address Postcard Created in Assessment 4.1

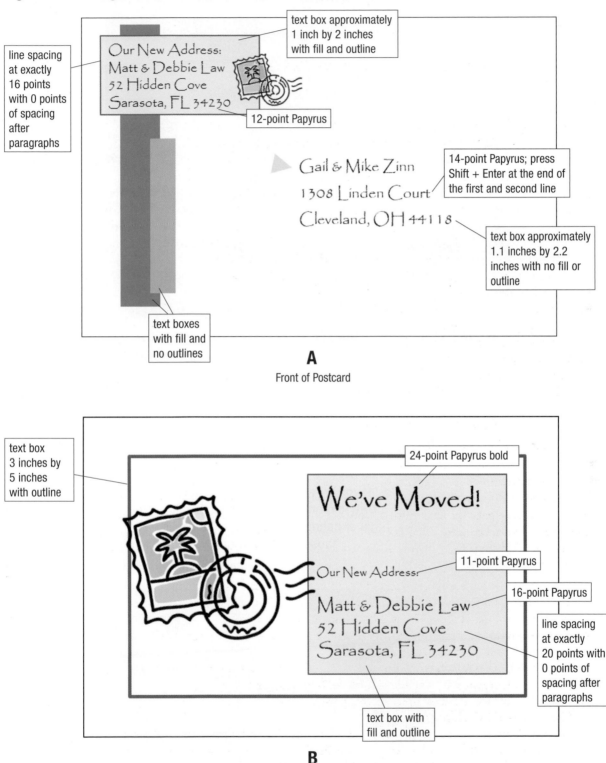

line spacing at exactly 16 points with 0 points of spacing after paragraphs

text box approximately 1 inch by 2 inches with fill and outline

12-point Papyrus

Our New Address:
Matt & Debbie Law
52 Hidden Cove
Sarasota, FL 34230

14-point Papyrus; press Shift + Enter at the end of the first and second line

Gail & Mike Zinn
1308 Linden Court
Cleveland, OH 44118

text box approximately 1.1 inches by 2.2 inches with no fill or outline

text boxes with fill and no outlines

A
Front of Postcard

text box 3 inches by 5 inches with outline

24-point Papyrus bold

We've Moved!

11-point Papyrus

Our New Address:

16-point Papyrus

Matt & Debbie Law
52 Hidden Cove
Sarasota, FL 34230

line spacing at exactly 20 points with 0 points of spacing after paragraphs

text box with fill and outline

B
Back of Postcard

Figure 4.29 Sample Invitation for Assessment 4.2

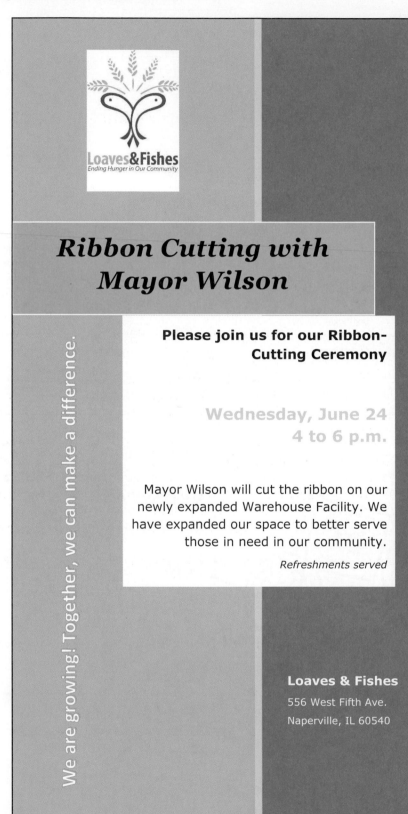

Assessment 4.3   Create a Certificate of Completion for a Course

Create a certificate of completion for the course you are currently taking.

1. Create the certificate at a blank document or use a predesigned template and then customize the template.
2. Include your name as the certificate recipient, the course name and number, and the course completion date.
3. Include a line for your instructor's signature.
4. Include any additional features to enhance the appearance of the certificate, such as graphics, shapes, or a page border.
5. Save the certificate with the name **C04-A03-ClassCertificate**.
6. Print and then close **C04-A03-ClassCertificate.docx**.

Assessment 4.4   Create a Hanging Name Tag and Agenda

As a virtual event planner, you run your business from your home. One of your clients, Global Network, is a network of accounting firms with members from all over the world. You are organizing an annual meeting for this group in Beijing in 2016. You have already prepared a template for the hanging name tags that the attendees will wear to all of the activities. Along with the attendee's name, city, and country, the tag will include the conference agenda. Complete the following steps to format the hanging name tag and agenda as shown in Figure 4.30 on page 178:

1. Open a document based on the template by completing the following steps:
   a. Open File Explorer.
   b. Navigate to your Chapter04 folder.
   c. Double-click *HangingNameTagTemplate.dotx*.
   d. Save the document with the name **C04-A04-HangingNameTag**.
2. Type the text for the front and back of the name tag as shown in Figure 4.30 and according to the specifications given in the figure.
   a. Use text boxes with the fill and outline removed, or type the text directly into the document, adjusting the line spacing by pressing the Enter key and adjusting the values in the *Before* and *After* measurement boxes in the *Spacing* section of the Paragraph dialog box. Consider adjusting the line spacing setting from the default *1.08* to *Single* or type increments in the *Multiple*, *Exactly*, or *At least* measurement boxes at the Paragraph dialog box.
   b. Click the logo on the front of the tag and then drag a copy of the logo to the back side of the tag.
3. Type the agenda text for the inside left and inside right parts of the tag in the table cells of the template as shown in the figure.
   a. Use the tab settings shown in Figure 4.30.
   b. Insert an en dash in each of the time durations.
4. Save **C04-A04-HangingNameTag.docx**.
5. Print one side of the document, reload the document into your printer, and then print the other side.
6. Trim the tag and, if one is available, fold it to fit into a clear plastic holder.
7. Close **C04-E04-HangingNameTag.docx**.

Figure 4.30 Name Tag and Agenda Created in Assessment 4.4

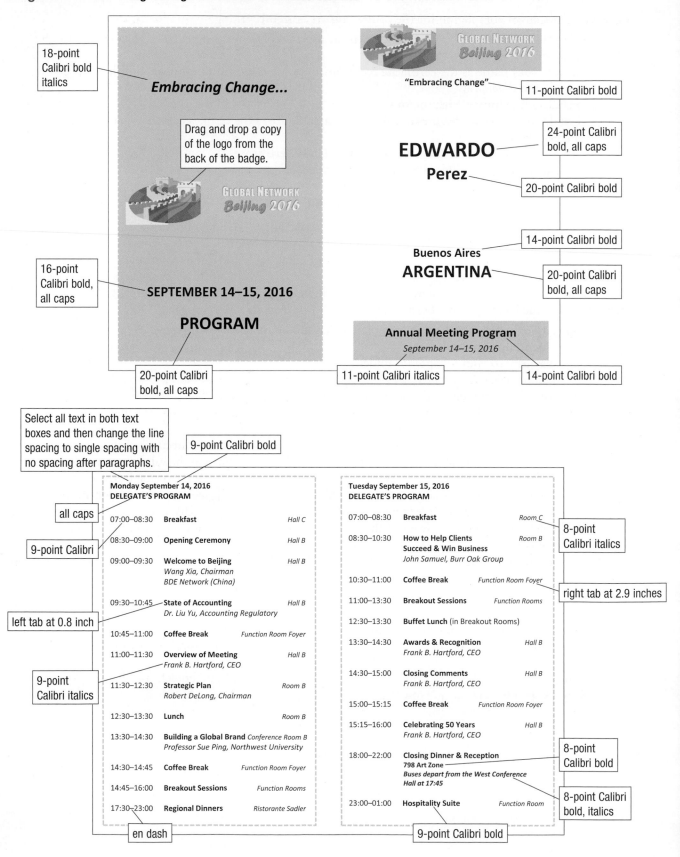

18-point Calibri bold italics

Embracing Change...

Drag and drop a copy of the logo from the back of the badge.

GLOBAL NETWORK Beijing 2016

"Embracing Change" — 11-point Calibri bold

EDWARDO — 24-point Calibri bold, all caps

Perez — 20-point Calibri bold

14-point Calibri bold

16-point Calibri bold, all caps

Buenos Aires
ARGENTINA — 20-point Calibri bold, all caps

SEPTEMBER 14–15, 2016

PROGRAM

Annual Meeting Program
September 14–15, 2016

20-point Calibri bold, all caps

11-point Calibri italics

14-point Calibri bold

Select all text in both text boxes and then change the line spacing to single spacing with no spacing after paragraphs.

9-point Calibri bold

Monday September 14, 2016
DELEGATE'S PROGRAM

all caps

9-point Calibri

07:00–08:30	**Breakfast**	*Hall C*
08:30–09:00	**Opening Ceremony**	*Hall B*
09:00–09:30	**Welcome to Beijing**	*Hall B*
	Wang Xia, Chairman	
	BDE Network (China)	
09:30–10:45	**State of Accounting**	*Hall B*
	Dr. Liu Yu, Accounting Regulatory	
10:45–11:00	**Coffee Break**	*Function Room Foyer*
11:00–11:30	**Overview of Meeting**	*Hall B*
	Frank B. Hartford, CEO	
11:30–12:30	**Strategic Plan**	*Room B*
	Robert DeLong, Chairman	
12:30–13:30	**Lunch**	*Room B*
13:30–14:30	**Building a Global Brand** *Conference Room B*	
	Professor Sue Ping, Northwest University	
14:30–14:45	**Coffee Break**	*Function Room Foyer*
14:45–16:00	**Breakout Sessions**	*Function Rooms*
17:30–23:00	**Regional Dinners**	*Ristorante Sadler*

left tab at 0.8 inch

9-point Calibri italics

en dash

Tuesday September 15, 2016
DELEGATE'S PROGRAM

07:00–08:30	**Breakfast**	*Room C*
08:30–10:30	**How to Help Clients**	*Room B*
	Succeed & Win Business	
	John Samuel, Burr Oak Group	
10:30–11:00	**Coffee Break**	*Function Room Foyer*
11:00–13:30	**Breakout Sessions**	*Function Rooms*
12:30–13:30	**Buffet Lunch** (in Breakout Rooms)	
13:30–14:30	**Awards & Recognition**	*Hall B*
	Frank B. Hartford, CEO	
14:30–15:00	**Closing Comments**	*Hall B*
	Frank B. Hartford, CEO	
15:00–15:15	**Coffee Break**	*Function Room Foyer*
15:15–16:00	**Celebrating 50 Years**	*Hall B*
	Frank B. Hartford, CEO	
18:00–22:00	**Closing Dinner & Reception**	
	798 Art Zone	
	Buses depart from the West Conference	
	Hall at 17:45	
23:00–01:00	**Hospitality Suite**	*Function Room*

8-point Calibri italics

right tab at 2.9 inches

8-point Calibri bold

8-point Calibri bold, italics

9-point Calibri bold

Assessment 4.5   Create and Format a Marketing Plan

As a team, create an attention-getting document advertising a spring promotion for a new line of products that your team chooses.

1. At a blank document, apply styles, an appropriate theme, a background color, gradients, pictures, or textures, and any other formatting elements to enhance the appearance of the document.
2. Save your document with the name **C04-A05-SpringPromotion**.
3. Print a copy of this document for each member of your class and then close the document.
4. Using PowerPoint, prepare a presentation to promote the line of products. Include at least five slides in the presentation. Save the presentation with the name **C04-A05-Products**. Print and then close **C04-A05-Products.pptx**.

Creating Letterheads, Envelopes, Business Cards, and Press Releases

Performance Objectives

Upon successful completion of Chapter 5, you will be able to:

- Produce letterheads, envelopes, business cards, and press releases
- Identify the purpose of a letterhead
- Customize a letterhead template
- Customize text boxes and shapes
- Create and format ruled lines
- Create and customize envelopes
- Create business cards using labels and quick parts
- Insert and format WordArt
- Refine letter, word, and line spacing

Desktop Publishing Terms

leading	logo	press release	tracking
line spacing	pixel	ruled lines	

Word Features Used

anchors	envelopes	quick parts	WordArt
borders and shading	kerning	shapes	
character spacing	labels	text boxes	
Click and Type	line spacing	text wrapping	

Note: Before beginning computer exercises for this chapter, copy to your storage medium the Chapter05 folder from the CD that accompanies this textbook and then make Chapter05 the active folder. Remember to substitute for graphics that may no longer be available.

Understanding the Purpose of Letterheads

DTP POINTER

A letterhead conveys specific information, establishes an identity, and projects an image.

In planning a letterhead design, think about its purpose. While the content of a letter may vary, the purpose of any letterhead is generally the same—to convey specific information, to establish an identity, and to project an image.

Conveying Information

Consider all of the necessary information you want to include in your letterhead. Also, consider what items your readers expect to find in your letterhead. Although the information provided may vary, letterheads commonly contain the following:

- Name of company or organization
- Logo
- Address
- Shipping or mailing address, if different from street address
- Telephone number, including area code (Include actual numbers if your phone number incorporates a catchy word as part of the number; include any extra phone numbers, such as a local number and/or a toll-free number.)
- Fax number, including area code
- Email address
- Web address
- Marketing statement or company slogan

The information in a letterhead tells the reader how to contact you by phone, by email, by regular mail, or in person. Omitting an important component in your letterhead projects a careless attitude and can negatively affect your business.

Establishing an Identity

A business relationship is often initiated through written communication. For example, a buyer from one company may write to another company inquiring about a certain product or asking for a price list; a real estate agent may send out a letter explaining his or her services to residents in surrounding communities; or a volunteer organization may send letters to local businesses soliciting their support. Whatever the reason for the letter, a letterhead with a specific design and layout helps to establish the identity of an organization. When readers are exposed to the same pattern of consistent elements in a letterhead over a period of time, they soon begin to establish a certain level of familiarity with the organization name, logo, colors, and so forth. Therefore, a letterhead should be immediately recognizable and identifiable.

You can further emphasize the identity of an organization by using some of the design elements from a letterhead in other business documents. If you do not want to create your own design, many direct-mail paper suppliers offer a line of attractively designed color letterheads, along with coordinating envelopes, business cards, fax cover sheets, press release forms, brochures, postcards, note cards, disc labels, and more. All you have to do is plan the layout of the letterhead text to complement the existing design and then print the text on the predesigned papers. Purchasing a coordinating line of predesigned papers can save on the high costs of professional designing and printing. It also provides a quick, convenient way to establish your identity among your readers.

Projecting an Image

Along with establishing an identity, letterheads help to project an image. In determining the image you want to project, assess your target audience. Who are they? What is their background, education, age, and so on? What image do you want your readers to form in their minds about your company, business, or organization? What does their experience tell them to expect?

Look at the two Financial Consultation letterheads in Figure 5.1. What image of the business do you form in your mind when you view each letterhead? The top letterhead projects a fun, casual, not-so-professional image, while the bottom letterhead conveys a more serious, businesslike attitude. Even though these images may not be accurate representations of the business, they affect the way you think about the business. On the other hand, giving your readers exactly what they expect can sometimes lead to boredom. Your challenge is to create a design that gives readers what they expect and, at the same time, sets your letterhead apart from the rest.

Printing your letterhead on high-quality paper can add to the cost, but it certainly presents a more professional image. You may have to go to a commercial printer to purchase this kind of paper. Many print shops let you buy paper by the sheet, along with matching envelopes.

◀ **DTP POINTER**
Printing on high-quality paper presents a professional image.

Figure 5.1 Comparing Letterhead Designs

Using Letterhead Templates

As discussed in Chapter 3, Word includes a variety of predesigned template documents, including letterheads. Search for letterhead templates by clicking the FILE tab and then clicking the *New* option. At the New backstage area, type *letterhead* in the search text box and then press the Enter key. A few sample letterhead templates are shown in Figure 5.2.

The descriptive names of the letterhead templates coordinate with the descriptive names for the memo, fax, report, and resume templates provided by Office.com. Using coordinating templates is an easy way for you to establish identity and consistency among your internal and external business documents.

Additional templates are available at http://office.microsoft.com/en-us/templates or the Microsoft Office templates partners website at http://office.microsoft.com/en-us /templates/templates-partners-FX010242583.aspx. At either website, type a search word or phrase in the search text box and then press the Enter key. At the templates partners website, click one of the company name hyperlinks in the *All Templates Partners* section (see Figure 5.3) to access other sites for business and personal templates.

DTP POINTER

Use coordinating templates to establish identity and consistency among your internal and external business documents.

Figure 5.2 Using Word Templates for Letterheads

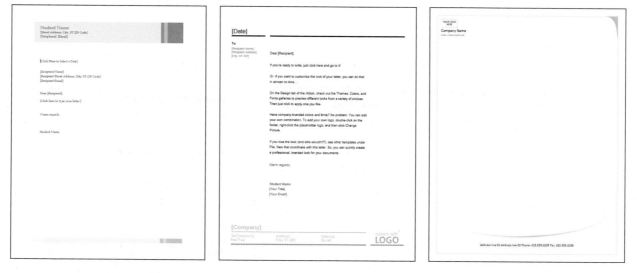

Figure 5.3 Using Other Online Sources for Business Templates

Click a hyperlink to access a partner site for additional business and personal templates.

Customizing a Logo Used in a Template

A *logo* is an image or symbol designed to represent a company or brand. In Exercise 5.1, you will customize a grouped drawing object that is used as a logo in a Word letterhead template. You will need to ungroup the object and change the color to match the colors of your company's brand. To ungroup and then regroup a drawing object, complete the following steps:

1. With the object selected, click the Group button in the Arrange group on the DRAWING TOOLS FORMAT tab or PICTURE TOOLS FORMAT tab and then click *Ungroup* at the drop-down list.
2. If a prompt displays to convert the picture to a drawing object, click Yes.
3. Customize an individual component of the object by clicking the component and then making changes with the options on the DRAWING TOOLS FORMAT tab or the PICTURE TOOLS FORMAT tab.
4. To regroup the components of the object, click in the object, click the HOME tab, click the Select button in the Editing group, and then click *Select All* at the drop-down list.
5. With all components in the object selected, click the DRAWING TOOLS FORMAT tab, click the Group button in the Arrange group, and then click *Group* at the drop-down list.

logo

An image or symbol designed to represent a company or brand

Select

Using the Selection Pane

Word includes the Selection pane to make working with layers a little easier. The Selection pane lists each item separately so you can apply custom effects to just that item, without having to click through the layers on the page. To access this feature, click the Select button in the Editing group on the HOME tab and then click *Selection Pane* at the drop-down list. Figure 5.4 shows a document with the Selection pane active.

In Exercise 5.1, you will customize a professionally designed letterhead template and then save the template. Figure 5.5A on page 186 shows the plain letterhead template and Figure 5.5B shows the letterhead template with all of the graphic elements used to create the design selected. Use the Selection pane to help you select these elements individually.

Figure 5.4 Using the Selection Pane

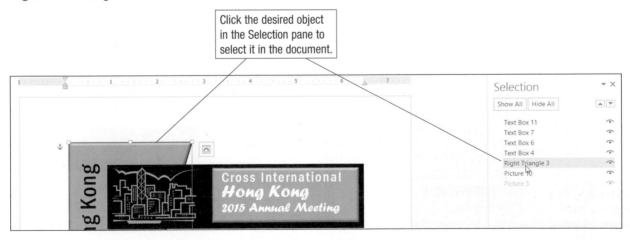

Figure 5.5 Formatting a Letterhead Template

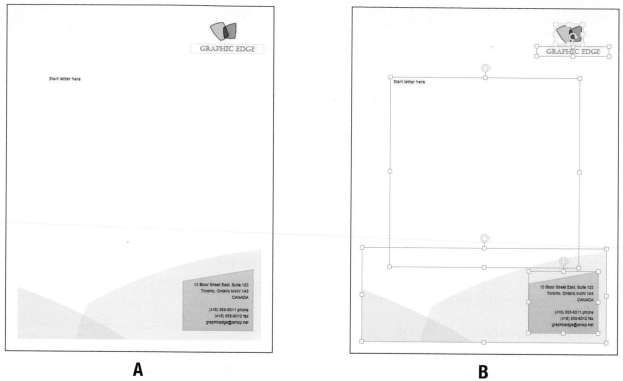

A
Letterhead Template

B
Letterhead Template with Design Elements Selected

Exercise 5.1 Creating a Letterhead Using a Template

1. In Word, open **GraphicEdgeTemplate.dotx** from your Chapter05 folder and then save the document with the name **C05-E01-GraphicEdgeTemplate**. Make sure *Word Template (*.dotx)* displays in the *Save as type* option box.
2. Display the Selection pane by clicking the Select button in the Editing group on the HOME tab and then clicking *Selection Pane* at the drop-down list. Notice the list of objects contained in the document that displays in the Selection pane.
3. Customize the logo graphic as shown in Figure 5.6 on page 187 by completing the following steps:
   a. Click *Picture 5* in the Selection pane to select the logo graphic.
   b. Click the PICTURE TOOLS FORMAT tab.
   c. Click the Group button in the Arrange group and then click *Ungroup* at the drop-down list.
   d. At the message asking if you want to convert the imported picture to a Microsoft Office drawing object, click the Yes button.

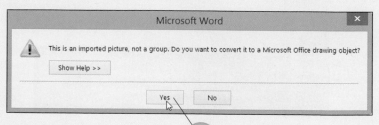

e. Drag the object back to its original position.

f. Click outside the object to deselect it and then click the red shape (left shape) of the logo.

g. Click the DRAWING TOOLS FORMAT tab.

h. Click the Shape Fill button arrow in the Shape Styles group and then click the *Light Green* color (fifth color in the *Standard Colors* section).

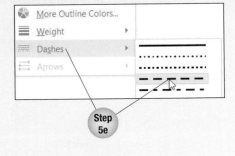

4. Close the Selection pane by clicking the Close button located in the upper right corner of the pane.

5. Format the text *Financial Consultation* and the text box containing it by completing the following steps:

a. Select the text *Financial Consultation* and then type **Graphic Edge**.

b. Select *Graphic Edge* and then change the font to 15-point Castellar.

c. Select the text box containing *Graphic Edge* by clicking the border of the text box.

d. With the text box selected, click the DRAWING TOOLS FORMAT tab.

e. Click the Shape Outline button arrow in the Shape Styles group, point to *Dashes* at the drop-down gallery, and then click the fourth option at the side menu.

f. Change the color of the dashed line by clicking the Shape Outline button arrow and then clicking the *Light Green* color (fifth option in the *Standard Colors* section).

6. Replace the text in the text box located in the bottom right corner of the template with the text shown in Figure 5.6 (the company address, telephone numbers, and email address).

7. Add an orange gradient fill and change the shape of the text box containing the address by completing the following steps:

a. Select the text box containing the address information.

b. Click the DRAWING TOOLS FORMAT tab if necessary to make it active.

c. Click the More button in the Shape Styles group.

d. Click the *Subtle Effect - Orange, Accent 2* shape style (third column, fourth row).

e. Click the Edit Shape button in the Insert Shapes group, point to *Change Shape* at the drop-down list, and then click the *Flowchart: Manual Input* shape in the *Flowchart* section.

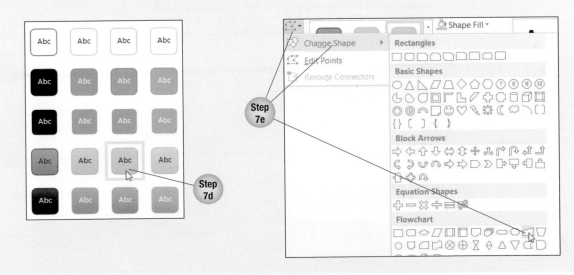

8. Save and then close **C05-E01-GraphicEdgeTemplate.dotx.**
9. Open File Explorer, navigate to your Chapter05 folder, and then double-click *C05-E01-GraphicEdgeTemplate.dotx.* (This opens a document based on the template.)
10. Select the text *Start letter here* (the text is inside a text box) and then insert a document by completing the following steps:
    a. Click the INSERT tab.
    b. Click the Object button arrow in the Text group and then click *Text from File* at the drop-down list.
    c. At the Insert File dialog box, navigate to your Chapter05 folder and then double-click *Graphic Text.docx.*
11. Save the document with the name **C05-E01-GELetter.**
12. Print and then close **C05-E01-GELetter.docx.**

Figure 5.6 Letterhead Created in Exercise 5.1

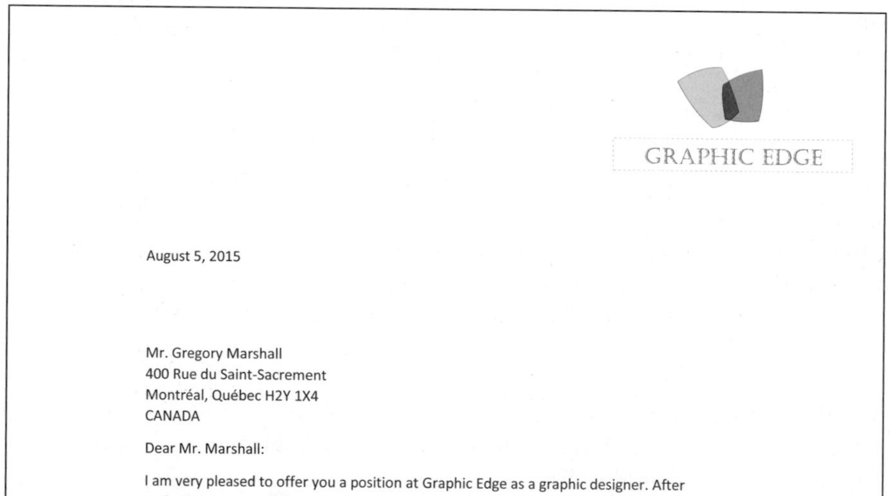

GRAPHIC EDGE

August 5, 2015

Mr. Gregory Marshall
400 Rue du Saint-Sacrement
Montréal, Québec H2Y 1X4
CANADA

Dear Mr. Marshall:

I am very pleased to offer you a position at Graphic Edge as a graphic designer. After reviewing your portfolio, considering your outstanding grades at Vancouver College, and discussing your creative contributions during your internship at CDP, I am excited about inviting you to join our team.

In addition to the salary we discussed, you will receive two weeks' paid vacation every 12 months, a bonus equaling two weeks' salary payable on the last pay check of the year, health benefits, and a $50,000 life insurance policy. This position is a two-year agreement, after which it may be renegotiated. Either party may terminate with a two-week notice.

I am positive that you will make a superb addition to our firm. If you have any questions, please call me at the office.

Sincerely,

Georgiana Forrester
Art Director

10 Bloor Street East, Suite 120
Toronto, Ontario M4W 1A8
CANADA

(416) 555-6011 phone
(416) 555-6012 fax
graphicedge@emcp.net

Creating Custom Letterheads

Designing your own letterhead lets you create your own identity and saves you time and money. In upcoming exercises, you will have the chance to create a letterhead from scratch and then save the letterhead as a template. Before you practice creating a letterhead, you will learn about several useful Word features that will assist you in this process.

Incorporating Design Concepts in Letterheads

When designing your letterhead, it is a good idea to start by creating thumbnail sketches to try out your ideas. While working on your sketches and, ultimately, when creating your letterhead, consider the following design concepts:

- Focus—create a focal point in the letterhead to draw in your audience.

- Balance—use a symmetrical layout where similar elements are distributed evenly on the page, or use an asymmetrical layout where dissimilar elements are distributed unevenly on the page in such a way as to balance one another.

- Proportion—design elements sized in proportion to their relative importance to the intended message. Your letterhead should not take up any more than 2 inches at the top of the page, preferably less.

- Contrast—use enough contrast to make it noticeable, and make sure there is enough surrounding white space assigned to darker elements on the page.

- Directional flow—group related items close to each other and establish a visual connection between items on the page by using a strong alignment.

- Consistency—use a typeface consistently in your letterhead even though it may vary in type size, typestyle, or color. Repeat elements that tie the letterhead to subsequent pages, such as a ruled horizontal line that is repeated as a footer on each page.

- Color—use color sparingly to provide emphasis and contrast, and use a color that meets your readers' expectations for the mood, tone, and image of your organization and your message.

Using the Click and Type Feature

The Click and Type feature can be used to insert text, graphics, tables, or other items into a blank area of a Word document. In Print Layout view, drag the mouse pointer across the document to view the Click and Type pointer with different alignment options, as shown in Figure 5.7. Double-clickc to move the insertion point to the location of the mouse pointer. Word will automatically change the paragraph alignment. Once the insertion point is in the desired location, begin typing or insert a graphic or other item. If the Click and Type feature does not work, check to see that it is enabled by displaying the Word Options dialog box, clicking *Advanced* in the left panel, and then making sure a check mark displays in the *Enable click and type* check box in the *Editing options* section.

Figure 5.7 Using Click and Type Alignment

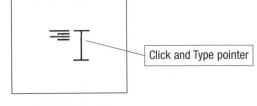

Left Alignment   Center Alignment   Right Alignment   Click and Type pointer

Figure 5.8 Using Vertical Page Position

Customize Status Bar	
Formatted Page Number	1
Section	1
✓ Page Number	Page 1 of 1
✓ Vertical Page Position	9.4"
Line Number	
Column	20

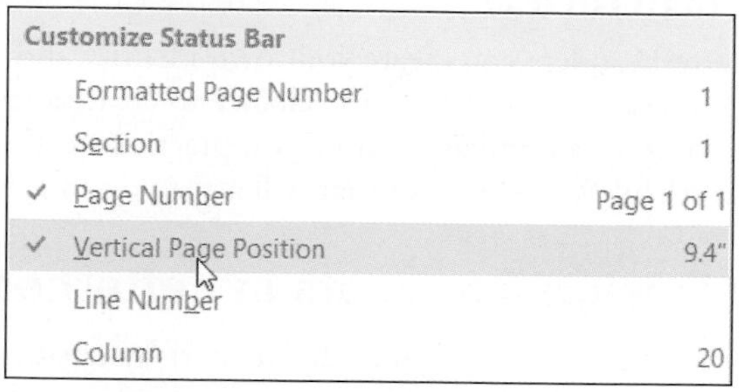

Using the Vertical Page Position Feature

DTP POINTER

Turn on the Vertical Page Position feature to view the exact location of your insertion point relative to the top of the document.

To add the vertical location of your insertion point to the items displayed on the Status bar, right-click the Status bar and then click the *Vertical Page Position* option at the Customize Status Bar pop-up list, as shown in Figure 5.8. This feature is helpful when you need to position text at an exact distance from the top of the page. For example, if you are printing a letter on predesigned letterhead stationery, you will need to set the text approximately 2 inches from the top of the page to make room for the preprinted letterhead.

Using Text Boxes in Design

Text boxes are useful in desktop publishing because they can be dragged to any position on the page using the mouse, or by specifying exact horizontal and vertical locations at the Layout dialog box. Another important feature of text boxes is that they are created in the drawing (foreground) layer and are considered drawing objects. Like any other object in Word, a text box can be placed above or below the text layer in a Word document. Text can be wrapped around a text box in a variety of ways, the direction of the text within a text box can be changed, and text boxes can be linked to one another.

Additionally, text boxes, as well as other Word objects, can be formatted with options on the DRAWING TOOLS FORMAT tab, as shown in Figure 5.9. Attributes such as shape fill, outline, and effects can be used to customize a text box.

Setting Text Box Margins

By default, a text box has left and right internal margins of 0.1 inch, and top and bottom internal margins of 0.05 inch. To adjust these margins, click the desired text box to access the DRAWING TOOLS FORMAT tab and then click the Shape Styles group task pane launcher. When the Format Shape task pane appears, click the Layout & Properties icon and then click the *TEXT BOX* option. Adjust the values in the measurement boxes for the internal margins, as shown in Figure 5.10.

Figure 5.9 Formatting Options on the DRAWING TOOLS FORMAT Tab

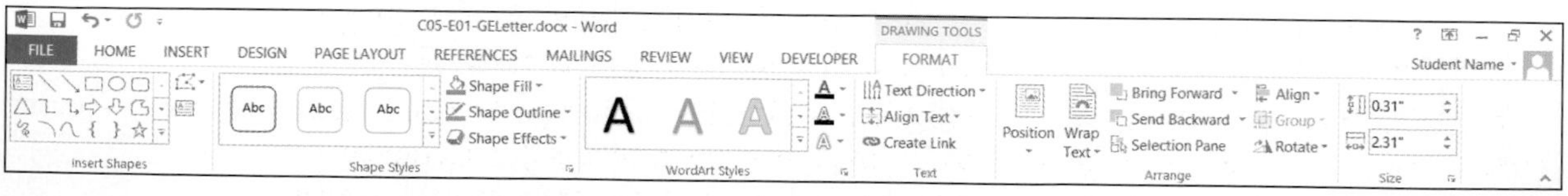

Figure 5.10 Adjusting Text Box Properties at the Format Shape Task Pane

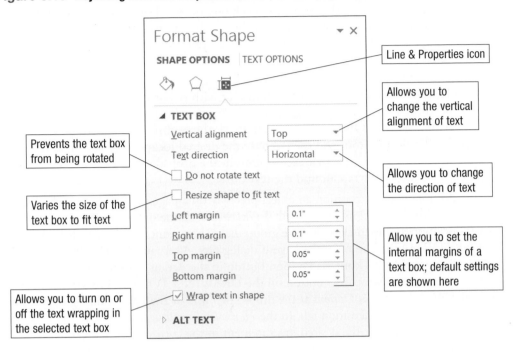

Sizing a Text Box

Change the size of a text box with the sizing handles located at its edges or with the *Shape Height* and *Shape Width* measurement boxes on the DRAWING TOOLS FORMAT tab. To size a text box with the sizing handles, select the text box and then position the mouse pointer on a sizing handle until it turns into a double-headed arrow. Hold down the mouse button, drag the outline of the text box toward or away from the center of the text box until it is the desired size, and then release the mouse button. To maintain the proportions of the existing text box dimensions, use one of the corner sizing handles to change both the width and the height at the same time. Hold down the Ctrl key as you drag one of the corner sizing handles and the text box will remain centered in the same position on the page.

To size a text box with the *Shape Height* and *Shape Width* measurement boxes on the DRAWING TOOLS FORMAT tab, select the text box and then type the desired measurement in each measurement box.

Positioning a Text Box

One of the biggest advantages to using a text box is the ability to position it anywhere on the page. Word provides several ways of positioning text boxes: using the move handle on the text box, using the keyboard, using the Position button in the Arrange group on the DRAWING TOOLS FORMAT tab, or using options at the Layout dialog box with the Position tab selected. To move a text box using the move handle (four-headed arrow), click the outline of the text box, hold down the mouse button, drag the outline of the text box to the new location, and then release the mouse button.

To move a text box using the keyboard, click the outline of the text box and then press the arrow keys to nudge the text box in small increments across the document page. When you nudge a text box, it moves one space over on the drawing grid, which is a set of intersecting lines used to align objects. The drawing grid is not visible in your document and the lines do not print. To view the gridlines, click the VIEW tab and then insert a check mark in the *Gridlines* check box in the Show group. If you hold down the Ctrl key as you nudge a text box, the text box moves one pixel at a time. A *pixel* is a single unit of measurement that your computer monitor uses to paint images on your screen. These units, which often appear as tiny dots, compose the pictures displayed by your screen.

Besides moving a text box with the mouse or with the arrow keys on the keyboard, you can position a text box on a page using the Position button in the Arrange group on the DRAWING TOOLS FORMAT tab. Click the outline of the text box to select it, click the Position button, and then choose the desired location for your text box, as shown in Figure 5.11. Notice that each option in the drop-down gallery depicts how the document text will wrap around the text box.

In addition, you can position an object precisely on a page with options at the Layout dialog box with the Position tab selected. To do this, click the outline of the text box you want to position and then click the Size group dialog box launcher on the DRAWING TOOLS FORMAT tab to open the Layout dialog box. Alternatively, you can open the Layout dialog box by clicking the Position button in the Arrange group on the PAGE LAYOUT tab or the Wrap Text button on the DRAWING TOOLS FORMAT tab, and then clicking *More Layout Options* at the drop-down list. At the Layout dialog box, shown in Figure 5.12, click the Position tab. In the *Horizontal* section, make sure *Absolute position* is selected, and then type the desired measurement in the corresponding measurement box. In the *to the right of* option box, select the point (*Margin, Page, Column, Character, Left Margin, Right Margin, Inside Margin,* or *Outside Margin*) from which you want to horizontally position the selected text box. Follow the same process in the *Vertical* section. This method provides precise control over the placement of the text box.

Copying a Text Box

In some situations you may want to make an exact copy of a text box and place it in a different location in a document. To do this, position the insertion point on the text box outline until the I-beam turns into a pointer with a four-headed arrow attached. Press the left mouse button, hold down the Ctrl key, and then drag a copy of the text box to the desired location.

Figure 5.11   Positioning a Text Box Using the Position Button Drop-down Gallery

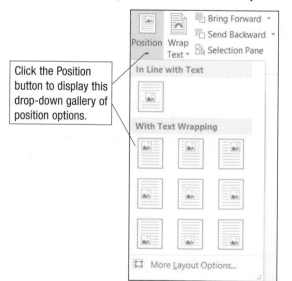

pixel

A single unit of measurement that your monitor uses to paint images on your screen

Position

Figure 5.12 Using the Layout Dialog Box to Precisely Position a Text Box Horizontally and Vertically

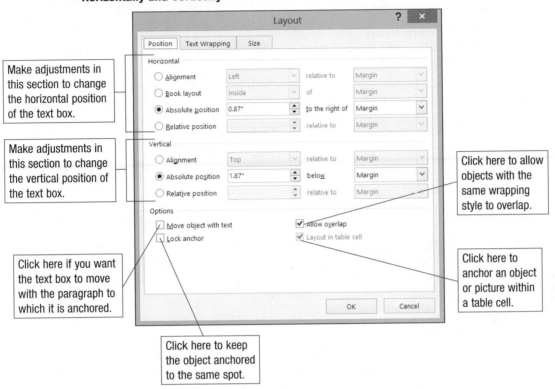

Make adjustments in this section to change the horizontal position of the text box.

Make adjustments in this section to change the vertical position of the text box.

Click here if you want the text box to move with the paragraph to which it is anchored.

Click here to keep the object anchored to the same spot.

Click here to allow objects with the same wrapping style to overlap.

Click here to anchor an object or picture within a table cell.

Anchoring a Text Box

Every object, including a text box, is automatically anchored, or attached, to the paragraph closest to the object. To see the paragraphs to which objects are anchored, the display of object anchors feature must be enabled. To turn on the display of object anchors, click the FILE tab, click *Options*, click *Display* in the left panel of the Word Options dialog box, click the *Object anchors* check box to insert a check mark, and then click OK to close the dialog box. Figure 5.13 shows a paragraph and text box with the object anchor displayed.

Figure 5.13 Viewing an Object Anchor

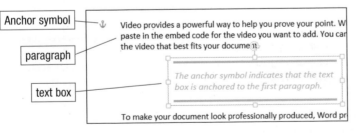

Anchor symbol

paragraph

text box

DTP POINTER

If you do not want a text box to move with the paragraph to which it is anchored, click the *Move object with text* check box at the Layout dialog box with the Position tab selected to remove the check mark.

When you reposition a text box, the anchor moves to the paragraph closest to the new position of the text box. The following points provide more information about object anchors in Word:

- A text box always appears on the same page as the paragraph to which it is anchored. By default, the text box moves with the paragraph to which it is anchored, but the paragraph will not move with the text box.

- If you do not want a particular text box to move with the paragraph to which it is anchored, click the outline of the text box to select it, display the Layout dialog box, click the Position tab, and then remove the check mark from the *Move object with text* check box.

- To keep the text box on the same page as the paragraph to which it is anchored, click the *Lock anchor* check box to insert a check mark. If the paragraph is moved to another page, the text box will be moved to that page as well.

- To make an object remain stationary at a specific location on a page regardless of the text that surrounds it, display the Layout dialog box and click the Position tab. Enter specific measurements at the *Absolute position* measurement box in the *Horizontal* section and in the *Vertical* section, and make selections in the *to the right of* and *below* option boxes. Lastly, remove the check mark from the *Move object with text* check box.

Wrapping Text around a Text Box

Wrap Text

By default, a text box displays in the layer above, or in front of, the text. To wrap text around, behind, or in front of a text box, select the text box, display the DRAWING TOOLS FORMAT tab, and then click the Wrap Text button in the Arrange group. Several wrapping options are available, and the way text boxes appear with each of these options applied is illustrated in Figure 5.14. The wrapping styles available at the Wrap Text button drop-down list are summarized in Table 5.1.

At the Layout dialog box with the Text Wrapping tab selected, you can use the *Wrap text* section to modify the way text wraps around a text box. The options available in the *Wrap text* section are described in Table 5.2.

Figure 5.14 Comparing Text Wrapping Styles

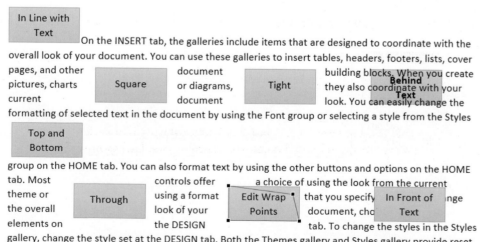

Table 5.1 Text Wrapping Styles Available at the Wrap Text Button Drop-down Gallery

In Line with Text	The object is placed in the text layer at the insertion point in a line of text.	In Line with Text
Square	Text wraps around all four sides of the selected text box or object.	Square
Tight	Text wraps tightly around the shape of an object rather than the box holding the object. (This style is more apparent when applied to a shape other than a square or rectangle.)	Tight
Through	This option is similar to *Tight*. Text not only wraps around the shape of an object, but it also flows through any open areas of the object box. This option may produce a visible change with certain graphic images, but no changes will occur when applied to a text box.	Through
Top and Bottom	Text wraps around the top and bottom of the text box (object) but not on both sides. Text stops at the top of the text box (object) and restarts on the line below the object.	Top and Bottom
Behind Text	Text wrapping is removed and the text box or object is placed behind the text layer in the document.	Behind Text
In Front of Text	Text wrapping is removed and the text box or object is placed in front of the text. This is the default setting.	In Front of Text
Edit Wrap Points	This option allows you to wrap text closer to the object.	Edit Wrap Points

Table 5.2 Advanced Wrapping Styles Available on the Text Wrapping Tab of the Layout Dialog Box

Both sides	Text wraps on both sides of the text box.
Left only	Text wraps along the left side of the text box but not on the right side.
Right only	Text wraps along the right side of the text box but not on the left side.
Largest only	Text wraps along the largest side of the object. This does not produce any changes when applied to a text box.

Customizing Text Boxes

By default, a text box has a black single-line outline around all sides and contains a white background fill. However, a text box can be customized in a variety of ways, including changing outline style and color and changing the background fill color.

Changing Text Box Outlines and Effects

The following methods, along with your own creativity, can be used to customize the outline of a text box (or other objects).

Shape Outline

To add, remove, or change the color, weight, or style of a text box outline, select the text box and then click the Shape Outline button arrow in the Shape Styles group on the DRAWING TOOLS FORMAT tab. At the Shape Outline button drop-down gallery, click a color in the *Theme Colors* or *Standard Colors* section or click the *More Outline Colors* option to pick from an extended selection of standard colors or create your own custom colors. Click *Weight* or *Dashes* to change the thickness or style of the text box outline. Click *No Outline* to remove the outline from around the text box. A colored outline can also be applied to a text box by clicking one of the shape style thumbnails in the Shape Styles group. You can also click the Shape Styles group task pane launcher to access outline options at the Format Shape task pane. Three examples of outlines are shown in Figure 5.15.

Shape Effects

To add shape effects to a text box, select the text box, click the Shape Effects button in the Shape Styles group, point to *Preset, Shadow, Reflection, Glow, Soft Edges, Bevel,* or *3-D Rotation* and then click an option at the side menu. Figure 5.16 illustrates examples of these shape effects.

Figure 5.15 Changing Text Box Outlines

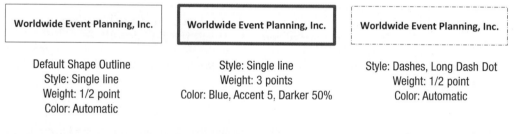

Figure 5.16 Changing Text Box Effects

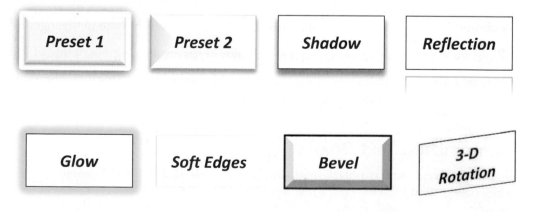

Changing Text Box Fill

Shape Fill

Customize the text box fill with the Shape Fill button in the Shape Styles group on the DRAWING TOOLS FORMAT tab. Click the Shape Fill button arrow and then choose a fill color in the *Theme Colors* or *Standard Colors* section of the drop-down gallery, or choose the *No Fill*, *More Fill Colors*, *Picture*, *Gradient*, or *Texture* options, as shown in Figure 5.17.

Fill colors can also be added to a text box with the second through sixth rows of shape styles that are available by clicking the More button at the right side of the shape style thumbnails in the Shape Styles group.

Add a transparent effect to the text box fill color by clicking the Shape Fill button arrow, clicking the *More Fill Colors* option, and then dragging the slider in the *Transparency* section of the Colors dialog box as shown in Figure 5.18. You can also change the transparency by adjusting the percentage in the measurement box at the right side of the *Transparency* section.

Figure 5.17 Changing Shape Fill

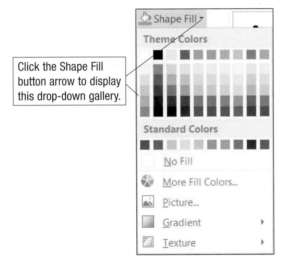

Click the Shape Fill button arrow to display this drop-down gallery.

Figure 5.18 Adding Transparency to a Color

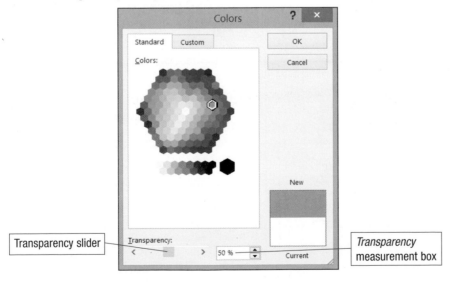

Transparency slider

Transparency measurement box

Inserting Predesigned Text Boxes

Word 2013 includes several predesigned text boxes that can be used in your documents. Simply insert the text box and then replace the placeholder text with a picture, a graphic, or text. To access predesigned text boxes, click the Text Box button in the Text group on the INSERT tab and then click an option at the drop-down list, as shown in Figure 5.19. Figure 5.20 illustrates a few predesigned text boxes used in documents.

Figure 5.19 Inserting Predesigned Text Boxes

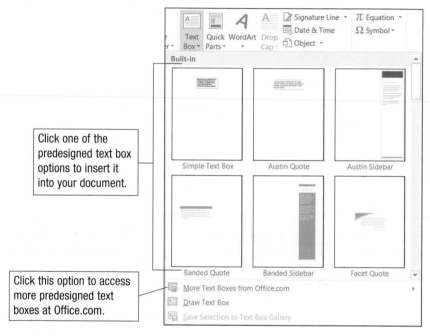

Click one of the predesigned text box options to insert it into your document.

Click this option to access more predesigned text boxes at Office.com.

Figure 5.20 Using Predesigned Text Boxes

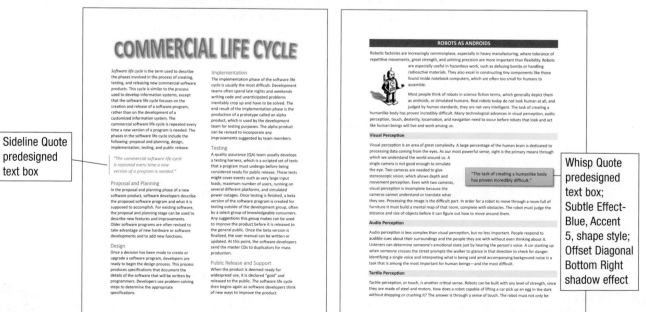

Sideline Quote predesigned text box

Whisp Quote predesigned text box; Subtle Effect-Blue, Accent 5, shape style; Offset Diagonal Bottom Right shadow effect

Creating Horizontal and Vertical Ruled Lines

Horizontal and vertical lines can be drawn in a document by using line options at the Shapes button drop-down list or by using paragraph borders. As with text boxes, you can adjust the weight, length, position, color, and shading of the lines you create. In typesetting, these horizontal and vertical lines are called **ruled lines** (also known as rules or ruling lines) to distinguish them from lines of type.

Horizontal and vertical ruled lines are used to guide a reader's eyes across and down the page, to separate sections or columns of text, to add visual interest, and to act as boundaries to the surrounding text. A thicker line serves as a stronger visual barrier than a thinner line. Make sure ruled lines in a document are consistent in both purpose and appearance.

Drawing Horizontal and Vertical Lines

To insert a horizontal or vertical line, click the INSERT tab, click the Shapes button in the Illustrations group, click the desired line option in the *Lines* section of the drop-down list, and then click and drag in the document to create the line. To create a straight horizontal, vertical, or diagonal line, hold down the Shift key as you drag to create the line.

Shapes

Sizing and Formatting Lines

Sizing a drawn line is similar to sizing a text box. Select the line to be sized, position the mouse pointer on either sizing handle until it turns into crosshairs (hold down the Shift key if you want to make sure the line retains its shape and direction), drag the crosshairs in the appropriate direction until the line is the desired length, and then release the mouse button. For precise measurements, select the line and then enter a measurement in the *Shape Width* measurement box in the Size group on the DRAWING TOOLS FORMAT tab.

Format a drawn line with options on the DRAWING TOOLS FORMAT tab. Select different weights, such as those shown in Figure 5.21, from the side menu that displays when you point to *Weight* at the drop-down gallery that displays when you click the Shape Outline button arrow in the Shape Styles group. Choose colors, such as those shown in the figure, by selecting options in the *Theme Colors* or *Standard Colors* section of the drop-down gallery. You can also point to the *Dashes* or *Arrows* option and then choose an option from the side menu that displays.

Figure 5.21 Customizing the Weight and Color of Lines

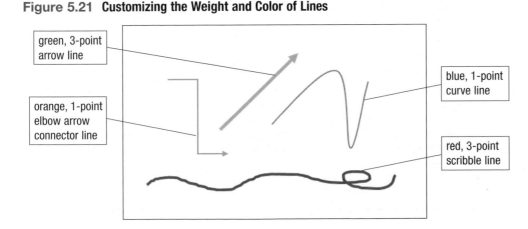

Positioning Horizontal and Vertical Lines

Position horizontal and vertical lines in the same way you position a text box. Select a line and then use the mouse, the arrow keys on the keyboard, options on the DRAWING TOOLS FORMAT tab, or options at the Layout dialog box with the Position tab selected to reposition the line.

Creating Horizontal Lines Using Paragraph Borders

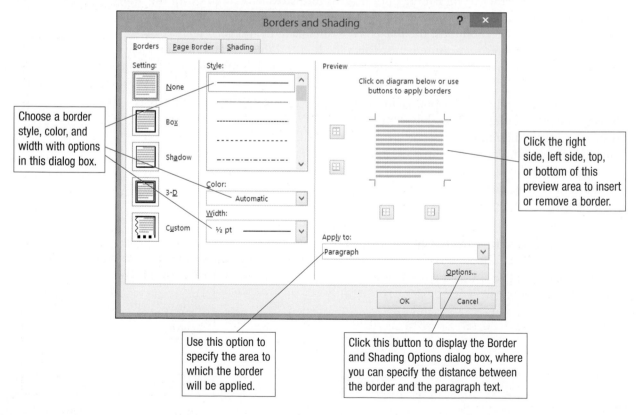

Borders

Every paragraph you create in Word is surrounded by an invisible frame. (Remember that a paragraph may contain text or consist of only a hard return.) To add a border to the top, bottom, or sides of your paragraph, use the options at the Borders button drop-down gallery in the Paragraph group on the HOME tab. To change the position of the border, click the Borders button arrow and then click the desired border location at the drop-down gallery.

Border lines can be created and customized with options at the Borders and Shading dialog box with the Borders tab selected, as shown in Figure 5.22. Display this dialog box by clicking the Borders button arrow and then clicking *Borders and Shading* at the drop-down gallery. The dialog box contains options for changing the border settings, line style, line color, line width, border location, and distance between borders and text.

In Exercise 5.2, you will create a letterhead for an event planning firm. You will use grouped images, text boxes, ruled lines, and text effects to enhance your letterhead design.

Figure 5.22 Customizing in the Borders and Shading Dialog Box with the Borders Tab Selected

Choose a border style, color, and width with options in this dialog box.

Click the right side, left side, top, or bottom of this preview area to insert or remove a border.

Use this option to specify the area to which the border will be applied.

Click this button to display the Border and Shading Options dialog box, where you can specify the distance between the border and the paragraph text.

1. Open **WEPLetterhead.docx** from your Chapter05 folder and then save the document with the name **C05-E02-WEPLetterhead**.
2. Arrange the pictures to create the letterhead as shown in Figure 5.23 on page 204 by completing the following steps:
   a. Click each picture and then drag each image to form a straight, tight line of pictures. *Hint: The images have already been sized appropriately and their text wrapping has been changed to Tight. To get a better view to align the picture objects, zoom in.*

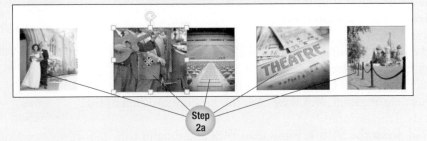

Step 2a

   b. Once the images have been positioned appropriately, hold down the Shift key and then click each image.
   c. With all five images selected (their sizing handles should be displayed), click the PICTURE TOOLS FORMAT tab, click the Align button in the Arrange group, and then click *Align Top* at the drop-down list.

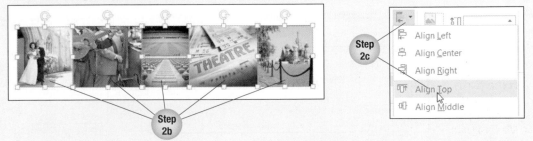

Step 2b

Step 2c

   d. With the images still selected, click the Group button in the Arrange group and then click *Group* at the drop-down list.
3. Position the grouped image by completing the following steps:
   a. With the grouped image selected, click the Position button in the Arrange group on the PICTURE TOOLS FORMAT tab and then click *More Layout Options* at the drop-down list.
   b. Click the *Alignment* option in the *Horizontal* section of the Layout dialog box.
   c. Click the down-pointing arrow to the right of the option box containing the word *Left* and then click *Centered* at the drop-down list.
   d. Click the down-pointing arrow at the right of the option box to the right of the *relative to* option in the *Horizontal* section and then click *Page* at the drop-down list.

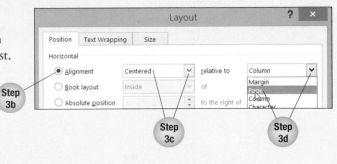

Step 3b

Step 3c

Step 3d

e. Make sure the *Absolute position* option in the *Vertical* section is selected.

f. Select the current measurement in the *Absolute position* measurement box and then type **0.5**.

g. Click the down-pointing arrow to the right of the option box to the right of the *below* option and then click *Page* at the drop-down list.

h. Click OK.

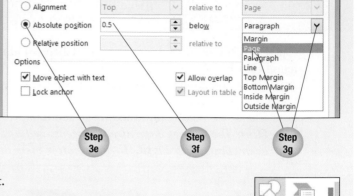

4. Draw the blue horizontal line shown below the grouped image in Figure 5.23 by completing the following steps:

a. Click the INSERT tab, click the Shapes button in the Illustrations group, and then click the *Line* option (first option in the *Lines* section).

b. Hold down the Shift key and then click and drag in the document to create a horizontal line.

c. With the line selected, click the More button in the Shape Styles group on the DRAWING TOOLS FORMAT tab and then click the *Subtle Line - Accent 5* style (sixth column, first row).

d. Click in the *Shape Width* measurement box in the Size group, type **6.5**, and then press Enter.

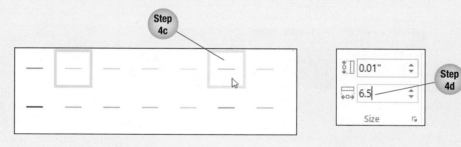

e. Drag the line so it is positioned under the grouped image, as shown in Figure 5.23.

f. With the line selected, click the Position button in the Arrange group and then click *More Layout Options* at the drop-down list.

g. At the Layout dialog box, click the *Alignment* option in the *Horizontal* section and then change the alignment to centered relative to the page. (See image at right.)

h. Click OK to close the dialog box.

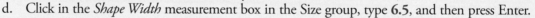

5. Insert the globe clip art image by completing the following steps:
   a. Turn on the display of nonprinting characters, position the insertion point to the left of the fifth paragraph symbol from the top, and then turn off the display of nonprinting characters.
   b. Click the INSERT tab and then click the Online Pictures button in the Illustrations group.
   c. At the Insert Pictures window, type **globe sun** in the *Office.com Clip Art* text box and then press Enter.
   d. When the search results display, double-click the image shown at the right. (If this image is not available, you can use the file **globesun.png** located in your Chapter05 folder.)
   e. With the image selected, click in the *Shape Height* measurement box in the Size group on the PICTURE TOOLS FORMAT tab, type **0.7**, and then press Enter. (Word will automatically change the shape width to 0.7 inch.)
   f. Click the Wrap Text button in the Arrange group and then click *In Front of Text* at the drop-down list.
   g. Drag the image so it is positioned as shown in Figure 5.23.

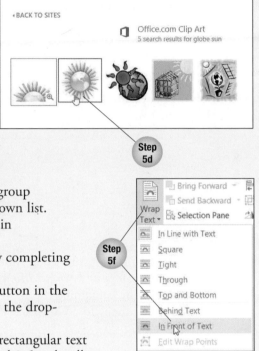

6. Create the *Worldwide Event Planning, Inc.* text by completing the following steps:
   a. Click the INSERT tab, click the Text Box button in the Text group, and then click *Draw Text Box* at the drop-down list.
   b. Click and drag in the document to create a rectangular text box that is approximately 5.0 inches wide and 0.6 inch tall.
   c. Type **Worldwide Event Planning, Inc.**
   d. Select the text, click the HOME tab, click the Text Effects and Typography button in the Font group, and then click the *Fill - Blue, Accent 1, Shadow* option (second column, first row).
   e. Change the font to 24-point Palatino Linotype and then apply bold and italic formatting.
   f. Display the Font dialog box with the Advanced tab selected, turn on kerning at 24 points and above, and then click OK to close the dialog box.

7. Customize the text box by completing the following steps:
   a. Click the text box border to select it.
   b. Click the DRAWING TOOLS FORMAT tab.
   c. Click the Shape Fill button arrow in the Shape Styles group and then click *No Fill* at the drop-down gallery.
   d. Click the Shape Outline button arrow and then click *No Outline* at the drop-down gallery.
   e. Drag the text box so it is positioned as shown in Figure 5.23.

8. Select the blue line you previously created. Hold down the mouse button and the Ctrl key and drag a copy of the line below the *Worldwide Event Planning, Inc.* text.
9. With the line selected, click the DRAWING TOOLS FORMAT tab, click the Shape Outline button arrow, point to *Weight*, and then click *1¹/₂ pt* at the side menu.

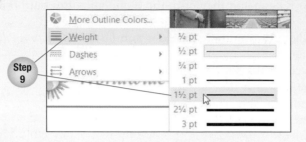

10. Click the Shape Outline button arrow again and then click the *Green, Accent 6* option (last column, first row in the *Theme Colors* section).

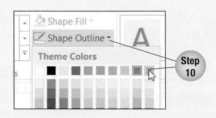

11. Drag the line so it is positioned as shown in Figure 5.23. **Hint: With the line selected, use the arrow keys on your keyboard to nudge it into correct position.**
12. Select the text box containing the address and then position it as shown in Figure 5.23.
13. Save, print, and then close **C05-E02-WEPLetterhead.docx**.

Figure 5.23 Letterhead Created in Exercise 5.2

Creating Envelopes

Let your company letterhead be the starting point for the design of your other business documents. Using an envelope designed in coordination with a letterhead is another way of projecting a professional image and establishing your identity with your target audience. Using some of the same design elements in both the letterhead and the envelope contributes to continuity and consistency among your documents. These same elements can be carried over into memo and fax templates, business cards, invoices, and brochures.

Designing an Envelope

When planning your envelope design, remember that it does not have to be an exact replica of the letterhead—you just need to select common elements to establish a visual link between the two documents. Keep in mind that the design area of your envelope is smaller and shaped differently than that of your letterhead. For example, using the same typeface and typestyles in a smaller type size and repeating a graphic element may be just enough to establish that link.

Changing the Text Direction

Because designing an envelope requires working within a small area, you often need to come up with creative ways to incorporate various design elements. For example, you may want to change the direction of certain text elements to add interest to your design and make use of wasted space. You can change the direction of the text within a text box by clicking the Text Direction button in the Text group on the DRAWING TOOLS FORMAT tab. Rotating the text can add focus and contrast to your text. Figure 5.24 shows the options available at the Text Direction button drop-down list.

Using the Envelope Feature

Word's envelope feature makes creating professional-looking envelopes easy and inexpensive. This feature displays in the document screen a blank envelope that already contains appropriate formatting for margins and a text box in the mailing address position.

◀ **DTP POINTER**

Use your company letterhead as the starting point for the design of all your business documents.

◀ **DTP POINTER**

Use consistent elements to establish a visual connection between your envelope and letterhead.

◀ **DTP POINTER**

Consider the actual size of the design area.

Text Direction

Figure 5.24 Using the Text Direction Button Drop-down List

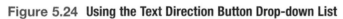

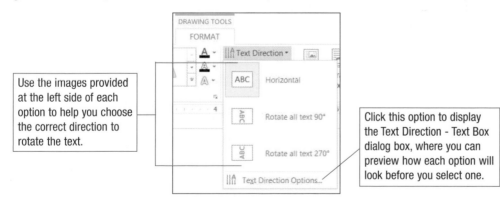

Use the images provided at the left side of each option to help you choose the correct direction to rotate the text.

Click this option to display the Text Direction - Text Box dialog box, where you can preview how each option will look before you select one.

To create a customized envelope for a particular document and insert a logo in the envelope, complete the following steps:

1. Open the document for which you want to create an envelope and then click the MAILINGS tab.
2. Click the Envelopes button in the Create group.
3. At the Envelopes and Labels dialog box with the Envelopes tab selected, click the Options button.
4. At the Envelope Options dialog box, make sure the desired envelope displays in the *Envelope size* option box. If it does not, select the desired size. (If the size you want is not listed, click *Custom size* at the drop-down list and then enter the dimensions of your envelope.)
5. Select a desired font for the delivery address and the return address.
6. Click the Printing Options tab in the Envelope Options dialog box, select the feed method required by your printer, and then click OK. ***Note: Printer feed methods are discussed in the next section of this chapter.***
7. At the Envelopes and Labels dialog box with the Envelopes tab selected, click the Add to Document button to display your envelope at the top of the document window.
8. Position the insertion point inside the envelope, insert a logo, and then drag to position the logo.

Envelopes

Word adds the envelope to the beginning of the current document and numbers the envelope as page 1 and the first page of the document as page 2. To print just your envelope (without the rest of the document), select page 1 in the preview pane at the Print backstage area, click *Print Current Page* in the *Settings* section, and then click the Print button.

The envelope feature also includes an option to add electronic postage to envelopes and labels. You must install electronic postage software before you can use this feature. The Microsoft Office website provides information about electronic postage add-ins.

Checking Envelope Printing Options

To determine the best way to feed an envelope into your printer, display the Envelopes and Labels dialog box with the Envelopes tab selected and then view the information. If the feed method displayed in the *Feed* section of the Envelopes and Labels dialog box does not work for your printer, click the Options button and then choose the correct options in the *Feed method* section and the *Feed from* option box at the Envelope Options dialog box with the Printing Options tab selected. Feed methods are visually displayed at this dialog box, as shown in Figure 5.25.

Figure 5.25 Selecting Feed Methods at the Envelope Options Dialog Box

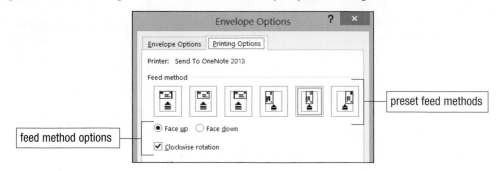

In Exercise 5.3, you will design a coordinating envelope template for the letterhead you created in Exercise 5.2.

Exercise 5.3   Designing a Coordinating Envelope

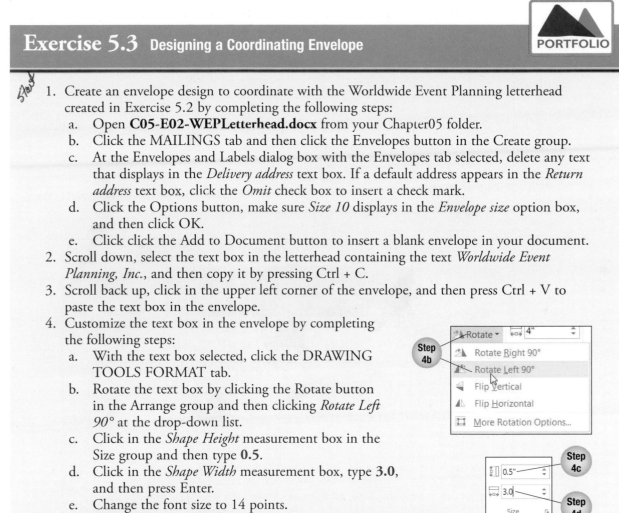

1. Create an envelope design to coordinate with the Worldwide Event Planning letterhead created in Exercise 5.2 by completing the following steps:
    a.   Open **C05-E02-WEPLetterhead.docx** from your Chapter05 folder.
    b.   Click the MAILINGS tab and then click the Envelopes button in the Create group.
    c.   At the Envelopes and Labels dialog box with the Envelopes tab selected, delete any text that displays in the *Delivery address* text box. If a default address appears in the *Return address* text box, click the *Omit* check box to insert a check mark.
    d.   Click the Options button, make sure *Size 10* displays in the *Envelope size* option box, and then click OK.
    e.   Click click the Add to Document button to insert a blank envelope in your document.
2. Scroll down, select the text box in the letterhead containing the text *Worldwide Event Planning, Inc.*, and then copy it by pressing Ctrl + C.
3. Scroll back up, click in the upper left corner of the envelope, and then press Ctrl + V to paste the text box in the envelope.
4. Customize the text box in the envelope by completing the following steps:
    a.   With the text box selected, click the DRAWING TOOLS FORMAT tab.
    b.   Rotate the text box by clicking the Rotate button in the Arrange group and then clicking *Rotate Left 90°* at the drop-down list.
    c.   Click in the *Shape Height* measurement box in the Size group and then type **0.5**.
    d.   Click in the *Shape Width* measurement box, type **3.0**, and then press Enter.
    e.   Change the font size to 14 points.
    f.   Move the text box to the left side of the envelope as shown in Figure 5.26 on page 208.
5. Copy the globe image from the letterhead and then paste it into the envelope.
6. Size and position the image in the envelope as shown in Figure 5.26.
7. Copy the text box containing the address in the letterhead and then paste it into the envelope.
8. Select the address text and then change the paragraph alignment to left.
9. Delete the website and phone number from the address.
10. Drag the return address text box to the location shown in Figure 5.26.
11. Position the insertion point in the text box in the middle of the envelope and then type **[Type address here.]**.
12. Save your envelope and letterhead as a template by completing the following steps:
    a.   Press F12 to display the Save As dialog box.
    b.   At the Save As dialog box, click the *Save as type* option box and then click *Word Template (*.dotx)* at the drop-down list.
    c.   Type **C05-E03-WEPLetterhead+Envelope** in the *File name* text box.
    d.   Navigate to your Chapter05 folder and then click the Save button.
13. Close **C05-E03-WEPLetterhead+Envelope.dotx**.

Figure 5.26 Letterhead with Envelope Created in Exercise 5.3

Creating Business Cards

A business card includes your name, title, company or organization name, address, telephone number, fax number, email address, and web address. You can also include a one-sentence description of your business, business philosophy, or slogan. Your business card is one of your best personal marketing opportunities, so it is important to design it thoughtfully.

Designing Business Cards

To establish your identity and to stay consistent with other business documents such as letterheads and envelopes, you should include your company logo on your business card. Most business cards are created with sans serif typefaces because the characters are easier to read. The type sizes vary from 12 to 14 points for important words such as your name and title and 8 to 10 points for telephone and fax numbers. Vary the appearance by using bold, italics, small caps, or text effects. Figure 5.27 illustrates two similar business cards that include all of the necessary information but are slightly different in design. The one on the right is the best choice as it reinforces a consistent strong right alignment. The photograph adds a more updated, professional feel than the clip art image used in the first example.

Business cards should be printed on high-quality cover stock paper. Specially designed full-color papers and forms for creating business cards more easily and professionally are available at office supply stores and paper companies. Printing your own business cards saves you the expense of having to place a large minimum order with an outside printer. This is especially helpful to a new small business. You may decide to design your own card and then take it to a professional printer to be printed in large quantities or contact an online printing source for convenient, efficient printing. Be sure to contact the printer first to confirm whether a Word file saved in PDF format will be acceptable.

◀DTP POINTER
Keep your business card design simple and elegant.

◀DTP POINTER
For better printing results, make sure your images are at least 300 dpi.

◀DTP POINTER
Use your favorite search engine to locate an online printing source for your documents.

Figure 5.27 Evaluating Business Card Design

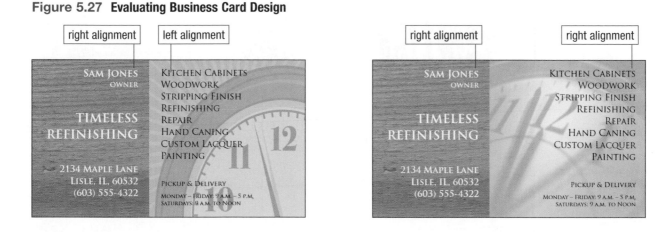

Using the Labels Feature to Create Business Cards

You can use Word's labels feature and a business card label option to create business cards similar to the ones shown in Figure 5.28. You can also use a business card label option to create membership cards, name tags, coupons, placeholders, or friendly reminder cards. Most label options will produce 10 business cards—two columns of labels with five rows in each column. The columns and rows are set up automatically in a Word table and each label (business card) appears in a cell in the table.

When creating business cards, use the label option that matches the labels you have purchased. A common business card label option is Avery 5371 or 8371 Business Cards. The only difference between these two label product numbers is the paper type of the product. The 5371 is made to be used in a laser printer, and the 8371 is made to be used in an inkjet printer. In both cases, the business cards will be 2 inches by 3.5 inches and the sheet containing the business cards will be 8.5 inches by 11 inches.

One method for creating business cards with the labels feature is to insert blank labels in the document, create the first label, and then save the elements of the label to the Quick Part gallery. Then, display the Envelopes and Labels dialog box with the Labels tab selected, type your quick part name in the *Address* text box, press F3, and then click the New Document button.

DTP POINTER

Do not use more than two or three fonts in the business card design; one font is preferable. Change the font size and other font effects for interest.

Figure 5.28 Creating Your Own Business Cards

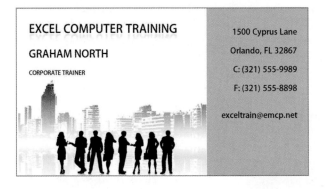

Using Online Templates to Create Business Cards

As an alternative to designing your own business cards, an array of professionally designed business card templates are available for download at Office.com. In addition to Office.com, the Microsoft Office templates partners website at http://office.microsoft.com/en-us/templates/templates-partners-FX010242583.aspx also provides business card templates. Figure 5.29 illustrates some of the business card templates available online.

To download a business card template from Office.com, click the FILE tab and then click the *New* option. At the New backstage area, type *business cards* in the search text box and then press Enter. Double-click to download the desired business card template.

◀ DTP POINTER

Use a generous amount of white space in your business card.

Figure 5.29 Using Online Business Card Templates

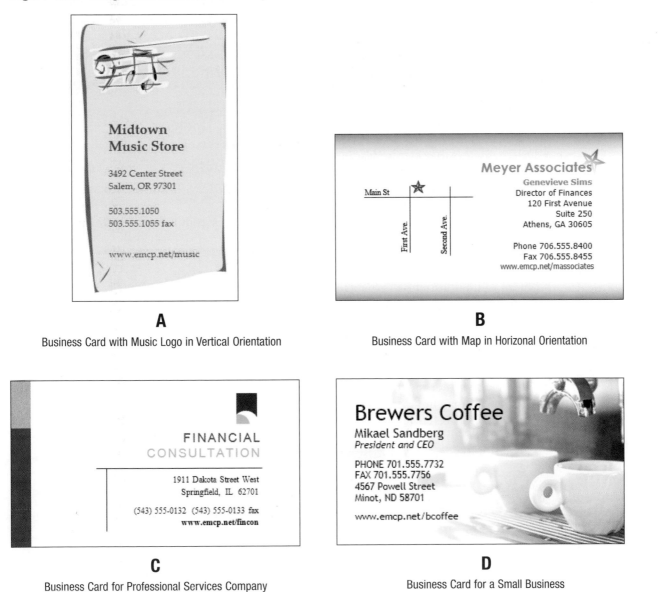

A

Business Card with Music Logo in Vertical Orientation

B

Business Card with Map in Horizonal Orientation

C

Business Card for Professional Services Company

D

Business Card for a Small Business

In Exercise 5.4, you will create business cards using the labels feature, shapes, text boxes, and the Quick Part gallery.

1. At a blank document, create the business cards shown in Figure 5.30 on page 215 by completing the following steps:
   a. Click the MAILINGS tab.
   b. Click the Labels button in the Create group.
   c. At the Envelopes and Labels dialog box, with the Labels tab selected, click the Options button.
   d. At the Label Options dialog box, change the option in the *Label vendor* option box to *Avery US Letter*, select *8371 Business Cards* in the *Product number* list box, and then click OK.
   e. Delete any text that may appear in the *Address* list box and then click the New Document button.
   f. If the table gridlines do not display, click the TABLE TOOLS LAYOUT tab and then click the View Gridlines button in the Table group.

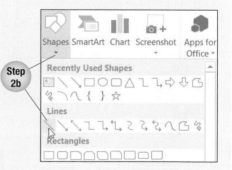

2. Create the blue line that appears at the top of the business card by completing the following steps:
   a. Click the INSERT tab.
   b. With the insertion point positioned in the first cell of the table in the document, click the Shapes button in the Illustrations group and then click the first line shape in the *Lines* section of the drop-down list.
   c. Hold down the Shift key as you drag the crosshairs to draw a horizontal line that is 2.75 inches in length. With the line selected, verify the length of the line with the *Shape Width* measurement box in the Size group on the DRAWING TOOLS FORMAT tab.
   d. With the line still selected, apply the Subtle Line - Accent 5 style from the Shape Styles gallery (sixth column, first row).

   e. Position the line as shown in Figure 5.30.

3. Create a text box that will contain the company name by completing the following steps:
   a. Click the INSERT tab, click the Text Box button in the Text group, and then click *Draw Text Box* at the drop-down list.

   Banded Quote   *Banded Sidebar*
   More Text Boxes from Office.com
   Draw Text Box
   Save Selection to Text Box Gallery

   Step 3a

   b. Position the crosshairs in the first label (cell) and then draw a text box that is approximately the same size and in the same location as the *Worldwide Event Planning, Inc.* text box shown in Figure 5.30.
   c. With the text box selected, change the height to 0.4 inch and the width to 3 inches.
   d. Remove the shape outline and the shape fill.
   e. Change the font to 14-point Palatino Linotype, apply bold and italic formatting, and then apply the Fill - Blue, Accent 1, Shadow style using the Text Effects and Typography button drop-down gallery (second column, first row).
   f. Type **Worldwide Event Planning, Inc.** and then right align the text within the text box.
   g. Display the Format Shape task pane by clicking the Shape Styles group task pane launcher on the DRAWING TOOLS FORMAT tab.
   h. Click *TEXT OPTIONS* in the Format Shape task pane, click the Layout & Properties icon, click *TEXT BOX* (if necessary to expand the list of options), and then change the right margin to 0 inches.

   Format Shape   ▾ ✕

   SHAPE OPTIONS   TEXT OPTIONS

   A   A   A≡

   Step 3h

   ◢ TEXT BOX
   Vertical alignment   Top   ▾
   Text direction   Horizontal   ▾
   ☐ Do not rotate text
   ☐ Resize shape to fit text
   Left margin   0.1" ▴▾
   Right margin   0 ▴▾
   Top margin   0.05" ▴▾

   i. Close the task pane.
   j. Select the text in the text box and then display the Font dialog box with the Advanced tab selected.
   k. At the dialog box, turn on kerning at 12 points and above, select *Standard and Contextual* in the *Ligatures* option box drop-down list, and then click OK to close the dialog box.
4. Make a copy of the blue line and then format it by completing the following steps:
   a. Select the blue line, hold down the Ctrl key, and then drag a copy of the line below the text box containing the text *Worldwide Event Planning, Inc.*
   b. With the new line selected, use the Shape Outline button on the DRAWING TOOLS FORMAT tab to change the color of the line to *Green, Accent 6,* (last column, first row in the *Theme Colors* section) and to change the weight to $1^1/_2$ pt.
5. Create another text box to contain the address text by completing the following steps:
   a. Draw a text box that measures 1 inch in height by 2.75 inches in width.
   b. Remove the shape outline and the shape fill.
   c. With the insertion point positioned inside the text box, press Ctrl + R to change to right alignment.
   d. Display the Format Shape task pane, change the right margin to 0 inches (refer to Step 3h), and then close the task pane.
   e. Type the following text:
      421 Lexington Avenue, Suite 500 (Press Shift + Enter.)
      New York, NY 10170-0555 (Press Enter.)
      www.worldwideevent.emcp.net (Press Shift + Enter.)
      917.555.9055

f. Remove the hyperlink from the website text by right-clicking the website address and then clicking *Remove Hyperlink* at the shortcut menu.

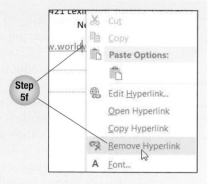

g. Select the text in the text box you just typed, change the font size to 9 points, apply bold formatting, and then apply the Green, Accent 6 font color.

h. Select the web address and telephone number and then change the font size to 8 points.

i. Position the text box as shown in Figure 5.30.

6. Create another text box to contain the text *Corporate Meetings*, etc. as shown in Figure 5.30 by completing the following steps:

a. Draw a text box that measures 0.25 inch by 3.5 inches.

b. Remove the shape outline and the shape fill.

c. Position the insertion point inside the text box and then press Ctrl + E to change to center alignment.

d. Change the font size to 7 points, change the font color to *Blue, Accent 1, Darker 25%* (fifth column, fifth row in the *Theme Colors* section), and then type the following text:
    Corporate Meetings | Weddings | Holiday Parties | Group Tours | Cultural Events
    (Press the spacebar before and after each bar character.)

e. Position the text box as shown in Figure 5.30.

7. Position the insertion point in the upper left corner of the table cell (not in a text box) and then insert the globe sun clip art image (you can copy it from the letterhead or insert it from your Chapter05 folder or Office.com).

8. Change the height of the globe sun image to 0.8 inch, change the text wrapping to *In Front of Text*, and then position the image as shown in Figure 5.30.

9. Group the objects in the business card and then save the grouped object as a quick part by completing the following steps:

a. Select the two lines.

b. Hold down the Shift key and then select the remaining text boxes and globe sun image. (All six objects should be selected.)

c. Click the DRAWING TOOLS FORMAT tab.

d. Click the Group button in the Arrange group and then click *Group* at the drop-down list.

e. Click the INSERT tab.

f. Click the Quick Parts button in the Text group and then click *Save Selection to Quick Part Gallery* at the drop-down list.

g. At the Create New Building Block dialog box, type **XXX-Worldwide** in the *Name* text box (type your initials in place of the *XXX*) and then click OK.

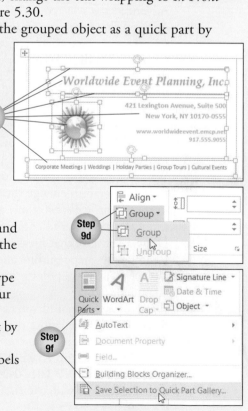

10. Create a full sheet of business cards using your quick part by completing the following steps:

a. Click the MAILINGS tab and then click the Labels button in the Create group.

b. At the Envelopes and Labels dialog box with the Labels tab selected, click the Options button.

c. At the Label Options dialog box, make sure *Avery US Letter* is selected in the *Label vendors* option box and *8371 Business Cards* is selected in the *Product number* list box and then click OK to close the dialog box.

d. At the Envelopes and Labels dialog box with the Labels tab selected, delete any text that may appear in the *Address* list box, type **XXX-Worldwide** (type your initials in place of the *XXX*) and then press F3.

e. At the same dialog box, make sure *Full page of the same label* is selected and then click the New Document button. (A full sheet of business cards will display on your screen.)

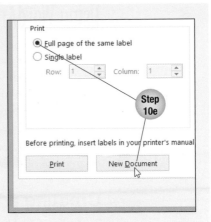

11. Save the full sheet of business cards with the name **C05-E04-WEPBusinessCards**.

12. Print and then close **C05-E04-WEPBusinessCards.docx**. Printing the business cards on thick cardstock made especially for your type of printer is preferable. If you print the business cards on plain paper, you may want to print the table gridlines as shown in Figure 5.30 so you can see the business card borders and use them for trimming. (To print the gridlines, display the TABLE TOOLS DESIGN tab and then click the *Table Grid* option in the Table Styles gallery.)

13. Close the document that you used for creating the sample label without saving it.

Figure 5.30 Business Cards Created in Exercise 5.4

Using WordArt

WordArt can be used to create compelling text effects. You can use it to distort or modify text or cause the text to conform to a variety of shapes. This is useful for creating company logos and headings and can be easily incorporated into a company letterhead. It is also useful for headlines in flyers and announcements. WordArt is a powerful tool for creating a focal point in a document.

Type *logos* in the *Office.com Clip Art* text box at the Insert Pictures window to view shapes that may be used to create logos. Add your company name, formatted in WordArt, to any one of these images to create a simple logo, as shown in Figure 5.31.

Creating a WordArt Object

WordArt

To insert WordArt in a document, click the INSERT tab and then click the WordArt button in the Text group. This displays the WordArt drop-down gallery. Click the desired option at the gallery, and a WordArt text box is inserted in the document containing the words *Your text here*. The DRAWING TOOLS FORMAT tab becomes active. Type the desired WordArt text.

Formatting WordArt Text

Apply formatting to WordArt text with options in the WordArt Styles group on the DRAWING TOOLS FORMAT tab. You can apply a predesigned WordArt style, change the WordArt text color and text outline color, and apply a text effect such as shadow, reflection, glow, bevel, 3-D rotation, and transform. With the transform option, you can mold the WordArt text to a specific shape. To do this, click the Text Effects button, point to *Transform*, and then click the desired shape at the side menu. Use options in the Arrange group to specify the position, text wrap, document layer, alignment, and rotation of the WordArt text. Specify the size of the WordArt with options in the Size group.

Formatting a WordArt Text Box

WordArt text is inserted in a text box, and this text box can be customized with options in the Shape Styles group on the DRAWING TOOLS FORMAT tab. Use options in this group to apply a predesigned style to the WordArt text box, change the text box fill color and outline color, and apply an effect to the WordArt text box such as shadow, reflection, glow, soft edges, bevel, and 3-D rotation.

Figure 5.31 Using WordArt to Design a Logo

Refining Letter, Word, and Line Spacing

Manually adjusting the kerning, tracking, and leading in your documents can help them to look more polished and professional. You will learn more about these tools and how to work with them in the following sections.

Kerning Character Pairs

As you learned in Chapter 2, the process of decreasing or increasing the white space between specific character pairs is called *kerning*. Generally, the horizontal spacing of typefaces is designed to optimize body text, which is usually set at 9 to 13 points. At larger sizes, the same relative horizontal space can appear loose, especially when uppercase and lowercase letters are combined. Kerning visually equalizes the space between specific characters and is usually used in headlines and other blocks of large type (14 points and larger). Figure 5.32 illustrates common character pairs that are affected by using the kerning feature. In Word, kerning can be accomplished automatically, or character pairs can be selected and kerned manually.

Using Automatic Kerning

When automatic kerning is turned on, Word adjusts the space between certain pairs of letters above a specific point size. Not all character pairs are affected with automatic kerning. Some common character pairs that may be automatically kerned are *Ta, To, Ty, Vi,* and *WA*. The amount of space that is adjusted for specific character pairs is defined in a kerning table, which is part of the printer definition. The printer definition is a preprogrammed set of instructions that tells the printer how to perform various features.

To turn on automatic kerning, display the Font dialog box with the Advanced tab selected. Click the *Kerning for fonts* check box to insert a check mark. In the *Points and above* measurement box, type or use the up- and down-pointing arrows to specify the minimum point size for kerning to take effect.

Using Manual Kerning

When you kern letters manually, you get to make the decision as to which letters to kern. Manual kerning is especially helpful if you need to increase or decrease space between letters to improve legibility, to create a special effect, or to fit text in a specific amount of space.

Figure 5.32 Comparing Examples of Character Pair Kerning

WA (kerned)	Ta (kerned)
WA (not kerned)	Ta (not kerned)
Ty (kerned)	Vi (kerned)
Ty (not kerned)	Vi (not kerned)

To manually kern a pair of letters, select the pair of characters you want to kern, and then access the Font dialog box with the Advanced tab active. Click the down-pointing arrow at the right of *Spacing* option box and then click *Expanded* (if you want to increase the spacing between the selected character pair) or *Condensed* (if you want to decrease the spacing). In the *By* measurement box, click the up or down arrows to specify the amount of space by which the selected character pair is to be increased or decreased.

Tracking Text

tracking

Equally reducing or increasing the horizontal space between all characters in a selected block of text

In traditional typesetting, equally reducing or increasing the horizontal space between all characters in a block of text is called ***tracking***. Tracking affects all characters, while kerning affects only specific character pairs. The purpose of tracking is the same as kerning: to produce more attractive, easy-to-read type. In addition, you can use tracking to create unusual spacing for a specific design effect or to fit text into a certain amount of space.

In Word, tracking is virtually the same as manual kerning because both processes involve condensing or expanding character spacing at the Font dialog box. Whereas manually kerning involves adjusting the character spacing of selected character pairs, tracking involves adjusting the character spacing of a selected block of text, such as a heading, a subheading, or a phrase. Adjust tracking by selecting the text and then expanding or condensing text at the Font dialog box with the Advanced tab selected. Refer to Figure 5.33 to see how adjusting tracking affects text.

Setting Line Spacing

line spacing

The vertical spacing between lines; expressed in points or in a percentage of the line height

Line spacing is the vertical spacing of the lines within a paragraph expressed as a fixed amount in points or as a percentage of the line height. Line spacing includes ***leading*** (pronounced *ledd-ing*), which is the amount of white space between lines. The height of the characters plus the leading equals the line spacing. By clicking the Line Spacing button on the HOME tab, you can set line spacing at 1.0, 1.15, 1.5, 2.0, 2.5, or 3.0, as shown in Figure 5.34. The default setting for body text is 1.08 line spacing with 8 points of spacing after paragraphs. Leading depends on the font size selected; the larger the font size, the larger the amount of leading between the lines. Most leading is set at 20 percent of the size of the font. That means that there will be 2 points of leading between text that is set at 10 points and 2.4 points of leading if the font is set for 12 points.

leading

The amount of white space between lines

Line Spacing

Figure 5.33 Comparing Tracking (Normal, Condensed, and Expanded Character Spacing)

22-point font size
normal
— *Desktop Publishing Using Word 2013*

22-point font size
condensed by 1.5 points
— *Desktop Publishing Using Word 2013*

22-point font size
expanded by 2 points
— *Desktop Publishing Using Word 2013*

Figure 5.34 Adjusting Line and Paragraph Spacing

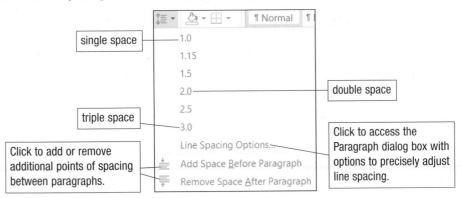

single space

triple space

Click to add or remove additional points of spacing between paragraphs.

double space

Click to access the Paragraph dialog box with options to precisely adjust line spacing.

Setting Leading

In Word, you cannot specifically set leading. However, the *At least* and *Exactly* options at the *Line spacing* option box in the Paragraph dialog box, as shown in Figure 5.35, are the closest thing to it. Both of these settings express values that are in total line height, not blank space height. For instance, if you set the *Exactly* setting to 16 points, when used on a paragraph containing 12-point text, this would result in 4 points of leading between lines. If you used the same setting with 20-point text, there would be no leading, and the tops of the larger letters would be cut off. Experiment with using the *At least* and *Exactly* options to get a better feel for using them. Any extra space that you add to a line of text is added below the text. Table 5.3 on page 220 explains all of the options at the *Line spacing* option box.

Figure 5.35 Adjusting Line Spacing (Including Leading) at the *Line Spacing* Option Box

Choose the *At least* option or the *Exactly* option at this drop-down list to set specific line spacing that includes leading.

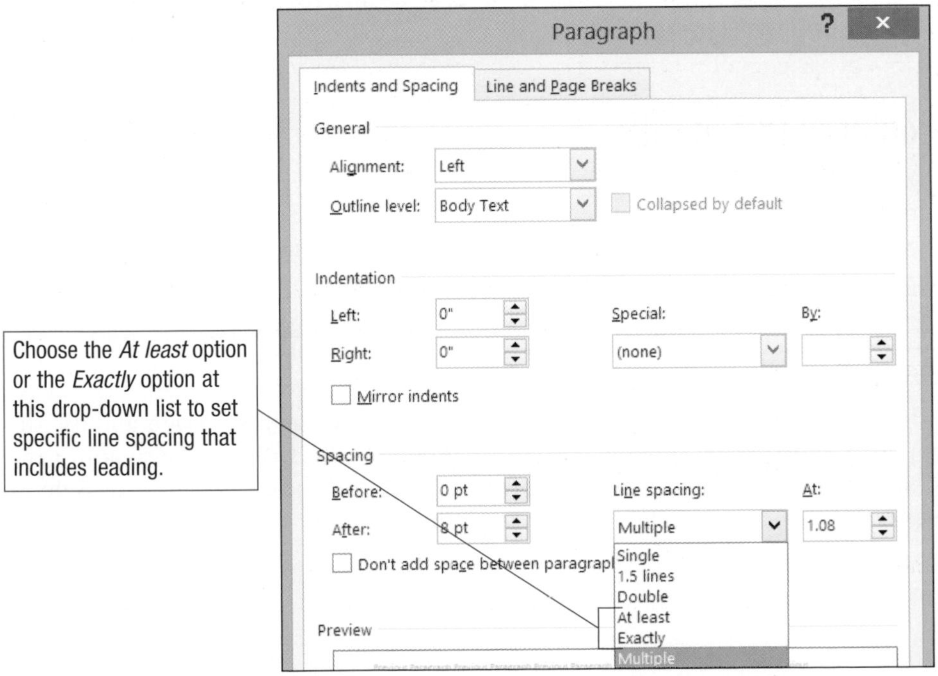

Table 5.3 Line Spacing Options Available at the Paragraph Dialog Box

Single	No extra space between lines
1.5 Lines	An extra half-height blank line between each printed line of the paragraph
Double	An extra blank line between each printed line of the paragraph
At Least	A minimum line height that you specify in point value
Exactly	A precise line height that you specify. If you specify a size that is smaller than the largest font size used in the paragraph, the large letter will be truncated on top
Multiple	Any value from 0 to 132, in decimal increments of 0.01

Setting Spacing Before or After a Paragraph

One way to add space before or after a paragraph is to choose the *Add Space Before Paragraph* option or the *Remove Space After Paragraph* option at the Line and Paragraph Spacing button drop-down list in the Paragraph group on the HOME tab. The PAGE LAYOUT tab also contains *Before* and *After* measurement boxes that work like their counterparts in the Paragraph dialog box. Of course, you can add line spacing between paragraphs by pressing the Enter key, but each Enter is considered a paragraph in itself and this can make things difficult when you are trying to apply styles to paragraphs of text. By adding line spacing before or after, you make the line spacing a part of that paragraph.

Paragraph spacing can also be adjusted by clicking the Paragraph Spacing button in the Document Formatting group on the DESIGN tab. At the drop-down list that displays, click one of these options: *No Paragraph Space, Compact, Tight, Open, Relaxed, Double,* or *Custom Paragraph Spacing.*

DTP POINTER ❯

Press Shift + Enter (line break) to start a new line within the same paragraph. Inserting a line break forces the insertion point to the next line without adding 8 points of spacing after the paragraph.

press release

A written or recorded communication directed to the news media for the purpose of announcing something newsworthy

Creating a Press Release

In Exercise 5.5, you will create a **press release**, which is a written or recorded communication directed to the news media for the purpose of announcing something newsworthy. Typically, press releases are mailed, faxed, or emailed to newspapers, radio stations, and television stations, but they may also be posted on the Internet. Press releases can announce a range of news items such as scheduled events, personal promotions, awards, new products and services, sales and other financial data, accomplishments, or new office or store openings.

In Exercise 5.5, you will include WordArt in the press release design and use the Snipping Tool to create a graphic file from a grouped object. You will also adjust the tracking, kerning, and line spacing of the text in the press release document. Refer to Chapter 1 to review information about the Snipping Tool.

1. Open **C05-E02-WEPLetterhead.docx**, which was created in Exercise 5.2.
2. Save the grouped image in the letterhead as a graphic file in PNG format by completing the following steps:
   a. Display the Windows Charms bar (do this by hovering your mouse in the lower right corner of the screen) and then click the Search button.
   b. At the Apps screen with the insertion point positioned in the *Search Apps* text box, type **snip**.
   c. Click the Snipping Tool tile in the search results.

   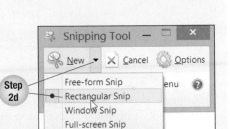

   d. Click the New button arrow at the Snipping Tool window and then click the *Rectangular Snip* option.
   e. Drag the crosshairs to create a box around the grouped image in the letterhead.

   f. At the Snipping Tool window, click the Save Snip button.
   g. At the Save As dialog box, type **WEPGraphic** in the *File name* text box.
   h. Click the down-pointing arrow at the right of the *Save as type* option box and then click *Portable Network Graphic file (PNG) (*.PNG)* at the drop-down list.
   i. Navigate to your Chapter05 folder and then click the Save button.
   j. Close the Snipping Tool window.
   k. Close **C05-E02-WEPLetterhead.docx**.
3. Open **PressRelease.docx** from your Chapter05 folder and then save the document with the name **C05-E05-PressRelease**.
4. Select the text in the upper left cell of the table and then apply the following formatting:
   a. Change the font to 7.5-point Century Gothic.
   b. Change the line spacing to 1.15.
   c. Select the text *Contact: Margo Hamel* and then apply bold formatting.
5. Insert WordArt with a graphic background in the upper right cell by completing the following steps:
   a. Position the insertion point in the upper right cell of the table and then click the INSERT tab.

   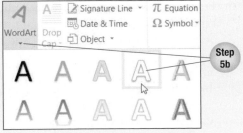

   b. Click the WordArt button in the Text group and then click the *Fill - White, Outline - Accent 1, Shadow* option (fourth column, first row).
   c. Type **Worldwide Event Planning, Inc.**
   d. Select the text you just typed and then change the font to 18-point Bookman Old Style and, if necessary, apply bold formatting.

e. With the text still selected, display the Font dialog box with the Advanced tab selected.

f. Turn on kerning at 12 points and above, select *Standard and Contextual* at the *Ligatures* option box drop-down list, and then click OK to close the dialog box.

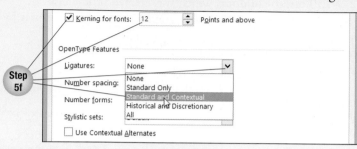

g. With the text in the top right cell still selected, click the Text Effects button in the WordArt Styles group on the DRAWING TOOLS FORMAT tab, point to *Transform*, and then click the *Chevron Down* option (second column, second row in the *Warp* section).

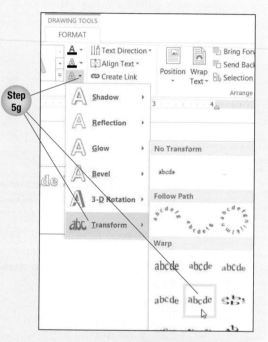

h. Click the Text Outline button arrow in the WordArt Styles group and then click *Dark Blue* (ninth color in the *Standard Colors* section).

i. Using the mouse, drag the corner sizing handles to increase the size of the WordArt object to fill the cell.

j. With the WordArt object selected (the outline on the object will be a solid line and the sizing and rotation handles will be visible), click the Shape Fill button arrow in the Shape Styles group and then click the *Picture* option at the drop-down gallery.

k. At the Insert Pictures window, click the Browse button that displays to the right of *From a file*.

l. At the Insert Picture window, navigate to your Chapter05 folder and then double-click **WEPGraphic.PNG**.

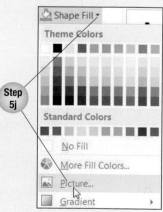

6. Press Ctrl + End to position the insertion point below the table, type **PRESS RELEASE**, and then press the Enter key.

7. Select the text *PRESS RELEASE* and then apply the following formatting:

a. Change the font to 42-point Century Gothic.

b. Click the Font Color button arrow in the Font group on the HOME tab and then click the *More Colors* option.

c. At the Colors dialog box, click the Custom tab.

d. Make sure the *RGB* color model is selected and then type **42** in the *Red* measurement box, **90** in the *Green* measurement box, and **120** in the *Blue* measurement box.

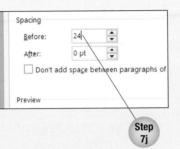

Step 7d

e. Click OK to close the dialog box.
f. Display the Font dialog box with the Advanced tab selected.
g. Change the *Spacing* option to *Condensed* by 0.25 points and turn on kerning at 14 points and above.
h. Click OK to close the dialog box.
i. Display the Paragraph dialog box.
j. Change the value in the *Before* measurement box in the *Spacing* section to *24*.
k. Click OK to close the dialog box.

Step 7j

8. Press Ctrl + End and then press the Enter key.
9. Change the font to 14-point Century Gothic and then apply the blue color used in Step 7d to the text.
10. Type **Worldwide Event Planning, Inc. Announces Global Expansion** and then press Shift + Enter.
11. Type **London will serve Eastern European region.** and then press the Enter key twice.
12. Select the text *London will serve Eastern European region.*, change the font size to 11 points, and then apply italic formatting.
13. Press Ctrl + End, change the font to 10-point Century Gothic, and then change the font color to *Black, Text 1* (second column, first row in the *Theme Colors* section).
14. Type the three paragraphs of text shown in the press release in Figure 5.36 on page 224. For the fourth paragraph, type the three # symbols with a space after the first and second symbols and then center the paragraph.
15. Select the three paragraphs of text you typed, display the Paragraph dialog box, and then apply the following formatting:
    a. Change the line spacing to *Single*.
    b. Change the value in the *After* measurement box in the *Spacing* section to 18 points.
    c. Click OK to close the dialog box.

Step 15b   **Step 15a**

16. Replace the text in the footer as shown in Figure 5.36 by completing the following steps:
    a. Click the INSERT tab, click the Footer button in the Header & Footer group, and then click *Edit Footer* at the drop-down list.
    b. Select the text *Type release date and time here* and then type **For release 9 a.m. EST, July 27, 2015, USA - 14:00, U.K.**
    c. Select the text you just typed and then change the font to 10-point Century Gothic.
    d. Click the date picker that displays in the left margin.
    e. Click the date picker down-pointing arrow and then click the *July 27, 2015* option in the calendar (you will need to navigate to the year 2015 and the month of July).
    f. Double-click in the document to close the Footer pane.

Step 16e

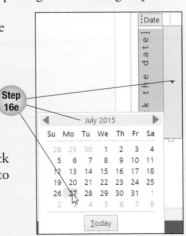

17. Save, print, and then close **C05-E05-PressRelease.docx**.

Figure 5.36 **Press Release Created in Exercise 5.5**

Contact: Margo Hamel
Worldwide Event Planning
421 Lexington Avenue, Suite 500
New York, NY 10170-0555
www.worldwideevent.emcp.net
Phone 917.555.9055
Fax 917.555.9060

PRESS RELEASE

Worldwide Event Planning, Inc. Announces Global Expansion
London will serve Eastern European region.

New York, July 27, 2015: Today, Worldwide Event Planning, Inc. is proud to announce the opening of their new office in London, U.K. The office is located at Earl Street, SW7 near the Liverpool Street Station, telephone # 020 7985 7650.

A few years ago, the average profit margin for Worldwide Event Planning, Inc., a New York–based event planning entrepreneur, was approximately 15 percent. Worldwide today announced a profit margin between 30 and 40 percent. Worldwide Event Planning, Inc. attributes the industry's good health to several factors including the improved economy and the trend of corporate America to outsource their meeting and planning functions.

A key factor to the success of Worldwide Event Planning, Inc. is its thorough research of all its vendors and suppliers. Its dedicated research also involves keeping current with customs and etiquette in unfamiliar markets. Worldwide conducts research; creates an event design; finds a suitable site; arranges food, décor, and entertainment; plans transportation to and from the event; and sends invitations to attendees.

# # #

July 27, 2015

For release 9 a.m. EST, July 27, 2015, USA - 14:00, U.K.

Chapter *Summary*

➤ A letterhead contains a design and layout that conveys specific information, establishes an identity, and projects an image for a business. Designing and producing your own letterhead can be a less costly alternative to having it designed and produced through a professional designer and printer.

➤ A number of letterhead templates are available for download at Office.com or a template partner.

➤ Objects can be grouped, ungrouped, and regrouped. Group objects by selecting each object and then clicking the Group button in the Arrange group on the PAGE LAYOUT tab.

➤ The Selection pane lists each item in a document. Display the Selection pane by clicking the Select button in the Editing group on the HOME tab and then clicking *Selection Pane* at the drop-down list.

➤ Use the Click and Type feature to insert text, graphics, tables, or other items into a blank area of a document.

➤ To view the vertical location of your insertion point, position your mouse pointer on the Status bar, right click, and then click the *Vertical Page Position* option at the Customize Status Bar pop-up menu.

➤ A text box is used as a container for text and graphics. Text boxes are extremely useful in desktop publishing because text and graphics can be placed at exact horizontal and vertical locations on the page. They can also serve as placeholders for items such as illustrations and photos.

➤ Adjust text box margins with options at the Format Shape task pane with the Layout & Properties icon selected and the TEXT BOX options expanded.

➤ Position a text box precisely on a page using options at the Layout dialog box with the Position tab selected.

➤ A pixel is a single unit of measurement that your monitor uses to paint images on your screen.

➤ All objects, including text boxes, are automatically anchored or attached to the paragraph closest to the object.

➤ Format a text box with buttons and options on the DRAWING TOOLS FORMAT tab.

➤ Specify how you want text to wrap around, behind, or in front of a text box with options at the Wrap Text button drop-down gallery.

➤ Word includes predesigned text boxes you can insert in a document by clicking the Text Box button in the Text group on the INSERT tab and then clicking an option at the drop-down list.

➤ Ruled lines act as boundaries to the surrounding text. Ruled lines can be used in a document to create a focal point, draw the eye across or down the page, separate columns and sections, or add visual appeal.

➤ Lines can be created using the Line button in the Shapes group on the INSERT tab. To create a straight line, hold down the Shift key as you drag the crosshairs to draw the line. Format a drawn line with buttons and options on the DRAWING TOOLS FORMAT tab.

➤ To create lines around a paragraph, click the down-pointing arrow at the right of the Border button in the Paragraph group on the HOME tab and then click the desired option at the drop-down gallery.

➤ When creating a design for an envelope, select enough common elements from the letterhead so that a link is established in the viewer's mind between the letterhead and the envelope.

➤ Create an envelope by clicking the MAILINGS tab, clicking the Envelopes button in the Create group, and then clicking the Add to Document button. Customize an envelope with options at the Envelope Options dialog box. Display this dialog box by clicking the Options button at the Envelopes and Labels dialog box with the Envelopes tab selected.

➤ Business cards are another way to establish identity among a target audience. Establish an identifying connection between a business card and a letterhead by repeating some of the design elements from the letterhead.

➤ Save frequently used text and graphics, such as a letterhead or company logo, as a building block in the Quick Part gallery.

➤ Create business cards using a Word business card label template. Choose a business card label at the Envelopes and Labels dialog box with the Labels tab selected. Choose a label vendor and product number at the Label Options dialog box.

➤ With the WordArt feature, you can distort or modify text to conform to a variety of shapes. Use options in the WordArt Styles group on the DRAWING TOOLS FORMAT tab to customize your WordArt text.

➤ Kerning is the process of decreasing or increasing the white space between specific character pairs To automatically kern characters pairs, insert a check mark in the *Kerning for fonts* check box at the Font dialog box with the Advanced tab selected. Manually kern character pairs by selecting the character pair and then using the *Spacing* option box at the Font dialog box with the Advanced tab selected to expand or condense the space between the pair.

➤ In traditional typesetting, tracking is equally reducing or increasing the horizontal space between all characters in a block of text. Tracking affects all characters, while automatic kerning affects only specific character pairs.

➤ Adjust line spacing by clicking the Line Spacing button in the Paragraph group on the HOME tab and then selecting an option at the drop-down gallery. Adjust line spacing, including leading, by using the *At least* or *Exactly* options from the *Line spacing* option box on the Indents and Spacing tab of the Paragraph dialog box.

➤ Press Shift + Enter (line break) to start a new line within the same paragraph. A line break forces the insertion point to the next line without adding the default 8 points of spacing after the paragraph.

➤ Spacing adjustments can be made to text by adding points of space before or after paragraphs of text. Do this with options from the Line and Paragraph Spacing button in the Paragraph group on the HOME tab, the *Before* and *After* measurements boxes on the PAGE LAYOUT tab, or with options from the Paragraph Spacing button in the Document Formatting group on the DESIGN tab.

➤ A press release is a written or recorded communication directed to the news media to announce something having news value. Create a press release to inform the public of scheduled events, personal promotions, awards, news products and services, sales and other financial data, accomplishments, or new office or store openings.

Commands Review

FEATURE	RIBBON TAB, GROUP/OPTION	BUTTON
envelopes	MAILINGS, Create	
group	PAGE LAYOUT, Arrange	
kerning	HOME, Font	
labels	MAILINGS, Create	
Layout dialog box	DRAWING TOOLS FORMAT, Size	
line spacing	HOME, Paragraph	
position	DRAWING TOOLS FORMAT, Arrange	

FEATURE	RIBBON TAB, GROUP/OPTION	BUTTON
quick parts	INSERT, Text	
select	HOME, Editing	
shape effects	DRAWING TOOLS FORMAT, Shape Styles	
shape fill	DRAWING TOOLS FORMAT, Shape Styles	
shape outline	DRAWING TOOLS FORMAT, Shape Styles	
shapes	INSERT, Illustrations	
templates	FILE, *New*	
text box	INSERT, Text	
view table gridlines	TABLE TOOLS LAYOUT, Table	
WordArt	INSERT, Text	

Key Points *Review*

Multiple Choice: Fill in the blanks with the correct term from the choices listed below each question.

1. By default, a text box has left and right internal margins of _____ inch(es).
   a. 0.05   b. 0.1
   c. 0.5   d. 1.0

2. In typesetting, the thickness of a line is called its weight and is measured in _____.
   a. points   b. pixels
   c. inches   d. dots per inch

3. Press the _____ key while drawing a line with the Line Shape to create a straight line.
   a. Ctrl   b. Shift
   c. spacebar   d. Alt

4. To transform the shape of WordArt text, click this button on the DRAWING TOOLS FORMAT tab.
   a. Text Outline   b. Text Effects
   c. Text Fill   d. Transform

5. Save frequently used text or graphics as a building block in this gallery.
   a. Document Formatting   b. Text
   c. Styles   d. Quick Part

6. Use this feature to distort or modify text to create a variety of shapes.
   a. Clip Art   b. Shapes
   c. WordArt   d. Picture

7. Use this feature to position the insertion point in a blank area of the document or to change paragraph alignment for text to be typed.
   a. Click and Type
   b. AutoText
   c. AutoFormat
   d. Smart Tags

8. Equally reducing or increasing the horizontal space between all characters in a selected block of text is called _____.
   a. kerning
   b. nudging
   c. aligning
   d. tracking

9. Position an object precisely on a page with options at this dialog box.
   a. Layout
   b. DRAWING TOOLS FORMAT
   c. Styles
   d. Paragraph

10. To apply a shadow effect to a text box, click the _____ button arrow in the Shape Styles group on the DRAWING TOOLS FORMAT tab.
    a. Shadow
    b. Position
    c. Shape Effects
    d. Shape Fill

Chapter Assessments

Assessment 5.1   Create and Use a Letterhead for a Foreign Hotel

The Isar Hotel in Munich, Germany, has just opened and you are responsible for designing the hotel letterhead. Look at the letterhead in Figure 5.37 and then create the letterhead and letter with the following specifications:

1. At a blank document, insert the text WILLKOMMEN ZUM *er* ISAR HOTEL MÜNICH as WordArt text using the Gradient Fill - Blue, Accent 1, Reflection WordArt option, as shown in Figure 5.37. (Insert the Ü symbol at the Symbol dialog box with the (normal text) font selected [character code 00DC] and insert the *er* symbol with the Wingdings font selected [character code 106].)

2. Select the WordArt text box containing the text you just typed and then make the following changes:
   a. Change the font to 11-point Segoe UI Semibold.
   b. Change the font color to *Orange, Accent 2, Darker 50%* (sixth column, bottom row in the *Theme Colors* section).
   c. Expand the spacing of the text by 4.7 points. (Do this at the Font dialog box with the Advanced tab selected.)

3. Insert a text box in the document and then type the hotel address and phone and fax numbers, as shown in the figure. Press Shift + Enter and then type the web address. Select the text box and then apply the following formatting:
   a. Change the paragraph alignment to right.
   b. Change the font to 8-point Microsoft JhengHei and then apply bold formatting.
   c. Apply the Dark Blue font color (ninth color in the *Standard Colors* section).
   d. Select the web address, apply italic formatting, and then change the font size to 7 points.
   e. Remove the text box shape fill and outline.
   f. Size the text box to accommodate the text and then position the text box as shown in Figure 5.37.

4. Align the WordArt text box above the address text box as shown in Figure 5.37.

5. Insert **IsarHotel.png** from your Chapter05 folder and then apply the following formatting:
   a. Change the height of the image to 0.8 inch.
   b. Change the text wrapping to *Tight*.
   c. Position the image as shown in Figure 5.37.
6. Select both text boxes and the image and then group the objects.
7. With the objects grouped, use the Position button on the PICTURE TOOLS FORMAT tab to change the position to *Position in Top Center with Square Text Wrapping*.
8. Press Ctrl + End to move the insertion point below the grouped objects, click the HOME tab, and then click the *No Spacing* style in the Styles group.
9. Save the document as a template into your Chapter05 folder with the name **C05-A01-HotelLtrhd**.
10. Close **C05-A01-HotelLtrhd.dotx**.
11. Open File Explorer, navigate to your Chapter05 folder, and then double-click **C05-A01-HotelLtrd.dotx.** (This opens a document based on the template.)
12. Type text in the letter as shown in Figure 5.37. (Insert the ä in the word *Sächlich* at the Symbol dialog box with the (normal text) font selected [character code 00E4].)
13. Save the completed letter with the name **C05-A01-HotelLetter**.
14. Print and then close **C05-A01-HotelLetter.docx**.

Figure 5.37 Letterhead and Letter Created in Assessment 5.1

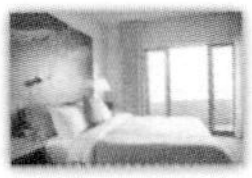

WILLKOMMEN ZUM & ISAR HOTEL MÜNICH

Wilenmayerstrade 10, 803 München, GERMANY, TEL +49 (0) 89 55544 0, FAX +49 (0) 89 55544 1000

www.ISARHOTEL@emcp.net

Herzlich Willkommen Im Isar Sächlich Münich

May 12, 2015

Dear Guest,

I am very pleased that you have chosen Isar Hotel Münich for your stay in Münich.

As part of the Schöenfeld Luxury Hotels, we offer top-class surroundings for your stay. Our staff is dedicated to making your stay an enjoyable experience. Every Schöenfeld Hotel is uniquely designed for guests who expect excellence and value individuality. Whether your stay is a business-related event, a luxury holiday, or a relaxing vacation experience, we invite you to discover our chain of hotels.

Please contact us immediately, at any time, with any special requests, questions, or concerns. We want your stay to be luxurious and carefree.

I wish you a successful and enjoyable stay.

Sincerely,

Gerhard Kohl
General Manager

Assessment 5.2   Create a Hotel Envelope

Use some of the letterhead elements you created in Assessment 1 to create an envelope for the hotel (as shown in Figure 5.38) with the following specifications:

1. Insert an envelope in a new, blank document.
2. Insert in the envelope **IsarHotel.png** from your Chapter05 folder.
3. Change the height of the image to 0.9 inch.
4. Change the text wrapping to *Tight*.
5. Insert a text box with no fill and no outline. Type the hotel address in the text box, select the text you just typed, and then change the font to 9-point Microsoft JhengHei and apply the Dark Blue font color. Apply bold formatting and change the paragraph alignment of the text to right.
6. Insert a text box with no fill and no outline and then type **ISAR HOTEL MÜNICH**.
7. Select the text you just typed and then apply the Gradient Fill - Blue, Accent 1, Reflection text effect (use the Text Effects and Typography button in the Font group on the HOME tab).
8. With the text still selected, change the font to 11-point Segoe UI Semibold; the font color to Orange, Accent 2, Darker 50%; and expand the spacing of the text by 6 points.
9. Size and position the elements so your envelope is similar to the envelope in Figure 5.38.
10. Save the envelope document with the name **C05-A02-HotelEnvelope**.
11. Print and then close **C05-A02-HotelEnvelope.docx**. (Manual feed of the envelope may be necessary.)

Figure 5.38 Envelope Created in Assessment 5.2

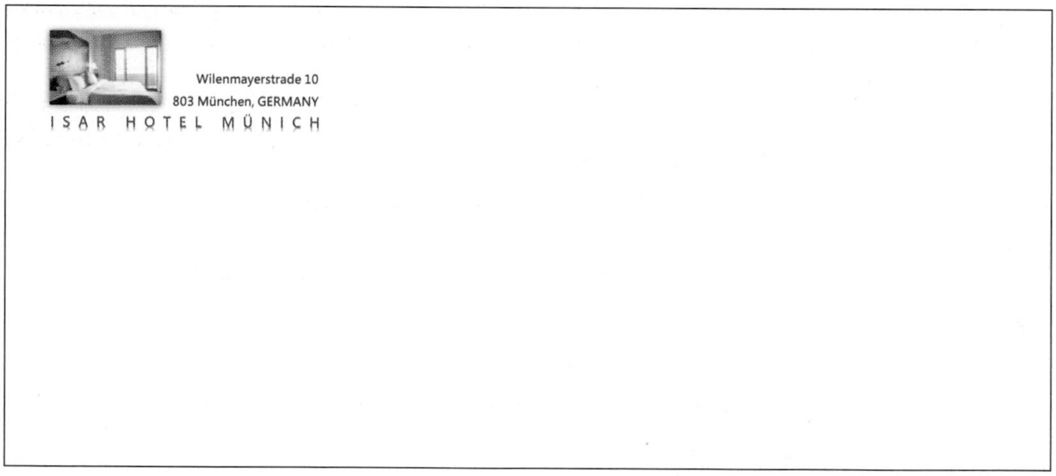

Assessment 5.3   Create Business Cards

Create business cards for the general manager of the Isar Hotel as shown in Figure 5.39 with the following specifications:

1. At a blank document, insert blank labels using the Avery US Letter label vendor and the 8371 Business Cards product number.
2. Insert **IsarHotel.png** in the first label, change the height of the image to 1.1 inches, apply Tight text wrapping, and then position the image as shown in Figure 5.39.
3. Create a text box for the hotel address, telephone number, and web address. Remove the text box shape fill and outline and then type the text in the text box as shown in Figure 5.39. Select the text you just typed, change the line spacing to *Single*, change the spacing after paragraphs to *0*, change the font to 9-point Microsoft JhengHei, apply bold formatting, change the text color to *Dark Blue*, and change the paragraph alignment to right. Select the web address, change the font size to 8 points, and then apply italic formatting. Size and position the text box as shown in Figure 5.39.
4. Create a text box for the name and title, *Gerhard Kohl, General Manager*. Remove the text box shape fill and outline and then type **Gerhard Kohl, General Manager**. Select the text you just typed, change the font to 11-point Microsoft JhengHei, apply bold formatting, and change the font color to Dark Blue. Size and position the text box as shown in Figure 5.39.
5. Create WordArt using the Gradient Fill - Blue, Accent 1, Reflection option. Type **ISAR HOTEL MÜNICH** in the WordArt text box. Select the text you just typed, change the font to 14-point Segoe UI Semibold, change the font color to *Orange, Accent 2, Darker 50%*, and expand the text by 6 points. Size and position the WordArt as shown in Figure 5.39.
6. Select the image, the two text boxes, and the WordArt text box and then group the objects. Save the grouped objects in the Quick Part gallery and name the quick part *XXX-IsarHotel* (use your initials in place of the *XXX*).
7. Click the MAILINGS tab and then click the Labels button. At the Envelopes and Labels dialog box with the Labels tab selected, type **XXX-IsarHotel** (type your initials in place of the *XXX*) in the *Address* text box, press F3, and then click the New Document button.
8. Save the labels document with the name **C05-A03-BusinessCards**.
9. Print and then close **C05-A03-BusinessCards.docx**.
10. Close the document containing the single label without saving the document.

Figure 5.39 Business Card Created in Assessment 5.3

Assessment 5.4 Download Word and PowerPoint Templates

You are responsible for creating letterhead and business card templates in Word and a presentation template in PowerPoint for Redline Products. You will search for and then download templates with a red theme.

1. In Word, search for and then download a letterhead template with a red theme. Use the company name, Redline Products, and then fill in the remaining placeholders in the letterhead with information of your choosing. Save the completed letterhead as a template into your Chapter05 folder with the name **C05-A04-RPLetterhead**. Print and then close the letterhead template.
2. In Word, search for and then download a business card template with a red theme. Insert the appropriate information in the placeholders using the same information you inserted in the letterhead. Save the completed business card as a template into your Chapter05 folder and name it **C05-A04-RPBusinessCards**. Print and then close the business card template.
3. Open PowerPoint, display the New backstage area, and then search for and download a presentation template with a red theme. Save the downloaded presentation as a template into your Chapter05 folder and name it **C05-A04-RPPresentation**. Print and then close the presentation template.

Assessment 5.5 Design Documents for a Hotel

As a group project, create a fictitious hotel in a city that interests you. For this hotel, prepare the following documents:

GROUP PROJECT

1. Create an attractive and well-designed letterhead for the hotel. Save the letterhead as a template with the name **C05-A05-LtrhdTemplate**. Print and then close **C05-A05-LtrhdTemplate.dotx**.
2. Open a document based on the letterhead template you created and then type a document that includes a SmartArt graphic that provides information to guests on times for check in, continental breakfast, afternoon snack, and check out. Figure 5.40 illustrates a sample solution. Save the completed document with the name **C05-A05-HotelInfo**. Print and then close **C05-A05-HotelInfo.docx**.
3. Use the Internet to search for points of interest in and around the city you have chosen for your hotel. Create a document sheet with information about at least five points of interest. Figure 5.41 illustrates a sample solution. Include a predesigned text box, use WordArt text, and consider other design elements such as clip art, photographs, and design themes when creating your document. Save the completed document with the name **C05-A05-PointsofInterest**. Print and then close **C05-A05-PointsofInterest.docx**.

Figure 5.40 Sample Letter for Assessment 5.5

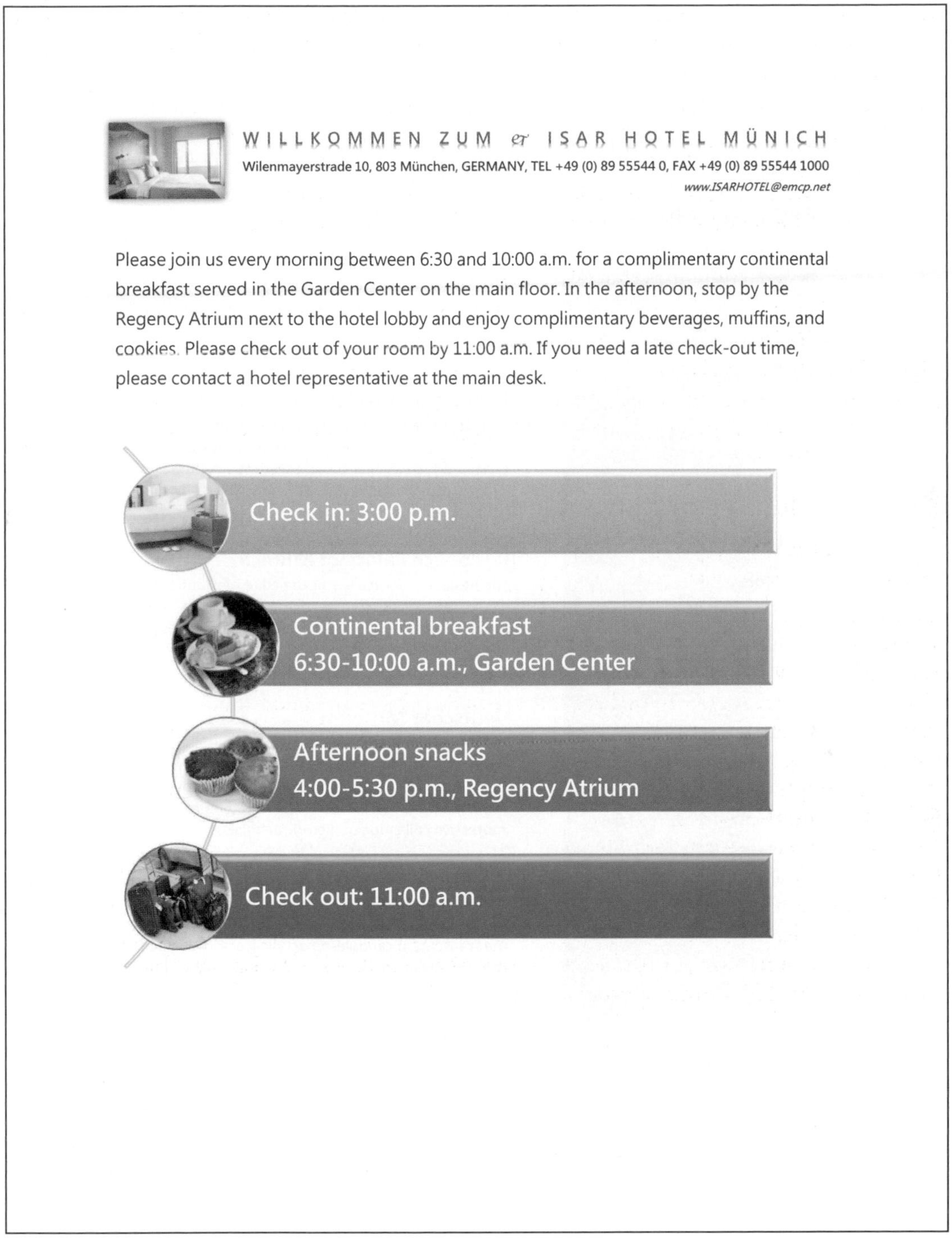

WILLKOMMEN ZUM *&* ISAR HOTEL MÜNICH

Wilenmayerstrade 10, 803 München, GERMANY, TEL +49 (0) 89 55544 0, FAX +49 (0) 89 55544 1000

www.ISARHOTEL@emcp.net

Please join us every morning between 6:30 and 10:00 a.m. for a complimentary continental breakfast served in the Garden Center on the main floor. In the afternoon, stop by the Regency Atrium next to the hotel lobby and enjoy complimentary beverages, muffins, and cookies. Please check out of your room by 11:00 a.m. If you need a late check-out time, please contact a hotel representative at the main desk.

Check in: 3:00 p.m.

Continental breakfast
6:30-10:00 a.m., Garden Center

Afternoon snacks
4:00-5:30 p.m., Regency Atrium

Check out: 11:00 a.m.

Figure 5.41 Sample Information Sheet for Assessment 5.5

MÜNICH

MÜNICH, GERMANY

Münich is the capital and largest city of the German state of Bavaria and the third largest city in Germany. Münich is located in southern Germany and was founded in 1158 by Henry the Lion, the duke of Saxony and Bavaria. Spread out over 310 square kilometers, Münich has a population of approximately 1.4 million. Münich is known as the gateway to the Bavarian Alps and is considered the silicon valley of Europe.

Marienplatz

Marienplatz is the central square in the center of Münich. In the square, you can explore a variety of buildings, churches, and landmarks. Mariensäule, the Marian Column topped with the golden statue of the Virgin Mary, is located in Marienplatz.

The English Garden

Münich's largest park, The English Garden, is a wonderful place to explore. The park provides a variety of recreational activities—rent a paddle boat, stroll along the wooded paths, and visit a traditional beer garden.

Residence Palace of Münich

The Residence Palace lies at the edge of Münich's old town and is the former royal palace of the Bavarian monarchs. Today the Residence houses one of the best European museums of interior decoration.

Deutsches Museum

The Deutsches Museum is located on an island in the Isar river that runs through Münich's city center. The museum is one of the oldest and largest science and technology museums in the world and boasts an impressive collection of historic artifacts.

Olympic Stadium

The site for the 1972 Summer Olympics, the Olympic Stadium was revolutionary and futuristic for its time. The transparent canopies of acrylic glass, modeled after the Alps, are the signature characteristic of the stadium.

http://en-wikipedia.org/wiki/Munich
http://gogermany.about.com/od/citiesandregions/tp/Munich

Chapter 6

Creating Basic Elements of a Newsletter

Performance Objectives

Upon successful completion of Chapter 6, you will be able to:

- Understand, create, and format the basic elements of a newsletter
- Review and apply design concepts to a newsletter
- Set margins in a newsletter
- Create and format columns in a newsletter
- Create borders and ruled lines in a newsletter
- Create drop caps
- Create, modify, and apply styles to a newsletter
- Apply the Widow/Orphan control feature
- Use Windows Paint to edit images
- Use Windows Fax and Scan
- Mail a newsletter

Desktop Publishing Terms

body text	folio	nameplate	subhead
byline	graphic image	orphan	subtitle
columns	gutter	pull quote	tombstoning
drop cap	headline	rivers	widow
em space	mirror margin	self-mailer	

Word Features Used

column break	margins	section break
columns	page borders	styles
mail merge	save as template	Widow/Orphan control

Note: Before beginning computer exercises for this chapter, copy to your storage medium the Chapter06 folder from the CD that accompanies this textbook and then make Chapter06 the active folder. Remember to substitute for graphics that may no longer be available.

Understanding the Basic Elements of a Newsletter

Newsletters are used to communicate information to a group of people, such as members of a club or employees within an organization. Successful newsletters contain consistent elements in every issue. This makes it easy for readers to find what they need, and the ultimate goal of any newsletter is to effectively communicate the content. The basic elements of a newsletter are as follows:

- **Nameplate:** Contains the newsletter's title and is usually located on the front page. Nameplates (also known as banners) can include the company logo, a unique typeface, or a graphic image to help reinforce an organization's identity.

- **Logo:** A name, symbol, trademark, or graphic image used to create or reinforce an organization's identity. Logos are often used in the nameplate of a newsletter.

- **Subtitle:** A short phrase describing the purpose or audience of the newsletter. The subtitle (or tagline) is usually located below the nameplate, near the folio.

- **Folio:** Contains the publication information, including the volume number, issue number, and the current date of the newsletter. The folio usually appears near the nameplate, but it can also be displayed at the bottom or side of a page. In desktop publishing, *folio* can also be used to refer to the page number.

- **Headlines:** Titles of articles meant to attract the reader's attention. Headlines can be set in 22- to 72-point type or larger, generally in a sans serif typeface.

- **Subheads:** Secondary headings that provide the transition from headline to body text. Subheads may also be referred to as section headings because they are sometimes used to break up the text into sections. Subheads are usually set in bold and in a larger type size than the body text.

- **Byline:** Identifies the author of an article. A byline is usually located under the headline.

- **Body text:** The main text of an article (also known as body copy).

- **Graphic images:** Photographs or illustrations added to newsletters to support the body text and add interest to the document.

Figure 6.1 displays these elements in a sample newsletter page. While additional newsletter elements and enhancements will be presented in Chapter 7, this chapter will cover the basics of planning, designing, and creating a newsletter.

Planning a Newsletter

DTP POINTER ❯

Examine as many publications as you can to get design ideas.

Before beginning to create a newsletter, you must determine a plan. When you know who you are creating your newsletter for, as well as how and why you are creating it, it will be easier to determine what content to include and what to leave out. This will give your newsletter a clear focus, which will more effectively hold your readers' interest. Consider the following questions as you plan your newsletter:

- What is the purpose or goal of your newsletter? Are you trying to sell, inform, explain, or announce?

- Who will be the audience of your newsletter? What do they need to know? What do they want to know?

- What image do you want your newsletter to project? How will you achieve this?

- Will your newsletter contain graphic images, such as photos, illustrations, or advertisements?

Figure 6.1 Identifying Basic Elements in a Newsletter Page

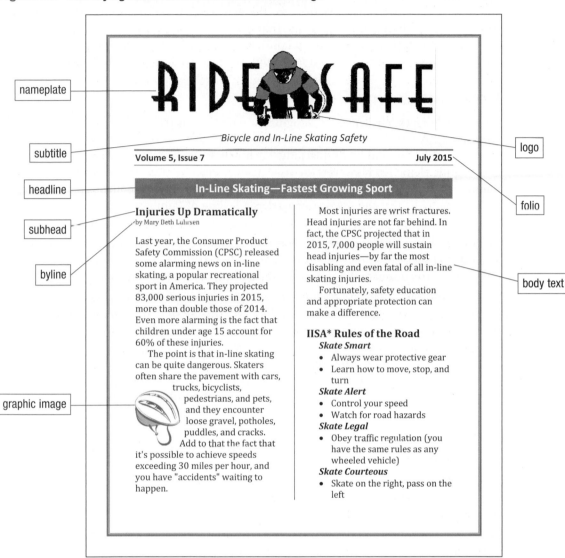

- How often will your newsletter be published? What items do you need or want to repeat in each issue?

- What is your budget for creating your newsletter? How much time can you devote to creating it? Will you be working on it alone, or will you have help?

Designing the Page Layout of a Newsletter

The desktop publishing concepts and guidelines discussed in previous chapters provide good starting points for designing your newsletter. These guidelines emphasize the use of consistency, balance, proportion, contrast, white space, focus, directional flow, and color. As always, if you are designing a newsletter for a company or another organization, make sure the design coordinates with the organization's identity by using the same logos, typefaces, type sizes, column arrangements, and color choices that are used in other correspondence.

Typically, page layout begins with choosing the size and orientation of the paper and determining the margins desired for the newsletter. Next, decisions on the number, length, and width of columns become imperative. Typefaces, type sizes, and typestyles must also be considered, as well as graphic images, ruled lines, and shading and coloring. This section will walk you through the process of making these decisions.

Applying Design Concepts

One of the biggest challenges in designing a newsletter is balancing change with consistency. A newsletter is a document that is typically reproduced on a regular basis—often monthly, bimonthly, or quarterly. Each new issue contains new ideas, articles, and graphic elements. However, for your newsletter to be effective, each issue must also maintain a consistent organization and appearance. Consistency contributes to your publication's identity and gives your readers a feeling of familiarity.

DTP POINTER

Newsletter design should be consistent from issue to issue.

Newsletter features that may be kept consistent among issues include size of margins; column layout; nameplate formatting and location; logos; color; ruled lines; and formatting of headlines, subheads, and body text. Later in the chapter, you will create styles to automate the process of formatting consistent elements.

Focus and balance can be achieved through the design and size of the newsletter's nameplate; the arrangement of text on the page; the use of graphic images and photographs; and the careful placement of lines, borders, and backgrounds. When including graphic images or photos, use restraint. A single, large, well-placed illustration is usually preferred over many small images scattered throughout the document. Size graphic images or photos according to their relative importance to the content. Headlines and subheads can serve as secondary focal points as well as provide balance to the document as a whole.

DTP POINTER

Use no more than one or two images per page if possible.

As you already know, white space creates contrast and attracts the reader's eyes. Surround text with white space to make it stand out. If you want to draw attention to the nameplate or headline of the newsletter, you may want to choose a bold typestyle, a larger type size, or a WordArt style in addition to surrounding the text with white space. Use sufficient white space throughout your newsletter to break up blocks of text and offer the reader visual relief.

DTP POINTER

Use graphic accents with discretion.

Good directional flow can be achieved by using ruled lines that guide the reader's eyes through the document. Graphic elements placed strategically throughout a newsletter can also provide a pattern for the reader's eyes to follow. If you decide to use color in a newsletter, do so sparingly. Establish focus and directional flow by using color to highlight key information or elements in your publication.

Analyze how the design concepts discussed above were achieved in Figure 6.1 on page 237. What does this newsletter design do well? How could it be improved?

Choosing Paper Size and Type

The first considerations in designing a newsletter page layout are the type of paper and the paper size. The number of copies needed and the equipment available for creating, printing, and distributing the newsletter can affect this decision. Most newsletters are created on standard 8.5-by-11-inch paper, although some are printed on larger sheets such as 8.5-by-14-inch paper. The most economical choice for printing is the standard 8.5-by-11-inch paper. This size of paper is easier to hold and read, is cheaper to mail, and fits easily in standard file folders.

When deciding on the weight of the paper for your newsletter, consider the cost, the quality desired, and the graphics or photographs to be included. Typically, the heavier the stock, the more expensive the paper. In terms of color, note that white paper can create glare, making reading more difficult. If possible, investigate other, more subtle colors. Another option is to purchase predesigned newsletter paper from a paper supply company. These papers come in many colors and designs and often contain differently shaded areas on a page to help separate and organize your text.

Setting Margins in a Newsletter

After considering the paper you will use for the newsletter, determine the margins of the newsletter pages. The margin size is linked to the number of columns needed, the formality desired, the visual elements to be used, the amount of text to be included, and the type of binding, if any. Keep the margins consistent throughout your newsletter. The following are a few general rules for newsletter margins:

- A wide right margin is considered formal. This approach positions the text at the left side of the page—the side where most readers tend to look first. If the text is justified, the newsletter will appear even more formal.

- A wide left margin is less formal. A table of contents or marginal subheads can be placed in the left margin to give the newsletter an airy, open appearance and make it easier for the reader to find what he or she needs.

- Equal left and right margins tend to create an informal look.

If you plan to create a multiple-page newsletter with facing pages, you may want to use ***mirror margins***, which means that the outside margins of the page are equal and the inside margins are equal, creating a mirror image, as shown in Figures 6.2 below and 6.3 on page 240. Often, the inside margin is wider than the outside margin; however, this may depend on the amount of space taken up by the binding. To create facing pages with mirror margins, click the Margins button in the Page Setup group on the PAGE LAYOUT tab and then click *Custom Margins* at the drop-down list. At the Page Setup dialog box with the Margins tab selected, click the down-pointing arrow at the right of *Multiple pages* in the *Pages* section and then click *Mirror margins* at the drop-down list. If you plan to include page numbering, position the numbers on the outside edges of each page.

When creating a multiple-page newsletter, you may need to increase the inside margins to create a ***gutter*** to accommodate the binding. Gutter space can be added to the left side or top of a page. To bind a document like a book with facing pages, you need to add gutter space to the inside margins. This means adding space to the left

DTP POINTER
Be generous with your margins. Do not crowd text.

mirror margins
Created when the outside and inside margins of two facing pages are equal to each other, creating a mirror image

Margins

gutter
Additional space added to inside margins to accommodate the binding

DTP POINTER
Place page numbers on the outside edges when using mirror margins.

Figure 6.2 Understanding Mirror Margins with a Wider Outside Margin

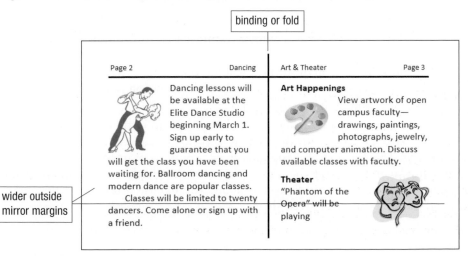

Figure 6.3 Understanding Mirror Margins with a Wider Inside Margin

gutters

| Page 2 | Dancing | Art & Theater | Page 3 |

Dancing lessons will be available at the Elite Dance Studio beginning March 1. Sign up early to guarantee that you will get the class you have been waiting for. Ballroom dancing and modern dance are popular classes.
Classes will be limited to twenty dancers. Come alone or sign up with a friend.

Art Happenings
View artwork of open campus faculty— drawings, paintings, photographs, jewelry, and computer animation. Discuss available classes with faculty.

Theater
"Phantom of the Opera" will be playing

wider inside mirror margins

DTP POINTER
Use extra wide gutters or margins to counteract dense text.

margin of odd pages and the right margin of even pages. To add gutters, display the Page Setup dialog box with the Margins tab selected, specify whether you want to add gutter space to the left or top margin with the *Gutter position* option, and then enter the gutter measurement in the *Gutter* measurement box. To add gutter space to facing pages, first specify mirror margins by clicking the Margins button in the Page Setup group and then clicking the *Mirrored* option at the drop-down list or by displaying the Page Setup dialog box with the Margins tab selected, clicking the down-pointing arrow at the right of the *Multiple pages* option box, and then clicking *Mirror margins* at the drop-down list. With mirror margins selected, enter a measurement in the *Gutter* measurement box.

Creating Columns in a Newsletter

When preparing newsletters, an important consideration is the readability of the document. The line length of text can enhance or detract from this. Setting the text in columns can make reading the text easier for your audience. **Columns** are vertically oriented blocks of text with short line lengths in which text flows from the bottom of one to the top of the next. You will use columns to format the newsletter created throughout this chapter; however, keep in mind that you can also use linked text boxes to position text within a newsletter. This method is used in most of the newsletter templates available at Office.com and will be introduced in Chapter 7.

columns

Vertically oriented blocks of text with short line lengths; text flows from the bottom of one to the top of the next

DTP POINTER
Columns added to newsletters improve readability.

Columns

Using columns in a newsletter promotes text organization and helps guide the reader's eyes. As discussed earlier, the columns feature allows text to flow from column to column in the document. When the first column on the page is filled with text, the insertion point moves to the top of the next column on the same page in a snaking pattern. When the last column on the page is filled, the insertion point moves to the beginning of the first column on the next page.

Columns can be created by clicking the Columns button in the Page Setup group on the PAGE LAYOUT tab. At the drop-down list, click *One, Two, Three, Left, Right,* or *More Columns*. The *Left* and *Right* options enable columns of unequal width to create an asymmetrical layout. Clicking the *More Columns* option displays the Columns dialog box, as shown in Figure 6.4. This dialog box allows you to customize the widths of the columns and the white space between them.

Figure 6.4 Customizing Columns at the Columns Dialog Box

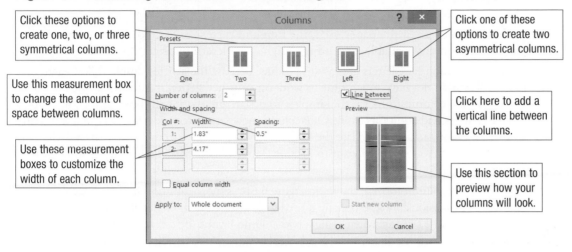

Click these options to create one, two, or three symmetrical columns.

Use this measurement box to change the amount of space between columns.

Use these measurement boxes to customize the width of each column.

Click one of these options to create two asymmetrical columns.

Click here to add a vertical line between the columns.

Use this section to preview how your columns will look.

Using Balanced and Unbalanced Columns

Word automatically lines up (balances) columns by filling every column to the last line. On the last page of a newsletter, there may not be enough text for Word to balance the columns. For example, in a two-column layout, the text in the first column may flow to the bottom of the page, while the text in the second column may end near the top. Columns can be manually balanced by completing the following steps:

1. Position the insertion point at the end of the text in the last column of the section you want to balance.
2. Click the PAGE LAYOUT tab and then click the Breaks button.
3. At the Breaks button drop-down list, click *Continuous* in the *Section Breaks* section.

Breaks

Figure 6.5A shows the last page of a document containing unbalanced columns. Figure 6.5B shows the same page after the columns have been balanced. If you want to force a new page to start after the balanced columns, click after the continuous break and then manually insert a page break by pressing Ctrl + Enter.

Figure 6.5 Comparing Unbalanced and Balanced Columns

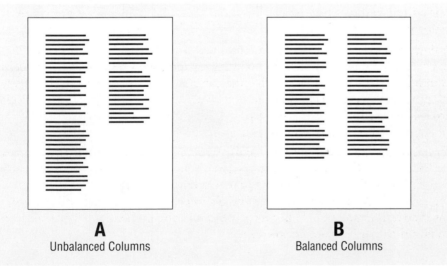

A
Unbalanced Columns

B
Balanced Columns

Determining the Number of Columns

The number of columns used in newsletters may vary from one column to two or more columns. The size of the paper used, the font and type size selected, the amount of text and other content available, and other design considerations affect this decision.

One-column newsletters are easy to produce because the articles simply follow each other. If you do not have much time to work on your newsletter, this format is the one to use. The one-column format is the simplest to design and work with because it allows you to make changes and additions easily. One-column newsletters require a larger type size (usually 11 or 12 points) to accommodate the long line length. Be sure to use wide margins with this column layout. You may also want to include a table of contents, a schedule, or some other text box feature on one side of a one-column newsletter, as shown in Figure 6.6A

The two-column format, shown in Figure 6.6B, is most common for newsletters. It conveys a professional look, especially if used with justified text. Generally, use type sizes between 10 and 11 points when using a two-column layout. Be careful to avoid *tombstoning*, which occurs when headlines or subheads display side by side in adjacent columns. Adding graphic enhancements will make this classic two-column format more interesting.

tombstoning

Occurs when headings display side by side in adjacent columns

Figure 6.6 Comparing One-Column and Two-Column Newsletters

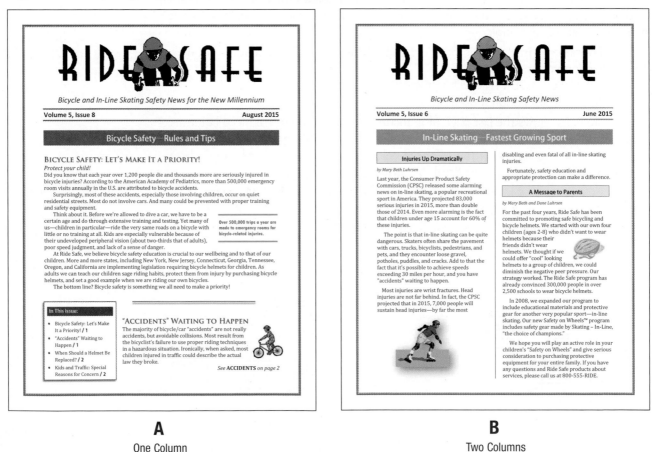

A

One Column

B

Two Columns

A three-column format can be successful if you avoid using too much text on the page. This popular format is more flexible for adding interesting design elements. You may use a smaller type size (9 to 11 points) and fit more information on a page. Placing headlines, subheads, text, or graphics across one, two, or three columns can create a distinctive flow. Often, one column on the first page of the newsletter is reserved for a table of contents, marginal subheads, or other design elements, thus allowing for more white space in the document and more visual interest.

A four-column design gives you even more flexibility than the three-column layout; however, it may be more time consuming to lay out. Leaving one column fairly empty with a great deal of white space to offset more text-intensive columns is a visually appealing solution. This format gives you many opportunities to display headlines, subheads, graphics, and other design elements across one or more columns. You will need to use a small type size for your text (9 to 10 points). Also, consider printing on larger-sized paper when using this layout.

Using Varying Numbers of Columns

Section breaks can be used to vary the page layout within a single newsletter. For example, you can use a section break to separate a one-column nameplate from text that is created in three columns, as shown in Figure 6.7. There are three methods for inserting section breaks in documents. The first method involves selecting break options at the Breaks button drop-down list. For the second method, insert a section break by selecting the *This point forward* option at the *Apply to* option box at the Columns dialog box. In the third method, select the text first, and then apply column formatting.

To move the insertion point between columns, use the mouse or press Alt + Up Arrow to move the insertion point to the top of the previous column, or press Alt + Down Arrow to move the insertion point to the top of the next column.

Figure 6.7 Using Section Breaks in a Newsletter

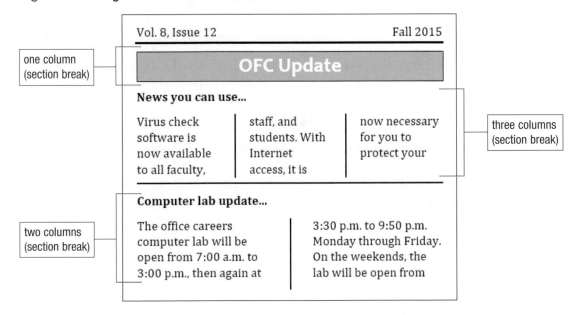

In addition, when formatting text in columns, Word automatically breaks the columns to fit the page. If a column breaks in an undesirable location, you can insert a column break in the document to control where the columns end and begin on the page. To insert a column break, position the insertion point where you want the new column to begin and then press Ctrl + Shift + Enter, or click the Breaks button on the PAGE LAYOUT tab and then click *Column* in the *Page Breaks* section of the drop-down list.

Changing the Number of Columns

Select

To change the number of columns for an entire newsletter, press Ctrl + A, or click the Select button in the Editing group on the HOME tab and then click *Select All* at the drop-down list. To change the number of columns for a portion of a document, select the text or sections you want to change first. After selecting the text, click the Columns button and then select the number of desired columns at the drop-down list. If you want to remove column formatting altogether, select the sections you want to change, click the Columns button, and then click *One* at the drop-down list.

Changing Column Width

If your newsletter is divided into sections, click in the section you want to change and then drag the column marker on the horizontal ruler. If an adjacent column is hampering your efforts to change the width of another column, change the width of the adjacent column first. If the column widths are equal, all of the columns will change. If the column widths are unequal, only the column you are adjusting will change. To specify exact measurements for column widths, hold down the Alt key to display the column width measurements as you drag the column marker on the ruler, or display the Columns dialog box and then type exact measurements in the measurement boxes.

Adding Vertical Ruled Lines between Columns

Position the insertion point in the section where you want to add a vertical ruled line, display the Columns dialog box, click to add a check mark in the *Line between* check box (see Figure 6.4 on page 241), and then close the dialog box.

Adding Borders and Horizontal Lines to Newsletter Pages

You can add page borders, paragraph borders, borders around images, borders around text boxes, and horizontal lines between paragraphs to change the appearance of your newsletters. To add a page border, click the Page Borders button in the Page Background group on the DESIGN tab. At the Borders and Shading dialog box with the Page Border tab selected, select a particular line style, color, and width, or select a predesigned art border. Make sure *Whole document* displays in the *Apply to* option box.

Page Borders

To create a border around a paragraph of text, click the Borders tab at the Borders and Shading dialog box and then make desired changes to the line style, color, or width. Make sure *Paragraph* displays in the *Apply to* option box.

Add a horizontal line to a document by clicking the Online Pictures button in the Illustrations group on the INSERT tab, using the search text *horizontal line* at the Insert Pictures window, and then double-clicking the desired horizontal line. Format the horizontal line with options on the PICTURE TOOLS FORMAT tab.

You can also add a horizontal or vertical line to your newsletter by clicking the Shapes button in the Illustrations group on the INSERT tab, clicking a line in the *Lines* section, and then drawing a line in your document. Customize the line with options on the DRAWING TOOLS FORMAT tab.

Using Drop Caps in a Newsletter

A ***drop cap*** is created by setting the first letter of the first word in a paragraph in a larger font size, dropped down into the paragraph or extended into the margin. Drop caps identify the beginning of major sections or parts of a document, and they can be used to enhance the appearance of publications such as magazines, brochures, and newsletters.

Drop caps look best within a paragraph of text set in a proportional font. The drop cap can be set in the same font as the paragraph text, or it can be set in a complementary font. For example, you may set a drop cap in a sans serif font, while the paragraph text is set in a serif font. A drop cap can be limited to one character, or it can be the entire first word of a paragraph.

Create a drop cap with options at the Drop Cap button drop-down list in the Text group on the INSERT tab. You can choose to set the drop cap in the paragraph or in the margin. Click *Drop Cap Options* at the Drop Cap button drop-down list to display the Drop Cap dialog box. At this dialog box, you can specify the font, the number of lines you want the letter to drop, and the distance you want the letter to be positioned from the text of the paragraph.

drop cap
Created by setting the first letter of the first word in a paragraph in a larger font size, dropped down into the paragraph or extended into the margin

Drop Cap

Using Styles in a Newsletter

Styles are especially valuable for saving time, effort, and keystrokes in creating newsletters. Newsletters contain elements that must remain consistent from page to page as well as from issue to issue, and styles reinforce this consistency by saving formatting instructions with a name so they can be applied over and over.

One method for creating a customized style is to apply formatting to text and then create a style based on the formatting. To create a style based on existing formatting, select the text or object, click the More button in the Styles group on the HOME tab, and then click *Create a Style* at the drop-down gallery. At the Create New Style from Formatting dialog box, type a name for the style and then click OK.

Creating a Newsletter

Now that you are familiar with the basic elements of a newsletter and the considerations that go into planning and designing one, you are ready to begin creating a newsletter of your own. The following sections will guide you through creating and placing each element of the Loaves & Fishes newsletter shown in Figure 6.8 on page 246.

Figure 6.8 Loaves & Fishes Newsletter Created in Exercises 6.1–6.7

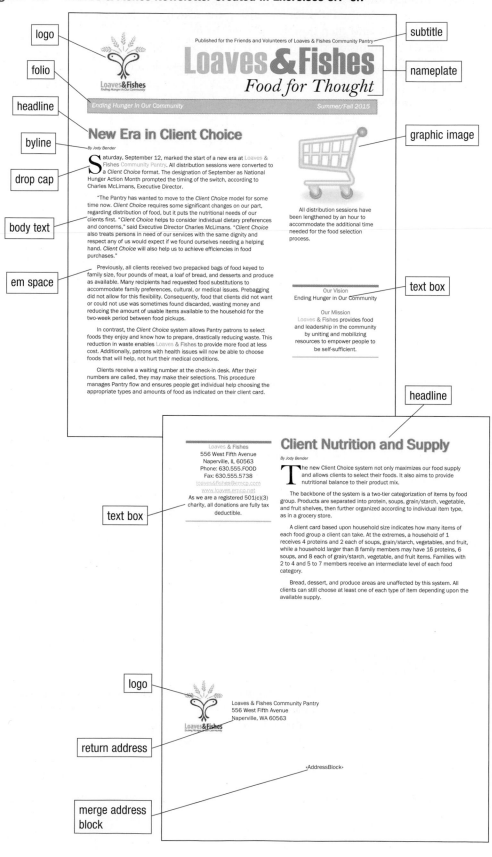

logo

folio

headline

byline

drop cap

body text

em space

subtitle

nameplate

graphic image

text box

headline

text box

logo

return address

merge address block

Creating a Nameplate

Creating a nameplate is the first step in building the Loaves & Fishes newsletter. A *nameplate* (also known as a banner) is the artwork (graphic, logo, scanned image, or cropped image) and/or type that includes the name of the publication and is usually placed at the top of the first page of a newsletter. It captures the reader's eyes and immediately identifies the newsletter. The choice of fonts, type sizes, and the designs of the name are important because they help the reader form his or her first impression of the newsletter and because they are used in every issue.

The nameplate you will create in Exercise 6.1A consists of the organization's logo, the organization's name, and the newsletter name set in the same colors as those used in the logo. Loaves & Fishes uses two different logo designs in most of its publications. The Loaves & Fishes logos may display in black and white or in green and gold. Most nameplates remain unchanged from issue to issue; therefore, saving them as a style (as you will do with other newsletter elements in the exercises in this chapter) is not necessary, but the nameplate should be saved in the newsletter template.

Figure 6.9 illustrates several examples of nameplates. Examine them for the use and different location of elements. Looking at the work of others can help you develop your own skills in design and layout.

nameplate

A newsletter element, also known as a banner, that first captures the reader's eyes and immediately identifies the newsletter

◀ **DTP POINTER**
Your nameplate should sell the contents of your newsletter.

Figure 6.9 Illustrating Sample Nameplates

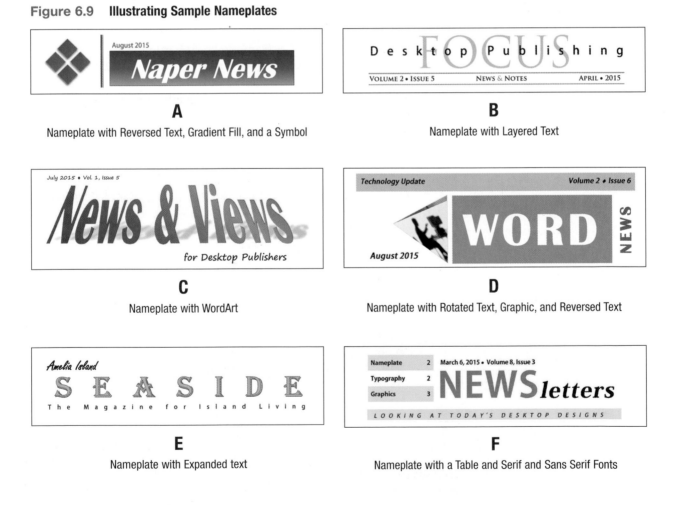

A

Nameplate with Reversed Text, Gradient Fill, and a Symbol

B

Nameplate with Layered Text

C

Nameplate with WordArt

D

Nameplate with Rotated Text, Graphic, and Reversed Text

E

Nameplate with Expanded text

F

Nameplate with a Table and Serif and Sans Serif Fonts

1. Display a blank document and then save it with the name **C06-E01-Nameplate**.
2. Change the top, bottom, left, and right document margins to 0.5 inch. *Hint: Click the* **Narrow** *option at the Margins button drop-down list.*
3. Apply the Organic theme and the Franklin Gothic theme fonts.
4. With the insertion point positioned at the beginning of the document, press the Enter key 10 times. Press Ctrl + Home to position the insertion point back at the top of the document and then insert **Loaves&FishesColor.png** from your Chapter06 folder.
5. Format, size, and position the logo as shown in Figure 6.8 on page 246 by completing the following steps:
   a. With the logo selected, click the Color button in the Adjust group on the PICTURE TOOLS FORMAT tab, click *Set Transparent Color* at the drop-down gallery, and then click any section of the logo to the right or left of the fish to remove the light gray background.
   b. Change the text wrapping of the logo to *Square*.
   c. Resize the logo by typing **1.8** in the *Shape Height* measurement box in the Size group on the PICTURE TOOLS FORMAT tab.
   d. Position the logo as shown in Figure 6.8.
6. Draw a text box to the right of the logo that measures approximately 1 inch in height and 5.5 inches in width and then format the text box and the text within the text box by completing the following steps:
   a. With the text box selected, type **1.1** in the *Shape Height* measurement box in the Size group on the DRAWING TOOLS FORMAT tab, type **5.6** in the *Shape Width* measurement box, and then press Enter.
   b. Position the insertion point inside the text box, change the paragraph alignment to right, and then type **Loaves&Fishes**.
   c. Select *Loaves*, change the font to 72-point Haettenschweiler, and then apply the Gold, Accent 6 font color (last column, first row in the *Theme Colors* section).
   d. Select the text *&Fishes* and then change the font to 72-point Haettenschweiler.
   e. Click the Font Color button arrow and then click *More Colors* at the drop-down gallery. At the Colors dialog box, click the Custom tab, type **56** in the *Red* measurement box, **140** in the *Green* measurement box, and **78** in the *Blue* measurement box. Click OK to close the dialog box.

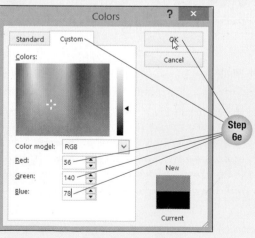

f. Select *Loaves&Fishes* and then click the Font dialog box launcher.

g. At the Font dialog box, click the Advanced tab, change the *Spacing* option to *Expanded*, and make sure *1 pt* displays in the *By* measurement box at the right of the *Spacing* option box.

h. Click the *Kerning for fonts* check box to insert a check mark, type **14** in the *Points and above* measurement box, and then click OK.

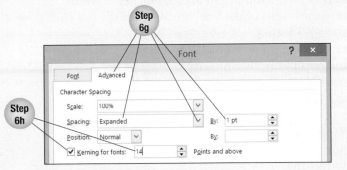

i. Select the *&* (ampersand) and then change the font to 72-point Eras Bold ITC.

j. Drag the text box containing *Loaves&Fishes* to a position similar to that shown in Figure 6.8.

k. Remove the shape fill and shape outline.

7. Draw a text box and then format the text box and the text within it by completing the following steps:

a. With the text box selected, type **0.7** in the *Shape Height* measurement box in the Size group on the DRAWING TOOLS FORMAT tab, type **5** in the *Shape Width* measurement box, and then press Enter

b. Position the insertion point inside the text box, change the paragraph alignment to right, and then type **Food for Thought**.

c. Select *Food for Thought*, change the font to 36-point Bell MT, apply italic formatting, and then turn on kerning at 14 points and above.

d. Remove the shape fill and shape outline from the text box and then position it as shown in Figure 6.8.

8. Save **C06-E01-Nameplate.docx**. *Note: You do not need to print until you are finished with the entire newsletter.*

Creating a Folio

The *folio* in a newsletter consists of publishing information that changes from issue to issue, such as the volume number, issue number, and date. However, the formatting applied to the folio should remain consistent with each issue. Frequently, the folio is preceded or followed by a graphic that sets the folio information apart from the rest of the nameplate. The folio may appear above or below the nameplate. Reversed text can be used to add emphasis and interest—use a thick font or apply bold to make the font stand out against the shaded background, as shown in the Loaves & Fishes newsletter in Figure 6.8 on page 246. You will create this folio in Exercise 6.1B.

> **folio**
> Contains publishing information that changes from issue to issue, such as the volume number, issue number, and date

1. With **C06-E01-Nameplate.docx** open, save the document with the name **C06-E01-Folio**.
2. Create the folio for the newsletter in Figure 6.8 on page 246 by completing the following steps:
   a. Below the text box containing *Food for Thought*, draw a text box that measures approximately 0.3 inches in height and 7.5 inches in width.
   b. Change the shape height of the text box to 0.37 inch and the shape width to 7.5 inches.

   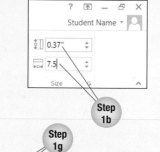

   c. Position the insertion point inside the text box and then type **Ending Hunger in Our Community**.
   d. With the insertion point still located inside the text box, set a right tab at 7.2 inches. ***Hint: Use the Tabs dialog box.***
   e. Press Tab and then type **Summer/Fall 2015**.
   f. Select *Ending Hunger in Our Community* and *Summer/Fall 2015*, change the font size to 12 points, and then apply bold and italic formatting.

   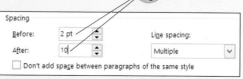

   g. With the insertion point positioned anywhere in the text in the text box, click the Paragraph dialog box launcher, type **2** in the *Before* measurement box and **10** in the *After* measurement box in the *Spacing* section, and then click OK.

   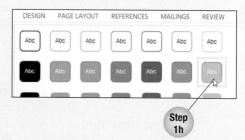

   h. Select the text box, click the More button in the Shape Styles group on the DRAWING TOOLS FORMAT tab, and then click the *Colored Fill - Gold, Accent 6* style option (last column, second row). The text should automatically display in white.
   i. Position the text box as shown in Figure 6.8.
3. Create a style from existing formatting by completing the following steps:
   a. Select the folio text box.
   b. Click the More button in the Styles group on the HOME tab and then click *Create a Style* at the drop-down gallery.
   c. At the Create New Style from Formatting dialog box, type **Folio** in the *Name* text box and then click OK. ***Hint: The Folio style is added to the list of styles in this document.***

4. Save **C06-E01-Folio.docx**.

Creating a Subtitle

A *subtitle* is a newsletter element that appears near the nameplate and emphasizes the purpose of the newsletter and/or identifies the intended audience. The text in the subtitle remains consistent from issue to issue, so creating a style for this element is not necessary because it should be saved as part of the newsletter template. A subtitle is usually set in a sans serif typeface of 14 to 24 points, and kerning should be turned on. You will create the subtitle for the Loaves & Fishes newsletter in Exercise 6.1C.

subtitle

Appears near the nameplate; emphasizes the purpose of the newsletter and/or identifies the intended audience

---

Exercise 6.1C Creating a Subtitle for a Newsletter   Part 3 of 8

---

1. With **C06-E01-Folio.docx** open, save the document with the name **C06-E01-Subtitle**.
2. Format the subtitle by completing the following steps:
    a. Above the text box containing *Loaves&Fishes*, draw a text box that measures approximately 0.3 inch in height and 5.25 inches in width.
    b. With the text box selected, change the shape height to 0.3 inch and the shape width to 5.25 inches.
    c. With the insertion point positioned inside the text box, change the font size to 10 points and the paragraph alignment to right.
    d. Type **Published for the Friends and Volunteers of Loaves & Fishes Community Pantry**.
    e. Remove the shape fill and shape outline from the text box and then position it as shown in Figure 6.8 on page 246. *Hint: Make sure the last characters in each of the text boxes align vertically near the right margin.*
3. Group all the nameplate elements by completing the following steps:
    a. Hold down the Shift key and click to select each of the elements.
    b. Click the Group button in the Arrange group on the DRAWING TOOLS FORMAT tab and then click *Group* at the drop-down list.

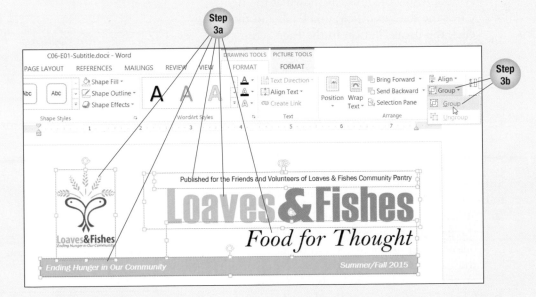

4. Save **C06-E01-Subtitle.docx**.

Creating a Headline

Headlines organize text and tell the reader what information an article will communicate. To set the headline apart from the text, use a larger type size, a heavier weight, and/or a different typeface than the body. When determining a type size for a headline, start with 18 points and then increase the size until you find an appropriate one. As a guideline, choose a sans serif typeface for a headline; however, this is not a hard-and-fast rule.

Headlines of more than one line often improve in readability and appearance if leading (the white space between lines) is reduced. Using all caps (sparingly) or small caps substantially reduces leading below headlines automatically because capital letters lack descenders. Headlines and subheads should have more space above than below. This indicates that the headline goes with the text that follows it rather than the text that precedes it.

Because headlines may be used several times in a newsletter, you will need to create a style to reinforce consistency and promote efficiency in formatting the document. In Exercise 6.1D, you will create a headline for the Loaves & Fishes newsletter and then create a style to save the headline formatting.

Exercise 6.1D Creating a Headline for a Newsletter   Part 4 of 8

1. With **C06-E01-Subtitle.docx** open, save the document with the name **C06-E01-Headline**.
2. Create a section break between the folio and the headline by completing the following steps:
   a. Turn on the display of nonprinting characters by clicking the Show/Hide ¶ button in the Paragraph group on the HOME tab.
   b. Position the insertion point on the paragraph symbol below the folio, as shown at the right.
   c. Click the the PAGE LAYOUT tab and then click the Breaks button in the Page Setup group.
   d. Click the *Continuous* option at the drop-down list. This will insert a continuous section break below the folio at the bottom of the nameplate. ***Hint: If you cannot see the continuous section break in your document, move the nameplate up until the break is visible.***
3. Turn on the columns feature by completing the following steps:
   a. With the insertion point still positioned at the paragraph symbol below the folio (and below the continuous section break), click the Columns button in the Page Setup group on the PAGE LAYOUT tab.
   b. Click *More Columns* at the drop-down list.

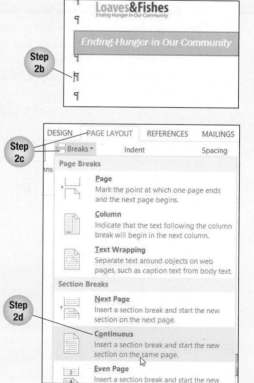

---

c. At the Columns dialog box, click *Right* in the *Presets* section. This will create two asymmetrical columns where the left column is twice as wide as the right one.

d. Type **0.4** in the *Spacing* measurement box for column 1 in the *Width and spacing* section.

e. Click OK to close the dialog box.

f. Click the Show/Hide ¶ button in the Paragraph group on the HOME tab to turn off the display of nonprinting characters.

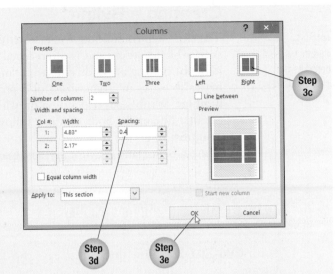

4. Create the headline by completing the following steps:

a. Change the font size to 28 points and turn on bold formatting.

b. Change the font color to the green color used in the banner (Red 56, Green 140, Blue 78).

c. Type **New Era in Client Choice**.

d. Select *New Era in Client Choice*, display the Font dialog box with the Advanced tab selected, and then turn on kerning at 14 points and above.

e. With the headline still selected, click the Text Effects and Typography button, point to *Shadow* at the drop-down list, and then click the *Offset Right* option at the side menu (first column, second row in the *Outer* section).

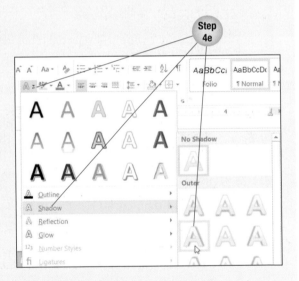

f. Position the insertion point anywhere in the headline and then click the Paragraph dialog box launcher.

g. At the Paragraph dialog box, type **12** in the *Before* measurement box and **0** in the *After* measurement box and then click OK.

5. Create a style from existing formatting by completing the following steps:

a. Position the insertion point anywhere in the headline text, click the More button in the Styles group on the HOME tab, and then click *Create a Style* at the drop-down gallery.

b. At the Create New Style from Formatting dialog box, type **Headline** in the *Name* text box and then click OK. ***Hint: The Headline style is added to the list of styles saved with this document.***

6. Save **C06-E01-Headline.docx**.

Creating a Byline

byline

A newsletter element that identifies the author of the article

The next step in building the newsletter is to create the byline. The **byline** identifies the author of the article and is often typed in the same typeface as the body text but with italic formatting applied. The byline may be the same size as the body typeface, but it may also be set in a type size 1 or 2 points smaller. The byline may appear below the headline or subhead, depending on which is the title of the article, or it may appear as the first line of the body text if it follows a headline or subhead that spans two or more columns. Align the byline at the left margin or at the right side of a column. You will create a byline and a byline style in Exercise 6.1E.

Exercise 6.1E Creating a Byline for a Newsletter   Part 5 of 8

1. With **C06-E01-Headline.docx** open, save the document with the name **C06-E01-Byline**.
2. Create a style to format the byline in the newsletter as shown in Figure 6.8 on page 246 by completing the following steps:
   a. Turn on the display of nonprinting characters.
   b. Position the insertion point on the paragraph symbol below the headline text.
   c. Type **By Jody Bender**.
   d. Press Enter once if a paragraph symbol does not display after the byline.
   e. Select the byline *By Jody Bender,* change the font size to 8 points, and then apply italic formatting.
   f. With the byline still selected, click the PAGE LAYOUT tab, type **6** in the *After* measurement box in the *Spacing* section in the Paragraph group, and then press Enter.
   g. Turn off the display of nonprinting characters.
3. Create a style from existing text by completing the following steps:
   a. With the byline text selected, click the More button in the Styles group and then click *Create a Style* at the drop-down gallery.
   b. At the Create New Style from Formatting dialog box, type **Byline** in the *Name* text box and then click OK. ***Hint: The byline style is added to the list of styles saved with this document.***
4. Save **C06-E01-Byline.docx**.

Formatting Body Text

body text

The main content of the newsletter

In this section you will format the **body text**, or the main content, of the newsletter you are creating. You will also change the font and font size, and create em spaces for paragraph indentations. Before doing so, take a look at some of the formatting options that can be applied to body text.

Changing Paragraph Alignment

The type of paragraph alignment you choose for a newsletter influences the tone of your publication. Paragraphs can be aligned in a variety of ways: at the left margin; at the right margin; at both the left and right margins (justified); or centered between the margins, causing both the left and right margins to be ragged.

Align Left   Center

Align Right   Justify

Justified text (text that aligns at both the left and right margins) is common in publications such as textbooks, newspapers, newsletters, and magazines. It is more formal than left-aligned text, but for justified text to convey a professional appearance, the line length must be appropriate. If the line length is too short, the words and/ or characters in a paragraph may be widely spaced. Several consecutive lines with widely spaced areas can cause *rivers* of white space. Remedying this situation requires increasing the line length, changing to a smaller type size, and/or hyphenating long words. Text aligned at the left is the easiest to read and is popular for publications of all kinds. Center alignment should only be used for small blocks of text.

rivers
Channels of white space caused by numerous lines of text that are too widely spaced

Indenting Paragraphs with Em Spaces

In typesetting, tabs are generally measured by em spaces rather than inch measurements. An *em space* is a space as wide as the point size of the type. For example, if the type size is 12 points, an em space is 12 points wide. You should typically indent newsletter text by one or two em spaces.

em space
A space as wide as the point size of the type

Em space indentations can be created in two ways. One way to create an em space is to type an increment at the *Left* or *Right* indent measurement boxes in the Paragraph group on the PAGE LAYOUT tab. Alternatively, you can create an em space at the Tabs dialog box. In Exercise 6.1F, you will change the default tab setting to one and one half em space indentations for each paragraph preceded with a tab. You will do this by typing *18 pt* in the *Default tab stops* measurement box at the Tabs dialog box. Word will convert this point measurement to 0.25 inch because a horizontal inch contains 72 points. Be sure to use em spaces for any paragraph indentations used in newsletters. Also, use em spaces for spacing around bullets and any other indented text in newsletters.

Generally, the first paragraph after a headline or subhead is not indented even though all remaining paragraphs will have an em space paragraph indentation. Notice the paragraph formatting in Figure 6.8 on page 246.

Applying the Widow/Orphan Control Feature

The Widow/Orphan control feature in Word is turned on by default. This feature prevents the first and last lines of paragraphs from being separated across pages. A *widow* is a single line of a paragraph, headline, or subhead that is pushed to the top of the next page. A single line of text that appears by itself at the bottom of a page is called an *orphan*. The Widow/Orphan control option is located in the *Pagination* section of the Paragraph dialog box with the Line and Page Breaks tab selected.

widow
A single line of a paragraph or heading that is pushed to the top of the next page

Even with the Widow/Orphan control feature on, you should still watch for subheads that are inappropriately separated from text at the end of a column or page. To keep a heading or subhead with the text that follows it, consider inserting a check mark in the *Keep with next* check box in the Paragraph dialog box with the Line and Page Breaks tab selected. You can also select the text you want to keep together and then insert a check mark in the *Keep lines together* check box.

orphan
A single line of text appearing by itself at the bottom of a page

You will add body text to the Loaves & Fishes newsletter in Exercise 6.1F.

Exercise 6.1F **Creating Body Text for a Newsletter** **Part 6 of 8**

1. With **C06-E01-Byline.docx** open, save the document with the name **C06-E01-Body**.
2. Position the insertion point on the blank line below the byline text. Insert the text file **ClientChoice.docx** located in your Chapter06 folder.

3. Format the body text by completing the following steps:
   a. Select the text from *Saturday, September 12* to the end of the document and then verify that the font is 11-point Franklin Gothic Book.
   b. With the text still selected, click the Paragraph group dialog box launcher to display the Paragraph dialog box.
   c. Click the Tabs button located in the bottom left corner of the Paragraph dialog box.
   d. At the Tabs dialog box, type **18 pt** in the *Tab stop position* text box, make sure *Left* is selected in the *Alignment* section, and then click the Set button. (Eighteen points is one and one half em spaces, which is equal to approximately 0.25 inch.)
   e. Click OK to close the Tabs dialog box.
   f. Position the insertion point in front of each of the paragraphs (except the first paragraph) and then press the Tab key.
4. Create a style to format the body text by completing the following steps:
   a. Position the insertion point in one of the indented paragraphs in the body of the newsletter. ***Hint: Do not position the insertion point in the first paragraph, as this paragraph is not indented.***
   b. Click the More button in the Styles group and then click *Create a Style* at the drop-down gallery.
   c. At the Create New Style from Formatting dialog box, type **Body** in the *Name* text box, and then click OK. ***Hint: The Body style is added to the list of styles saved with this document.***
5. Add a drop cap to the first paragraph by completing the following steps:

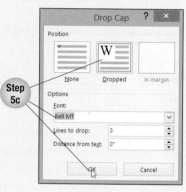

   a. Position the insertion point in the word *Saturday* in the first paragraph.
   b. Click the INSERT tab, click the Drop Cap button in the Text group, and then click *Drop Cap Options* at the drop-down list.
   c. At the Drop Cap dialog box, click the *Dropped* option in the *Position* section, change the *Font* option in the *Options* section to *Bell MT*, and then click OK.
6. Save **C06-E01-Body.docx**.

Creating Subheads for Newsletters

Subheads organize text and expand on headlines, giving readers more information or clues about the text. In addition, subheads also provide contrast on text-intensive pages. Marginal subheads are sometimes placed in the left margin or in a narrow column to the left of the body text, providing an airy, open appearance. Subheads can be set in a larger type size, different typeface, or heavier weight than the text. They can be centered, left aligned, right aligned, or formatted in shaded boxes.

Inserting and Editing Graphic Images in Newsletters

Graphic images are pictures or clip art added to a newsletter to support or expand on points made in the text. Choose graphic images carefully and use them sparingly. You can edit graphic images to make them more suitable for your particular newsletter, as you will do in Exercise 6.1G. Along with using buttons on the PICTURE TOOLS FORMAT tab to customize a picture (which you will learn more about in Chapter 8), you can also modify clip art by ungrouping it using Word as a picture editor or by using Windows Paint. You can also scan images by using Microsoft Fax and Scan.

Using Windows Paint for Images

Paint is a feature in Windows 8 that you can use to create drawings on a blank drawing area or in existing pictures. Many of the tools you use in Paint are found on the ribbon, which is near the top of the Paint window, as shown in Figure 6.10. Open Paint by displaying the Windows 8 Start screen, right-clicking anywhere in the Start screen background (not on a tile), clicking the All apps button located at the bottom right side of the Start screen, and then clicking the Paint tile located in the *Windows Accessories* section.

Using Windows Fax and Scan

You may want to scan predesigned company logos (with permission) or photographs that relate to the subject of your newsletter using Windows Fax and Scan, which is optimized for scanning, viewing, and storing text documents, as shown in Figure 6.11. Open Windows Fax and Scan by displaying the Windows 8 Start screen, right-clicking anywhere in the Start screen background (not on a tile), clicking the All apps button located at the bottom right side of the Start screen, and then clicking the Windows Fax and Scan tile located in the *Windows Accessories* section.

Figure 6.10 Using Windows Paint

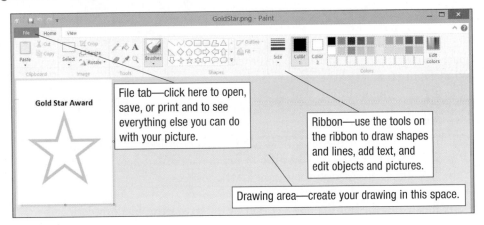

Figure 6.11 Using Windows Fax and Scan

1. With **C06-E01-Body.docx** open, save the document with the name **C06-E01-Graphics**.
2. Position the insertion point at the beginning of the second column of text. (If necessary, turn on the display of nonprinting characters to determine where the column begins.)
3. Insert the image of a shopping cart, as shown in Figure 6.8 on page 246, by completing the following steps:

    a. Click the INSERT tab and then click the Online Pictures button in the Illustrations group.

    b. Type **shopping cart** in the *Office.com Clip Art* text box, press the Enter key, and then double-click the image shown at the right. (Insert a similar image if this one is not available.)

    c. With the image selected, click the Color button in the Adjust group on the PICTURE TOOLS FORMAT tab and then click *Gold, Accent color 6 Light* (last column, last row in the *Recolor* section).

    d. With the image selected, click the Rotate button in the Arrange group and then click *Flip Horizontal* at the drop-down gallery. ***Note: You almost always want graphics to face the text.***

    e. Change the height and width of the image to 2.1 inches.

    f. Apply Square text wrapping to the image and then position it as shown in Figure 6.8.

    g. Turn on the display of nonprinting characters and then make sure a paragraph symbol displays below the image. If not, move the image up until the paragraph symbol displays below it.

    h. Position the insertion point at the beginning of the paragraph located below the image, click the PAGE LAYOUT tab, type **18** in the *Before* measurement box in the *Spacing* section in the Paragraph group, and then press Enter.

    i. Turn off the display of nonprinting characters.

4. Insert the text box located in the bottom right corner of the newsletter by completing the following steps:

    a. With the insertion point positioned on the line below the image, click the INSERT tab, click the Text Box button in the Text group, click the *Draw Text Box* option at the drop-down list, and then click in the document immediately to the right of the insertion point.

    b. Change the height of the text box to 2 inches and the width to 2.4 inches.

    c. With the insertion point positioned in the text box, change the spacing after paragraphs to 0 points, change the paragraph alignment to center, and then type the following:

    Our Vision (Press Enter.)
    Ending Hunger in Our Community (Press Enter two times.)
    Our Mission (Press Enter.)
    Loaves & Fishes provides food and leadership in the community by uniting and mobilizing resources to empower people to be self-sufficient.

    d. Select *Our Vision,* hold down the Ctrl key and select *Our Mission,* apply bold formatting, and then change the font color to the green color used earlier in the newsletter (Red 56, Green 140, Blue 78).

e. Select *Loaves*, apply bold formatting, and then change the font color to *Gold, Accent 6*.

f. Select *& Fishes*, apply bold formatting, and then change the font color to the green color used in Step 4d.

g. Click the text box border to select the text box, click the Borders button arrow in the Paragraph group on the HOME tab, and then click *Borders and Shading* at the drop-down list.

h. At the Borders and Shading dialog box, change the *Color* option to the green color used in this newsletter, change the *Width* option to *4 ½ pt*, and then click the top border in the *Preview* section.

i. Change the *Color* option to *Gold, Accent 6*, change the *Width* to *2 ¼ pt*, click the bottom border in the *Preview* section, and then click OK to close the dialog box.

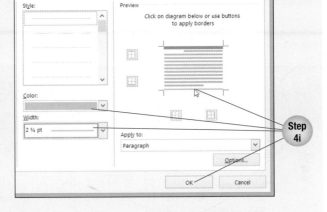

j. Remove the shape outline from the text box.

k. Apply Square text wrapping to the text box.

l. Position the image near the center of the right column, as shown in Figure 6.8.

5. Insert a column break by completing the following steps:

a. Position the insertion point at the beginning of the last paragraph in the left column (begins *All distribution sessions*). Make sure the insertion point is positioned at the left margin (before the tab) rather than in the first word.

b. Click the PAGE LAYOUT tab, click the Breaks button in the Page Setup group, and then click the *Column* option in the *Page Breaks* section of the drop-down list. The last paragraph of text should now display just below the shopping cart image in the right column. If necessary, reposition the shopping cart image and text box so that they appear as shown in Figure 6.8.

6. Save **C06-E01-Graphics.docx**.

Mailing a Newsletter

In Exercise 6.1H, you will format the back of the newsletter you created in this chapter to create a self-mailer. A **self-mailer** is a document that can be mailed without the use of an envelope. After you create the self-mailer, you will insert merge codes into the self-mailer section of the newsletter and then merge the newsletter with an existing data source file. Use options on the MAILINGS tab to merge a newsletter with a data source file. After completing the merge, fold the newsletter to send it through the mail. Before mailing a self-mailer newsletter, fold the newsletter in half and attach a label to bind the halves together. Figure 6.12 on page 260 illustrates a label option, measuring 1.5 inches by 1.5 inches, that can be used as a bind for a folded newsletter. Even though the USPS allows some staples in mail, it is better not to use staples to close your mail pieces. Staples can slow down sorting and delivery; they may require the mail piece to be handled manually instead of automatically, and therefore increase the cost of processing the mailing.

self-mailer
A document that can be mailed without the use of an envelope

Figure 6.12 Creating Round Labels to Bind a Folded Newsletter

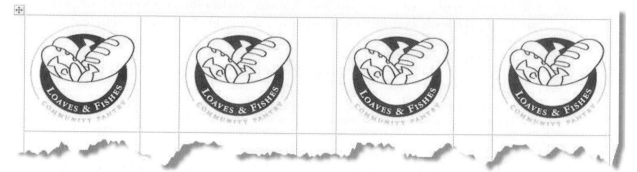

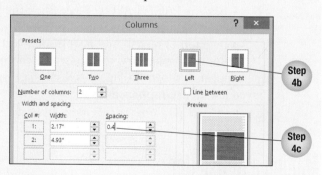

Exercise 6.1H Changing the Newsletter Layout
and Merging to a Data Source   Part 8 of 8

PORTFOLIO

1. With **C06-E01-Graphics.docx** open, save the document with the name **C06-E01-Loaves&FishesNewsletter**.
2. Press Ctrl + End to position the insertion point at the end of the document (above the vision text box), click the INSERT tab, and then click the Page Break button in the Pages group. *Hint: If the hard returns at the bottom of the first page automatically generate another page, you will not need to insert a page break.*
3. Click the PAGE LAYOUT tab, click the Breaks button in the Page Setup group, and then click the *Continuous* option in the *Section Breaks* section of the drop-down list.
4. Change the column layout by completing the following steps:
   a. Click the Columns button in the Page Setup group and then click *More Columns* at the drop-down list.
   b. Click *Left* in the *Presets* section.
   c. Type **0.4** in the *Spacing* measurement box for column 1 in the *Width and spacing* section.
   d. Click OK to close the dialog box.
5. Insert the text box shown in the left column of page 2 in Figure 6.8 on page 246 by completing the following steps:
   a. With the insertion point positioned in the left column of the second page, click the INSERT tab, click the Text Box button in the Text group, scroll down the drop-down list, click *Draw Text Box*, and then click in the document to the right of the insertion point.
   b. Change the height of the text box to 2.2 inches and change the width to 2.4 inches.

   c. With the insertion point positioned in the text box, change the spacing after paragraphs to 0 points, change the paragraph alignment to center, and then type the following text:

> **Loaves & Fishes** (Press Enter.)
> **556 West Fifth Avenue** (Press Enter.)
> **Naperville, IL 60563** (Press Enter.)
> **Phone: 630.555.FOOD** (Press Enter.)
> **Fax: 630.555.5738** (Press Enter.)
> **loaves&fishes@emcp.com** (Press Enter.)
> **www.loaves.emcp.net** (Press Enter.)
> **As we are a registered 501(c)(3) charity, all donations are fully tax deductible.**
> *Hint: If the (c) changes automatically to a copyright symbol, immediately press Ctrl + Z to undo the change. Also, allow the email address and web address to display automatically as hyperlinks (light green text with an underline).*

   d. Apply the green and gold font colors and then apply bold formatting, as shown in Figure 6.8.

   e. Apply the green 4 ½ point border to the top of the text box and the gold 2 ¼ point border to the bottom of the text box, as instructed in Steps 4g through 4i in Exercise 6.1G.

   f. Remove the shape outline from the text box.

   g. Apply Square text wrapping to the text box and then position it as shown in Figure 6.8.

6. Create the text in the next column by completing the following steps:

   a. Position the insertion point below the text box on the second page and then press Ctrl + Shift + Enter to move the insertion point to the top of the next column. If necessary, move the text box back to the left side of the document and make sure it is positioned above the column break. You may need to turn on the display of nonprinting characters to view the column break.

   b. At the top of the right column, type **Client Nutrition and Supply** and then press Enter.

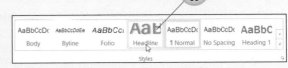

Step 6c

   c. Position the insertion point in *Client Nutrition and Supply* and then click the *Headline* option in the Styles group.

   d. Click below the heading and then insert **NutritionandSupply.docx**, located in your Chapter06 folder.

   e. Select *By Jody Bender* and then apply the Byline style in the Styles group.

   f. Select the article text and then apply the Body style in the Styles group.

   g. Position the insertion point in the word *The*, the first word in the first paragraph, and then insert a drop cap in the Bell MT font that is dropped into the paragraph.

7. Create the mailing text by completing the following steps:

   a. Position the insertion point at the end of the nutrition and supply text (after the period that follows *upon the available supply*).

   b. Click the PAGE LAYOUT tab, click the Breaks button in the Page Setup group, and then click the *Continuous* option in the *Section Breaks* section.

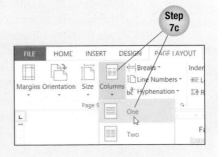

Step 7c

   c. Click the Columns button in the Page Setup group and then click *One* at the drop-down list.

   d. Insert **Loaves&FishesColor.png** from your Chapter06 folder.

   e. With the logo selected, click the Color button in the Adjust group on the PICTURE TOOLS FORMAT tab, click *Set Transparent Color* at the drop-down gallery, and then click to the left or right of the fish images to remove the light gray background.

f. Change the text wrapping to *Square* and then size and position the logo as shown on the second page in Figure 6.8.

g. Draw a text box for the Loaves & Fishes return address as shown in Figure 6.8.

➥ h. Type the return address text in the text box. (Refer to Figure 6.8 for the return address text or see Step 5c of this exercise. Press Shift + Enter at the end of each line of the address.)

i. Remove the shape fill and shape outline from the text box.

j. Position the text box to the right of the logo, as shown in the figure.

k. Draw another text box for the merged mailing addresses in a location similar to that shown in Figure 6.8.

8. Insert the merge codes by completing the following steps:

a. Position the insertion point inside the mailing address text box, click the MAILINGS tab, and then click the Start Mail Merge button in the Start Mail Merge group.

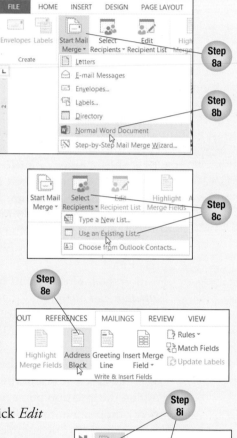

b. Click *Normal Word Document* at the drop-down list.

c. Click the Select Recipients button in the Start Mail Merge group and then click *Use an Existing List* at the drop-down list.

d. Select **NaperGrovePatients.mdb** from your Chapter06 folder.

e. Click in the empty mailing address text box, if necessary, and then click the Address Block button in the Write & Insert Fields group.

f. At the Insert Address Block dialog box, click OK.

g. Select the «Address Block» merge code in the text box, click the PAGE LAYOUT tab, type **0** in the *After* measurement box in the *Spacing* section in the Paragraph group, and then press Enter. (This results in single spacing the addresses.)

h. Remove the shape fill and shape outline from the text box.

i. Click the Finish & Merge button in the Finish group on the MAILINGS tab and then click *Edit Individual Documents* at the drop-down list.

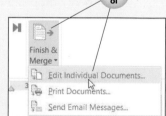

j. Make sure *All* is selected in the *Merge records* section of the Merge to New Document dialog box and then click OK.

9. Save the merged newsletter with the name **C06-E01-MergedNewsletter**.

10. Print only the merged newsletter addressed to Jansen Dell and then close **C06-E01-MergedNewsletter.docx**.

11. Save **C06-E01-Loaves&FishesNewsletter.docx**.

12. *Optional:* Create a circular label to be used when the newsletter is folded in half and sent through the mail. At a blank document, display the Label Options dialog box, choose the Avery US Letter - 8293 High Visibility Round Labels, and then insert the **Loaves&Fishes .png** black and white circular logo from your Chapter06 folder. Save the label as **C06-E01-MailingLabel**. Print and then attach the label to the folded newsletter.

Saving a Newsletter as a Template

To save time in creating future issues of your newsletter, save your newsletter as a template. To do this, delete all text, pictures, and objects that will not stay the same for future issues. Conversely, leave the nameplate and all of its text, pictures, symbols, and so on, that will remain the same (or use the same style) in each issue of your newsletter. For example, to save the Loaves & Fishes newsletter as a template, leave the following items and delete the rest:

- Folio (The month and volume/issue numbers will change, but the titles will remain—use the folio text as placeholder text.)

- Nameplate

- Subtitle

- Headlinc (The headline text will change, but the position and formatting will remain—use the headline text as placeholder text.)

- Byline (The byline text will change, but the position and formatting will remain—use the byline text as placeholder text.)

- Body text (The body text will change, but the formatting will remain—leave a paragraph as placeholder text.)

After you have deleted the text and elements that will change with each issue and replaced them with placeholders (if desired), press F12 to display the Save As dialog box. At the Save As dialog box, change the *Save as type* option to *Word Template (*.dotx)*. Navigate to the folder in which you want to save your newsletter template (consult your instructor as to where to save your template) type a name for your template, and then click the Save button.

Chapter Summary

➤ Newsletter elements divide the newsletter into organized sections to help the reader understand the text. Basic newsletter elements include a nameplate, logo, subtitle, folio, headline, subhead, byline, body text, and graphic image.

➤ The nameplate, or banner, consists of the newsletter's title and is usually located on the front page.

➤ A subtitle is a short phrase describing the purpose or audience of the newsletter.

➤ A folio is the publication information, including the volume number, issue number, and the current date of the newsletter.

➤ Headlines are titles to articles and are frequently created to attract the reader's attention.

➤ Subheads, or subheadings, are secondary headings that provide the transition from headlines to body text.

➤ The byline identifies the author of an article.

➤ The main part of the newsletter is the body text or body copy.

➤ Graphic images are added to newsletters to help stimulate ideas and add interest to the document.

➤ The margin size for a newsletter is linked to the number of columns needed, formality desired, visual elements used, and amount of text available. Keep margins consistent in a newsletter.

➤ If you plan to create a multiple-paged newsletter with facing pages, you may want to use the Word mirror margins feature, which accommodates wider inside or outside margins.

➤ Focus and balance can be achieved in a newsletter through the design and size of the nameplate; use of graphic images; and careful use of lines, borders, and backgrounds.

➤ The line length of text in a newsletter can enhance or detract from the readability of the text.

➤ Setting text in columns may improve the readability of newsletters.

➤ The columns on the last page of a document can be balanced by inserting a continuous section break at the end of the text.

➤ Section breaks are used to vary the page layout within a single newsletter.

➤ Tombstoning occurs when headings display side by side in adjacent columns.

➤ Styles assist in maintaining consistency in recurring elements.

➤ Styles are created for a particular document and are saved with the document.

➤ Indent paragraphs in a newsletter with em spaces. An em space is as wide as the point size of the type.

➤ Create a newsletter as a self-mailer, which is is document that can be mailed without the use of an envelope.

➤ To establish consistency from one issue to the next and to save time, save your newsletter as a template.

Commands Review

FEATURE	RIBBON TAB, GROUP	BUTTON	KEYBOARD SHORTCUT
align center	HOME, Paragraph		Ctrl + E
align left	HOME, Paragraph		Ctrl + L
align right	HOME, Paragraph		Ctrl + R
column break	PAGE LAYOUT, Page Setup	, *Column*	
columns	PAGE LAYOUT, Page Setup		
continuous section break	PAGE LAYOUT, Page Setup	, *Continuous*	
justify	HOME, Paragraph		Ctrl + J
margins	PAGE LAYOUT, Page Setup		
styles	HOME, Styles		

Key Points Review

True or False: Select the correct answer by circling T or F.

1. A folio provides information that describes the purpose of the newsletter and/or the intended audience of the newsletter. T F

2. Column formatting affects the entire document unless your document is divided into sections. T F

3. The columns on the last page can be balanced by inserting a column break at the end of the text. T F

4. Tombstoning occurs when headings display side by side in adjacent columns. T F

5. Word's mirror margins feature accommodates wider inside and outside margins. T F

6. If the type size in a document is 12 points, then an em space is 24 points wide. T F

7. After a style has been created, the only way to change the style is to rename it and create it again. T F

8. A byline identifies the author of an article. T F

9. A template is a document that can be mailed without the use of an envelope. T F

10. A graphic image is a newsletter element that organizes text and expands on headlines. T F

11. The headline in a newsletter organizes text and helps readers decide whether they want to read the article. T F

12. Paint is a feature in Windows 8 that you can use to create drawings on a blank drawing area or in existing pictures. T F

13. A single line of a paragraph that displays on the top of the next page is referred to as an orphan. T F

14. The banner is a lead-in to the content of the paragraph following it. T F

15. When you save existing formatting as a style, it is added to the list of styles for that document. T F

Chapter *Assessments*

Assessment 6.1 Create Original Nameplates

Design and then create two nameplates (including subtitle, folio, graphics, and/or logo) for two newsletters for organizations, schools, or businesses (real or fictional).

1. Prepare thumbnail sketches of your designs. Create one nameplate using an asymmetrical design. Also, include a graphic image, WordArt, or special character symbol in at least one of the nameplates.
2. Save the first nameplate document with the name **C06-A01-NameplateA**.
3. Print and then close **C06-A01-NameplateA.docx**. Attach your thumbnail sketch of this design to the printout.
4. Save the second nameplate document with the name **C06-A01-NameplateB**.
5. Print and then close **C06-A01-NameplateB.docx**. Attach your thumbnail sketch of this design to the printout.

Assessment 6.2 Create a Newsletter for an Optometrist

In Assessment 6.2, you will create a newsletter for Naper Grove Vision Care that will be distributed to patients. Figure 6.13 on page 268 is provided as a sample newsletter. Create a newsletter using your own design ideas and knowledge of newsletter concepts and Word features presented in this chapter. Include the following specifications:

1. Prepare a thumbnail sketch of your design.
2. Create an attention-getting nameplate.
3. Use appropriate fonts and text effects.
4. Insert **FocalPoints.docx** located in your Chapter06 folder.
5. Consider using a photo and adding picture effects.
6. *Optional:* Include an inspirational, popular, or thought-provoking quotation at the end of your newsletter. Books of popular quotations are available at your public library, school library, and on the Internet (use a search engine and search for quotes).
7. Save your newsletter with the name **C06-A02-Eyes**.
8. Print and then close **C06-A02-Eyes.docx**. Attach your thumbnail sketch.

Figure 6.13 Sample Solution for Assessment 6.2

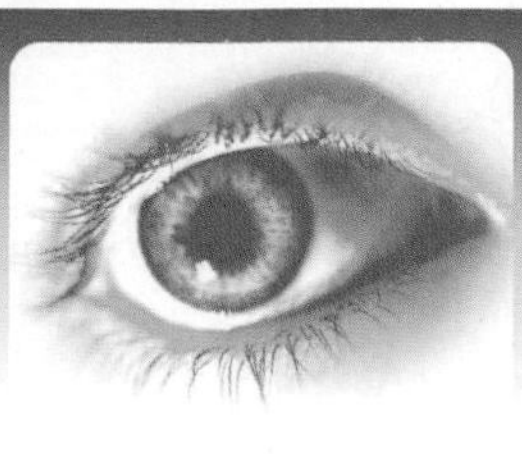

FOCAL POINTS

An informative newsletter from Drs. Sims, Giancola, Kampschroeder, and Halkias

Fall 2015

DON'T LOSE SIGHT OF DIABETIC EYE DISEASE

As part of National Diabetes Month in November, the Federal government's National Eye Institute and the American Academy of Optometry are continuing their efforts to focus upon the importance of yearly-dilated eye exams for people with diabetes. These efforts are part of an ongoing campaign called "Don't Lose Sight of Diabetic Eye Disease," sponsored by the National Eye Health Education Program Partnership.

During their lifetime, nearly half of the nation's estimated 16 million people with diabetes will develop some degree of diabetic retinopathy, the most common form of diabetic eye disease. Diabetic retinopathy damages the tiny blood vessels in the retina, the light-sensitive tissue that lines the back of the eye. As many as 25,000 people annually go blind from the disorder, making it a leading cause of blindness among working-age Americans. Diabetic eye disease can be detected through a dilated eye examination, which is recommended at least once a year. If discovered in time, severe vision loss or blindness can be prevented.

For more information or to learn more about diabetic eye disease call our office or write: National Eye Health Education Program, 2020 Vision Place, Bethesda, MD 20892-3655.

LASER VISION CORRECTION NEWS

Of all the Refractive Surgery options available currently, the two most common and most successful are PRK (Photo Refractive Keratectomy) and Lasik (Laser Assisted In-Situ Keratomileusis). PRK is a refractive surgery that attempts to surgically correct myopia (nearsightedness) at the corneal plane by laser removal of corneal tissue. PRK has been performed since 1992 and is gaining worldwide acceptance.

Lasik is a laser procedure, which can reshape the surface of the eye in order to reduce the amount of refractive error and is most advantageous for patients who have moderate to high levels of myopia. Documentation and research is available to substantiate the effectiveness of Lasik.

Our doctors will gladly meet with you to discuss laser vision options and answer any questions you may have. If you are a candidate for laser surgery; we will refer you to a prominent surgeon for the procedure and co-manage all post-operative care with you and the surgeon.

"WHEN A MAN IS OUT OF SIGHT, IT IS NOT TOO LONG BEFORE HE IS OUT OF MIND."

-VICTOR HUGO

5018 Fairview Avenue
Downers Grove, IL 60515
(630) 555-3268

Naper Grove Vision Care
29 S. Webster, Suite 200
Naperville, IL 60540
(630) 555-3511

Assessment 6.3 Complete a Mail Merge in a Newsletter

INTEGRATED

In this assessment, you will open a Word document and then merge it with a data source file (Access database). You will print two copies of the Naper Grove newsletter created in Assessment 6.2 and then print the first page of the merged document on the back of one copy, and the last page of the merged document on the back of the second copy. Figure 6.14 on page 270 shows how the back of the first copy will look when you are finished. To create the merged document and print the necessary pages, complete the following steps:

1. Print two copies of the Naper Grove newsletter, **C06-A02-Eyes.docx**. You will print on the back of these copies in Step 8.
2. Open **NGAddressMain.docx** from your Chapter06 folder and save it with the name **C06-A03-NGAddressMain**.
3. Click the MAILINGS tab, click the Select Recipients button in the Start Mail Merge group, and then click *Use an Existing List* at the drop-down list. At the Select Data Source dialog box, navigate to your Chapter06 folder and then double-click ***NaperGrovePatients.mdb***.
4. Position your insertion point inside the text box that displays at the right of the clip art image located toward the bottom of the document and then click the Address Block button in the Write & Insert Fields group on the MAILINGS tab. At the Insert Address Block dialog box, click OK.
5. Remove the address text box shape outline.
6. Click the Finish & Merge button in the Finish group on the MAILINGS tab. At the Merge to New Document dialog box, make sure *All* is selected and then click OK.
7. Save the merged letters with the name **C06-A03-NGAddresses**.
8. Print the first merged letter to the back of one copy of **C06-A02-Eyes.docx** and the last merged letter to the back of the second copy of that document.
9. Close **C06-A03-NGAddresses.docx** and then fold each newsletter with the address displaying on the outside so that they are ready to mail.
10. Save and then close **C06-A03-NGAddressMain**.

Figure 6.14 Completed Back of First Copy in Assessment 6.3

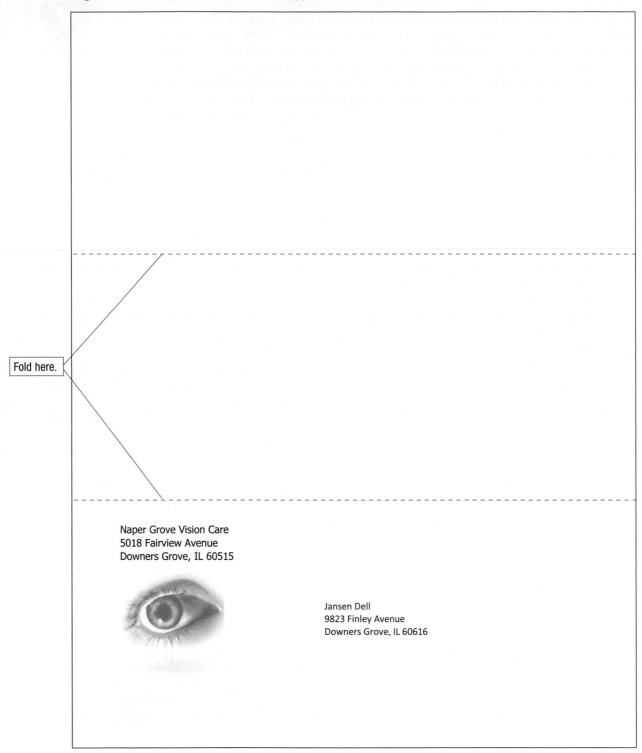

Fold here.

Naper Grove Vision Care
5018 Fairview Avenue
Downers Grove, IL 60515

Jansen Dell
9823 Finley Avenue
Downers Grove, IL 60616

Assessment 6.4   Re-create a Newsletter

Open and then print a copy of **ButterfieldGardens.docx**, located in your Chapter06 folder. As a group project, assign tasks for each of the members of your group to evaluate the newsletter in this assessment, discuss the necessary changes, and then re-create the document. Assume you received this newsletter in the mail as a marketing promotional document. The newsletter looks relatively neat and organized, but with closer inspection, you notice there are a few errors in spelling, formatting, layout, and design. Re-create the newsletter according to the following specifications, using your own ideas for an interesting newsletter layout and design:

1. Prepare a thumbnail sketch of your design.
2. Re-create the nameplate or create a nameplate (logo, subtitle, folio) of your own for this company; consider using WordArt in your nameplate design. ***Hint: The Butterfield Gardens logo is located in your Chapter06 folder.***
3. Create a different layout and design for the newsletter using newspaper columns. Use more than one column in an asymmetrical design or consider using a template from Office.com.
4. Correct all spelling and formatting errors. ***Hint: The document contains several errors.***
5. Use any graphics that support your design. Consider using a graphic or photo from the Internet.
6. Consider inserting a shape or chart.
7. Use any newsletter elements and enhancements that will improve the effectiveness and appeal of this newsletter. ***Hint: Remember to kern character pairs and condense or expand characters if necessary.***
8. Save the publication with the name **C06-A04-Butterfield**.
9. Print and then close **C06-A04-Butterfield.docx**. Attach the thumbnail sketch to the back of the newsletter.

Chapter 7

Using Design Elements to Enhance Newsletters

Performance Objectives

Upon successful completion of Chapter 7, you will be able to:

- Define and create design elements that enhance newsletter content
- Create headers and footers
- Create a table of contents
- Insert sidebars and pull quotes
- Create kickers and end signs
- Create linked text boxes
- Insert a jump line

- Use scanned or downloaded images
- Add captions to pictures
- Create a masthead
- Use copyfitting techniques
- Send a newsletter as an email attachment
- Save a newsletter in HTML and view it in an Internet browser

Desktop Publishing Terms

caption	jump line	pull quote	sidebar
copyfitting	kicker	scanner	spot color
end sign	masthead	screening	table of contents
HTML	MHTML		

Word Features Used

borders and shading	linked text boxes	quick parts	templates
building blocks	page numbers	styles	text boxes
captions	pictures	symbols	Web Page Preview
headers and footers			

Note: Before beginning computer exercises for this chapter, copy to your storage medium the Chapter07 folder from the CD that accompanies this textbook and then make Chapter07 the active folder. Remember to substitute for graphics that may no longer be available.

Understanding Newsletter Design and Formatting Techniques

Chapter 6 introduced the basic design elements and formatting techniques used in creating a newsletter. In this chapter, you will learn about additional design elements to include in a newsletter, as well as new ways to format the content of a newsletter to maximize its impact on the intended audience.

Understanding Advanced Newsletter Design Elements

The most effective newsletters contain an appealing and well-positioned blend of text and visual elements. As illustrated in Figure 7.1, visual elements such as a table of contents, kicker, and sidebar can be used as focal points to draw the reader into the content of the newsletter. Other design elements such as headlines, subheads, ruled lines, jump lines, and end signs can be used to indicate the directional flow of information in the document, and still others, such as page borders and pull quotes, can be used to provide balance, proportion, and contrast in a newsletter. All of these elements, if used in a consistent format and manner, can create unity within a single newsletter and among different issues of a newsletter.

Formatting a Newsletter Using Columns, Text Boxes, and Tables

The majority of newsletters are formatted in a two- or three-column layout. As discussed in Chapter 6, these columns can be equal in width, providing a symmetrical design, or they can be of varying widths, providing an asymmetrical design. In Word, three methods are available for creating the appearance of columns in a newsletter layout—columns, text boxes, and tables. Your challenge is to determine which method (or combination of methods) will work best to achieve the desired results in your newsletter.

Using the columns feature may seem like the simplest choice, especially when laying out a newsletter similar to those created in Chapter 6. However, placing text within text boxes or tables can allow you to more easily change the position or dimensions of an article, as is often required when trying to arrange elements in a newsletter. Another benefit to using text boxes is that they can be linked to one another, a feature you will learn more about later in this chapter.

In the newsletter in Figure 7.1, a text box with a shadow border was used to create the sidebar, and a table with a top border was used to create the table of contents. The second column of the newsletter was created by placing each article within a separate table. The dark blue line between the articles was created using a line shape, and it acts as a visual separator between the blocks of text (tables). In this case, tables were chosen over text boxes because of the graphics and pull quote that accompany the articles. In a table, text will wrap around a graphic or text box inserted in a cell, whereas text will not wrap around elements, such as shapes and additional text boxes, if the original text is also contained within a text box. Compared with text boxes, however, tables are not as easy to position and they may produce unpredictable results if you try to insert a text box within the table.

As another example, look at Figure 7.6 on page 281. To accommodate the bicycle safety article (on page 1 of the newsletter) and the text wrapping around the pull quote, the columns feature was used to create an asymmetrical two-column layout. All of the remaining articles and features are contained in text boxes.

Figure 7.1 Identifying Design Elements in a Newsletter

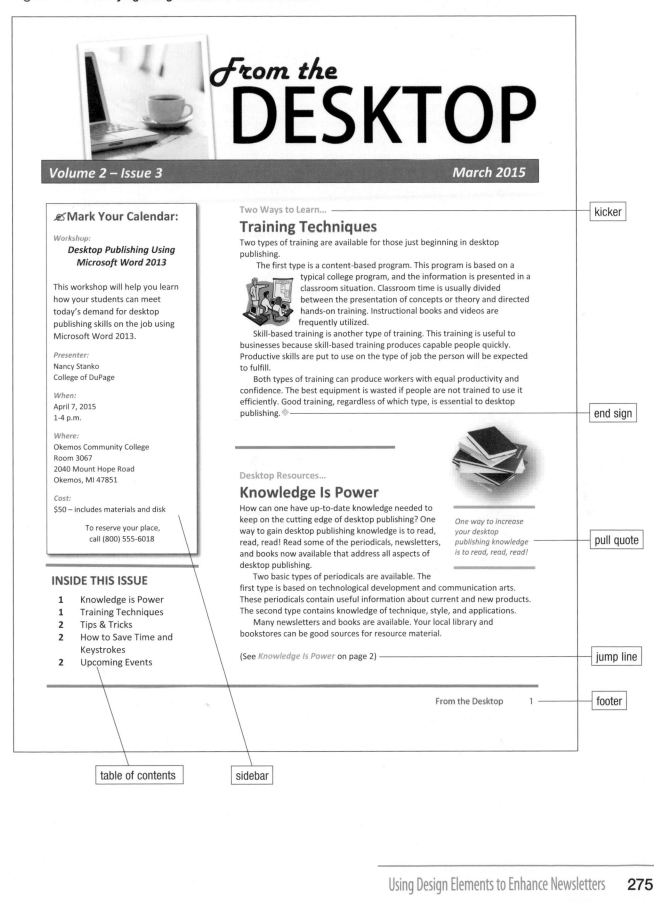

From the DESKTOP

Volume 2 – Issue 3   March 2015

✍ **Mark Your Calendar:**

Workshop:
Desktop Publishing Using Microsoft Word 2013

This workshop will help you learn how your students can meet today's demand for desktop publishing skills on the job using Microsoft Word 2013.

Presenter:
Nancy Stanko
College of DuPage

When:
April 7, 2015
1-4 p.m.

Where:
Okemos Community College
Room 3067
2040 Mount Hope Road
Okemos, MI 47851

Cost:
$50 – includes materials and disk

To reserve your place,
call (800) 555-6018

INSIDE THIS ISSUE

1   Knowledge is Power
1   Training Techniques
2   Tips & Tricks
2   How to Save Time and Keystrokes
2   Upcoming Events

Two Ways to Learn... ———————————————— kicker

Training Techniques

Two types of training are available for those just beginning in desktop publishing.

The first type is a content-based program. This program is based on a typical college program, and the information is presented in a classroom situation. Classroom time is usually divided between the presentation of concepts or theory and directed hands-on training. Instructional books and videos are frequently utilized.

Skill-based training is another type of training. This training is useful to businesses because skill-based training produces capable people quickly. Productive skills are put to use on the type of job the person will be expected to fulfill.

Both types of training can produce workers with equal productivity and confidence. The best equipment is wasted if people are not trained to use it efficiently. Good training, regardless of which type, is essential to desktop publishing. ◈ ———————————————— end sign

Desktop Resources...

Knowledge Is Power

How can one have up-to-date knowledge needed to keep on the cutting edge of desktop publishing? One way to gain desktop publishing knowledge is to read, read, read! Read some of the periodicals, newsletters, and books now available that address all aspects of desktop publishing.

One way to increase your desktop publishing knowledge is to read, read, read! ———————————————— pull quote

Two basic types of periodicals are available. The first type is based on technological development and communication arts. These periodicals contain useful information about current and new products. The second type contains knowledge of technique, style, and applications.

Many newsletters and books are available. Your local library and bookstores can be good sources for resource material.

(See *Knowledge Is Power* on page 2) ———————————————— jump line

table of contents   sidebar

Using Newsletter Templates from Office.com

While creating your own newsletter template gives you more control over the design and layout of the document, it can be a time-consuming process. To save time, you may choose to use one of the newsletter templates from Office.com that are available at the New backstage area, as shown in Figure 7.2. (Note that the number of available newsletter templates may vary, because new ones are occasionally added to the collection.)

When you preview the Office.com templates in Word, you will find that most of them use linked text boxes as their underlying structure. The newsletter templates are also formatted using styles to reinforce consistency. In addition, the basic design and colors used in each newsletter stay consistent from page to page, and each newsletter includes many preformatted design elements such as nameplates, tables of contents, pull quotes, picture captions, headers and footers, and sidebars, as shown in Figure 7.3.

Figure 7.2 Choosing Newsletter Templates at the New Backstage Area

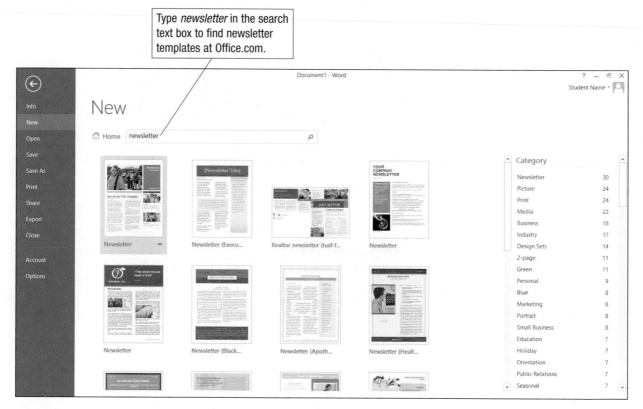

Type *newsletter* in the search text box to find newsletter templates at Office.com.

Figure 7.3 Viewing Design Elements in Word Newsletter Templates from Office.com

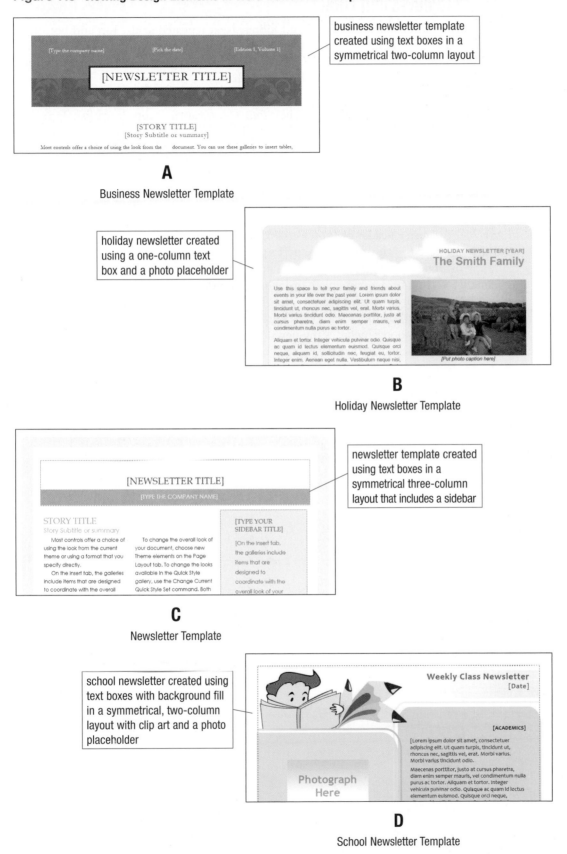

business newsletter template created using text boxes in a symmetrical two-column layout

A

Business Newsletter Template

holiday newsletter created using a one-column text box and a photo placeholder

B

Holiday Newsletter Template

newsletter template created using text boxes in a symmetrical three-column layout that includes a sidebar

C

Newsletter Template

school newsletter created using text boxes with background fill in a symmetrical, two-column layout with clip art and a photo placeholder

D

School Newsletter Template

Creating Headers and Footers

As you learned in Chapter 3, headers and footers (text repeated at the top and bottom of every page) are commonly used in newsletters, manuscripts, textbooks, reports, and other publications. A predesigned header or footer can be inserted in a document or you can create your own header or footer from scratch.

To create a header from scratch, click the INSERT tab, click the Header button in the Header & Footer group, and then click *Edit Header* at the drop-down list. Type text or insert objects in the Header pane and then click the Close Header and Footer button in the Close group on the HEADER & FOOTER TOOLS DESIGN tab. Complete similar steps to create a footer from scratch.

In a newsletter, information such as the page number, a slogan, the name of the newsletter, the issue number or date of the newsletter, and the name of the organization producing the newsletter are commonly placed in the header or footer, as illustrated in Figure 7.4. Because a header or footer is commonly repeated on every page (starting with the second page), it provides the perfect place to reinforce the identity of a company or organization. For example, including the company or organization name or a smaller version of the nameplate or logo in a header or footer can increase the reader's awareness of the brand identity. In Figure 7.4A, the Ride Safe header (the third header from the top) includes both the company logo and slogan. In Figure 7.4B, the Community News footer includes the newsletter name and the page number set in reversed text in a green bar that ties in the colors used throughout the newsletter.

DTP POINTER
Use a header or footer to reinforce company or organizational identity.

DTP POINTER
Consistent formatting of a header and footer helps to establish unity in a publication.

Figure 7.4 Illustrating Examples of Headers and Footers

A
Header Examples

B
Footer Examples

Creating Different Headers and Footers within a Newsletter

By default, Word inserts a header and/or footer on every page in the document. However, you can create different headers and footers within the same document. For example, you can:

- create a unique header or footer on the first page
- omit a header or footer on the first page
- create different headers or footers for odd and even pages
- create different headers or footers for different sections in a document

To create a different header or footer on the first page of a multiple-page document, position the insertion point anywhere in the header or footer on the first page and then click the *Different First Page* check box in the Options group on the HEADER & FOOTER TOOLS DESIGN tab to insert a check mark. The Header pane on the first page will be labeled *First Page Header,* and the Footer pane on the first page will be labeled *First Page Footer.* If you do not want a header or footer on the first page, leave the First Page Header and First Page Footer panes blank. If you do want a header or footer on the first page, type the text for the header or footer and then click the Next button in the Navigation group to move to the Header or Footer pane on the second page of the document. (Click the Previous button if you need to edit the first page header or footer after moving to the second page.) Type the text you want to include in the header or footer for all other pages in the document. Use the Go to Header or Go to Footer button in the Navigation group to move back and forth between the Header and Footer panes. When you are finished creating and editing headers and footers, click the Close Header and Footer button in the Close group.

The ability to use different headers and footers on odd and even pages is useful when inserting page numbers in a multiple-page newsletter that has spreads (pages that face one another). Odd page numbers can be placed on the right side of the page, and even page numbers can be placed on the left side of the page. To create different odd and even page headers and footers, insert a check mark in the *Different Odd & Even Pages* check box in the Options group on the HEADER & FOOTER TOOLS DESIGN tab. Remember to keep the formatting consistent for both the odd and even page headers and footers.

When starting a new section of your newsletter, you may want to create a new header or footer just for that section. If you want a header or footer to print in only a specific section and not on pages in the previous sections, you must turn off the Link to Previous feature. This tells Word that the new header or footer only applies to this section and not to any previous sections. Break a section link by clicking the Link to Previous button in the Navigation group on the HEADER & FOOTER TOOLS DESIGN tab.

Next

Previous

Close Header and Footer

◀ **DTP POINTER**

Right pages should have odd page numbers and left pages should have even page numbers.

Link to Previous

Saving Headers and Footers

A header you create from scratch is saved with the document. If you want to make the header available for future documents, save the header as a building block in the Header gallery. To do this, select the header, click the Header button on the HEADER & FOOTER TOOLS DESIGN tab, and then click *Save Selection to Header Gallery* at the drop-down list. At the Create New Building Block dialog box, type a name for the header in the *Name* text box and then click OK. Complete similar steps to save a footer in the Footer gallery. A header you save to the Header gallery is available at the Header button drop-down list or at the Building Blocks Organizer dialog box. A footer you save to the Footer gallery is available at the Footer button drop-down list or at the Building Blocks Organizer dialog box.

Adding Spot Color to a Newsletter

spot color

One color added as an accent in a black-and-white publication

Adding **spot color** refers to using one color as an accent in a black-and-white publication. Spot color can be applied to such elements as ruled lines, graphic images, borders, background fill, headings, special characters, and end signs, as shown in Figure 7.5A. You can also apply spot color to the background of a text box or to a drop cap. If your logo or organizational seal contains a particular color, you may choose to use that color as a unifying element throughout your publication. Variations of a spot color can be obtained by **screening**, or producing a lighter shade of the same color. Refer to Figure 7.5 to see how spot color can add to the visual appeal of a publication.

screening

Decreasing the intensity of a color to produce a lighter shade

Another way to incorporate spot color into a newsletter is by adding color to all or part of a black-and-white image. Add color to the entire image by selecting the image, clicking the Color button in the Adjust group on the PICTURE TOOLS FORMAT tab to display a drop-down gallery of different colors and effects, and then clicking an option. To add color to a specific part of an image, select the image, click the Group button in the Arrange group on the PICTURE TOOLS FORMAT tab, and then click *Ungroup*. For most images, this will make it possible for you to select and apply color to each part of the image individually.

Figure 7.5 Comparing Versions of a Newsletter with and without Spot Color

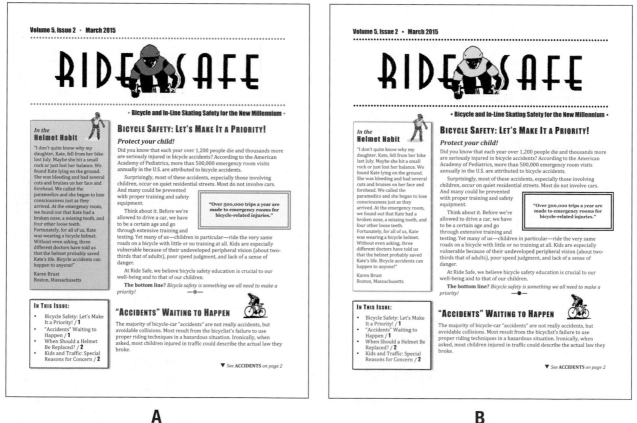

A

With Spot Color

B

Without Spot Color

Some image formats, such as bitmap (.bmp) will not allow you to ungroup the image. However, you can make some changes to the image by using the *Set Transparent Color* option at the Color button drop-down list, as shown in Figure 7.6A. After you click the *Set Transparent Color* option, click the desired area of the image to make it transparent, as shown in Figure 7.6B. With the image selected, apply the new color by clicking the Shading button in the Paragraph group on the HOME tab and then clicking the desired color, as shown in Figure 7.6C. To make more sophisticated changes to a bitmap image, use a photo-editing program.

Make sure to use spot color sparingly. Just as an all black-and-white page may appear gray, using too much spot color can change the whole "color" of the document and detract from any emphasis or contrast that using the spot color created.

Using spot color can make a black-and-white publication look brighter and more appealing, but keep in mind that using color always adds to the cost of printing. Be sure to price out the cost of color printing during the planning stages of your project.

Figure 7.6 **Using the *Set Transparent Color* Option to Change the Color in a Bitmap Image**

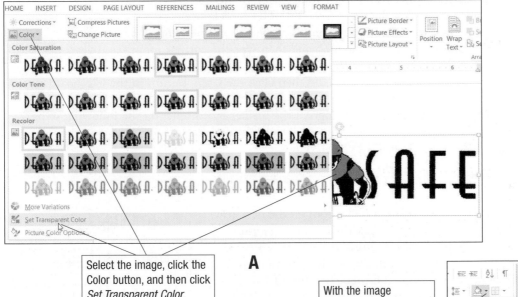

Select the image, click the Color button, and then click *Set Transparent Color*.

A

Click the area you want to recolor.

B

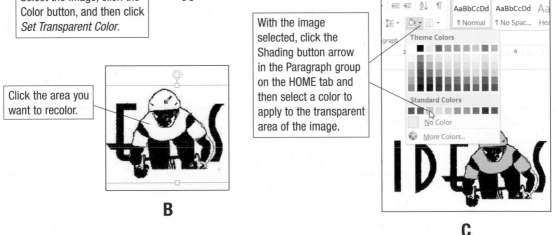

With the image selected, click the Shading button arrow in the Paragraph group on the HOME tab and then select a color to apply to the transparent area of the image.

C

In Exercise 7.1A, you will create a header and footer for a newsletter. In Figure 7.7 on page 286, notice how the triangular logo in the header repeats the image of the bicyclist in the nameplate. In addition, the dotted line in the header on page 2 of the newsletter is consistent in style and color with the dotted lines located within the nameplate on page 1. The slogan text is set in a fun font that reinforces the youthful message of the biking newsletter. The footer repeats the round bullet symbols found in the nameplate, the header, and the end signs, which will later be used within the body text to indicate the end of an article. As you can see, headers and footers help to provide a visual connection between the separate pages in a multiple-page publication.

Exercise 7.1A Creating a Header and Footer with Spot Color in a Newsletter   Part 1 of 9

1. Add a header and footer to the beginning stages of a newsletter, as shown on the second page of the Ride Safe newsletter in Figure 7.7 on page 286, by completing the following steps:
   a. Open **NewsletterBanner.docx** from your Chapter07 folder.
   b. Save the document with the name **C07-E01-Header&Footer**.
   c. Change the zoom to 75% and turn on the display of nonprinting characters.
   d. Select the month and year in the folio and then type the current month and year.
   e. Select one of the dotted lines in the banner, click the Clipboard task pane launcher to display the Clipboard task pane, and then click the Copy button in the Clipboard group. (The line will be pasted into the header later.)
2. Change the spot color in the Ride Safe logo in the banner by completing the following steps:
   a. Select the Ride Safe logo (cyclist with dark teal shirt and *RIDE SAFE* text) and then click the PICTURE TOOLS FORMAT tab.
   b. Click the Color button in the Adjust group.
   c. Click the *Set Transparent Color* option located toward the bottom of the drop-down gallery.
   d. Position the Set Transparent Color tool on the dark teal shirt in the logo and then click the left mouse button. *Hint: The dark teal shirt should become transparent.*
   e. Click the HOME tab, click the Shading button arrow in the Paragraph group, and then click the *Blue, Accent 5, Darker 25%* option (ninth column, fifth row in the *Theme Colors* section).

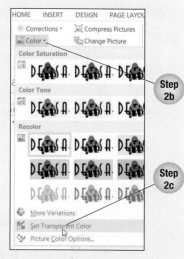

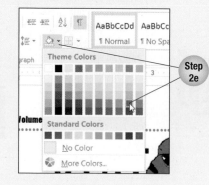

3. Create two uneven columns using the columns feature by completing the following steps. (These columns are being set up for steps in future exercises and to avoid potential problems.)

   a. Press Ctrl + End to position the insertion point below the newsletter banner, click the PAGE LAYOUT tab, click the Columns button in the Page Setup group, and then click *More Columns* at the drop-down list.

   b. At the Columns dialog box, click *Left* in the *Presets* section, change the spacing after column 1 in the *Widths and spacing* section to 0.4 inch, change the *Apply to* option to *This point forward*, and then click OK.

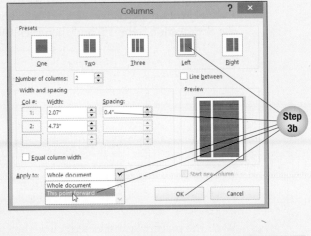

   c. Click the Breaks button in the Page Setup group on the PAGE LAYOUT tab and then click the *Column* option in the *Page Breaks* section of the drop-down list.

   d. With the insertion point positioned at the top of the column at the right, repeat the previous step to insert one more column break. This will produce a second page, which is necessary to create the headers and footers as described in Steps 4 and 5.

   e. Press Ctrl + Home to position the insertion point at the beginning of the document.

4. Create a different first page header and footer by completing the following steps:

   a. Click the INSERT tab, click the Header button in the Header & Footer group, and then click *Edit Header* at the drop-down list.

   b. On the HEADER & FOOTERS TOOLS DESIGN tab, click in the *Different First Page* check box in the Options group to insert a check mark. **Hint: *The Header pane should be labeled* First Page Header -Section 1-.**

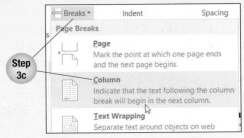

5. Create the header for the rest of the newsletter by completing the following steps:

   a. Click the Next button in the Navigation group. **Hint: *The Header pane should be labeled* Header -Section 2-.**

   b. Click the Link to Previous button in the Navigation group to turn off this feature. **Hint: *If a prompt displays asking you to delete this header/footer and connect to the header/footer in the previous section, click No. You should not see* Same as Previous *displayed in the upper right corner of the header.***

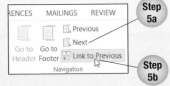

   c. Click the Pictures button in the Insert group.

   d. At the Insert Picture dialog box, navigate to your Chapter07 folder and then double-click **Ridesf2teal.bmp. Hint: *This is a BMP (bitmapped) graphic file.***

6. Format the picture by completing the following steps:
   a. With the picture selected, click the Size group dialog box launcher on the PICTURE TOOLS FORMAT tab.
   b. At the Layout dialog box with the Size tab selected, click in the *Height* measurement box in the *Scale* section, type **35**, and then click OK. (The width will automatically adjust to 35%.)

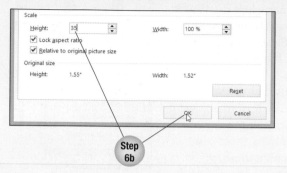

Step 6b

c. With the picture still selected, click the Color button in the Adjust group and then click the *Blue, Accent color 5 Light* color at the drop-down gallery (sixth column, third row in the *Recolor* section).
   d. Click once to the right of the image to deselect it.
7. In the Header pane on page 2, draw a text box to the right of the Ride Safe logo that will accommodate the dotted line and slogan shown on page 2 of the newsletter in Figure 7.7. The text box should measure approximately 0.4 inches high by 6.75 inches wide.
8. On the DRAWING TOOLS FORMAT tab, make the following changes to the text box:
   a. Click the Shape Outline button arrow in the Shape Styles group and then click *No Outline* at the drop-down list.
   b. Click the Position button in the Arrange group and then click *More Layout Options* at the drop-down gallery.
   c. At the Layout dialog box with the Position tab selected, change the *Absolute position* measurement in the *Horizontal* section to 1.1 inches and then change the *to the right of* option to *Page*.
   d. Change the *Absolute position* measurement in the *Vertical* section to 0.7 inch, change the *below* option to *Page*, and then click OK.
   e. Click the Shape Styles group task pane launcher.
   f. At the Format Shape task pane, make sure *SHAPE OPTIONS* is selected at the top of the task pane, click the Layout & Properties icon, and then click *TEXT BOX* to display the options.
   g. Change the *Left margin* and *Right margin* measurements to 0 inches and then close the task pane.

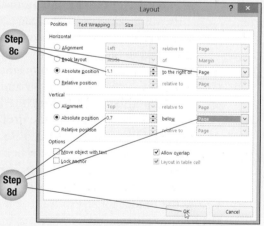

Step 8c

Step 8d

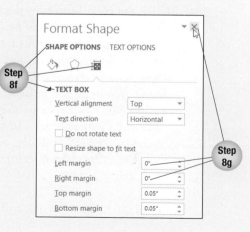

Step 8f

Step 8g

9. Insert the dotted line and slogan by completing the following steps:
   a. Make sure the insertion point is positioned inside the text box.
   b. If necessary, display the Clipboard task pane, click once on the dotted line item to insert it inside the text box, and then close the task pane. (The line length will be adjusted in the following steps.)
   c. Position the insertion point in the middle of the dotted line and then press the Delete key until the paragraph symbol displays at the end of the dotted line within the text box. Continue pressing the Delete key until there is enough space at the end of the line to type the slogan within the text box.
   d. Position the insertion point at the end of the dotted line and then type **Winners wear helmets!** If some of the text disappears, delete more of the dotted line until the entire slogan is visible. If you need to insert more blue dots, select a dot, click the Copy button, click to the right of the selected dot, and then click the Paste button to paste as many dots as needed to ensure the text displays at the right margin.
   e. Select the slogan text and then change the font to 11-point Tempus Sans ITC. Apply bold formatting and the Black, Text 1 font color.
   f. With the slogan text still selected, display the Font dialog box with the Advanced tab selected.
   g. Click the down-pointing arrow at the right of the *Position* option box in the *Character Spacing* section and then click *Raised* at the drop-down list. Make sure *3 pt* displays in the *By* option box. (This raises the slogan to be in alignment with the dotted line.)

   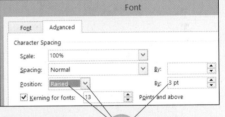

   h. Click OK to close the dialog box.
   i. If the slogan wraps to the next line, delete more of the dotted line until the slogan fits in the text box. If you delete more than necessary, copy and paste more dots.

10. Create the footer that will begin on the second page by completing the following steps:
    a. Click the HEADER & FOOTER TOOLS DESIGN tab and then click the Go to Footer button in the Navigation group.
    b. Verify that the left side of the Footer pane is labeled *Footer -Section 2*. If *Same as Previous* displays at the right side of the Footer pane, click the Link to Previous button in the Navigation group to turn off this feature.
    c. Click the Page Number button in the Header & Footer group, point to *Bottom of Page*, scroll down the side menu, and then click the *Dots* option.

    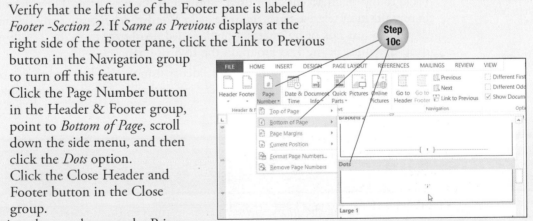

    d. Click the Close Header and Footer button in the Close group.

11. Preview the newsletter at the Print backstage area, comparing both pages against the illustrations in Figure 7.7. Make sure no header or footer text displays on page 1 and the header and footer text correctly displays on page 2. ***Hint: You may need to adjust the bottom margin if the footer does not print properly.***

12. Save **C07-E01-Header&Footer.docx**.

Figure 7.7 Header and Footer Created in Exercise 7.1A

Creating Sidebars

sidebar

Information or a related story set off from the body text in a graphics box

A *sidebar* is a block of information or a related story that is set off from the body text using some type of box or border. A sidebar may include a photograph or a graphic image along with the text. Frequently, a sidebar contains a shaded or screened background in an accent color used throughout the newsletter. The sidebar can be set in any position relative to the body text. In Word, sidebars can easily be created by drawing a text box or by inserting predesigned text boxes from the Text Box button drop-down list in the Text group on the INSERT tab.

In Exercise 7.1B, you will create a sidebar using a text box and then position the text box at the left margin. In later exercises, you will add more visual enhancements to the same newsletter.

Exercise 7.1B Inserting a Sidebar into a Newsletter   Part 2 of 9

1. Insert a sidebar (containing the *In the Helmet Habit* feature) in the newsletter you started in Exercise 7.1A by completing the following steps:
   a. With **C07-E01-Header&Footer.docx** open, save the document with the name **C07-E01-Sidebar**.
   b. Make sure the zoom is set to 75% and that nonprinting characters display.
   c. Position the insertion point to the left of the first column break in the left column on page 1 and then turn on kerning at 14 points and above.

d. Draw a text box just below the column break in the left column that is approximately the same size and in the same position as the sidebar shown in Figure 7.8 on page 289.

e. Change the height of the text box to 4.7 inches and the width to 2.2 inches.

f. Position the insertion point in the text box and then insert **HelmetHabitText.docx**. located in your Chapter07 folder. Do not be concerned if all of the text is not visible at this point.

g. Make sure the font size of the sidebar text is 10 points.

h. Select the text box, click the Position button in the Arrange group on the DRAWING TOOLS FORMAT tab, and then click *More Layout Options* at the drop-down gallery.

i. At the Layout dialog box with the Position tab selected, click the *Alignment* option in the *Horizontal* section to select it, make sure *Left* displays in the *Alignment* option box, and then change the *relative to* option to *Margin*.

j. In the *Vertical* section, verify that the *Absolute position* option is selected, change the *Absolute position* measurement to 3.3 inches, change the *below* option to *Page*, and then click OK.

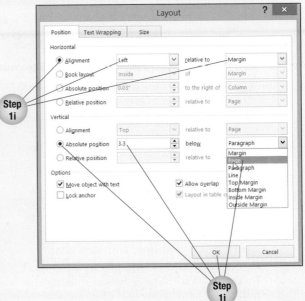

k. With the text box still selected, click the More button in the Shape Styles group, and then click the *Subtle Effect - Blue, Accent 1* option (second column, fourth row).

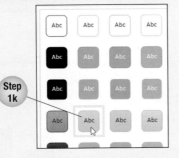

l. With the text box still selected, click the Shape Effects button in the Shape Styles group, point to *Shadow*, and then click the *Offset Right* option (first column, second row in the *Outer* section).

m. Click the Shape Outline button arrow in the Shape Styles group and then click the *Dark Blue* option (ninth option in the *Standard Colors* section).

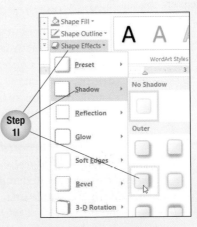

2. Format the text inside the sidebar by completing the following steps:

a. Position the insertion point at the beginning of the title *In the Helmet Habit* and then press Enter.

b. Select *In the* and then change the font to 12-point Cambria. Apply bold and italic formatting and change the font color to *Dark Blue*.

c. Position the insertion point in front of *Helmet* in the title, delete the space before *Helmet*, and then press Enter.

d. Select *Helmet Habit*, change the font to 14-point Impact, apply the Dark Blue font color, and then expand the character spacing by 1.2 points.

e. Position the insertion point within the title text *In the*, display the Paragraph dialog box, change the *Line spacing* option to *Exactly*, type **10** in the *At* measurement box, and then click OK.

f. Position the insertion point within the title text *Helmet Habit* and then change the spacing after paragraphs to 6 points.

3. For use in future issues, create styles for the sidebar heading by completing the following steps:

a. Position the insertion point within the title text *In the*, and then click the HOME tab if necessary to make it active.

b. Click the More button in the Styles group.

c. Click *Create a Style* at the drop-down gallery.

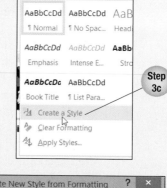

d. At the Create New Style from Formatting dialog box, type **Sidebar Heading-1** in the *Name* text box and then click OK.

e. Position the insertion point anywhere within the title text *Helmet Habit* and then follow Steps 3b–3d, naming this style *Sidebar Heading-2*.

4. Position the insertion point after *. . . anyone!"* in the last line of the article text, press the Delete key to eliminate the extra hard return below that line, and then change the spacing after paragraphs to 6 points.

5. Insert the skater image by completing the following steps:

a. Deselect the text box and then make sure the insertion point is not positioned in the text box containing the sidebar text.

b. Click the INSERT tab and then click the Online Pictures button.

c. At the Insert Pictures window, type **in-line skating** in the *Office.com Clip Art* text box and then press Enter.

d. Double-click the image shown at the right to insert it into your newsletter. **Hint: Substitute a different clip art image if necessary or desired. Do not be concerned if parts of your newsletter move out of place. Adjustments will be made in the next step.**

6. Format the skater image by completing the following steps:

a. With the skater image selected, click the Wrap Text button in the Arrange group on the PICTURE TOOLS FORMAT tab and then click the *In Front of Text* option at the drop-down list.

b. Use the corner sizing handles to reduce the size of the image so that it is similar to the skater image shown in Figure 7.8.

c. Click and drag the image so that it is overlapping the upper right corner of the sidebar text box, as shown in Figure 7.8.

7. Save **C07-E01-Sidebar.docx**.

Figure 7.8   Sidebar Created in Exercise 7.1B

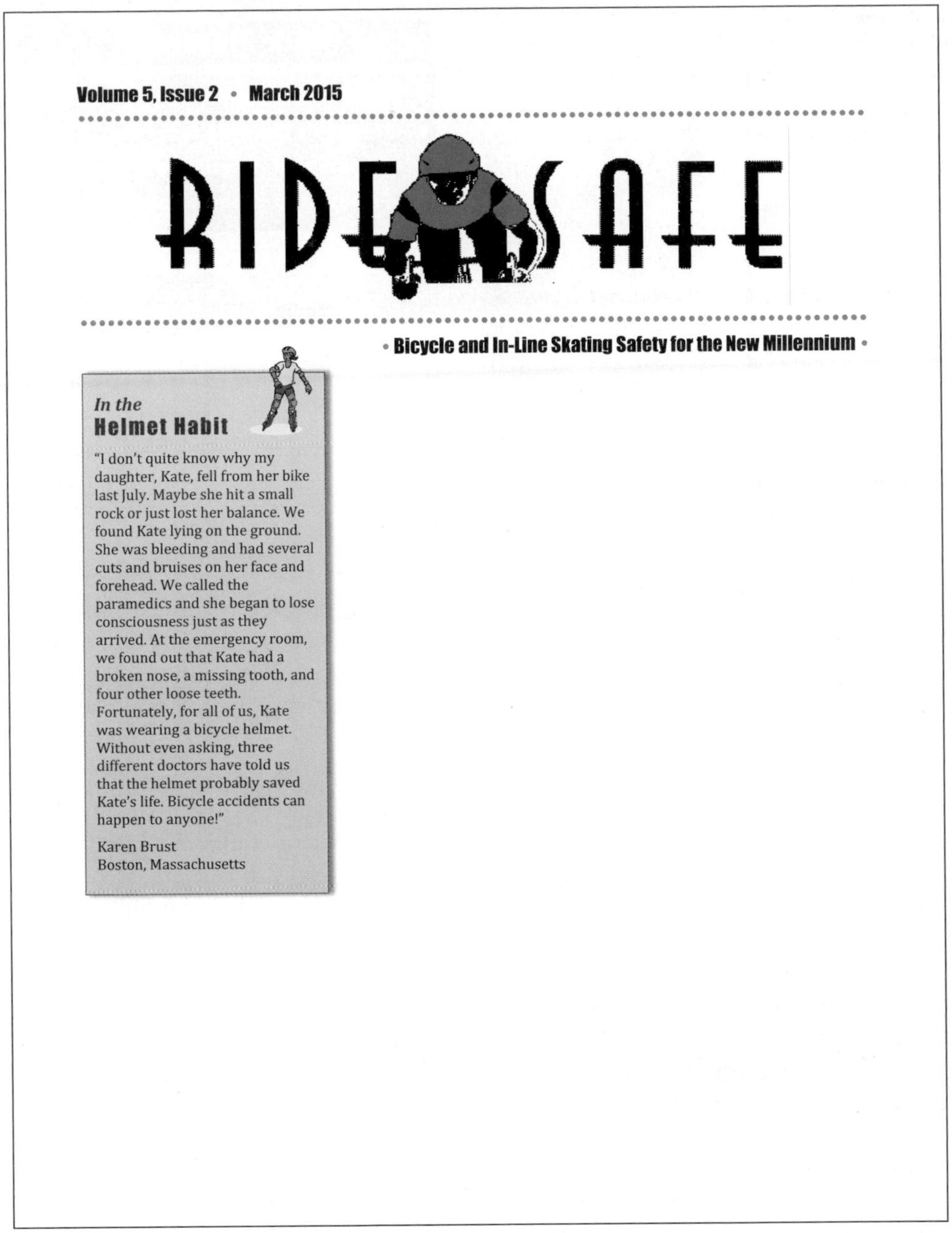

Volume 5, Issue 2   •   March 2015

RIDE SAFE

• Bicycle and In-Line Skating Safety for the New Millennium •

In the
Helmet Habit

"I don't quite know why my daughter, Kate, fell from her bike last July. Maybe she hit a small rock or just lost her balance. We found Kate lying on the ground. She was bleeding and had several cuts and bruises on her face and forehead. We called the paramedics and she began to lose consciousness just as they arrived. At the emergency room, we found out that Kate had a broken nose, a missing tooth, and four other loose teeth. Fortunately, for all of us, Kate was wearing a bicycle helmet. Without even asking, three different doctors have told us that the helmet probably saved Kate's life. Bicycle accidents can happen to anyone!"

Karen Brust
Boston, Massachusetts

Creating a Table of Contents

A *table of contents* is a list of the articles, features, and other major elements of a newsletter and their corresponding page numbers. A table of contents is optional in a one- or two-page newsletter, but in multiple-page newsletters, a table of contents is an important and necessary element. The information in the table of contents greatly influences whether the reader will read beyond the front page of the newsletter. Consequently, the table of contents should stand out from the surrounding information and be legible and easy to follow. Figure 7.9 on page 290 shows a few examples of tables of contents in newsletters.

table of contents

A list of articles and features and their page numbers

Figure 7.9   Understanding Tables of Contents in Newsletters

A table of contents is usually located on the front page of a newsletter. It is often placed in the lower left or right corner of the page. It can, however, be placed closer to the top of the page—on either side of, or even within, an asymmetrically designed nameplate. If a newsletter is designed to be a self-mailer (no envelope), the table of contents can be placed near the mailing address so the reader is invited into the newsletter before he or she even opens it.

The table of contents in Figure 7.10 on page 293 is located in the lower left corner. The blue border, bullets, bold title, and numbers make the table of contents easily identifiable while adding visual interest to the page. The table of contents, along with the drop-shadowed text box that contains it, will also add weight to the left side of the page and balance to the page as a whole once the body text is added to the right side of the page. You will create this table of contents in Exercise 7.1C.

Exercise 7.1C Inserting a Table of Contents in a Newsletter   **Part 3 of 9**

1. With **C07-E01-Sidebar.docx** open, save the document with the name **C07-E01-TableofContents**.
2. Insert the table of contents text in a text box by completing the following steps:
   a. Draw a text box that is approximately the same size and in the same position as the table of contents text box shown in Figure 7.10 on page 293.
   b. Position the insertion point in the text box and then insert **TableofContentsText.docx** from your Chapter07 folder.
   c. With the text box selected, click the DRAWING TOOLS FORMAT tab to make it active and then apply the Dark Blue shape outline.
   d. Change the weight of the outline to 1½ points.
   e. Change the height of the text box to 1.9 inches and the width to 2.2 inches.
   f. Click the Position button in the Arrange group and then click *More Layout Options* at the drop-down list.

g. At the Layout dialog box with the Position tab selected, click the *Alignment* option in the *Horizontal* section to select it, make sure *Left* displays in the *Alignment* option box, and then change the *relative to* option to *Margin*.

h. In the *Vertical* section, verify that the *Absolute position* option is selected, change the *Absolute position* measurement to 7.63 inches, change the *below* option to *Margin*, and then click OK.

i. Click the Shape Effects button in the Shape Styles group, point to *Shadow*, and then click the *Offset Right* option at the side menu (first column, second row in the *Outer* section).

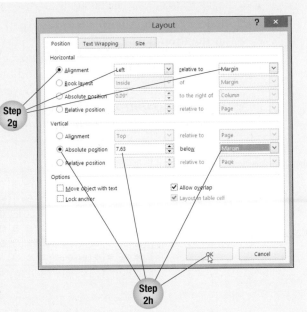

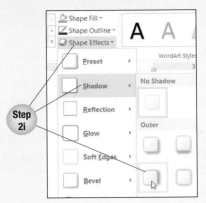

3. Select the title text *In This Issue:* and then apply the following formatting:
   a. Apply the Subtle Reference style.
   b. Change the font to 12-point Impact and apply the Dark Blue font color.
   c. Expand the text by 1.2 points.
   d. Change the spacing after paragraphs to 8 points.

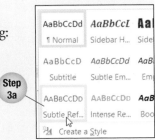

4. Select the remaining text below the title and then apply the following formatting:
   a. Change the font to 11-point Cambria. ***Hint: Do not be concerned if some of the text is not visible at this point.***
   b. Display the Paragraph dialog box, type **2** in the *After* measurement box in the *Spacing* section, change the *Line Spacing* option to *Exactly*, type **12** in the *At* measurement box (if necessary), and then click OK.

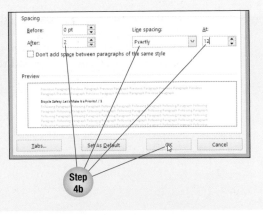

c. Click the Bullets button arrow in the Paragraph group and then click *Define New Bullet* at the drop-down gallery.

d. At the Define New Bullet dialog box, click the Symbol button, select *Wingdings* in the *Font* option box, click the round bullet shown in the image below (character code 159, located in approximately the seventh row), and then click OK to close the Symbol dialog box. ***Hint: Type 159 in the* Character code *text box at the Symbol dialog box to quickly locate the bullet symbol.***

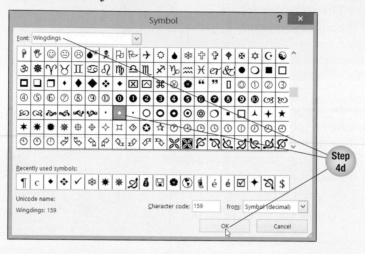

e. At the Define New Bullet dialog box, click the Font button to display the Font dialog box, change the bullet color to *Dark Blue*, and then click OK two times to close both dialog boxes.

f. Change the bullet position by displaying the Paragraph dialog box, typing **0** in the *Left* measurement box in the *Indentation* section, changing the *Special* option to *Hanging*, typing **0.3** in the *By* measurement box and then clicking OK.

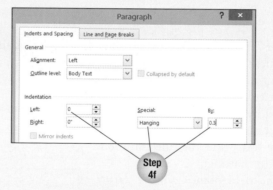

g. Select each page number in the table of contents text box and change the font to Impact.

5. Save **C07-E01-TableofContents.docx**.

Figure 7.10 Table of Contents Created in Exercise 7.1C

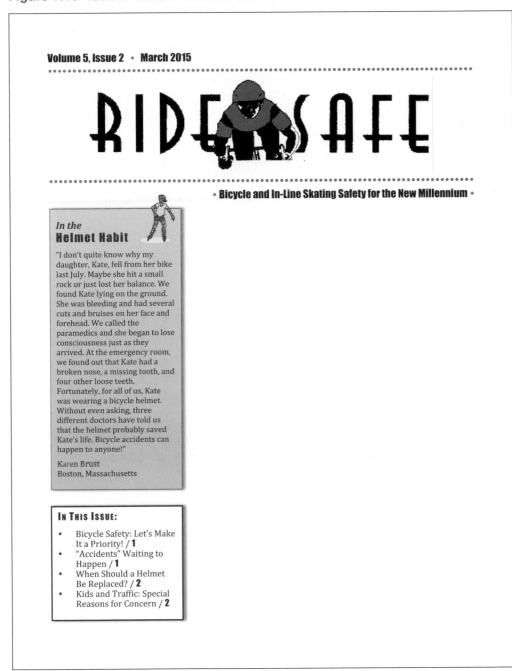

Volume 5, Issue 2 • **March 2015**

RIDE SAFE

• **Bicycle and In-Line Skating Safety for the New Millennium** •

In the Helmet Habit

"I don't quite know why my daughter, Kate, fell from her bike last July. Maybe she hit a small rock or just lost her balance. We found Kate lying on the ground. She was bleeding and had several cuts and bruises on her face and forehead. We called the paramedics and she began to lose consciousness just as they arrived. At the emergency room, we found out that Kate had a broken nose, a missing tooth, and four other loose teeth. Fortunately, for all of us, Kate was wearing a bicycle helmet. Without even asking, three different doctors have told us that the helmet probably saved Kate's life. Bicycle accidents can happen to anyone!"

Karen Brust
Boston, Massachusetts

IN THIS ISSUE:

Creating Pull Quotes

pull quote

A short, direct phrase, statement, or important point formatted to stand out from the rest of the body copy

DTP POINTER

Pull quotes should be brief and interesting and stand out from the rest of the text.

A *pull quote* (also called a pullout or callout) is a direct phrase, summarizing statement, or important point associated with the body copy of a newsletter. A pull quote acts as a focal point, helps to break up lengthy blocks of text, and provides visual contrast. Using pull quotes is an excellent way to draw readers into an article.

Effective pull quotes are interesting, brief, and formatted to stand out from the rest of the body copy. Keep in mind the following tips when creating pull quotes for a newsletter:

- Include relevant and interesting text in a pull quote. Edit any direct quotes so they will not be taken out of context when read individually as a pull quote.
- Keep pull quotes brief—approximately 10 to 15 words, and never longer than a few lines.
- Choose a font or font style that contrasts with the font used for the article text.
- Increase the type size to make the pull quote text stand out from the body text.
- Apply bold and/or italic formatting to the pull quote text.
- Set off the pull quote from the body text with ruled lines or a graphics box.
- Use at least one element in your pull quote design that establishes a visual connection with the rest of your newsletter.
- Be consistent. Use the same format for all pull quotes throughout the newsletter and throughout future issues of the same newsletter.

In Exercise 7.1D, you will insert the first newsletter article, format the article heading and article text, and create a pull quote. Because these particular elements may be repeated throughout the newsletter, you will also create styles for them.

Exercise 7.1D Creating Styles and a Pull Quote in a Newsletter   Part 4 of 9

1. With **C07-E01-TableofContents.docx** open, save the document with the name **C07-E01-PullQuote**.
2. Position the insertion point to the left of the column break in the right column and then insert **BicycleSafetyText.docx**, located in your Chapter07 folder.
3. Select the article heading *Bicycle Safety: Let's Make It a Priority!* and then make the following changes:
   a. Change the font to 18-point Impact, change the font color to *Dark Blue*, and apply small caps formatting (Ctrl + Shift + K).
   b. Expand the character spacing by 1.2 points.
   c. Change the spacing after paragraph to 6 points.
4. Create a style from this formatting for use with future article headings by completing the following steps:
   a. Position the insertion point in the article heading.
   b. Click the More button in the Styles group on the HOME tab and then click *Create a Style* at the drop-down gallery.
   c. At the Create New Style from Formatting dialog box, type **Article Head** in the *Name* text box and then click OK.

Step 4c

Create New Style from Formatting

Name:
Article Head

Paragraph style preview:

STYLE1

OK   Modify...   Cancel

5. Format the article text by completing the following steps:
   a. Position the insertion point at the beginning of the line *Did you know* and then select all of the article text.
   b. Change the font to 11-point Cambria.
   c. Display the Paragraph dialog box, type **3** in the *After* measurement box in the *Spacing* section, change the *Special* option to *First line*, type **0.2** in the *By* measurement box, and then click OK.

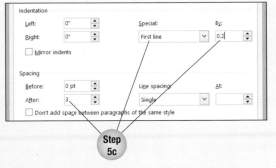

Step 5c

6. With the article text still selected, create a style and name it **Article Text**.
7. Create a style for the first paragraph of the article that eliminates the first line indentation by completing the following steps:
   a. Position the insertion point within the first paragraph of article text.
   b. Display the Paragraph dialog box, make sure the Indents and Spacing tab is selected, change the *Special* option to *(none)* in the *Indentation* section, and then click OK.
   c. Create a style and name it **1st Paragraph**.
8. Create a pull quote by completing the following steps:
   a. Click the INSERT tab, click the Text Box button in the Text group, scroll down the drop-down list, and then click the *Grid Quote* option.

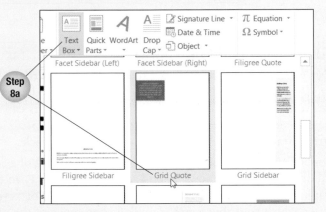

Step 8a

   b. With the text placeholder selected in the pull quote text box, type **"Over 500,000 trips a year are made to emergency rooms for bicycle-related injuries."**
   c. Select the text in the pull quote text box, change the font to 9-point Georgia, apply bold formatting, remove italic formatting, change the font color to *Black, Text 1*, and then change the case to *Sentence case*. **Hint: Use the Change Case button in the Font group.**
   d. Select the pull quote text box, change the shape fill to *Gold, Accent 4, Lighter 80%* and then change the shape outline to *Blue, Accent 5*.
   e. Change the height of the pull quote text box to 1 inch and the width to 2.5 inches.
   f. Drag the pull quote to a position similar to that shown in Figure 7.11 on page 296.
9. In the last paragraph of the article text, select *The bottom line?* and then apply bold formatting. Select the last sentence, *Bicycle safety is something we all need to make a priority!*, and then apply italic formatting.
10. Save **C07-E01-PullQuote.docx**.

Figure 7.11 Article and Pull Quote Formatted in Exercise 7.1D

Creating Kickers and End Signs

kicker

A lead-in phrase or sentence that precedes the beginning of an article

end sign

A symbol or special character indicating the end of an article

A *kicker* is a brief sentence or phrase that leads into an article. Generally, a kicker is set in a size smaller than the headline but larger than the body text. It is often stylistically distinct from both the headline and the body text. Kickers can be placed above or below the headline or article heading. In Figure 7.1 on page 275, a kicker is placed above the first article heading and serves as a lead-in to the first article.

Symbols or special characters used to indicate the end of a section of text, such as the end of an article, are known as *end signs*. In Figure 7.1, an end sign follows the last paragraph in the first article. The end sign is the same color as the accent color in the newsletter, which contributes to the unified appearance of the publication. The end sign in the Ride Safe newsletter shown in Figure 7.12 mimics the dots in the nameplate and footer and the colors coordinate with the newsletter color scheme. Appropriate special characters or combinations of these characters—such as ℞, ◎, ✳, ❖, ✪, and ✕, from the Wingdings and Webdings fonts—may be used as end signs.

In Exercise 7.1E, you will add a kicker and an end sign to the Ride Safe newsletter.

Exercise 7.1E Creating a Kicker and an End Sign in a Newsletter   Part 5 of 9

1. With **C07-E01-PullQuote.docx** open, save the document with the name **C07-E01-EndSign**.
2. Create the kicker by completing the following steps:
   a. Position the insertion point at the beginning of the first paragraph below the *Bicycle Safety* article heading.
   b. Type **Protect your child!** and then press Enter.

c. Select *Protect your child!* and then change the font to 14-point Cambria and apply bold and italic formatting.

3. Create a style for the kicker formatting by completing the following steps:
   a. Position the insertion point anywhere within the kicker.
   b. Create a style and name it *Kicker*.

4. Create the end sign by completing the following steps:
   a. Position the insertion point before the paragraph mark at the end of the first article (to the right of the exclamation point located after the word *priority*) and then press the Tab key three times. ***Hint: Make sure italic formatting is turned off.***

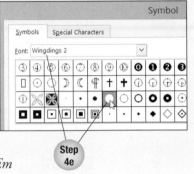

   b. Click the INSERT tab, click the Symbol button in the Symbols group, and then click *More Symbols* at the drop-down list.
   c. At the Symbol dialog box, click the Special Characters tab.
   d. Double-click the *Em Dash* option and then click the Symbols tab.
   e. Change the *Font* option to *Wingdings 2* and then double-click the round bullet located in approximately the seventh row (character code 152).

Step 4e

   f. Click the Special Characters tab again, double-click the *Em Dash* option, and then click the Close button.
   g. Select the end sign (the three new symbols you inserted) and then change the font to 11-point Impact.
   h. Select the round bullet and then change the color to *Blue, Accent 5*.

5. Save **C07-E01-EndSign.docx**.

Figure 7.12 Kicker and End Sign Created in Exercise 7.1E

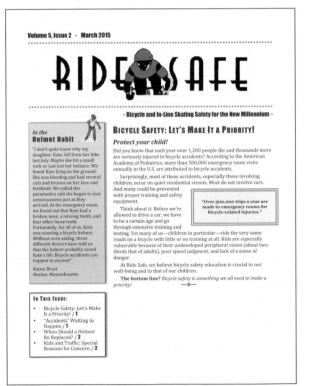

Using Linked Text Boxes in Newsletters

DTP POINTER

Including the first part of several different articles on the first page of a newsletter helps spark reader interest in the content.

Featuring the beginning of several articles on the front page of a newsletter increases the chance of attracting readers. Also, some articles may be too lengthy to fit on one page, so it is necessary to continue them on another page. This can be hard to manage when you set the body text of your newsletter in columns or a table, but it is easy when you use text boxes, due to the text box linking feature in Word. This feature allows text to flow from one text box to another, even if the text boxes are not adjacent or even on the same page.

You need at least two text boxes to create a link; however, any number of text boxes can be added to the chain of linked text boxes. When the first text box is filled, the text automatically flows into the second text box, and then into the third text box in the chain. If you add or delete text in one of the text boxes, the remaining article text in the other text boxes adjusts to the change.

You can establish as many chains of linked text boxes in a document as you need. For example, you can create one chain of linked text boxes for an article that begins on page 1 and then continues on pages 3 and 4. For a different article that begins on page 2 and continues on page 4 of the same newsletter, you can create another chain of linked text boxes.

Creating and Breaking the Link

To link text boxes, you must first create two or more text boxes. For example, if you have an article that begins on page 1 and is to be continued on page 2 of a newsletter, create a text box on page 1 and then create another text box on page 2. Size the text boxes to fit within the allotted column width and then position the text boxes as desired. If necessary, you can readjust the size and position later, after the text has been added.

To create a link between the two text boxes, complete the following steps:

1. Select the text box that is to be the first in the chain of linked text boxes.
2. Click the DRAWING TOOLS FORMAT tab, if necessary, to select it.
3. Click the Create Link button in the Text group. The mouse pointer will display as a small upright pitcher.
4. Position the mouse pitcher over the text box to be linked. The pitcher appears tipped with letters spilling out of it when it is over a text box that can receive the link, as shown in Figure 7.13. Click once to complete the link.

Create Link

Figure 7.13 Linking Text Boxes

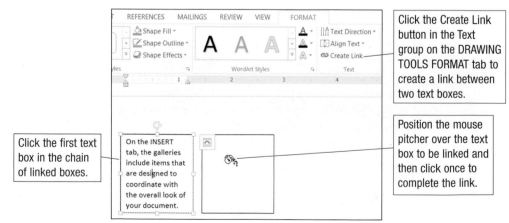

Click the first text box in the chain of linked boxes.

On the INSERT tab, the galleries include items that are designed to coordinate with the overall look of your document.

Click the Create Link button in the Text group on the DRAWING TOOLS FORMAT tab to create a link between two text boxes.

Position the mouse pitcher over the text box to be linked and then click once to complete the link.

5. To create a link from the second text box to a third text box, select the second text box and then repeat Steps 2–4. Repeat these steps to add more links to the chain.
6. To break the chain of linked text boxes, click in the text box that precedes the text box to which you want to break the link and then click the Break Link button in the Text group on the DRAWING TOOLS FORMAT tab.

Break Link

Creating Jump Lines

When you start an article on one page and continue it on another, you have to direct the reader as to where he or she can go to read the rest of the text. A *jump line* in a newsletter is used to indicate that an article or feature continues on another page or is being continued from another page. As an aid in the directional flow of information in a document, a jump line must be easily distinguishable from the surrounding text so the reader can find it. A jump line is commonly set in small italic type, approximately 2 points smaller than the body text. Jump lines can also be enclosed in parentheses.

In Exercise 7.1F, you will create linked text boxes within the Ride Safe newsletter and add jump lines so that the reader knows the text boxes are connected.

jump line

Text informing the reader that an article continues on another page or is being continued from another page

Exercise 7.1F Creating Linked Text Boxes and a Jump Line in a Newsletter **Part 6 of 9**

1. With **C07-E01-EndSign.docx** open, save the document with the name **C07-E01-JumpLine**.
2. Insert linked text boxes by completing the following steps:
   a. Make sure nonprinting characters display and then scroll to the bottom of page 1.
   b. Draw a text box below the column break to hold the beginning of the second article. Adjustments will be made to the size and position of the text box in future steps so that it displays as shown in Figure 7.14 on page 302.
   c. Click to position the insertion point at the top of the left column on page 2 and then draw a text box to hold the remaining article text. Using the horizontal ruler as a guide, limit the width of the text box to the column width in the left column. Adjustments will be made to the formatting, size, and position of this text box in Exercise 7.1I
3. Create a link between the two text boxes so that text will automatically flow from one text box to another by completing the following steps:
   a. Select the first text box, located on page 1, click the DRAWING TOOLS FORMAT tab, and then click the Create Link button in the Text group.
   b. Position the mouse pointer, which now displays as an upright pitcher, over the second text box, located on page 2, until it displays as a pouring pitcher and then click once to complete the link.
   c. Remove the shape outline in the first text box that is linked (at the bottom of page 1, second column).
   d. Change the height of the first text box to 1.8 inches and the width to 4.7 inches.
   e. Move the first text box to a position similar to that shown in Figure 7.14.

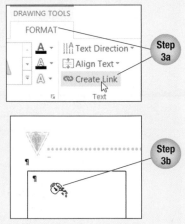

f. Click the Shape Styles group task pane launcher, click *SHAPE OPTIONS* if necessary to select it at the Format Shape task pane, click the Layout & Properties icon, and then click *TEXT BOX* to display the options.

g. Change the left, right, top, and bottom margins to 0 inches and then close the task pane.

h. Click once inside the first text box to position the insertion point and then insert **AccidentText.docx** from your Chapter07 folder.

i. Check the text box on page 2 and make sure the remaining article text is visible. If not, use the sizing handles to enlarge the text box.

j. Position the insertion point anywhere in the title *"Accidents" Waiting to Happen* in the first text box and then apply the Article Head style. **Hint: If the Article Head style does not display in the Styles gallery, click the More button in the Styles group.**

4. Format the article text by completing the following steps:

a. Double-click to select the word *The* at the beginning of the line *The majority of bicycle-car "accidents"*, hold down the Shift key, and then press Ctrl + End to select all of the article text in both text boxes. **Hint: The text in the second text box will not be highlighted, even though it is selected.**

b. With the text selected, apply the Article Text style from the Styles gallery.

c. Position the insertion point anywhere in the first paragraph and then apply the 1st Paragraph style.

5. Create a jump line by completing the following steps:

a. Position the insertion point at the end of the first paragraph and press Enter twice.

b. Change the paragraph alignment to right.

c. Display the Symbol dialog box, change the font to Wingdings 3, insert the triangle symbol shown in the image at the right (character code 113, located in approximately the fifth row), and then click the Close button.

d. Press the spacebar once and then type **See ACCIDENTS on page 2**. If the beginning of the second paragraph is visible below the jump line, press Enter to force this text to appear at the beginning of the linked text box on page 2.

e. Select *See* in the new jump line on page 1 and apply italic formatting.

f. Select *ACCIDENTS* and apply bold formatting.

g. Select *on page 2* and apply italic formatting.

h. Select the entire jump line text (not the triangle symbol) and then change the font to 10-point Cambria.

i. Click the PAGE LAYOUT tab and then make sure the *After* option in the *Spacing* section in the Paragraph group is set to *3 pt*.

6. Save the formatted jump line as a quick part by completing the following steps. ***Note: You are saving the jump line as a quick part instead of creating a style because the jump line contains mixed formatting and text that can be used in other jump lines.***

   a. Select the entire jump line, including the triangle symbol.

   b. Click the INSERT tab, click the Quick Parts button in the Text group, and then click *Save Selection to Quick Part Gallery* at the drop-down list.

   c. At the Create New Building Block dialog box, type **jump line** in the *Name* text box and then click OK.

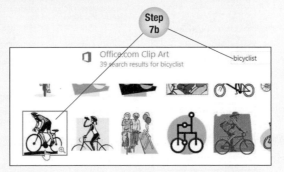

Step 6c

7. Insert the image of the man riding a bicycle in the article subhead by completing the following steps:

   a. Position the insertion point above the column break on page 1.

   b. Display the Insert Pictures window, type **bicyclist** in the *Office.com Clip Art* text box, press the Enter key, and then double-click the image shown below. (Choose a similar image if this one is not available.)

Step 7b

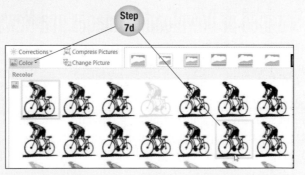

   c. With the image selected, change the text wrapping to *In Front of Text*.

   d. Click the Color button in the Adjust group and then click the *Blue, Accent color 5 Dark* option (sixth column, second row in the *Recolor* section).

Step 7d

   e. Size and position the image as shown in Figure 7.14.

8. Save **C07-E01-JumpLine.docx**.

Figure 7.14 Linked Text Boxes and Jump Line Created in Exercise 7.1F

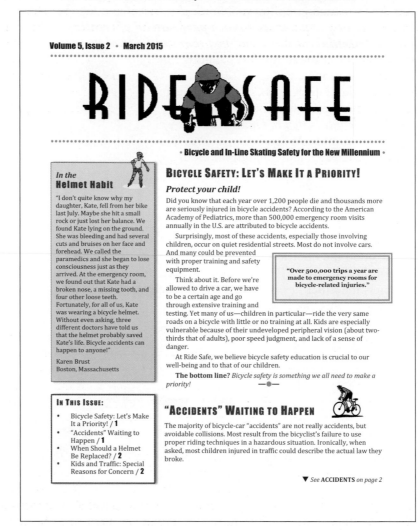

Using Scanned or Downloaded Images in a Newsletter

Noncomputer-generated images, such as traditional photographs, illustrations, and diagrams, can be included in a newsletter through the use of a scanner and compatible scanner software. A *scanner* and its associated software convert a photograph, drawing, or text into a compatible digital file format that can be inserted into a Word document.

You can scan images yourself using a standard desk model scanner or digital camera, or you can have the images professionally scanned if you need a very high-quality output (for example, if the image is going to be printed in a much larger size than the original).

scanner

Device that converts a hard copy into a compatible digital file format

One important factor to keep in mind is that you must get permission to use artwork, photos, or illustrations before you can legally scan them. You must also get permission to use artwork from the Web, even if you do not see the traditional copyright symbol. You can type the keywords *free graphics* or *free clip art* into a search engine to find a large selection of graphics that you are free to use. When you purchase clip art and stock photography, you generally buy the right to use it and even modify it, but you may not resell the images themselves as hard copy or computer images. When purchasing these items, read the copyright information provided in the accompanying documentation.

If you want to include a photograph in a newsletter but the one you want to use is not immediately available, you can insert a placeholder, such as a text box, in your newsletter. You can then insert the image whenever you have it. If you want to include an image that you only have in hard copy (such as an old photograph, a map, or a hand-drawn diagram) and no scanner is available, you can print your newsletter, tape or glue the image into the area reserved by the text box, and have a commercial printer duplicate your newsletter.

◀ **DTP POINTER**

Find out about copyright restrictions on any images you want to use and request permission, if necessary.

Creating Captions

Think of all the times you have picked up a newspaper or magazine, looked at a photograph, and immediately read the accompanying explanation. While some images can stand on their own, most photographs, illustrations, diagrams, and charts need to be explained to the reader through a short description known as a ***caption***. Readers' eyes are drawn to elements, such as images, that stand out on the page. Adding a descriptive caption to an image quickly gives your reader an idea of what it is about, as shown in Figure 7.15. A well-written caption can entice your reader to read the corresponding article and maybe even the rest of the newsletter.

Captions should explain their associated images while at the same time establishing a connection to the body text. Make the caption text look different from the body text by applying bold or italic formatting, changing the font color, or decreasing the type size. As always, legibility is key. Keep captions as short as possible, and focus on explaining the things that readers will immediately see and wonder about. Make sure to write and format your captions in a consistent manner throughout your document.

caption

An accompanying description or explanation of a graphic image, illustration, or photograph

Figure 7.15 Understanding Captions

Figure 1 Mt. Rainier, Washington State

Table 1 The Greek Alphabet

Letter name	Uppercase	Lowercase	Letter name	Uppercase	Lowercase
Alpha	A	α	Nu	N	ν
Beta	B	β	Xi	Ξ	ξ
Gamma	Γ	γ	Omicron	O	o
Delta	Δ	δ	Pi	Π	π
Epsilon	E	ε	Rho	P	ρ
Zeta	Z	ζ	Sigma	Σ	σ
Eta	H	η	Tau	T	τ
Theta	Θ	θ	Upsilon	Υ	υ
Iota	I	ι	Phi	Φ	φ
Kappa	K	κ	Chi	X	χ
Lambda	Λ	λ	Psi	Ψ	ψ
Mu	M	μ	Omega	Ω	ω

captions

Insert Caption

The easiest way to insert a caption is by using the captions feature. To do this, select the image and then click the Insert Caption button in the Captions group on the REFERENCES tab, or right-click the image and then click *Insert Caption* at the shortcut menu. This will display the Caption dialog box, where you can adjust several different settings for the caption, as shown in Figure 7.16.

When you display the Caption dialog box for the first time in a document, you will notice that the text *Figure 1* has already been inserted in the *Caption* text box. A caption label like *Figure 1* or *Table 1* comes in handy when creating more detailed, technical newsletters that may contain tables, SmartArt graphics, or even an Excel worksheet or PowerPoint slide. These elements should be captioned with labels and either numbers or letters (Figure 3, Table C, etc.) so that you can easily reference them within the text. The caption feature automatically numbers the figures in a document for you. You can change the type of label (Figure, Table, etc.) by clicking the down-pointing arrow next to the *Label* option box and then selecting a new label, and you can add label options to this option box by clicking the New Label button. Change the style of numbering by clicking the Numbering button, and change the position of the caption by clicking the down-pointing arrow at the right of the *Position* option box. Once you have selected the appropriate label and position for the caption, you can add a title, description, or other text in the *Caption* box and then click OK to close the dialog box. You can also add or edit the caption text in the text box that appears near the image after you close the Caption dialog box.

DTP POINTER

Including labels in captions makes it much easier for the reader to find images referenced within the main text of a document.

If the images in your newsletter do not need to be labeled, you can create captions without labels by clicking the *Exclude labels from caption* check box in the Caption dialog box to insert a check mark. This will remove the label from the *Caption* text box so that you can type caption text without a label.

Another option is to create a caption from scratch. To do this, simply insert a text box, type the desired caption text, and then size and position the text box near the image as desired. This option is best used in documents that contain only a few images, because it can be much more time consuming than using the captions feature.

In Exercise 7.1G, you will add a picture and a corresponding caption to the Ride Safe newsletter.

Figure 7.16 Using the Caption Dialog Box

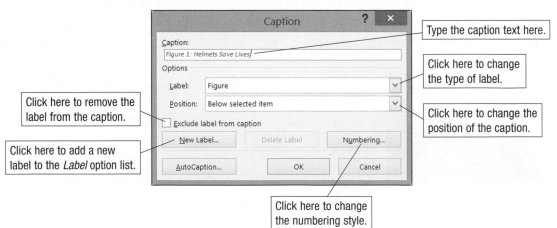

1. With **C07-E01-JumpLine.docx** open, save the document with the name **C07-E01-Picture**.
2. Insert a picture title, as shown in Figure 7.17 on page 306, by completing the following steps:
    a. Press Ctrl + End to position the insertion point at the top of page 2 and then press Ctrl + Shift + Enter to position the insertion point at the top of the right column.
    b. Draw a text box at the top of the right column that is 0.5 inch in height and 4.5 inches in width. *Note: You may have to resize the linked text box in the left column on the second page.*
    c. Remove the shape outline from the new text box.
    d. Click once in the new text box to position the insertion point inside it.
    e. Type **Who Says Helmets Aren't Cool?**
    f. Insert the arrow symbols at the beginning and end of the heading as shown in Figure 7.17 using the arrows shown at the right (Wingdings font, character codes 201 and 202).

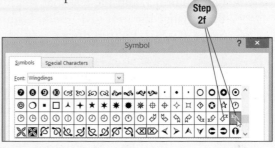

    g. Apply the Article Head style to *Who Says Helmets Aren't Cool?* and the arrow symbols and then change the paragraph alignment of the text in the text box to center.
    h. Drag and position the text box as shown in Figure 7.17.
    i. If the text box in the left column and the text box you just inserted in the right column overlap each other, reduce the width of the text box in the left column so that it is approximately the same width as the column. Use the horizontal ruler as a guide.
3. Insert a picture as shown in Figure 7.17 by completing the following steps:
    a. Position the insertion point at the top left corner of page 2, and then insert a picture similar to the one displayed in Figure 7.17. *Hint: Type cyclist in the* **Office.com Clip Art** *text box.*
    b. Change the text wrapping to *In Front of Text*.
    c. Change the width of the picture to 4.5 inches.
    d. Click the Crop button in the Size group, drag the top left corner border of the cropping tool down approximately 0.25 inch and right approximately 0.25 inch (see image at right), and then click the Crop button to turn off the cropping feature.

    e. Change the width of the picture to 4.5 inches. (Since you cropped the image in the previous step, you need to make the image wider again.)
    f. Click the Compress Pictures button in the Adjust group.
    g. Make sure a check mark displays in the *Delete cropped areas of pictures* check box in the *Compression options* section of the Compress Pictures dialog box, and then click OK.
    h. Position the image as shown in Figure 7.17.

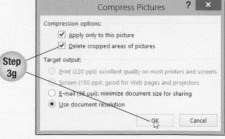

4. Create a picture caption by completing the following steps:
   a. With the picture selected, right-click the picture and then click *Insert Caption* at the shortcut menu.
   b. At the Caption dialog box, make sure *Figure 1* displays in the *Caption* text box and then click OK.
   c. With the insertion point positioned inside the caption text box and to the right of *Figure 1*, type a colon and then press the spacebar.
   d. Insert **PictureText.docx** from your Chapter07 folder at the location of the insertion point.
5. Select the entire caption, including the figure label, the figure number, and the text that you just inserted and then change the font to 10-point Cambria and apply bold and italic formatting.
6. Save **C07-E01-Picture.docx**.

Figure 7.17 Picture and Caption Formatted in Exercise 7.1G

Creating a Newsletter Masthead

The ***masthead*** is a newsletter element that contains the publication information. A masthead usually contains the following items (see Figure 7.18):

- Name and address of the company or organization producing the newsletter
- Newsletter publication schedule, such as weekly, monthly, or biannually
- Names of those contributing to the production of the newsletter, such as editors, authors, and graphic designers
- Copyright information
- A list of persons contributing to the production of the newsletter

The masthead may also contain a small logo, seal, or other graphic identifier. Although a masthead is commonly located on the back page of a newsletter, you will sometimes find it on the first page. Wherever you decide to place the masthead, be consistent from issue to issue in the masthead design, layout, and location.

masthead

A newsletter element that contains the publication information

◀**DTP POINTER**

Be consistent in the design, layout, and placement of the masthead from issue to issue.

Figure 7.18 Illustrating Examples of Masthead Designs

Desktop Designs

Editor:
Martha Ridoux

Design and Layout:
Grace Shevick

Contributing Authors:
Jonathan Dwyer
Nancy Shipley
Christine Johnson

Published Monthly by:
DTP Training, Inc.
4550 North Wabash St.
Chicago, IL 60155
(312) 555-9366
www.emcp.net/dtp

© *Copyright 2015 by:*
DTP Training, Inc.
All rights reserved.

Desktop Designs

Editor:
Martha Ridoux

Design and Layout:
Grace Shevick

Contributing Authors:
Jonathan Dwyer
Nancy Shipley
Christine Johnson

Published Monthly by:
DTP Training, Inc.
4550 North Wabash St.
Chicago, IL 60155
(312) 555-9366
www.emcp.net/dtp

© Copyright 2015 by:
DTP Training, Inc.
All rights reserved.

---

1. With **C07-E01-Picture.docx** open, save the document with the name **C07-E01-Masthead**.
2. Insert a predesigned text box to hold the masthead text by completing the following steps:
    a. Position the insertion point at the beginning of the second page of the newsletter.
    b. Click the INSERT tab, click the Text Box button in the Text group, and then scroll down and click the *Simple Quote* option at the drop-down list.

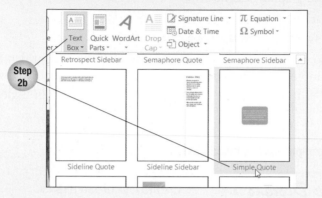

    c. With the new text box selected, type **2.2** in the *Shape Height* measurement box in the Size group on the DRAWING TOOLS FORMAT tab, type **3.1** in the *Shape Width* measurement box, and then press Enter.
    d. Drag the text box to the bottom left corner of page 2 to a location similar to that shown in Figure 7.19.
    e. With the text box selected, apply the Subtle Effect - Blue, Accent 1 effect in the Shape Styles gallery on the DRAWING TOOLS FORMAT tab.

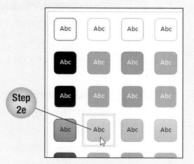

    f. Change the shape outline color to *Dark Blue*.
    g. Click once inside the text box to select the placeholder and then insert **MastheadText .docx** from your Chapter07 folder.
    h. Press Ctrl + A to select all the masthead text in the text box, click the PAGE LAYOUT tab, type **0** in the *After* option in the *Spacing* section in the Paragraph group, and then press Enter.
    i. Click in the title of the text box, *Ride Safe*, and change the spacing after paragraphs to 6 points.
3. Save **C07-E01-Masthead.docx**.

Figure 7.19   Masthead Created in Exercise 7.1H

⋯⋯⋯⋯⋯⋯⋯⋯⋯⋯⋯⋯⋯⋯⋯⋯⋯⋯⋯⋯⋯⋯⋯⋯•Winners wear helmets!

Research indicates that 60% of all U.S. bicycle-car collisions occur among bicyclists between the ages of 8 and 12. Children are permitted to travel with only *"look both ways before you cross the street"* and *"make sure you stop at all stop signs"* warnings. Obviously, these "warnings" are not enough.

⇐ WHO SAYS HELMETS AREN'T COOL? ⇒

Figure 1: Certainly not the children of Silverton, Oregon! One of the biggest reasons children don't wear bicycle helmets is because their friends don't wear them. By getting all the children in your school or neighborhood to order bicycle helmets at the same time, you can help turn this peer pressure from negative to positive. Suddenly, wearing a bicycle helmet becomes the "cool" thing to do. With your support, your kids can be "cool," too!

Ride Safe

Editor:
Brandon Keith
Design and Layout:
Cassie Lizbeth
Authors:
Chris Urban
Justine Youssef
Amanda Knicker
Published quarterly by:
Ride Safe, Inc.
P.O. Box 888
Warrenville, IL 60555
800-555-RIDE
Fax: 630-555-9068
© Copyright 2015 by:
Ride Safe, Inc.
All rights reserved.

2

Understanding Copyfitting

Publications such as magazines and newsletters contain information that varies from issue to issue. Though there is structure in how the articles or stories are laid out on the page (such as the asymmetrical two-column format in the Ride Safe newsletter), there may be times when an article takes up more or less space than is allotted to it. Arranging text and design elements so that they fit in a fixed amount of space is referred to as *copyfitting*.

copyfitting

Arranging text and design elements so that they fit in a fixed amount of space

There are many methods you can use to copyfit a newsletter, depending on the challenges you encounter. Some of the most common methods are listed below.

When you need to create more space for text, try the following:

- Reduce the margins.
- Change the alignment.
- Change the typeface, typestyle, or size, but limit body type size to a minimum of 9 points, preferably 10 or 11 points.
- Reduce the spacing before and after paragraphs (or hard returns) to reduce the spacing around the nameplate, headlines, subheads, frames, or text boxes.
- Reduce the spacing between paragraphs.
- Turn on hyphenation.
- Condense the spacing between characters.
- Reduce the line spacing in the body text.
- Remove a sidebar, pull quote, kicker, or end sign.
- Edit the text, including rewriting and eliminating sections.

When you need to fill more space, try the following:

- Increase the margins.
- Change the alignment.
- Change font size, but limit body type size to a maximum of 12 points.
- Increase the spacing between paragraphs.
- Adjust the character spacing.
- Increase the line spacing in the body text.
- Increase the spacing around the nameplate, headlines, subheads, text boxes, or graphic images.
- Add a sidebar, pull quote, kicker, end sign, graphic lines, clip art, photo, etc.
- Add text.

Be consistent when making any copyfitting adjustments. For example, if you increase the white space after one headline, increase the white space after all headlines. Alternatively, if you decrease the type size of the body text in an article, decrease the type size of body text in all articles. Adjustments are less noticeable when completed uniformly. Also, small adjustments can often make a big difference. For instance, rather than reducing type size by a whole point, try reducing it by 0.25 or 0.5 point.

In the Ride Safe newsletter created in the previous exercises, you made copyfitting adjustments to the typeface, type size, typestyle, spacing above and below the article headings, spacing between paragraphs, spacing within the paragraphs, and size and position of text boxes. In Exercise 7.1I, you will reposition the linked text box and add two more articles to the second page of the Ride Safe newsletter. You will also apply styles and insert a clip art image.

DTP POINTER

Don't go overboard when making copyfitting changes—small adjustments can make a big difference.

1. With **C07-E01-Masthead.docx** open, save it with the name **C07-E01-Newsletter**.
2. Add content to the second page of the newsletter, as shown in Figure 7.20 on page 313, by completing the following steps, making your own minor adjustments if necessary to fit the articles in their respective locations:
   a. To make room for the article THE LIGHT BULB TEST at the beginning of page 2, click and drag the linked text box located on page 2 that contains the remaining text from the ACCIDENTS article to just above the Ride Safe masthead. (This text box will be formatted in future steps.)
   b. Position the insertion point at the top left side of page 2 (at the beginning of column 1) and then draw a text box to hold the article THE LIGHT BULB TEST.
   c. Remove the shape outline and shape fill from the text box.
   d. Change the size of the text box to 4.0 inches in height and 2.4 inches in width.
   e. Drag the text box to a position similar to that shown in Figure 7.20.
   f. Change the left, right, top, and bottom margins of the text box to 0 inches.
      Hint: Change the internal margins at the Format Shape task pane with the Layout & Properties icon selected.
   g. Click once inside the text box to position the insertion point and then insert **LightBulbText.docx** from your Chapter07 folder.
   h. Position the insertion point in the heading *The Light Bulb Test* and then apply the Article Head style.
   i. Position the insertion point in the first paragraph and then apply the 1st Paragraph style.
   j. Position the insertion point in the second paragraph and then apply the Article Text style.
3. Insert the light bulb image in the article heading by completing the following steps:
   a. Position the insertion point between LIGHT and BULB in the heading and then delete the space between the words.
   b. With the insertion point positioned between the two words, display the Insert Pictures window, type **glowing light bulb** in the *Office.com Clip Art* text box, press the Enter key, and then double-click the image shown at the right. (Select a similar image if this one is not available; you may need to broaden your search by using the keywords *light bulb*.)

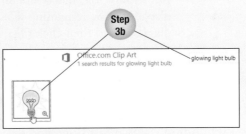

   c. With the light bulb image selected, size it similarly to the image shown in Figure 7.20. Make sure the light bulb is small enough so that your article heading fits on one line, and the article text fits within the text box.
4. Create the end sign at the end of the article by completing the following steps:
   a. On page 1, select the end sign at the end of the first article and then press Ctrl + C to copy the end sign.
   b. Position the insertion point to the right of the period in the last sentence at the end of the article THE LIGHT BULB TEST, press the spacebar three times, and then press Ctrl + V to paste the end sign into the text box.

5. Select the linked text box that contains the remaining text from the *Accidents* article and then make the following changes with options on the DRAWING TOOLS FORMAT tab:
   a. Remove the shape outline and shape fill.
   b. Change the size of the text box to 2 inches in height and 2.4 inches in width.
   c. Change the internal text box margins to 0 inches at the Format Shape task pane.
   d. Drag the text box to a position similar to that shown in Figure 7.20.
6. Insert and format the "continued" jump line at the beginning of the text in the linked text box on page 2 by completing the following steps:

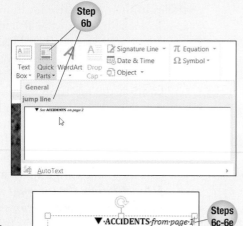

Step 6b

   a. Position the insertion point at the beginning of the text in the linked text box on page 2.
   b. Click the INSERT tab, click the Quick Parts button in the Text group, and then click the *jump line* option located in the *General* section of the drop-down list.
   c. Delete the word *See* in the jump line.
   d. Select the word *on* and then type **from**.
   e. Select the number *2* and then type **1**.
7. Insert the horizontal line above the jump line by completing the following steps:

Steps 6c-6e

   a. Position the insertion point in the jump line, click the HOME tab, click the Borders button arrow in the Paragraph group, and then click *Borders and Shading* at the drop-down gallery.
   b. At the Borders and Shading dialog box with the Borders tab selected, change the *Width* option to *1 pt*, click the top border of the diagram in the *Preview* section, make sure no borders display on the remaining sides of the diagram, and then click OK.

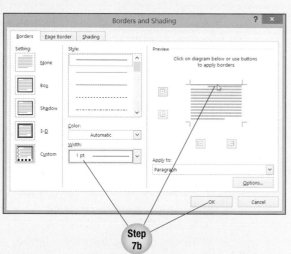

8. Copy and paste the end sign from the article *THE LIGHT BULB TEST* three spaces after the end of this article. (Drag the masthead text box downward slightly if necessary.)
9. Adjust the two text boxes and the masthead as necessary so that they display as shown in Figure 7.20.

Step 7b

10. Save **C07-E01-Newsletter.docx**.
11. Insert an article in the remaining space in the right column of page 2 by completing the following steps:
    a. Draw a text box to hold the article *WHEN SHOULD A HELMET BE REPLACED?* that is approximately the same size and in the same location as that shown in Figure 7.20.
    b. Remove the shape outline and shape fill from the text box.
    c. Change the size of the text box to 4.1 inches in height and 4.5 inches in width.
    d. Change the left, right, top, and bottom margins to 0 inches at the Format Shape task pane.
    e. Click once inside the text box to position the insertion point and then insert **ReplaceHelmetText.docx** from your Chapter07 folder.
    f. Drag the box to a position similar to that shown in Figure 7.20.

12. Apply styles to the article text you just inserted by completing the following steps:
    a. Position the insertion point in the title *When Should a Helmet Be Replaced?* and then apply the Article Head style.
    b. Select all of the paragraph text and then apply the 1st Paragraph style.
13. Insert a bullet and emphasize the text at the beginning of each paragraph by completing the following steps:
    a. Select all of the article text paragraphs (excluding the title).
    b. Click the Bullets button in the Paragraph group on the HOME tab.
    c. Click the Decrease Indent button in the Paragraph group to move the bullets to the edge of the text box.
    d. Select the first sentence in each bulleted paragraph and then change the font to Impact.
14. Scroll through the newsletter and make any copyfitting adjustments that may be necessary.
15. Turn off the display of nonprinting characters and change the zoom to 100%.
16. Save and then print **C07-E01-Newsletter.docx**.

Figure 7.20   Final Newsletter Created in Exercises 7.1A–7.1I

Distributing Newsletters

In Chapter 6, you learned how to add addresses to newsletters and distribute them through the mail. If you are concerned about the cost of printing and mailing a newsletter, there are other methods of distribution available. Two such methods are sending a newsletter as an email attachment and posting a newsletter on the Web.

Sending a Newsletter as an Email Attachment

Imagine that you are the owner of a small business and would like to inform your customers of new products, upcoming sales or special promotions, and articles that may be of interest to them. You are thinking of preparing a monthly newsletter; however, you do not want the added expense of printing and mailing the newsletter. An inexpensive, easy, and effective alternative for you is to send the newsletter as an email attachment.

While you could send the Word document itself as an email attachment, a better option is to save your newsletter in PDF format and then send it as an email attachment. The PDF file format captures all of the elements of a printed document as an electronic image that anyone can view, print, and forward, even if they do not have Word or any other word processing software installed on their computer. Save a Word document in PDF format by clicking the FILE tab, clicking the *Export* option, clicking the Create PDF/XPS button, making sure *PDF (*.pdf)* displays in the *Save as type* option box at the Publish as PDF or XPS dialog box, and then clicking the Publish button.

Viewing a Newsletter on the Web

A newsletter created in Word can be saved in a web format, such as ***HTML*** or ***MHTML***, that allows you to view the document in a web browser. If the newsletter is formatted in a table, the structure of the newsletter will stay in place when it is viewed on the Web.

To save a newsletter in HTML, click the FILE tab and then click the *Export* option. At the Export backstage area, click the *Change File Type* option, click the *Single File Web Page (*.mht, *.mhtml)* option, and then click the Save As button, as shown in Figure 7.21. At the Save As dialog box, type the file name and then specify where you want to save the document. Click the Change Title button, type a page title, which will display in the title bar of the browser, at the Enter Text dialog box, and then click OK. Click the Save button at the Save As dialog box and, if necessary, click the Continue button at the Microsoft Word Compatibility Checker.

To view the newsletter in a web browser, add the Web Page Preview button to the Quick Access toolbar. Begin by clicking the Customize Quick Access Toolbar button at the right of the Quick Access toolbar and then clicking the *More Commands* option at the drop-down list. At the Word Options dialog box with the *Quick Access Toolbar* option selected, click the down-pointing arrow at the right of the *Choose commands from* option box, click *All Commands*, scroll down and click the *Web Page Preview* option from the list, click the Add button, and then click OK, as shown in Figure 7.22. Open the newsletter in Word and then click the Web Page Preview button to view the document as it would display on a web page in your chosen browser. Depending on the formatting applied to the newsletter in Word, the newsletter elements may not appear in the same location when saved in Single File Web Page format.

Figure 7.21 Saving a Document as a Single File Web Page

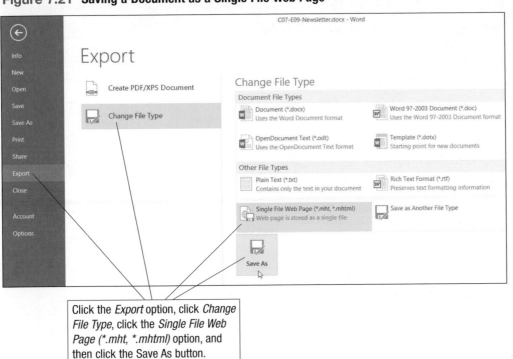

Click the *Export* option, click *Change File Type*, click the *Single File Web Page (*.mht, *.mhtml)* option, and then click the Save As button.

Figure 7.22 Adding the Web Page Preview Button to the Quick Access Toolbar

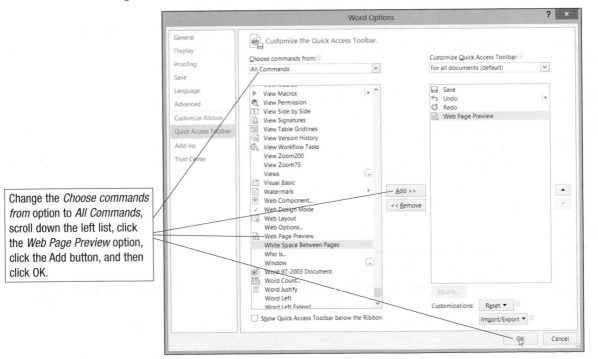

Change the *Choose commands from* option to *All Commands*, scroll down the left list, click the *Web Page Preview* option, click the Add button, and then click OK.

Exercise 7.2 Saving a Newsletter as a Web Page and as a PDF

1. With **C07-E01-Newsletter.docx** open, add the Web Page Preview button to the Quick Access toolbar by completing the following steps:

   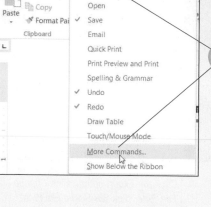

   a. Click the Customize Quick Access Toolbar button located on the Quick Access toolbar and then click *More Commands* at the drop-down list.

   b. At the Word Options dialog box with *Quick Access Toolbar* selected in the left panel, click the down-pointing arrow at the right of the *Choose commands from* option box and then click *All Commands* at the drop-down list.

   c. Scroll down the list box on the left and then click the *Web Page Preview* option.

   d. Click the Add button and then click OK to close the dialog box.

2. Save the newsletter as a single file web page by completing the following steps:

   a. Click the FILE tab and then click the *Export* option.

   b. Click the *Change File Type* option in the middle panel, click *Single File Web Page (*.mht, *.mhtml)* option in the *Other File Types* section, and then click the Save As button.

   c. Navigate to your Chapter07 folder and then type **C07-E02-NewsletterWebPage** in the *File name* text box.

   d. Click the Change Title button located at the bottom right of the Save As dialog box, type **Ride Safe** in the *Page title* text box at the Enter Text dialog box, and then click OK.

   e. Click the Save button.

   f. Click Continue at the compatibility checker dialog box.

3. View the newsletter in a web browser by clicking the Web Page Preview button on the Quick Access toolbar. Notice that many of the newsletter elements do not appear in the same location when saved in the Single File Web Page format.

4. Close your web browser and then close **C07-E02-NewsletterWebPage.mht**.

5. Open **C07-E01-Newsletter.docx** and display the newsletter in Print Layout view by clicking the Print Layout button in the view area on the Status bar.

6. Save the newsletter as a PDF by completing the following steps:

   a. Click the FILE tab and then click the *Export* option.

   b. Click the Create PDF/XPS button in the *Create a PDF/XPS Document* section.

   c. At the Publish as PDF or XPS dialog box, navigate to your Chapter07 folder and then type **C07-E02-NewsletterPDF** in the *File name* text box.

   d. Insert a check mark in the *Open file after publishing* check box and then click the Publish button.

   e. View the newsletter in PDF format and then close Adobe Reader.

7. Save and then close **C07-E01-Newsletter.docx**.

Chapter Summary

➤ Elements that can be added to a newsletter to enhance the visual impact include tables of contents, headers and/or footers, mastheads, kickers, sidebars, pull quotes, captions, ruled lines, jump lines, page borders, and end signs.

➤ Newsletters can be formatted in columns, tables, or text boxes.

➤ Headers and footers are commonly used in newsletters. Headers and footers can be placed on specific pages, only odd pages, or only even pages, and they can include page numbering, a slogan, a logo, or a horizontal ruled line.

➤ Use spot color—a color in addition to black—in a newsletter as an accent to such features as graphic lines, graphic images, borders, backgrounds, headings, and end signs.

➤ A sidebar is set off from the body text in a text box and can include a photograph or graphic image along with text.

➤ A sidebar can be created from scratch by drawing and then enhancing a text box, or you can insert a predesigned sidebar from the Text Box button drop-down list or the Building Blocks Organizer dialog box.

➤ In multiple-page newsletters, a table of contents is an important element and is generally located on the front page in the lower left or right corner.

➤ A pull quote acts as a focal point, helps to break up lengthy blocks of text, and provides visual contrast.

➤ A kicker is typically set in a smaller type size than the headline but larger than the body text and is placed above or below the headline or article heading.

➤ Symbols or special characters used to indicate the end of a section of text are called end signs.

➤ If an article begins on one page and continues onto another page, link the text boxes containing the article text to help the text flow from one text box to another.

➤ In a newsletter, jump lines indicate a continuation of an article or feature on another page, which enables the newsletter to feature the beginning of several articles on the front page.

➤ Noncomputer-generated images such as photographs and illustrations can be scanned and inserted into a newsletter.

➤ Captions can be added to images to establish a connection to the copy. Bold or italicize caption text and set it in a smaller point size to make it different from the body text.

➤ Predesigned Word captions can be added to an image, table, or graphic, or you can create your own design from scratch using a text box.

➤ A masthead is a repeating element that usually contains the company address, newsletter publication schedule, names of those contributing to the production, and copyright information. It is generally located on the back page of a newsletter.

➤ Copyfitting refers to making varying amounts of text or typographical enhancements fit in a fixed amount of space.

➤ A newsletter can be saved and then sent as an email attachment. If the recipient does not have Word, the newsletter can be saved in PDF file format.

➤ Newsletters can be saved in HTML and then viewed in Web Page Preview.

➤ Formatting a newsletter in a table structure holds the newsletter design elements in place when viewed in a web page.

Commands Review

FEATURE	RIBBON TAB, GROUP	BUTTON, OPTION	KEYBOARD SHORTCUT
break link	DRAWING TOOLS FORMAT, Text		
caption	REFERENCES, Captions		
column break	PAGE LAYOUT, Page Setup	, *Column Break*	Ctrl + Shift + Enter
columns	PAGE LAYOUT, Page Setup		
footer	INSERT, Header & Footer		
go to footer	HEADER & FOOTER TOOLS DESIGN, Navigation		
go to header	HEADER & FOOTER TOOLS DESIGN, Navigation		
header	INSERT, Header & Footer		
link text boxes	DRAWING TOOLS FORMAT, Text		
link to previous	HEADER & FOOTER TOOLS DESIGN, Navigation		
next section	HEADER & FOOTER TOOLS DESIGN, Navigation		
page numbers	HEADER & FOOTER TOOLS DESIGN, Header & Footer		
previous section	HEADER & FOOTER TOOLS DESIGN, Navigation		
quick parts	INSERT, Text		
symbol	INSERT, Symbols		
Web Page Preview	Quick Access toolbar		

Key Points *Review*

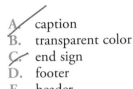

A. caption
B. transparent color
C. end sign
D. footer
E. header

F. jump line
G. kicker
H. masthead
I. pull quote
J. scanner

K. sidebar
L. spot color
M. copyfitting

Matching: In the space at the left, provide the correct letter or letters from the above list that match each definition.

____H____ 1. A repeating element that can add consistency among newsletter issues and that contains the company address, newsletter publication schedule, names of those contributing to the production of the newsletter, and copyright information

____A____ 2. A feature that describes or explains an image, table, illustration, or photograph

____E____ 3. Text that is repeated at the top of every page

____K____ 4. A block of information or a related story that is set off from the body text in a graphic box

____L____ 5. A color in a newsletter, other than black, used as an accent

____M____ 6. Making varying amounts of text or typographical enhancements fit in a fixed amount of space

____C____ 7. A symbol or special character used to indicate the end of a section of text

____F____ 8. A feature that is used to indicate that an article or feature continues on another page

____G____ 9. A brief sentence or phrase that is a lead-in to an article

____J____ 10. A device that converts a photograph, drawing, or text into a compatible digital file format

Short Answer: On a blank sheet of paper, provide the correct answer for each question.

1. List at least three formatting features that can be applied to a table of contents in a newsletter to make it visually interesting and stand out from the article text.
2. What is a caption and why are captions useful in a newsletter?
3. List at least four copyfitting ideas to create more space in a document.
4. What is the purpose of linking text boxes, and why is this feature advantageous in a newsletter?
5. What is copyfitting? List three suggestions to create more space in a newsletter and three suggestions to fill extra space in a newsletter.

Chapter *Assessments*

Assessment 7.1   Identify the Parts of a Newsletter

In this assessment, you will open a newsletter and identify specific elements of the newsletter.

1. Open **DownbeatWeekly.docx** from your Chapter07 folder and save it with the name **C07-A01-DownbeatWeekly.docx**.
2. Review the newsletter for the items listed below. Label those items that you find in the newsletter by inserting text boxes with lines drawn from the text boxes to the items directly into the newsletter document. (Not all elements are included in the newsletter.)

caption	jump line	spot color
end sign	kicker	subheads
folio	masthead	subtitle
footer	nameplate	table of contents
header	pull quote	
headlines	sidebar	

3. Save, print, and then close **C07-A01-DownbeatWeekly**.

Assessment 7.2   Use a Word Newsletter Template

PORTFOLIO

In this assessment, you will incorporate your copyfitting skills and your knowledge of Word templates to create a business newsletter based on a Word template. A sample solution is shown in Figure 7.23.

1. Open **CapeTownMeetingText.docx**, located in your Chapter07 folder.
2. Open File Explorer, navigate to your Chapter07 folder, and then double-click *NewsletterTemplate.dotx*. (This opens a document based on the template.)
3. Save the document with the name **C07-A02-McAfeeNewsletter**.
4. Copy and paste the text from **CapeTownMeetingText.docx** to the placeholder in **C07-A02-McAfeeNewsletter.docx**. You will need to do a considerable amount of copyfitting and reformatting of text. The placeholder objects may not accommodate your text and graphics properly. Replace the graphics as needed. *Hint: Change the view to View Side by Side by clicking the VIEW tab and then clicking the View Side by Side button in the Window group. Copy and paste between the two documents at one screen.*
5. Apply appropriate styles to the text.
6. Save, print, and then close **C07-A02-McAfeeNewsletter.docx**.
7. Close the **CapeTownMeetingText.docx** file.

Assessment 7.3   Save a Newsletter as a PDF and in HTML Format

In this assessment, you will open a Word newsletter template that was created in a table format. You will save and view the newsletter as a PDF. You will then save it in HTML format and then view the document in Web Page Preview. Create the newsletter by completing the following steps:

1. Open File Explorer, navigate to your Chapter07 folder, and then double-click *WebPageTemplate.dotx*. (This opens a document based on the template.)
2. Scroll through the template to understand how it was created and read the placeholder text for helpful hints.
3. Save the document as a PDF by completing the following steps:
   a. Click the FILE tab and then click the *Export* option.
   b. Click the Create PDF/XPS button in the *Create a PDF/XPS Document* section.

Figure 7.23 Sample Solution for Assessment 7.2

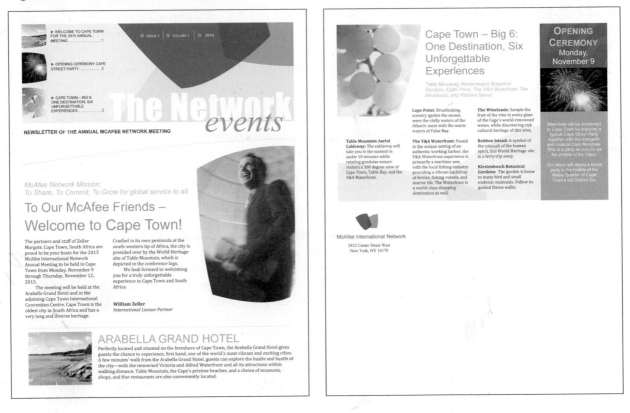

c. At the Publish as PDF or XPS dialog box, navigate to your Chapter07 folder and then type **C07-A03-PDFNewsletter** in the *File name* text box.

d. Insert a check mark in the *Open file after publishing* check box and then click the Publish button.

e. View the newsletter in PDF format and then close Adobe Reader.

4. Save the document in HTML format by completing the following steps:

a. Click the FILE tab and then click the *Export* option.

b. At the Export backstage area, click the *Change File Type* option, click the *Single File Web Page (*.mht, *.mhtml)* option in the *Other File Types* section, and then click the Save As button.

c. At the Save As dialog box, navigate to your Chapter07 folder, type **C07-A03-WebPageNewsletter** in the *File name* text box, and then click the Save button.

5. Make sure the Web Page Preview button displays on the Quick Access toolbar. If the button does not display, add the button to the Quick Access toolbar. (See Exercise 7.2 on page 316 for instructions on how to add the button to the Quick Access toolbar.)

6. Click the Web Page Preview button on the Quick Access toolbar.

7. View the document in your Internet browser.

8. Press the Home key to display the beginning of the newsletter in your Internet browser and then press the Print Screen key to capture a picture of the newsletter in your browser.

9. Open a blank document and then click the Paste button to paste a copy of the screen capture.

10. Save the document as **C07-A03-NewsletterCapture**.

11. Print and then close **C07-A03-NewsletterCapture.docx**. Close the Internet browser window.

12. Close **C07-A03-WebPageNewsletter.mht**.

Optional: Replace the placeholder text in the newsletter with your own text. Customize the graphics and other design elements in the newsletter to complement your message.

Assessment 7.4   Insert an Excel Worksheet as a Visual Aid in a Newsletter

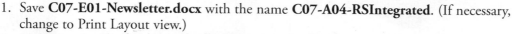

Open **C07-E01-Newsletter.docx**, which you created in Exercises 7.1A through 7.1I, and then format and embed a worksheet created in Excel on page 2 of the newsletter as shown in Figure 7.24. Include the following specifications:

1. Save **C07-E01-Newsletter.docx** with the name **C07-A04-RSIntegrated**. (If necessary, change to Print Layout view.)
2. Minimize the Word document and then open Excel 2013.
3. At the Excel opening screen, open **RideSafeProducts.xlsx**, located in your Chapter07 folder.
4. Enhance the Excel worksheet by completing the following steps:
   a. With cell A1, which contains *Ride Safe Products – 2015*, selected (a thick green border should display around the cell), click the Fill Color button arrow in the Font group on the HOME tab and then click the *Blue, Accent 5* option (ninth column, first row in the *Theme Colors* section).
   b. With cell A1 still selected, click the Borders button arrow in the Font group and then click *More Borders* at the bottom of the drop-down list. At the Format Cells dialog box with the Border tab selected, click the sixth line style in the right column in the *Style* list box, change the *Color* option to *Orange* (third option in the *Standard Colors* section), click the Outline button in the *Presets* section to add the borders to the preview diagram, and then click OK.
   c. With cell A1 still selected, change the font to 22-point Forte and change the font color to *White, Background 1*.
   d. Select cells A2:C2, change the font to 11-point Impact, and then change the font color to *Orange*.
   e. Select cells A3:C11 and then change the font to 10-point Franklin Gothic Book.
   f. Select cell A13, click the Format button in the Cells group, click *Row Height* at the drop-down list, type **28**, and then click OK.
   g. With cell A13 still selected, change the font to 8-point Franklin Gothic Book and then apply italic formatting.
   h. With cell A13 still selected, click the Wrap Text button in the Alignment group.
   i. Select cells C3:C11, click the Number Format list box arrow in the Number group, and then click the *Currency* option.

   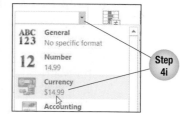

   j. Select cells A1:C13 and then apply the same thick orange border you applied in Step 4b.
5. Save the Excel worksheet as **C07-A04-RideSafeProducts**.
6. Select cells A1:C13 and then click the Copy button in the Clipboard group.
7. Minimize Excel and then maximize Word.
8. Delete the last article text within the text box at the bottom of **C07-A04-RSIntegrated.docx** (the *WHEN SHOULD A HELMET BE REPLACED?* article).
9. With the insertion point positioned inside the text box, click the Paste button arrow in the Clipboard group on the HOME tab and then click *Paste Special* at the drop-down list. Click *Microsoft Excel Worksheet Object* in the Paste Special dialog box and then click OK.
10. If necessary, resize the text box to display the entire Excel object.
11. Save, print, and then close **C07-A04-RSIntegrated.docx**.
12. Close **C07-A04-RideSafeProducts.xlsx** and then close Excel.

Figure 7.24 Excel Worksheet Inserted on Page 2 of the Ride Safe Newsletter in Assessment 7.4

•••Winners wear helmets!

THE LIGHT 💡 BULB TEST

To illustrate the effectiveness of a bicycle helmet, try the following. Wrap a light bulb in plastic wrap, seal the bottom with a rubber band and place it in a bicycle helmet. Secure the light bulb with tape and drop the helmet onto a flat, hard surface from above your head. The light bulb will not break. In most cases, it will even still light. Now, drop the light bulb without the protection of the helmet. The light bulb will produce a sick thud as it breaks. Helmets *can* make a difference.

    Caution: This experiment is meant to be done under close supervision. —●—

▼ **ACCIDENTS** *from page 1*

    Research indicates that 60% of all U.S. bicycle-car collisions occur among bicyclists between the ages of 8 and 12. Children are permitted to travel with only *"look both ways before you cross the street"* and *"make sure you stop at all stop signs"* warnings. Obviously, these "warnings" are not enough. —●—

Ride Safe

Editor:
Brandon Keith
Design and Layout:
Cassie Lizbeth
Authors:
Chris Urban
Justine Youssef
Amanda Knicker
Published quarterly by:
Ride Safe, Inc.
P.O. Box 888
Warrenville, IL 60555
800-555-RIDE
Fax: 630-555-9068
© **Copyright 2015 by:**
Ride Safe, Inc.
All rights reserved.

☞ WHO SAYS HELMETS AREN'T COOL? ☜

Figure 1: Certainly not the children of Silverton, Oregon! One of the biggest reasons children don't wear bicycle helmets is because their friends don't wear them. By getting all the children in your school or neighborhood to order bicycle helmets at the same time, you can help turn this peer pressure from negative to positive. Suddenly, wearing a bicycle helmet becomes the "cool" thing to do. With your support, your kids can be "cool," too!

Ride Safe Products - 2015		
Product	**Description**	**Cost**
RS1000	Helmet, choice of colors, 3 sizes	$14.99
XSAir	Helmet, Tattoo design, 1 size	$16.99
RS4000	In-Line Skating Helmet, 6 colors, 2 sizes	$22.99
SL100	Flashing Helmet Safety Light	$5.99
SL200	Night Eye Flashing Bicycle Safety Light	$7.99
PG200	In-Line Skating Protective Gear	$32.99
W300	Ride Safe Four Water Bottle	$2.99
S100	Reflective Sweatshirts, 4 sizes	$28.99
T100	Reflective T-Shirts, 5 sizes	$22.99

*All of the Ride Safe bicycle and in-line skating helmets are independently certified to the stringent A.N.S.I. and A.S.T.M standards.

• • •
2

Assessment 7.5   Create and Revise a Newsletter Based on Peer Feedback

GROUP PROJECT

In this assessment, you will work with another student in your class to create a newsletter from existing content and new content you find and create yourselves. Start by opening **ButterfieldGardens.docx** in your Chapter07 folder.

1. Select a Word newsletter template or design the newsletter from scratch. Incorporate all of the existing document content onto the first page of the newsletter. Use the columns feature, linked text boxes, and/or a table as the underlying structure for your newsletter. Be creative and remember to use plenty of white space. Use the Butterfield Gardens logo (**ButterfieldGardenLogo.png**), located in your Chapter07 folder.

2. Insert several appropriate photographs or clip art images to enhance the first page of the document.

3. Add a second page to the newsletter and discuss with your partner what content you want to include on this page. Keep in mind the topic of the newsletter and the intended audience.

4. Search the Internet to find interesting articles about gardening to include on the second page of your newsletter. Type **gardening** in the search text box at www.google.com, www.bing.com, or any search engine of your choosing. Make sure to create bylines to give credit for the articles you choose to insert. Search for and select images that reinforce the message.

5. Correct any spelling and grammatical errors or formatting inconsistencies in the Butterfield Gardens document. Create and apply styles to reinforce consistency.

6. Save your document and name it **C07-A05-Butterfield**.

7. Print your newsletter and then close **C07-A05-Butterfield.docx**.

8. In class, conduct a peer review of the newsletters by completing the following steps:

   a. Work with your partner to choose a name for your team. Do not share it with the rest of the class.

   b. Print your newsletter and write your team name somewhere on the document.

   c. Your instructor will collect all of the printed newsletters and randomly distribute a newsletter to each class participant.

   d. When you and your partner receive a newsletter to review, look it over carefully and, on the back of the newsletter, write editorial comments addressing such items as target audience, visual appeal, overall layout and design, font selection, graphic image selection, focus, balance, proportion, contrast, directional flow, consistency, and use of color. Make sure to point out what has been done well, as well as what still needs work.

   e. Exchange newsletters with other groups until you have had an opportunity to write comments on the back of each newsletter.

   f. Review the comments on the back of your own newsletter and revise your newsletter based on the suggestions.

9. Save and name the revised version of your newsletter **C07-A05-ButterfieldRevised**.

10. Print and then close **C07-A05-ButterfieldRevised.docx**.

11. Evaluate your revised newsletter with the document evaluation checklist (**DocumentEvaluationChecklist.docx**) located in your Chapter07 folder.

Performance *Assessments*

Preparing Personal and Business Documents

ASSESSING PROFICIENCIES

In this unit, you have learned to apply design concepts to create personal documents, letterheads, envelopes, business cards, press releases, and newsletters.

Note: Before beginning computer exercises for this unit, copy to your storage medium the Unit02 folder from the CD that accompanies this textbook and then make Unit02 the active folder. Remember to substitute for graphics that may no longer be available.

Assessment U2.1   **Use a Template to Create a Certificate**

1. Open File Explorer, navigate to your Unit02 folder, and then double-click **F&LCertificate.dotx**. (This opens a document based on the template.)
2. Modify the award certificate as shown in Figure U2.1 by completing the following steps:
   a. Type the text in the placeholders. (Use your name in place of *Student Name*.)
   b. Insert **L&F-ColorLogo.png** from your Unit02 folder, change the height of the image to 2 inches, and then position the image in the lower right corner of the certificate, as shown in the figure.
3. Save the completed certificate and name it **U2-PA01-L&FCertificate**.
4. Print and then close **U2-PA01-L&FCertificate.docx**.

Figure U2.1 Certificate Created in Performance Assessment U2.1

1. At a blank document, create a letterhead similar to the one shown in Figure U2.2 by completing the following steps:
   a. Complete a search for the keyword *eagles* at the Insert Pictures window.
   b. Insert, size, format, and position the eagle image as shown in Figure U2.2.
   c. Apply the Fill - Black, Text 1, Outline - Background 1, Hard Shadow - Accent 1 WordArt style to the text *Blue Eagle Airlines*, apply the Cascade Up transform effect, and then change the font size to 24 points.
   d. Draw a text box and then type **On the Wings of Eagles** in 13-point Book Antiqua (substitute another font if necessary), apply italic formatting, expand the text by 1.5 points, and turn on kerning at 13 points and above. Change the font color to a color that coordinates with the eagle image. Position the text box as shown in the figure.
   e. Create the blue arrow extending from the graphic image to the text box containing *On the Wings of Eagles*.
   f. Create a text box that contains the name *Dallas Love Field* set in 10-point Book Antiqua with bold formatting and then add the following address information in 9-point Book Antiqua (substitute a different font if necessary):

      22 Mockingbird Lane
      Dallas, TX 75235
      www.emcp.net/beair
      214.555.6073
      1.800.555.6033
      214.555.6077 (Fax)

   g. Change the paragraph alignment in the text box to right. Adjust the line spacing and color as desired and position the text box as shown in Figure U2.2.
   h. Create another arrow that extends from *Eagles* to the text box containing the address, as shown in Figure U2.2. Use the same arrow style and color used in the figure. (Both arrows in the document should be the same style and color.)
2. Create a coordinating envelope using the company name, address, and contact information as shown in Figure U2.2 by completing the following steps:
   a. To add an envelope to the document, display the Envelopes and Labels dialog box with the Envelopes tab selected and then click the Add to Document button.
   b. Insert the letterhead graphics in the envelope by copying and pasting, and then resize the graphics as necessary to fit the envelope.
   c. Add the stamp graphic to the envelope and then change the color of the graphic to match the color scheme of the envelope.
3. Save the completed letterhead and envelope document with the name **U2-PA02-BEAirlines**.
4. Print and then close **U2-PA02-BEAirlines.docx**.

Figure U2.2 Letterhead and Envelope Created in Performance Assessment U2.2

Blue Eagle Airlines —————→ *On the Wings of Eagles*

Dallas Love Field
22 Mockingbird Lane
Dallas, TX 75235
www.emcp.net/beair
214.555.6073
1.800.555.6033
214.555.6077 (Fax)

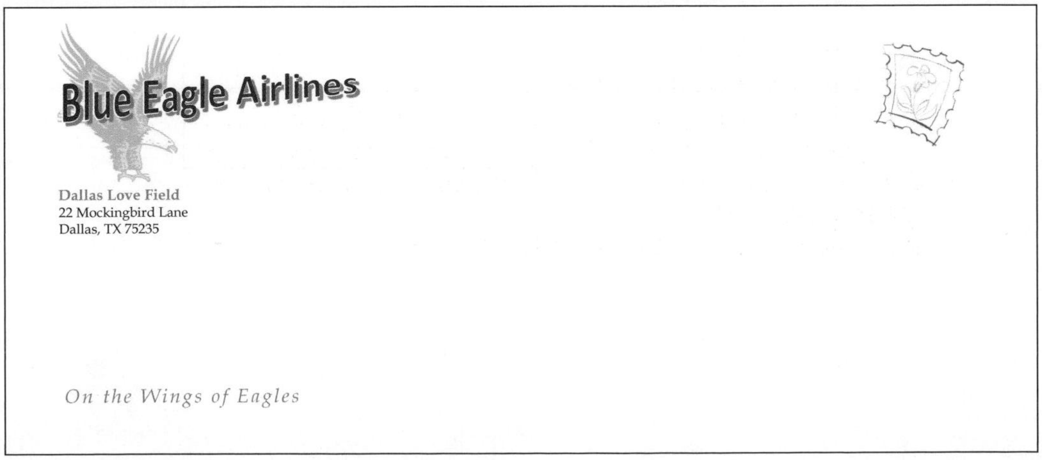

Blue Eagle Airlines

Dallas Love Field
22 Mockingbird Lane
Dallas, TX 75235

On the Wings of Eagles

1. At a blank document, insert Avery US Letter 8371 Business Cards labels. *Hint: Use the Labels button in the Create group on the MAILINGS tab.*
2. In the first label on the sheet, create the business card shown in Figure U2.3 by completing the following steps:
    a. Insert **L&F-ColorLogo.png** at the left side of the cell, change the height to 1.9 inches, change the text wrapping to *Square*, and then position the image as shown in the figure.
    b. Create a text box for the information about Jody Bender. Format the text in the text box so it appears similar to what is shown in Figure U2.3. (Use the Calibri font for the text.)
    c. Create a text box for the slogan *Together we can make a difference!* Apply formatting so that the text appears similar to what is shown in Figure U2.3 and then rotate and position the text box.
3. Group the logo and the two text boxes in the label and then save the grouped object as a quick part named **XXX-L&FBusinessCard**. (Use your initials in place of *XXX*.)
4. Save the label document with the name **U2-PA03-L&FBusCardLabel** and then close the document.
5. At a blank document, display the Envelopes and Labels dialog box with the Labels tab selected, make sure the *Avery US Letter, 8371 Business Cards* label is selected in the *Label* section, type **XXX-L&FBusinessCard** in the *Address* list box (type your initials in place of the *XXX*), press F3, and then click the New Document button.
6. Save the business cards document and name it **U2-PA03-L&FBusCards**.
7. Print and then close **U2-PA03-L&FBusCards.docx**.

Figure U2.3 Business Card Created in Performance Assessment U2.3

Assessment U2.4   Create the Back Side of a Business Card

1. Use Avery US Letter 8371 Business Cards labels to create the back sides of the business cards you created in Assessment U2.3. Include in the label the text *Be a part of it!* and *Volunteer today at Loaves & Fishes*. Include any additional elements you think will enhance the appearance of the card. You determine the formatting and positioning of the elements on the label.
2. Group the elements in the label and then save the grouped object as a quick part named **XXX-L&FBusCardBack**. (Use your initials in place of the *XXX*.)
3. Save the label document with the name **U2-PA04-L&FBusCardBackLabel** and then close the document.
4. At a blank document, create a sheet of Avery US Letter 8371 Business Cards labels and then insert the **XXX-L&FBusCardBack** quick part.
5. Save the business cards document and name it **U2-PA04-L&FBusCardsBack**.
6. Print and then close **U2-PA04-L&FBusCardsBack.docx**.

Assessment U2.5   Prepare a Volunteer Newsletter

1. Create a newsletter to be sent to the Loaves & Fishes volunteers using a table and/or text boxes (see Figure U2.4 on page 330 for a sample solution) by completing the following steps:
   a. For the text of the newsletter articles, insert the following text files from your Unit02 folder:
      DonationsNeeded.docx
      VolunteerOpportunities.docx
      DietaryChanges.docx
      HealthierChoices.docx
   b. Insert the Loaves & Fishes logo, **L&F-ColorLogo.png**.
   c. Insert an appropriate image in at least one of the articles.
2. Save the document and name it **U2-PA05-L&FNewsletter**.
3. Print **U2-PA05-L&FNewsletter.docx**.
4. Save the document again in PDF format.
5. Close both documents.

DTP CHALLENGE

Take your skills to the next level by completing this more challenging assessment:

Assessment U2.6   Research and Create Files for a New Business

1. Create a fictional small business that sells a product or provides a service that interests you. Use the design concepts and Word features you have learned in this unit to create the following for your business:
   - Letterhead template (Save the template document as **LtrhdTemplate.dotx**.)
   - Envelope (Save the envelope document as **BusEnv.docx**.)
   - Business cards (Save the business cards document as **BusCards.docx**.)
2. Save each of the files you create and then print and close the files.
3. Using the **LtrhdTemplate.dotx** template you created, prepare a press release announcing the grand opening of your business. Include information such as dates and times, address, and contact numbers.
4. Save the press release and name it **PressRelease**.
5. Print and then close **PressRelease.docx**.

Figure U2.4 Sample Solution for Performance Assessment U2.5

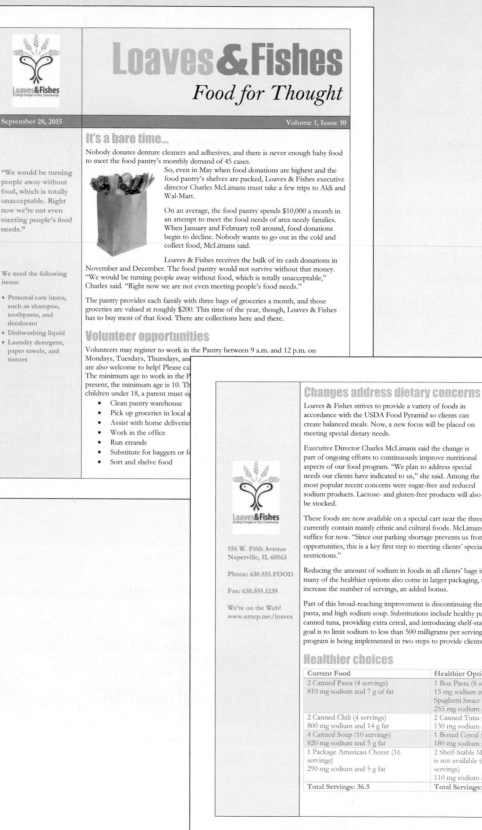

Loaves & Fishes
Food for Thought

September 28, 2015   Volume 1, Issue 10

It's a bare time...

Nobody donates denture cleaners and adhesives, and there is never enough baby food to meet the food pantry's monthly demand of 45 cases.

So, even in May when food donations are highest and the food pantry's shelves are packed, Loaves & Fishes executive director Charles McLimans must take a few trips to Aldi and Wal-Mart.

On an average, the food pantry spends $10,000 a month in an attempt to meet the food needs of area needy families. When January and February roll around, food donations begin to decline. Nobody wants to go out in the cold and collect food, McLimans said.

Loaves & Fishes receives the bulk of its cash donations in November and December. The food pantry would not survive without that money. "We would be turning people away without food, which is totally unacceptable," Charles said. "Right now we are not even meeting people's food needs."

The pantry provides each family with three bags of groceries a month, and those groceries are valued at roughly $200. This time of the year, though, Loaves & Fishes has to buy most of that food. There are collections here and there.

Volunteer opportunities

Volunteers may register to work in the Pantry between 9 a.m. and 12 p.m. on Mondays, Tuesdays, Thursdays, an[d]
are also welcome to help! Please ca[ll]
The minimum age to work in the P[antry]
present, the minimum age is 10. Th[e]
children under 18, a parent must si[gn]

- Clean pantry warehouse
- Pick up groceries in local a[rea]
- Assist with home deliveries
- Work in the office
- Run errands
- Substitute for baggers or f[or]
- Sort and shelve food

"We would be turning people away without food, which is totally unacceptable. Right now we're not even meeting people's food needs."

We need the following items:

- Personal care items, such as shampoo, toothpaste, and deodorant
- Dishwashing liquid
- Laundry detergent, paper towels, and tissues

Changes address dietary concerns

Loaves & Fishes strives to provide a variety of foods in accordance with the USDA Food Pyramid so clients can create balanced meals. Now, a new focus will be placed on meeting special dietary needs.

Executive Director Charles McLimans said the change is part of ongoing efforts to continuously improve nutritional aspects of our food program. "We plan to address special needs our clients have indicated to us," she said. Among the most popular recent concerns were sugar-free and reduced sodium products. Lactose- and gluten-free products will also be stocked.

These foods are now available on a special cart near the three self-serve carts that currently contain mainly ethnic and cultural foods. McLimans said this would have to suffice for now. "Since our parking shortage prevents us from offering shopping opportunities, this is a key first step to meeting clients' special dietary needs and restrictions."

Reducing the amount of sodium in foods in all clients' bags is another goal. Since many of the healthier options also come in larger packaging, the shift would also increase the number of servings, an added bonus.

Part of this broad-reaching improvement is discontinuing the purchase of chili, canned pasta, and high sodium soup. Substitutions include healthy pasta sauce, doubling the canned tuna, providing extra cereal, and introducing shelf-stable, low-fat milk. Our goal is to limit sodium to less than 500 milligrams per serving, she added. The program is being implemented in two steps to provide clients with a smooth transition.

Loaves & Fishes

556 W. Fifth Avenue
Naperville, IL 60563

Phone: 630.555.FOOD

Fax: 630.555.1239

We're on the Web!
www.emcp.net/loaves

Healthier choices

Current Food	Healthier Option
2 Canned Pasta (4 servings) 810 mg sodium and 7 g of fat	1 Box Pasta (8 servings) 15 mg sodium and 3 g fat Spaghetti Sauce (5 servings) 255 mg sodium and .8 g fat
2 Canned Chili (4 servings) 800 mg sodium and 14 g fat	2 Canned Tuna (5 servings) 130 mg sodium and 0 g fat
4 Canned Soup (10 servings) 820 mg sodium and 5 g fat	1 Boxed Cereal (11 servings) 180 mg sodium and 1 g fat
1 Package American Cheese (16 servings) 290 mg sodium and 5 g fat	2 Shelf-Stable Milk (or cheese when milk is not available through NIFB) (8 servings) 110 mg sodium and 5 g fat
Total Servings: 36.5	**Total Servings: 40**

UNIT 3

Preparing Promotional Documents

Creating Flyers and Announcements

Performance Objectives

Upon successful completion of Chapter 8, you will be able to:

- Produce promotional documents such as flyers and announcements
- Review and apply design concepts
- Use tables to guide the layout of design elements
- Understand graphic formats and color terminology
- Apply page color

- Apply shape and picture effects
- Adjust image brightness, contrast, sharpness, and softness
- Adjust image color saturation, color tone, and recolor
- Apply artistic effects to images
- Remove backgrounds from pictures
- Use SmartArt graphics in documents

Desktop Publishing Terms

announcement	color tone	flyer	raster graphics
bitmapped graphics	crop marks	gradient	RGB
brightness	dpi	grayscale	transparent
CMYK	fill	HSL	vector graphics

Word Features Used

artistic effects	group	rotate	text wrapping
brightness	page color	shape effects	ungroup
contrast	picture effects	shape fill	WordArt
corrections	picture styles	shape outline	
crop to shape	position	shape styles	
drawing grid	recolor	SmartArt	
gradient	remove background	tables	

Note: Before beginning computer exercises for this chapter, copy to your storage medium the Chapter08 folder from the CD that accompanies this textbook and then make Chapter08 the active folder. Remember to substitute for graphics that may no longer be available.

Planning and Designing Flyers and Announcements

flyer

Promotional document used to advertise a product or service that is available for a limited amount of time

Flyers and announcements are two types of promotional documents. **Flyers** generally advertise a product or service that is available for a limited amount of time. You may find a flyer stuffed into a grocery bag; attached to a mailbox, door handle, or windshield; or in a stack on a countertop in a store. The basic purpose of a flyer is to communicate a message at a glance, so the contents of a flyer should be brief and to the point. For the flyer to be effective, the basic layout and design should be free of clutter, without too much text or too many graphics. Use white space generously to set off an image or text and to help promote good directional flow.

announcement

Promotional document used to inform an audience of an upcoming event

An **announcement** informs an audience of an upcoming event. An announcement may create interest in an event but does not necessarily promote a product or service. For instance, you may receive an announcement of new course offerings at your local community college or an announcement of an upcoming community gathering, sporting event, concert, race, contest, raffle, or new store opening.

As with any other desktop publication, planning should be the first step in the process of creating a flyer or announcement. Because you have a limited amount of space to work with when creating these documents, it is especially important to prepare a thumbnail sketch, which is like thinking on paper. Clearly define your purpose and assess your target audience. You should consider your target audience even when making design decisions such as choosing type sizes—for example, the older your audience, the larger the print might need to be. Remember to consider your budget as well. Generally, producing flyers and announcements is one of the least expensive means of advertising.

DTP POINTER

Preparing a thumbnail sketch is especially helpful when creating flyers and announcements.

DTP POINTER

Consider your audience when choosing type sizes.

DTP POINTER

The upper left corner of a document is usually read first.

Successful promotional documents attract the reader's attention and keep it. Consider how you can attract the reader's eyes by using interesting headlines, dynamic graphics, and pops of color for emphasis. Keep in mind that readers generally look at graphics first, then the headline, and, finally, the company logo. Your goal is to hold their attention long enough to see all three!

Using Tables for Page Layout

After you have created a thumbnail sketch for a flyer or announcement, you can draw a table in a Word document to block off areas of the page and reflect the layout you have sketched in your thumbnail. Figure 8.1 shows how a table can serve as a framework for creating an announcement.

Table

Draw Table

To create a table layout like the one shown in Figure 8.1A, use the *Draw Table* option. To access this option, click the INSERT tab, click the Table button in the Tables group, and then click *Draw Table* at the drop-down list. This causes the mouse pointer to display as a pen. Draw table lines in the document by holding down the left mouse button as you drag in the document. When you are finished creating the table, click the Draw Table button in the Draw group on the TABLE TOOLS LAYOUT tab to turn the drawing feature off. If you need to remove lines from your table, click the Eraser button in the Draw group. This causes the mouse pointer to display as an eraser. Drag the eraser along the lines you want to remove.

Eraser

With the measurement boxes in the Cell Size group on the TABLE TOOLS LAYOUT tab, you can change row height and column width within your table. You can also change row height in a table by dragging the row border up or down and change column width by dragging the column border left or right.

Figure 8.1 Using a Table to Create an Announcement

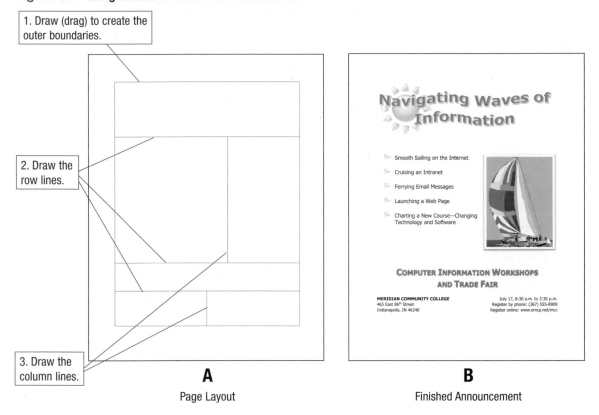

1. Draw (drag) to create the outer boundaries.

2. Draw the row lines.

3. Draw the column lines.

A

Page Layout

B

Finished Announcement

The TABLE TOOLS LAYOUT tab also contains many other buttons you can use to adjust and format your table. You can customize table properties, insert or delete rows and columns, merge or split cells, specify text alignment within cells, and sort data in the table. The TABLE TOOLS DESIGN tab appears next to the TABLE TOOLS LAYOUT tab and contains buttons and options that allow you to apply and customize a table style, apply shading and border lines to a table or cells, and customize table borders.

In Exercise 8.1A, you will draw a table to create the layout for an announcement. You will add text and images to the announcement in subsequent exercises.

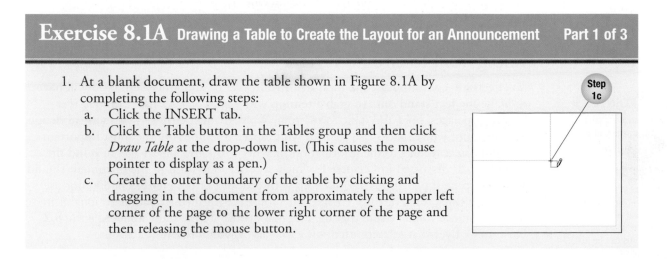

Exercise 8.1A Drawing a Table to Create the Layout for an Announcement   Part 1 of 3

1. At a blank document, draw the table shown in Figure 8.1A by completing the following steps:
   a. Click the INSERT tab.
   b. Click the Table button in the Tables group and then click *Draw Table* at the drop-down list. (This causes the mouse pointer to display as a pen.)
   c. Create the outer boundary of the table by clicking and dragging in the document from approximately the upper left corner of the page to the lower right corner of the page and then releasing the mouse button.

Step 1c

d. Position the pen at the left boundary line approximately 2 inches below the top boundary line of the table and then drag to create a horizontal line from the left boundary line to the right boundary line.

e. Position the pen at the left boundary line approximately 2 inches above the bottom boundary line and then drag to create a horizontal line from the left boundary line to the right boundary line.

f. Position the pen at the left boundary line approximately 0.75 inch below the line you just drew in Step 1e and then drag to create a horizontal line from the left boundary line to the right boundary line.

g. In the second row, position the pen approximately 2.5 inches from the right boundary line and then drag down to create a vertical line.

h. In the bottom row, position the pen at the approximate center of the row and then drag to create a vertical line.

i. Click the Draw Table button in the Draw group on the TABLE TOOLS LAYOUT tab to turn off the drawing feature.

2. Click the table move handle that displays in the upper left corner of the table (a four-headed arrow inside a square) to select the entire table and then change the font to Tahoma.

3. With the table still selected, remove border lines by clicking the TABLE TOOLS DESIGN tab, clicking the Borders button arrow in the Borders group, and then clicking *No Border* at the drop-down gallery. (Dashed gridlines should display the table lines. If these gridlines are not visible, click the TABLE TOOLS LAYOUT tab and then click the View Gridlines button in the Table group.)

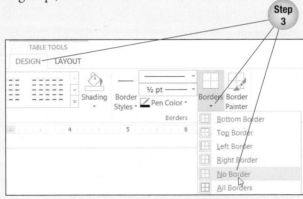

4. Save the document with the name **C08-E01-Announcement**.

Using Text to Create Focus

DTP POINTER

White space creates a clean page that is easy to read.

DTP POINTER

Remember the rule of thirds—one-third of the document should be white space and two-thirds can be text or graphics.

To effectively communicate the message of your flyer or announcement, you will have to make the text stand out. To grab attention with text, consider using unique (yet legible) typefaces, bold and italic formatting, WordArt, text effects, asymmetrical design, and plenty of white space. Use color or white space to emphasize the most important text and direct readers to the information they need to know first. Keep in mind the rule of thirds discussed in Chapter 1, which says that one-third of the document should be white space if two-thirds are taken up with text and/or design objects. Do not use more than three fonts or three colors. After you have finished a document, look at it from a distance to make sure that the essential details are the most visible. Figure 8.2 illustrates a flyer that attracts attention with varying fonts and font attributes.

Figure 8.2 Using Text to Create Focus in an Announcement

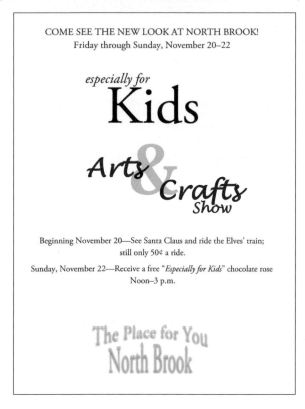

Using Graphics for Emphasis

Graphics can add excitement to a publication and generate enthusiasm. Well-placed graphics can transform a plain page into a compelling visual document, as shown in Figure 8.3 on page 338. However, it is effective only if the graphic enhances the subject of the document. While clip art illustrations tend to create a fun, playful, or whimsical appearance, photographs can convey a more professional, sophisticated, or serious tone. If you are deciding among many graphics, select the simplest. A simple graphic demands more attention and has more impact; graphics that are too complicated can create clutter and confusion. Use a graphic to aid in directional flow, and use white space generously around graphics. Use your thumbnail sketch as a tool to help you make decisions on position, size, and orientation of graphics.

Search for clip art images and photographs at Office.com by clicking the INSERT tab and then clicking the Online Pictures button in the Illustrations group. At the Insert Pictures window, type a keyword, phrase, or category in the *Office.com Clip Art* text box and then press Enter. When the search results display in the Insert Pictures window, double-click the desired image.

Consider using clip art images and/or photographs as a base to create your own unique graphics. For example, combine clip art images with other clip art images and then crop, size, or color different areas of the combined image. Alternatively, edit a photograph by using tools within Word, Paint, or, if you have access to it, a photo-editing program such as Adobe Photoshop. You will learn more about customizing images later in this chapter.

◀ DTP POINTER

Choose images that relate to the message.

◀ DTP POINTER

Leave plenty of white space around a graphic.

◀ DTP POINTER

Do not overuse clip art; use one main visual element per page.

Figure 8.3 Using Graphics for Emphasis in a Flyer

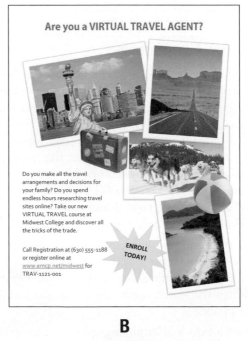

Are you a VIRTUAL TRAVEL AGENT?

Do you make all the travel arrangements and decisions for your family? Do you spend endless hours researching travel sites online? Take our new VIRTUAL TRAVEL course at Midwest College and discover all the tricks of the trade.

Call Registration at (630) 555-1188 or register online at www.emcp.net/midwest for TRAV-1121-001

ENROLL TODAY!

A

Flyer without Graphics

Are you a VIRTUAL TRAVEL AGENT?

Do you make all the travel arrangements and decisions for your family? Do you spend endless hours researching travel sites online? Take our new VIRTUAL TRAVEL course at Midwest College and discover all the tricks of the trade.

Call Registration at (630) 555-1188 or register online at www.emcp.net/midwest for TRAV-1121-001

ENROLL TODAY!

B

Flyer with Graphics

In Exercise 8.1B, you will add text and images to the announcement you started in Exercise 8.1A. You will insert WordArt to create focus on the headline of your announcement and insert clip art from Office.com to add emphasis to the message of the document.

1. With **C08-E01-Announcement.docx** from Exercise 8.1A open, click in the first cell in the table and then insert WordArt text in the cell by completing the following steps (refer to Figure 8.4 on page 341):

    a. Click the INSERT tab, click the WordArt button in the Text group, and then click the *Fill - Blue, Accent 1, Outline - Background 1, Hard Shadow - Accent 1* option (third column, bottom row).

    b. Type **Navigating Waves of Information**.

    c. Click in the *Shape Height* measurement box in the Size group on the DRAWING TOOLS FORMAT tab, type **1.35**, and then press Enter.

    d. Click the Text Effects button in the WordArt Styles group, point to *Transform*, and then click the *Double Wave 2* option (last column, fifth row in the *Warp* section).

    e. Click the Text Fill button arrow in the WordArt Styles group and then click the *Blue* option at the drop-down gallery (eighth color in the *Standard Colors* section).

    f. Drag the WordArt text box so it is centered vertically and horizontally in the first cell.

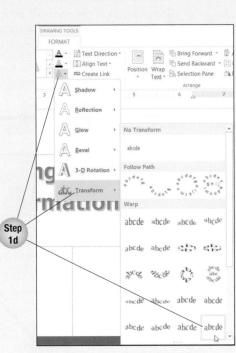

2. Click in the first cell outside the WordArt text box and then insert the image of the sun as shown in Figure 8.4 by completing the following steps:

    a. Click the INSERT tab and then click the Online Pictures button in the Illustrations group.

    b. At the Insert Pictures window, type **sun** in the *Office.com Clip Art* text box and then press Enter.

    c. Double-click the sun image shown below.

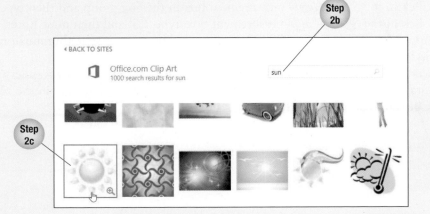

    d. With the sun image selected, click in the *Shape Height* measurement box on the PICTURE TOOLS FORMAT tab, type **2**, and then press Enter.

3. Click in the second cell in the second row and then insert the image of the sailboat by completing the following steps:

 a. Click the INSERT tab and then click the Online Pictures button.

 b. At the Insert Pictures window, type **sailboat** in the *Office.com Clip Art* text box and then press Enter.

 c. Double-click the sailboat image shown below.

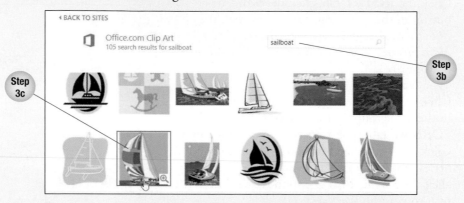

 d. With the sailboat image selected, click the Size group dialog box launcher on the PICTURE TOOLS FORMAT tab. At the Layout dialog box with the Size tab selected, click the *Lock aspect ratio* check box in the *Scale* section to remove the check mark and then click OK to close the dialog box.

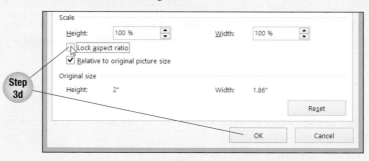

 e. Click in the *Shape Height* measurement box in the Size group and then type **3.3**.

 f. Click in the *Shape Width* measurement box, type **2.5**, and then press Enter.

 g. Apply the Simple Frame, White picture style (first picture style thumbnail in the Picture Styles group).

 h. Click the Wrap Text button and then click *Square* at the drop-down gallery.

 i. Drag the sailboat image so it is centered horizontally and vertically in the cell.

4. Save **C08-E01-Announcement.docx**.

Figure 8.4 Text and Graphics Added to the Announcement in Exercise 8.1B

Inserting Images from a Scanner or Digital Camera

You are not limited to using only Microsoft Office clip art and photographs in your documents. You can insert images from a scanner or digital camera into a document in a manner similar to inserting an image from Office.com. If you are scanning an image, save the image to a folder on your computer or another storage medium. If you want to use an image from a digital camera, transfer the image file to a folder on your computer or another storage medium. Once the desired image file has been placed in a folder on your computer or other storage medium, insert the image by clicking the INSERT tab and then clicking the Pictures button to open the Insert Picture dialog box. Navigate to the folder where the image is located and then double-click the image to insert it.

Understanding and Selecting Scanner Resolution

dpi

Dots per inch (dpi); unit of measurement for resolution

A scanner is a device that converts hard copies of text or images into digital form so that they can be stored on your computer. Recall from Chapter 1 that resolution refers to the clarity of an image. Resolution is measured in dots per inch, or **dpi**. The higher the dpi, the clearer the image will appear, so higher resolution images are usually more desirable. However, one of the most common mistakes made when using a scanner is overscanning. Most scanners are capable of scanning up to 1200 dpi or more, so it may be tempting to scan at the highest resolution. However, if you scan a 5-by-7-inch image at 1200 dpi, the resulting digital image will take up 140 MB of memory. A good rule of thumb is to scan your images at 300 dpi. This is the resolution required for most print publications. If you later want to use the image for a digital purpose, such as embedding it in an email or posting it on a website, you should save it down to 72 dpi so that it will take less time to load.

Understanding Graphic File Formats

bitmapped or raster graphics

Images composed of individual pixels of color that can be edited one by one or as a group

Two major types of graphic images exist today—bitmap (or raster) graphics and vector graphics. **Bitmapped graphics**, or **raster graphics**, are composed of pixels in a grid. Remember from Chapter 5 that a pixel is each individual dot or square of color in a picture or graphic. Each pixel, or "bit," in the image contains information about the color to be displayed. These graphics are a collection of individual pixels of color that can be edited one by one or as a group. An enlarged bitmap image appears jagged around the edges. Bitmap images have a fixed resolution and cannot be resized without losing image quality. Enlarging the bitmap image enlarges the size of the pixels used to create it and causes the image to appear jagged or blurry around the edges. Photographs are a kind of bitmap image, and common bitmap file formats are JPEG, GIF, TIFF, PNG, and BMP. Most bitmap images can be converted easily to other bitmap-based formats.

vector graphics

Images made up of mathematically defined lines and curves

Vector graphics are made up of shapes (lines and curves) that are mathematically defined. You can resize a vector graphic by dragging the sizing handles surrounding the image, and the edges will remain smooth because the shapes in the image resize accordingly. If a software program has the word *draw* or *illustrate* in its name, the images and drawings you create in it will be vector graphics. Images imported using a scanner cannot typically be saved in a vector graphics file format.

Choosing Graphic File Formats

After you scan an image or import it from a digital camera, you can save it in several different file formats. The most common formats are JPEG (Joint Photographic Experts Group), TIFF (Tagged Image File Format), GIF (Graphics Interchange Format), PNG (Portable Network Graphics), and BMP (Bitmap Image). Choosing the right format depends on how you will use your image.

When choosing an image format, consider that the GIF format allows only 256 colors (8-bit), so it may not be as desirable as TIFF or JPEG formats, which allow for more colors. The PNG format is the successor to GIF, and it supports True Color (16 million colors). The PNG and GIF formats are typically used for online viewing. The general rule is to use JPEG for photographic images and GIF or PNG for images that have text, sharp lines, or large areas of solid colors.

Using Color to Enhance Promotional Documents

Color is a powerful tool in communicating information. You can incorporate color into a document through text or images; by using colored paper or a colored page background; by adding lines, shapes, or borders; or through special graphics such as charts and graphs. You will learn more about the different ways to add color to your document throughout the remainder of this chapter.

Understanding Color Terms Used in Desktop Publishing

When working on desktop publishing projects in Word 2013 or any other program, you may encounter some specialized terms that are used to explain color. The following is a list of some of these terms and their definitions, many of which have been defined in previous chapters:

- *Balance* is the amount of light and dark in a picture.
- **Brightness** or *value* is the amount of light in a color.
- *Contrast* is the amount of gray in a color.
- **CMYK** is an acronym for cyan, magenta, yellow, and black. A color printer combines these colors to create all other colors.
- **Gradient** is a gradual varying of color.
- **Grayscale** is a range of shades from black to white.
- *Hue* is a variation of a primary color, such as green-blue.
- *Luminescence* is the brightness of a color, that is, of the amount of black or white added to a color. The larger the luminescence number, the lighter the color.
- **RGB** is an acronym for red, green, and blue. Each pixel on your computer monitor is made up of some combination of these three colors.
- *Saturation* is the purity of a color. A color is completely pure, or saturated, when it is not diluted with white.

brightness
The relative lightness of a picture

CMYK
Stands for cyan, magenta, yellow, and black—the colors that combine to create all other colors

gradient
An effect created by a gradual varying of color

grayscale
A range of shade from black to white

RGB
Stands for the colors red, green, and blue

Adding and Printing Page Color

Page Color

Add page color to a Word document with the Page Color button in the Page Background group on the DESIGN tab. Page color, by default, displays on the screen but does not print. If you want to print the page color in a document, click the FILE tab and then click *Options*. At the Word Options dialog box, click *Display* in the left panel. In the *Printing options* section of the dialog box, click the *Print background colors and images* check box to insert a check mark and then click OK to close the dialog box.

When you apply page color to a document, the color will appear to extend to the edge of the page on the screen, but pages may print with a white border along the edge of the paper. Recall from Chapter 4 that this border is a limitation of the printer hardware known as the nonprinting area, and it may measure approximately 0.25 inch. Most inkjet and laser printers do not allow printing to the edge of the page. You may want to print to a larger paper size and then trim to the desired size to create the look of a bleed (content printed to the edge of the paper). Determine the nonprinting area of your desktop printer by setting the left, right, top, and bottom margins to zero. The margins will automatically reset to the minimum margin that is supported by the printer. You may want to make a note of the size of your printer's nonprinting area.

Showing Document Content

Options for turning on or off the display of certain content in a document are available in the *Show document content* section of the Word Options dialog box with *Advanced* selected in the left panel. To turn on an option, insert a check mark in the option's check box.

To view the margin boundaries in your document, insert a check mark in the *Show text boundaries* check box (see Figure 8.5). The boundaries that display in the document do not print. Use boundary lines to position design elements on the page.

Crop marks show where a publication page will be trimmed. In Word, these marks display on the screen when the *Show crop marks* option at the Word Options dialog box has been selected (see Figure 8.5). Crop marks only show on a printed page when the content has been printed to a paper size that is larger than the document page.

Figure 8.5 Showing Boundaries and Crop Marks at the Word Options Dialog Box

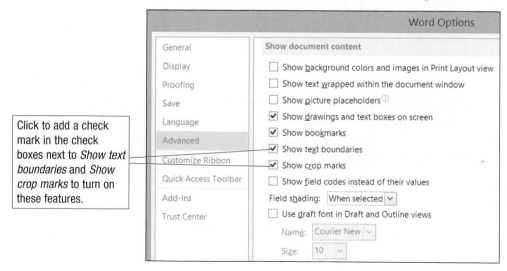

Click to add a check mark in the check boxes next to *Show text boundaries* and *Show crop marks* to turn on these features.

In Exercise 8.1C, you will add the body text to your announcement. You will also add a page background color and then adjust the settings at the Word Options dialog box so that the background color prints and crop marks display.

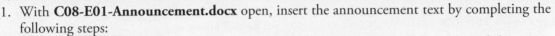

1. With **C08-E01-Announcement.docx** open, insert the announcement text by completing the following steps:
   a. Position the insertion point in the first cell of the second row of the table and then use the Object button in the Text group on the INSERT tab to insert **Sailing.docx** located in your Chapter08 folder.
   b. Position the insertion point in the cell in the third row of the table and then insert **TradeFair.docx** located in your Chapter08 folder. Press the Backspace key one time to delete the extra line after the inserted text. Make sure that the text is centered horizontally and vertically. Resize the row if necessary.
   c. Position the insertion point in the first cell in the fourth row and insert **Midwest.docx** located in your Chapter08 folder. Press the Backspace key one time to delete the extra line after the inserted text.
   d. Position the insertion point in the second cell in the fourth row and insert **Register.docx** located in your Chapter08 folder. Press the Backspace key one time to delete the extra line after the inserted text.
   e. With the insertion point positioned in the second cell in the fourth row, click the Align Top Right button in the Alignment group on the TABLE TOOLS LAYOUT tab.
   f. Make sure that the table fits on one page. If not, make slight adjustments to row heights until the table fits on one page and the document does not contain a second page. *Hint: When you position the mouse pointer on a line in the table, the mouse pointer should display as a left-and-right-pointing arrow with two vertical lines in the middle or as an up-and-down-pointing arrow with two horizontal lines in the middle. Drag to move the line and then release the left mouse button when you are satisfied with the position.*

2. Add a page color by clicking the DESIGN tab, clicking the Page Color button in the Page Background group, and then clicking the *Gold, Accent 4, Lighter 80%* option (eighth column, second row in the *Theme Colors* section).

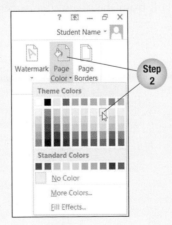

3. Turn on the printing of background colors and the display of crop marks by completing the following steps:
   a. Click the FILE tab and then click *Options*.
   b. At the Word Options dialog box, click *Display* in the left panel.
   c. Click the *Print background colors and images* check box to insert a check mark.
   d. Click *Advanced* in the left panel.
   e. Scroll down the dialog box to the *Show document content* section and then click the *Show crop marks* check box to insert a check mark.

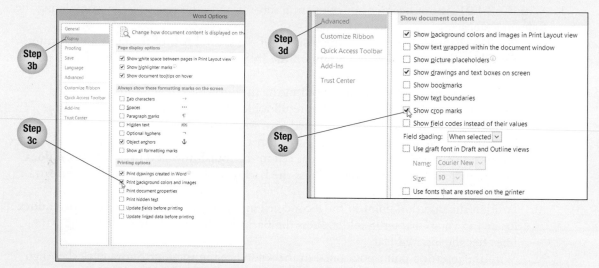

   f. Click OK to close the dialog box.
4. View the entire page by clicking the VIEW tab and then clicking the One Page button in the Zoom group. If any of the items are not positioned as shown in Figure 8.6, drag any boundary line in the table to adjust the size of the cell. If the flyer displays too high or low on the page, change the top and/or bottom margins to center the flyer vertically on the page. Use the crop marks as a reference for aligning the flyer in the center of the page.
5. Change the view back to 100% by clicking the 100% button on the VIEW tab.
6. Save, print, and then close **C08-E01-Announcement.docx**.
7. Display the Word Options dialog box with *Display* selected in the left panel and then remove the check mark from the *Print background colors and images* option. Click *Advanced* in the left panel, remove the check mark from the *Show crop marks* check box, and then close the dialog box.

Figure 8.6 Announcement Created in Exercise 8.1

Navigating Waves of Information

- Smooth Sailing on the Internet
- Cruising an Intranet
- Ferrying Email Messages
- Launching a Web Page
- Charting a New Course—Changing Technology and Software

COMPUTER INFORMATION WORKSHOPS AND TRADE FAIR

MERIDIAN COMMUNITY COLLEGE
465 East 86th Street
Indianapolis, IN 46240

July 17, 8:30 a.m. to 3:30 p.m.
Register by phone: (317) 555-8909
Register online: www.emcp.net/mcc

Modifying Document Elements to Enhance Promotional Materials

Word provides a variety of features you can use to modify document elements to better support the message of an announcement or flyer. As discussed in Chapter 5, ruled lines can be used to create a focal point, draw the eye across or down the page, separate columns and sections, or add visual appeal. Borders can be used to frame text or an image. Shading can be used to create visual interest in the background of a table, a paragraph, selected text, or a drawing object. Shape and picture effects can be added to graphics to create depth and movement. Examples of lines, borders, shading, and effects are displayed in Figure 8.7.

Figure 8.7 Illustrating Lines, Borders, Shading, Shadow, and Bevel Effects

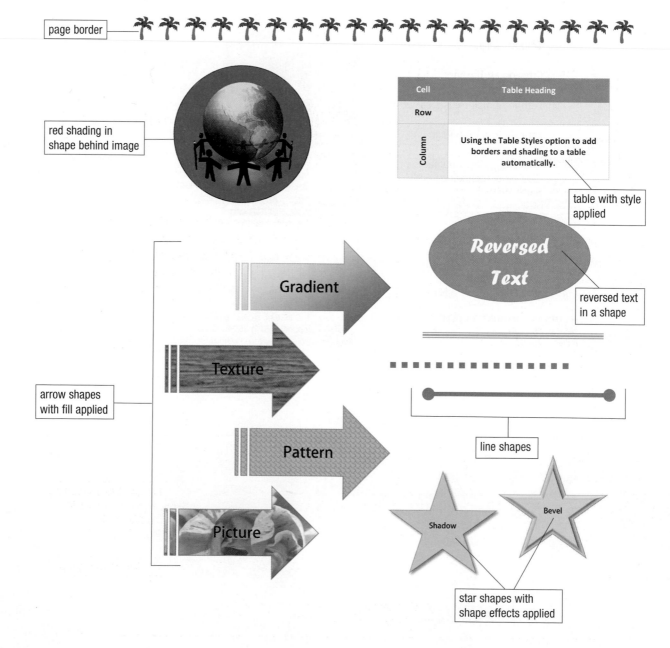

Adding Fill to Document Elements

A background, or *fill*, can be added to a table, paragraph, selected text, shapes, objects, and some images. You can fill drawing objects with solid colors or a gradient, a pattern, a texture, or even a picture. Shapes can be filled with photographs or clip art to create an interesting focal point. In Exercise 8.2, you will fill an arrow shape with a picture as a means of reinforcing the theme of the document. To add an image as fill, insert a shape, click the Shape Fill button arrow in the Shape Styles group on the DRAWING TOOLS FORMAT tab, and then click *Picture* at the drop-down gallery. At the Insert Pictures window, search for and then insert the desired image.

Another method for filling a shape with an image is to insert the image, make sure the image is selected, click the Crop button arrow in the Size group on the PICTURE TOOLS FORMAT tab, point to *Crop to Shape* at the drop-down list, and then click the desired shape at the side menu. The image will conform to the design shape. This method is shown in Figure 8.8.

Using the Drawing Grid

The Word drawing grid is a network of lines that help you align drawing objects, such as shapes, text boxes, clip art, and pictures. As you draw an object, Word pulls it into alignment with the nearest intersection of gridlines. By default, the gridlines of the drawing grid are not visible, but you can display gridlines by clicking the VIEW tab and then clicking the *Gridlines* check box in the Show group to insert a check mark. You can adjust settings for the drawing grid at the Grid and Guides dialog box, as shown in Figure 8.9 on page 350. Display this dialog box by clicking the PAGE LAYOUT tab, clicking the Align button in the Arrange group, and then clicking *Grid Settings* at the drop-down list.

The horizontal and vertical spacing between the gridlines defaults to 0.13 inch. This vertical spacing can be changed with the options in the *Grid settings* section of the Grid and Guides dialog box. The dialog box also contains options for specifying the types of gridlines to display and how often the gridlines show on the screen. To temporarily move an object without it snapping to a gridline, press the Alt key as you drag the object.

Figure 8.8 Adding a Picture Fill to a Shape

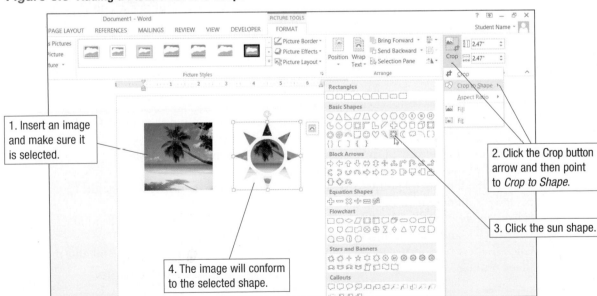

1. Insert an image and make sure it is selected.

2. Click the Crop button arrow and then point to *Crop to Shape*.

3. Click the sun shape.

4. The image will conform to the selected shape.

Figure 8.9 Customizing the Drawing Grid at the Grid and Guides Dialog Box

When the *Snap objects to other objects* check box contains a check mark, you will see the objects pull toward the nearest gridline.

Click to add a check mark next to *Use margins* to establish the horizontal and vertical starting points for the drawing grid.

Click to add a check mark next to *Display gridlines on screen* to enable this feature.

Use these measurement boxes to specify the spacing settings for the horizontal and vertical grids.

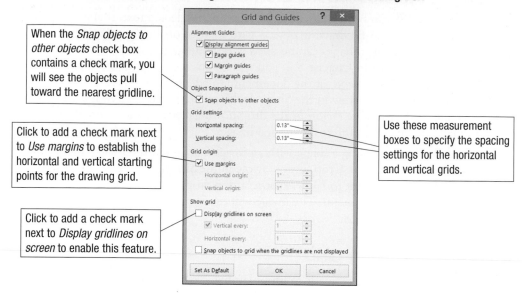

In Exercise 8.2, you will create an announcement for the Brighton Health & Fitness Center promoting a new summer program. Keep the theme of the flyer in mind as you decide on photos to use in the document.

Exercise 8.2 Creating an Announcement with Shapes and Picture Fill Using the Drawing Grid

PORTFOLIO

1. Open **Health.docx** from your Chapter08 folder and then save the document with the name **C08-E02-Health**.
2. Click the Show/Hide ¶ button in the Paragraph group on the HOME tab to turn on the display of nonprinting characters.
3. Apply formatting to text by completing the following steps (refer to Figure 8.10 on page 354):
   a. Select the text *Healthy choices point to healthy lives....*
   b. Change the font to 36-point Papyrus and apply bold formatting.
   c. Select the text *Healthy*, hold down the Ctrl key, and then select the text *healthy*.
   d. Apply the Green, Accent 6, Darker 25% font color (last column, fifth row in the *Theme Colors* section).
   e. Select the word *point* and then apply italic formatting.
4. Position the insertion point in the text box below *Healthy choices…* and then insert **Cardio.docx** from your Chapter08 folder.
5. Apply formatting to the text in the text box by completing the following steps:
   a. Select all of the text you just inserted in the text box.
   b. Change the font to 14-point Arial, apply italic formatting, and then change the paragraph alignment to right.
   c. Select *Summer Cardio Mix*, remove italic formatting, change the font to 18-point Bauhaus 93, and then apply the Green, Accent 6, Darker 25% font color.
   d. Click the text box border to select the text box and then remove the shape fill and the shape outline.

6. Apply formatting to the text in the *Brighton Health* text box by completing the following steps:
   a. Select all of the text in the text box and then change the paragraph alignment to center.
   b. Select *Brighton Health & Fitness Center* and then change the font to 16-point Bauhaus 93 and apply the Green, Accent 6, Darker 25% font color.
   c. Select both lines of the address and then change the font to 10-point Arial and apply the Green, Accent 5, Darker 25% font color.
   d. Select the text box containing the text you just formatted and then remove the shape fill and the shape outline.

7. Position the insertion point in the text box behind the *Brighton* text and then insert the symbol (logo) as shown in Figure 8.10 by completing the following steps:
   a. Click the INSERT tab, click the Symbol button in the Symbols group, and then click *More Symbols* at the drop-down list.
   b. At the Symbol dialog box with the Symbols tab selected, change the font to Webdings.
   c. Click the symbol shown at the right (approximately the seventh symbol in the seventh row). **Hint: Type 134 in the Character code *text box to locate the symbol.***
   d. Click the Insert button and then click the Close button.
   e. Select the symbol, change the font size to 115 points, and then apply the White, Background 1, Darker 15% font color (first column, third row in the *Theme Colors* section).
   f. Center the symbol in the text box and then, if necessary, position the text box as shown in Figure 8.10.
   g. Remove the shape fill and shape outline from the text box.

8. Turn on the display of the drawing grid to help in aligning the arrow shapes shown in Figure 8.10 by completing the following steps:
   a. Click the PAGE LAYOUT tab, click the Align button in the Arrange group, and then click *Grid Settings* at the drop-down list.
   b. At the Grid and Guides dialog box, make sure a check mark displays in the *Snap objects to other objects* check box.
   c. Select the current measurement in the *Horizontal spacing* measurement box in the *Grid settings* section and then type **0.22**.
   d. Select the current measurement in the *Vertical spacing* measurement box in the *Grid settings* section and then type **0.22**.
   e. Make sure a check mark displays in the *Use margins* check box in the *Grid origin* section.
   f. Click the *Display gridlines on screen* check box in the *Show grid* section to insert a check mark.
   g. Select the current number in the *Vertical every* measurement box and then type **2**.
   h. Select the current number in the *Horizontal every* measurement box, type **2**, and then click OK to close the dialog box.

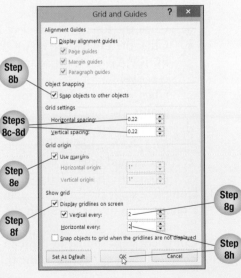

9. Create the top arrow by completing the following steps:
   a. Click the INSERT tab, click the Shapes button in the Illustrations group, and then click the *Striped Right Arrow* option in the *Block Arrows* section.

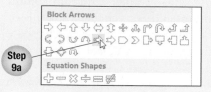

Step 9a

   b. Drag the crosshairs to create an arrow similar to the one at the right and the top arrow shown in Figure 8.10.
   c. Click in the *Shape Height* measurement box in the Size group on the DRAWING TOOLS FORMAT tab and then type **2.4**.
   d. Click in the *Shape Width* measurement box, type **3**, and then press Enter.
   e. Click the Shape Effects button in the Shape Styles group, point to *Shadow*, scroll down the side menu, and then click the *Perspective Diagonal Upper Left* option (first option in the *Perspective* section).
   f. Position the arrow as shown at the right and in Figure 8.10.

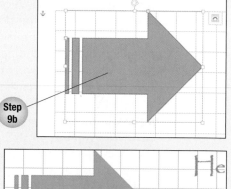

Step 9b

10. With the arrow selected, copy it by holding down the Ctrl key and then dragging the copy of the arrow below the first arrow as shown at the right and in Figure 8.10.

11. Create another copy of the arrow and position it as shown at the right and in Figure 8.10.

12. Insert a picture fill in the top arrow by completing the following steps:
   a. Click the top arrow to select it.
   b. Click the DRAWING TOOLS FORMAT tab if necessary to make it active.
   c. Click the Shape Fill button arrow in the Shape Styles group and then click *Picture* at the drop-down gallery.
   d. At the Insert Pictures window, click in the *Office.com Clip Art* text box, type **vegetables**, and then press Enter.
   e. Locate and insert a vegetable photograph similar to the picture in the top arrow shown in Figure 8.10.

13. Complete steps similar to those in Step 12 to insert a photograph of citrus fruit in the second arrow (see Figure 8.10).

14. Complete steps similar to those in Step 12 to insert a photograph of exercising in the third arrow (see Figure 8.10).

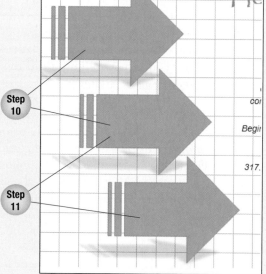

Step 10

Step 11

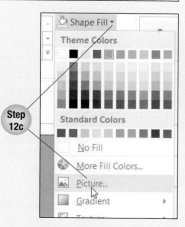

Step 12c

15. Select the three arrows, change the shape outline to *Green, Accent 6, Darker 25%* (last column, fifth row in the *Theme Colors* section), and then deselect the arrows.
16. Turn off the display of the drawing grid by clicking the VIEW tab and then clicking the *Gridlines* check box in the Show group to remove the check mark.
17. Turn off the display of nonprinting characters.
18. Insert a page border from the *Art* option box by completing the following steps:
    a. Click the DESIGN tab and then click the Page Borders button in the Page Background group.
    b. At the Borders and Shading dialog box with the Page Border tab selected, click the down-pointing arrow at the right of the *Art* option box.
    c. Scroll to the end of the drop-down list, scroll back up the list, and then click the fifteenth page border from the bottom (a thin-thick line). Verify that you have chosen the correct line by comparing its appearance in the *Preview* section of the dialog box with the preview image shown below.
    d. Click the *Color* option box arrow and then click the *Green, Accent 6, Darker 25%* option (last column, fifth row in the *Theme Colors* section).
    e. Click OK to close the dialog box.

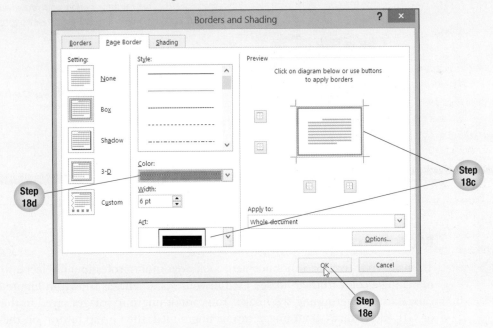

19. Save, print, and then close **C08-E02-Health.docx**.

Figure 8.10 Announcement Created in Exercise 8.2

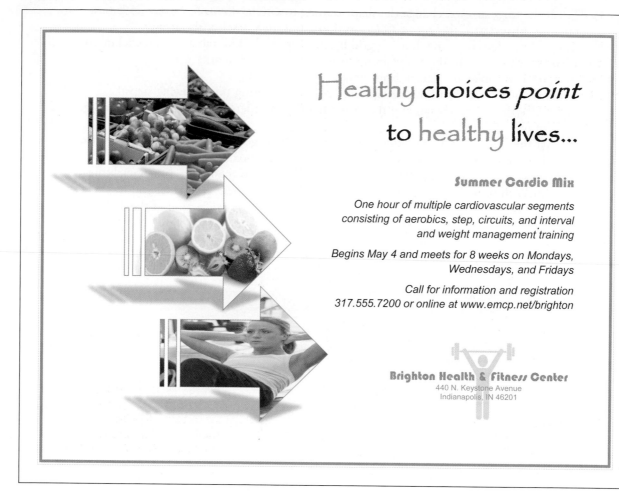

Matching Colors within a Document

To make your flyer or announcement look even more professional, select a font color by matching a color from an image used in your document, as shown in Figure 8.11. To do this, start by ungrouping the image. You cannot ungroup images saved in the PNG, JPG, or GIF file formats. If an image can be ungrouped, the Group button on the PICTURE TOOLS FORMAT tab will be active. Select a segment of the ungrouped image that contains the color you want to use, display the Colors dialog box with the Custom tab selected, click the *More Fill Colors* option at the drop-down gallery, and then write down the values from the *Red*, *Green*, and *Blue* measurement boxes. Or, click the down-pointing arrow at the right of the *Color model* option box on the Custom tab in the Colors dialog box, click *HSL* at the drop-down list, and then record the **HSL** values in the *Hue*, *Saturation*, and *Luminescence* measurement boxes. Use the same values to apply color to selected fonts and drawing objects.

HSL

Stands for hue, saturation, and luminescence

Figure 8.11 Matching Colors from an Ungrouped Image

Select a desired color in the ungrouped image, click the Shape Fill button arrow in the Shape Styles group on the DRAWING TOOLS FORMAT tab, and then click *More Fill Colors*.

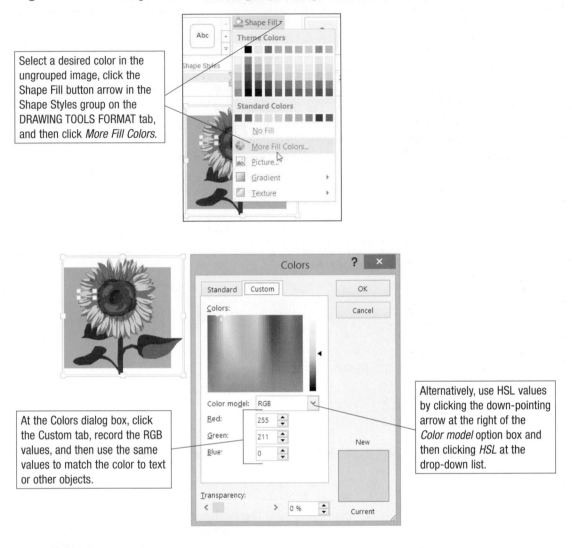

At the Colors dialog box, click the Custom tab, record the RGB values, and then use the same values to match the color to text or other objects.

Alternatively, use HSL values by clicking the down-pointing arrow at the right of the *Color model* option box and then clicking *HSL* at the drop-down list.

To apply the same color to text, select the text, click the Font Color button arrow, and then click More Colors at the drop-down gallery. At the Colors dialog box with the Custom tab selected, type the same values from the selected area of the image into the measurement boxes.

Applying Shape and Picture Effects

Add depth to lines, text boxes, drawing objects, and pictures using either shape effects or picture effects, as shown in Figure 8.12. Many of these effects have been discussed in earlier chapters. Display shape effects by selecting the drawing object and then clicking the Shape Effects button in the Shape Styles group on the DRAWING TOOLS FORMAT tab. Display picture effects by selecting the picture object and then clicking the Picture Effects button in the Pictures Styles group on the PICTURE TOOLS FORMAT tab.

Effects are also available at the Format Shape task pane, as shown in Figure 8.13A. Display this task pane by selecting the drawing object and then clicking the Shape Styles group task pane launcher on the DRAWING TOOLS FORMAT tab. Picture effects are available at the Format Picture task pane, as shown in Figure 8.13B. Display this task pane by selecting the picture object and then clicking the Picture Styles group task pane launcher on the PICTURE TOOLS FORMAT tab.

Shape Effects

Picture Effects

Figure 8.12 Adding Interest with Picture Effects

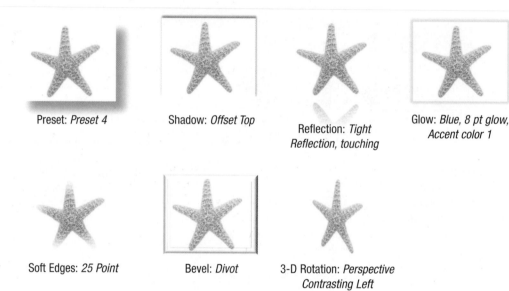

Preset: *Preset 4*

Shadow: *Offset Top*

Reflection: *Tight Reflection, touching*

Glow: *Blue, 8 pt glow, Accent color 1*

Soft Edges: *25 Point*

Bevel: *Divot*

3-D Rotation: *Perspective Contrasting Left*

Figure 8.13 Using the Format Shape Task Pane and Format Picture Task Pane

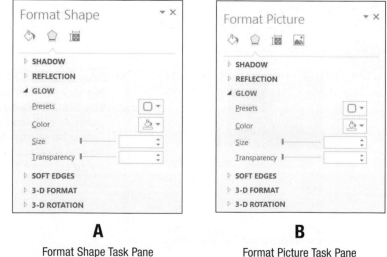

A

Format Shape Task Pane

B

Format Picture Task Pane

In Exercise 8.3, you will create a flyer using the techniques you have learned for inserting and modifying document elements. You will create and customize a page border using a picture, create a text box with fill, apply text effects, and more.

Exercise 8.3 Creating a Flyer Using a Picture Border and Text Effects

1. At a blank document, change the theme colors to *Violet II* by clicking the DESIGN tab, clicking the Theme Colors button in the Document Formatting group, and then clicking *Violet II* at the drop-down gallery.
2. Insert a flower border as shown in Figure 8.14 on page 359 by completing the following steps:
   a. Click the INSERT tab and then click the Pictures button in the Illustrations group.
   b. At the Insert Picture dialog box, navigate to your Chapter08 folder and then double-click *FlowerBorder.wmf*.
3. Customize the flower border by completing the following steps:
   a. With the flower border selected, right-click in the border image and then click *Edit Picture* at the shortcut menu.
   b. Click each segment of the flowers and apply a variation of the purple color in the *Theme Colors* section of the Shape Fill button drop-down gallery. Use Figure 8.14 as a guide, but feel free to make your own choices.
   c. Select the flower border image (not a segment of the image), click the Position button in the Arrange group on the DRAWING TOOLS FORMAT tab, and then click the *Position in Middle Center with Square Text Wrapping* option at the drop-down gallery.
4. Create a text box inside the graphic border and insert text by completing the following steps:
   a. Click the INSERT tab, click the Text Box button in the Text group, and then click *Draw Text Box* at the drop-down list.
   b. Drag the crosshairs to draw a box inside the graphic border.
   c. Remove the shape fill and shape outline from the text box.
   d. With the insertion point positioned inside the text box, insert **Design.docx** from your Chapter08 folder.
   e. Select all of the text and then change the font to Tempus Sans ITC.
5. Select *Details by Design* in the text box and then apply the following formatting:
   a. Change the font to 48-point Gabriola.
   b. Apply the Purple, Accent 2, Darker 25% font color (sixth column, fifth row in the *Theme Colors* section).

c. Display the Font dialog box with the Advanced tab selected. Expand the spacing by 0.5 points, choose *Standard and Contextual* from the *Ligatures* option box drop-down list, choose *6* from the *Stylistic sets* option box drop-down list, and then click OK to close the dialog box.

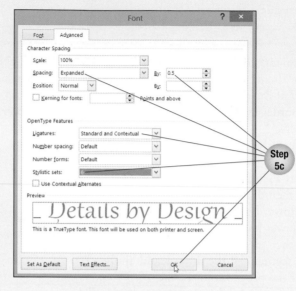

6. Position the insertion point in front of *RESIDENTIAL AND* and then press the Tab key.
7. Position the insertion point in front of *COMMERCIAL DESIGN* and then press the Tab key twice.
8. Select *RESIDENTIAL AND COMMERCIAL DESIGN* and then make the following changes:
   a. Click the Text Effects and Typography button in the Font group on the HOME tab and then click the *Gradient Fill - Blue, Accent 1, Reflection* option (second column, second row).
   b. Change the font size to 16 points.
   c. Apply bold formatting.
   d. Change the font color to a green color of some of the leaves by clicking the Font Color button arrow and then clicking *More Colors*. At the Colors dialog box, click the Custom tab. Type **51** in the *Red* measurement box, **153** in the *Green* measurement box, and **102** in the *Blue* measurement box and then click OK.

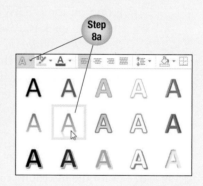

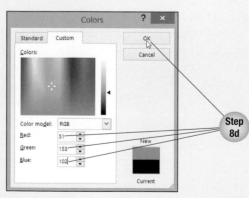

9. Position the insertion point in front of *Think spring!*, press Ctrl + Shift + End to select the text from the insertion point to the end of the text in the text box, and then click the Center button in the Paragraph group on the HOME tab. (Make sure the text fits inside the picture border, similar to the way it appears in Figure 8.14.)

10. Select *Think spring!*, change the font size to 26 points, apply bold formatting, and then apply the Purple, Accent 2, Darker 25% font color (sixth column, fifth row in the *Theme Colors* section).

11. Select the text from the paragraph that begins *Plan a new look* through the end of the text in the text box, apply bold formatting, and then change the font color to the green color you applied in Step 8d. (The green color you previously applied will display in the *Recent Colors* section of the drop-down gallery.)

12. Resize the text box and make any other needed adjustments so your document displays similar to what is shown in Figure 8.14.

13. Save the document with the name **C08-E03-Design**.

14. Print and then close **C08-E03-Design.docx**.

Figure 8.14 Flyer Created in Exercise 8.3

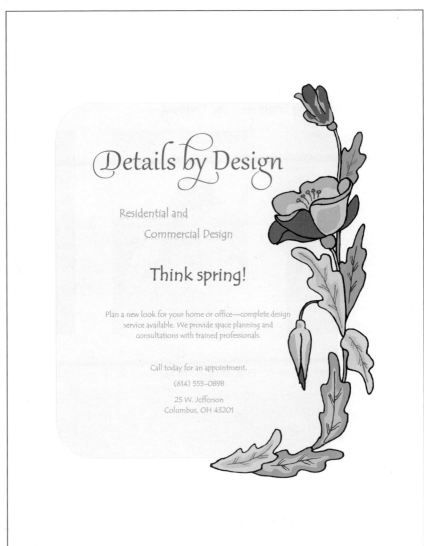

Adjusting Pictures

The PICTURE TOOLS FORMAT tab contains numerous options for customizing pictures. Whether adjusting the brightness or contrast of a picture, applying distinctive picture styles with depth and dimension, or selecting unique picture effects, you will be amazed by all of the creative opportunities.

Adjusting Brightness, Contrast, Sharpness, and Softness

Corrections

You can adjust the brightness, or relative lightness, of a picture; the contrast (difference between the darkest and lightest areas of a picture); and the sharpness or softness of a picture by clicking the Corrections button in the Adjust group on the PICTURE TOOLS FORMAT tab. Figure 8.15A shows an original image of two penguins. Figure 8.15B shows the same image with brightness increased by 20 percent and contrast decreased by 20 percent. Notice the lighter overall color of the image and the way the foreground and background images blend together. Figure 8.15C shows the original image with the brightness decreased by 20 percent and the contrast increased by 20 percent. This image is darker than images A and B, and the penguins' dark heads clearly stand out against the lighter background.

To enhance finer details in an image or blur any slight imperfections, you can adjust the image clarity in the *Sharpen/Soften* section of the Corrections button drop-down gallery. Figure 8.16 depicts an original image, one that has been sharpened by 50 percent, and one that has been softened by 50 percent.

Figure 8.15 **Adjusting Brightness and Contrast**

A	B	C
Original Picture	Brightness: +20% Contrast: -20%	Brightness: -20% Contrast: +20%

Figure 8.16 Sharpening and Softening an Image

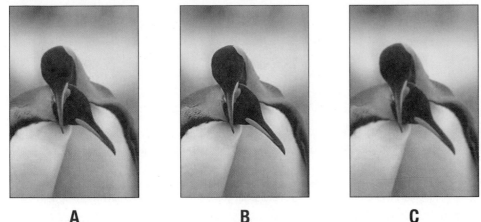

A
Original Picture

B
Sharpen: 50%

C
Soften: 50%

Adjusting Color Saturation, Color Tone, and Recolor

Clicking the Color button in the Adjust group on the PICTURE TOOLS FORMAT tab allows you to adjust three picture qualities: saturation, color tone, and recolor. Recall from Chapter 2 that saturation is the purity or intensity of a color. Increasing the saturation makes an image appear more vivid, while reducing the saturation causes the image colors to turn more gray (for example, selecting 0 percent saturation makes a colored image appear black and white). Figure 8.17B on page 362 depicts an image in which the saturation has been increased by 300 percent and Figure 8.17C shows an image in which the saturation has been decreased by 33 percent.

Color

Color tone refers to the overall color of an image and is also known as color temperature. The original color temperature of an image is created by the light source used when the picture is taken, but you can adjust this value to achieve the desired look in the image. The options in the *Color Tone* section of the Color button drop-down gallery are labeled with temperatures ranging from *4700K* to *11200K*, where K stands for *kelvin*. Blue and green tones are considered cool, or lower in temperature, and red and yellow are considered warm, or higher in temperature. For example, selecting the *11200K* option gives your image an overall red/yellow tone, as shown in Figure 8.17D.

color tone
The overall color temperature of an image, where reds and yellows are warm and blues and greens are cool

The *Recolor* section of the Color button drop-down gallery allows you to apply an overall color to an image. The image in Figure 8.17E has been recolored using the *Green, Accent color 6 Dark* option.

Using the Format Picture Task Pane

While the Corrections and Color buttons in the Adjust group on the PICTURE TOOLS FORMAT tab allow you to make many different adjustments, you may want to make adjustments to an image that are not provided by one of these predesigned options. If this is the case, you can display the Format Picture task pane by clicking *Picture Corrections Options* at the bottom of the Corrections button drop-down gallery or *Picture Color Options* at the bottom of the Color button drop-down gallery. The *PICTURE CORRECTIONS* and *PICTURE COLOR* sections of the Format Picture task pane contain sliders and measurement boxes you can use to more precisely adjust values. These sections each also contain a Presets button that you can click to view and choose from popular adjustment options, as shown in Figure 8.18 on page 362.

Figure 8.17 Adjusting Saturation, Color Tone, and Recolor at the Color Gallery

A

Original Picture

B

Saturation: 300%

C

Saturation: 33%

D

Color Tone: 11200K

E

Recolor: Green,
Accent color 6 Dark

Figure 8.18 Choosing from the Most Common Preset Color Saturation and Color Tone Options

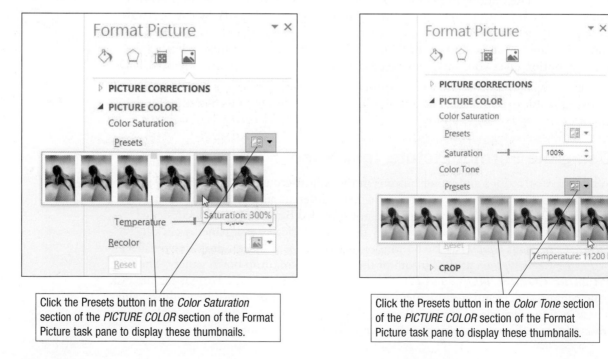

Click the Presets button in the *Color Saturation* section of the *PICTURE COLOR* section of the Format Picture task pane to display these thumbnails.

Click the Presets button in the *Color Tone* section of the *PICTURE COLOR* section of the Format Picture task pane to display these thumbnails.

Making a Color Transparent

You can make one color in a picture *transparent*, or see-through, to better show any text that is layered on top of it, to layer pictures on top of each other, or to remove or hide parts of a picture as desired. To make a color in a picture transparent, select the picture, click the Color button in the Adjust group on the PICTURE TOOLS FORMAT tab, and then click the *Set Transparent Color* option. The mouse pointer changes to an eraser with an arrow at the end. Point the arrow at the color in the picture you want to make transparent and click. Word only allows you to make one color in an image transparent. If you need to remove more than one color, you should do so in another image-editing program and then insert the image into the Word document. See Figure 8.19 for an example of the transparency feature.

Applying Artistic Effects

Use the Artistic Effects button in the Adjust group on the PICTURE TOOLS FORMAT tab to make a picture look like a sketch, drawing, or painting. Note that you can only apply one artistic effect at a time to a picture, so applying a different artistic effect will remove the previously applied artistic effect. Figure 8.20 shows the effects of applying the Photocopy and Pencil Grayscale effects to a picture.

Artistic Effects

Figure 8.19 Setting Transparent Color

A

Original Graphic

B

Graphic with Transparency Applied
to the Light Green Background Color

Figure 8.20 Applying Artistic Effects

A

Original Graphic

B

Photocopy Effect

C

Pencil Grayscale Effect

Compressing Pictures

One way to reduce the file size of an image is to compress it. To do this, select the image and then click the Compress Pictures button in the Adjust group on the PICTURE TOOLS FORMAT tab. Make the desired selections at the dialog box and then click OK. As you learned in Chapter 4, compressing a picture after cropping can be especially helpful, as it removes the unwanted areas of the picture from the file.

Compressing a picture can change the amount of detail retained in the original picture. This means that after compression, the picture can look different than it did before. You should compress your picture and save the file before you apply any adjustments or artistic effects.

Removing the Background of a Picture

Remove Background

Use the Remove Background button in the Adjust group on the PICTURE TOOLS FORMAT tab to remove unwanted portions of a picture. If you select an image and then click the Remove Background button, the BACKGROUND REMOVAL tab displays with three options in the Refine group and two options in the Close group (see Figure 8.21). The background area that will be removed displays in a magenta color. Click the Mark Areas to Keep button to draw lines marking areas to keep in your picture. Click the Mark Areas to Remove button to draw lines marking areas to remove from the picture. Use the Delete Mark button to delete lines you have drawn marking areas to keep or remove. Use the Discard all Changes button to close the BACKGROUND REMOVAL tab and discard all of the changes. Finally, click the Keep Changes button to close the BACKGROUND REMOVAL tab and keep all of the changes.

Using Pictures Styles

Approximately 30 borders and effects can be added to a picture to enhance the appeal of the image. Picture styles are available in the Picture Styles group on the PICTURE TOOLS FORMAT tab. The options in the Picture Styles gallery are enabled with the live preview feature, so you can simply hover the mouse over each effect to see how it will look when applied to your picture.

Figure 8.21 Removing the Background of a Picture

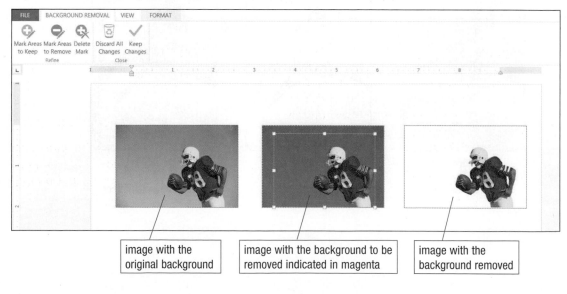

image with the original background

image with the background to be removed indicated in magenta

image with the background removed

In Exercise 8.4, you will create the front side of an announcement that will promote an auction to benefit a local zoo. The document will be trimmed to a page size of 5 inches by 7 inches. You will use a picture border and insert a photograph that reinforces the overall theme of the document. You will also make several picture adjustments and remove the background of the image.

Exercise 8.4 Creating the Front Side of an Announcement with a Border, a Text Box, WordArt, and an Image

1. Open **SafariBall.docx** from your Chapter08 folder and then save the document with the name **C08-C04-SafariBall.**
2. Customize the zebra border by completing the following steps:
   a. Click the zebra border to select it.
   b. Click the PICTURE TOOLS FORMAT tab.
   c. Change the height of the image to 5.1 inches and the width to 7.1 inches.
   d. Click the Rotate button in the Arrange group and then click *Rotate Right 90°* at the drop-down gallery.
   e. Click the Position button in the Arrange group and then click the *Position in Middle Center with Square Text Wrapping* option.
3. Create a text box containing the document text as shown in Figure 8.22 on page 367 by completing the following steps:
   a. Draw a text box in the document.
   b. Change the height of the text box to 5.5 inches and the width to 3.5 inches.
   c. Click the Position button and then click the *Position in Middle with Square Text Wrapping* option.
   d. With the insertion point positioned in the text box, insert **SafariText.docx** from your Chapter08 folder.
   e. With the insertion point still positioned in the text box, apply the Facet theme.
   f. Click the DRAWING TOOLS FORMAT tab, click the More button in the Shape Styles group, and then click the *Subtle Effect - Green, Accent 1* option (second column, fourth row).
4. Insert WordArt in the text box as shown in Figure 8.22 by completing the following steps:
   a. Position the insertion point in the first blank line below the text *Please join us for the.*
   b. Click the INSERT tab, click the WordArt button in the Text group, and then click the *Gradient Fill - Red, Accent 1, Reflection* option (second column, second row).

c. Type **SIXTH ANNUAL**, press Shift + Enter, and then type **SAFARI BALL**.

d. Click the border of the WordArt text box to select it.

e. Click the Text Fill button arrow in the WordArt Styles group on the DRAWING TOOLS FORMAT tab and then click the *Dark Green, Accent 2, Darker 25%* option (sixth column, fifth row in the *Theme Colors* section).

f. Change the font size of the WordArt text by clicking the HOME tab, clicking the Font Size button arrow, and then clicking *28* at the drop-down gallery.

g. Drag the WordArt so that it is positioned as shown in Figure 8.22.

h. Click outside the WordArt text box to deselect it.

5. Insert the zebra picture shown in Figure 8.22 by completing the following steps:

a. With the insertion point still positioned outside of the WordArt text box, click the INSERT tab and then click the Pictures button in the Illustrations group.

b. At the Insert Picture dialog box, navigate to your Chapter08 folder and then double-click *zebra.png*.

c. With the zebra image selected, click the Wrap Text button in the Arrange group and then click the *In Front of Text* option at the drop-down gallery.

d. Make sure all of the zebra image is visible. If not, adjust the position of the image.

e. Click the Remove Background button in the Adjust group.

f. Position the mouse pointer on the bottom middle sizing handle of the zebra image background and then drag the bottom border of the background down to the bottom of the image.

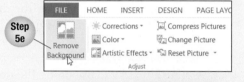

g. Drag the left middle sizing handle until the left border of the background is just left of the zebra's left ear.

h. Drag the top middle sizing handle up until the top border of the background is just above the zebra's ears.

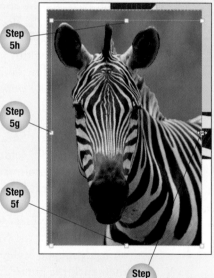

i. Drag the right middle sizing handle until the right border of the background is at the right border of the image. (Make sure the parts of the image that remain match what you see in the image to the right and in Figure 8.22. You may need to continue to adjust the borders to ensure the background is removed completely.)

j. Click the Keep Changes button in the Close group on the BACKGROUND REMOVAL tab.

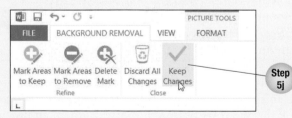

k. Change the height of the zebra image to 1.8 inches.

l. Drag the zebra image so it is positioned as shown in Figure 8.22.

6. Save, print, and then close **C08-E04-SafariBall.docx**.

Figure 8.22 Front of Announcement Created in Exercise 8.4

In Exercise 8.5, you will create the back side of the announcement promoting the auction to benefit the Brookfield Zoo. You will create and format a text box with information about auction items and insert and format two pictures and a clip art image that reinforce the overall theme of the announcement.

1. At a blank document, insert a text box and then modify it with the following specifications:
   a. Change the height of the text box to 7.1 inches and the width to 5.1 inches.
   b. Change the position to *Position in Middle Center with Square Text Wrapping*.
   c. Apply the Facet theme.
   d. Make the DRAWING TOOLS FORMAT tab active, click the More button in the Shape Styles group, and then click the *Subtle Effect - Green, Accent 1* option (second column, fourth row).
   e. With the insertion point positioned in the text box, insert **SafariAuction.docx** from your Chapter08 folder.
2. Insert the WordArt as shown in Figure 8.23 with the following specifications:
   a. Click the INSERT tab if necessary to make it active, click the WordArt button in the Text group, and then click the *Gradient Fill - Red, Accent 1, Reflection* option (second column, second row).
   b. Type **LIVE AUCTION ITEMS:**.
   c. Click the border of the WordArt text box to select it.
   d. Click the Text Fill button arrow in the WordArt Styles group on the DRAWING TOOLS FORMAT tab and then click the *Dark Green, Accent 2, Darker 25%* option (sixth column, fifth row in the *Theme Colors* section).
   e. Change the font size of the WordArt to 26 points.
   f. Position the WordArt as shown in Figure 8.23.
   g. Click outside the WordArt text box to deselect it.
3. Insert the image of the leopard with the following specifications:
   a. Click in the upper left corner of the document, outside the announcement text box, and then insert **leopard.png** from your Chapter08 folder using the Insert Picture dialog box. ***Hint: Make sure the insertion point is not positioned inside the text box.***
   b. Change the height of the image to 2 inches.
   c. Apply Tight text wrapping.
   d. Apply the Drop Shadow Rectangle picture style (located in the Pictures Styles group).
   e. Position the leopard image as shown in Figure 8.23.
4. Click in the upper left corner of the document, outside the announcement text box, and then insert the image of the lion with the following specifications:
   a. Insert **lion.png** from your Chapter08 folder using the Insert Picture dialog box.
   b. Change the height of the image to 2 inches.
   c. Apply Tight text wrapping.
   d. Apply the Center Shadow Rectangle picture style (located in the Pictures Styles group).
   e. Click the Send Backward button in the Arrange group on the PICTURE TOOLS FORMAT tab.
   f. Position the lion image as shown in Figure 8.23.
5. Insert the paws graphic shown in Figure 8.23 by completing the following steps:
   a. Click in the document outside the text box and the images.
   b. Click the INSERT tab and then click the Online Pictures button.

c. At the Insert Pictures window, type **paws** in the *Office.com Clip Art* text box and then press Enter.

d. Double-click the paws image that displays at the right.

e. Change the text wrapping for the image to *In Front of Text*.

f. Apply the Orange, Accent color 4 Dark color (fifth column, second row in the Color button drop-down gallery).

g. Move the paws image to the bottom of the text box, as shown in Figure 8.23.

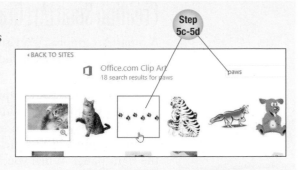

6. Save the document with the name **C08-E05-SafariBall**.

7. Print the document on the back of **C08-E04-SafariBall.docx**. Trim the page to 5 inches by 7 inches.

8. Close **C08-E05-SafariBall.docx**.

Figure 8.23 Back of Announcement Created in Exercise 8.5

Creating SmartArt Graphics

A SmartArt graphic is a visual representation of information and ideas. SmartArt graphics are useful to include in promotional materials because they can communicate complex ideas in a simple, visual manner.

SmartArt

Create a SmartArt graphic by clicking the INSERT tab and then clicking the SmartArt button in the Illustrations group. The Choose a SmartArt Graphic dialog box will display, as shown in Figure 8.24. Select a category in the left panel, select a graphic in the middle panel, and then view the graphic and read a description of it in the right panel. When you find the graphic you want to use, click OK to insert it in the document. The information in Table 8.1 will help you decide on the type of SmartArt graphic that will best serve your needs.

Figure 8.24 Using the Choose a SmartArt Graphic Dialog Box

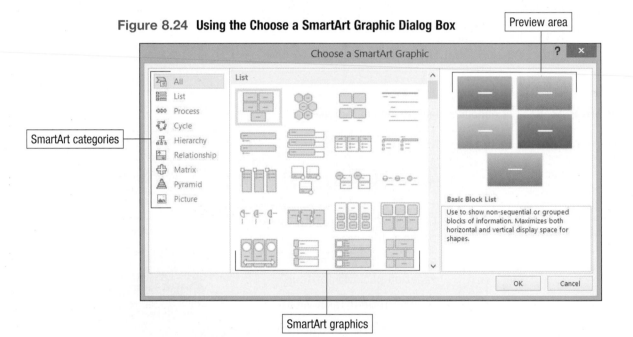

Table 8.1 Categories of SmartArt Graphics

Use this type of SmartArt	To do this
List	Show nonsequential information.
Process	Show steps in a process or timeline.
Cycle	Show a continual process.
Hierarchy	Create an organizational chart or decision tree.
Relationship	Illustrate connections.
Matrix	Show how parts relate to a whole.
Pyramid	Show proportional relationships with the largest component on the top or bottom.
Picture	Contain placeholders for pictures.

Using the Text Pane

The text pane displays at the left side of your SmartArt graphic and is used to enter and edit the text that appears in your graphic. When you first insert a SmartArt graphic, placeholder text displays in the text pane as well as in the graphic, as shown in Figure 8.25. If the text pane is not visible, turn on the display by clicking the Text Pane button in the Create Graphic group on the SMARTART TOOLS DESIGN tab or by clicking the small, square button containing a right-pointing arrow that displays in the middle center of the left border of the SmartArt graphic. As you type text in the text pane, the SmartArt graphic is automatically updated.

Using the SMARTART TOOLS DESIGN Tab

Use buttons and options on the SMARTART TOOLS DESIGN tab, shown in Figure 8.26, to add shapes, move shapes, change the layout, change colors, and apply a style. SmartArt styles provide a quick and easy way to add professional effects to your SmartArt graphic. When you insert a SmartArt graphic into your document, it will match the theme applied to the document. If you change the theme of the document, the look of the SmartArt graphic will be updated automatically.

Using the SMARTART TOOLS FORMAT Tab

Further customizations can be applied to your SmartArt graphic by using the buttons and options on the SMARTART TOOLS FORMAT tab, shown in Figure 8.27. You can change the look of your SmartArt graphic by changing the fill of its shape or text; by adding effects such as shadows, reflections, glows, or soft edges; or by adding 3-D effects such as bevels or rotations. WordArt formatting choices and preformatted shape styles are also available on this tab.

Figure 8.25 Using the Text Pane

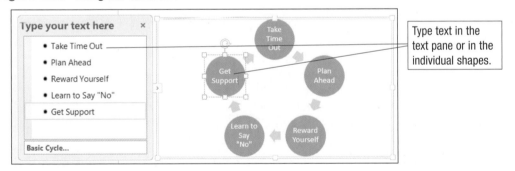

Figure 8.26 Customizing a SmartArt Graphic Using the SMARTART TOOLS DESIGN Tab

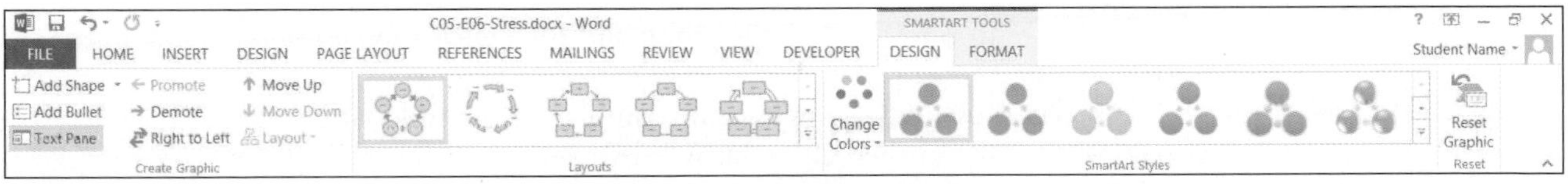

Figure 8.27 Formatting a SmartArt Graphic Using the SMARTART TOOLS FORMAT Tab

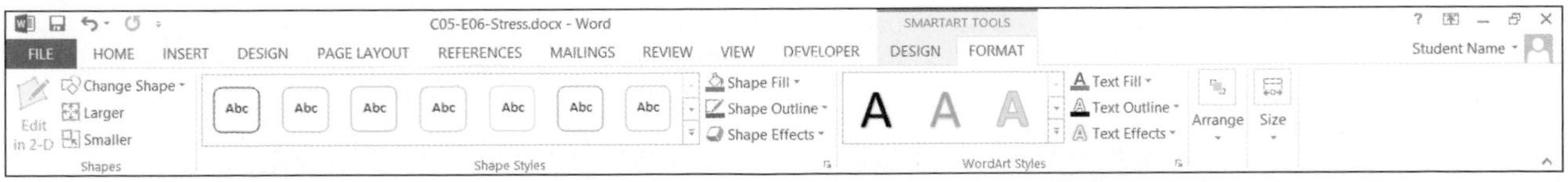

In Exercise 8.6, you will create a flyer and insert and format an image and WordArt text. You will also insert a list SmartArt graphic and then add shapes to the SmartArt graphic, change the colors, apply a style, and then size and position the graphic.

1. At a blank document, apply the Retrospect theme.
2. Insert the stress image in your document and format the image as shown in Figure 8.28 on page 375 by completing the following steps:
   a. Click the INSERT tab and then click the Pictures button in the Illustrations group.
   b. At the Insert Picture dialog box, navigate to your Chapter08 folder and then double-click **stress.png**.
   c. Change the width of the image to 6.5 inches.
   d. Apply a reflection to the image by clicking the Picture Effects button in the Picture Styles group on the PICTURE TOOLS FORMAT tab, pointing to *Reflection* at the drop-down list, and then clicking the *Half Reflection, touching* option (second column, first row in the *Reflection Variations* section).
   e. Apply a glow to the image by clicking the Picture Effects button, pointing to *Glow,* and then clicking the *Orange, 11 pt glow, Accent color 1* option (first column, third row in the *Glow Variations* section).
   f. Change the transparency of the glow color by clicking the Picture Effects button, pointing to *Glow,* and then clicking *Glow Options* at the bottom of the side menu. At the Format Picture task pane, with the Effects icon selected, select the current percentage in the *Transparency* measurement box, type **30**, press Enter, and then close the task pane.
   g. Apply an artistic effect to the image by clicking the Artistic Effects button in the Adjust group and then clicking the *Film Grain* option (third column, third row).
   h. Click the Position button in the Arrange group and then click the *Position in Top Center with Square Text Wrapping* option.
3. Create the WordArt text shown in Figure 8.28 by completing the following steps:
   a. Click the INSERT tab and then click the WordArt button in the Text group.
   b. Click the *Fill - White, Outline - Accent 2, Hard Shadow - Accent 2* option (fourth column, bottom row).
   c. Type **Five Ways to De-Stress**.
   d. Change the height of the WordArt to 1.8 inches and the width to 6 inches.

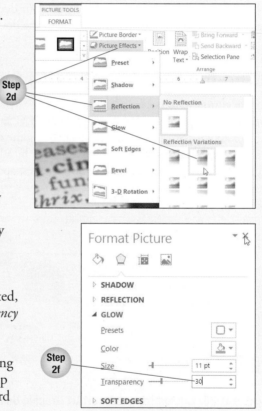

e. Click the Text Effects button in the WordArt Styles group, point to *Transform*, and then click the *Triangle Up* option (third column, first row in the *Warp* section).

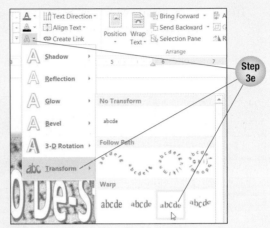

Step 3e

4. Insert the SmartArt shown in Figure 8.28 by completing the following steps:
   a. Click the INSERT tab and then click the SmartArt button in the Illustrations group.
   b. Click *List* in the left panel of the Choose a SmartArt Graphic dialog box.
   c. Scroll down the list box in the middle panel and then double-click the *Vertical Picture Accent List* option.

5. Add two additional shapes to the SmartArt graphic by clicking the Add Shape button in the Create Graphic group on the SMARTART TOOLS DESIGN tab twice.

6. Change the color of the SmartArt by clicking the Change Colors button in the SmartArt Styles group and then clicking the *Colorful Range - Accent Colors 2 to 3* option (second option in the *Colorful* section).

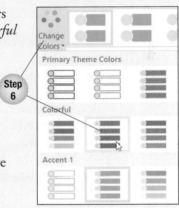

Step 6

7. Apply a SmartArt style by clicking the More button in the SmartArt Styles group and then clicking the *Inset* option (second option in the *3-D* section).

8. Change the size of the SmartArt by completing the following steps:
   a. Click the outside border of the SmartArt to select the entire SmartArt graphic and not an element in the SmartArt.
   b. Click the SMARTART TOOLS FORMAT tab.
   c. Click the Size button.
   d. Change the shape height to 4.5 inches and the shape width to 6.5 inches.

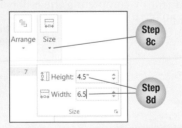

Step 8c

Step 8d

9. Change the position of the SmartArt by clicking the Arrange button, clicking the Position button at the drop-down list, and then clicking the *Position in Middle Center with Square Text Wrapping* option (second column, second row in the *With Text Wrapping* section).

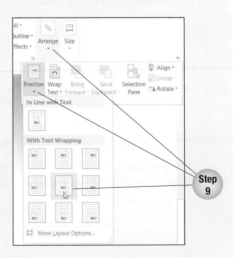

Step 9

10. If the text pane is not visible, turn on the display by clicking the small, square button containing a right-pointing arrow that displays in the middle center of the left border of the SmartArt.

11. Type text in the text pane as shown in Figure 8.28 and in the image below.

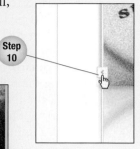

Step 10

Step 11

12. Close the text pane by clicking the Close button located in the upper right corner of the text pane.

13. Insert a picture in the top circle shape of the SmartArt graphic (the circle shape that displays to the left of *Take time out*) by completing the following steps:
    a. Click the picture icon that displays in the top circle shape.
    b. At the Insert Pictures window, click in the *Office.com Clip Art* text box, type **clock**, and then press Enter.
    c. Double-click the clock image shown in Figure 8.28. (If this image is not available, choose a similar picture.)

14. Complete steps similar to those in Step 13 to insert a picture of a to-do list in the second circle shape, a picture of ice cream cones in the third circle shape, a picture of a stoplight in the fourth circle shape, and a picture of a family in the fifth circle shape.

15. Click outside of the SmartArt graphic, press Ctrl + End to move the insertion point to the end of the document, and then insert text in the document by completing the following steps:
    a. Insert **Stress.docx** from your Chapter08 folder.
    b. Select the text *Help is on the way!*.
    c. Click the HOME tab, click the More button in the Styles group, and then click the *Intense Reference* option at the drop-down gallery.
    d. With the text still selected, change the font size to 14 points.

Step 15c

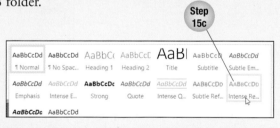

16. Save the document with the name **C08-E06-Stress**.

17. Print and then close **C08-E06-Stress.docx**.

Figure 8.28 Flyer Created in Exercise 8.6

Chapter Summary

- Flyers and announcements are considered to be among the least expensive means of advertising.

- A flyer advertises a product or service that is available for a limited amount of time. An announcement informs an audience of an upcoming event.

- In planning a flyer or announcement, use a table to organize text, graphics, and other design elements on the page.

- Graphics added to a flyer or announcement can add excitement and generate enthusiasm for the product, service, or event. A simple graphic demands more attention and has more impact than a complex one.

- When you scan a picture, consider the destination for the picture and the necessary resolution and file format.

- A bitmapped, or raster, image is created by pixels of color. A vector graphic is created using mathematical equations.

- Use color in a publication to elicit a particular feeling, emphasize important text, attract attention, organize data, or create a pattern. Limit the color to small areas so it attracts attention but does not create visual confusion.

- Borders and lines added to a document aid directional flow, add color, and organize text to produce professional-looking results.

- The drawing grid is a network of lines that help align drawing objects. Turn on the display of gridlines by clicking the *Gridlines* check box in the Show group on the VIEW tab, and adjust gridlines settings with options at the Grid and Guides dialog box.

- Using one of the colors from an image in text throughout your document is a good way to create unity. Ungroup the image, select the portion that displays in the color you want, display the Color dialog box to discover the color formula, and then apply that color where desired.

- Apply effects to lines, text boxes, and shapes with options on the DRAWING TOOLS FORMAT tab and the Format Shape task pane. Apply effects to images such as pictures and clip art with options on the PICTURE TOOLS FORMAT tab and the Format Picture task pane.

- Use options on the PICTURE TOOLS FORMAT tab to change the brightness and contrast of an image; soften or sharpen the image; change the color and color saturation, tone, and transparency; or apply an artistic effect.

- Apply creative borders and effects to a picture with picture styles, available on the PICTURE TOOLS FORMAT tab.

- Compress a picture to reduce the size of the file and to permanently remove any cropped areas.

- Use the Remove Background button on the PICTURE TOOLS FORMAT tab to remove unwanted portions of a picture, to highlight the subject of the picture, or to remove distracting details.

- A SmartArt graphic is a visual representation of information and ideas. Create a SmartArt graphic at the Choose a SmartArt Graphic dialog box. Display this dialog box by clicking the INSERT tab and then clicking the SmartArt button in the Illustrations group.

- Customize and format a SmartArt graphic with options on the SMARTART TOOLS DESIGN tab and the SMARTART TOOLS FORMAT tab.

Commands Review

FEATURE	RIBBON TAB, GROUP	BUTTON, OPTION
artistic effects	PICTURE TOOLS FORMAT, Adjust	
compress pictures	PICTURE TOOLS FORMAT, Adjust	
corrections	PICTURE TOOLS FORMAT, Adjust	
crop	PICTURE TOOLS FORMAT, Size	
draw table	TABLE TOOLS LAYOUT, Draw	, Draw Table
drawing grid	VIEW, Show	
Grid and Guides dialog box	PAGE LAYOUT, Arrange	, Grid Settings
eraser	TABLE TOOLS LAYOUT, Draw	
page borders	DESIGN, Page Background	
page color	DESIGN, Page Background	
picture color	PICTURE TOOLS FORMAT, Adjust	
picture effects	PICTURE TOOLS FORMAT, Picture Styles	
remove background	PICTURE TOOLS FORMAT, Adjust	
shape effects	DRAWING TOOLS FORMAT, Shape Styles	
SmartArt	INSERT, Illustrations	
table	INSERT, Tables	

Key Points Review

A.	announcement	F.	fill	K.	Remove Background
B.	balance	G.	flyer	L.	saturation
C.	Corrections	H.	gradient	M.	SmartArt
D.	crop marks	I.	hue	N.	thumbnail
E.	drawing grid	J.	pixel	O.	WordArt

Completion: In the space at the left, provide the correct letter or letters from the above list that match each definition.

_____G_____ 1. Advertises a product or service that is available for a limited amount of time

_____A_____ 2. Informs an audience of an upcoming event

_____N_____ 3. A rough sketch used in planning layout and design

_____B_____ 4. The amount of light and dark in a picture

_____H_____ 5. A gradual varying of color

_____L_____ 6. Purity or intensity of color

_____E_____ 7. Network of lines that help align drawing objects

_____D_____ 8. Used to show where a publication will be trimmed

_____C_____ 9. Button on the PICTURE TOOLS FORMAT tab containing brightness and contrast options

_____K_____ 10. Button on the PICTURE TOOLS FORMAT tab used to remove unwanted portions of a picture

_____F_____ 11. Shading added to drawing objects

_____M_____ 12. A graphic that is a visual representation of information and ideas in the form of a diagram or organizational chart

Chapter *Assessments*

Assessment 8.1   Create a Community Announcement

1. At a blank document, insert **sun.jpg** from your Chapter08 folder.
2. Make the following changes to the image:
   a. Apply Tight text wrapping.
   b. Click the Copy button.
   c. Use the Crop button on the PICTURE TOOLS FORMAT tab to crop off the bottom half of the image.
   d. Deselect the image.
3. Click the Paste button to paste a copy of the original sun into your document and then make the following changes:
   a. Crop off the top half of the copy to the point where you cropped off the bottom half of the original.
   b. Click the Color button in the Adjust group and then click the *Washout* option in the *Recolor* section.
   c. Apply Tight text wrapping.
4. Use the Align Objects button on the PICTURE TOOLS FORMAT tab to center align the top image and then the bottom image. Make any necessary adjustments to either image so they display as shown in Figure 8.29 on page 380.
5. Draw a text box that measures 6.75 inches in height and 6.25 inches in width. Center the top of the text box with the top of the lightened part of the image. ***Hint: It should look like the sun is peeking over the text box.***
6. Remove the shape fill from the text box.
7. Use the *Dashes* option at the Shape Outline button drop-down gallery to add a round dotted orange border to the text box and use the *Weight* option to increase the weight to 4½ points.
8. With the insertion point positioned in the text box, insert **GoodMorning.docx** from your Chapter08 folder.
9. Select the text box, change the font to Tekton Pro, and then change the font color to *Blue, Accent 5, Darker 50%*. ***Note: If the Tekton Pro font is not available, substitute the Poor Richard font.***
10. Select the text *Good Morning Naperville*, change the font size to 40 points, expand the spacing by 0.3 point, and turn on kerning at 40 points and above.
11. Insert white space between the groups of text as shown in Figure 8.29. Make sure the text appears in the text box as shown in the figure. If necessary, make adjustments to the size of the text box. ***Hint: Adjust the spacing using specific line spacing options or insert additional spacing before and after each paragraph with the* Before *and* After *measurement boxes in the Paragraph group on the PAGE LAYOUT tab.***
12. Save the document with the name **C08-A01-GoodMorning**.
13. Print and then close **C08-A01-GoodMorning.docx**.

Figure 8.29 Announcement Created in Assessment 8.1

Good Morning Naperville

If daytime luncheons and meetings don't work for you,
mark your calendar now for the second in a series of
general membership breakfast meetings.

Start your day off with a breakfast full of
networking that will surely get you on the right track.

Monday, September 28, 2015
7:00 – 8:30 a.m.
Holiday Inn Select
1801 N. Naper Blvd.
Naperville, IL

Topic: Mergers & Acquisitions—How Do
They Impact Our Community?
$15 for members, $20 for non-members

RSVP to the Naperville Chamber of Commerce
by Thursday, September 10, 2015
(630) 555-4141 or chamber@emcp.net

Assessment 8.2   Create a Heart Health Flyer

1. At a blank document, change the page orientation to landscape.
2. Insert **heart.png** (see Figure 8.30) from your Chapter08 folder and then apply the following formatting:
   a. Change the width to 9 inches.
   b. Change the position to *Position in Middle Center with Square Text Wrapping.*
   c. Change the text wrapping to *Behind Text.*
   d. Apply the Blur artistic effect.
3. Insert the Basic Radial SmartArt diagram (located in the third column, third row with *Cycle* selected in the left panel).
4. Make the following changes to the SmartArt graphic (refer to Figure 8.30):
   a. Add five additional shapes.
   b. Select the SmartArt graphic (not an element in the graphic).
   c. Apply the Colorful Range - Accent Colors 2 to 3 colors.
   d. Apply the Metallic Scene 3-D SmartArt Style.

e. Change the height of the SmartArt graphic to 5.5 inches and the width to 9 inches.

f. Change the position to *Position in Middle Center with Square Text Wrapping*.

g. Change the text wrapping to *Through*.

h. Press Ctrl + B to apply bold formatting.

i. Type the text in each of the shapes as shown in Figure 8.30. Type **Risk Factors** in the middle shape and then type the following text in the outside shapes, beginning with the shape at the top and moving clockwise to the next shape:

Smoking

Gender

Age

Stress

Alcohol and drug abuse

Family history

High cholesterol

Obesity

Hypertension

5. Insert the text *Heart Attack Risk Factors* as WordArt text with the following specifications:

a. Use the Fill - White, Outline - Accent 1, Glow - Accent 1 WordArt style.

b. Apply the Square transform effect.

c. Change the height to 0.5 inches.

d. Position the WordArt as shown in Figure 8.30.

6. Insert the text *Groves Memorial Hospital* as WordArt text with the following specifications:

a. Use the Fill - White, Outline - Accent 1, Glow - Accent 1 WordArt style.

b. Change the font size of the WordArt text to 18 points.

c. Position the WordArt as shown in Figure 8.30.

7. Save the document with the name **C08-A02-Heart**.

8. Print and then close **C08-A02-Heart.docx**.

Figure 8.30 Flyer Created in Assessment 8.2

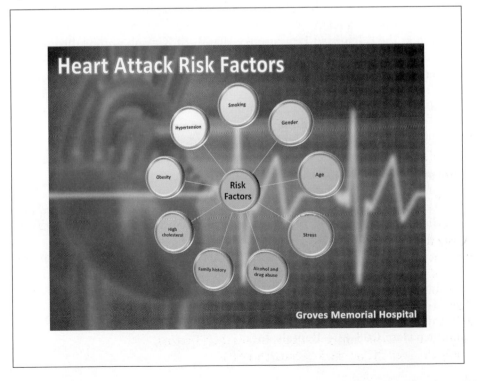

Assessment 8.3   Create a College Flyer

1. At a blank document, create a flyer promoting the spring session of classes at Midwest College in Oak Park, Illinois, similar to the sample shown in Figure 8.31. Use text boxes, shapes, photographs, WordArt, and any applicable formatting techniques that you have learned. *Hint: You may use an appropriate template, but make sure to customize it.*
2. Type **SUMMER, 2015**, and **Midwest** in three separate text boxes and arrange them attractively. *Hint: You may want to layer your design objects and change the text wrapping.*
3. Include the following text in the flyer:

   Midwest College, 567 Main Street, Oak Park, IL 60305-8019 708.555.0148 (or use the name and address of your college)

   Dates to note: Summer Session, May 26 to July 30, call 708.555.0148 or register online at www.emcp.net/midwest/summer

   Summer is a chance to: Learn new skills. Complete a required course. Take one course at a time. Have time to work while taking a class.
4. Insert a photograph related to college by searching using the keyword *college* at the Insert Pictures window. *Hint: You may want to crop the image and resize it appropriately.*
5. Use at least one of each of the following picture adjustments: correction, color, and artistic effects.
6. Create a logo for Midwest College using WordArt.
7. Save the completed document with the name **C08-A03-College**.
8. Print and then close **C08-A03-College.docx**.

Assessment 8.4   Create a Flyer That Promotes Island Rentals

1. At a blank document, create a flyer advertising a rental program for island vacation condominiums. (Figure 8.32 displays a sample document. Use your own design ideas for the flyer.) Include the following text and specifications:

   a. The name of the rental company is Beach Time Rentals, Inc.
   b. Prepare a logo with WordArt and possibly a clip art image.
   c. Insert an appropriate number of beach scene photographs.
   d. Include the following text:

      Vacation at the celebrated Lowcountry islands of Kiawah and Seabrook near historic Charleston, South Carolina. Beach Time Rentals, Inc. offers a variety of unique condos, villas, and homes on Kiawah and Seabrook. For more information on our short- and long-term rental programs, call 843.555.1150 or 1.800.555.4765. Office hours: 9 a.m. to 5 p.m. Monday through Friday 9 a.m. to 6 p.m. Saturdays. Visit us online at www.emcp.net/beachtime
2. Embed an Excel table of temperatures by completing the following steps:
   a. Open Excel and then open **Temperatures.xlsx** from your Chapter08 folder.
   b. Select cells A1:D16 and then click the Copy button on the HOME tab.
   c. In your Word flyer document, click the Paste button arrow in the Clipboard group on the HOME tab and then click *Paste Special* at the drop-down list. At the Paste Special dialog box, click *Microsoft Excel Worksheet Object* in the *As* list box, make sure the *Paste* option is selected, and then click OK.
   d. Right-click the temperature table, click *Format Object*, click the Layout tab at the Format Object dialog box, click *In Front of text* in the *Wrapping style* section, and then click OK.
   e. Position the table as desired.
3. Close Excel.
4. In Word, save the document with the name **C08-A04-Rentals**.
5. Print and then close **C08-A04-Rentals.docx**.

Figure 8.31 Sample Solution for Assessment 8.3

Figure 8.32 Sample Solution for Assessment 8.4

Assessment 8.5   Create a Hospital Organizational Chart

GROUP PROJECT

1. Create an organizational chart using SmartArt showing a hospital administrative structure. (Figure 8.33 displays a sample solution. Use your own design ideas when creating the organizational chart.) As a group, assign individual responsibilities, which may include the following:

   - Defining the purpose of the document
   - Creating thumbnail sketches
   - Outlining layout and design objectives
   - Collecting images
   - Creating a logo

2. Include at least one photograph of the hospital and/or personnel and hospital activities.
3. Save the completed document with the name **C08-A05-OrganizationalChart**.
4. Print and then close **C08-A05-OrganizationalChart.docx**.

Figure 8.33 Sample Solution for Assessment 8.5

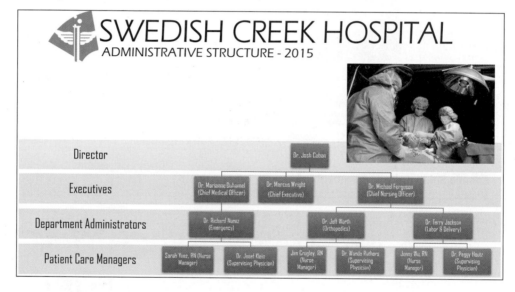

Chapter 9

Creating Brochures and Booklets

Performance Objectives

Upon successful completion of Chapter 9, you will be able to:

- Produce brochures and booklets
- Understand various folding styles and brochure layouts
- Use columns, text boxes, tables, and the book fold and 2 pages per sheet features as the underlying design for brochures and booklets

- Understand and practice duplex printing
- Modify and save a style
- Modify and save a style set

Desktop Publishing Terms

booklet	duplex printing	map fold
brochure	gate fold	panels
dummy	letter fold	parallel folds

Word Features Used

book fold	Draft view	section breaks	2 pages per sheet
column breaks	manual duplex	styles	
columns	orientation	style sets	

Note: Before beginning computer exercises for this chapter, copy to your storage medium the Chapter09 folder from the CD that accompanies this textbook and then make Chapter09 the active folder. Remember to substitute for graphics that may no longer be available.

Planning Brochures and Booklets

brochure

A short informational or promotional publication; created on one sheet that is later folded to create multiple pages

A **brochure** is a small informational or promotional pamphlet that often contains both text and images or graphics. A brochure is produced on one sheet of paper that is then folded to create different pages. A **booklet** is similar to a brochure in content and length, but its pages are bound (with staples, stitches, glue, etc.) rather than folded. As with any other desktop publication, it is important to plan a brochure or booklet before you begin to create it.

Defining the Purpose

booklet

A short informational or promotional publication; differs from a brochure in that it is bound rather than folded

The purpose of a brochure or booklet can be to inform, educate, promote, or sell. Which of these purposes is each of the following brochures or booklets trying to accomplish?

- A city agency mails brochures to the community explaining a local recycling program.
- A doctor displays brochures on childhood immunizations in the patient waiting room.
- A car salesperson hands out a brochure on a current model to a potential buyer.
- A new management consulting firm sends out brochures introducing its services.
- A professional organization mails booklets to its members listing membership information—addresses, telephone numbers, fax numbers, email addresses, and so on.
- A homeowners association prepares a directory of names, addresses, and services provided by residents (babysitting, pet sitting, garage cleaning, and so on).
- Volunteers for a local theater prepare a playbill (formatted as a booklet) for distribution during theatrical production.

If you noticed that some brochures and booklets have more than one purpose, you are correct. For example, the goals of a brochure on childhood immunizations may be to inform and educate, and the goals of a brochure about a car model may be to inform and promote the sale of the car. Alternatively, the goals of a playbill (booklet) may be to inform an audience of facts about a play, introduce people who are playing the roles, and promote organizations that support the community theater.

Keep in mind that brochures and booklets are yet another means of establishing your organization's identity and image. Incorporating design elements from your other business documents into the design of your brochure or booklet reinforces your brand among your readers.

Determining the Content

Before creating the layout and design of your brochure or booklet, determine what the content will be. You should include the following items:

- A clearly stated description of the topic, product, service, or organization
- A description of the people or company doing the informing, educating, promoting, or selling
- A description of how the reader will benefit from this information, product, service, or organization
- A clear indication of what action you want your audience to take after reading the brochure or booklet
- An easy way for readers to carry out the desired action, such as a phone number to call, a detachable postcard to send in for more information, or a form to fill in

Creating Brochures

Before you start typing the copy for a brochure, you have to make a few key decisions regarding page layout and printing. These decisions include determining the size and type of paper, deciding on the page layout, setting the margins, and determining the panel widths.

Determining the Size and Type of Paper

Determining the paper size is an important first step in planning a brochure because it helps to determine the number and size of panels the brochure will have. *Panels* are the "pages" of a brochure that are created by the folds in the paper.

Brochures can be folded in a number of different ways. The manner in which a brochure is folded determines the order in which the panels are set on the page and read by the recipient. All brochures are folded using *parallel folds*, or folds that run in the same direction. The most common brochure fold is called a *letter fold*, also known as a trifold. A letter fold creates a three-panel brochure, as shown in Figure 9.1A. Other brochure folds that can easily be created on standard-size 8.5-by-11-inch paper in landscape orientation include an accordion fold and a single fold (see Figures 9.1B and 9.1C). Standard legal-size paper (8.5 by 14 inches) can be used to create a brochure with a *map fold* or a *gate fold*, as shown in Figures 9.1D and 9.1E. Different paper sizes can be used to create variations of these folds. In addition, folds do not always have to create equal panel sizes. Experiment with different paper sizes and brochure folds to find the one that is best suited to your content and audience.

Brochures are usually printed on both sides of the page and can be printed on a variety of paper stocks. The paper stock may vary in size, weight, color, and texture. Some papers made especially for brochures also contain guidelines that tell you where to fold. The type of paper you select for your brochure affects the total production cost. When selecting the paper stock for a brochure, consider the following factors:

- Standard-size brochures, such as a three-panel brochure created from 8.5-by-11-inch paper stock, can fit easily in a #10 business envelope.
- Standard-size brochures designed as self-mailers satisfy postal regulations and are therefore less costly to mail.
- Paper stocks in nonstandard sizes may be more expensive to purchase and to mail.
- Heavier-weight papers are more expensive to purchase and more costly to mail.
- Higher-quality paper stocks are more expensive to purchase.
- Colored paper is more costly than standard white, ivory, cream, or gray.
- Paper stocks with preprinted designs are more expensive than plain paper stock.

panels
Pages in a brochure created by folds

parallel folds
Folds that run in the same direction

letter fold
Fold that creates a three-panel brochure where the sides of the paper fold in toward the middle; paper is folded two times

map fold
Paper is folded three times—the first two folds face inward and the third faces outward

gate fold
Paper is folded three times—all three folds face inward

Figure 9.1 **Understanding Brochure Folds**

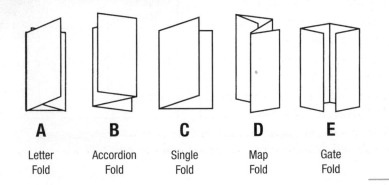

A	B	C	D	E
Letter Fold	Accordion Fold	Single Fold	Map Fold	Gate Fold

Although cost is an important factor when choosing paper stock, you should also take into account how the brochure will be distributed, how often each copy will be handled, and the level of quality you require. If you expect your target audience to keep your brochure for a period of time or to handle it often, plan to purchase a higher-quality, heavier paper stock. Similarly, choose a paper within your budget that enhances the image you want to leave in the reader's mind.

If you intend to print the brochure yourself, run a sample of the paper you intend to use through your printer. Some papers are better suited for laser and inkjet printers than others. If you are unsure about what type of paper to purchase, take a master copy of your brochure to a printer for advice on the best type of paper for the situation. You can also take your printed brochure to a print shop and have it folded on commercial folding equipment. If you plan to design the brochure as a self-mailer, take a sample of the paper stock to the post office to see if it meets USPS mailing regulations.

Understanding Brochure Page Layout

The folds within your brochure create distinct sections within which you can place specific blocks of text. For example, a three-panel brochure layout actually has six panels available for text—three panels on one side of the paper and three more on the other side. The way a brochure is folded determines the order in which the reader will view each panel, and thus how the content should be organized. Notice how the panels are labeled in the letter-fold brochure layout illustrated in Figure 9.2. Panels 1, 2, and 3 are located on the inside of the brochure, moving from left to right. Panel 4 is the page you see when the cover is opened. Panel 5 is the back of the folded brochure, which may be used for mailing purposes, if desired. Panel 6 is the cover of the brochure. The main content of the brochure is contained in panels 1, 2, and 3.

It can be confusing to figure out how to arrange the content in your Word document to achieve the final brochure layout. Because of this, it is a good idea to create a mockup, or *dummy*, of your brochure. A dummy is created using the same size paper as the final document and is folded in the same manner. A dummy can be as simple or as detailed as you would like. If you simply need visual verification that you are placing the correct text in the correct panel, fold the paper in the style you have chosen and then label each panel (similar to what is shown in Figure 9.2). If you want to plan the placement of text within each panel, the margins, and the white space between columns, make a more detailed dummy with specific margin, column, and spacing settings.

Figure 9.2 Understanding Panel Layout in a Letter-fold Brochure

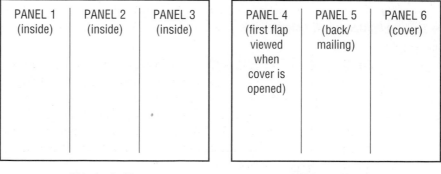

PANEL 1 (inside)	PANEL 2 (inside)	PANEL 3 (inside)		PANEL 4 (first flap viewed when cover is opened)	PANEL 5 (back/ mailing)	PANEL 6 (cover)

Side 1—Inside   Side 2—Outside

DTP POINTER
View mailing regulations at www.usps.gov.

DTP POINTER
The way a brochure is folded helps to determine how the content should be organized.

dummy
A mockup document that is laid out, folded, trimmed, and/or labeled in the same way as the actual publication

While you can create a simple brochure dummy by hand, it is best to create more complex dummies in Word. A brochure dummy can be created in Word using columns, tables, text boxes, or the 2 pages per sheet feature (applicable only to single-fold brochures). For example, to create a standard-size, three-panel brochure, create a dummy by changing the page orientation to landscape and then dividing the page into three columns using the columns feature, or into three columns and one row using the table feature. Alternatively, three text boxes can be sized and positioned on the page to represent three panels. Once you understand the order in which the different panels of your brochure will be seen, you can start to plan the content that will go on each one.

◀DTP POINTER
Keep a dummy of the folded brochure by your side and refer to it when creating the content for each panel.

Setting Page Margins for a Brochure

Because brochure panels are small, it is desirable to set the page margins as narrow as possible to create more space for content. Many home and office printers require a minimum of a 0.5-inch left or right margin (depending on page orientation) because a certain amount of space is needed for the printer to grab the paper and eject it from the printer. If you set margins less than the minimum, Word will prompt you with the following message: *One or more margins are set outside the printable area of the page. Choose the Fix button to increase the appropriate margins.* Click the Fix button to change the margins to the printer's minimum setting. Check the new margin setting by clicking the Margins button in the Page Setup group on the PAGE LAYOUT tab. If landscape is the selected paper orientation, the right margin will be the only margin "fixed" by Word because that is the side of the paper the printer grabs to eject the paper.

Even if Word only fixes one margin in your document, you should still adjust the opposite side margin to match. For example, if your printer requires a minimum of 0.5 inch for the right margin in landscape orientation, set the left and right margins at 0.5 inch.

If you click the Ignore button to respond to the prompt to fix the margins, the program will ignore the printer's minimum requirement and accept whatever margins you have set. However, the printer will not print anything in its nonprinting area, which will result in content that is cut off. Use the Print Preview area of the Print backstage area to view the results of setting margins that are less than the printer's minimum requirements.

Determining Panel Widths and Margins

In most brochure layouts, the widths of the panels cannot all be exactly equal, because one panel needs to fold and lay flat inside another. If equal panel sizes are used, the margins on some of the panels will appear uneven and the brochure folds will not fall properly in relation to the text. To solve this problem, individually size the text boxes for each panel to accommodate the appropriate placement of the text and the folds to achieve the desired result. You will have to experiment and make adjustments to find the appropriate widths.

Several methods can be used to create the panels of a brochure. The letter-fold brochure template shown in Figure 9.3 on page 390 uses a table as the underlying structure, as do most templates from Office.com. Other templates use text boxes for the panels, as shown in Figure 9.4 on page 390. Columns may also be used as the underlying structure of a brochure, as you will learn in Exercise 9.2. Choosing a method for structuring a letter-fold brochure depends on what is easiest for you to use and what is most appropriate for the design of the brochure.

Figure 9.3 Using a Brochure Template from Office.com (Formatted with a Table)

Figure 9.4 Using a Brochure Template from Office.com (Formatted with Text Boxes)

When designing a letter-fold brochure with three panels, as shown in Figure 9.5, consider the following steps for determining panel widths and the widths of the spaces between them:

◀DTP POINTER

Saving a blank brochure as a template will save time if you need to make a second brochure at a later date.

1. One way to determine the approximate width of each panel is to fold the brochure paper stock into the desired configuration, which, in this example, is a letter-fold layout. Measure the width of each panel. The width obtained will be approximate, because a ruler cannot measure hundredths of an inch, but it will be a good starting point.

2. Establish the left and right margins for the whole page. (See the previous section on setting page margins for a brochure.)

3. The left margin for the whole brochure page is also the left margin for panel 1. Therefore, subtract the left margin setting from the total width of panel 1. Estimate how much of the remaining amount is needed to allow for the text and other content and for an appropriate amount of white space on the right side of the panel. For example, if panel 1 measures approximately 3.7 inches, and the left page margin is 0.55 inch, subtract 0.55 inch from 3.7 inches. From the 3.15 inches that remain, estimate how much of that space will be occupied by text and how much needs to be allotted for the right margin of panel 1 (i.e., the white space before the fold). The method used to create the white space between columns depends on the method used to create the columns, as explained in Table 9.1 on page 392.

Figure 9.5 Determining Panel Widths for a Letter-fold Brochure

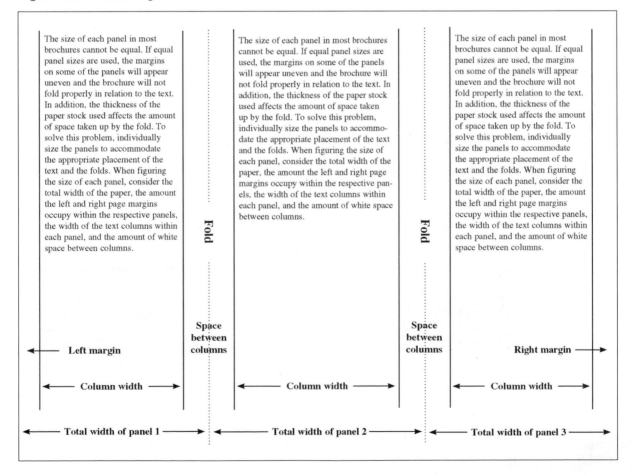

4. For panel 2, use the whole panel width to estimate how much space you will need for the content and an appropriate amount of white space on the left and right sides of the panel. The column width in panel 2 will be wider than the widths in panels 1 and 3.

5. For panel 3, you can use the same measurements you came up with for panel 1. Keep in mind that the margins are flipped from what they were in panel 1, though—the right margin for the whole brochure page is also the right margin for the panel.

6. After establishing text column widths and the amount of white space in between for panels 1, 2, and 3, reverse the measurements for panels 4, 5, and 6. For example, panels 1 and 6 will be the same measurement, panels 2 and 5 will be the same, and panels 3 and 4 will be the same. If you are using the columns feature, you will need to insert a section break to vary the column formatting on the second page. See the *Inserting and Removing Section Breaks* section later in this chapter for more information. If you are using the table feature, create another table for the second page of the brochure, reversing the column measurements from panels 1, 2, and 3. If you are using text boxes, remember to reverse the order as stated previously.

7. Use the previous suggestions to create a dummy. Insert random text in every panel and print. To insert random text, type *=rand()* and then press Enter. Fold the page as you would the brochure, and check the amount of space between columns. As illustrated in Figure 9.5 on the previous page, the space between panels is divided by the fold, allowing white space on either side of the fold. In other words, the space between columns serves as the margins for two different panels. Is the text positioned correctly within each panel? If not, adjust the space between columns and/or the column width settings, and then print and fold again.

Table 9.1   Methods Used to Create Spacing between Columns

Method used to create columns	Method used to create spacing between columns
columns	At the Columns dialog box in the *Width and spacing* section, adjust the amount in each *Spacing* text box.
table	Create blank columns in between the columns that contain the text for each panel.
text boxes	Size and position the text boxes containing the text for each panel, leaving the desired amount of white space between text boxes.
book fold	Adjust the margin settings and the gutter space.
2 pages per sheet	Adjust the margin settings. (2 pages per sheet is applicable only to single-fold brochures.)

Using Columns to Format Brochures and Booklets

Recall from Chapter 6 that columns are vertically oriented blocks of text with short line lengths in which text flows from the bottom of one column to the top of the next, as shown in Figure 9.6. Columns are used for text in newspapers, newsletters, brochures, booklets, and magazines.

By default, all Word documents are automatically set up in a one-column format. However, a document can include as many columns as you can fit on the page. Word determines the width of columns based on the number of columns you specify and the page width, margin settings, and spacing between columns. Column formatting can be assigned to a document before the text is typed, or it can be applied to existing text.

As mentioned earlier, dividing the page into columns is one method of creating the different panels of a brochure. The following sections will explain how to work with the columns feature in Word.

Creating Columns

To create columns, begin by clicking the Columns button in the Page Setup group on the PAGE LAYOUT tab to display the Columns button drop-down list, shown in Figure 9.7. From here, you can select preset column designs. When you select one of these designs, the column feature is applied to the whole document, to the section where your insertion point is located (if you have divided the document into sections), or to the selected text, if you have selected any. Remember that each column will contain the content for one panel of the brochure.

Columns

Using the Columns Dialog Box

For more control over customizing columns, click *More Columns* at the bottom of the Columns button drop-down list to display the Columns dialog box, as shown in Figure 9.8 on page 394. Experiment with changing the width between columns and note how the changes affect the text in each panel. For example, in a letter-fold brochure, increasing the space between columns 1 and 2 will cause the text in panel 2 to shift to the right, whereas decreasing the space between columns 1 and 2 will cause the text in panel 2 to shift to the left.

To remove column formatting, position the insertion point in the section containing columns and then change the column format to one column using either the Columns button drop-down list or the Columns dialog box.

Figure 9.6 Understanding Flow within Columns

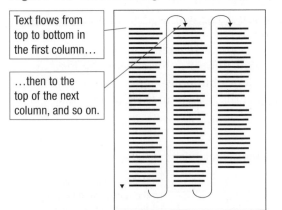

Figure 9.7 Choosing Preset Column Designs

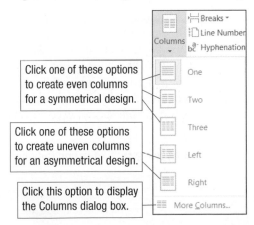

Figure 9.8 Reviewing Options at the Columns Dialog Box

Click or type the number of columns desired.

Enter a measurement for the width of each column.

Enter the amount of space you want between columns.

Remove the check mark to create columns of unequal width.

Insert a check mark to add a vertical line between the columns.

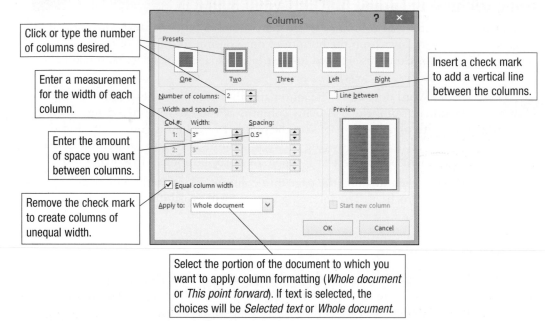

Select the portion of the document to which you want to apply column formatting (*Whole document* or *This point forward*). If text is selected, the choices will be *Selected text* or *Whole document*.

Using the Horizontal Ruler to Adjust Column Widths

After columns have been created, the width and spacing of the columns can be changed with the column markers on the horizontal ruler (see Figure 9.9). To do this, make sure the horizontal ruler is displayed (click to insert a check mark in the *Ruler* check box in the Show group on the VIEW tab). Position the arrow pointer in the middle of the Left Margin or Right Margin column marker on the horizontal ruler until it turns into a left-and-right-pointing arrow. Hold down the left mouse button, drag the column marker to the left or right to make the column narrower or wider, and then release the mouse button. Hold down the Alt key as you drag the column marker to view exact measurements on the ruler.

Inserting and Removing Section Breaks

By default, any column formatting you select is applied to the whole document. However, you can create different numbers or styles of columns within the same document if you divide the document into sections. For example, your brochure may contain a title or headline that you want to span the entire width of the page instead of just one column. To accomplish this, type and format the title, position the insertion point at the left margin of the first line of text to be formatted into columns, click the Breaks button in the Page Setup group on the PAGE LAYOUT tab, and then click one of the section break options, as shown in Figure 9.10. Additionally, you can use the Columns dialog box to apply a section break automatically from the location of the insertion point to the end of the document or until other column formatting is encountered by changing the *Apply to* option at the bottom of the Columns dialog box from *Whole document* to *This point forward*.

Breaks

Figure 9.9   Adjusting Column Widths on the Horizontal Ruler

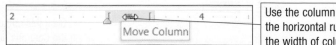

Use the column markers on the horizontal ruler to change the width of columns.

Figure 9.10 Inserting Section Breaks with Options at the Breaks Button Drop-down List

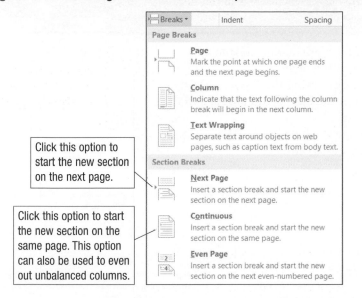

Click this option to start the new section on the next page.

Click this option to start the new section on the same page. This option can also be used to even out unbalanced columns.

As you learned in Chapter 6, section breaks are used to allow layout or formatting changes within a document. Use them between sections that have different margins, paper size or orientation, page borders, headers and footers, columns, page numbering, line numbering, footnotes, and endnotes.

Recall from Chapter 6 that section breaks can also be used to balance the text in columns. For example, if you have one full-length column and one very short one, you can insert a section break to divide the content evenly between the two columns. To do this, position the insertion point at the end of the last column, click the Breaks button and then click the *Continuous* option at the drop-down list.

To delete a section break, click the VIEW tab and then click the Draft View button in the Views group or click the Show/Hide ¶ button in the Paragraph group on the HOME tab to turn on the display of nonprinting characters. The section break will display as a dotted line with the text *Section Break*. Position the insertion point to the left of the section break and then press the Delete key to remove it. When you delete a section break, you also delete the formatting in the section of text before the break. That text becomes part of the following section, and it assumes the formatting of that section.

Inserting a Column Break

When formatting text into columns, Word automatically breaks the columns to fit the page. At times, text may wrap from one column to another in an undesirable way. For example, a heading may appear at the bottom of the column, while the text that follows the heading begins at the top of the next column. You can change these automatic column breaks by manually inserting column breaks at the desired locations.

To insert a column break, position the insertion point where you want the new column to begin and then press Ctrl + Shift + Enter, or click the Breaks button in the Page Setup group on the PAGE LAYOUT tab and then click *Column* in the *Page Breaks* section.

To familiarize yourself with the layout of panels in a letter-fold brochure, you will use Word to create a dummy like the one shown in Figure 9.2, on page 388, in the following exercise.

◄ DTP POINTER

As you create a brochure, continually evaluate the column breaks to make sure they occur in appropriate locations.

1. At a blank document, change the page orientation to landscape.
2. Change the left and right margins to 0.5 inch.
3. Change to a three-column format by clicking the PAGE LAYOUT tab, clicking the Columns button in the Page Setup group, and then clicking *Three* at the drop-down list.

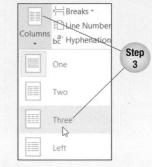

4. Insert the panel labels by completing the following steps:
   a. Change the paragraph alignment to center.
   b. Type **PANEL 1**, press Enter, and then type (**inside**) in the first panel (column 1).
   c. Click the Breaks button in the Page Setup group on the PAGE LAYOUT tab and then click *Column* in the *Page Breaks* section.
   d. Using Figure 9.2, on page 388, as a guide, repeat Steps 4b through 4c until all six panels are labeled as shown in Figure 9.2. ***Hint: Press Ctrl + Shift + Enter to insert a column break.***
5. Print the dummy by completing the following steps:
   a. Press Ctrl + Home to position the insertion point on the first page (containing panels 1, 2, and 3).
   b. Display the Print backstage area.
   c. At the Print backstage area, click the down-pointing arrow at the right of the first gallery in the *Settings* section (contains the text *Print All Pages*) and then click the *Print Current Page* option.
   d. Click the Print button.
   e. Put the first printed page back in the printer so the second page can be printed on the back of the first page. ***Note: You may need to experiment to find the proper way to put the page back into the printer so that the dummy prints as it should. You will learn more about printing on both sides of the paper later in the chapter.***
   f. Position the insertion point on the second page (containing panels 4, 5, and 6) and then print it.
6. Fold the dummy as you would the real brochure.
7. Save the dummy brochure with the name **C09-E01-Dummy**.
8. Close **C09-E01-Dummy.docx**.
9. *Optional:* Open the SampleBrochures folder located in your Chapter09 student data folder and then practice the different folds.

DTP POINTER

You can use a procedure similar to that in Exercise 9.1 to create a dummy using a table. Insert a table with five columns and one row—three columns for the panels and two columns for the spaces between them.

Now that you have a dummy of a letter-fold brochure, you can refer to it anytime you are unsure where content you add to your Word document will appear in the final printed brochure. In the chapter exercises that follow, you will have the opportunity to create a letter-fold brochure using three uneven newspaper columns and other formatting features such as text boxes, reversed text, color, and bulleted lists.

When working on a brochure, remember to save often. Creating even a simple brochure involves many steps, and you would not want to lose your work by failing to save. Also, view your document frequently to assess the overall layout and design. Adjustments often need to be made that can affect other parts of the document not visible in the document window.

1. At a blank document, change the page orientation to landscape. (You will be creating an informational brochure on a safari similar to the one shown in Figure 9.11 on page 400.)
2. Click the Margins button in the Page Setup group on the PAGE LAYOUT tab and then click *Narrow* to change the top, bottom, left, and right margins to 0.5 inch.

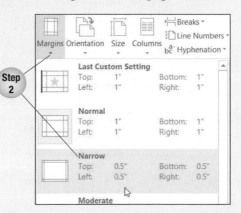

3. Apply the Facet theme.
4. Apply the Orange theme colors.

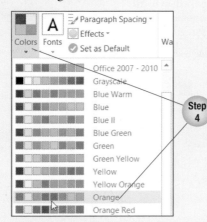

5. Apply the Casual style set.
6. With the insertion point positioned at the top of the page, insert **SafariIntro.docx** from your Chapter09 folder.
7. Position the insertion point anywhere in the heading *WHAT ARE THE BIG 5?* and then make the following changes:
   a. Apply the Heading 1 style and then change the paragraph alignment to center.
   b. Insert a bottom border by clicking the Borders button arrow in the Paragraph group on the HOME tab and then clicking *Bottom Border* at the drop-down gallery.

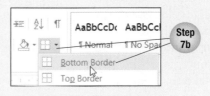

   c. Change the spacing before paragraphs to 0 points and the spacing after paragraphs to 10 points.
8. Select the paragraph of text that begins *The "Big 5" refers to*, apply the Intense Emphasis style, and then apply the Tan, Accent 5, Darker 50% font color (ninth column, bottom row in the *Theme Colors* section).
9. Press Ctrl + End to move the insertion point to the end of the document and then press the Enter key.
10. Click the *No Spacing* style option in the Styles group on the HOME tab.

11. Change to a three-column format by completing the following steps:
    a. Click the PAGE LAYOUT tab.
    b. Click the Columns button in the Page Setup group and then click *More Columns* at the drop-down list.
    c. At the Columns dialog box, click *Three* in the *Presets* section.
    d. Select the current measurement in the column 1 *Width* measurement box and then type **2.47**.
    e. Click in the column 1 *Spacing* measurement box and make sure that *1.29"* displays.
    f. Click the down-pointing arrow at the right of the *Apply to* option box and then click *This point forward* at the drop-down list.
    g. Click OK.

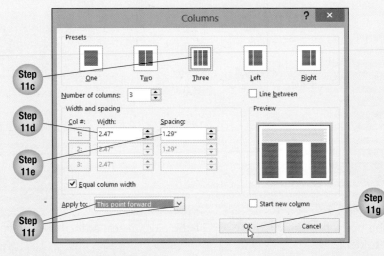

12. With the insertion point positioned at the end of the document, insert **Safari1.docx** from your Chapter09 folder.
13. Select the text from the paragraph that begins *Large, robust* through the paragraph that begins *Adolescent males roam*. Click the HOME tab and then click the Bullets button in the Paragraph group.
14. Position the insertion point at the beginning of the text *Lion* and then insert **lion.png** from your Chapter09 folder.
15. Make the following changes to the lion image:
    a. Apply Square text wrapping.
    b. Click the More button in the Picture Styles group and then click the *Rotated, White* option (third column, third row).

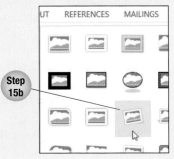

16. Position the insertion point in the text *Lion*, apply the Heading 2 style, and then insert a bottom border.
17. Position the insertion point at the end of the first column (in the blank line below the last bulleted item) and then insert a column break by pressing Ctrl + Shift + Enter.

18. Complete steps similar to Steps 12 through 17 to insert the following text files and images and then apply the picture styles. *Hint: Insert a column break after formatting each panel. After changing the text wrapping to* **Square**, *you will need to move down the image of the leopard and the rhinoceros as shown in Figure 9.11 to make sure that the animal names line up horizontally.*

	Text File	Graphic File	Picture Style
Panel 2	**Safari2.docx**	**leopard.png**	Beveled Matte, White
Panel 3	**Safari3.docx**	**rhino.png**	Bevel Perspective Left, White

19. Insert the safari graphic behind the text on the page as shown in Figure 9.11 by completing the following steps:
    a. Press Ctrl + Home.
    b. Click the INSERT tab and then click the Pictures button in the Illustrations group.
    c. Navigate to your Chapter09 folder and then double-click *safariborder.png*.
    d. Change the width of the image to 11 inches.
    e. Change the text wrapping to *Behind Text*.
    f. Drag the image so it is positioned approximately a quarter of an inch from the bottom edge of the page, as shown below.

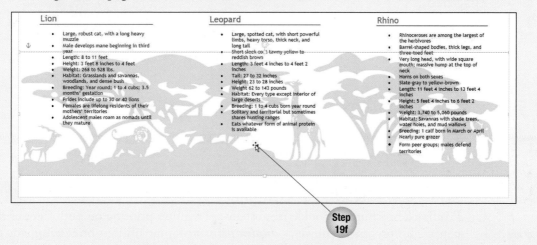

20. Make any necessary adjustments so that your document looks similar to the one shown in Figure 9.11.
21. Save the brochure with the name **C09-E02-Panels1-3**.

Figure 9.11 Front of Brochure Created in Exercise 9.2 (Panels 1–3)

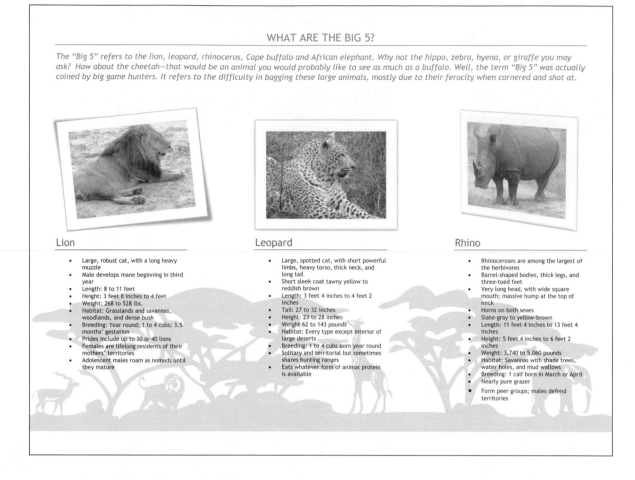

WHAT ARE THE BIG 5?

The "Big 5" refers to the lion, leopard, rhinoceros, Cape buffalo and African elephant. Why not the hippo, zebra, hyena, or giraffe you may ask? How about the cheetah—that would be an animal you would probably like to see as much as a buffalo. Well, the term "Big 5" was actually coined by big game hunters. It refers to the difficulty in bagging these large animals, mostly due to their ferocity when cornered and shot at.

Lion

- Large, robust cat, with a long heavy muzzle
- Male develops mane beginning in third year
- Length: 8 to 11 feet
- Height: 3 feet 8 inches to 4 feet
- Weight: 268 to 528 lbs.
- Habitat: Grasslands and savannas, woodlands, and dense bush
- Breeding: Year round; 1 to 4 cubs; 3.5 months' gestation
- Prides include up to 30 or 40 lions
- Females are lifelong residents of their mothers' territories
- Adolescent males roam as nomads until they mature

Leopard

- Large, spotted cat, with short powerful limbs, heavy torso, thick neck, and long tail
- Short sleek coat tawny yellow to reddish brown
- Length: 3 feet 4 inches to 4 feet 2 inches
- Tail: 27 to 32 inches
- Height: 23 to 28 inches
- Weight 62 to 143 pounds
- Habitat: Every type except interior of large deserts
- Breeding: 1 to 4 cubs born year round
- Solitary and territorial but sometimes shares hunting ranges
- Eats whatever form of animal protein is available

Rhino

- Rhinoceroses are among the largest of the herbivores
- Barrel-shaped bodies, thick legs, and three-toed feet
- Very long head, with wide square mouth; massive hump at the top of neck
- Horns on both sexes
- Slate-gray to yellow-brown
- Length: 11 feet 4 inches to 13 feet 4 inches
- Height: 5 feet 4 inches to 6 feet 2 inches
- Weight: 3,740 to 5,060 pounds
- Habitat: Savannas with shade trees, water holes, and mud wallows
- Breeding: 1 calf born in March or April
- Nearly pure grazer
- Form peer groups; males defend territories

Understanding Duplex Printing

duplex printing
Printing on both sides of a sheet of paper

Printing a brochure or booklet almost always requires printing on both sides of the paper. This process is known as **duplex printing**. Some printers offer automatic duplex printing, while others provide instructions so that you can manually reinsert pages to print on the second side. Some printers do not support duplex printing at all. To determine whether a specific printer supports duplex printing, check the printer manual or review the options in the *Settings* section of the Print backstage area. You can also display the printer properties by clicking the <u>Printer Properties</u> hyperlink below the Printer gallery.

DTP POINTER

When placing the printed first page in the printer tray, make sure to orient it so that the second page prints on the blank side of the paper.

If your printer supports duplex printing manually (not automatically), you can select the *Manually Print on Both Sides* option in the second gallery in the *Settings* section of the Print backstage area in Word, as shown in Figure 9.12. All pages that appear on one side of the paper will print, and then you will be prompted to turn the stack over and feed the pages into the printer again. You can also print on both sides by printing odd and then even pages. To do this, display the Print backstage area and then click the *Only Print Odd Pages* option at the first gallery in the *Settings* section. Once you are satisfied with the settings, click the Print button. After the odd pages are printed, flip the stack of pages over, click the *Only Print Even Pages* option, and then click the Print button. Depending on your printer, you might have to rotate and reorder the pages to print the other side of the stack.

Figure 9.12 Setting Up Manual Duplex Printing at the Print Backstage Area

Click the Print button after you have selected your desired print options.

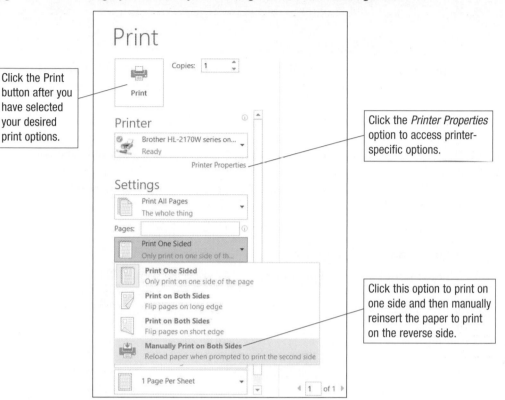

Click the *Printer Properties* option to access printer-specific options.

Click this option to print on one side and then manually reinsert the paper to print on the reverse side.

In addition, the order in which the pages print can be changed by clicking the FILE tab and then clicking *Options*. At the Word Options dialog box, click *Advanced* in the left panel and then add check marks next to options to print on the front or back of a page, as shown in Figure 9.13. If you change the settings in the Word Options dialog box, make sure you change them back before attempting to print a regular document.

In Exercise 9.2B, you will complete the brochure you started in Exercise 9.2A. As in the previous exercise, columns will be used to create the panels on the reverse side of the brochure. Refer to your dummy to see that panel 4 is the reverse side of panel 3, panel 5 is the reverse side of panel 2, and panel 6 is the reverse side of panel 1. As you progress through the exercise, remember to save your document often.

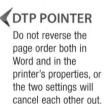

◀ DTP POINTER

Do not reverse the page order both in Word and in the printer's properties, or the two settings will cancel each other out.

Figure 9.13 Changing Printing Options at the Word Options Dialog Box

Select one of these options to determine which side of a page prints first during duplex printing.

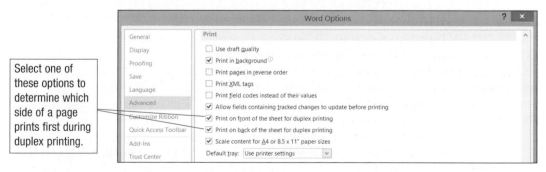

1. With **C09-E02-Panels1-3.docx** open, save the document with the name **C09-E02-Safari**.
2. Create panels 4, 5, and 6 of the safari brochure shown in Figure 9.14 by completing the following steps:
   a. Press Ctrl + End to position the insertion point at the end of the page containing panels 1, 2, and 3, and then press Ctrl + Shift + Enter to insert a column break.
   b. Complete steps similar to those in Steps 12 through 17 in Exercise 9.2A to format panels 4 and 5 as shown in Figure 9.14. Insert the following text files and photographs and then apply the following picture styles. ***Hint: Remember to insert a column break after formatting each panel.***

	Text File	Graphic File	Picture Style
Panel 4	**Safari4.docx**	**buffalo.png**	Rotated, White
Panel 5	**Safari5.docx**	**elephant.png**	Beveled Matte, White

   c. Move down the elephant image so the *African Elephant* heading aligns horizontally with the *Cape Buffalo* heading.

Cape Buffalo
- Massive animal with short neck, ox-like

African Elephant
- Largest land mammal

Step 2c

3. Create the title text in panel 6 (the cover) by completing the following steps:
   a. At the top of panel 6, press the Enter key six times. ***Hint: Make sure the No Spacing style is selected in the Styles gallery.***
   b. Type the following:
      > **Out of** (Press Enter.)
      > **Africa** (Press Enter.)
      > **Safari at** (Press Enter.)
      > **Kruger** (Press Enter.)
      > **National** (Press Enter.)
      > **Park** (Press Enter six times.)
   c. Select the text you just typed, change the font to 26-point Castellar, apply the Tan, Accent 5, Darker 50% font color (ninth column, bottom row in the *Theme Colors* section), and then change the paragraph alignment to center.
   d. Add a reversed text effect to *AFRICA* in panel 6 as shown in Figure 9.14 by selecting the text *AFRICA* (including the nonprinting paragraph symbol after the word) and then applying the Tan, Accent 5, Lighter 80% font color (ninth column, second row in the *Theme Colors* section).
   e. With *AFRICA* still selected, click the Shading button arrow in the Paragraph group on the HOME tab and then click the *Orange, Accent 1, Darker 25%* option (fifth column, fifth row in the *Theme Colors* section).

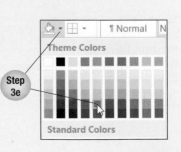

1 Normal N
Theme Colors

Step 3e

Standard Colors

4. Insert and format a text box on panel 6 by completing the following steps:
   a. Draw a text box in the document that is approximately 1 inch in height and 1.75 inches in width.
   b. With the insertion point inside the text box, type **In search of the BIG**.
   c. Select the text *In search of the BIG*, change the font to 24-point Gloucester MT Extra Condensed, and then apply the Orange, Accent 1, Darker 25% font color (fifth column, fifth row in the *Theme Colors* section).
   d. Change the paragraph alignment in the text box to right.
   e. Remove the shape fill and shape outline from the text box.
5. Insert and format another text box in panel 6 by completing the following steps:
   a. Draw a text box that is approximately 2 inches in height and 1 inch in width.
   b. With the insertion point inside the text box, type **5**.
   c. Select *5*, change the font to 100-point Papyrus, and then apply the Tan, Accent 5, Darker 50% font color (ninth column, bottom row in the *Theme Colors* section).
   d. Remove the shape fill and shape outline from the text box.
   e. Position the two text boxes as shown in Figure 9.14.
6. Copy the animal graphic located toward the bottom of the first page and paste it in the same location at the bottom of the second page (approximately a quarter of an inch above the bottom of the page).
7. Make any necessary adjustments so that your document looks similar to the one shown in Figure 9.14.
8. Save **C09-E02-Safari.docx** and then print the first page of the brochure (you may want to print the brochure on parchment or beige-colored paper). Reinsert the first page back into the printer and then print the second page on the back of the first page or print using the manual duplex feature at the Print backstage area.
9. Close **C09-E02-Safari.docx**.

Figure 9.14 Back of Brochure Created in Exercise 9.2 (Panels 4–6)

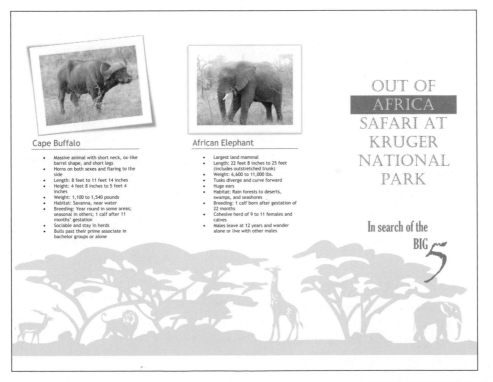

Creating Booklets

Recall that while booklets and brochures may have similar content, the major difference between the two is that booklets contain several pages that are bound together with staples, stitches, or glue, while brochures consist of one folded page. Booklets are often used for menus, manuals, directories, invitations, and programs. Various types of booklets can be created in Word. In this section, you will learn how to create a folded booklet, in which each sheet of standard-size 8.5-by-11-inch paper contains two pages of the booklet. You will then experiment with adding headers, footers, and page numbers to your booklet.

DTP POINTER

You can add a book fold to an existing document, but you may need to reposition some elements.

To create a folded booklet in Word, start at a blank document and then change the orientation to landscape. Display the Page Setup dialog box with the Margins tab selected, click the *Multiple pages* option box arrow, and then click *Book fold* at the drop-down list.

When you select *Book fold* at the Page Setup dialog box, Word sets up the document to print two pages on one side of the paper. You will then fold the paper so that it opens like a book. When planning the placement of your text, you must consider how the document will print and how the booklet will be assembled. For example, in an eight-page booklet, pages 8 and 1 are on the same side of the same sheet of paper, as are pages 2 and 7, pages 6 and 3, and pages 4 and 5, as shown in Figure 9.15. This can get confusing to keep track of, so as with a brochure, you may want to create a dummy booklet first. When you need to create additional pages for your booklet, insert a page break to create a new page with the existing book-fold setting.

When using the book-fold setting, your document will display with facing pages. This means that the margins of the left page are a mirror image of those of the right page (i.e., the inside margins are the same width, and the outside margins are the same width). The *Gutter* measurement box at the Page Setup dialog box is not available when you use the *Mirror margins, 2 pages per sheet,* or *Book fold* option. In Exercise 9.3, you will create an eight-page membership directory booklet that contains sequential page numbering.

Figure 9.15 Understanding Page Placement within an Eight-Page Booklet

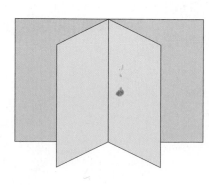

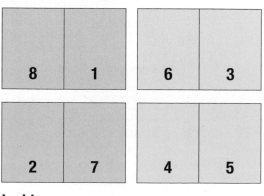

Outside

Inside

1. Open a blank document and save it with the name **C09-E03-GolfBookFold**.
2. Apply page formatting by completing the following steps:
   a. Click the PAGE LAYOUT tab, click the Margins button in the Page Setup group, and then click the *Custom Margins* option at the drop-down list.
   b. At the Page Setup dialog box with the Margins tab selected, change the top, bottom, right, and left margins to 0.5 inch.
   c. Change the gutter measurement to 0.25 inch.
   d. Click the down-pointing arrow at the right of the *Multiple Pages* option box in the *Pages* section and then click *Book fold* at the drop-down list. **Hint: When you select Book fold, the page orientation changes automatically to landscape.**
   e. Click the down-pointing arrow at the right of the *Sheets per booklet* option box and then click *8*.
   f. Click OK to close the dialog box.

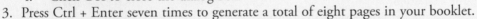

3. Press Ctrl + Enter seven times to generate a total of eight pages in your booklet.
4. Apply the Dividend theme.
5. Position your insertion point in the first page and then insert the images as shown on the cover in Figure 9.16 on page 408 by completing the following steps:
   a. Use the Pictures button in the Illustrations group on the INSERT tab to insert **womangolfer.png**, located in your Chapter09 folder.
   b. With the image selected, change the text wrapping to *In Front of Text*.
   c. Apply the Beveled Matte, White picture style (second option in the Picture Styles group) and then drag the image to a position similar to that shown in Figure 9.16.
   d. Use the Online Pictures button on the INSERT tab to insert the golf ball and club photograph as shown on the cover in Figure 9.16. At the Insert Pictures window, type **golf** in the *Office.com Clip Art* text box, press Enter, and then double click the image shown in the figure. *Hint: Substitute the image if necessary, but if you do, note that you may need to adjust the image dimensions.*
   e. Change the height of the image to 2.25 inches.
   f. Change the text wrapping to *Behind Text*.
   g. Click the Artistic Effects button in the Adjust group on the PICTURE TOOLS FORMAT tab and then click the *Texturizer* effect (second column, fourth row).

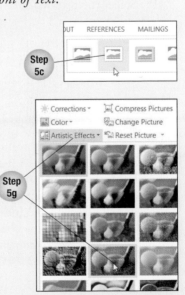

h. Click the More button in the Pictures Styles group and then click the *Rotated, White* option (third column, third row).

i. Drag the image to a position similar to that shown in Figure 9.16.

6. Add the text at the bottom of the cover page by completing the following steps:

a. Draw a text box that measures 1.25 inches by 3.5 inches.

b. Position the text box at the bottom of the cover page and then type the following:

Midwest Golf Club (Press Shift + Enter.)
Women's 9-Hole Directory (Press Shift + Enter.)
Summer 2015

c. Select the text *Midwest Golf Club* and then click the *Title* style option in the Styles group on the HOME tab.

d. Select the text *Women's 9-Hole Directory*, change the font to 14-point Trebuchet MS, and turn on kerning at 14 points and above.

e. Select the text *Summer 2015* and then change the font to 14-point Trebuchet MS.

f. With the text *Summer 2015* still selected, apply the Fill - White, Outline - Accent 2, Hard Shadow - Accent 2 text effect (fourth column, third row) using the Text Effects and Typography button in the Font group on the HOME tab.

g. Select the text box, click the DRAWING TOOLS FORMAT tab, click the More button in the Shape Styles group, and then click the *Subtle Effect - Plum, Accent 2* style (third column, fourth row).

h. With the text box still selected, change the paragraph alignment to center.

i. Save the document.

7. Position the insertion point at the top of page 2, press Ctrl + E, and then type **Notes**. ***Hint: Turn on the display of nonprinting characters and position the insertion point before the Page Break mark.***

8. Position the insertion point on page 3 (make sure the insertion point is positioned before the Page Break mark) and then insert **Welcome.docx** from your Chapter09 folder.

9. Select the text *Welcome to the 2015 golf season!* and then apply the Intense Quote style.

10. Select the text beginning with *All scores are to be posted* to the end of the text and then click the Bullets button in the Paragraph group.

11. With the text still selected, click the Paragraph dialog box launcher to display the Paragraph dialog box with the Indents and Spacing tab selected, remove the check mark from the *Don't add space between paragraphs of the same style* check box in the *Spacing* section, and then click OK.

12. Position the insertion point on page 4 (before the Page Break mark) and then insert **MemberNames.docx** from your Chapter09 folder.
13. Insert **MemberNames.docx** from your Chapter09 folder on page 5 and on page 6.
14. Position the insertion point on page 7 and then insert **Schedule.docx** from your Chapter09 folder.
15. Apply the Intense Quote style to the text *Ladies 9-Hole Golf Schedule*.
16. Position the insertion point at the top of page 8, press Ctrl + E, and then type **More Notes**.
17. Add page numbering by completing the following steps:
    a. Press Ctrl + Home to position the insertion point at the beginning of the document.
    b. Click the INSERT tab and then click the Page Number button in the Header & Footer group.
    c. Point to the *Bottom of Page* option at the Page Number button drop-down list and then click the *Plain Number 2* option in the *Simple* section of the side menu.
    d. Click the *Different First Page* check box in the Options group on the HEADER & FOOTER TOOLS DESIGN tab to insert a check mark.

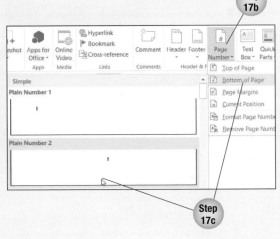

    e. Click the Close Header & Footer button in the Close group.
18. Print the document by completing the following steps:
    a. Display the Print backstage area.
    b. Click the second gallery in the *Settings* section (contains the text *Print One Sided*) and then click *Manually Print on Both Sides* at the drop-down list.
    c. Click the Print button.
    d. Word will print all of the pages that appear on one side of the paper and then prompt you to turn the stack over and feed the pages into the printer again. Once you have turned the stack of papers over, click the OK button. ***Hint: You may have to experiment with reloading your pages properly.***

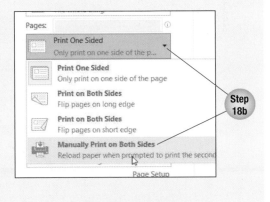

    e. Fold your pages to assemble your booklet.
19. Save and close **C09-E03-GolfBookFold.docx**.

Figure 9.16 Booklet Created in Exercise 9.3

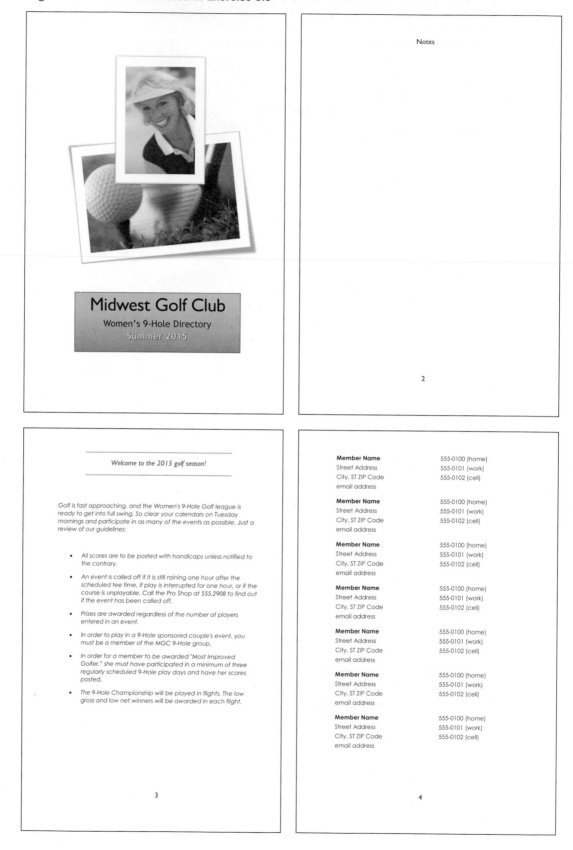

Figure 9.16 Booklet Created in Exercise 9.3 (continued)

Member Name Street Address City, ST ZIP Code email address	555-0100 (home) 555-0101 (work) 555-0102 (cell)
Member Name Street Address City, ST ZIP Code email address	555-0100 (home) 555-0101 (work) 555-0102 (cell)
Member Name Street Address City, ST ZIP Code email address	555-0100 (home) 555-0101 (work) 555-0102 (cell)
Member Name Street Address City, ST ZIP Code email address	555-0100 (home) 555-0101 (work) 555-0102 (cell)
Member Name Street Address City, ST ZIP Code email address	555-0100 (home) 555-0101 (work) 555-0102 (cell)
Member Name Street Address City, ST ZIP Code email address	555-0100 (home) 555-0101 (work) 555-0102 (cell)
Member Name Street Address City, ST ZIP Code email address	555-0100 (home) 555-0101 (work) 555-0102 (cell)

5

Member Name Street Address City, ST ZIP Code email address	555-0100 (home) 555-0101 (work) 555-0102 (cell)
Member Name Street Address City, ST ZIP Code email address	555-0100 (home) 555-0101 (work) 555-0102 (cell)
Member Name Street Address City, ST ZIP Code email address	555-0100 (home) 555-0101 (work) 555-0102 (cell)
Member Name Street Address City, ST ZIP Code email address	555-0100 (home) 555-0101 (work) 555-0102 (cell)
Member Name Street Address City, ST ZIP Code email address	555-0100 (home) 555-0101 (work) 555-0102 (cell)
Member Name Street Address City, ST ZIP Code email address	555-0100 (home) 555-0101 (work) 555-0102 (cell)
Member Name Street Address City, ST ZIP Code email address	555-0100 (home) 555-0101 (work) 555-0102 (cell)

6

Ladies 9-Hole Golf Schedule

Tuesday	April 21	Opening Luncheon
Tuesday	May 5	Opening Scramble
Tuesday	May 12	9-Hole Event, Front
Tuesday	May 19	9-Hole Event, Back
Friday	May 22	9-Hole Couple's Golf
Wednesday	May 27	Women's Rally for the Cure
Tuesday	June 2	9-Hole Event, Front
Tuesday	June 9	9-Hole Event, Back
Tuesday	June 12	9-Hole Event, Crazy Days
Tuesday	June 23	9-Hole Event, Front
Tuesday	June 30	9-Hole Guest Day
Tuesday	July 7	9-Hole, Championship
Friday	July 17	9-Hole, Couples Golf
Tuesday	July 21	Closing Lunch

7

More Notes

8

Modifying Styles and Style Sets

In Chapter 6 you created new styles using existing formatting. You can also create a style or style set by modifying an existing style or style set to fit your needs.

Modifying a Style

In Word 2013, styles are predesigned to work together to create an attractive, professional-looking document. The styles in the Styles group on the HOME tab are associated with the theme and style set you have applied to your document. You may want to experiment with selecting different themes and watching the changes in fonts, colors, and other attributes of text that has styles applied to it. Sometimes you may like certain aspects of a style, but need to modify other parts of it to suit your document.

To modify a predesigned style, complete the following steps:

1. Select text that is formatted with the attributes you want to change.
2. Format the selected text with the new attributes that you want.
3. Right-click the style you want to change in the Styles group on the HOME tab.
4. Click *Update to Match Selection*.

In addition, you can modify a style by completing the following steps:

1. Right-click the style you want to modify and then click *Modify* at the shortcut menu.
2. At the Modify Style dialog box, make the necessary changes.
3. Either give the modified style a new name (it will replace the original name), or save the style as originally named.
4. Click OK to close the Modify Style dialog box.
5. If the style has been previously used in the document, all occurrences will be updated with the changes you just made.

Modifying and Saving a Style Set

Style sets are predesigned combinations of styles, colors, and fonts. Style sets are available in the Document Formatting group on the DESIGN tab. When you hover the mouse pointer over a style set thumbnail in the Document Formatting group, the name of the style set will display, such as Basic (Elegant), Basic (Simple), Black & White (Capitalized), Black & White (Classic), Casual, Centered, Lines, Minimalist, and so forth. These style sets are predesigned to complement one another. Most of the time, you will not want to change these style sets. However, under certain circumstances, you might want to change the attributes of a style contained within a style set and then create a new style set that includes the modified style.

To create a new custom style set, complete the following steps:

1. Create or modify a style in the Styles group on the HOME tab.
2. Click the DESIGN tab and then click the More button at the right side of the style set thumbnails in the Document Formatting group.
3. Click *Save as a New Style Set*.
4. At the Save as a New Style Set dialog box, type a name for your new style set in the *File name* text box and then click the Save button.

To view the new style set, click the More button at the right side of the style set thumbnails in the Document Formatting group on the DESIGN tab. The new style set will display in the *Custom* section of the drop-down gallery.

Figure 9.17 Using the Organizer Dialog Box

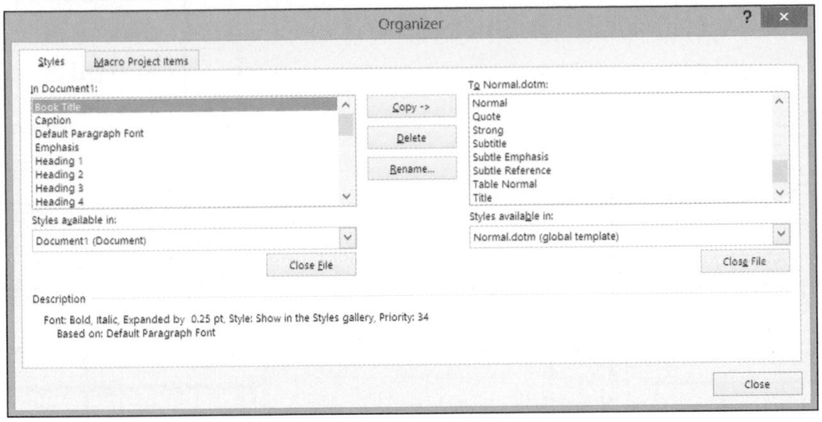

Copying Styles from Other Documents and Templates

If you have created new styles or modified existing styles in a document or template, you can make the styles available in other documents or templates by copying the styles. Copy styles from one document or template to another at the Organizer dialog box, shown in Figure 9.17. Display this dialog box by clicking the Styles group task pane launcher on the HOME tab and then clicking the Manage Styles button that displays at the bottom of the task pane. At the Manage Styles dialog box, click the Import/Export button that displays in the lower left corner of the dialog box.

At the Organizer dialog box, close the file on the right side by clicking the Close File button. Open the file containing the styles you want by clicking the Open File button, which was previously the Close File button. Click the style you want to copy in the list box on the right and then click the Copy button. This copies the style to the list box on the left side of the dialog box. Continue in this manner until you have copied all desired styles.

Using the 2 Pages per Sheet Feature to Create Brochures and Booklets

The 2 pages per sheet feature in Word can be used to create both brochures and booklets. This feature divides each page in half, as shown in Figure 9.18 on page 412. The printed page can then be folded in half and used as a single-fold brochure, or several pages can be folded and bound at the fold to create a booklet. Word displays and numbers each half page as a separate page. Any page formatting such as margins, paper size, and orientation can be applied to each half page. Headers and footers, page numbering, and page borders can also be inserted.

To use the 2 pages per sheet feature, click the PAGE LAYOUT tab and then click the Page Setup group dialog box launcher. At the Page Setup dialog box with the Margins tab selected, click the *Multiple pages* option box arrow and then click *2 pages per sheet* at the drop-down list. In addition, select *Portrait* or *Landscape* in the *Orientation* section and then enter the desired margin values. Refer to Figure 9.18 to see where the outside and inside margins are located when portrait or landscape orientation is selected.

In Exercise 9.4A, you will apply and modify styles and use the 2 pages per sheet feature to create a single-fold brochure in landscape orientation.

Figure 9.18 **Using the 2 Pages per Sheet Feature**

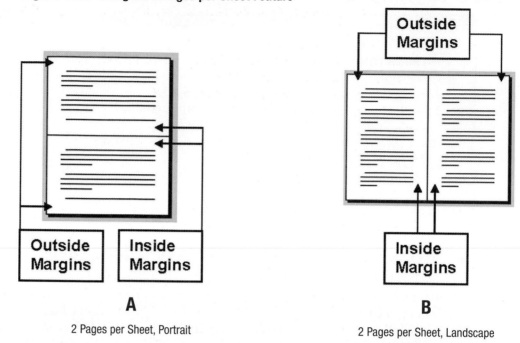

A

2 Pages per Sheet, Portrait

B

2 Pages per Sheet, Landscape

Exercise 9.4A   Creating the Inside Panels of a Single-fold Brochure Using 2 Pages per Sheet   Part 1 of 2

1. Open **SingleFoldLandscape.docx** located in the SampleBrochures folder in your Chapter09 folder and then print the document on both sides of a sheet of paper. Use this as a dummy for Exercise 9.4.

2. At a blank document, create the inside panels of a single-fold brochure as shown in Figure 9.19 on page 416 by completing the following steps:

   a. Click the PAGE LAYOUT tab and then click the Page Setup group dialog box launcher.

   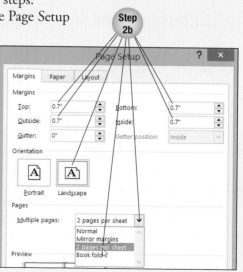

   Step 2b

   b. At the Page Setup dialog box with the Margins tab selected, change the top, bottom, left, and right margins to 0.7; change the page orientation to *Landscape*; and then click the down-pointing arrow at the right of the *Multiple pages* list box and click *2 pages per sheet*. (When you click the *2 pages per sheet* option, the left and right margins change to the outside and inside margins.)

   c. Click OK to close the dialog box.

   d. With the insertion point positioned at the beginning of the document, insert **HeartText.docx** from your Chapter09 folder.

   e. Press Ctrl + A to select all of the text in the document, click the HOME tab, and then click the No Spacing style.

3. Apply a style to the first paragraph of text and then modify the style by completing the following steps:
   a. Select the first paragraph of text.
   b. Click the Heading 1 style in the Styles group on the HOME tab.
   c. Change the font to 14-point Lucinda Sans Unicode, apply bold and italic formatting, and then apply the Blue, Accent 5, Darker 25% font color (ninth column, fifth row in the *Theme Colors* section).
   d. Right-click the Heading 1 style in the Styles gallery and then click *Update Heading 1 to Match Selection*.

4. Insert and format the drop cap paragraph as shown in Figure 9.19 by completing the following steps:
   a. Click anywhere in the first paragraph to deselect it and position the insertion point within it, and then click the INSERT tab.
   b. Click the Drop Cap button in the Text group and then click *Drop Cap Options* at the drop-down list.
   c. At the Drop Cap dialog box, click *Dropped* in the *Position* section, change the font to Harrington, make sure *3* displays in the *Lines to drop* measurement box, and change the value in the *Distance from text* measurement box to 0.1 inch.
   d. Click OK to close the dialog box.
   e. With the drop cap selected (gray sizing handles display around the letter), change the font color to *Orange, Accent 2, Darker 25%* (sixth column, fifth row in the *Theme Colors* section) and remove italic formatting.
   f. Click the Line and Paragraph Spacing button in the Paragraph group and then click *Remove Space Before Paragraph* at the drop-down list.

5. Apply a style and then modify the style by completing the following steps:
   a. Select the text *Diabetes: The Latest News* and apply the Heading 2 style.
   b. Right-click the Heading 2 style in the Styles group and click *Modify*.
   c. At the Modify Style dialog box, change the font to 16-point Cambria bold and apply the Orange, Accent 2, Darker 25% font color.

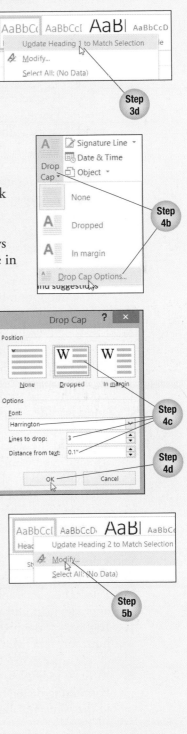

Step 3d

Step 4b

Step 4c

Step 4d

Step 5b

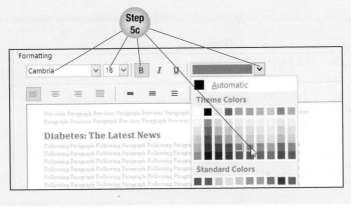

Step 5c

d. Apply small caps formatting by clicking the Format button in the lower left corner of the dialog box and then clicking *Font* at the pop-up list.

e. At the Font dialog box with the Font tab selected, insert a check mark in the *Small caps* check box and then click OK.

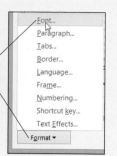

Step 5d

f. Add 18 points of spacing before the paragraph by clicking the Format button and then clicking *Paragraph* at the pop-up list. At the Paragraph dialog box, type **18** in the *Before* measurement box in the *Spacing* section and then click OK.

g. Click OK to accept the modifications to the Heading 2 style. (The modified Heading 2 style has replaced the previous Heading 2 style, which is saved with the document.)

6. Copy the Heading 3 and Heading 4 style from the **HeartTemplate.dotx** template into the current document by completing the following steps:

a. Click the Styles group task pane launcher.

b. Click the Manage Styles button at the bottom of the Styles task pane.

Step 6b

c. At the Manage Styles dialog box, click the Import/Export button located in the bottom left corner of the dialog box.

d. At the Organizer dialog box, click the Close File button below the option box containing the text *Normal.dotm (global template)*.

Step 6c

e. Click the Open File button (previously the Close File button), navigate to your Chapter09 folder, and then double-click **HeartTemplate.dotx** in the Content pane.

f. Select the Heading 3 and Heading 4 styles in the *In HeartTemplate.dotx* list box (hold down the Ctrl key as you click Heading 3 and Heading 4) and then click the Copy button.

g. If a Word message box displays asking if you want to override the Heading 3 style, click the Yes to All button. At the Organizer dialog box, click the Close button.

Step 6f

h. Close the Styles task pane.

7. Select the text *Tuesday, March 17, 2015* and then apply the Heading 3 style.

8. Select the text *Katherine Dwyer, M.D.* and then apply the Heading 4 style.

9. Create a style based on formatting by completing the following steps:

a. Select the paragraph beginning *One of the best ways*, change the font to 12-point Calibri, and add 12 points of spacing before the paragraph.

b. Right-click the text, click the Styles button on the Mini toolbar, and then click *Create a Style* at the side menu.

Step 9b

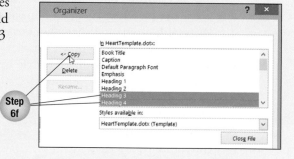

c. At the Create New Style from Formatting dialog box, type **HeartBody** in the *Name* text box and then click OK.

10. Apply the Heading 2, Heading 3, Heading 4, and HeartBody styles to the remaining headings and paragraphs as shown in Figure 9.19.

11. Position the insertion point before the text *All lectures:* and add 9 points of spacing before the paragraph.

12. Select the text from *All lectures:* to the end of the document and then change the font to 12-point Calibri and apply bold formatting and the Blue, Accent 5, Darker 25% font color.

13. Use tabs and the Tab key to align the lecture information (time and location) as displayed in Figure 9.19.

14. Position the insertion point before *The talk is* and then add 9 points of spacing before the paragraph.

15. Select the text *FREE* and then change the font color to *Orange, Accent 2, Darker 25%*.
    Note: If the text in the last paragraph at the bottom of the second page wraps to a third page, adjust the paragraph spacing to avoid creating the new page.

16. Save the modified style set by completing the following steps:
    a. Click the DESIGN tab.
    b. Click the More button in the Document Formatting group.
    c. At the drop-down gallery, click *Save as a New Style Set*.
    d. At the Save as a New Style Set dialog box, type **XXX-HeartStyles** (replacing the *XXX* with your initials) in the *File name* text box and then click the Save button.

17. Add the image on the first page of the brochure by completing the following steps:
    a. Position the insertion point before the text DIABETES: THE LATEST NEWS and then click the Online Pictures button in the Illustrations group on the INSERT tab.
    b. At the Insert Pictures window, type **health care professionals** in the *Office.com Clip Art* text box and then press Enter.
    c. Double-click the medical image shown in Figure 9.19. (If this image is not available, choose a similar image.)
    d. With the image selected, click the Crop button arrow in the Size group on the PICTURE TOOLS FORMAT tab, point to *Crop to Shape*, and then click the *Heart* option at the side menu (sixth column, third row in the *Basic Shapes* section).

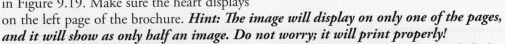

    e. Change the text wrapping to *In Front of Text* and then size and position the image as shown in Figure 9.19. Make sure the heart displays on the left page of the brochure. ***Hint: The image will display on only one of the pages, and it will show as only half an image. Do not worry; it will print properly!***
    f. With the image selected, click the Color button in the Adjust group, and then click the *Blue, Accent color 5 Light* option (sixth column, third row in the *Recolor* section).
    g. Click the Corrections button in the Adjust group and then click *Sharpen: 25%* in the *Sharpen/Soften* section.
    h. Change the text wrapping to *Behind Text*.

18. Save the document with the name **C09-E04-Panels1,2**.

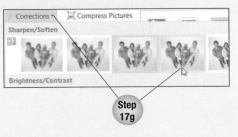

19. Print and then close **C09-E04-Panels1,2.docx**.

Figure 9.19 Inside Panels of the Brochure Created in Exercise 9.4

A fit heart can contribute to a long, healthy life for you and the ones you love. Join experts at the Edward Cardiovascular Institute to learn how to keep your heart beating strong.

DIABETES: THE LATEST NEWS
Tuesday, March 17, 2015
Katherine Dwyer, M.D.

One of the best ways to manage any medical condition is to keep abreast of the very latest information. Join endocrinologist Katherine Dwyer, M.D., for an up-to-the-minute discussion of the latest diabetes clinical trials, revised treatment guidelines, and new medical recommendations.

NEW ADVANCES IN CARDIAC SURGERY
Tuesday, March 24, 2015
Christine Johnson, M.D.

Advances in minimally invasive surgical procedures are helping patients get back to active, healthy lives more quickly—and more safely—than ever. Today, cardiac surgical procedures are marked by shorter hospital stays and recovery times, and lower costs. Learn more about these advances as Christine Johnson, M.D., leads an informative discussion.

EXERCISE—IS IT THE FOUNTAIN OF YOUTH?
Tuesday, March 31, 2015
Joan Perkins, M.D.

Everyone knows that exercise is good for your heart. Now, learn from a cardiologist exactly why it is good for you and what exercises provide the greatest benefits. Learn the specifics behind the "Just Do It" philosophy from Dr. Joan Perkins.

SETTING UP A HEART-HEALTHY KITCHEN
Tuesday, April 7, 2015
Kaitlin Anzalone, Registered Dietitian

A great start to beginning a heart-healthy diet is doing a heart-check of your kitchen. Join us for practical tips and suggestions for setting up your kitchen.

DIABETES AND CARDIOVASCULAR DISEASE
Tuesday, April 14, 2015
Wilma Schaenfeld, M.D.

During this session, we will discuss the clinical features of heart disease in the diabetic, as well as what you can do to reduce the likelihood of future problems.

All lectures: 7 to 8:30 p.m.
Edward Cardiovascular Institute
120 Spalding Drive
Naperville, Illinois 60540

The talk is FREE, but because space is limited, please register by calling (630) 555-4941.

In Exercise 9.4B, you will create the back and cover (panels 3 and 4) of the heart brochure you started in Exercise 9.4A. To make this brochure self-mailing, the back of the brochure will be used for the mailing address, return address, and postage. This newly created material will be printed on the reverse side of the content created in Exercise 9.4A and will appear as shown in Figure 9.20 on page 419.

Exercise 9.4B Creating the Back (Panel 3) and Cover (Panel 4) of a Single-fold Brochure   Part 2 of 2

1. Open **HeartCoverandBack.docx** from your Chapter09 folder and then save the document with the name **C09-E04-Panels3,4**.
2. Apply the style set you created in Exercise 9.4A by completing the following steps:
   a. Click the DESIGN tab.
   b. Click the More button in the Document Formatting group.

c. At the drop-down gallery, click the *XXX-HeartStyles* style set option in the *Custom* section (where *XXX* has been replaced with your initials).

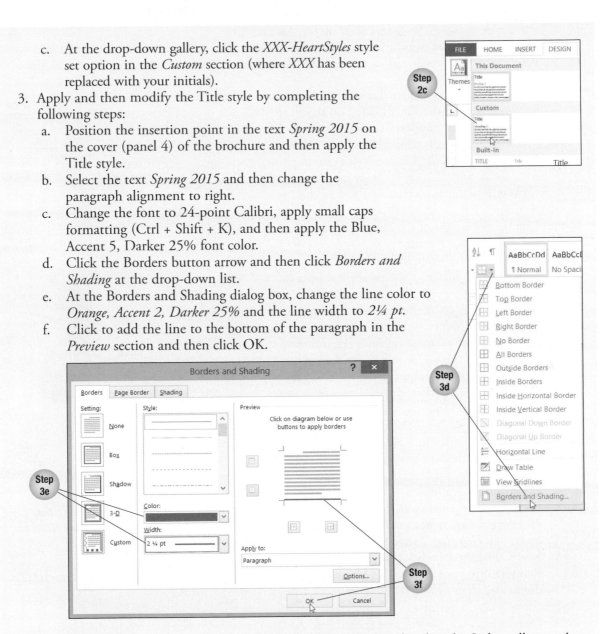

3. Apply and then modify the Title style by completing the following steps:

   a. Position the insertion point in the text *Spring 2015* on the cover (panel 4) of the brochure and then apply the Title style.

   b. Select the text *Spring 2015* and then change the paragraph alignment to right.

   c. Change the font to 24-point Calibri, apply small caps formatting (Ctrl + Shift + K), and then apply the Blue, Accent 5, Darker 25% font color.

   d. Click the Borders button arrow and then click *Borders and Shading* at the drop-down list.

   e. At the Borders and Shading dialog box, change the line color to *Orange, Accent 2, Darker 25%* and the line width to *2¼ pt.*

   f. Click to add the line to the bottom of the paragraph in the *Preview* section and then click OK.

   g. With the text still selected, right-click the Title style thumbnail in the Styles gallery and then click *Update Title to Match Selection* at the shortcut menu.

4. Remove the shape outline and shape fill from the title text box.

5. Select the text *Heart's*, change the font to 36-point Harrington, apply bold formatting, apply the Orange, Accent 2, Darker 25% font color, apply small caps formatting, and turn on kerning at 14 points and above.

6. With the text still selected, change the paragraph alignment to right.

7. Select the text *For your* and *Sake...,* change the font to 18-point Calibri, apply all caps formatting, and then change the paragraph alignment to right. **Hint: Select For Your, *hold down the Ctrl key, and then select Sake....***

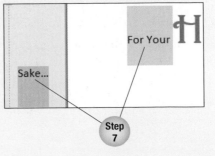

8. Press Ctrl + Home to position the insertion point at the beginning of the document and then insert the same health care professionals image used in Exercise 9.4A. (Substitute the image if necessary.)

9. Crop the image to a heart shape by making sure the image is selected, clicking the Crop button arrow on the PICTURE TOOLS FORMAT tab, pointing to *Crop to Shape*, and then clicking the *Heart* option in the *Basic Shapes* section of the drop-down list.

10. With the image still selected, click the Picture Effects button in the Picture Styles group, point to *Shadow*, and then click the *Inside Diagonal Top Right* effect (third column, first row in the *Inner* section).

11. Change the height of the image to 3.3 inches and the width to 4.13 inches.

12. Change the text wrapping to *In Front of Text* and then drag the image to the position shown in Figure 9.20.

13. Insert the logo on the front cover by completing the following steps:

    a. Press Ctrl + Home to move the insertion point to the beginning of the document.

    b. Use the Pictures button on the INSERT tab to insert **edwardcardio.png** from your Chapter09 folder.

    c. Change the height of the logo to 0.7 inch and the width to 1.88 inches.

    d. Change the text wrapping to *In Front of Text* and then drag the image to the position shown in Figure 9.20.

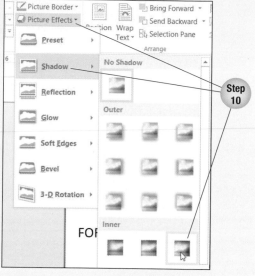

14. Select the text *EDWARD CARDIOVASCULAR INSTITUTE* in the return address (on the back cover, or panel 3, of the brochure) and then apply the Heading 3 style. ***Hint: If the Heading 3 style is not visible in the Styles group, click the More button. You may need to apply the Heading 2 style first to display the Heading 3 style in the Styles gallery.***

15. Save **C09-E04-Panels3,4.docx**.

16. Reinsert into your printer the document you printed in Exercise 9.4A (**C09-E04-Panels1,2. docx**) and then print **C09-E04-Panels3,4.docx** on the back side.

17. Close both documents.

18. Open a blank document and then delete the custom style set you created in the previous exercise by completing the following steps:

    a. Click the DESIGN tab.

    b. Click the More button in the Document formatting group.

    c. In the *Custom* section, right-click the style set containing your initials.

    d. Click *Delete* at the shortcut menu and then click the Yes button when a message box appears asking if you want to delete the style set.

    e. Close the blank document without saving changes.

Figure 9.20 Back and Cover of Brochure Created in Exercise 9.4

Chapter *Summary*

➤ Brochures and booklets can be used to inform, educate, promote, or sell. These documents can also be used to establish an organization's identity and image.

➤ The manner in which a brochure is folded determines the order in which the panels are set on the page. Folds create distinct sections in which to place blocks of text. The most common brochure fold is called a letter fold or single fold (portrait or landscape).

➤ A dummy is a mockup of a document used to visualize placement of text and objects to accommodate certain folds. Create a dummy to help determine the location of information on the brochure page layout.

➤ Because the panels in a brochure tend to be small, set the page margins as narrow as possible to create more space for content.

➤ Consistent elements are necessary to maintain continuity in a multiple-page brochure.

➤ When creating a brochure or booklet, you can use different methods to layout the page. The most common methods for creating a brochure or booklet are using text boxes, columns, or a table.

➤ Column formatting can be varied within the same document by using continuous section breaks to separate the sections that will be formatted with different column settings.

➤ Divide a document into sections to create different numbers or styles of columns within the same document with options at the Breaks button drop-down list or at the Columns dialog box.

➤ When printing a booklet, be sure to print on both sides of the paper. This is known as duplex printing.

➤ When you select *Book fold* at the Page Setup dialog box with the Margins tab selected, Word prints two pages on one side of the paper. When you fold the paper, it opens like a book.

➤ Repetitive formatting that is used to maintain consistency in a single publication or among a series of documents can be applied to text using a style.

➤ A style can be modified and any occurrence of the style in the document is automatically updated to reflect the changes.

➤ Modified styles can be saved to the Styles gallery as a replacement of the original style or they can be saved with a new name. Styles are saved in the document in which they are created.

➤ If the styles in a document have been created or modified, they can be saved as a style set. A saved style set can then be used in other documents.

➤ Styles can be copied from one document or template into another document or template with options at the Organizer dialog box.

Commands *Review*

FEATURE	RIBBON TAB, GROUP/OPTION	BUTTON	KEYBOARD SHORTCUT
breaks	PAGE LAYOUT, Page Setup		
columns	PAGE LAYOUT, Page Setup		
new style	HOME, Styles		
Print backstage area	FILE, *Print*		
styles	HOME, Styles		
style sets	DESIGN, Document Formatting		
Styles task pane	HOME, Styles		Alt + Ctrl + Shift + S

Key Points Review

A. all styles
B. book fold
C. booklet
D. Columns
E. Document Formatting
F. dummy
G. duplex printing

H. gate fold
I. gutter
J. landscape
K. letter fold
L. Manage Styles
M. Organizer
N. panels

O. parallel
P. right-angle
Q. style set
R. 2 pages per sheet

Matching: In the space at the left, provide the correct letter from the above list that matches each definition.

_F_ 1. A mockup of a brochure

_G_ 2. Option at the Print backstage area that allows you to print the document on both sides of the paper and prompts you to reload the paper

_O_ 3. Folds in a brochure that all run in the same direction

_D_ 4. Dialog box used to create columns of unequal width

_K_ 5. Feature that divides a physical page in half and may be used to create single-fold brochures

_Q_ 6. A combination of styles that are consistent with each other

_B_ 7. Word feature that prints two pages on one side of the paper so that when you fold the paper, it opens like a book

_L_ 8. To import or export styles from one document to another, display this dialog box

_C_ 9. A short informational or promotional publication that is bound

_H_ 10. When paper is folded three times with all three folds facing inward

_J_ 11. Page orientation that displays the page with the long side of the page on the top

_I_ 12. Feature that adds extra space to the side margin, top margin, or inside margin

_N_ 13. Sections of a brochure separated by folds

_E_ 14. Group on the DESIGN tab that includes buttons and options for choosing and saving a style set

_P_ 15. Folds in a brochure that intersect at a 90-degree angle

Chapter *Assessments*

Assessment 9.1   Create Inside Panels for a Letter-fold Brochure

As a supportive member of the Newport Volunteer Center, you have volunteered to use your desktop publishing skills to create a promotional brochure for the center. Your target audience includes the general public, but more specifically, volunteers, those in need of volunteers, and community organizers. Your audience will mainly consist of adults, but keep children in mind. Your purpose is to let your readers know what the volunteer center has to offer. The content of your brochure will include information on volunteer opportunities, various volunteer programs, scheduled events, and contact information.

In this first assessment, you will create panels 1, 2, and 3 (inside panels of the brochure) of the Newport Volunteer Center's brochure. In Assessment 9.2, you will create panels 4, 5, and 6 of the brochure. An example of a complete brochure is provided in Figures 9.21 on the next page and 9.22 on page 424; however, you are to create your own design (using text located in your Chapter09 folder). Complete your brochure according to the following specifications:

1. Create a letter-fold brochure. You can create your brochure layout from scratch using text boxes, columns, or tables. Alternatively, you can use one of the brochure templates at Office.com or at any other template source.
2. Include all of the information contained in the file **VolunteerText.docx**, located in your Chapter09 folder.
3. Create a thumbnail sketch of your design and then create a dummy to guide you in the placement of text.
4. Select an appropriate theme and then apply, create, and/or modify styles.
5. Use relevant graphics. A large selection of volunteer-related images can be viewed by displaying the Insert Pictures window and searching for images with the keywords *volunteer* and *community*. Viewing these images may help to inspire the design and color scheme of your brochure. Photographs tend to support sophisticated design.
6. Use a coordinated color scheme. Remember that you can customize text colors to match the color(s) in an image, customize the color(s) of an image to match a specific text color, or coordinate colors within another image.
7. Use appropriate typefaces. Make sure all text is legible. Turn on kerning for fonts over 14 points.
8. Make any necessary adjustments to the spacing before and after paragraphs.
9. As you work, evaluate your design for the concepts of focus, balance, proportion, contrast, directional flow, consistency, and color.
10. Save the document containing the inside panels of the brochure in your Chapter09 folder with the name **C09-A01-NVCPanels1-3**.
11. Print **C09-A01-NVCPanels1-3.docx**.

Figure 9.21 Sample Solution for Assessment 9.1 (Panels 1, 2, and 3 of a Letter-fold Brochure)

Assessment 9.2   Create Outside Panels for a Letter-fold Brochure

In this assessment, you will create panels 4, 5, and 6 of the brochure you started in Assessment 9.1. Include the following specifications:

1. With **C09-A01-NVCPanels1-3.docx** open, save the document with the name **C09-A02-NVCBrochure**.
2. Refer to the dummy you created in Assessment 9.1 to create the outside panels of the volunteer center brochure. A sample solution is provided in Figure 9.22 on page 424.
3. Apply any relevant styles according to the design you established in Assessment 9.1.
4. Make any necessary adjustments to the spacing or positioning of text.
5. After creating or modifying any styles, save the style set as **XXX-NVCStyles** (replace the *XXX* with your initials).
6. Save **C09-A02-NVCBrochure.docx**.
7. Print panels 4, 5, and 6 on the backside of the **C09-A01-NVCPanels1-3.docx** brochure that you completed in Assessment 9.1. Fold your brochure and check the placement of text and images in relation to the folds. Make any adjustments as necessary to produce a professional-looking finished product.
8. Open the **DocumentEvaluationChecklist.docx** located in your Chapter09 folder and then save the document with the name **C09-A02-Analysis**. Using the document evaluation checklist, evaluate your brochure design. Save, print, and then close **C09-A02-Analysis.docx**.
9. Close **C09-A02-NVCBrochure.docx**.

Figure 9.22 Sample Solution for Assessment 9.2 (Panels 4, 5, and 6 for a Letter-fold Brochure)

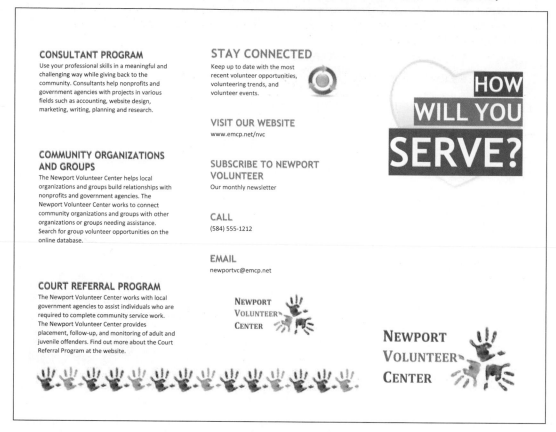

Assessment 9.3 Create a Brochure for Mailing

Using the same design style and content you used in Assessments 9.1 and 9.2, create a 2 pages per sheet brochure that will be mailed out to the local community. A sample brochure is provided in Figure 9.23. Your brochure should not match this sample, but should instead display design and style similarities to your own Assessment 9.1 and 9.2 documents. Include the following specifications in your design:

1. Starting at a blank document, modify the page setup to create a 2 pages per sheet page layout.
2. If you created a custom style set in Assessment 9.2, use the style set to keep the design and formatting consistent between brochures.
3. Create the inside panels before creating the outside panels.
4. Choose the text you want to include in the brochure from the **VolunteerText.docx** file located in your Chapter09 folder.
5. Use the sample solution shown in Figure 9.23 for ideas on the layout of the brochure. However, create your own design using elements from the previous assessments.
6. Use any shapes, text boxes, clip art, SmartArt, or other types of desktop publishing elements to enhance the appearance of the document. Reuse elements that you used in Assessments 9.1 and 9.2 to keep the appearance consistent between the brochures.
7. Type the following return address on the back cover of the brochure so that it can be mailed:

   Newport Volunteer Center
   2647 Saldago Drive East
   Newport, OR 97366
8. Save the document in your Chapter09 folder with the name **C09-A03-NVCMailer**.

9. Print the first page of the brochure and then print the second page on the back of the first page. Fold your brochure and check the placement of text and images in relation to the folds. Make any adjustments that are necessary to produce a professional and polished final product.

10. Close **C09-A03-NVCMailer.docx**.

Figure 9.23 Sample Solution for Assessment 9.3 (2 Pages per Sheet Layout)

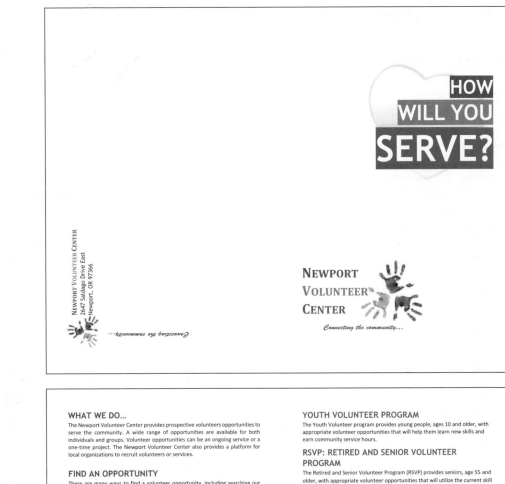

Assessment 9.4   Create a Fundraiser Brochure Containing a Chart

INTEGRATED

GROUP
PROJECT

You are a member of a fund-raising committee for the Loaves & Fishes Community Pantry. With the help of the other members of your group, plan an event to raise money and create a brochure that promotes the charity and advertises the event. A sample solution is shown in Figure 9.24. Your brochure may use similar elements and content but should not look exactly like the sample.

1. You can use the **loaveslogo.png** and **loavesbag.png** images located in your Chapter09 folder.
2. You may want to include a chart that illustrates the increase in the number of families served over the past three years. An example is shown in Figure 9.24. Use Excel to create the chart or use Word to create a column chart type as shown in the sample solution. In the sample solution, **loavesbag.png** was used as a fill for the data columns in the graph.
3. You can use the text in the sample document or, if it is difficult to read, you can open **LoavesText.docx** from your Chapter09 folder. Another option is to research a similar organization and fundraising event on the Internet for facts, information, goals, and so on, and then write the text yourself.
4. Save the completed brochure in your Chapter09 folder with the name **C09-A04-Fundraiser.docx**.
5. Print the brochure.
6. Open **DocumentEvaluationChecklist.docx** located in your Chapter09 folder and then save it with the name **C09-A04-Analysis**.
7. Use the document evaluation checklist to analyze your brochure and make any additional adjustments to the brochure, if necessary.
8. Save, print, and then close **C09-A04-Analysis.docx**.
9. Close **C09-A04-Fundraiser.docx**.
10. Staple the completed document evaluation to the back of your brochure.

Figure 9.24 Sample Solution for Assessment 9.4

Our Needs Have Increased

- 1,676 families (5,766 individuals)
- 160 seniors and disabled individuals
- 2,080 children, from infants to 18-year-olds

Number of Families Has Increased 63% since 2013

- 2013: 701
- 2014: 959
- 2015: 1140

How You Can Help

Cash donations are especially welcome. Your dollars go farther when we do the shopping. Any other food is welcome!

Help us help others this holiday season!

Loaves & Fishes Community Pantry
566 W. Fifth Avenue
Naperville, IL 60563

Please join us for our first annual

Picnic in December

Help us feed
Naperville's hungry

Loaves & Fishes
Ending Hunger in Our Community

Did You Know?

- There are over 4,000 individuals in Naperville living in poverty.
- A 2-bedroom apartment in Naperville costs a minimum of **$900/month.**
- A minimum wage-earner makes approximately **$1200/month** (gross) working a 40-hour week.
- This leaves less than **$300/month** for food, clothing, and utilities.

Loaves & Fishes:

- Distributes in excess of 770,000 pounds of food to families in need, annually.
- Has had a **250%** increase of families served over the last five years.
- Has provided food and personal care essentials to Naperville residents in need for **23 years.**
- Is a community-run pantry, operated by volunteers and supported by donations from the Naperville community at large.

When

Sunday, December 13, 2015

Open House, 6:30 p.m. to 10:00 p.m.

Where

Loaves & Fishes Community Pantry
566 W. Fifth Avenue
Naperville, IL 60563

Tickets

$50 per ticket ($30 tax deductible)

Events

- Cocktails
- Picnic, hot and cold hors d'oeuvres
- Silent auction
- Music and entertainment

Please respond by Monday, November 23

☐ I/we request _____ reservations at $50 per person ($30 tax deductible).

☐ I am unable to attend, but please accept my monetary donation to the food pantry.

☐ Enclosed is my check for $ _____ made payable to Loaves & Fishes.

☐ Please charge $ _____ to my credit card.

☐ Visa   ☐ Mastercard   ☐ Discover

Name: _____

Card number: _____

Expiration date: _____

Please use the enclosed envelope to mail your **RSVP** and payment by **Monday, November 23**.

You may also reply by telephone at **(630) 555-3663** or send email to **loaves@emcp.net**

Creating Specialty Promotional Documents

Performance Objectives

Upon successful completion of Chapter 10, you will be able to:

- Create specialty promotional documents
- Understand paper types
- Create lines on which to type using the underline feature, the shapes feature, a table, and tab leaders
- Create lines that align
- Insert field codes
- Create a data source and merge data
- Create crop marks using symbols and tabs

Desktop Publishing Terms

bond paper	cover paper	newsprint paper	tag paper
book paper	leaders	offset paper	

Word Features Used

field codes	Mail Merge	tables
headers and footers	shapes	tabs
labels	symbols	themes

Note: Before beginning computer exercises for this chapter, copy to your storage medium the Chapter10 folder from the CD that accompanies this textbook and then make Chapter10 the active folder. Remember to substitute for graphics that may no longer be available.

Creating Specialty Promotional Documents

In addition to newsletters, flyers, announcements, brochures, and booklets, the promotional documents category includes tickets, enrollment forms, gift certificates, postcards, bookmarks, name tags, invitations, and greeting cards, among many others. These types of documents can be considered promotional because they often display a business or organization name or promote an item or service that is for sale.

Whether creating tickets for a charitable event, discount coupons for a grocery store, bookmarks promoting reading at a public library, or coasters advertising a local restaurant, combining the desktop publishing features available in Word with a little imagination can produce endless possibilities. Figure 10.1 illustrates a few promotional documents created with the basic design concepts and Word features used in most of the exercises in this chapter. Figure 10.2 illustrates templates from Office.com that can be used to promote business interests.

DTP POINTER ›

Well-organized and clearly written promotional documents inspire confidence in the reader.

Throughout this chapter, you will practice creating a few different types of promotional documents: raffle tickets, a registration form, postcards and postcard labels, a greeting card, a promotional poster, and bookmarks. As with any other desktop publishing document, it is important to take time to plan and design your specialty promotional materials. Think about your purpose and audience and determine what content the document needs to communicate. Create thumbnail sketches and/or dummies to help visualize your plans before you start to work. Take time to carefully select fonts, images, and other design elements. Remember that the content is the most important part of any document.

Figure 10.1 Creating Specialty Promotional Documents in Word

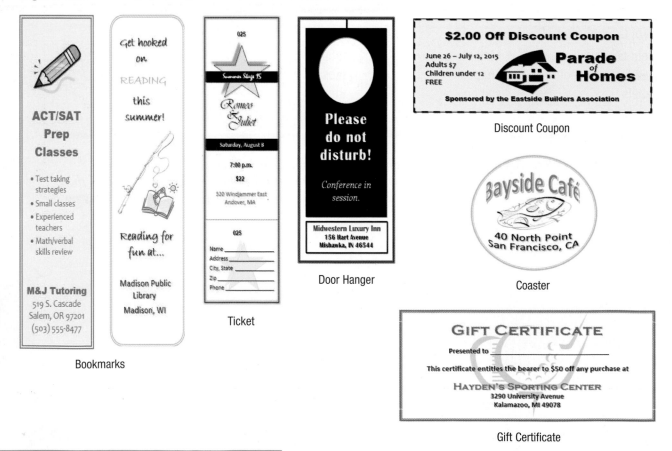

Bookmarks

Ticket

Door Hanger

Discount Coupon

Coaster

Gift Certificate

Figure 10.2 Using Word Templates to Create Specialty Promotional Documents

Bookmarks

Open House

Club Membership Card

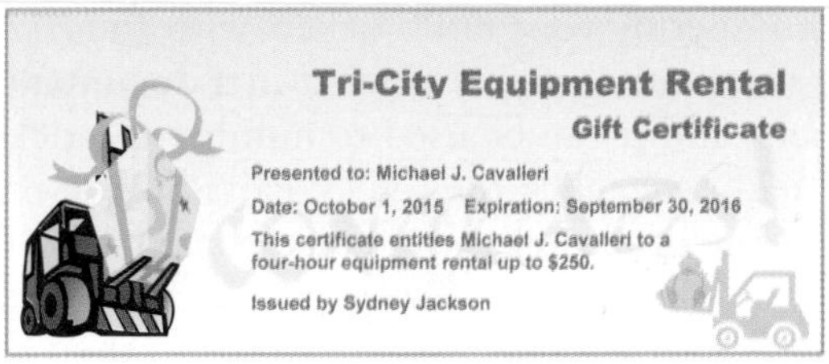

Gift Certificate

Punch Card

Thank You

Menu

Creating Raffle Tickets

Raffle tickets are considered specialty promotional documents because they are often used to help raise money for an organization or a cause. You can use the table feature in Word to quickly and easily create raffle tickets. Printing the tickets on a thicker paper stock will make them more substantial and durable.

Using Tables to Create Promotional Documents

Tables are useful in desktop publishing because they offer a precise, standardized layout that takes only a few minutes to create. Table layouts can be modified at any time, and the gridlines simplify the process of applying borders and shading to specific areas of the document.

Tables are especially well-suited to creating raffle tickets. You can adjust the sizes of the rows and columns to create uniformly sized tickets, and you can add an extra column to create the stub portion of the ticket. Word also simplifies the process of numbering your raffle tickets with the *AutoNum* field code. This field code is the same one that gets entered in a document when you insert automatic page numbers, and it can be used to number the tickets and stubs sequentially. To insert this field code, click the Quick Parts button on the INSERT tab and then click *Field* at the drop-down list. This opens the Field dialog box, as shown in Figure 10.3. Make sure *(All)* displays in the *Categories* option box and then click *AutoNum* in the *Field names* list box. You will then have an opportunity to choose a format (e.g., 1, 2, 3, ...) for your numbers. When you are finished making your selections, click OK to close the dialog box.

Figure 10.3 Inserting an AutoNum Field Code

At the Field dialog box, make sure *(All)* displays in the *Categories* option box, select *AutoNum* in the *Field names* list box, select a format in the *Format* list box, and then click OK.

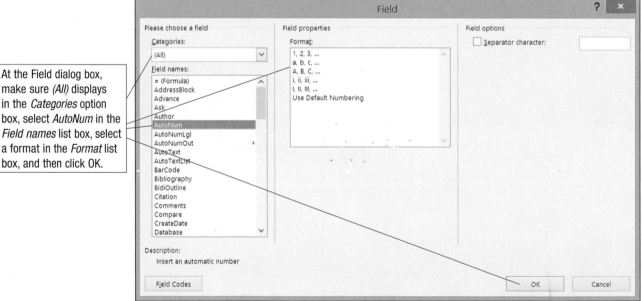

Understanding Paper Types

Picking the right paper for your project can be difficult. Each paper type has its own special characteristics. Two characteristics that vary from paper to paper are stiffness and grain. Stiffness refers to how easily the paper can bend, and grain is the direction in which wood fibers in the paper are aligned. It is important to notice the grain if you plan on folding the paper because folding against the grain in a stiff sheet can cause the paper to crack. Stiff paper is often scored so it is easier to fold.

One of the most common types of paper is **bond paper**, which is used for a variety of applications from business forms to home and office stationery. It is a strong type of paper, and its cotton fiber content, which usually ranges from 25 to 50 percent, contributes to its good ink absorption. However, bond paper is thin, and it does have a tendency to jam printers easily. **Book paper** is another common paper type. It is durable, inexpensive, and more opaque than bond paper, which makes it well-suited to two-sided printing.

Several other common types of paper are available. **Cover paper**, also known as cardstock, is a heavy, stiff sheet that is durable and folds easily in the direction of the grain. It is commonly used for folders, postcards, business cards, greeting cards, and book covers. **Newsprint paper** is used almost exclusively for newspapers and is generally inexpensive. **Offset paper** is used in offset printing because it is strong and resists tearing when used in large, fast printers. **Tag paper** is dense and strong and is used for merchandise tags. Other types of specialty papers include onionskin paper (also known as tissue paper) and rice paper.

In Exercise 10.1, you will create raffle tickets for a fundraiser for Loaves & Fishes Food Pantry. Each ticket will need a number printed twice—once on a ticket for the raffle entrants to keep and once on a stub to be placed in the raffle. The tickets should be printed on 65-lb. cover stock.

bond paper
Common paper type with good ink absorption

book paper
Durable, inexpensive, opaque paper well-suited for two-sided printing

cover paper
Heavy, durable paper that folds easily in direction of grain; also known as cardstock

newsprint paper
Inexpensive paper used for printing newspapers

offset paper
Strong paper that resists tears when used in fast printers

tag paper
Dense, strong paper used for merchandise tags

Exercise 10.1 Creating Raffle Tickets and Stubs with Sequential Numbering

PORTFOLIO

1. At a blank document, begin creating the tickets shown in Figure 10.4 on page 436 by changing the top and bottom margins to 0.75 inch.
2. Create a table with two columns and one row.
3. Change the row height and column widths in the table by completing the following steps:
   a. With the insertion point positioned in the first cell in the table, click the TABLE TOOLS LAYOUT tab.
   b. Select the current measurement in the *Height* measurement box in the Cell Size group, type **2**, and then press Enter.
   c. Select the current measurement in the *Width* measurement box in the Cell Size group, type **4**, and then press Enter.
   d. Click in the second cell (column) in the table.

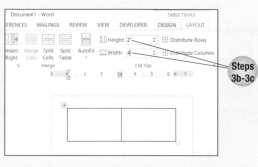

Steps 3b-3c

e. Select the current measurement in the *Width* measurement box in the Cell Size group, type **2.25**, and then press Enter.

4. Select the first column and then change the right cell border line to a dashed line by completing the following steps:

a. Click the TABLE TOOLS DESIGN tab.

b. Click the Borders button arrow in the Borders group and then click *Borders and Shading* at the drop-down list.

c. At the Borders and Shading dialog box with the Borders tab selected, make sure *Cell* is selected in the *Apply to* option box.

d. Click the right border line in the *Preview* box to remove the line.

e. Click the third line (dashed line) from the top in the *Style* list box and then click where the previous line displayed in the *Preview* box.

f. Click OK to close the dialog box.

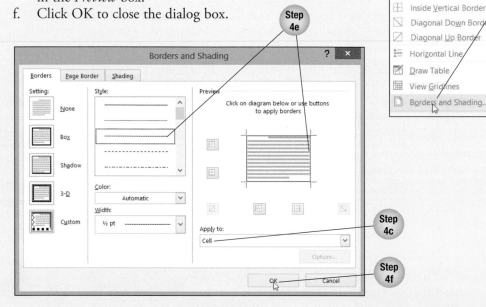

5. Save the document in your Chapter10 folder with the name **C10-E01-Raffle**.

6. Insert the ticket and stub text by completing the following steps:

a. Position the insertion point in the first cell and then insert **Raffle.docx**, located in your Chapter10 folder.

b. Press the Backspace key to remove a blank line.

c. Position the insertion point in the second cell and then insert **Stub.docx**, located in your Chapter10 folder.

d. Press the Backspace key to remove a blank line.

7. Insert the Loaves & Fishes Community Pantry logo by completing the following steps:

a. Position the insertion point in the first cell in the first row and then insert **L&F-Pantry.png**, located in your Chapter10 folder.

b. Apply Tight text wrapping.

c. Position the logo as shown in Figure 10.4.

d. With the logo selected, copy it to the stub section by holding down the Ctrl key as you drag and drop the logo to the stub section of the ticket.

e. Click the Color button in the Adjust group on the PICTURE TOOLS FORMAT tab and then click the *Washout* option in the *Recolor* section.

f. Apply Behind Text text wrapping.

g. Position the logo in the stub section as shown in Figure 10.4.

8. Insert sequential numbering by completing the following steps:

a. Position the insertion point at the right of *No.* in the first cell and then press the spacebar once.

b. Click the INSERT tab, click the Quick Parts button in the Text group, and then click *Field* at the drop-down list.

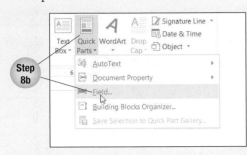

c. At the Field dialog box, make sure *(All)* displays in the *Categories* option box.

d. Click *AutoNum* in the *Field names* list box.

e. Click OK to close the dialog box.

f. Position the insertion point at the right of *No.* in the second cell (stub), press the spacebar once, and then insert the *AutoNum* field code as you did in Steps 8b–8e.

9. Copy the table row three times by completing the following steps:

a. Select the table row.

b. Press Ctrl + C to copy the row.

c. Press Ctrl + End to move the insertion point below the table.

d. Press Ctrl + V three times. (This inserts three additional rows in the table.)
Note: If the dashed right border of the first column does not copy to the next three rows, complete Step 4 again to apply the dashed right border to the first column.

10. Horizontally center the table by completing the following steps:

a. Select the entire table.

b. Click the TABLE TOOLS LAYOUT tab.

c. Click the Properties button in the Table group.

d. At the Table Properties dialog box make sure the Table tab is selected and then click the *Center* option in the *Alignment* section.

e. Click OK to close the dialog box.

11. Save, print, and then close **C10-E01-Raffle.docx**.

Figure 10.4 Raffle Tickets Created in Exercise 10.1

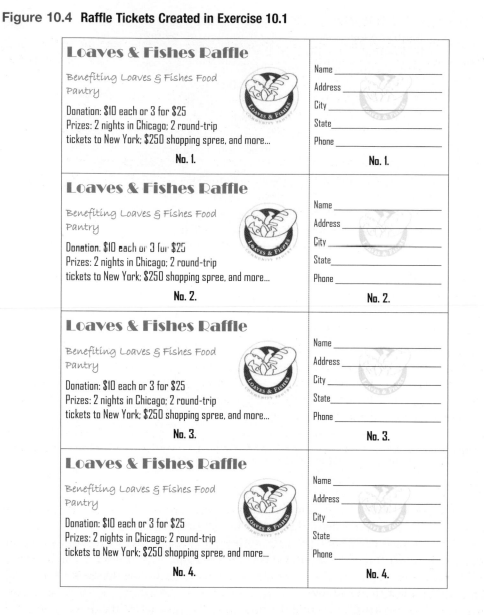

Creating Registration Forms

Registration forms and application forms can be used to gather information for promotional purposes such as a mailing, an event, or a contest. These forms can be printed and then filled in, or they can be completed electronically. While the most important part of these documents is to create space for all the information you need to gather, you can also add design elements to your form to create interest and anticipation among your audience.

If a form is to be filled in electronically, it is important that it be as user-friendly as possible. Have you ever opened an application form with the intention of typing on the lines that are provided, only to find that your text pushes the line forward or that you cannot position the insertion point anywhere on the line? Several methods can be used to create lines on which you can successfully type. These will be explained in the following sections. You will also learn a more complex method for creating forms in Chapter 11.

Creating Lines Using the Underline Feature

The first method for creating a line on which you can type requires the use of the Underline button and the Tab key. To create a line using the Tab key and the Underline button, complete the following steps:

1. Create tab stops at the points where you want the line to start and stop.
2. Press the Tab key to align the insertion point at the first tab.
3. Click the Underline button in the Font group on the HOME tab to turn on underlining.
4. Press the spacebar once. This creates a location (placeholder) where text can be entered on the line. (You may want to turn on the display of nonprinting characters so you can view the spacebar placeholder.)
5. Press the Tab key to create the line.
6. Click the Underline button to turn off underlining.
7. Press the Enter key to move to the next line or press the Tab key to move to the next column.

Figure 10.5 shows the tab settings on the horizontal ruler and the use of the Underline button and Tab key. To make sure you can type on the line you just created, move your insertion point to the position after the spacebar and then type some text. The text should appear typed above the line.

To type on the line that was created using the underline and tab method, turn on the display of nonprinting characters and then position the insertion point immediately right of the space you created as a placeholder (displays as a small dot in the middle of the line) and then type text. If the insertion point is placed before the placeholder, the line will be pushed to the right as you type. If you create a form using the Underline button, you should consider including a note instructing the person filling out the form to position the insertion point one space to the right of the beginning of the underline.

Creating Lines Using the Shapes Feature

The second method for creating a line on which you can type involves creating a line shape from the Shapes button drop-down list in the Illustrations group on the INSERT tab. When a line (or any other shape) is placed within a document, it can be moved around the document by selecting the shape and then pressing the arrow keys or using the mouse to drag it to the desired location. The shape will move along the lines of the invisible drawing grid that exists within each document, as discussed in earlier chapters. Each time you press an arrow key, the shape will move in that direction to the next line of the drawing grid. Often, the default spacing between the gridlines of a document is larger than desired for moving an object, but you can adjust the spacing setting to overcome that problem.

Figure 10.5 Using the Underline Button and Tab Key to Create Fill-in Lines

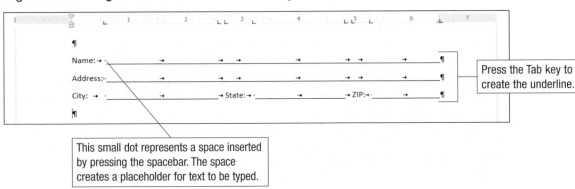

You can use the Align button in the Arrange group on the DRAWING TOOLS FORMAT tab to adjust the placement of the lines and make sure they all look uniform. For example, you can select two or more lines and then align them at the left by clicking the Align button and then clicking *Align Left* at the drop-down list or align them between the left and right margins by clicking *Align Center*. If you have three or more lines selected, you can distribute the lines vertically by clicking the *Distribute Vertically* option at the Align button drop-down list.

Creating Lines Using Tables

DTP POINTER❯

If you need to indent text within a table cell, press Ctrl + Tab to insert a tab inside the cell.

The third method for creating lines that you can type on is to insert a table into your document and then add and remove border lines. Tables allow for easy alignment and placement of the elements within a form. Whether you are creating a document that will be printed or one that will be filled in at a computer, you can use a table as an underlying structure for organizing your text. Type the labels (such as *Name:* or *Date:*) in cells and then remove any unnecessary border lines, such as the left, top, and right borders, as shown in Figure 10.6B.

Creating Lines Using Tab Leaders

leaders

Lines that lead the reader's eyes across a space on the page

Another method for creating lines that align is to use ***leaders***, which are lines that guide the reader's eyes across the page. Word allows you to create several types of leaders by using tabs. To do this, display the Tabs dialog box, set a tab where you want the lines to end, and then click the desired leader option. Click the Set button and then click OK to close the dialog box. In the document, type the label text and then press the Tab key. A leader will display from the text to the tab setting. You cannot insert text on a leader line because typed text will replace the leaders.

In Exercise 10.2, you will use three of the four methods discussed for creating lines in a form. While you are working through the exercise, form an opinion on which method is easiest to use. You would not typically use all four methods in one form.

Figure 10.6 **Using a Table to Create Lines in a Form**

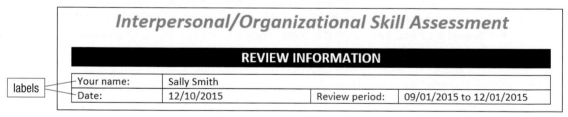

A

Table with Default Borders on All Sides of Cells

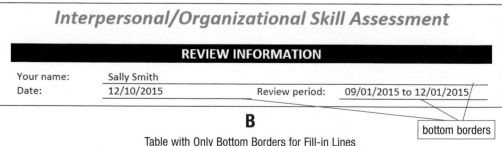

B

Table with Only Bottom Borders for Fill-in Lines

1. Open **Registration.docx** from your Chapter10 folder and then save the document with the name **C10-E02-Registration**. (You will customize the registration document so it appears as shown in Figure 10.7 on page 442.)

2. Position the insertion point at the left margin, two lines below the text *CONFERENCE REGISTRATION*.

3. Make sure the horizontal ruler is visible. (If it is not, click the VIEW tab and then click the *Ruler* check box in the Show group to insert a check mark.)

4. Display the Tabs dialog box, set left tabs at 0.75 inch and 6.5 inches, and then click OK to close the dialog box.

5. Type **Name:** and then press the Tab key to align the insertion point at the first tab setting. (This is where the underline will begin.)

6. Click the Underline button in the Font group on the HOME tab and then press the spacebar once. (This creates a placeholder for the starting point of the line.)

7. Press the Tab key. (A line is created between the insertion point and the tab marker at 6.5 inches.)

8. Click the Underline button to turn off underlining.

9. Press the Enter key and then type **Address:**.

10. Press the Tab key to align the insertion point at the first tab.

11. Click the Underline button and then press the spacebar once to create the placeholder.

12. Press the Tab key to create the line.

13. Click the Underline button to turn off underlining.

14. Press the Enter key.

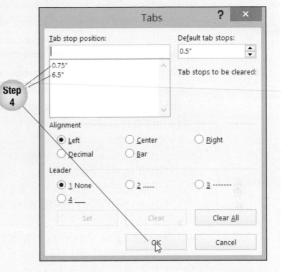

15. Use a table to create the *City*, *State*, and *Zip* lines by completing the following steps:

    a. Click the INSERT tab.

    b. Click the Table button in the Tables group and then drag over the grid to create a table with one row and six columns.

    c. Select the table.

    d. Click the Borders button arrow in the Borders group on the TABLE TOOLS DESIGN tab and then click *No Border* at the drop-down gallery. ***Hint: Make sure your table gridlines are turned on.***

    e. Type **City:** in the first cell.

    f. Type **State:** in the third cell.

    g. Type **ZIP:** in the fifth cell.

    h. Click in the cell containing *City:*, click the TABLE TOOLS LAYOUT tab, select the current measurement in the *Width* measurement box in the Cell Size group, type **0.75**, and then press Enter.

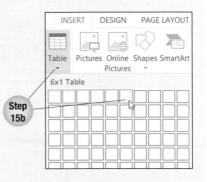

i. Change the widths of the remaining columns as follows:
    Column 2 = 2 inches
    Column 3 = 0.6 inch
    Column 4 = 1.75 inches
    Column 5 = 0.5 inch
    Column 6 = 0.9 inch
j. Position the insertion point inside the second cell and then click the TABLE TOOLS DESIGN tab.
k. Make sure the *Line Style* option box in the Borders group displays with a solid line. If it does not, click the *Line Style* option box arrow and then click the first line style option at the drop-down gallery. Choosing a line style makes the Border Painter button active. Click the Border Painter button to deactivate it.
l. Click the Borders button arrow and then click *Bottom Border* at the drop-down gallery.
m. Position the insertion point inside the fourth cell and then click the Borders button.
n. Position the insertion point inside the sixth cell and then click the Borders button.
o. Change the margin for the first cell by completing the following steps:
    1) Click in the first cell.
    2) Click the TABLE TOOLS LAYOUT tab.
    3) Click the Properties button in the Table group.
    4) At the Table Properties dialog box, click the Cell tab.
    5) Click the Options button that displays in the lower right corner of the dialog box.
    6) At the Cell Options dialog box, click the *Same as the whole table* check box to remove the check mark.
    7) Select the current measurement in the *Left* measurement box, type **0**, and then press Enter.

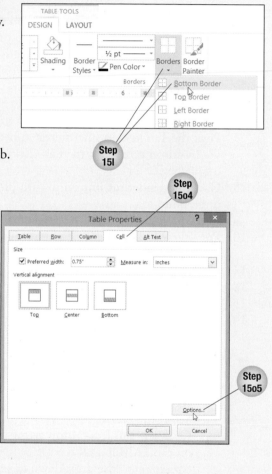

    8) Click OK to close the Table Properties dialog box.

16. Create the *Phone* and *Email* lines using line shapes by completing the following steps:
    a. Position the insertion point on the blank line below the table and then press Enter.
    b. Type **Phone:** and then press Enter.
    c. Type **Email:** and then press Enter.
    d. Click the INSERT tab, click the Shapes button in the Illustrations group, and then click the *Line* option (first option in the *Lines* section).
    e. Position the crosshairs to the right of *Phone:* and visually align it with the left edge of the *City:* fill-in line.
    f. Hold down the Shift key and then click and drag to create a line that is approximately 2 inches long (approximately the same length as the *City:* fill-in line).
    g. Click the *Subtle Line - Dark 1* thumbnail in the Shape Styles gallery on the DRAWING TOOLS FORMAT tab (the first thumbnail).

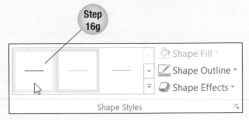

    h. Press Ctrl + D to duplicate the line.
    i. Drag the duplicated line so it is positioned after *Email* and visually align it with the left edge of the *Phone:* fill-in line.
    j. Check the position of your two drawn lines in the document and make any needed adjustments so your lines display as shown in Figure 10.7.
17. Position the insertion point on the blank line below the *Check one:* text.
18. Create and format a table by completing the following steps:
    a. Insert a table with three columns and three rows.
    b. Change the width of the first column to 0.3 inch, the width of the second column to 0.5 inch, and the width of the third column to 3 inches.
    c. Remove the border lines from the table. (Do this by selecting the entire table, clicking the TABLE TOOLS DESIGN tab, clicking the Borders button arrow, and then clicking *No Border* at the drop-down gallery.)
    d. Insert a bottom border in the three cells in the first column.
    e. Center the table horizontally by clicking the TABLE TOOLS LAYOUT tab and then clicking the Properties button. At the Table Properties dialog box, click the Table tab, click the *Center* option in the *Alignment* section, and then click OK.
    f. Type the text in the cells as shown in Figure 10.7.
19. Save and then print **C10-E02-Registration.docx**.
20. Save the document with the name **C10-E02-RegistrationComplete**.
21. Insert information in the form as shown in Figure 10.8 on page 443.
22. Save and then print **C10-E02-RegistrationComplete.docx**. (You may notice that the weight of the lines may not be consistent; therefore, choosing one method of creating lines throughout the document is a good idea. The three methods were used in this exercise for demonstration and practice purposes.)
23. Close **C10-E02-RegistrationComplete.docx**.

Figure 10.7 Registration Form Created in Exercise 10.2

Best Sellers of the Western Region

Spring Conference, March 14, 2015

CONFERENCE REGISTRATION

Name: _____

Address: _____

City: _____ State: _____ ZIP: _____

Phone: _____

Email: _____

Registration deadline: February 27, 2015

Check one:

_____	$100	Participant from member institution
_____	$125	Participant from non-member institution
_____	$150	Institutional membership dues

Your check must accompany registration

Make check payable to:

Storyteller Books

Mail registration to:

Storyteller Books
123 Main Street
Glen Ellyn, IL 60137

Figure 10.8 Completed Form Created in Exercise 10.2

Best Sellers of the Western Region

Spring Conference, March 14, 2015

CONFERENCE REGISTRATION

Name: Sasha Kovich

Address: 13442 South Elmhurst Drive

City: Chicago   State: IL   ZIP: 60605

Phone: (312) 555-4826

Email: skovich@emcp.net

Registration deadline: February 27, 2015

Check one:

x	$100	Participant from member institution
	$125	Participant from non-member institution
	$150	Institutional membership dues

Your check must accompany registration

Make check payable to:

Storyteller Books

Mail registration to:

Storyteller Books
123 Main Street
Glen Ellyn, IL 60137

Creating Postcards

If you have a brief message to get across to customers or prospective customers, postcards can be an appropriate means of delivering it. Postcards are inexpensive to create and mail. They can be used as appointment reminders, change-of-address notifications, reply cards, display cards, thank-you cards, or invitations. You can purchase predesigned, printed postcards with attractive borders and color combinations, in differing sizes and weights that meet U.S. Postal Service standards. You can also find blank, prestamped 3.5-by-5.5-inch postcards at any U.S. Postal Service location.

Word provides predesigned postcard templates that include placeholder text to instruct you on how to use the template. To locate these templates, click the FILE tab and then click the *New* option. Enter *postcard* in the search text box, press Enter, and then double-click the desired postcard template. Postcard templates can be customized to include promotional images and text by simply adding an appropriate photo, logo, or clip art, along with a promotional statement that reinforces the identity of the company or promotes a service or product provided by that organization. In addition, you can prepare postcards for mass mailing by using the Mail Merge feature.

Alternatively, you can create postcards using the labels feature, which provides postcard labels such as Avery US Letter 3256 Postcards, 5689 Postcards, or 8387 Postcards. Each of these options includes four postcards per page that measure 4.25 inches by 5.5 inches. The Avery US Letter 8386 Postcards label creates two labels per page that measure 4 inches by 6 inches each.

Most postcards are created on cover stock paper. The paper weight or thickness must be strong enough to hold up in the mail. The front side of the postcard is used for your return address and the recipient's address along with an area reserved for the postage. On the reverse, you can create a headline and use a graphic, photo, or watermark to emphasize the message. Make sure to leave room for your message and optional signature. You will practice creating postcards using the labels feature in Exercise 10.3.

Exercise 10.3 Creating Postcards Using the Labels Feature

1. At a blank document create postcards using a label (see Figure 10.9 on page 446) by completing the following steps:
   a. Click the MAILINGS tab and then click the Labels button in the Create group.
   b. At the Envelopes and Labels dialog box with the Labels tab selected, click the Options button that displays toward the bottom of the dialog box.
   c. At the Label Options dialog box, select *Avery US Letter* in the *Label vendors* option box, select *8386 Postcards* in the *Product number* list box, and then click OK.
   d. At the Envelopes and Labels dialog box, click the New Document button.

2. Insert the clip art image into the top postcard and format it as shown in Figure 10.9 by completing the following steps:
   a. Use the Pictures button on the INSERT tab to insert **visions.png** from your Chapter10 folder into the postcard.
   b. Change the width of the image to 4 inches.
   c. Apply Square text wrapping.
   d. Position the image as shown in Figure 10.9.
3. Insert the text by completing the following steps:
   a. Draw a text box in the top postcard that measures 2 inches in height and 3.5 inches in width.
   b. Type **See the world a little clearer and a little brighter with regular eye examinations.** in the text box.
   c. Select *See the world* and then change the font to 24-point Bauhaus 93 and the font color to *Blue* (eighth option in the *Standard Colors* section).
   d. Select the rest of the text, change the font to 24-point Harlow Solid Italic, and then change the font color to *Green, Accent 6* (last column, first row in the *Theme Colors* section).
   e. Select the text box, change the paragraph alignment to center, and then remove the shape fill and shape outline.
   f. Position the text box as shown in Figure 10.9.
4. Group the image and text box by completing the following steps:
   a. Click the image to select it.
   b. Hold down the Shift key and then click the text box. (The image and the text box should both be selected.)
   c. Click the PICTURE TOOLS FORMAT tab.
   d. Click the Group button in the Arrange group and then click *Group* at the drop-down list.

5. Copy the grouped object in the first postcard and paste it into the second postcard. Position the pasted object in the same position on the second postcard as the object in the first postcard (refer to Figure 10.9).
6. Save the document with the name **C10-E03-Postcards**.
7. Print two copies of **C10-E03-Postcards.docx** and then close the document.

Figure 10.9   Postcards Created in Exercise 10.3

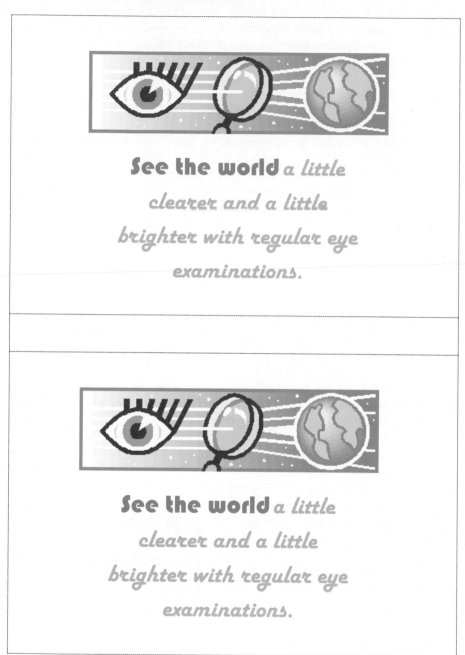

Merging Promotional Documents for Mailing

In Chapter 6, you merged a newsletter main document with an existing data source file. You can create your own data source file with the Select Recipients button in the Start Mail Merge group on the MAILINGS tab.

Creating a Data Source File

To create a data source file with the Select Recipients button, click the button and then click the *Type a New List* option at the drop-down list. At the New Address List dialog box, shown in Figure 10.10, use the predesigned fields offered by Word and type the required data, or edit the fields by deleting and/or inserting custom fields and then type the data. When you have entered all of the records, click OK. At the Save Address List dialog box, navigate to the desired folder, type a name for the data source file, and then click OK. Word saves a data source file as an Access database, but you do not need the Access application installed on your computer to complete a merge with a data source file.

Select Recipients

Merging Documents

When you have created the main document and the data source file, complete the merge by clicking the Finish & Merge button in the Finish group on the MAILINGS tab. At the drop-down list that displays, you can choose to merge the records and create a new document, send the merged documents directly to the printer, or send the merged documents by email.

Finish & Merge

To merge the documents and create a new document with the merged records, click the *Edit Individual Documents* option at the Finish & Merge button drop-down list. Identify specific records you want to merge with options at the Merge to New Document dialog box. Select the *All* option to merge all of the records in the data source. Select the *Current record* option if you want to merge only the current record. Use the *From* and *To* text boxes to specify a range of records for merging. For example, if you want to merge only records 1 through 3, you would enter *1* in the *From* text box and *3* in the *To* text box. When you have made your selections, click OK.

Figure 10.10   Using the New Address List Dialog Box

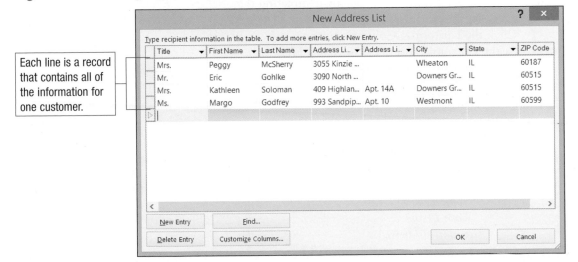

Merging Postcard Labels

Start Mail Merge

Update Labels

DTP POINTER

The United States Postal Service recommends typing addresses in ALL CAPS with no punctuation. To follow this recommendation, make sure to type the information in your data source file in all caps and leave out the punctuation.

To merge postcard labels, specify the data source file by clicking the MAILINGS tab, clicking the Select Recipients button, and then clicking *Use an Existing List* at the drop-down list. At the Select Data Source dialog box, navigate to the folder containing the data source file and then double-click the file. Next, create the postcard label main document, which is the front side of the postcard that contains mailing information (for example, see Figure 10.12 on page 451). To do this, click the Start Mail Merge button in the Start Mail Merge group and then click *Labels* at the drop-down list. At the Label Options dialog box that displays, select the desired label vendor and product number and then click the OK button. At the label document, type the any text in the first postcard, such as the return address, insert the «AddressBlock» field in the appropriate location in the postcard, and then click the Update Labels button in the Write & Insert Fields group on the MAILINGS tab to update the labels so each postcard contains the «AddressBlock» field. Merge the label main document with the specified data source file by clicking the Finish & Merge button in the Finish group, clicking *Edit Individual Documents*, selecting the desired option in the Merge to New Document dialog box, and then clicking OK to close the dialog box.

In Exercise 10.4, you will create a data source file containing customer names and addresses for Naper Grove Vision Care, create the front side of the postcard you started in Exercise 10.3, and then merge the postcard with the data source file.

Exercise 10.4 Creating a Data Source and Merging Labels for a Postcard Mailing

1. Create a data source for merging with a postcard label by completing the following steps:
   a. At a blank document, click the MAILINGS tab.
   b. Click the Select Recipients button in the Start Mail Merge group and then click *Type a New List* at the drop-down list.
   c. At the New Address List dialog box, predesigned fields display in the list box. Delete fields by completing the following steps:
      1) Click the Customize Columns button.
      2) At the Customize Address List dialog box, click *Company Name* to select it and then click the Delete button.
      3) At the message informing you that any information in the field will be deleted when you delete the field, click Yes.
      4) Complete steps similar to Steps 1c2 and 1c3 to delete the following fields:
         > *Country or Region*
         > *Home Phone*
         > *Work Phone*
         > *E-mail Address*
      5) Click OK to close the Customize Address List dialog box.

Step 1b

Step 1c2

d. At the New Address List dialog box, enter the information for the first customer listed in Figure 10.11 on page 451 by completing the following steps:

1) Type **Mrs.** in the *Title* field and then press the Tab key.
2) Type **Peggy** and then press the Tab key.
3) Type **McSherry** and then press the Tab key.
4) Type **3055 Kinzie Court** and then press the Tab key twice.
5) Type **Wheaton** and then press the Tab key.
6) Type **IL** and then press the Tab key.
7) Type **60187** and then press the Tab key. (This moves the insertion point to the *Title* field in the next record.)

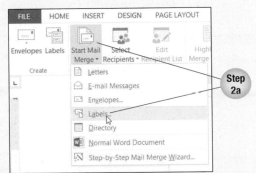

e. Type the information for the three remaining patients in Figure 10.11 in this order: Gohlke, Soloman, Godfrey. After entering the ZIP code for the last patient, Margo Godfrey, click OK to close the New Address List dialog box.

f. At the Save Address List dialog box, save the data source file to your Chapter10 folder with the name **NaperGrovePatientList**. (Word saves this document as a database file with the *.mdb* file extension.)

2. Create a postcard label main document by completing the following steps:

a. Click the Start Mail Merge button in the Start Mail Merge group on the MAILINGS tab and then click *Labels* at the drop-down list.

b. At the Label Options dialog box, make sure *Avery US Letter* is selected in the *Label vendors* option box, make sure *8386 Postcards* is selected in the *Product number* list box, and then click OK.

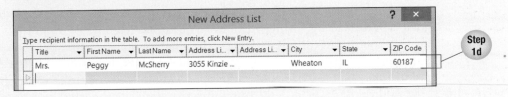

3. With the insertion point positioned in the top postcard, make the following changes:

a. Display the Paragraph dialog box, remove the spacing before paragraphs, make sure single line spacing is selected, and then click OK to close the dialog box.

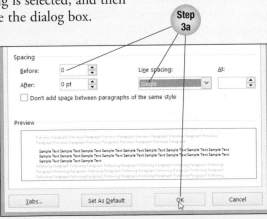

b. At the postcard, press the spacebar once and then press the Enter key. (If you do not press the spacebar before pressing the Enter key, the insertion point will be moved above the postcard label.) With the insertion point positioned in the label, type the following text:

> **Naper Grove Vision Care** (Press Enter.)
> **5018 Fairview Avenue** (Press Enter.)
> **Downers Grove, IL 60515** (Press Enter twice.)
> **Just a friendly reminder!** (Press Enter twice.)
> **Please call our office now for your** (Press Enter.)
> **appointment (630) 555-3932.**

c. Select *Naper Grove Vision Care*, change the font to 16-point Calibri, apply bold and small caps formatting, change the font color to *Blue* (eighth option in the *Standard Colors* section), and turn on kerning at 16 points and above.

d. Select *Just a friendly reminder!*, and then change the font to 16-point Harlow Solid Italic, and the font color to *Light Green* (fifth option in the *Standard Colors* section).

4. Insert the Address Block field in the top postcard and update the labels to copy the top label and paste its contents in the second label by completing the following steps:

a. Position the insertion point immediately to the right of the period located after the telephone number and then press Enter twice.

b. Click the PAGE LAYOUT tab, select the current measurement in the *Left* measurement box in the Paragraph group, type **2.5**, and then press Enter.

c. Click the MAILINGS tab and then click the Address Block button in the Write & Insert Fields group.

d. At the Address Block dialog box, click OK to accept the default settings.

e. Click the Update Labels button in the Write & Insert Fields group.

5. Merge the postcard main document with the **NaperGrovePatientList.mdb** data source file by completing the following steps:

a. Click the Finish & Merge button in the Finish group on the MAILINGS tab and then click *Edit Individual Documents* at the drop-down list.

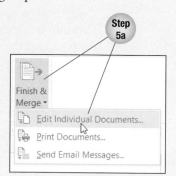

b. At the Merge to New Document dialog box, make sure *All* is selected and then click OK. (Your merged document should appear similar to what is shown in Figure 10.12.)

6. Save the merged postcard document with the name **C10-E04-MergedPostcards**.

7. Insert the two pages you printed of **C10-E03-Postcards.docx** correctly into the printer and then print **C10-E04-MergedPostcards.docx**.

8. Close **C10-E04-MergedPostcards.docx**.

9. Save the main document with the name **C10-E04-PostcardMainDoc**.

10. Close **C10-E04-PostcardMainDoc.docx**.

Figure 10.11 Information for Data Source Fields Used in Exercise 10.4

Title	=	Mrs.	*Title*	=	Mr.
First Name	=	Peggy	*First Name*	=	Eric
Last Name	=	McSherry	*Last Name*	=	Gohlke
Address Line 1	=	3055 Kinzie Court	*Address Line 1*	=	3090 North Orchard Road
Address Line 2	=		*Address Line 2*	=	
City	=	Wheaton	*City*	=	Downers Grove
State	=	IL	*State*	=	IL
ZIP Code	=	60187	*ZIP Code*	=	60515
Title	=	Mrs.	*Title*	=	Ms.
First Name	=	Kathleen	*First Name*	=	Margo
Last Name	=	Soloman	*Last Name*	=	Godfrey
Address Line 1	=	409 Highland Drive	*Address Line 1*	=	993 Sandpiper Lane
Address Line 2	=	Apt. 14A	*Address Line 2*	=	Apt. 10
City	=	Downers Grove	*City*	=	Westmont
State	=	IL	*State*	=	IL
ZIP Code	=	60515	*ZIP Code*	=	60599

Figure 10.12 Merged Postcards Created in Exercise 10.4

NAPER GROVE VISION CARE
5018 Fairview Avenue
Downers Grove, IL 60515

Just a friendly reminder!

Please call our office now for your
appointment (630) 555-3932.

Mrs. Peggy McSherry
3055 Kinzie Court
Wheaton, IL 60187

NAPER GROVE VISION CARE
5018 Fairview Avenue
Downers Grove, IL 60515

Just a friendly reminder!

Please call our office now for your
appointment (630) 555-3932.

Mrs. Kathleen Soloman
409 Highland Drive
Apt. 14A
Downers Grove, IL 60515

NAPER GROVE VISION CARE
5018 Fairview Avenue
Downers Grove, IL 60515

Just a friendly reminder!

Please call our office now for your
appointment (630) 555-3932.

Mr. Eric Gohlke
3090 North Orchard Road
Downers Grove, IL 60515

NAPER GROVE VISION CARE
5018 Fairview Avenue
Downers Grove, IL 60515

Just a friendly reminder!

Please call our office now for your
appointment (630) 555-3932.

Ms. Margo Godfrey
993 Sandpiper Lane
Apt. 10
Westmont, IL 60599

Creating Invitations and Greeting Cards

Invitations and greeting cards are typically one-page documents with either a horizontal or vertical book fold. Invitations are used to tell an audience about an event and ask them to attend, and greeting cards can be used for a variety of promotional purposes.

Planning Invitations and Greeting Cards

In planning a card, consider focus, balance, consistency, proportion, contrast, and directional flow. While including plenty of white space is always a good design practice, it is especially important when you are working within a small area, such as a card. If you are using a graphic image for focus, be sure that the image relates to the subject of the card. Promote consistency through the use of color, possibly picking out one or two colors from the graphic image used in your card to use in the text. Include the company logo, if one is available. Select one or two fonts that match the tone of the document.

DTP POINTER

Promote consistency among company documents by inserting a logo and using colors found in the logo.

Designing Invitations and Greeting Cards

Since cards are often smaller than a standard-size sheet of paper, it is possible to produce more than one card on each page. There are a few different ways to do this. You can use the 2 pages per sheet feature that you learned about in Chapter 9. You can also use a table to divide the Word document page into quadrants, as shown in Figure 10.13. These quadrants represent the front, back, and inside panels of the card. After you print the page, you would fold the page horizontally and vertically along the fold lines, as shown in the figure. A table can also be used to create two cards on one page in landscape orientation, as shown in Figure 10.14.

You can also use Word templates to create cards. Locate templates by entering *greeting cards* in the search text box in the New backstage area. You can then customize them to suit your organization's identity. Consider including your company's logo or one of the graphics from the card on the envelope as well.

Figure 10.13 Creating One Card per Sheet in Portrait Orientation

Figure 10.14 Creating Two Cards per Sheet in Landscape Orientation

Printing Invitations, Greeting Cards, and Custom Envelopes

When choosing the paper on which to print your cards, consider a heavier weight paper, such as 60- or 65-lb. uncoated cover stock paper. Professional-quality cardstock can be purchased at an office supply store for printing invitations and greeting cards. Greeting card envelopes can also be purchased and come in varying sizes, such as 5.75 inches by 8.75 inches and 4.38 inches by 5.75 inches.

To print a custom-size envelope, click the Envelopes button in the Create group on the MAILINGS tab, click the Options button at the Envelopes and Labels dialog box with the Envelopes tab selected, click the arrow to right of the *Envelope size* list box, and then scroll down and click *Custom size* at the bottom of the list box. Type the desired dimensions at the Envelope Size dialog box, as shown in Figure 10.15 on page 454. Refer to your printer documentation to determine the correct way to load envelopes for your specific printer.

If you have a long list of recipients, consider creating a master copy of your card and taking it to a commercial printer to have it reproduced and machine folded. For a mass mailing of an invitation or a holiday card, consider creating a data source consisting of names and addresses and then merging this information onto envelopes or mailing labels, as you did in Exercise 10.4.

Figure 10.15 Creating a Custom-Sized Envelope

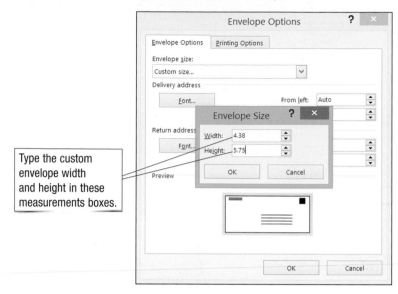

Type the custom envelope width and height in these measurements boxes.

In Exercise 10.5, you will change the margins and insert a border, picture, and text box to create the front and back of an invitation. You will then create another document containing the inside message of the invitation by changing the margins and inserting a text box and clip art image. Both of these documents are shown in Figure 10.16 on page 457.

Exercise 10.5 Creating the Cover, Back, and Inside of an Invitation

1. At a blank document, change the top margin to 6 inches and the left, bottom, and right margins to 0.7 inch.
2. Use the Pictures button in the Illustrations group on the INSERT tab to insert **blue-green-border.png** from your Chapter10 folder. (See Figure 10.16A on page 457.)
3. With the border selected, make the following changes:
   a. Click the Rotate button in the Arrange group on the PICTURE TOOLS FORMAT tab and then click *Rotate Left 90°* at the drop-down list.
   b. Click the Size group dialog box launcher.

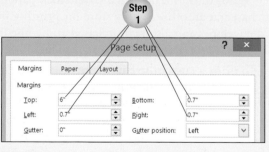

c. At the Layout dialog box with the Size tab selected, remove the check mark from the *Lock aspect ratio* check box in the *Scale* section.

d. Select the current measurement in the *Absolute* measurement box in the *Height* section and then type **6.6**.

e. Select the current measurement in the *Absolute* measurement box in the *Width* section, type **4.2**, and then click OK.

f. Click the Position button in the Arrange group and then click *Position in Bottom Center with Square Text Wrapping* at the drop-down gallery.

g. Click the Wrap Text button in the Arrange group and then click *Behind Text* at the drop-down gallery.

4. Use the Pictures button on the INSERT tab to insert **phonathon.png** from your Chapter10 folder.

5. With the picture selected, make the following changes:

   a. Change the width of the picture to 4 inches.

   b. Apply In Front of Text text wrapping.

   c. Drag the picture so it is positioned as shown at the right and in Figure 10.16A.

6. Create the text boxes located on the border by completing the following steps:

   a. Draw a text box that measures 0.8 inch in height and 2.9 inches in width.

   b. Apply the Facet theme.

   c. Type **Sharing, Inc.** in the text box.

   d. Select *Sharing, Inc.*, apply the Fill - Dark Green, Accent 2, Outline - Accent 2 effect using the Text Effects and Typography button on the HOME tab, and then change the font size to 32 points.

   e. With the text still selected, change the paragraph alignment to center.

   f. Click the DRAWING TOOLS FORMAT tab and then remove the shape outline from the text box.

   g. Click the Shape Fill button arrow, point to *Gradient*, and then click *More Gradients* at the bottom of the side menu.

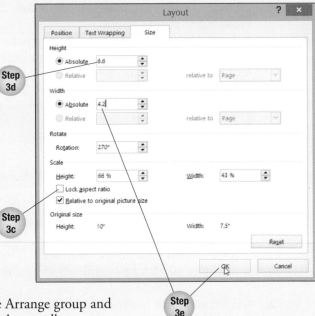

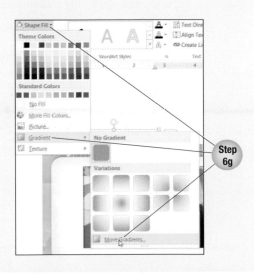

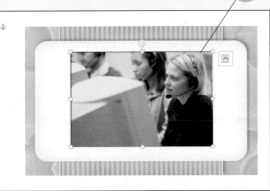

h. At the Format Shape task pane, click the *Gradient fill* option to select it.

i. Click the Direction button in the task pane and then click the *Linear Up* option (second column, second row).

j. Close the Format Shape task pane.

k. Drag the text box so it is positioned on the top border, as shown in Figure 10.16A.

l. Drag a copy of the text box and position it on the bottom border.

m. Change the text in the copied text box to *Phonathon 2015*.

n. Change the width of the text box to 3.7 inches.

o. Position the text box on the bottom border, as shown in Figure 10.16A.

7. Create the WordArt logo on the back of the cover as shown in Figure 10.16A by completing the following steps:

a. Click the INSERT tab, click the Header button in the Header & Footer group, and then click *Edit Header* at the drop-down gallery.

b. Click the INSERT tab, click the WordArt button in the Text group, and then click *Fill - Dark Green, Accent 2, Outline - Accent 2* (third column, first row).

c. Type **Desktop Designs**.

d. Click the Text Effects button in the WordArt Styles group, point to *Transform*, and then click the *Triangle Up* option (third column, first row in the *Warp* section).

e. Change the height of the WordArt to 0.7 inch and the width to 2.2 inches.

f. Click the Align button in the Arrange group on the DRAWING TOOLS FORMAT tab and then click *Align Center* at the drop-down gallery.

g. Rotate the WordArt image by clicking the Rotate button and then clicking *Flip Vertical* at the drop-down gallery.

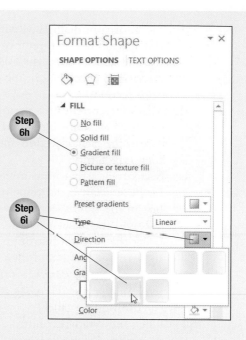

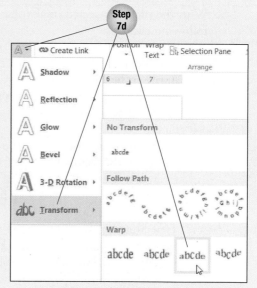

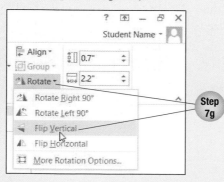

8. Save the document with the name **C10-E05-Cover**.
9. Print and then close **C10-E05-Cover.docx**.
10. Open **Sharing.docx** from your Chapter10 folder and then save it with the name **C10-E05-InsideText**.
11. Insert and format the clip art image shown in Figure 10.16B by completing the following steps:
    a. Use the Pictures button on the INSERT tab to insert **family.png** from your Chapter10 folder.
    b. Change the height of the image to 1.7 inches.
    c. Apply Square text wrapping.
    d. Crop the bottom of the image as shown at the right.
    e. Position the image as shown in Figure 10.16B.
12. Save **C10-E05-InsideText.docx**.

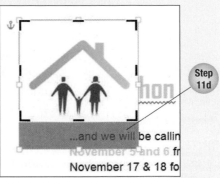

13. Place the printed cover into your printer. *Hint: Be careful to position the paper correctly so the inside document will print on the reverse side of the cover, with the text appearing right-side up when you lift up the cover.*
14. Print and then close **C10-E05-InsideText.docx**.
15. Finish the invitation by folding the top of the page to the bottom of the page.

Figure 10.16 Card Created in Exercise 10.5

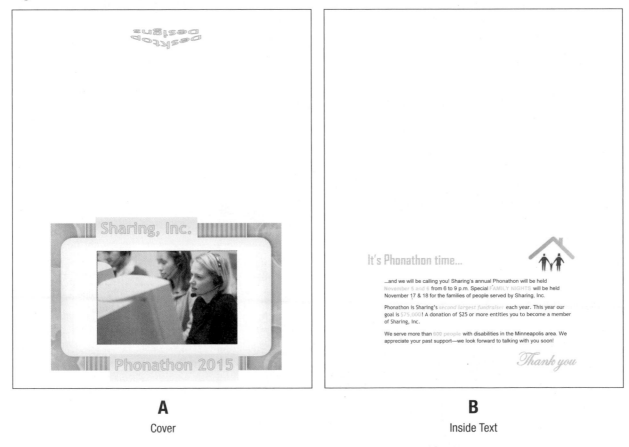

A

Cover

B

Inside Text

Creating and Printing a Promotional Poster

A poster is generally a large, illustrated sheet of paper designed to advertise or publicize an event or activity. Posters vary in size and are usually attached to a wall or some other vertical surface. Before creating a poster, take the time to determine the theme or subject matter. Your poster should convey information clearly without a lot of clutter. Consider the following guidelines when creating a poster:

DTP POINTER

Do not let the graphics in a poster overpower the message.

- Written content should be edited so that it explains the important points of your subject matter without being wordy.

- Include graphics if they help to spark interest and illustrate or complement the information in the poster.

DTP POINTER

Resist using fancy typefaces in a poster, as they make content hard to read.

- Use no more than two or three fonts in the poster, and make sure they are legible both close up and from a distance.

- Carefully check and correct any spelling or grammatical errors.

In Exercise 10.6, you will create a promotional document for a golf club. The document will be formatted in the same manner as a standard-sized Word document, but it will be printed as a poster on four pages that, when assembled, will measure approximately 15 inches by 19 inches.

DTP POINTER

Spelling and grammar errors in a poster can cause it to lose credibility with the reader.

Printing a Promotional Poster

The directions for printing the poster created in Exercise 10.6 are given using a Brother color laser printer. You will need to follow the directions for printing this exercise based on the printer options for your specific printer. Some experimentation may be necessary.

Figure 10.17 shows the Brother printer advanced options dialog where you can access the appropriate poster size for printing. To display a dialog box similar to the one shown in Figure 10.17, click the FILE tab and then click the *Print* option. At the Print backstage area, click the *Printer Properties* option located directly below the name of your printer in the *Printer* section. Select the appropriate tab or click an Advanced button to display options for printing poster-sized documents. Select an option that will print the poster at the desired size. To create a poster measuring 15 inches by 9 inches

Figure 10.17 Printing a Promotional Poster

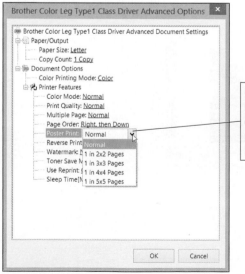

Click the *Poster Print* option box arrow to display this drop-down list of poster printing options for a Brother color laser printer.

on letter-sized paper, which is 8.5 inches by 11 inches, you will need to select an option that prints the poster in four parts on four separate sheets of paper. Select the desired orientation for your poster and then click OK.

Trimming and Assembling a Poster

As you learned in Chapter 4, most printers have a nonprinting area, which means that text and graphics cannot be printed to the very edge of the page. Because of this, you will most likely have to trim the pages of your poster before taping them together. As an alternative to cutting off the edges, you can fold them toward the back of the paper and then tape the pages together. This may provide more support for the taped area, but it may also make your poster heavier and bulkier.

If you want the poster to print on one page so that you do not have to assemble it, consider having the poster professionally printed at a print shop, office supply store, or similar type of business.

Exercise 10.6 Creating and Printing a Poster

1. Open **Poster.docx** located in your Chapter10 folder and then save the document with the name **C10-E06-Poster**.
2. With the insertion point positioned at the beginning of the document, insert and format the clip art image shown in Figure 10.18 on page 461 by completing the following steps:
   a. Use the Pictures button on the INSERT tab to insert **Chicago.png** from your Chapter10 folder.
   b. Change the width of the image to 4.5 inches.
   c. Change the position of the image to *Position in Top Center with Square Text Wrapping*.
3. Create a text box that measures 0.8 inch in height and 3 inches in width and then type **Sweet Home** in the text box.
4. Select *Sweet Home* and then change the font to 36-point Bauhaus 93 and apply the Red font color.
5. Remove the shape fill and shape outline from the text box and then drag the text box so it is positioned as shown in Figure 10.18.
6. Drag a copy of the text box (you will use it for the word *Chicago*) to a position similar to that shown in Figure 10.18. Select *Sweet Home* in the new copy of the text box and then type **Chicago**.

7. Select the text in the text box below the Chicago skyline image, change the font to 18-point Calibri, and then change the paragraph alignment to center.

8. Select *Midwest Golf Club Ladies 9-Hole Guest Day* and then apply the following formatting:

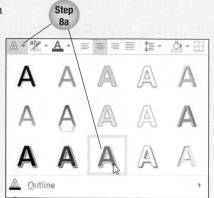

Step 8a

a. Use the Text Effects and Typography button in the Font group on the HOME tab to apply the Fill - Blue, Accent 1, Outline - Background 1, Hard Shadow - Accent 1 effect (third column, bottom row).

b. Change the font size to 26 points.

c. Display the Font dialog box with the Advanced tab selected, turn on kerning at 26 points and above, expand the spacing by 0.5 points, and then close the dialog box.

9. Save **C10-E06-Poster.docx**.

10. Print the document by completing the following steps: ***Hint: These steps may vary depending on your printer. If your printer does not include a poster printing option, check with your instructor.***

Step 10b

a. Click the FILE tab and then click the *Print* option.

b. At the Print backstage area, click the *Printer Properties* option.

c. At the printer document properties dialog box, click the Advanced button. (Or, click a tab that provides an option to print a poster in four parts, on four separate pages.)

d. Click the *Poster Print* option, click the down-pointing arrow, and then click *1 in 2x2 Pages*. (This step will vary depending on your printer.)

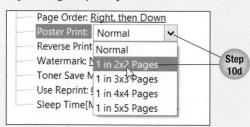

Step 10d

e. Click OK to close the dialog box pages and, if necessary, click OK to close the printer document properties dialog box.

f. At the Print backstage area, click the Print button.

11. Trim and then tape the pages of your poster together.

12. Return your printer settings back to the default settings.

13. Close **C10-E06-Poster.docx**.

Figure 10.18 **Poster Created in Exercise 10.6**

Creating Bookmarks

Creating and distributing promotional bookmarks to your customers and potential customers is a good way to constantly remind them of your company or brand. Because a bookmark is something they can potentially use over and over again, your advertisement can continue to be effective long after you have created it.

Creating Crop Marks Using Tab Settings

Since a bookmark is smaller in size than a standard sheet of paper, several bookmarks can be created on one page. You can insert crop marks on the printed page to act as guides for trimming the bookmarks. In Chapter 8, you learned how to turn on the crop marks feature at the Word Options dialog box with *Advanced* selected in the left panel. However, these crop marks only display at the left and right margins and do not print, so they cannot act as guides for trimming your bookmarks.

You can manually insert crop marks in a document by creating tab settings at designated areas along the top and/or bottom of the document and then inserting a crop mark symbol at the left margin and at each tab. Notice the crop mark symbols that display along the top of the pages in Figure 10.19 on page 464.

Printing Bookmarks

As mentioned above, the crop marks that Word adds to a document display only on the screen and do not print. However, if you create your own crop marks in the Header pane or Footer pane, they will print and be available to use as a guide for trimming. You may want to print your bookmarks on cardstock and then laminate them before trimming. This will increase their durability and give them a professional appearance.

In Exercise 10.7, you will insert crop mark symbols at the left margin and at tab settings in the Header pane, which will cause the crop marks to display at the top of both pages.

Exercise 10.7 Creating Bookmarks with Crop Marks

1. Open **Bookmarks.docx** located in your Chapter10 folder and then save the document with the name **C10-E07-Bookmarks**.
2. Create the crop marks as shown in Figure 10.19 on page 464 by completing the following steps:
   a. Click the INSERT tab, click the Header button in the Header & Footer group, and then click *Edit Header* at the drop-down gallery.
   b. Change the left and right margins to 0.6 inch.
   c. At the Tabs dialog box, set center tabs at 2.5 inches, 4.9 inches, and 7.3 inches and set a right tab at 9.8 inches. Click OK to close the dialog box.
   d. With the insertion point positioned at the left margin in the Header pane, click the INSERT tab, click the Symbol button in the Symbols group, and then click *More Symbols* at the drop-down list.

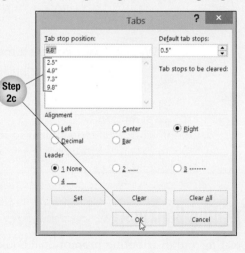

e. At the Symbol dialog box, click the down-pointing arrow at the right side of the *Font* option box and then click *SimSun* at the drop-down list.

f. Select the text in the *Character code* text box and then type **2518** to select the symbol that resembles a reversed capital *L*.

g. Click the Insert button and then click the Close button.

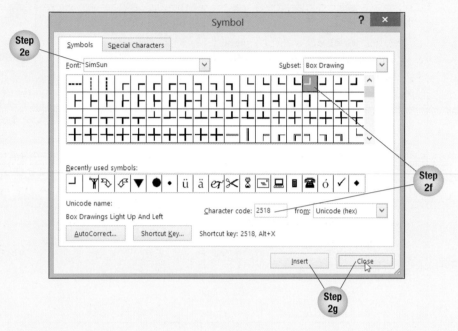

h. Press the Tab key to move the insertion point to the 2.5-inch center tab and then insert the crop mark symbol that displays as an upside down capital *T* by displaying the Symbol dialog box, typing **2534** as the character code, clicking the Insert button, and then clicking the Close button.

i. Press the Tab key to move the insertion point to the 4.9-inch center tab and then insert the same symbol as the one inserted at the 2.5-inch center tab. ***Hint: This symbol will now display as the first option in the Symbol button drop-down list.***

j. Press the Tab key to move the insertion point to the 7.3-inch center tab and then insert the same symbol as the one inserted at the 2.5-inch and 4.9-inch center tabs.

k. Press the Tab key to move the insertion point to the 9.8-inch right tab and then insert the crop mark symbol that displays as a capital *L* by displaying the Symbol dialog box, typing **2514** as the character code, clicking the Insert button, and then clicking the Close button.

3. Double-click in the document to make the document active.

4. Save and then print the first page of **C10-E07-Bookmarks**.

5. Turn over the page you printed, reinsert it into the printer (so the second page prints on the back of the first page) and then print page 2. ***Hint: You may want to laminate the bookmarks and then cut them using the crop marks as guides.***

6. Close **C10-E07-Bookmarks.docx**.

Figure 10.19 Bookmarks Created in Exercise 10.7

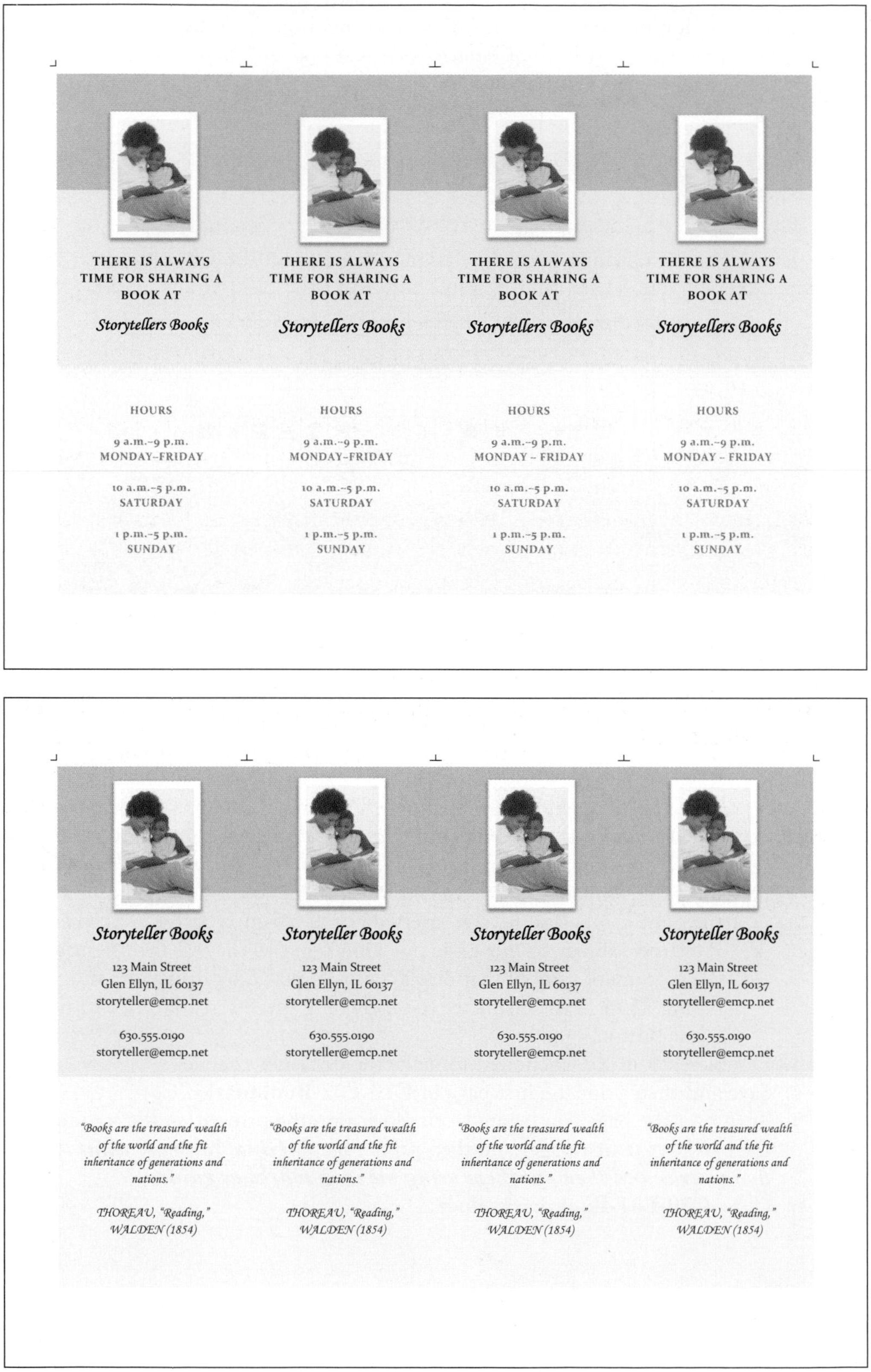

Chapter *Summary*

➤ Create and format promotional documents using templates or create and format them from scratch using tables or text boxes.

➤ The table feature is one of the most efficient tools for designing and creating promotional documents and forms.

➤ Insert an automatic numbering command in a ticket document by adding an AutoNum field code.

➤ Create lines that you can type on by designing a document using tables, inserting fields, drawing a line shape, drawing lines using the Underline command and tab settings, or using tab leaders.

➤ Postcards can be used to get a brief message across to customers or prospective customers.

➤ Create a postcard using a predesigned postcard template or use the labels feature, which provides predefined postcard labels.

➤ The labels feature formats documents so that they can be printed on designated label sheets.

➤ Create a data source file with the Select Recipients button in the Start Mail Merge group on the MAILINGS tab.

➤ When creating a data source file, use predesigned fields offered by Word at the New Address List dialog box. Delete predesigned fields not needed for a data source file and create custom fields, if necessary.

➤ Word saves a data source file as an Access database with the *.mdb* file extension.

➤ Merge a main document with a data source file to create a new document, send the merged documents directly to the printer, or send the merged documents by email.

➤ When merging postcards labels, insert the «AddressBlock» field in the appropriate location in the postcard main document and then click the Update Labels button so each postcard contains the «AddressBlock» field.

➤ Create cards by inserting text in text boxes or using a table to create each panel of a card.

➤ A poster can be printed by accessing your specific printer properties dialog box and selecting an option to print the poster on four sheets of paper or more. The number of pages selected will determine the size of the overall poster.

➤ Crop marks to assist in trimming a document can be created by setting tabs in the Header or Footer pane and then inserting cropping symbols from the Symbol dialog box.

Commands Review

FEATURE	RIBBON TAB, GROUP /OPTION	BUTTON, OPTION
Address Block field	MAILINGS, Write & Insert Fields	
align	DRAWING TOOLS FORMAT, Arrange	
borders	TABLE TOOLS DESIGN, Borders	
Field dialog box	INSERT, Text	, *Field*
finish merge	MAILINGS, Finish	
labels	MAILINGS, Create	
New Address List dialog box	MAILINGS, Start Mail Merge	, *Type a New List*
New backstage area	FILE, *New*	
select recipients	MAILINGS, Start Mail Merge	
start mail merge	MAILINGS, Start Mail Merge	
Symbol dialog box	INSERT, Symbols	Ω
table	INSERT, Table	
Table Properties dialog box	TABLE TOOLS LAYOUT, Table	
update labels	MAILINGS, Write & Insert Fields	
Word Options dialog box	FILE, *Options*	

Key Points Review

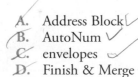

A. Address Block
B. AutoNum
C. envelopes
D. Finish & Merge

E. labels
F. New Address List
G. printer
H. Printer Properties

I. Select Recipients
J. tab
K. tab leaders
L. table

Matching: In the space at the left, provide the correct letter or letters from the above list that match each definition.

_L_ 1. Feature that provides a framework for creating forms

_B_ 2. Form field that allows you to add automatic numbering to a ticket document

_K_ 3. One method for creating lines on which to type

_G_ 4. The data source and the main document can be merged to a new document or to this

_F_ 5. Dialog box used to delete predesigned fields in a data source file

_A_ 6. Button on the MAILINGS tab used to insert a formatted address field into a main document

_D_ 7. Button on the MAILINGS tab used to merge the main document with the data source

_E_ 8. Feature used to create postcards

_H_ 9. Option at the Print backstage area used to display a dialog box with specific information about your printer

_I_ 10. Click this button on the MAILINGS tab and then click *Type a New List* to display the New Address List dialog box

Chapter Assessments

Assessment 10.1　Create a Promotional Gift Certificate

1. At a blank document, create a gift certificate similar to the ones shown in Figure 10.20 with the following specifications:
   a. Change the top, bottom, left, and right margins to 0.65 inch.
   b. Create a table with two columns and one row.
   c. Change the row height to 2.65 inches, the width of the first column to 4.75 inches, and the width of the second column to 2.25 inches.
   d. Change the top, left, bottom, and right default cell margins to 0.1 inch.
   e. Display the Borders and Shading dialog box, click the middle column border in the *Preview* section to remove the border, and then click OK.
   f. Center the table horizontally on the page.
   g. With the insertion point positioned in the first cell, type **Gift Certificate** and then press Enter twice.
   h. Select *Gift Certificate*, change the font to 36-point French Script MS, and then apply the Blue, Accent 5, Darker 25% font color (ninth column, fifth row in the *Theme Colors* section).
   i. Position the insertion point on the blank line below *Gift Certificate* and then set left tabs at 0.5 inch, 1.75 inches, 2.75 inches and 4.3 inches.
   j. Using the tabs you set in the previous step, type the text in the first cell as shown in Figure 10.20. To create the underlines, press the spacebar once after typing a text label, click the Underline button on the HOME tab, press the spacebar again, and then press Ctrl + Tab to move to the next tab and create the underline. (You may need to press Ctrl + Tab more than once to create an underline of the correct length.) Once you have typed an underline, turn off the underline feature, press Enter twice, and then type the next text label. Continue in this manner until you have typed all the text and underlines in the first cell.
   k. Type the text in the second cell as shown in Figure 10.20. Center the text and set *Butterfield Gardens* in 24-point French Script MS in the Blue, Accent 5, Darker 25% font color. Remove the hyperlink from the web address.
2. Insert the Butterfield Gardens logo (**ButterfieldGardenLogo.png**), located in your Chapter10 folder. Change the color of the logo to *Blue, Accent color 5 Light*, the text wrapping to *Tight*, and then resize and position the logo as shown in Figure 10.20.
3. Create two more certificates on the same page by copying and pasting the table. ***Hint: Insert one hard return between each certificate.***
4. Save the document with the name **C10-A01-Certifcate**.
5. Print and then close **C10-A01-Certificate.docx**.

Assessment 10.2　Create and Merge Name Tags

1. At a blank document, create the name tag main document shown in Figure 10.21 on page 470. Begin by clicking the MAILINGS tab, clicking the Start Mail Merge button, and then clicking *Labels* at the drop-down list.
2. At the Label Options dialog box, choose *Avery US Letter* as the label vendor, select *5393 Hanging Name Badges* in the *Product number* list box, and then click OK to close the dialog box.
3. Select the data source file by clicking the Select Recipients button and then clicking *Use an Existing List* at the drop-down list. At the Select Data Source dialog box, navigate to your Chapter10 folder and then double-click *FloralDataSource.mdb*.

Figure 10.20 Gift Certificates Created in Assessment 10.1

Gift Certificate

Date _____

This certificate entitles _____

To _____ Dollars $ _____

Presented by _____

Authorized signature _____

Butterfield Gardens
29 W 036 Butterfield Road
Warrenville, IL 60555
(630) 555-1062

www.emcp.net/butterfield

Butterfield GARDENS

Gift Certificate

Date _____

This certificate entitles _____

To _____ Dollars $ _____

Presented by _____

Authorized signature _____

Butterfield Gardens
29 W 036 Butterfield Road
Warrenville, IL 60555
(630) 555-1062

www.emcp.net/butterfield

Butterfield GARDENS

Gift Certificate

Date _____

This certificate entitles _____

To _____ Dollars $ _____

Presented by _____

Authorized signature _____

Butterfield Gardens
29 W 036 Butterfield Road
Warrenville, IL 60555
(630) 555-1062

www.emcp.net/butterfield

Butterfield GARDENS

4. With the insertion point positioned inside the first name tag, make the following changes:
   a. Change the spacing before paragraphs to 0 points.
   b. Press the spacebar once, press the Enter key, and then change the font to 11-point Arial Black.
   c. Type the text and insert the field codes in the cell as shown in Figure 10.21. Insert the field codes by clicking the Insert Merge Field button arrow on the MAILINGS tab and then clicking the desired field code at the drop-down list.
   d. Select the fields *«FirstName»*, *«LastName»*, and *«JobTitle»* and then change the font size to 14 points.
   e. Select from the blank line above the fields *«FirstName» and «LastName»* through the blank line below *«JobTitle»* and then apply Dark Blue shading.
   f. Align the lines of text as shown in Figure 10.21.
   g. Click the Update Labels button in the Write & Insert Field group on the MAILINGS tab.
5. Merge the main document with the data source by clicking the Finish & Merge button, clicking *Edit Individual Documents* at the drop-down list, making sure *All* is selected in the Merge to New Document dialog box, and then clicking OK.
6. Save the merged document with the name **C10-A02-NameTags**.
7. Print and then close **C10-A02-NameTags.docx**. (These name tags are designed to be inserted into a holder, which is a clear plastic sleeve with a clip or pin on the reverse side. Holders are usually available through mail order paper companies or office supply companies.)
8. Save the name tags main document with the name **C10-A02-NameTagsMainDoc**.
9. Close **C10-A02-NameTagsMainDoc.docx**.

Figure 10.21 Name Tag Main Document and Merged Document Created in Assessment 10.2

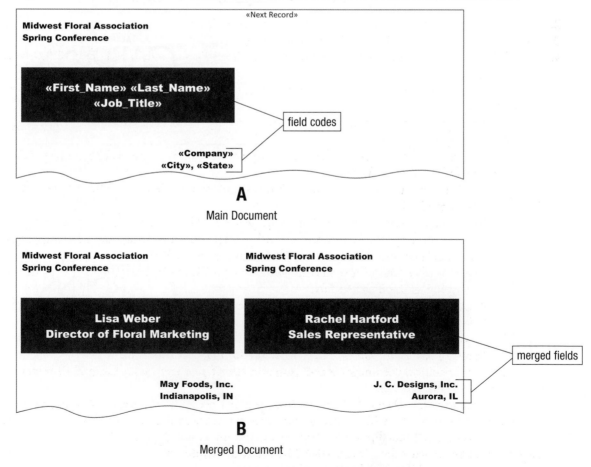

A

Main Document

B

Merged Document

Assessment 10.3   Create an Event Invitation

1. At a blank document, create the front panels of the invitation shown in Figure 10.22A on page 472 with the following specifications:
   a. Change the orientation to landscape and change the top, bottom, left, and right margins to 0.5 inch.
   b. Insert a table with two columns and two rows and then select the entire table and change the row height to 3.6 inches.
   c. Insert the shading fill color in the bottom two cells using the following custom color: Red = 51, Green = 51, and Blue = 153. *Hint: Use options at the Colors dialog box with the Custom tab selected to apply the custom color.*
   d. Type the text **An evening out on the town!** in the location indicated in the figure and then change the font to 16-point Harrington with bold formatting and the font color to *Gold, Accent 4, Lighter 60%* (eighth column, third row in the *Theme Colors* section).
   e. Position the insertion point at the beginning of the cell containing the text you just typed and then insert **conductor.png** from your Chapter10 folder. Change the text wrapping for the image to *In Front of Text* and then position the image as shown in Figure 10.22A.
   f. Insert **stars1.png** from your Chapter10 folder. Use the Set Transparent Color tool (located in the Color button drop-down gallery in the Adjust group on the PICTURE TOOLS FORMAT tab) to remove the white background fill from the image. Change the text wrapping to *In Front of Text*, change the width of the image to 2.5 inches, and then position the image as shown in Figure 10.22A.
   g. Copy the images and the text from the first cell in the bottom row to the second cell in the bottom row. Make any adjustments necessary so the text and images in the second cell match the text and images in the first cell.
2. Save the document with the name **C10-A03-InvitationCover**.
3. Print and then close **C10-A03-InvitationCover.docx**.
4. At a blank document, create the inside panels of the invitation as shown in Figure 10.22B with the following specifications:
   a. Change the orientation to landscape and change the top, bottom, left, and right margins to 0.5 inch.
   b. Insert a table with two columns and two rows and then select the entire table and change the row height to 3.6 inches.
   c. Type the text in the first cell in the bottom row as shown in Figure 10.22B on page 472 with the following specifications:
      1) Set the first four lines of text in 14-point Candara and the last two lines of text in 12-point Candara.
      2) Insert the five lines of text starting with *Trattoria 8* inside a text box and set the text in 13-point Candara. Remove the text box shape outline, change the text wrapping to *Tight*, and position the text box as shown in Figure 10.22B.
      3) Insert the five lines of text starting with *Chicago Theater* inside a text box with the same formatting as the first text box.
      4) Apply bold formatting, italic formatting, and center alignment to text as shown in Figure 10.22B.
      5) Apply the Gradient Fill - Gold, Accent 4, Outline - Accent 4 text effect to the text *"Evening out on the town"* and increase the font size to 18-points.
   d. Insert and position the images **stars2.png** and **stars3.png** from your Chapter10 folder as shown in Figure 10.22B.
   e. Copy the text, text boxes, and images from the first cell in the bottom row to the second cell in the bottom row. Make any adjustments necessary so the text, text boxes, and images in the second cell match the text, text boxes, and images in the first cell.
5. Save the document with the name **C10-A03-InvitationInside**.
6. Print and then close **C10-A03-InvitationInside.docx**.

Figure 10.22 Invitation Created in Assessment 10.3

A

Invitation Cover

B

Invitation Inside Text

Assessment 10.4 Create an Integrated Application Form

In this exercise, you will create a scholarship application form using a Word table. You will insert information from an Excel worksheet into the Word table. You will see that integrating Excel (with its automatic calculating features) into the Word form makes it easier to calculate totals.

PORTFOLIO

INTEGRATED

1. At a blank document, using Figure 10.23 as a guide, create the scholarship application form shown in Figure 10.24, on page 474. Insert a table and use the cells as placeholders for the information. Complete the form as shown in Figure 10.24 *except* do not insert the Community Services chart or the clip art image in the row below the *Eligibility requirements* paragraph. ***Hint: Resize the column widths and row heights before merging cells for the headings.***
2. Save the application form document that you created in Step 1 with the name **C10-A04-ScholarshipApplicationForm**. Leave the form open as you complete the following steps.
3. Open Excel and then open **CommunityServiceHours.xlsx**, located in your Chapter10 folder.
4. Add the AutoSum formula in cell B8 by positioning the insertion point in the cell, clicking the AutoSum button in the Editing group on the HOME tab, typing **B2:B7** in the formula, and then pressing Enter.
5. Select and then copy cells A1 through B8.
6. Click the Word button on the taskbar. (This should display **C10-A04-ScholarshipApplication Form.docx** on the screen). Position the insertion point in the cell below the *Eligibility requirements* paragraph, click the Paste button arrow in the Clipboard group on the HOME tab, and then click *Paste Special* at the drop-down list. At the Paste Special dialog box, click *Microsoft Excel Worksheet Object* in the *As* list box and then click OK.
7. Click the Excel button on the taskbar, close **CommunityServiceHours.xlsx**, and then close Excel.
8. Insert an image similar to the one shown in Figure 10.24.

Figure 10.23 Using a Table to Create a Scholarship Form

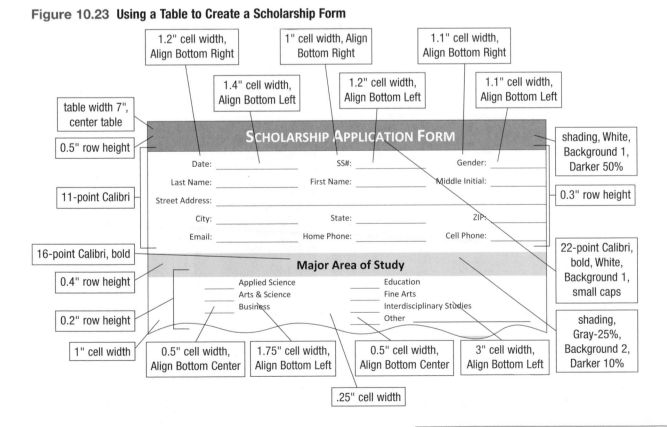

9. Save **C10-A04-ScholarshipApplicationForm.docx**.
10. Save the document with Save As with the name **C10-A04-ScholarshipApplicationFormCompleted**.
11. Fill in the application form as shown in Figure 10.25. (Press the Tab key to move from one cell to the next.) To fill in the numbers in the Excel worksheet, double-click the worksheet and then type the numbers as shown in Figure 10.25. The total amount should automatically recalculate. Click outside the object to return to the Word editing functions.
12. Save, print, and then close **C10-A04-ScholarshipApplicationFormCompleted.docx**.

Figure 10.24 Application Form for Assessment 10.4

SCHOLARSHIP APPLICATION FORM

Date: _____   SS#: _____   Gender: _____

Last Name: _____   First Name: _____   Middle Initial: _____

Street Address: _____

City: _____   State: _____   ZIP: _____

Email: _____   Home Phone: _____   Cell Phone: _____

Major Area of Study

_____ Applied Science   _____ Education
_____ Arts & Science   _____ Fine Arts
_____ Business   _____ Interdisciplinary Studies
                              _____ Other _____

High School Class Standing	**Intended Student Status**
_____ Junior	_____ Full-time (12 hours or more)
_____ Senior	_____ Half-time (9 to 11 hours)
_____ Graduate	_____ Half-time (6 to 8 hours)

Eligibility requirements include a minimum of 40 hours of community service throughout your four years of high school. Double-click the chart below and then fill in the number of hours you have volunteered in each category. The total hours will be calculated automatically.

Community Services	
Day camp	
Fund-raising	
Government	
High school	
Homeless shelter	
Other	
Total	0

Thank you for your application. Please return to Kelly Cavanaugh, 22 Parrot Way, St. Paul, MN 55102.

Figure 10.25 Completed Application Form for Assessment 10.4

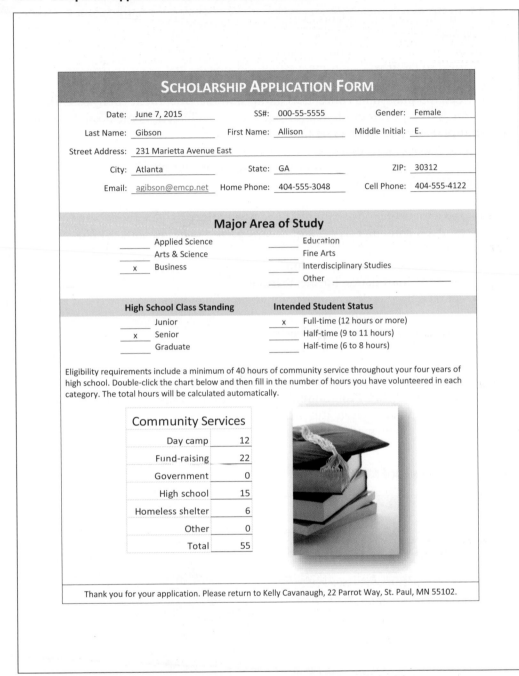

SCHOLARSHIP APPLICATION FORM

Date: June 7, 2015　　SS#: 000-55-5555　　Gender: Female

Last Name: Gibson　　First Name: Allison　　Middle Initial: E.

Street Address: 231 Marietta Avenue East

City: Atlanta　　State: GA　　ZIP: 30312

Email: agibson@emcp.net　　Home Phone: 404-555-3048　　Cell Phone: 404-555-4122

Major Area of Study

_____ Applied Science　　_____ Education
_____ Arts & Science　　_____ Fine Arts
__x__ Business　　_____ Interdisciplinary Studies
　　　　　　　　　　_____ Other _____

High School Class Standing　　Intended Student Status

_____ Junior　　__x__ Full-time (12 hours or more)
__x__ Senior　　_____ Half-time (9 to 11 hours)
_____ Graduate　　_____ Half-time (6 to 8 hours)

Eligibility requirements include a minimum of 40 hours of community service throughout your four years of high school. Double-click the chart below and then fill in the number of hours you have volunteered in each category. The total hours will be calculated automatically.

Community Services	
Day camp	12
Fund-raising	22
Government	0
High school	15
Homeless shelter	6
Other	0
Total	55

Thank you for your application. Please return to Kelly Cavanaugh, 22 Parrot Way, St. Paul, MN 55102.

Assessment 10.5   Design and Create a Promotional Document

1. Form groups of three or four students. Assign necessary group tasks to create a promotional document of your own design based on a sample document you have found or a template located on the Internet. Use any of the Word features you have learned so far. If you are using a sample document, first evaluate the document for good layout and design, a clear and concise message, and proper use of other desktop publishing concepts as outlined in the **Document Analysis Guide** (refer to **DocumentAnalysisGuide.docx** located in your Chapter10 folder). Some possible promotional documents include the following examples:
   - Invitation to a new store opening
   - Introduction of a new course at your local community college
   - Invitation to a class reunion
   - Business greeting card or company party invitation
   - Postcard as a follow-up or one promoting a new business (coffee shop, party planner, attorney's office, computer services, or health spa as shown in Figure 10.26)
   - Membership card
   - Ticket with a company or organization name or logo
   - Form requesting information for membership
   - Document used by a service company promoting e-Bill—paying your account balance online
   - Postcard advertising a sample sale
   - Poster advertising services at a travel agency
2. Create the document using a size other than 8.5-by-11-inch paper, or print the document with multiple pages as a poster.
3. Save the completed document with the name **C10-A05-Promotional**.
4. Print and then close **C10-A05-Promotional.docx**. (Attach the original document if one was used.)
5. Discuss the approach used to create this document with the rest of the class. Each member should participate in the presentation.

Figure 10.26 Sample Solution for Assessment 10.5

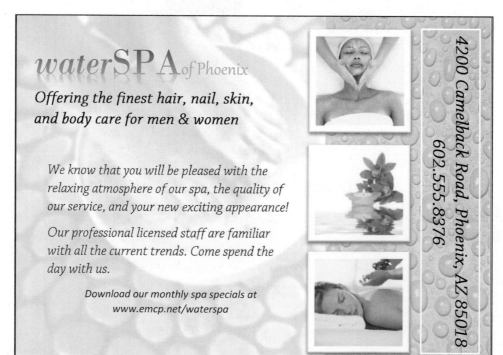

Preparing Promotional Documents

ASSESSING PROFICIENCIES

In this unit, you have learned to apply the design concepts to create flyers, brochures, booklets, and other specialty promotional documents.

Note: Before beginning computer exercises for this section, copy to your storage medium the Unit03 folder from the CD that accompanies this textbook and then make Unit03 the active folder. Remember to substitute for graphics that may no longer be available.

Assessment U3.1   Create a Dental Flyer

You work for a dental clinic and are responsible for creating a flyer promoting clinic services. Using the table feature in Word, create the flyer shown in Figure U3.1 on page 478 by completing the following steps:

1. At a blank document, change the top margin to 1.25 inches.
2. Insert a table with two columns and four rows and then make the following modifications to the table (refer to Figure U3.1):
   a. Change the height of the first row to 1.7 inches, the second row to 3.9 inches, the third row to 1.1 inches, and the fourth row to 1.4 inches.
   b. Merge the cells in the first row and then use the Shading button in the Tables Styles group on the TABLE TOOLS DESIGN tab to apply Blue, Accent 1, Darker 25% shading (fifth column, fifth row in the *Theme Colors* section) to the cell, as shown in Figure U3.1.
   c. Apply Blue, Accent 1, Darker 25% shading to the second cell in the second row and the two cells in the bottom row.
   d. Merge the two cells in the third row and then apply Blue, Accent 1, Lighter 40% shading (fifth column, fourth row in the *Theme Colors* section) to the cell, as shown in Figure U3.1.
   e. Click in the first row and then change the alignment to Align Center. ***Hint: This button is located on the TABLE TOOLS LAYOUT tab.***
   f. Click in the third row and then change the alignment to Align Center Left.
   g. Change the cell alignment of both cells in the fourth (bottom) row to Align Center Left.
3. Type the text shown in Figure U3.1 in the cells and apply formatting by completing the following steps:
   a. Type **Need a new smile?** in the first row, change the font size to 56 points, and then use the Text Effects and Typography button to apply the Fill - White, Outline - Accent 1, Glow - Accent 1 text effect.
   b. Type the text in the second cell in the second column and then change the font size to 18 points and the font color to *White, Background 1*. ***Hint: You will need to press the Enter key one time before typing the text.***

c. Type **Call today! 800.555.1225** in the third row, change the font size to 36 points, and then use the Text Effects and Typography button to apply the Fill - White, Outline - Accent 1, Shadow text effect.

d. Type the text in the two cells in the bottom row, change the font size to 14 points, and change the font color to *White, Background 1*.

4. Insert **dentist.png** from your Unit03 folder, change the text wrapping to *In Front of Text*, and then position the image in the first cell in the second row as shown in Figure U3.1.

5. Insert **tooth.png** from your Unit03 folder, change the height to 1.3 inches, change the text wrapping to *In Front of Text*, and then position the image in the third row as shown in Figure U3.1.

6. Save the document with the name **U3-PA01-BriteSmileFlyer**.

7. Print and then close **U3-PA01-BriteSmileFlyer.docx**.

Figure U3.1 Flyer Created in Performance Assessment U3.1

Assessment U3.2 Create a Flyer with a SmartArt Graphic

You work for Global Enterprises, and you have been asked to create a flyer that shows the company's branch locations and contains the company slogan. Create the flyer shown in Figure U3.2 on page 480 by completing the following steps:

1. At a blank document, change the orientation to landscape and change the top, bottom, left, and right margins to 0.5 inch.
2. Insert **GEglobe.png** from your Unit03 folder and then make the following changes:
   a. Change the height of the image to 7.5 inches.
   b. Crop the image so it appears similar to what is shown in Figure U3.2 on page 480.
   c. Change the color of the image to *Blue, Accent color 5 Light*.
   d. Change the position of the image to *Position in Middle Left with Square Text Wrapping*.
3. Apply the Blue, Accent 5, Darker 25% page color.
4. Insert the text *Global Enterprises* as WordArt with the following specifications:
   a. Use the Fill - White, Outline - Accent 1, Shadow WordArt option.
   b. Change the height to 1 inch and the width to 7.3 inches.
   c. Apply the Square transform effect.
   d. Position the WordArt as shown in Figure U3.2.
5. Insert the SmartArt graphic as shown in Figure U3.2 with the following specifications:
   a. Use the Vertical Curved List SmartArt graphic.
   b. Add two additional shapes.
   c. Change the colors to *Colorful Range - Accent Colors 5 to 6*.
   d. Change the height of the SmartArt graphic to 5 inches and the width to 6.5 inches.
   e. Type the text in the shapes as shown in Figure U3.2.
   f. Change the position of the SmartArt graphic to *Position in Middle Right with Square Text Wrapping*.
6. Insert the text *Providing goods and services around the globe!* in a text box. Change the font size of the text to 26 points, change the font color to *White, Background 1*, change the paragraph alignment to right, change the height of the text box to 1 inch and the width to 4.3 inches, remove the shape fill and outline, and then position the text box as shown in Figure U3.2.
7. Save the document with the name **U3-PA02-GEFlyer**.
8. Specify that you want page color to print (do this at the Word Options dialog box with *Display* selected in the left panel) and then print the document.
9. Specify that you do not want page color to print and then close **U3-PA02-GEFlyer.docx**.

Figure U3.2 Flyer Created in Performance Assessment U3.2

Assessment U3.3   Create a Fact Sheet

Using the text in **FactSheetText.docx**, create a fact sheet highlighting the services offered by Winston & McKenzie's Executive Search Services Department according to the following specifications (refer to Figure U3.3 for a sample solution, but use your own design and formatting):

1. Create a thumbnail sketch of your proposed page layout and design. You will need to experiment with the layout and design.
2. Insert **WMLogo.png** into the document.
3. Vary the fonts, type sizes, typestyles, and text effects to emphasize the relative importance of items.
4. Use bullets to list the services offered. You choose the bullet style.
5. Include any relevant pictures, symbols, borders, colors, and so on, in your fact sheet. Size and position the page elements however you see fit, and apply shading, borders and fill, spacing, alignment, and so forth as desired. ***Hint: Photographs tend to look more professional than clip art.***
6. Save the document with the name **U3-PA03-W&MFactSheet**.
7. Print and then close **U3-PA03-W&MFactSheet.docx**.
8. Open **DocumentEvaluationChecklist.docx** located in your Unit03 folder and save the document with the name **U3-PA03-Analysis**. Use the checklist to evaluate your fact sheet.
9. Save, print, and then close **U3-PA03-Analysis.docx**. Hand in both items.

Figure U3.3 Sample Solution for Performance Assessment U3.3

Winston & McKenzie, CPA Executive Search

About Executive Search Services...

Winston & McKenzie Executive Search consultants are both highly qualified and highly professional. Many have advanced degrees in personnel administration, psychology, organization development, marketing, and communications. This interdisciplinary dynamism within Winston & McKenzie, coupled with the insight and vision of your management team, turn the problem of finding a new executive into an opportunity to plan and act strategically.

You select the services that meet your needs...

- ➢ Defining the position
- ➢ Handling internal candidates
- ➢ Assessing candidates
- ➢ Conducting interviews
- ➢ Testing candidates
- ➢ Performing reference and background checks
- ➢ Assisting with employment offers

For more information about Executive Search...

Please call Janet Rankins at (317) 555-6342 or Bill Brockman at (317) 555-8989.

Winston & McKenzie Executive Search Services—working with you and for you in selecting the right management team.

**Winston & McKenzie, CPA
Executive Search**

Using the text in **WMText1.docx**, **WMText2.docx**, and **WMText3** **.docx**, located in your Unit03 folder, create a self-mailing trifold brochure according to the following specifications (refer to Figure U3.4 for a sample solution, but use your own design and formatting).

Reminder: Save periodically as you work through this assessment.

1. Create a dummy of the brochure layout so you know exactly which panel will be used for each section of text.
2. Prepare a thumbnail sketch of your proposed layout and design.
3. At a blank document, set up the page by completing the following steps:
   a. Change the orientation to landscape.
   b. Change the top and bottom margins to 0.5 inch and the left and right margins to 0.45 inch.
   c. Change the gutter measurement to 0.25 inch.
4. Create the inside panels of the brochure according to the following specifications:
   a. Use columns, text boxes, or a table as the underlying structure for the brochure.
   b. Insert **WMText1.docx** in panel 1, **WMText2.docx** in panel 2, and **WMText3.docx** in panel 3.
   c. Choose appropriate typefaces, type sizes, and text effects that best reflect the mood or tone of the brochure and the company it represents. ***Hint:*** ***If you are using columns, insert column breaks to begin each new panel.***
   d. Consider using a drop cap, SmartArt, shape, watermark, or any other design element that creates focus.
   e. Create new styles or modify existing styles to save time and keystrokes. You may want to create styles for headings, body text, and bulleted items.
   f. Apply bullets to lists. You decide on the bullet symbol, size, color, spacing, and so forth.
   g. Use text boxes to specifically position text or to highlight text in a unique way.
   h. Include ruled lines. Choose an appropriate line style, thickness, placement, and color.
5. To make the brochure a self-mailer, create the mailing address side of the request for information (created in panel 3) and insert the mailing information into panel 4 by completing the following steps:
   a. Insert the mailing address into a text box and then use the Text Direction button to rotate the mailing address 90 degrees. You decide on an appropriate font, type size, and color. Type the following address:
      Winston & McKenzie, CPA
      Executive Search Services
      4600 North Meridian Street
      Indianapolis, IN 46208
   b. Size and position the text box containing the mailing address in an appropriate position.
   c. Leave panel 5 blank since it will be the backside of the self-mailer. Once a person fills out the information in panel 3, he or she will refold the brochure so that panel 4, the self-mailer panel, will display on top.
6. Create the cover of the brochure in panel 6 by completing the following steps:
   a. Type **You Can't Afford to Make the Wrong Hiring Decision!** as the title of the brochure.
   b. Insert **WMLogo.png** from your Unit03 folder and then size and position the logo.

c. Decide on an appropriate location for the company name, address, and the following phone and fax numbers and then type the information in that location:

Phone: (317) 555-8900
Fax: (317) 555-8901
Email: winmck@emcp.net
Web: www.emcp.net/winmck

7. Save the brochure with the name **U3-PA04-Brochure**.
8. Print and then close **U3-PA04-Brochure.docx**.
9. Open **DocumentEvaluationChecklist** from your Unit03 folder and then save the document with the name **U3-PA04-Analysis**. Use the checklist to evaluate your brochure. Make any changes that are necessary.
10. Save, print, and then close **U3-PA04-Analysis.docx**. Hand in both items.

Figure U3.4 Sample Solution for Performance Assessment U3.4

Identifying, Assessing, and Hiring Senior Officers

Your executive management team is critical to your institution's success. However, selecting the right individuals is not easy. Hiring the wrong candidates can cost your institution as much as two times their salary in wasted recruiting and training expenses, lost productivity, and lowered morale.

Winston & McKenzie, CPA, can help you make more effective staffing decisions. We do more than simply take job specs over the phone and send you a stack of résumés. We work with you to initially evaluate the position to determine whether it should be filled, altered, or eliminated. Once the decision to fill a position is made, we can conduct the entire search, parts of the process, or simply coach you through the process. Your needs determine our level of involvement.

Our search consultants utilize Winston & McKenzie's full range of specialized financial institution resources to enhance your search.

You Select the Services that Meet Your Needs

✓ Defining the position
✓ Handling internal candidates
✓ Generating candidates
✓ Assessing candidates
✓ Conducting interviews
✓ Testing candidates
✓ Performing reference and background checks
✓ Assisting with employment offers

I Would Like More Information...

on how Winston & McKenzie can help my institution find and hire the right management team.

For more information about our Executive Search Services please call:

Janet Ronkins at (317) 555-6342
Email: winmck@emcp.net

Visit our website at:

www.emcp.net/winmck

or complete the information request card below.

Name: _____
Institution: _____
Address: _____
City: _____
State: _____
ZIP: _____
Email: _____
Telephone: _____
Cell: _____

Winston & McKenzie, CPA
Executive Search Services
4600 North Meridian Street
Indianapolis, IN 46240

You Can't Afford to Make the Wrong Hiring Decision!

Winston & McKenzie, CPA
Executive Search

Winston & McKenzie, CPA
Executive Search Services
4600 North Meridian Street
Indianapolis, IN 46208

Phone: (317) 555-8900
Fax: (317) 555-6901
Email: winmck@emcp.net
Web: www.emcp.net.winmck

Assessment U3.5   Create an Invitation

In this assessment, you will use the table feature to create an invitation for a fashion show.

1. Use the Word table feature to create the cover of an invitation in landscape orientation. If you can find an appropriate template, feel free to use and customize it.
2. Type the following information on the cover of the invitation: **Act II Theater's Fifth Annual Fashion Show**. Add graphics, watermarks, lines, borders, symbols, or other enhancements to the invitation cover (see Figure U3.5A for a sample solution).
3. Save the completed cover with the name **U3-PA05-InvitationCover**.
4. Print and then close **U3-PA05-InvitationCover.docx**.
5. Use the Word table feature to create the inside of the invitation. Type the following information on the inside of the invitation:
   > **Please join us for the fifth annual Fashion Show fund-raising event for Act II Theater, Friday, May 8.**
   > **Benaroya Hall, 300 Connor Street**
   > **Social hour: 6:30 to 7:30 p.m.**
   > **Fashion show: 7:30 to 8:30 p.m.**
   > **All proceeds fund the youth community theater project.**
6. Add graphics, watermarks, lines, borders, symbols, or other enhancements to the inside of the invitation (see Figure U3.5B for a sample solution).
7. Save the completed invitation with the name **U3-PA05-InvitationInside**.
8. Print and then close **U3-PA05-InvitationInside.docx**.

DTP CHALLENGE

Take your skills to the next level by completing this more challenging assessment.

Assessment U3.6   Create a Virtual Office Resource Guide

1. Create a resource guide for a virtual office. Research information on helpful websites, commercial printers, computer repair companies, office supply companies, airports, limousine or taxi companies, local conference centers (hotels with conference room availability), restaurants for business meetings, community clubs or organizations for entrepreneurs, community college virtual office courses, temporary office employment companies, and any other resources you think would be valuable to a person operating a company from home.
2. Format the resource information in either a manual or booklet format. ***Hint: Use the 2 pages per sheet or book fold features to format the manual or booklet***.
3. Allow enough space to add additional resources to your document in the future.
4. Use appropriate graphics, fonts, tables, footers, and so on.
5. Use styles to reinforce consistency in the design.
6. Save the document with the name **U3-PA06-VirtualResourceGuide**.
7. Print and then close **U3-PA06-VirtualResourceGuide.docx**.

A

Cover of Invitation

B

Inside of Invitation

UNIT 4

Producing Web Pages, Microsoft Publisher Publications, and PowerPoint Presentations

Creating Web Pages and Forms

Performance Objectives

Upon successful completion of Chapter 11, you will be able to:

- Understand Internet and intranet terminology
- Apply basic desktop publishing concepts to the layout and design of a web page
- Use the *Document Location* text box to access the Internet and other files
- Create a web page with bookmarks and hyperlinks
- Create forms using content controls and legacy tools
- Save and protect a form as a template

Desktop Publishing Terms

hyperlink	Internet Service	storyboard	World Wide Web
Hypertext Transfer	Provider (ISP)	Uniform Resource	XML
Protocol (HTTP)	intranet	Locator (URL)	
Internet	round-trip	web page	

Word Features Used

bookmarks	DEVELOPER tab	hyperlinks	tables
bullets	*Document Location*	legacy tools	templates
content controls	text box	page color	themes
content control	images	restrict editing	Web Layout view
properties	fill effects	split cells	Web Page Preview
design mode	form fields		

Note: Before beginning computer exercises for this chapter, copy to your storage medium the Chapter11 folder from the CD that accompanies this textbook and then make Chapter11 the active folder. Remember to substitute for graphics that may no longer be available.

Understanding and Accessing Web Pages

web page

A computer file created in HTML and viewed with a web browser

A *web page* is a computer file containing information in the form of text or graphics along with commands written in Hypertext Markup Language (HTML). Once a web page has been created, it can be placed on a server to be accessed by anyone on the Internet. A collection of web pages creates a *website*.

website

A collection of web pages

Word 2013 can save a document as a web page by converting it into an HTML file, which is a type of file that can be published on the Internet. A web browser such as Microsoft Internet Explorer, Mozilla Firefox, or Google Chrome can read the HTML code and display the text and graphics in the web page. Although Word 2013 is a viable program for creating web pages, professional web designers usually choose to use applications such as Microsoft Expression Web or Adobe Dreamweaver, especially if the website will have several pages and complex linking requirements.

A web page created in Word is basically the same as a regular document in terms of typing, formatting, and layout. However, a few Word features such as passwords, headers and footers, and columns do not transfer when you save in HTML format. Most Word documents to be converted into web pages are created in table format. The table structure provides good boundary lines for text and images.

Internet

Worldwide network of computers connected together to share information

Understanding Internet and Intranet Terminology

The *Internet* is a worldwide network of commercial, educational, governmental, and personal computers connected together for the purpose of sharing information. The *World Wide Web* (often called the Web) is the most commonly used application on the Internet and is a set of standards and protocols used to access information available on the Internet. An *intranet* is an "internal Internet" within an organization that uses the same web technology and tools as the Internet and is also used to share information. Intranets are usually only accessible to the members of an organization. An intranet may provide employees with online access to reference material, job postings, phone and address lists, company policies and procedures, enrollment in and updates on benefit plans, company newsletters, and other human resources information.

World Wide Web

A set of standards and protocols used to access information on the Internet, often called the Web

intranet

An "internal Internet" within an organization that uses Internet technology and tools

Throughout this chapter, you will simulate creating web pages for both the Internet and an organization's intranet. These web pages will be saved as HTML files to a flash drive or hard drive. You will view each web page with the Internet Explorer web browser in read-only view.

Uniform Resource Locator (URL)

The address used to identify locations on the Internet

Accessing Web Pages Using URLs

A *Uniform Resource Locator* (*URL*) is used to identify a location on the Internet. A URL is the address that you enter to access a web page or website. An example of a URL is http://www.microsoft.com. The first part of the URL, *http://*, identifies the protocol. The letters *http* stand for *Hypertext Transfer Protocol*, which is one of the protocols or languages used to transfer data within the Web. The colon and slashes separate the protocol from the server name. The server name is the second component of the URL—for example, in http://www.microsoft.com, the server name is identified as www.microsoft. The last part of the URL specifies the domain to which the server belongs—for example, .com refers to "commercial," .edu refers to "educational," .gov refers to "government," and .mil refers to "military." If the protocol displays with an *s* in the acronym https://, the website is thought to be secured.

Hypertext Transfer Protocol (HTTP)

One of the languages used to transfer data within the World Wide Web

If you know the URL for a specific website and want to visit that site, type the URL in the Address bar in your browser. The home page is the starting point for viewing any website. From the home page, you can access other pages within the website or jump to other websites. You do this by clicking hyperlinks that are embedded in the web pages. A *hyperlink* is text or a graphic that you click to go to a file, a location in a file, a web page on the Internet, or a web page on an intranet. Move the mouse pointer over a hyperlink and the mouse pointer becomes a hand. This is one method for determining if something is a hyperlink. Most pages contain a variety of hyperlinks. Using these links, you can move quickly to the content you want to view. Later in this chapter, you will learn how to include hyperlinks within a web page you create in Word.

hyperlink

Text or a graphic in a web page that will connect you to other pages or websites in different locations

Accessing Web Pages Using the *Document Location* Text Box

Besides accessing websites from your browser, you can also access websites from within Word by using the *Document Location* text box. To add the *Document Location* text box to the Quick Access toolbar, complete the following steps:

1. Click the Customize Quick Access Toolbar button that displays at the right side of the Quick Access toolbar and then click *More Commands*.
2. With *Quick Access Toolbar* selected in the left panel, click the down-pointing arrow at the right of the *Choose commands from* option box and then click *All Commands*.
3. Scroll down the list box, click *Document Location*, and then click the Add button as shown in Figure 11.1.
4. Click OK to close the dialog box.

After the *Document Location* text box has been added to the Quick Access toolbar, it will display as shown in Figure 11.2. To access other files and websites without leaving your open document, you can type a URL in the *Document Location* text box or click the down-pointing arrow next to the text box and click an option at the drop-down list, and then press Enter to connect to the desired destination.

Figure 11.1 Using the Word Options Dialog Box to Customize the Quick Access Toolbar

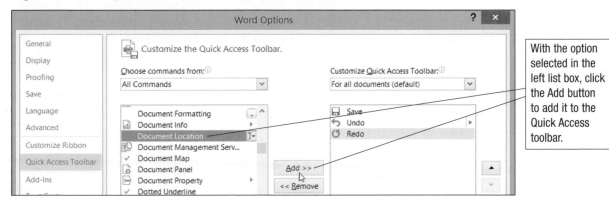

With the option selected in the left list box, click the Add button to add it to the Quick Access toolbar.

Figure 11.2 Using the *Document Location* Text Box

Type the URL or desired document location and then press Enter.

Planning and Designing a Web Page

Like any other document you create in Word, web pages require careful planning and design. While many of the same visual design principles that apply to printed documents also apply to web pages, there are a few other, more specialized, design tips to keep in mind.

Using Design Tips When Creating Web Pages

As you plan your web page, consider the following design tips:

DTP POINTER>

Remember that just because your web page looks good in one browser doesn't mean that it will look good in all browsers.

storyboard

A diagram or blueprint that defines the elements that appear on each web page and shows how pages are interrelated.

DTP POINTER>

Too many graphics or large graphics can slow down your web page.

- Determine the goal of your website and continually evaluate your page to make sure you are accomplishing your goal.
- Identify and focus on your intended audience.
- Review and critique specific aspects of other web pages.
- Determine an appropriate horizontal width for the web page so that users don't have to scroll horizontally.
- Do not overuse italics or bold.
- Determine elements to be emphasized. Keep the design simple. Use white space effectively.
- Be consistent with hyperlinks so that visitors know where they are, where they came from, and where they can go.
- Create a ***storyboard***, which is a diagram or blueprint that defines the elements that appear on each web page and shows how pages are interrelated.
- If using animated graphics, keep them simple so as not to annoy your reader.
- Make sure your page fits within a standard browser window (1024 × 768 pixels).
- Do not use large graphics that take forever to download.
- Use graphics that relate to the content and do not distract from the message.
- Use clean and clear navigation.
- Maintain a consistent color scheme. (Consider using predesigned themes.)
- Keep the background simple, making sure the text can be seen clearly. Make sure there is enough contrast between the text and background.
- Avoid small text and all caps.
- If you include bulleted lists, make sure each one includes at least two items. Do not use more than two levels of bullets. Use consistent wording in bulleted text.
- Keep charts and graphs simple. The most effective graphs are pie charts with three or four slices and column charts with three or four columns.
- Design your site so that it is accessible by individuals who may have hearing or visual impairments. For the visually impaired, consider increasing the text size, providing more text contrast, and allowing keyboard shortcuts for navigation. For the hearing impaired, consider adding a script for any audio clips on the website.
- Remember that a web page is often the first impression you are giving the world about your product or yourself. Offering a poorly designed web page can be worse for your business than having none at all.
- Include a plan for maintaining your website and keeping it current.

Planning Your Web Page

Consider using a thumbnail sketch to organize your page layout before actually creating it. Include space for text, photographs, graphics, headlines, ruled lines, and so on. Instead of including everything on one huge home page, use hyperlinks to other pages.

Remember that the front door of a website is its home page. This page should contain elements to achieve the goals an organization (or individual) has set for the website. Understand what your goals are before you design the site. Are you creating a website on an intranet to share information among employees or a web page on the Internet to market a product or service? Know your budget before starting. There are things you can do on any budget, but some things (such as videos and animation) may cost more than you can afford.

You may want to create a nameplate or banner to display a logo and company name in an interesting way. Include your company logo to reinforce your company's identity. The site should also include a variety of ways to contact the company such as an address, telephone number, email address, and fax number.

Graphics are probably the simplest way to make your web page look interesting. Be sure to choose a graphic that is appropriate to the subject of the page. Animation, video, and words that scroll across the screen are eye-catching devices that can entice your audience to return to your website, but they can take a while to load. Make sure the graphics, animations, and/or videos you choose do not detract from the user friendliness of your site.

◀ DTP POINTER

Create a folder to save your web page.

◀ DTP POINTER

Use a company logo to reinforce company recognition.

Previewing in Web Layout View and Web Page Preview

To begin building from a blank web page, start a new document in Word and then switch to Web Layout view. To do this, click the VIEW tab and then click the Web Layout button in the Views group or click the Web Layout button in the view area on the Status bar. In Web Layout view, you can view the page similar to how it will display on a web page.

However, if you need more realism, you may want to access Web Page Preview to examine the page in an actual web browser. Click the Web Page Preview button on the Quick Access toolbar to open the current Word document in your favorite browser. (If the Web Page Preview button does not display on the Quick Access toolbar, add it by completing similar steps to those you used for adding the *Document Location* text box.)

Web Layout

Web Page Preview

Using Tables in Web Page Design

Tables provide a good framework for a web page. You can control where text, pictures, and white space display in a web page by using cells in a table. Empty cells are often used to visually separate table information. When inserting pictures inside a cell, make sure the text wrapping has been set to *In Line With Text* so that you can use the alignment buttons on the TABLE TOOLS FORMAT tab.

When you use a table to format the page, you will generally apply the *No Border* option (using the Borders button in the Borders group on the TABLE TOOLS DESIGN tab) so that viewers do not see the borders. In Web Layout view, the table structure will display with light gray gridlines as shown in Figure 11.3 on page 494.

Figure 11.3 Viewing a Table Structure in Web Layout View

Caring4Pets Animal Clinic	6340 Main Street Lisle, IL 60532 caring4pets@emcp.net Office Phone: (630) 555-8874 Office Fax: (630) 555-9841

You are the most important person in your pet's life; our goal is to support you in keeping your pets happy and healthy.

| General Information:
    Services
    Staff Members

Cat Care Info
Dog Care Info
Other Pets
Client Service Survey | Business Hours:

Monday:
Tuesday:
Wednesday:
Thursday:
Friday:
Saturday:
Sunday: |

7:30 a.m.–7:00 p.m.
7:30 a.m.–7:00 p.m.
7:30 a.m.–7:00 p.m.
7:30 a.m.–7:00 p.m.
7:30 a.m.–7:00 p.m.
8:00 a.m.–2:30 p.m.
Closed |
| Animals treated:
Cats, Dogs, Exotics | Travel Directions:
View Google Maps | |

Using Other Office Applications to Create Web Pages

A web page can be created using each of the applications in Office 2013. Excel web pages are useful when you want to use the worksheet formatting, calculation, and data analysis capabilities in creating electronic order forms, demographic information, testing or survey information, or a cost comparison. The Excel Save As dialog box looks similar to the Word Save As dialog box. You will have an option to save the worksheet in HTML or with the *XML* format, which is a flexible format recommended if the page will be published and if the data are meant to be manipulated or acted on by other programs and scripts. Keep in mind that PowerPoint and Access can also be used in a website. All of these Office files can be customized to reinforce a uniform web page design by using consistent themes, logos, fonts, colors, and images.

In Exercise 11.1, you will visit a website by typing the URL in the *Document Location* text box that you added to the Quick Access toolbar in Word. This opens the Internet Explorer browser window and displays the home page for the website. The Internet Explorer browser window contains many features similar to the Word window. As you view each of the websites listed in the exercise, pay attention to their layout and design.

XML

A language format that marks and organizes content to allow it to be easily read on different computer platforms; short for Extensible Markup Language

1. Make sure you are connected to the Internet. Start Word and then open a blank Word document.
2. Add the *Document Location* text box and the Web Page Preview button (if it was not added in Chapter 7) to the Quick Access toolbar by completing the following steps:

   a. Click the Customize Quick Access Toolbar button that displays at the right side of the Quick Access toolbar and then click *More Commands* at the drop-down list.
   b. At the Word Options dialog box with *Quick Access Toolbar* selected in the left panel, click the down-pointing arrow at the right of the *Choose commands from* option box and then click *All Commands*.
   c. Scroll down the list box on the left, click *Document Location,* and then click the Add button.
   d. Scroll down the list box, click *Web Page Preview*, and then click the Add button.
   e. Click OK to close the dialog box.
3. Explore several locations on the Internet from within Word by completing the following steps:
   a. Click in the *Document Location* text box located on the Quick Access toolbar.
   b. Type **www.newmountainlearning.com** and then press Enter.

   Step
   3b

   c. The New Mountain Learning home page will display similar to the image shown below. Notice that the layout is fairly simple, which makes it easy to understand and use. Each company logo contains a link to one of the five divisions of New Mountain Learning. The overall look of the page is simple and free of clutter.
   d. Close the web page by clicking the Close button in the upper right corner of the web browser.

e. In Word, click in the *Document Location* text box, type **www.cityofchicago.org**, and then press Enter.
f. Scroll down the home page for the city of Chicago, studying the layout and design elements.
g. Click in the Address bar in Internet Explorer (located in the upper left corner of the screen), type **www.nps.gov/yell**, and then press Enter. The Yellowstone National Park home page should display.
h. Click the <u>Support Your Park</u> hyperlink that displays in the left navigation pane. Review the information displayed on this page.
i. Close the Yellowstone National Park web page

Creating a Web Page

DTP POINTER❯

Choose a design and theme that match the content of your web page.

Now that you have spent some time viewing various web pages, you are ready to begin creating your own. While adding interesting features and design elements may be one of the most fun parts of creating a web page, the most important thing is to make sure that it works. The following sections will teach you how to successfully create the basic elements of a web page in Word.

Saving a Word Document as a Web Page

To save a Word document as a web page, follow the steps you normally would to save a document, but at the Save As dialog box, click the down-pointing arrow at the right of the *Save as type* option box and then select one of the following Web formats:

- Click the *Single File Web Page (*.mht;*mhtml)* option when you are planning to send the web page via email. This format is easy to download and manipulate.

round-trip

To convert an HTML file back to a Word document

- Click the *Web Page (*.htm;*.html)* option when you are planning to **round-trip** the page between Word and a web browser. That is, if you save a Word document in HTML, you can later reopen the HTML file and convert it back to a Word document. This format is not recommended for emailing the page to others.

- Click the *Web Page, Filtered (*.htm;*.html)* format option when you need the resulting saved file to be plain HTML. Use this format if you intend to integrate the page into a larger website that was created with Dreamweaver or another web design program. Do not use this format if you plan to edit the page in Word in the future.

In this chapter, you will be saving your web pages to your Chapter11 folder. If you want your page to be available on the Internet, you must have an *Internet Service Provider (ISP)* place it on a server. These Web hosting services usually charge a monthly or annual fee, but they can be relatively inexpensive depending on your needs. Some schools or colleges allow students space on a server to host student-created web pages.

Internet Service Provider (ISP)

A hosting service that places web pages on a server so they are viewable from the Internet

Creating and Editing Hyperlinks

The websites you visited in Exercise 11.1 included hyperlinks to connect you to other web pages or websites. You can create hyperlinks in your document that a reader can click to jump to a web page, a different location in the document, a different Word document, or a file created in a different application, such as an Excel workbook. The destination document or file you create can be saved on your hard drive, on your organization's network (intranet), or on the Internet. You can create hyperlinks from selected text or graphic objects such as buttons and pictures. By default, hyperlink text displays in blue and is underlined. When you return to the document after following a hyperlink, the hyperlink text color changes. You do not have to be connected to the Internet to use hyperlinks between Word documents.

To create a hyperlink from text in a Word document, select the text, click the INSERT tab, and then click the Hyperlink button in the Links group. At the Insert Hyperlink dialog box, shown in Figure 11.4, you can do the following:

Hyperlink

- Specify the type of location to which your hyperlink will lead—*Existing File or Web Page, Place in This Document, Create New Document*, or *E-mail Address*.
- Type a web URL to which you want the text to link in the *Address* text box.
- Use the folder list in the *Look in* option box drop-down list to browse for a file.
- Select the place in the current document to which you want to link. Note that if you want to link to any location other than the top of the page, you will need to create bookmarks or apply heading styles within the document before doing this. You will learn about creating bookmarks in the next section.
- Add a screen tip.

If you include an email address anywhere on your web page, Word will automatically create a hyperlink that opens a new, blank email message in the user's default email program when he or she clicks it.

To edit an existing hyperlink, right-click the hyperlink and then click *Edit Hyperlink* at the shortcut menu. Other options available in this menu are *Select Hyperlink, Open Hyperlink, Copy Hyperlink*, and *Remove Hyperlink*. Clicking *Remove Hyperlink* removes the link to the URL from the text or image but does not delete the text or image itself.

Figure 11.4 Investigating the Insert Hyperlink Dialog Box

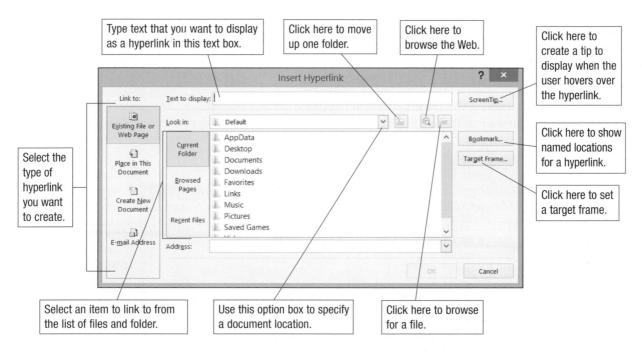

Creating Bookmarks

Creating a bookmark in Word is similar to folding down the corner of a page in a book to mark the place where you stopped reading. Bookmarks save locations that you want to easily be able to return to. Complete the following steps to create a bookmark in Word:

Bookmark

1. Position the insertion point or select the text at the location where you want to insert a bookmark.
2. Click the INSERT tab and then click the Bookmark button in the Links group.
3. At the Bookmark dialog box, shown in Figure 11.5, type a name for the bookmark in the *Bookmark name* text box. (Spaces are not allowed in bookmark names.)
4. Click the Add button.

Once you have created a bookmark, you can access that location in the document by clicking the Bookmark button to open the Bookmark dialog box, clicking the bookmark in the list box, and then clicking the Go To button. Bookmarks are helpful when creating hyperlinks within a document as well. When you click the *Place in This Document* option in the left panel of the Insert Hyperlink dialog box, all of the bookmarks you have created will display. Click a bookmark name to create a hyperlink to it from another location in the document.

Adding Bullets and Horizontal Lines to a Web Page

You can add bullets to your web page document by clicking the Bullets button on the HOME tab. You can also change regular bullets to special graphical bullets for your web page. To do this, click the Bullets button arrow and then click *Define New Bullet* at the drop-down gallery. At the Define New Bullet dialog box, click the Picture button. At the Insert Pictures window, click the Browse button to locate a file on your computer or type a search phrase in the *Office.com Clip Art* text box to search for a clip art image or illustration.

You can use horizontal or vertical ruled lines to separate the sections of a web page. Insert a horizontal line by selecting the text you want to appear immediately above the line, clicking the Borders button arrow in the Paragraph group on the HOME tab, and then clicking *Horizontal Line* at the drop-down gallery. If the text is located inside a table, you can insert a horizontal line in a table by clicking the Borders button arrow in the Borders group on the TABLE TOOLS DESIGN tab and then clicking *Horizontal Line* at the drop-down gallery. Complete similar steps to insert vertical lines at the desired locations.

Figure 11.5 Using the Bookmark Dialog Box

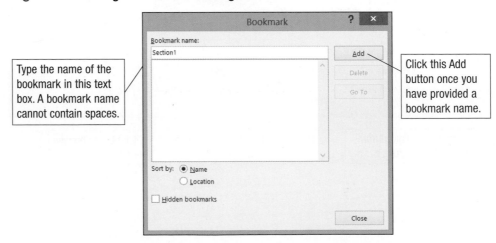

Adding Background Color to a Web Page

Consider adding background colors and other effects to make your documents more visually appealing to read online. To add a background color to your web page, click the DESIGN tab, click the Page Color button in the Page Background group, and then choose a color from the drop-down gallery or click *More Colors* if the color you want is not available in the *Theme Colors* or *Standard Colors* sections. To add a design or texture to the background of your page, click *Fill Effects* at the drop-down gallery. At the Fill Effects dialog box, shown in Figure 11.6, choose the desired gradient and color, texture, pattern, or picture background fill.

Page Color

◀DTP POINTER
Enhance your document with a background

Printing a Background from Your Browser

To print a web page background from Microsoft Internet Explorer, click the Print button arrow on the Command bar and then click *Page setup*. (If the Command bar is not visible, right-click in a blank area toward the top of the Internet Explorer window and then click *Command bar* at the shortcut menu.) At the Page Setup dialog box, shown in Figure 11.7 on page 500, click in the *Print Background Colors and Images* check box to insert a check mark. Click OK to close the dialog box. Note that changing these settings means that the page background will print from Internet Explorer, not from Word. For instructions on printing a page background from Word, see Chapter 8.

Figure 11.6 Adding a Background Fill Effect Using the Fill Effects Dialog Box

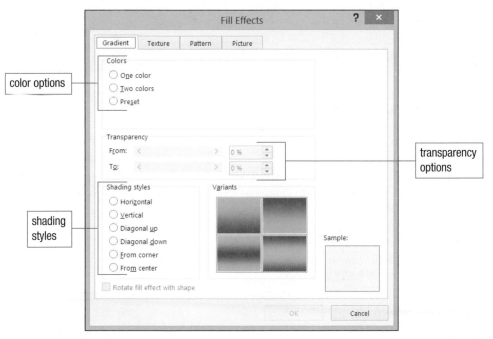

Figure 11.7 Printing a Web Page Background from Internet Explorer

Insert a check mark in this check box to print the background of the web page.

Page Setup

Paper Options
Page Size:
Letter

● Portrait   ○ Landscape
☑ Print Background Colors and Images
☑ Enable Shrink-to-Fit

Margins (inches)
Left: 0.75
Right: 0.75
Top: 0.75
Bottom: 0.75

Headers and Footers
Header:
Title

-Empty-

Page # of total pages

Footer:
URL

-Empty-

Date in short format

Change font

OK   Cancel

In Exercise 11.2, you will use the knowledge of web pages that you have gained so far in this chapter to create a personal home page. Figure 11.8 on page 504 shows a sample solution for this exercise—your result will appear differently.

Exercise 11.2 Creating a Personal Home Page

PORTFOLIO

1. At a blank document, change the margins to *Narrow* and then apply the Dividend theme.
2. Click the VIEW tab and then click the Web Layout button in the Views group.
3. Insert a table with one column and seven rows.
4. Select the table and then remove the borders by clicking the Borders button arrow in the Borders group on the TABLE TOOLS DESIGN tab and then clicking *No Border* at the drop-down gallery. ***Hint: Make sure table gridlines are turned on so you can see each cell of the table.***
5. Position the insertion point in the first cell and then split the cell by completing the following steps:
   a. Click the TABLE TOOLS LAYOUT tab.
   b. Click the Split Cells button in the Merge group.
   c. At the Split Cells dialog box, make sure *2* displays in the *Number of columns* measurement box and *1* displays in the *Number of rows* measurement box, and then click OK.
6. Position the insertion point in the first cell and then insert an image of yourself, or an image similar to the one shown in Figure 11.8 on page 504. Change the size of the image so that it is approximately 2 inches in height, similar to what is shown in Figure 11.8.
7. With the image selected, make sure the text wrapping is set to *In Line with Text.*

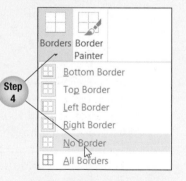

Step 4

Borders Border Painter

Bottom Border
Top Border
Left Border
Right Border
No Border
All Borders

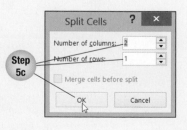

Step 5c

Split Cells   ? ×

Number of columns: 2
Number of rows: 1

☐ Merge cells before split

OK   Cancel

8. With the image still selected, click the HOME tab and then click the Center button in the Paragraph group.

9. Click the PICTURE TOOLS FORMAT tab and then click the *Simple Frame, White* option in the Picture Styles gallery.

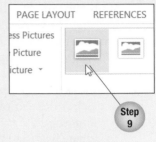

10. Position the insertion point in the second cell in the first row and then add your name by completing the following steps:
    a. Type your first and last names.
    b. Select your name and then increase the font size, change the font color, apply bold formatting, and center the text both horizontally and vertically in the cell. (Refer to Figure 11.8.)

11. Click the DESIGN tab, click the Page Color button in the Page Background group, and then click a color at the drop-down gallery. You can also click *Fill Effects* at the drop-down gallery to display the Fill Effects dialog box, where you can select a color or fill effect that complements the image you selected for your page.

12. Position the insertion point in the row below your image, press Enter and then change the style to a quote style of your choosing. ***Hint: Use the options in the Styles gallery on the HOME tab.***

13. If necessary, click the Center button in the Paragraph group on the HOME tab, type a sentence about yourself or type a favorite quote, and then press Enter.

14. With the insertion point positioned one space after the sentence or quote in the second row, insert a horizontal line below the sentence or quote by clicking the Borders button arrow in the Paragraph group and then clicking *Horizontal Line* at the drop-down list.

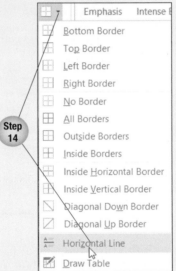

15. Position the insertion point in the row below the sentence or quote and then press Enter. Type **Experience | Education | Contact** and then press Enter. ***Hint: Press Shift + Backslash to insert the bar character (|).***

16. Select the text *Experience | Education | Contact*, apply a desired style, and then center the text if necessary.

17. Position the insertion point in the next (fourth) row, type **Professional Experience**, and then press Enter. Apply a desired heading style and alignment to the text *Professional Experience*.

18. Position the insertion point on the blank line below the *Professional Experience* subhead in the fourth row and then type a list highlighting your professional experience, pressing Enter after each item in the list, and pressing Enter twice after the last item. ***Hint: Figure 11.8 contains sample text.***

19. Select the list and then apply bullets of your choosing. ***Hint: Try using picture bullets.***

20. Position your insertion point in the next (fifth) row, type **Educational Background**, and then press Enter. Apply the same heading style to the text *Educational Background* that you applied to the text *Professional Experience*.

21. Type information about your educational background, pressing Enter after each item in the list and then pressing Enter twice after the last item.

22. With the insertion point positioned a double-space below the last item in the *Educational Background* list, insert a horizontal line.

23. Select the list you typed in Step 21 and then apply the same style of bullets you used in Step 19.

24. Position the insertion point in the next (sixth) row, type **Contact**, and then press Enter. Apply the same heading style to the text *Contact* that you applied to the headings *Professional Experience* and *Educational Background*.

25. Type your contact information. ***Hint: Press Ctrl + Tab to insert default tabs within the cell. Align the contact information using tabs, not spaces.***

26. Insert hyperlinks to employers, colleges, and so on, where appropriate, by completing the following steps:

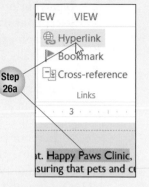

   a. Select the text of the first business or organization in the *Professional Experience* section, click the INSERT tab, and then click the Hyperlink button in the Links group.

   b. At the Insert Hyperlink dialog box, click the Existing File or Web Page button in the *Link to* section.

   c. Type the complete web address of the business or company in the *Address* text box.

   d. Click the ScreenTip button in the upper right corner of the Insert Hyperlink dialog box.

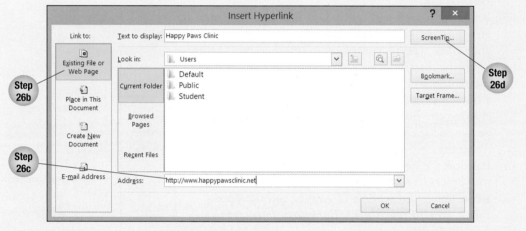

   e. Type the company or organization name in the *ScreenTip text* text box. Click OK twice. ***Hint: Test the link by holding down the Ctrl key and clicking the hyperlink.***

   f. Continue creating hyperlinks to employers, colleges, and so forth, by following steps similar to Steps 26a through 26e.

27. Insert a bookmark at the top of the page by completing the following steps:

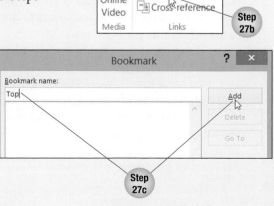

   a. Select the image at the top of the page.

   b. Click the Bookmark button in the Links group on the INSERT tab.

   c. At the Bookmark dialog box, type **Top** in the *Bookmark name* text box and then click the Add button.

28. Position the insertion point in the last (seventh) row of the table, press Enter, type **Top of Page**, press Enter again, and then insert a horizontal line. Select the text *Top of Page* and then change the paragraph alignment to center.

29. Insert hyperlinks in your web page by completing the following steps:
    a. Select the text *Experience* in the third row of the table (do not include the space after the word) and then click the Hyperlink button in the Links group on the INSERT tab.
    b. At the Insert Hyperlink dialog box, click the Place in This Document button in the *Link to* section.
    c. Click the *Professional Experience* heading in the *Select a place in this document* list box.
    d. Click OK.

e. Follow the steps above to hyperlink the headings *Educational Background* and *Contact* to the appropriate places in the document.
f. Select the text *Top of Page* located in the bottom row of the table and then click the Hyperlink button.
g. At the Insert Hyperlink dialog box, click the bookmark name *Top* and then click OK.

30. Save the document by completing the following steps:
    a. Press F12.
    b. At the Save As dialog box, click the *Save as type* option box arrow and then click *Single File Web Page (*.mht; *.mhtml)* at the drop-down list.
    c. Click in the *File name* text box and then type **C11-E02-MyWebPage**.
    d. Navigate to your Chapter11 folder and then click the Save button. ***Hint: If you get a message about some features not being supported by Web browsers, click Continue.***

31. Close **C11-E02-MyWebPage.mht**.

32. Open File Explorer, navigate to your Chapter11 folder, and then double-click **C11-E02-MyWebPage.mht**. This will open the web page in Internet Explorer. Print the page by pressing Ctrl + P and then clicking the Print button at the Print dialog box. ***Hint: Make sure the background color prints.***

33. Close Internet Explorer.

Figure 11.8 Sample Solution for Exercise 11.2

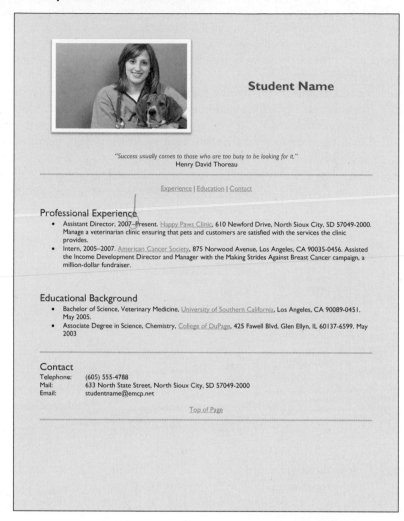

Student Name

"Success usually comes to those who are too busy to be looking for it."
Henry David Thoreau

Experience | Education | Contact

Professional Experience
- Assistant Director, 2007–Present. Happy Paws Clinic, 610 Newford Drive, North Sioux City, SD 57049-2000. Manage a veterinarian clinic ensuring that pets and customers are satisfied with the services the clinic provides.
- Intern, 2005–2007. American Cancer Society, 875 Norwood Avenue, Los Angeles, CA 90035-0456. Assisted the Income Development Director and Manager with the Making Strides Against Breast Cancer campaign, a million-dollar fundraiser.

Educational Background
- Bachelor of Science, Veterinary Medicine, University of Southern California, Los Angeles, CA 90089-0451. May 2005.
- Associate Degree in Science, Chemistry, College of DuPage, 425 Fawell Blvd, Glen Ellyn, IL 60137-6599. May 2003

Contact
Telephone: (605) 555-4788
Mail: 633 North State Street, North Sioux City, SD 57049-2000
Email: studentname@emcp.net

Top of Page

Creating a Form Using Content Controls and Legacy Tools

A form is a protected document that includes designated areas into which users enter specific data. Forms can be filled out electronically, or they can be printed and completed using a hard copy. Two kinds of fields can be entered into forms created in Word—the Word 2013 content controls and the legacy tools that have been carried over from earlier versions of Word.

Recall from Chapter 4 that content controls are fields within the form document where the person completing the form either enters text or selects information from a drop-down box, places a check mark in a check box, or picks a date. If you decide to insert content controls into your form, keep in mind that you can add instructional text (e.g., *Type your full name here.*) in a content control. To do this, select the content control and then type the text you want the content control to display.

Legacy tools are similar to content controls, but there are only three types of legacy form fields—Text Form Field, Checkbox Form Field, and Drop-down Form Field. Three additional tools are available, but they serve other purposes. Use the Legacy Tools button in the Controls group on the DEVELOPER tab to access legacy tools.

Legacy Tools

When you insert content controls or legacy tools, you must first turn on design mode. Click the DEVELOPER tab and then click the Design Mode button to make it active. Click the button again to turn design mode off.

Using Content Controls and Legacy Tools

Content controls in Word 2013 have great capabilities, but they also have a few drawbacks. For one, content controls do not work in versions of Word earlier than 2007. You can combine content controls and legacy form fields in a single form, but be aware that the content controls and legacy fields work very differently. For instance, you can use the Tab key to advance from one legacy field to the next, but you must use the mouse and click to activate a content control. You may want to stick to one type of field if you only want to save the data or if the form will be filled out by people using earlier versions of Word.

Advantages of using content controls include the following:

- More content controls are available than legacy tools.
- The document does not have to be protected for the form to function properly if completed in Word.
- Content controls can be set so that they cannot be deleted.
- Content controls are useful in connecting to XML data sources.

Disadvantages of using content controls include the following:

- A macro cannot be linked to a content control.
- Predefined number formats are not available.
- Content controls cannot perform calculations.
- The length of an entry cannot be limited.

Designing the Form

When designing your form, consider first where the fixed text should be placed on the page. Consider typing the label followed by a colon and then the placeholder text for the fill-in data. This will help you visualize the layout of the form. As an alternative, you may want to use tabs to align the input data. Use a table as the underlying structure for the labels and fill-in data as shown in Figure 11.9. The table may be the most efficient solution for organizing the information.

Figure 11.9 Visualizing the Layout of a Form

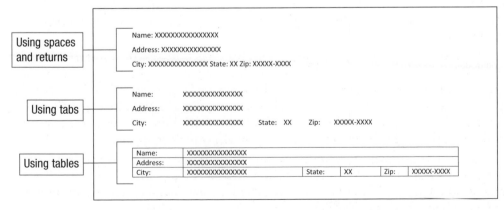

After determining the basic layout of your form, consider arranging the fields in logical groups, using labels that are easy to understand, placing fields in expected order, varying the types of fields, and leaving enough space for user input.

Protecting the Form

Restrict Editing

If you want users to enter information in the form template but not edit the template itself, then protecting the template is important. To do this, click the Restrict Editing button in the Protect group on the DEVELOPER tab. This displays the Restrict Editing task pane as shown in Figure 11.10. At this task pane, click in the *Allow only this type of editing in the document* check box to insert a check mark. Click the down-pointing arrow at the right side of the option box in the *Editing restrictions* section and then click *Filling in forms* at the drop-down list. Click the Yes, Start Enforcing Protection button in the task pane. You will be prompted to type a password; however, adding one to the protected template is not necessary. If you do not want to include a password, click OK without typing a password.

With or without a password, a legacy form will not work properly unless it is protected. When unprotected, the form treats the fields as static text, and you cannot enter anything into them. On a protected form, you can click in a field or press the Tab key to move from field to field, or use Shift + Tab to move to a previous field.

To unprotect a form, open it and then click the Restrict Editing button in the Protect group on the DEVELOPER tab. At the Restrict Editing task pane, click the Stop Protection button at the bottom of the task pane. If you created a password for the form, you will be required to enter it in order to unprotect the document.

Figure 11.10 Protecting a Form Template

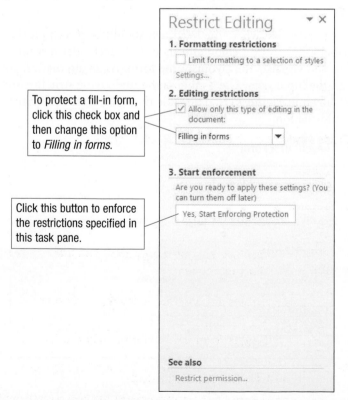

To protect a fill-in form, click this check box and then change this option to *Filling in forms*.

Click this button to enforce the restrictions specified in this task pane.

Determining Which Form Fields or Content Controls to Use

Content controls work in Word 2007, 2010, and 2013 documents and templates. You can apply formatting styles to them, and you can prevent them from being edited or deleted. Nine content controls are available, and they are summarized in Table 11.1.

Legacy form fields are the field types that were available in earlier versions of Word. You can continue to use them in Word 2013, and you must use them for forms saved in the Word 97–2003 formats. Table 11.2 explains each of the form fields.

Table 11.1 Content Controls Available on the DEVELOPER Tab in Word

Control	Icon	Description
Rich Text	Aa	Holds text that can optionally be formatted by the user (bold, italics, etc.).
Plain Text	Aa	Holds plain text that the user cannot format.
Picture		Holds a picture that the user inserts.
Building Block Gallery		Inserts a placeholder from which the user can select a building block.
Check Box		Displays a check box that the user can click to insert a check mark.
Combo Box		Displays a list of values that the user can select; the user can add other values.
Drop-Down List		Displays a list of values; the user cannot add more values.
Date Picker		Displays a calendar from which the user can pick a date.
Repeating Section		Contains other controls and repeats the contents of the control.

Table 11.2 Legacy Form Fields Available on the DEVELOPER Tab in Word

Field	Icon	Description
Text Form Field	abl	Holds text.
Check Box Form Field		Creates an on/off check box.
Drop-Down Form Field		Displays a list of values from which the user can choose.
Insert Frame		Creates a frame that holds static content.
Form Field Shading	a	Toggles form field shading on and off.
Reset Form Fields		Clears all entries in fields.

Filling in a Form

To fill in a form containing legacy form fields, open File Explorer and then open a document based on the template containing the legacy form fields. When you open a document based on the template, the insertion point is automatically inserted in the first form field. Type the information in the form field and then press the Tab key to move to the next field or press Shift + Tab to move to the previous field. To insert a check mark in a check box, press the spacebar or click in the field with the mouse.

Editing a Protected Form

If you want to edit your protected template, do the following:
1. Display the DEVELOPER tab.
2. Click the Restrict Editing button in the Protect group.
3. Click the Stop Protection button at the bottom of the Restrict Editing task pane as shown in Figure 11.11.
4. Close the task pane.
5. Click the Design Mode button in the Controls group to turn this feature on and then add any desired controls or remove any unwanted controls.

Printing a Form

After filling in a form, you can print the form in the normal manner. However, you also have the option to print just the data (not the entire form) or print the form and not the fill-in data. To print just the data in a form, display the Word Options dialog box, click *Advanced* in the left panel, and then click the *Print only the data from a form* in the *When printing this document* section as shown in Figure 11.12.

Figure 11.11 **Editing a Protected Form**

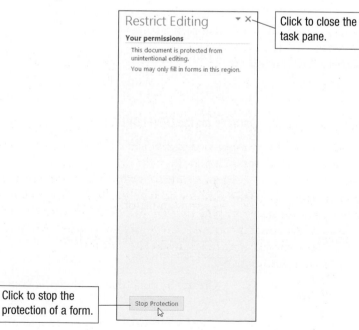

Click to close the task pane.

Click to stop the protection of a form.

Figure 11.12 Printing Data Only

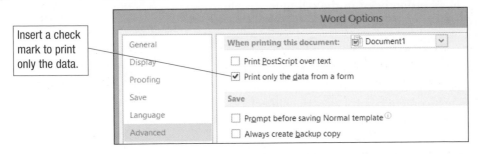

Insert a check mark to print only the data.

In Exercise 11.3, you will create a real estate client information form that contains fields for text such as name, spouse's name, address, and so on. The form will also contain fields with drop-down lists, date pickers, and check boxes. You will be inserting only content controls in this form. You will save the form as a protected template, open File Explorer, open a document based on the template (as described in Chapter 3), and then fill in the form in Word. Pressing the Tab key will not allow you to advance from one content control to the next; you will need to click to enter text in each field. You will also need to click inside the check box that corresponds to your desired response. The form you will create is shown in Figure 11.13 on page 512.

Exercise 11.3 Creating a Form with Content Controls

1. Open **MREFormTemplate.dotx** located in your Chapter11 folder.
2. Add content controls to the form by completing the following steps:

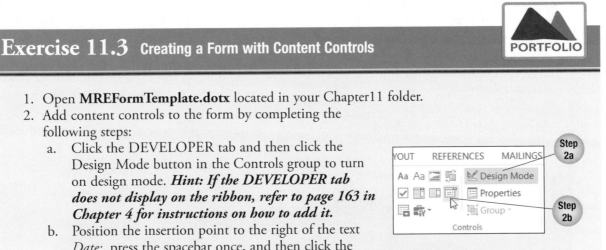

   a. Click the DEVELOPER tab and then click the Design Mode button in the Controls group to turn on design mode. ***Hint: If the DEVELOPER tab does not display on the ribbon, refer to page 163 in Chapter 4 for instructions on how to add it.***
   b. Position the insertion point to the right of the text *Date:*, press the spacebar once, and then click the Date Picker Content Control button in the Controls group. ***Hint: The date field will display a calendar when design mode is off and the field is clicked.***
   c. Position the insertion point to the right of *Name:*, press the spacebar once, and then click the Rich Text Content Control button. ***Hint: Rich text content controls allow the user to apply bold and italics and type multiple paragraphs. Plain text controls limit how much the user can type and do not allow the user to apply formatting to the text.***
   d. Add rich text content controls next to each of the following labels. (Press the spacebar once after each colon and then insert the control.)
      Spouse's name:
      Address:
      Phone:
      Cell:
      Email:

e. Position the insertion point in the cell immediately to the left of the cell containing *Home email* and then insert a check box by clicking the Check Box Content Control button in the Controls group.

f. Insert check box content controls at the left of the remaining labels in the *Preferred method of communication* section, but add a rich text content control after the *Other* label.

g. Insert rich text content controls in both cells in the row below the *Best time to call* cell.

h. Position the insertion point in the cell at the right of *Housing preference* and then click the Drop-Down List Content Control button in the Controls group.

i. Click the Properties button in the Controls group on the DEVELOPER tab.

j. At the Content Control Properties dialog box, type **Housing preference** in the *Title* and *Tag* text boxes and then click the Add button. At the Add Choice dialog box, type **Own** in the *Display Name* text box and then click OK. Click the Add button again, type **Rent**, and then click OK. Click the Add button a third time, type **Lease**, and then click OK. Click OK to close the Content Control Properties dialog box.

k. Insert the following controls next to the labels listed below and type the contents of the drop-down lists as indicated. For each label, type the label text in the *Title* and *Tag* text boxes in the Content Control Properties dialog box, as you did in Step 2j.

Label:	Type of content control:	Type this text to add to list:
Number of bedrooms:	drop-down list	2, 3, 4, 5, 6+
Number of stories:	drop-down list	Ranch, Bi-level, Tri-level, 2-story
Number of baths:	drop-down list	1, 2, 3, 4+
Number of garages:	drop-down list	1, 2, 3, 4
Square footage:	rich text	

Finished basement:	drop-down list	**Yes, No**
Price range in thousands:	drop-down list	**100-220**
		221-350
		351-500
		501-650
		651-800
		801+
Formal living room:	drop-down list	**Yes, No**
Formal dining room:	drop-down list	**Yes, No**

3. In the *Housing financial information* section, insert a check box content control in the cell to the left of the cell containing *Yes* and a check box content control in the cell to the left of the cell containing *No*.

4. Position the insertion point to the right of *Type of financing:*, press the spacebar, and then insert a rich text content control.

5. Position the insertion point to the right of *Mortgage per month:*, press the spacebar, and then insert a rich text content control.

6. Click the Design Mode button in the Controls group on the DEVELOPER tab to turn it off.

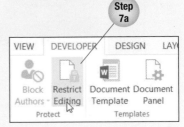

7. Protect the form by completing the following steps:

   a. Click the Restrict Editing button in the Protect group on the DEVELOPER tab.

   b. At the Restrict Editing task pane, click in the *Allow only this type of editing in the document* check box to insert a check mark.

   c. Click the down-pointing arrow at the right side of the option box in the *Editing restrictions* section and then click *Filling in forms* at the drop-down list.

   d. Click the Yes, Start Enforcing Protection button in the task pane.

   e. You will be prompted to type a password; however, it is not necessary to add one to the protected template. Click OK without typing a password.

   f. Close the Restrict Editing task pane.

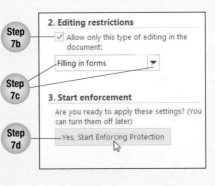

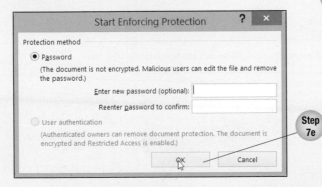

8. Save the form as a template with the name **C11-E03-MREFormTemplate**.

9. Close **C11-E03-MREFormTemplate.dotx**.
10. Using File Explorer, open a document based on **C11-E03-MREFormTemplate.dotx** and then fill in all the data fields with relevant information of your choosing. *Hint: You will need to click inside each content control to fill in the data.*
11. Save the completed form as a Word document (not a template) with the name **C11-E03-CompletedMREForm**.
12. Print and then close **C11-E03-CompletedMREForm.docx**

Figure 11.13 Form Created in Exercise 11.3

MIDWEST REAL ESTATE
1308 Ogden Avenue, Lisle, IL 60532
(630) 555-2313 ❖ midwest@emcp.net ❖ Virtual tours: www.emcp.net/midwest

Real Estate Client Information

Profile

Name: Click here to enter text.	Spouse's name: Click here to enter text.	Date: Click here to enter a date.

Address: Click here to enter text.

Phone: Click here to enter text.	Cell: Click here to enter text.	Email: Click here to enter text.

Preferred method of communication

☐	Home email	☐	Work email	☐	Home phone
☐	Work phone	☐	Cell phone	Other:	Click here to enter text.

Best time to call (include preferred phone numbers)

Click here to enter text.	Click here to enter text.

Housing preferences

Housing preference:	Choose an item.	Number of bedrooms:	Choose an item.
Number of stories:	Choose an item.	Number of baths:	Choose an item.
Number of garages:	Choose an item.	Square footage:	Click here to enter text.
Finished basement:	Choose an item.	Price range in thousands:	Choose an item.
Formal living room:	Choose an item.	Formal dining room:	Choose an item.

Housing financial information

Do you have a prequalified letter?	☐	Yes	☐	No

Type of financing: Click here to enter text.	Mortgage per month: Click here to enter text.

In Exercise 11.3, you created a real estate client information form using content controls. In Exercise 11.4, you will insert legacy form fields in an evaluation form. Your completed form will look like the one shown in Figure 11.14 on page 515.

Exercise 11.4 Creating an Evaluation Form with Legacy Tools

PORTFOLIO

1. Open **CCEvaluationForm.docx** located in your Chapter11 folder.
2. Save the document as a template in your Chapter11 folder with the name **C11-E04-CCEvaluationForm**. *Hint: Make sure the* **Save as type** *option is set to* **Word Template (*.dotx)** *and that the file is saved in your Chapter11 folder.*
3. Create a drop-down list for the Topic section of the form by completing the following steps:
   a. Position the insertion point one space after the text *Topic:*.
   b. Click the DEVELOPER tab.
   c. Click the Design Mode button.
   d. Click the Legacy Tools button and then click the Drop-Down Form Field button.
   e. Click the Properties button in the Controls group.
   f. At the Drop-Down Form Field Options dialog box, type **Getting Organized** in the *Drop-down item* text box and then click the Add button. Type **How Far Is Too Far?** and then click the Add button. Type **Communicate with Confidence**, click the Add button, and then click OK.
4. Create a drop-down list for the Facilities section of the form by completing the following steps:
   a. Position the insertion point one space after the text *Facilities:*.
   b. Click the Legacy Tools button and then click the Drop-Down Form Field button.
   c. Click the Properties button in the Controls group.
   d. At the Drop-Down Form Field Options dialog box, type **Artzen Hall** in the *Drop-down item* text box and then click the Add button. Type **Parks Hall** and then click the Add button. Type **Ross Building**, click the Add button, and then click OK.
5. Insert text fields for entering comments for questions 12 through 14 by completing the following steps:
   a. Position the insertion point in the cell to the right of the twelfth question cell, click the Legacy Tools button, and then click the Text Form Field button.
   b. Position the insertion point in the cell to the right of the thirteenth question cell, click the Legacy Tools button, and then click the Text Form Field button.
   c. Position the insertion point in the cell to the right of the fourteenth question cell, click the Legacy Tools button, and then click the Text Form Field button.

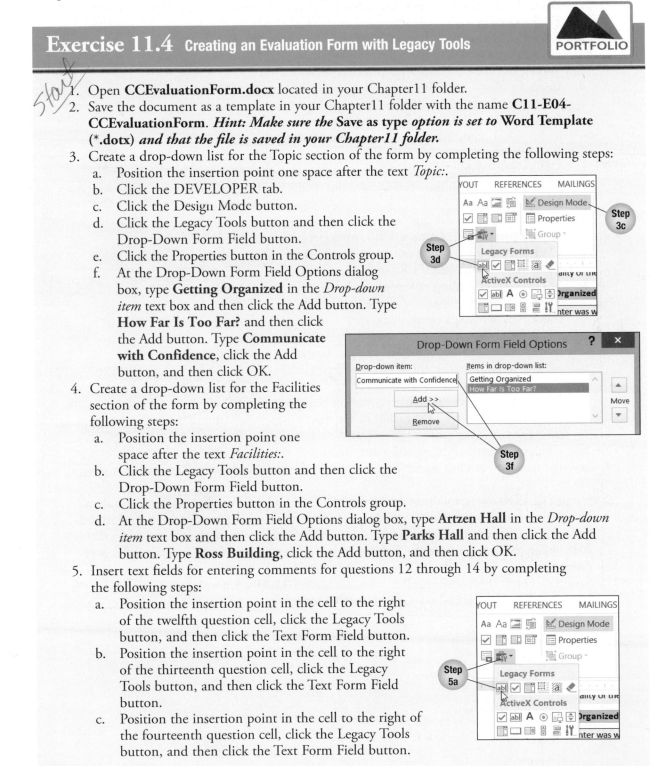

6. Insert check boxes in the Evaluation column, as shown in Figure 11.14, by completing the following steps:
   a. Position the insertion point in the first cell below the heading *Evaluation*.
   b. Click the Legacy Tools button, click the Check Box Form Field button, and then press the spacebar once.
   c. Type **3** and then press the spacebar 10 times.
   d. Insert another Check Box Form Field, press the spacebar once, type **2**, and then press the spacebar 10 times.
   e. Insert another Check Box Form Field, press the spacebar once, type **1**, and then press the spacebar 10 times.
   f. Insert another Check Box Form Field, press the spacebar once, and then type **NA**.
   g. Select the cell containing the four option buttons, click the Copy button in the Clipboard group on the HOME tab, and then paste this information to the rows shown in Figure 11.14.
   h. Turn off design mode.

7. Protect the form by completing the following steps:
   a. Click the Restrict Editing button in the Protect group on the DEVELOPER tab.
   b. At the Restrict Editing task pane, click the *Allow only this type of editing in the document* check box to insert a check mark.
   c. Click the down-pointing arrow to the right of the option box below the *Allow only this type of editing in the document* check box and then click *Filling in forms* at the drop-down list.
   d. Click the Yes, Start Enforcing Protection button.
   e. At the Start Enforcing Protection dialog box, click OK.
   f. Close the Restrict Editing task pane.
8. Save the template by clicking the Save button on the Quick Access toolbar and then close the template.
9. Using File Explorer, open a new document based on **C11-E04-CCEvaluationForm.dotx**.
10. Fill in the form as if you were evaluating a presentation named *How Far Is Too Far?* in the Parks Hall facility. ***Hint: Use the drop-down form fields to choose the topic and facility. Remember that you can use the Tab key to move from one field to the next with legacy form fields.***
11. Save the completed form document with the name **C11-E04-CompletedCCForm**.
12. Print and then close **C11-E04-CompletedCCForm.docx**.

Figure 11.14 Form Created in Exercise 11.4

Cooper Consulting, Inc.

Conference: Pride and Professionalism

Evaluation Form	Please tell us what you think about the conference. Use the following scale:
3 Strongly Agree/Excellent	2 Agree/Good	1 Disagree/Needs Improvement	NA

	Questions	Evaluation			
1	The conference was interesting.	☐ 3	☐ 2	☐ 1	☐ NA
2	The topics and subjects covered were relevant.	☐ 3	☐ 2	☐ 1	☐ NA
3	I was energized or stimulated by the conference.	☐ 3	☐ 2	☐ 1	☐ NA
4	I would recommend this format for future events.	☐ 3	☐ 2	☐ 1	☐ NA
5	Overall quality of the conference:	☐ 3	☐ 2	☐ 1	☐ NA

Topic: Getting Organized

6	The presenter was well informed and interesting.	☐ 3	☐ 2	☐ 1	☐ NA
7	I am interested in different presentation on this topic with more information.	☐ 3	☐ 2	☐ 1	☐ NA
8	Overall quality of the presentation:	☐ 3	☐ 2	☐ 1	☐ NA

Facilities: Artzen Hall

9	The meeting events were well organized.	☐ 3	☐ 2	☐ 1	☐ NA
10	The facilities were satisfactory.	☐ 3	☐ 2	☐ 1	☐ NA
11	The meeting room arrangements were comfortable.	☐ 3	☐ 2	☐ 1	☐ NA

Additional Comments

12	What is the most useful thing you learned at this conference?	
13	What other topics are you interested in having presented?	
14	Comments and suggestions on this conference:	

Chapter *Summary*

- A web page is a computer file containing information in the form of text or graphics along with commands written in Hypertext Markup Language (HTML). A collection of web pages creates a website.
- The Internet is a worldwide network of commercial, educational, governmental, and personal computers connected together for the purpose of sharing information.
- An intranet is an "internal Internet" within an organization that uses the same web technology and tools as the Internet and is also used for sharing information.
- The World Wide Web (www) is the most commonly used application on the Internet and is a set of standards and protocols used to access information available on the Internet.
- Uniform Resource Locators, or URLs, are the method used to identify locations on the Internet.
- Word provides the ability to jump to the Internet from the Word document screen by adding the *Document Location* text box to the Quick Access toolbar.
- A web page document can be previewed by adding the Web Page Preview button to the Quick Access toolbar.
- Web pages should be carefully planned and designed. Review other web pages for design ideas.
- Tables can be used as the underlying structure of a web page.
- Home pages are the starting point for viewing websites. Home pages usually describe and provide basic information about a company, school, government, or individual and provide hyperlinks to other related web pages.
- A hyperlink is text or a graphic that you click to go to a file, a location in a file, a web page on the Internet, or a web page on an intranet.
- One method for creating a hyperlink is to select the text and then click the Hyperlink button in the Links group on the INSERT tab.
- Bookmarks are created to mark a specific location within a document. You can create a hyperlink to take you to a bookmark from a different location in the document.
- Add horizontal lines to a web page by clicking the *Horizontal Line* option at the Borders button drop-down list.
- Add background color or textures to a web page with options at the Page Color button and Fill Effects dialog box. Display the Fill Effects dialog box by clicking the DESIGN tab, clicking the Page Color button in the Page Background group, and then clicking *Fill Effects* at the drop-down gallery.
- Display the DEVELOPER tab by clicking the FILE tab and then clicking *Options*. At the Word Options dialog box with the *Customize Ribbon* selected in the left panel, click in the *Developer* check box to insert a check mark and then click OK.
- Content controls are fields within a form document where text can be entered or information can be selected from a drop-down box, check box, or date picker. Insert content controls with buttons on the DEVELOPER tab.
- Use options at the Restrict Editing task pane to protect a form document or template. Display the Restrict Editing task pane by clicking the Restrict Editing button in the Protect group in the DEVELOPER tab.
- Legacy tools are available for creating form fields in a form document or template. Access legacy form fields by clicking the Legacy Tools button in the Controls group on the DEVELOPER tab.
- A form document or template can be edited by unprotecting the document or template, making desired changes, and then protecting the document or template.

Commands *Review*

FEATURE	RIBBON TAB, GROUP/OPTION	BUTTON
bookmark	INSERT, Links	
building block gallery content control	DEVELOPER, Controls	
bullets	HOME, Paragraph	
check box content control	DEVELOPER, Controls	
combo box content control	DEVELOPER, Controls	
date picker content control	DEVELOPER, Controls	
design mode	DEVELOPER, Controls	
Document Location text box	Quick Access toolbar	
drop-down list content control	DEVELOPER, Controls	
hyperlink	INSERT, Links	
legacy tools	DEVELOPER, Controls	
page color	DESIGN, Page Background	
picture content control	DEVELOPER, Controls	
plain text content control	DEVELOPER, Controls	
properties	DEVELOPER, Controls	
restrict editing	DEVELOPER, Protect	
rich text content control	DEVELOPER, Controls	
Web Layout view	VIEW, Views	
Web Page Preview	Quick Access toolbar	

Key Points *Review*

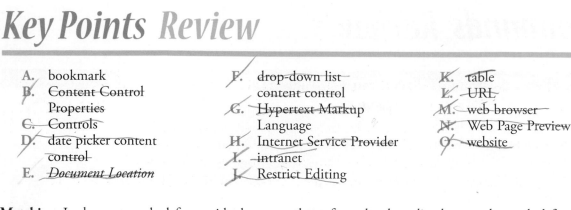

A. bookmark
B. Content Control Properties
C. Controls
D. date picker content control
E. *Document Location*

F. drop-down list content control
G. Hypertext Markup Language
H. Internet Service Provider
I. intranet
J. Restrict Editing

K. table
L. URL
M. web browser
N. Web Page Preview
O. website

Matching: In the space at the left, provide the correct letter from the above list that matches each definition.

_M_   1. An application used to view web pages

_H_   2. A hosting service that places web pages on a server so they are viewable from the Internet

_L_   3. Method used to identify locations on the Internet

_I_   4. A network used to share information within an organization

_A_   5. Feature used to move to another location within a document

_K_   6. Word feature that can be used as the underlying structure of a web page

_N_   7. Word preview screen at which a web page can be viewed

_G_   8. A World Wide Web language protocol

_E_   9. Text box used to access websites within Word

_O_   10. A collection of web pages

_J_   11. Button on the DEVELOPER tab that restricts how a form can be edited

_D_   12. Button on the DEVELOPER tab used to insert a date content control

_F_   13. Type of control used in a form if the person entering information needs to choose from a specific list of options

_B_   14. Dialog box that contains options to customize a content control

_C_   15. Group on the DEVELOPER tab in which the Legacy Tools button is located

Chapter Assessments

Assessment 11.1   Format a Real Estate Form and Excel Mortgage Calculator

In this assessment, you will open a Word form template and create a hyperlink from this form to an Excel spreadsheet. The spreadsheet includes automatic calculations for a mortgage loan (see Figure 11.15 on page 520). Include the following specifications:

1. Using File Explorer, open a document based on **C11-E03-MREFormTemplate.dotx**, which you created in Exercise 11.3.
2. Unprotect the form by clicking the DEVELOPER tab and then clicking the Restrict Editing button in the Protect group. Click the Stop Protection button at the bottom of the Restrict Editing task pane.
3. Position the insertion point in the cell that contains the text *Housing financial information*, click the TABLE TOOLS LAYOUT tab, and then click the Split Cells button in the Merge group. At the Split Cells dialog box, verify that *2* displays in the *Number of columns* measurement box and *1* displays in the *Number of rows* measurement box and then click OK.
4. Position the insertion point in the new cell to the right of *Housing financial information* and then type **Loan Calculator**. Select *Loan Calculator* and change the font size to 12 points. With the text still selected, click the Hyperlink button in the Links group on the INSERT tab and then create a hyperlink to the Excel file **LoanCalculator.xlsx**, located in your Chapter11 folder. *Hint: Change the* Look in **option at the Insert Hyperlink dialog box to your Chapter11 folder to locate the Excel file.**
5. Protect the form again, without setting a password, and then close the Restrict Editing task pane.
6. Save the form as a template in your Chapter11 folder, using the name **C11-A01-MREFormCalc.dotx**. Leave the template open.
7. Hold down the Ctrl key and then click the <u>Loan Calculator</u> hyperlink to access the Excel spreadsheet (loan calculator) located in your Chapter11 folder.
8. Fill in the Excel loan application worksheet for a loan of $200,000, at a 6% interest rate, and a 30-year loan period, using the current date.
9. Save the completed Excel worksheet with the name **C11-A01-LoanCalculator**.
10. Print the first page of **C11-A01-LoanCalculator.xlsx**.
11. Close **C11-A01-LoanCalculator.xlsx** and then close Excel.
12. Print and then close **C11-A01-MREFormCalc.dotx**.

Assessment 11.2   Format a Dental Insurance Form

Create a dental insurance form similar to the one shown in Figure 11.16 on page 521. Insert form fields and content controls where needed in the form. Include the following specifications:

1. Open **Dental.docx** from your Chapter11 folder.
2. Save the form in your Chapter11 folder as a template with the name **C11-A02-Dental**.
3. Insert an appropriate image in the first cell of the form.
4. Insert your choice of content controls or legacy form fields in the cells of the form.
5. Format the form to enhance its appearance.
6. When you are satisfied with the layout of the form, protect it.
7. Save **C11-A02-Dental.dotx** and then close it.

8. Send the template form to another student in your classroom. Ask him or her to do the following:
   - Use File Explorer to open a Word document based on the template.
   - Complete the form.
   - Save the form with the name **C11-A02-DentalFormCompleted**.
   - Print and then close **C11-A02-DentalFormCompleted.docx**.
   - Evaluate the form based on how easy it was to complete.

Figure 11.15 Form Template Created in Assessment 11.1

MIDWEST REAL ESTATE

1308 Ogden Avenue, Lisle, IL 60532

(630) 555-2313 ❖ midwest@emcp.net ❖ Virtual tours: www.emcp.net/midwest

Real Estate Client Information

Profile

Name: Click here to enter text.	**Spouse's name:** Click here to enter text.	**Date:** Click here to enter a date.
Address: Click here to enter text.		
Phone: Click here to enter text.	**Cell:** Click here to enter text.	**Email:** Click here to enter text.

Preferred method of communication

☐	Home email	☐	Work email	☐	Home phone
☐	Work phone	☐	Cell phone	Other:	Click here to enter text.

Best time to call (include preferred phone numbers)

Click here to enter text.	Click here to enter text.

Housing preferences

Housing preference	Choose an item.	Number of bedrooms:	Choose an item.
Number of stories:	Choose an item.	Number of baths:	Choose an item.
Number of garages:	Choose an item.	Square footage:	Click here to enter text.
Finished basement:	Choose an item.	Price range in thousands:	Choose an item.
Formal living room:	Choose an item.	Formal dining room:	Choose an item.

Housing financial information — **Loan Calculator**

Do you have a prequalified letter?	☐	Yes	☐ No
Type of financing: Click here to enter text.		Mortgage per month: Click here to enter text.	

Figure 11.16 Sample Solution for Assessment 11.2

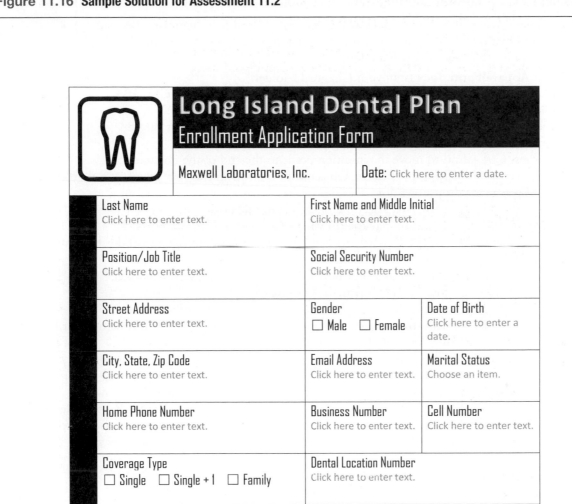

Long Island Dental Plan
Enrollment Application Form

| Maxwell Laboratories, Inc. | Date: Click here to enter a date. |

Last Name	First Name and Middle Initial
Click here to enter text.	Click here to enter text.

Position/Job Title	Social Security Number
Click here to enter text.	Click here to enter text.

Street Address	Gender	Date of Birth
Click here to enter text.	☐ Male ☐ Female	Click here to enter a date.

City, State, Zip Code	Email Address	Marital Status
Click here to enter text.	Click here to enter text.	Choose an item.

Home Phone Number	Business Number	Cell Number
Click here to enter text.	Click here to enter text.	Click here to enter text.

Coverage Type	Dental Location Number
☐ Single ☐ Single +1 ☐ Family	Click here to enter text.

Assessment 11.3   Format an Integrated Merchandise Order Form

In this assessment, you will insert an Excel worksheet into a Word form template. Because of the Excel automatic calculating features, you will see that integrating Excel into the Word form makes it easier to make the computations.

1. Open **ApparelForm.docx** from your Chapter11 folder.
2. Save the form in your Chapter11 folder as a template with the name **C11-A03-ApparelForm**.
3. Insert an Excel workbook with calculations below the email address at the end of the form, by completing the following steps:
    a. Press Ctrl + End to move the insertion point to the end of the document.
    b. Click the INSERT tab, click the Object button arrow in the Text group, and then click *Object* at the drop-down list.
    c. At the Object dialog box, select the Create from File tab.
    d. Click the Browse button, navigate to your Chapter11 folder, double-click **ExcelApparelForm.xlsx**, and then click OK. This inserts the Excel worksheet as an object, allowing you to use the Excel features from within Word.
    e. Protect the form so that users can only fill in fields. Do not set a password.
    f. Save and then close **C11-A03-ApparelForm.dotx**.
4. Using File Explorer, open a document based on **C11-A03-ApparelForm.dotx**.
5. Open **ApparelData.docx** from your Chapter11 folder and then add the information for Barbara Regel to the Swimming Apparel Order Form in the appropriate form fields at the top of the form. Stop entering information after you have typed the child's name. *Hint: Size and position the two documents so that you can view them at the same time.*
6. When you are finished filling in the top part of the form, unprotect the document.
7. Double-click inside the Excel object to open it for editing. Enter the data for Barbara Regel from **ApparelData.docx** in the appropriate cells. (Notice that the number of each item ordered, the total price for each item, and the total price for the order calculate automatically as you fill in the form.) When you are done entering information in the Excel object, click outside the object to close it.
8. Save the form with the name **C11-A03-CompletedApparelForm1**.
9. Print and then close **C11-A03-CompletedApparelForm1.docx**.
10. Follow Steps 4 through 9 to complete a second apparel form. Make sure you open a new document based on **C11-A03-ApparelForm.dotx** to type the information in the second form.
11. Save the second form with the name **C11-A03-CompletedApparelForm2**.
12. Print and then close **C11-A03-CompletedApparelForm2.docx**. (Refer to the sample solution shown in Figure 11.17.)

Assessment 11.4   Create a Web Page

As a group, assign individual tasks for each member of your group and then design and create a web page on a topic of your group's choosing. Suggested topics include gardening, favorite sport or team, community project, volunteer project, hobby, or vacation spot. Look at other websites for ideas and layouts. Research your topic on the Internet and include at least three hyperlinks and one bookmark. Use appropriate graphics, borders, buttons, dividers, and background. Name your web page **C11-A04-GroupWebPage**. *Optional:* Include an audio file and/or video file. Figure 11.18 on page 524 displays a sample solution.

Figure 11.17 Sample Solution for Assessment 11.3

Swimming Apparel
Order Form

We will place our River Rats apparel order immediately following registration this year to ensure that the swimmers have their items for the summer swim season. Please note: All swimmers registered for summer swim will receive a complimentary team T-shirt.

Name:	Joseph Larabee
Address:	455 Ridgeland Circle
City: Wheaton **ST:** IL **ZIP:** 60187	
Phone:	(630) 555-1288
Child's Name:	Jerrad

Order forms must be received by May 15 along with registration. Please make checks payable to River Rats. If you have any questions, please call Kerry Swimmer at (630) 555-1212 or email at kswimmer@emcp.net.

Item	Small	Medium	Large	X-Large	Quantity	Price	Total
Team T-Shirt					0	$8	$0
Zip Hoodie Sweatshirt					0	$24	$0
Micro-Poly Full Zip Jacket		1			1	$37	$37
Micro-Poly Fully Lined Pants w/zipper on lower leg		1			1	$30	$30
Cotton Cheer Shorts					0	$10	$0
Plaid Flannel PJ Pant					0	$20	$0
Heavy Duty Sports Bag (w/child's name)					1	$32	$32
Total Number of Items Ordered					3		
Total Price							$99

Figure 11.18 Sample Solution for Assessment 11.4

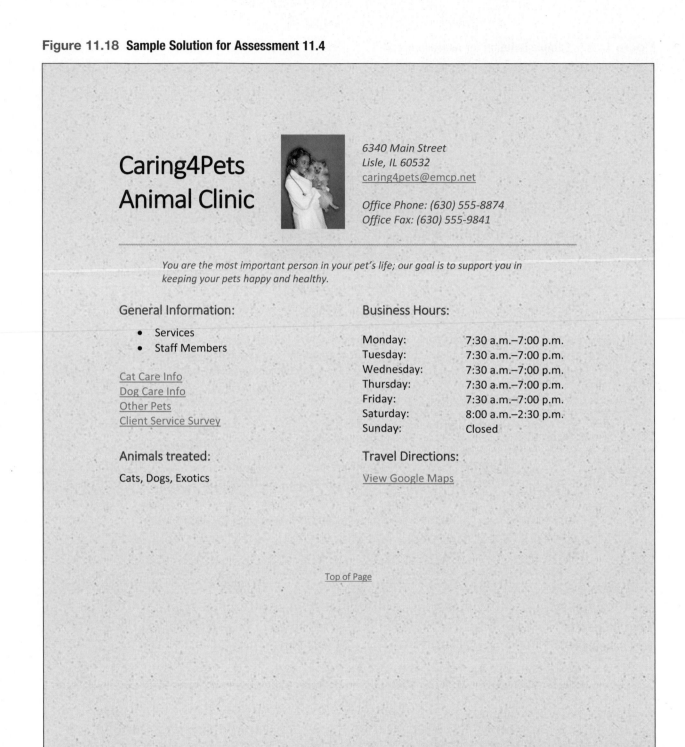

Caring4Pets
Animal Clinic

6340 Main Street
Lisle, IL 60532
caring4pets@emcp.net

Office Phone: (630) 555-8874
Office Fax: (630) 555-9841

You are the most important person in your pet's life; our goal is to support you in keeping your pets happy and healthy.

General Information:

- Services
- Staff Members

Cat Care Info
Dog Care Info
Other Pets
Client Service Survey

Animals treated:

Cats, Dogs, Exotics

Business Hours:

Monday:	7:30 a.m.–7:00 p.m.
Tuesday:	7:30 a.m.–7:00 p.m.
Wednesday:	7:30 a.m.–7:00 p.m.
Thursday:	7:30 a.m.–7:00 p.m.
Friday:	7:30 a.m.–7:00 p.m.
Saturday:	8:00 a.m.–2:30 p.m.
Sunday:	Closed

Travel Directions:

View Google Maps

Top of Page

Introducing Microsoft Publisher 2013

Performance Objectives

Upon successful completion of Chapter 12, you will be able to:

- Create a variety of different publications using Microsoft Publisher
- Determine when to use Word and when to use Publisher
- Apply desktop publishing design concepts to publications in Publisher
- Customize Publisher templates and create publications from scratch
- Insert, edit, and update a Business Information set
- Use master pages and layout guides
- Insert preformatted building blocks
- Share publications and prepare them for commercial printing

---

Desktop Publishing Terms

embedded picture	linked picture	Pantone color
hyphenation zone	overflow	story

Publisher Features Used

building blocks	Graphics Manager	Pack and Go Wizard	styles
Business Information set	hyphenation	Page Navigation pane	Text Fit
color schemes	layout guides	page numbers	
Design Checker	linked text boxes	rotate or flip	
font schemes	master pages	Smart Tags	

Note: Before beginning computer exercises for this chapter, copy to your storage medium the Chapter12 folder from the CD that accompanies this textbook and then make Chapter12 the active folder. Remember to substitute for graphics that may no longer be available.

Understanding the Capabilities of Microsoft Publisher 2013

Microsoft Publisher 2013 is an easy-to-use desktop publishing program designed for small business users and individuals who want to create their own high-quality, professional-looking business documents without the assistance of professional designers. Publisher 2013 provides hundreds of customizable templates, flexible page layout guides, improved picture features, and a full range of desktop publishing tools. With Publisher, you can create, design, and publish professional marketing and communication materials for print and email.

DTP POINTER

Use Publisher if your publication requires a commercial printer.

Pantone color

A popular color matching system used by the printing industry

DTP POINTER

Publisher provides features to help you manage complex, precise page layouts.

While Word provides sufficient features and capabilities for most desktop publishing processes, consider using Publisher if your documents (called *publications* in Publisher) require commercial printing. Publisher offers full support for commercial printing, including four-color separation and spot color processing. ***Pantone color***, a popular color matching system used by the printing industry, is also available to Publisher. You can also work with Word from inside Publisher to edit a publication, or you can select a Publisher design template and then import a Word document.

Also consider using Publisher if your document layouts are complex or need to be especially precise. Publisher includes more advanced but still easy-to-use layout guides, ruler guides, baseline guides, and snap options to align objects to ruler marks, guides, or other objects. Publisher includes hundreds of template options for common business publications and more complex design tasks, including color schemes, font schemes, and predesigned layouts and publication designs. Additional templates are available from Office.com at http://office.microsoft.com/templates.

Applying Design Concepts When Working in Publisher 2013

Throughout this text, you have learned that to create professional-looking publications, it is important to carefully plan and organize all content and design elements. This is as important when using Publisher as when using Word. If you use a Publisher template as the underlying structure of your customized publication, many of the design decisions will have already been made for you; however, you will still need to make critical choices as to the type of publication that best conveys your message, the color scheme that best reinforces the feel of your publication, and the design elements that best enrich your message and promote readability.

DTP POINTER

At least one-third of your document should contain white space.

If you are creating a publication or template from scratch to fit your company's design needs, it is especially important to apply the design concepts discussed in earlier chapters. Remember to keep the overall look of your publication simple and use plenty of white space. Reinforce consistency through spacing, fonts, alignment, repetition, color, and decorative elements such as borders, drop caps, and so on. Draw readers into your publication by using strong contrast, alignment, and focus. Achieve balance and proportion and establish smooth directional flow in a publication by organizing and positioning elements in such a way that the reader's eyes scan through the text and find particular words or images that you want to emphasize. The use of color and other design elements should work together to reflect the nature of the business being represented in the publication.

Getting Started with Publisher 2013

To open Publisher, click the Publisher tile at the Windows 8 Start screen. When you first open Publisher, the Publisher opening screen displays. At the opening screen, you can choose from or search for featured or built-in templates, or you can choose a blank page in a specific size, as shown in Figure 12.1. You can also click the <u>Open Other Publications</u> hyperlink to open files you have already created and saved.

Starting from a Template

You may choose to start your publication from a blank publication or from a template. Selecting one of the hundreds of professionally designed templates that are frequently updated and added to the Office.com template home page is a good option when you are first learning to use Publisher. After becoming familiar with the Publisher features, you may decide to start certain publications from scratch so that you can incorporate more of your own designs and ideas.

As illustrated in Figure 12.1, you can choose a template from the *FEATURED* section or the *BUILT-IN* section of the Publisher opening screen. The *FEATURED* section displays options for blank publication templates as well as new, featured templates. Click the *BUILT-IN* option to display categories of templates, such as award certificates, brochures, business cards, calendars, flyers, newsletters, and so on. When you click a category thumbnail, a variety of templates for that type of document display

◀ **DTP POINTER**

It is helpful to use Publisher templates when you are first starting out with the program. When you feel more comfortable using Publisher, you may decide to begin some of your publications from scratch.

Figure 12.1 Investigating the Publisher Opening Screen

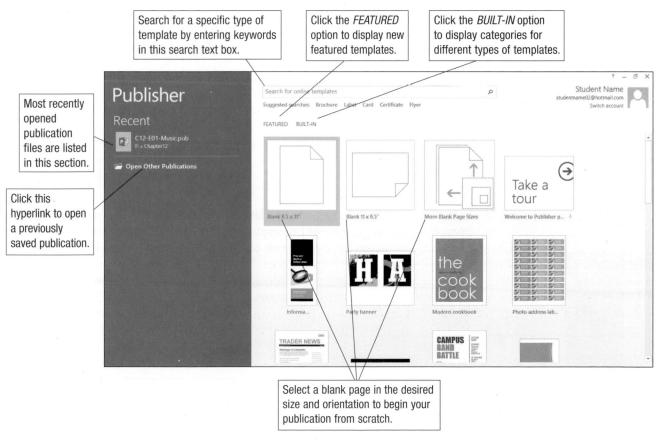

Most recently opened publication files are listed in this section.

Click this hyperlink to open a previously saved publication.

Search for a specific type of template by entering keywords in this search text box.

Click the *FEATURED* option to display new featured templates.

Click the *BUILT-IN* option to display categories for different types of templates.

Select a blank page in the desired size and orientation to begin your publication from scratch.

in the New backstage area. After selecting one of the templates, a task pane will display at the right side of the screen with options for customizing the template, including changing the color scheme, font scheme, and business information. After you have made the desired customizations, click the Create button located at the bottom of the task pane, as shown in Figure 12.2.

Starting from Scratch

If you choose to start your publication from a blank page, make sure the *FEATURED* section is selected and then click the *Blank 8.5 × 11"* option, the *Blank 11 × 8.5"* option, or the *More Blank Page Sizes* option. If you click the *More Blank Page Sizes* option, blank page templates in various sizes will display, as shown in Figure 12.3. Click the page that best fits your needs, determine a color scheme and font scheme in the task pane at the right side of the screen, and then click the Create button.

Exploring the Publisher 2013 Interface

Once you open a new template or blank page, you will see that Publisher offers a user interface consistent with the other Office programs, as shown in Figure 12.4. You can choose commands on the ribbon to help you create the publication from scratch. When you insert various objects, contextual tabs will become available in the ribbon. You will notice that one difference between the Word interface and the Publisher interface is that in Publisher, you can see the pages of your document in the Page Navigation pane at the left side of the screen and click the thumbnails to navigate among the pages. You will learn more about beginning to create and format a publication in the next section.

Figure 12.2 Selecting a Template from the *Newsletters* Category in the *BUILT-IN* Section

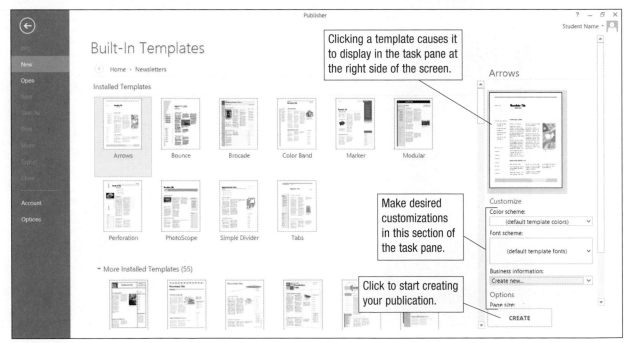

Figure 12.3 Selecting Blank Pages from the *FEATURED* Section

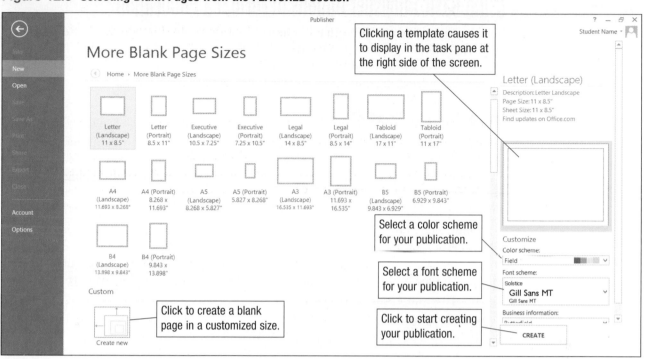

Figure 12.4 Investigating the Microsoft Publisher Window with the TEXT BOX TOOLS FORMAT Tab Selected

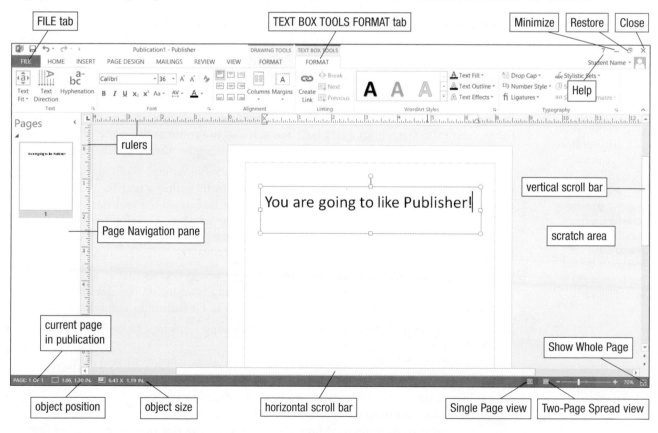

Using Basic Publisher Options to Format a Publication

In Exercise 12.1, you will begin a publication using a Publisher flyer template. The template contains placeholder text, design objects, and graphics. You will be instructed to insert a Word file, AutoFit the text, replace the picture, delete a design object, and apply other formatting options to enhance your publication.

Inserting a Text Box

One of the main differences between Publisher and Word is that in Publisher you must place all objects, such as text, graphics, pictures, WordArt, and shapes, inside a frame in order to include them in your publication. In Word, you simply begin typing your text in a blank document in a linear manner, but in Publisher, text is considered an object, which must be placed in a frame or text box first.

Draw a text box in a publication by clicking the Draw Text Box button in the Objects group on the HOME tab and then click or drag in the page to create the text box. If you draw a text box in a blank publication page, the Normal style will be applied to text you type in the text box. The Normal style contains the following default settings:

- 10-point Calibri font
- Black text color
- kerning at 14 points and above
- left alignment
- 1.19 line spacing
- 0.083 inch spacing after paragraphs

You can customize these default settings using options in the Font group and the Paragraph group on the HOME tab or in the Font dialog box or the Paragraph dialog box.

Inserting Text and Copyfitting with the Text Fit Feature

When you insert a text box in a page, the DRAWING TOOLS FORMAT tab and TEXT BOX TOOLS FORMAT tab are added to the ribbon. These tabs contain buttons you can use to customize text within a text box. You can also use commands on the HOME tab to apply styles, change text alignment, change fonts, and apply other text enhancements.

overflow
Text that does not fit within a text box; it is hidden until it is flowed into a new text box or the text box is resized to accommodate it

If the text box you create to hold your text is not big enough to fit all of the text, it will create overflow. ***Overflow*** is text that does not fit within a text box. Overflow text is hidden until it can be flowed into a new text box, until the text box is resized to include it, or until the text is resized to fit inside the text box. Overflow text is indicated by an ellipsis icon at the right side of the text box, as shown in Figure 12.5A. The sizing handles around the text box will also display in red.

The Text Fit feature in Publisher automatically resizes text so that it will fit into the allotted space. Recall from Chapter 7 that copyfitting is adjusting the size and spacing of text to make it fit within a specific space. The Text Fit feature is a copyfitting tool.

To use the Text Fit feature, complete the following steps (see Figure 12.5B):

1. Click in the text box.
2. Click the Text Fit button in the Text group on the TEXT BOX TOOLS FORMAT tab.
3. Select one of the following options at the drop-down list:
   a. To tell Publisher to automatically increase or decrease the font size of text to fit in the text box when you resize the box or type additional text, click *Best Fit*.

Text Fit

Figure 12.5 Using the Text Fit Feature to Handle Text in Overflow

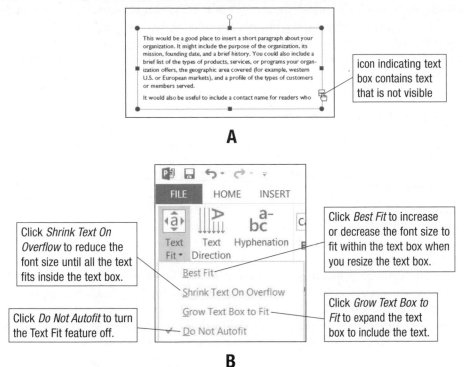

A

B

b. To reduce the font size of text until all of the text fits inside the text box, click *Shrink Text On Overflow*. To tell the text box to expand to include all of the text, click *Grow Text Box to Fit*.

c. To turn the Text Fit feature off, click *Do Not Autofit*. With automatic copyfitting turned off, the font size remains the same whenever you resize the text box or type additional text.

Changing Text Direction

When you create a new text box, by default, the direction of the text is horizontal. Click the Text Direction button in the Text group on the TEXT BOX TOOLS FORMAT tab to change the orientation of the text to vertical. Click the Text Direction button again to return the text to the default horizontal direction. If you create your text using WordArt, you will have more versatility in changing text direction, such as rotating text at 90 degrees to the right or left, flipping vertically or horizontally, or rotating it using the free rotate handle.

Text Direction

Adjusting Hyphenation Settings

Microsoft Publisher 2013 automatically hyphenates text as it is typed or pasted into text boxes. Control hyphenation settings in your publication at the Hyphenation dialog box. Display the Hyphenation dialog box by clicking the Hyphenation button in the Text group on the TEXT BOX TOOLS FORMAT tab (or by pressing Ctrl + Shift + H). At the Hyphenation dialog box, if the *Automatically hyphenate this story* check box contains a check mark, the **story** (a series of connected text boxes) will be automatically hyphenated. Publisher will choose when to hyphenate words based on grammatical rules and the

Hyphenation

story
Connected text boxes in a series

hyphenation zone—the amount of space that can be left between the end of the last word in a line and the right margin. To reduce the number of hyphens in a story, make the hyphenation zone wider. Do this by displaying the Hyphenation dialog box and increasing the amount in the *Hyphenation zone* measurement box. To reduce the raggedness of the right margin in a story, make the hyphenation zone narrower. For maximum control over hyphenation settings, click the Manual button at the Hyphenation dialog box to display the Hyphenate dialog box. At this dialog box, you can determine where a hyphen appears in a word.

Changing Font Colors

Font Color

Change the font color in Publisher in much the same way you would in Word. After you have drawn a text box (or clicked or selected text inside an existing text box), click the Font Color button arrow in the Font group on the TEXT BOX TOOLS FORMAT tab or in the Font group on the HOME tab and then click a color in the *Theme Colors* or *Standard Colors* section. To apply a color other than those included in the drop-down gallery, click *More Colors* at the drop-down gallery to open the Colors dialog box. Choose a color from the Standard tab or create one at the Custom tab. The Colors dialog box in Publisher has an additional tab, PANTONE®, where you can locate and select specific Pantone colors for your publication, as shown in Figure 12.6. When you have selected the desired color, click OK to close the dialog box. Publisher applies the color to the selected text and adds it to the Font Color and Fill Color palettes. ***Note: Pantone Colors displayed on the PANTONE® tab may not match Pantone-identified standards. Consult current Pantone color publications for accurate color.***

You can change the color of text and then fine-tune that color with tinting or shading. To apply a tint or shade, complete the following steps:

1. Select the text whose color you want to tint or shade.
2. Click the Font Color button arrow on the TEXT BOX TOOLS FORMAT tab or the HOME tab.
3. Click the *Tints* option at the drop-down gallery.
4. Click the tint or shade that you want in the *Tint/Shade* section of the Fill Effects dialog box, as shown in Figure 12.7.
5. Click OK. Publisher applies the tint or shade to the selected text and adds it to the *Recent Colors* section of the Font Color button drop-down gallery.

Figure 12.6 Using the Colors Dialog Box with the PANTONE® Tab Selected

Figure 12.7 Applying a Tint to Text at the Fill Effects Dialog Box

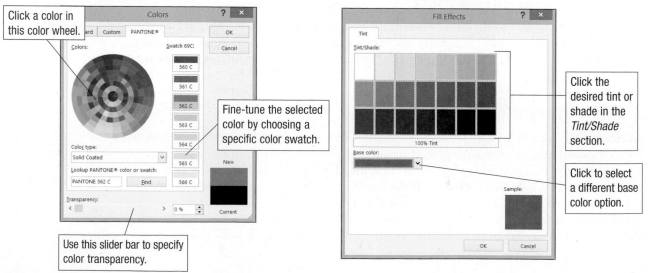

You can also change the font color in a publication to match part of an existing image or object. Publisher 2013 allows you to grab the color from one object and then paint it onto another object by using the Sample Font Color eyedropper tool. To use the tool, select the text to which you want to apply the sample color and then click *Sample Font Color* at the bottom of the Font Color button drop-down gallery. The mouse pointer will display as an eyedropper. Click the area of the picture or object from which you want to grab the color, as shown in Figure 12.8A. The text you selected will change to that color and the color you grabbed will display in the *Recent Colors* section of the Font Color button drop-down gallery, as shown in Figure 12.8B. The Sample Font Color eyedropper tool is also available at other button drop-down lists, such as Shape Fill and Shape Outline.

Using the Font Dialog Box

Specify how you want text to appear in your publication by selecting options in the Font dialog box, as shown in Figure 12.9 on page 534. The availability of some options depends on the languages and fonts that are installed and enabled for editing. Most of the general options such as *Font*, *Font style*, *Font Size*, and *Font Color*, along with other text effects such as *Underline* and *Small caps*, are similar to the same options available at Word's Font dialog box. Click the Fill Effects button in the *General* section to display a dialog box where you can apply text fill, text outlines, and text effects such as shadow, reflection, glow, and 3-D format.

OpenType fonts, such as Gabriola and Calibri, support a range of features that enable you to transform ordinary text into fine typography. If the font you choose does not support the OpenType features, this section will be unavailable. Change typography effects with options in the Font dialog box or in the Typography group on the TEXT BOX TOOLS FORMAT tab. Some fonts support advanced typography features similar to those available in Word, such as number styles, stylistic alternates, contextual alternatives, ligatures, and stylistic sets.

Figure 12.8 Using the Sample Font Color Tool

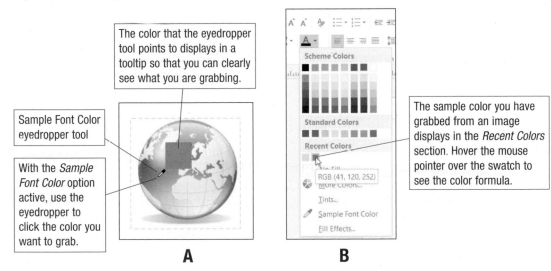

The color that the eyedropper tool points to displays in a tooltip so that you can clearly see what you are grabbing.

Sample Font Color eyedropper tool

With the *Sample Font Color* option active, use the eyedropper to click the color you want to grab.

The sample color you have grabbed from an image displays in the *Recent Colors* section. Hover the mouse pointer over the swatch to see the color formula.

A   **B**

Figure 12.9 **Adjusting Font Formatting at the Font Dialog Box**

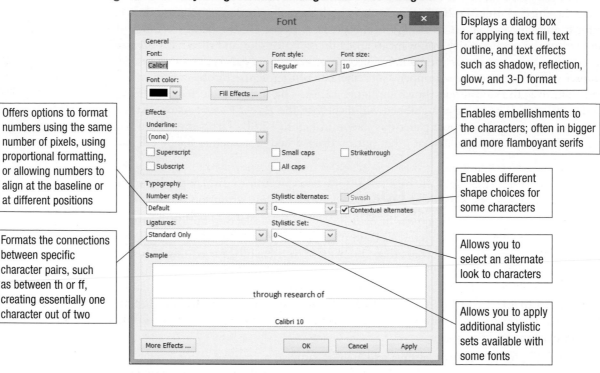

Offers options to format numbers using the same number of pixels, using proportional formatting, or allowing numbers to align at the baseline or at different positions

Formats the connections between specific character pairs, such as between th or ff, creating essentially one character out of two

Displays a dialog box for applying text fill, text outline, and text effects such as shadow, reflection, glow, and 3-D format

Enables embellishments to the characters; often in bigger and more flamboyant serifs

Enables different shape choices for some characters

Allows you to select an alternate look to characters

Allows you to apply additional stylistic sets available with some fonts

Applying Styles

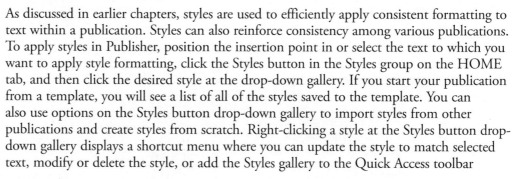

Styles

As discussed in earlier chapters, styles are used to efficiently apply consistent formatting to text within a publication. Styles can also reinforce consistency among various publications. To apply styles in Publisher, position the insertion point in or select the text to which you want to apply style formatting, click the Styles button in the Styles group on the HOME tab, and then click the desired style at the drop-down gallery. If you start your publication from a template, you will see a list of all of the styles saved to the template. You can also use options on the Styles button drop-down gallery to import styles from other publications and create styles from scratch. Right-clicking a style at the Styles button drop-down gallery displays a shortcut menu where you can update the style to match selected text, modify or delete the style, or add the Styles gallery to the Quick Access toolbar

Using Business Information Sets

Business Information sets are customized groups of information about an individual or an organization that can be used to quickly fill in appropriate places in publications such as business cards and flyers. A Business Information set can include components such as an individual's name, job position or title, organization name, address, phone and fax numbers, email address, tagline or motto, and logo. You can create as many different Business Information sets as you want. The data in each Business Information set is stored on the hard drive of the particular computer you are using.

When you create a publication, the Business Information set that you have used most recently is used to populate the new publication by automatically inserting the business information in place of the standard placeholder text that displays in the template. If you have not yet created any Business Information sets, the user and organization names are inserted from the information provided when Microsoft Office 2013 was installed.

To create a new Business Information set, click the FILE tab and then click the Edit Business Information button at the Info backstage area to display the Business Information dialog box. Click the New button in the Business Information dialog box to display the Create New Business Information Set dialog box. Alternatively, you can display the Business Information dialog box by clicking the Business Information button in the Text group on the INSERT tab and then clicking *Edit Business Information* at the drop-down list.

Business Information

At the Create New Business Information Set dialog box, type all pertinent information, add a logo if you want to, and then click the Save button. Figure 12.10 shows a partially completed Business Information set with a logo uploaded.

You can go back and edit a Business Information set whenever you like. Click the FILE tab and then click the Edit Business Information button to display the Business Information dialog box. Click the *Select a Business Information set* option box arrow, select the set you want to edit, click the Edit button to display the Edit Business Information Set dialog box with the information for the set you selected, make your changes, and then click the Save button. At the Business Information dialog box, click the Update Publication button to incorporate your changes into the publication you are currently creating.

In addition to inserting entire Business Information sets in a publication, you can also insert specific fields from those sets. To insert Business Information placeholders anywhere in your publication, click the Business Information button in the Text group on the INSERT tab and then click the field you want to add to your publication.

Figure 12.10 Creating a New Business Information Set at the Create New Business Information Set Dialog Box

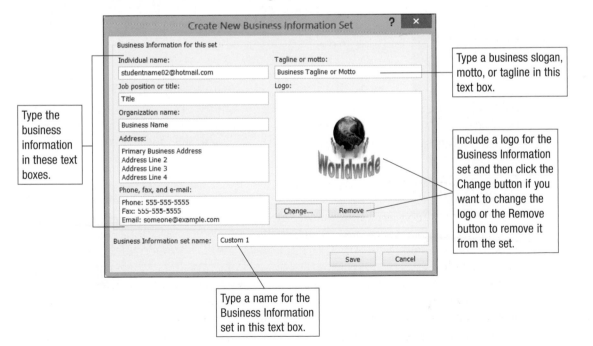

If you hover the mouse over a placeholder that uses information from a Business Information set, a Smart Tag button displays. Click this button to display a drop-down list with the following options: *Edit Business Information*, *Save to Business Information Set*, *Update from Business Information Set*, or *Convert to Plain Text*.

If you are working on a shared computer in a classroom or lab, make sure you delete the Business Information sets that you create for the exercises in this book (after you have saved, printed, and carefully proofread the publications that you create). If you do not delete your Business Information sets, they will automatically populate the publication of the next student who uses that computer. Delete a Business Information set by clicking the Business Information button in the Text group on the INSERT tab, clicking *Edit Business Information* at the drop-down list, selecting the desired business information set in the *Select a Business Information set* option box at the Business Information dialog box, clicking the Delete button, and then clicking the Yes button at the dialog box asking if you want to delete the Business Information set.

In Exercise 12.1, you will use a Publisher template to create the flyer shown in Figure 12.11 on page 540. You will create a new Business Information set to populate the flyer as well as add text and apply formatting to the publication.

Exercise 12.1 Creating a Flyer Using a Publisher Template

1. Open Publisher.
2. At the Publisher opening screen, click the *BUILT-IN* option.
3. Scroll down and then click the *Flyers* option.

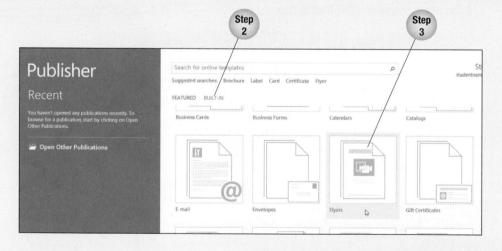

4. In the *Built-In Templates* section, click the *All Marketing* folder in the *Marketing* section.

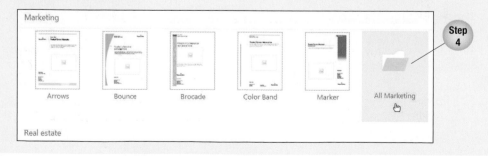

5. Scroll down and then click the *Eclipse* flyer template in the *More Installed Templates Informational* section. The Eclipse template will display in the task pane at the right side of the screen.

6. Customize the Eclipse template by completing the following steps:

a. In the task pane at the right side of the screen, click the down-pointing arrow at the right of the *Color scheme* option box and then click the *Harbor* option at the drop-down list.

b. Click the down-pointing arrow at the right of the *Font scheme* option box and then click the *Equity* option at the drop-down list.

c. Click the down-pointing arrow at the right of the *Business information* option box and then click the *Create new* option.

d. At the Create New Business Information Set dialog box, make the following changes, replacing any text that currently appears in each text box:

1) Type your first and last names in the *Individual name* text box.

2) Type **May your home be filled FOREVER with love and MUSIC.** in the *Tagline or motto* text box.

3) Click the Add Logo button and then insert **ForeverMusicLogo.png** from your Chapter12 folder.

4) Type the remaining text in the *Organization name*, *Address*, and *Phone, fax, and e-mail* text boxes as shown in the image below.

5) Type **Music** in the *Business Information set name* text box.

6) Click the Save button.

Step 5

Eclipse

Customize

Color scheme:
Harbor — Step 6a

Font scheme:
Equity
Franklin Gothic Book
Perpetua — Step 6b

Business information:
Create new...
Create new... — Step 6c
Options

Create New Business Information Set

Business Information for this set

Individual name: — Step 6d1
Student Name

Job position or title:
Title

Organization name: — Step 6d4
Forever Music Teaching Studio

Address:
1234 Third Street
Bloomington, IN 47406

Phone, fax, and e-mail:
Phone: 812.555.9843
Fax: 812.555.9845
Email: forevermusic@emcp.net

Tagline or motto: — Step 6d2
home be filled FOREVER with love and MUSIC.

Logo:

Change... Remove — Step 6d6

Business Information set name: Music — Step 6d5

Save Cancel

e. In the *Options* section of the task pane, click to add a check mark in the *Include mailing address* check box and make sure a check mark displays in the *Include graphic* check box.

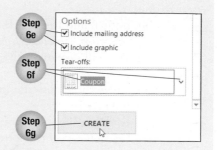

f. Click the down-pointing arrow at the right of the *Tear-offs* option box and then click *Coupon*.

g. Click the CREATE button at the bottom of the task pane.

7. Save the flyer with the name **C12-E01-Music**.

8. Click the page 1 thumbnail in the Page Navigation pane at the left side of the screen.

9. Press the F9 key or click the Zoom In button to zoom to 100%.

10. Replace the placeholder text by completing the following steps:

a. Select the text *Forever Music Teaching Studio* in the placeholder at the top of the flyer and then type **Michael Costanza**.

b. Hover the mouse pointer over *Michael Costanza*, click the Smart Tag button that displays, and then click *Convert to Plain Text* at the drop-down list.

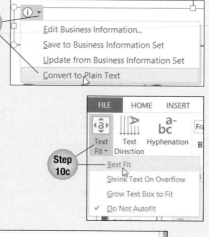

c. Click in the text box containing *Product/ Service Information*, click the TEXT BOX TOOLS FORMAT tab, click the Text Fit button in the Text group, and then click *Best Fit* at the drop-down list.

d. With the placeholder text *Product/Service Information* selected, apply bold formatting, type **Forever Music**, press Enter, and then type **Teaching Studio**.

e. Select *Forever Music Teaching Studio* and then change the font to Bodoni MT Condensed.

f. With the text still selected, click the HOME tab, click the Paragraph group dialog box launcher, select the current measurement in the *Between lines* measurement box in the *Line spacing* section, type **0.8sp**, and then press Enter.

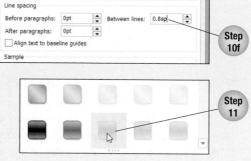

11. Add a gradient fill to the text frame containing *Forever Music Teaching Studio* by selecting the text box, clicking the DRAWING TOOLS FORMAT tab, clicking the More button at the right of the shape style thumbnails in the Shape Styles group, and then clicking the *Horizontal Gradient - Accent 2* option (third column, seventh row).

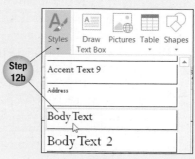

12. Replace the placeholder text below *Forever Music Teaching Studio* with text from a Word document by completing the following steps:

a. Select the placeholder text that begins *Place text here that introduces*, click the INSERT tab, click the Insert File button in the Text group, and then insert **Lessons.docx**, located in your Chapter12 folder.

b. With the insertion point positioned in the text box, press Ctrl + A to select all of the text in the text box, click the HOME tab, click the Styles button in the Styles group, scroll down the drop-down gallery, and then click *Body Text*. Change the font size to 14 points.

c. With the text selected, turn off automatic hyphenation by clicking the TEXT BOX TOOLS FORMAT tab, clicking the Hyphenation button in the Text group, clicking the *Automatically hyphenate this story* check box in the Hyphenation dialog box to remove the check mark, and then clicking OK.

d. Remove the text box fill by clicking the DRAWING TOOLS FORMAT tab, clicking the Shape Fill button arrow in the Shape Styles group, and then clicking *No Fill* at the drop-down gallery.

13. Select the *Tagline* placeholder text (*May your home be filled FOREVER with love and MUSIC.*) and then apply the Organization Name 2 style.

14. Apply bold formatting to the words *FOREVER* and *MUSIC*.

15. Select the telephone placeholder and then type **Phone: 812.555.9843**.

16. Make sure the company name, primary business address, phone, fax, and email in the lower left corner of the flyer are all correct. (Refer to the image below Step 6d on page 537.) If an error exists, click the Business Information button in the Text group on the INSERT tab, click *Edit Business Information* at the drop-down list, make sure *Music* displays in the *Select a Business Information set* option list box, click the Edit button, make the necessary changes at the Edit Business Information Set dialog box, click the Save button, and then click the Update Publication button.

17. Customize the coupon object in the bottom right corner of the page by completing the following steps:
    a. Type the following text to replace the current placeholder text:

Name of Item or Service:	**Any instrument lesson**
00% OFF	**50% Off**
ORGANIZATION NAME:	**FOREVER MUSIC TEACHING STUDIO**
Describe your location...	**Downtown Bloomington**
Tel: 555-555-5555	**Phone: 812.555.9843**
00/00/00	**January 1, 2016**

    b. Click two separate times (do not double-click) on the text box border containing the coupon text and then apply the Solid Fill, Compound Outline - Accent 1 fill (second column, eighth row) in the Shape Style group on the DRAWING TOOLS FORMAT tab. ***Hint: When you select the coupon text box, black Xs should display in the sizing handles.***

18. Add a picture to the center of the flyer by completing the following steps:
    a. Right-click the picture placeholder in the middle of the flyer and then click *Delete Object* at the shortcut menu.
    b. Click the INSERT tab and then click the Online Pictures button in the Illustrations group.
    c. Type **grand piano** in the *Office.com Clip Art* text box, press Enter, and then double-click the image similar to the one shown in Figure 12.11 on page 540.
    d. Size and position the image as shown in Figure 12.11.

19. Click once on the computer image in the coupon and then click again to select the image (sizing handles with black *Xs* display around the image), right-click the image, point to *Change Picture* at the shortcut menu, and then click *Remove Picture* at the side menu.

20. Click the picture icon that displays in the placeholder and then insert the same piano image from the Insert Pictures window.
21. Click the page 2 thumbnail in the Page Navigation pane at the left side of the screen and then insert **ForeverMusicLogo.png** from your Chapter12 folder. (Do this with the Pictures button on the INSERT tab.)
22. With the image selected, click the *Shape Width* measurement box in the Size group on the PICTURE TOOLS FORMAT tab, type **2**, and then press Enter.
23. Position the logo below the return address.
24. Save and then print **C12-E01-Music.pub**. *Hint: Print the second page on the back of the flyer.*
25. Ask your instructor if you should delete the Business Information set named *Music*. To delete the set, complete the following steps:
    a. Click the INSERT tab and then click the Business Information button in the Text group.
    b. Click *Edit Business Information* at the drop-down list.
    c. Click the Delete button at the Business Information dialog box.
    d. Click the Yes button to delete the set and then click the Close button.
26. Close **C12-E01-Music.pub**.

Figure 12.11 Flyer Created in Exercise 12.1

Working with Font and Color Schemes

Font schemes and color schemes are professionally predesigned combinations of fonts and colors chosen to complement the overall look of a publication. Font schemes and color schemes are generally saved within each Publisher template.

Applying Font Schemes

If you are not satisfied with the fonts in a template, you have the option to select a different combination of fonts, create your own personalized font scheme, or turn on or off font scheme options to update custom text styles, override applied text settings, and adjust font sizes.

To change the font scheme, click the PAGE DESIGN tab, click the Fonts button in the Schemes group, and then click a desired font scheme at the drop-down gallery. If you cannot find a scheme that matches your company branding or supports your design, click *Create New Font Scheme* at the bottom of the drop-down gallery as shown in Figure 12.12. After selecting a Font scheme, you can always override the Font scheme choices and apply a desired font, font size, and font style to selected text at the Font dialog box or by choosing options in the Font group on the HOME tab.

Aa

Fonts

Applying Color Schemes

As shown in Figure 12.13, Publisher 2013 provides a gallery of professionally designed color schemes—sets of coordinating colors that you can apply to text and objects. Text and objects set in a color from the color scheme will change automatically when you

Figure 12.12 Displaying Built-in Font Schemes   **Figure 12.13 Displaying Built-in Color Schemes**

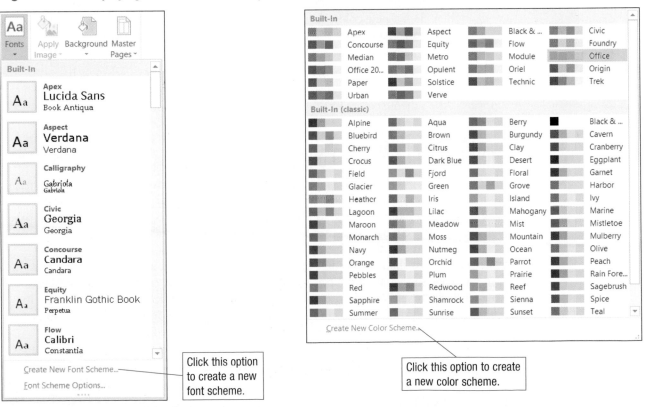

Figure 12.14 Creating a New Color Scheme at the Create New Color Scheme Dialog Box

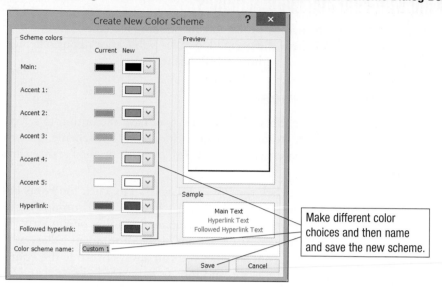

Make different color choices and then name and save the new scheme.

switch to a new color scheme or modify the current color scheme. You can select one of the color schemes, customize a selected scheme, or create a new custom color scheme. To create and save a custom color scheme, complete the following steps:

1. Click the PAGE DESIGN tab and then click the More button in the Schemes group.
2. Click *Create New Color Scheme* at the drop-down gallery.
3. At the Create New Color Scheme dialog box, shown in Figure 12.14, click the arrow next to each color that you want to change in the *New* column and then click a new color. To see more color choices, click *More Colors* at the drop-down gallery.
4. Type a name for your custom color scheme and then click the Save button.

All objects in your publication that were set in colors from the color scheme are now set in the colors of your custom color scheme. The colors that you select also appear as the scheme colors in the Font Color button drop-down gallery.

Working with a Master Page

Every page in a publication has a foreground layer and a background layer. The foreground layer is where you insert text and design objects that will appear on that particular page. The background layer is known as the master page. Any objects placed on the master page will appear on every page that uses that master page. For instance, if you place a watermark on a master page of a three-page publication that uses only that one master page, the watermark will display on all three pages. You might also insert a page numbering code in a master page so that all of the pages in the publication will be automatically numbered consecutively. In addition, layout guides and rulers may be added to the master page. In Publisher 2013, you can use multiple master pages in a single publication. This allows you to create different master pages for different parts of a publication.

To view the master page(s) for a publication, click the VIEW tab and then click the Master Page button in the Views group, or press Ctrl + M. The master page thumbnails will display in the Page Navigation pane at the left side of the screen, as shown in Figure 12.15. Master pages are identified by names such as Master Page (A)

Master Page

Figure 12.15 Viewing the Master Page

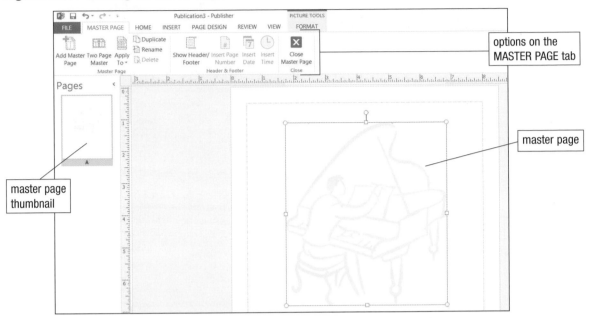

options on the
MASTER PAGE tab

master page

master page
thumbnail

or Master Page (B). You can also create a two-page master, which is useful when you are creating a publication that displays in a two-page spread. A two-page master allows you to insert page numbering on the left for an even page and on the right for an odd page.

Aligning Objects with Layout Guides

Layout guides create a framework or grid for aligning text boxes, columns, graphics, headings, and other objects used in a publication. Layout guides include margin guides (boundaries), grid guides (such as column and row guides), baseline guides, and ruler guides.

Layout guides can be customized by clicking the PAGE DESIGN tab and then clicking the Guides button in the Layout group to display a drop-down list of predesigned guides. In the *Built-In Ruler Guides* section, shown in Figure 12.16 on page 544, select a predesigned ruler guide or add new horizontal and/or vertical ruler guides to your current page layout. You can also customize margin, grid, and baseline guides by clicking the Guides button, clicking *Grid and Baseline Guides* at the drop-down list, and then making desired changes at the Layout Guides dialog box, shown in Figure 12.17 on page 544.

Guides

Using Margin Guides

Use margin guides to set the amount of white space that you want to appear around the edges of a publication. Margin guides display as blue, dotted lines on the page, as shown in Figure 12.18 on page 545. These margin guides do not display when you print your publication, but they help you lay out the page.

Using Grid Guides and Baseline Guides

Grid guides are lines used to set the number of columns and rows that you want on a page. Grid guides are useful in visualizing where columns and rows are inserted in a publication. Any objects or grids set on a master page show on all pages but can be edited only on the master page. At the Layout Guides dialog box with the Grid Guides

Figure 12.16 Choosing Built-in Ruler Guides

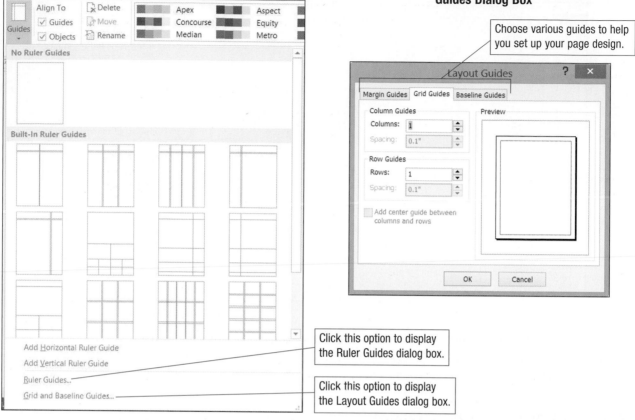

Figure 12.17 Adjusting Guides in the Layout Guides Dialog Box

Choose various guides to help you set up your page design.

Click this option to display the Ruler Guides dialog box.

Click this option to display the Layout Guides dialog box.

tab selected, enter the number of columns that you want between the left and right margin guides and adjust the amount of space between columns. You can also enter the number of rows that you want between the top and bottom margin guides and enter the amount of space between rows.

Use the baseline guides to align the baselines of your text. You can enter the amount of space that you want between horizontal baseline guides. The number that you enter is the amount of line spacing that will be applied to the paragraphs that you have set to align to the baseline guides.

Using Ruler Guides

Ruler guides are individual guides that you can use to measure or align objects. Ruler guides display as green dotted lines, as shown in Figure 12.18, and they are useful when you want to align several objects or position an object at an exact location on the page. At the Guides button drop-down list, click the *Add Horizontal Ruler Guide* or *Add Vertical Ruler Guide* option, position the insertion point on one of the green guides outside of any text box until the insertion point displays as a double-headed arrow with two vertical or horizontal bars, and then drag the green guide to a new location. Hold down the Ctrl key as you drag the double-pointed arrow to create additional ruler guides. Click the *Ruler Guides* option at the Guides button drop-down list to access the Ruler Guides dialog box, shown in Figure 12.19. Click options to set, clear, or clear all vertical or horizontal ruler guides.

Figure 12.18 **Illustrating Layout Guides for a Brochure**

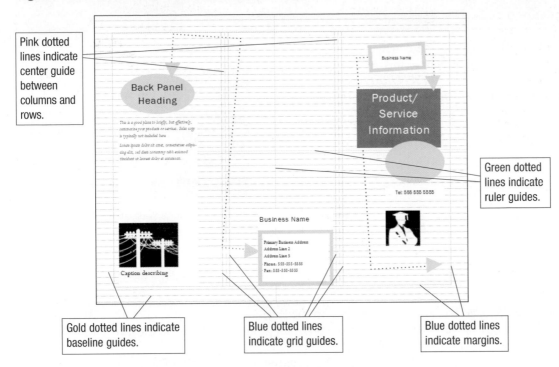

Pink dotted lines indicate center guide between columns and rows.

Green dotted lines indicate ruler guides.

Gold dotted lines indicate baseline guides.

Blue dotted lines indicate grid guides.

Blue dotted lines indicate margins.

Figure 12.19 **Adjusting Guides in the Ruler Guides Dialog Box**

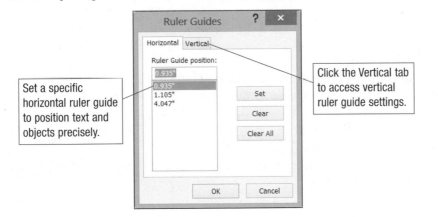

Set a specific horizontal ruler guide to position text and objects precisely.

Click the Vertical tab to access vertical ruler guide settings.

Align objects to rulers, guides, or other objects by clicking to insert a check mark in the *Guides* check box and/or *Objects* check box in the Layout group on the PAGE DESIGN tab. When you move an object near another object, ruler, or guide, you will see the object being pulled toward it.

To view the rulers, guides, boundaries, baselines, Page Navigation pane, scratch area, fields, and the Graphics Manager, display the VIEW tab and check these options in the Show group. The scratch area is the gray area that appears outside the publication page.

In Exercise 12.2A, you will create the brochure shown in Figure 12.20 on page 448 using a Publisher template. You will create a new color scheme for the flyer and use guides to align objects within it.

1. With Publisher open and the New backstage area displayed, click the <u>Brochure</u> link to the right of *Suggested searches* in the *FEATURED* section.
2. Double-click the *Informational brochure (Business design)* template option, as shown below.

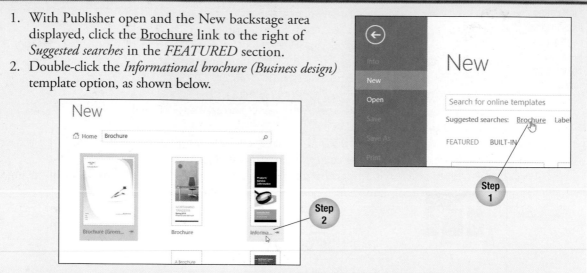

3. Make sure the page 1 thumbnail is selected in the Page Navigation pane, click the PAGE DESIGN tab, click the More button in the Schemes group, and then click *Create New Color Scheme* at the drop-down gallery.
4. At the Create New Color Scheme dialog box, click the down-pointing arrow at the right of *Followed hyperlink* in the *Scheme colors* section and then click the *Orange* option in the second row.
5. Type **My Scheme** in the *Color scheme name* text box and then click the Save button.
6. Click the Guides button in the Layout group on the PAGE DESIGN tab and then click the *3 Columns with Heading* option in the *Built-In Ruler Guides* section at the drop-down list.

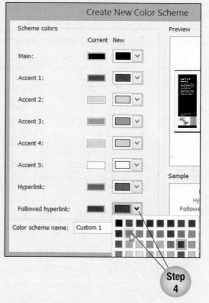

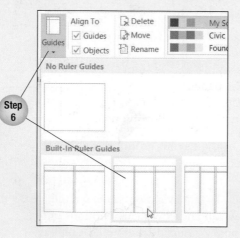

7. Click to select the *Product/Service Information* placeholder text in the cover panel on page 1 and then type **Worldwide Events Planning**.

8. Press Ctrl + A to select *Worldwide Events Planning*, click the TEXT BOX TOOLS FORMAT tab, click the Text Fit button in the Text group, and then click *Best Fit* at the drop-down list.

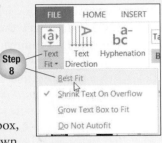

9. Select the picture placeholder (magnifying glass) in the same panel, click the PICTURE TOOLS FORMAT tab, click the Change Picture button in the Adjust group, and then click *Change Picture* at the drop-down list.

10. At the Insert Pictures window, click in the *Office.com Clip Art* text box, type **globe hands**, press Enter, and then double-click the image shown in Figure 12.20 on page 548, or a similar image if this one is no longer available.

11. Click outside of the image to deselect the image, click the original image that Publisher moved to the scratch area at the right of the publication, and then press the Delete key.

12. Select the *Organization Name* placeholder text below the image, press F9 to zoom in, change the font size to 9 points, and then type **Worldwide Events Planning, Inc.**

13. Select the tagline placeholder text in the brochure cover panel (*Your business tag line here.*) and then type **Corporate Meetings | Weddings | Holiday Parties | Cultural Events**.

14. Position the insertion point in the new corporate tagline text, click the HOME tab if necessary to make it active, click the Paragraph Spacing button in the Paragraph group, click *Paragraph Spacing Options* at the drop-down list, type **3** in the *Before paragraphs* measurement box in the *Line spacing* section, and then click OK.

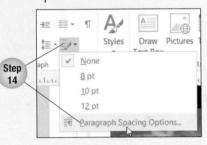

15. Select the telephone placeholder text, change the font size to 9 points, and then type **Phone: 212.555.9999**.

16. Save the publication with the name **C12-E02-BrochurePage1**.

17. Select the Organization logo placeholder in the middle panel, right-click the logo, and then click *Delete Object* at the shortcut menu.

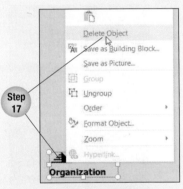

18. Insert the logo in the middle panel as shown in Figure 12.20 by clicking the INSERT tab, clicking the Pictures button in the Illustrations group, navigating to your Chapter12 folder, and then double-clicking ***WorldwideLogo.png***.

19. Drag the new logo to the location shown in the middle panel in Figure 12.20. As you drag the image, use the vertical object alignment bar (displays as a pink dashed line) to center align the logo horizontally in the panel.

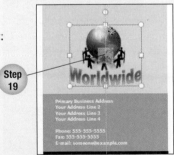

20. Replace the *Primary Business Address*, *Phone*, *Fax*, and *E-mail* placeholder text in the middle panel by typing the following text:

    421 Lexington Avenue, Suite 500
    New York, NY 10170-0555 [Press Enter twice.]
    Phone: 212.555.9999
    Fax: 212.555.9888
    Email: worldwide@emcp.net

21. Select the *Back Panel Heading* placeholder text in the left panel and then type **We are organized....**

22. Click the placeholder text in the text box below *We are organized* and then insert **OrganizedText.docx** from your Chapter12 folder. ***Hint: The text from the Word document will not display against the black fill in the text box. When you apply the style in the next step, the text will display in white against the black fill.***

23. Press Ctrl + A to select the text you just inserted, click the HOME tab, click the Styles button in the Styles group, scroll down the drop-down gallery, and then click *Body Text 4*.

24. If necessary, resize the text box containing the text you just inserted so that all of the text is visible. ***Hint: A small box containing an ellipsis will display on the text box border if all text is not visible.***

25. Select the caption placeholder text at the bottom of the left panel and then type **Our event planners are CSEP or CMP certified planners.** Position the caption as shown in Figure 12.20.

26. Right-click the key image below the caption text box, point to *Change Picture* at the shortcut menu, and then click *Change Picture* at the side menu. At the Insert Pictures window, click in the *Office.com Clip Art* text box, type **planners**, and then press Enter. Insert the image shown in Figure 12.20 (or a similar image). Resize and position the image as shown in the figure.

27. Delete the old key image from the scratch area. ***Hint: Make sure only the image in the scratch area is selected before deleting the image.***

28. Save **C12-E02-BrochurePage1.pub**.

Figure 12.20 Brochure Created in Exercise 12.2A

Using the Design Checker

The Design Checker reviews your publication for a variety of design and layout issues, identifies potential problems, and suggests options to fix them. For example, if your message has many large, high-resolution photos or it contains bitmapped text, the Design Checker will indicate that the file size may be too large for some email recipients' mailboxes.

To run the Design Checker, click the FILE tab and then click the Run Design Checker button at the Info backstage area. This displays the Design Checker task pane, as shown in Figure 12.21. At this task pane, click options to customize how the checker will review your publication. Click an item in the *Select an item to fix* list box to select the item in the publication and then, if necessary, make changes to address the problems identified by the Design Checker. Once an item has been fixed, it will be removed from the list.

In Exercise 12.2B, you will format the back of the brochure you started in Exercise 12.2A. You will then review your publication by running the design checker.

Figure 12.21 Using the Design Checker

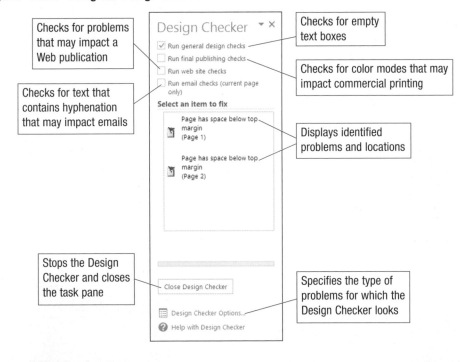

Checks for problems that may impact a Web publication

Checks for text that contains hyphenation that may impact emails

Checks for empty text boxes

Checks for color modes that may impact commercial printing

Displays identified problems and locations

Stops the Design Checker and closes the task pane

Specifies the type of problems for which the Design Checker looks

---

Exercise 12.2B Creating a Brochure Using a Publisher Template and the Design Checker   Part 2 of 2

1. With **C12-E02-BrochurePage1.pub** open, save it with the name **C12-E02-EventPlanner**.
2. Format the left panel on page 2 by completing the following steps:
   a. Click the page 2 thumbnail in the Page Navigation pane.
   b. Select the pushpin placeholder graphic, click the PICTURE TOOLS FORMAT tab, click the Change Picture button in the Adjust group, and then click *Change Picture* at the drop-down list.

c. At the Insert Pictures window, click in the *Office.com Clip Art* text box, type **worldwide** or **around the world** and then press Enter. Insert the image similar to Figure 12.22 on page 553. ***Hint: Select a similar image if the image is no longer available.***

d. Delete the original pushpin picture from the scratch area.

e. Select the *Main Inside Heading* placeholder text and then type **Why pick Worldwide?**

f. Select the placeholder text in the text box below *Why pick Worldwide?* and then insert **KeyFactor.docx** from your Chapter12 folder.

g. Press Ctrl + A to select the inserted text, click the HOME tab, click the Styles button in the Styles group, and then click the *Body Text* style. Resize the text box if the overflow button displays.

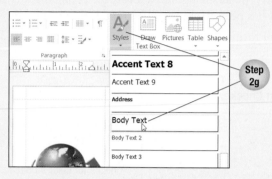

h. With the text still selected, click the Font Color button arrow in the Font group on the HOME tab and then click *Sample Font Color*. (The mouse pointer changes to the eyedropper tool.)

i. Drag the eyedropper tool to the green area of one of the continents in the globe image and then click the left mouse button. ***Hint: The green color from the image will automatically change the text color of the selected text.***

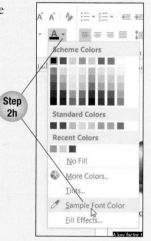

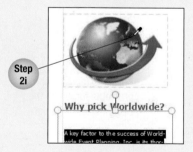

j. Drag and position the globe image and the text box below the title *Why pick Worldwide?* so they display as shown in Figure 12.22.

3. Select the first *Secondary Heading* placeholder text in the middle panel and then type **Corporate Events**.

4. Select the placeholder text in the text box below *Corporate Events* and then insert **CorporateEvents.docx** from your Chapter12 folder.

5. Select the *Secondary Heading* placeholder text below the *Corporate Events* heading and text and then type **Personal Events**.

6. Select the placeholder text below *Personal Events* and then insert **PersonalEvents.docx** from your Chapter12 folder.

7. Select the last *Secondary Heading* placeholder and then type **Special Events**.
8. Select the placeholder text below *Special Events* and then insert **SpecialEvents.docx** located from your Chapter12 folder. ***Hint: The two side-by-side text boxes give the appearance of two columns of text.***
9. Decrease the bottom border of the text box in the middle panel to make the *Special Events* heading begin at the top of the third panel (see Figure 12.22). Make any other necessary adjustments so that the panel displays similar to the figure. ***Hint: You may need to insert an extra line space above the* Personal Events *heading.***
10. Right-click the text box object at the bottom of the page and then click *Delete Object* at the shortcut menu.
11. Right-click the lightbulb graphic at the bottom of the page and then click *Delete Object* at the shortcut menu.
12. Click the Pictures button in the Illustrations group on the INSERT tab and then insert **EventGraphic.png** from your Chapter12 folder.
13. With the image selected, increase the size using the sizing handles and then drag it to the bottom of the page and center it at the top of the black bar as shown to the right and in Figure 12.22. ***Hint: Notice the pink vertical and horizontal guides as you drag the image to the bottom of the page.***

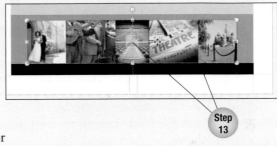

Step 13

14. Save **C12-E02-EventPlanner.pub**.
15. Apply a page background and change the color scheme by completing the following steps:
    a. Click the PAGE DESIGN tab, click the Background button in the Page Background group, and then click the *Accent 3 Horizontal Gradient* option (third column, first row in the *Gradient Background* section).

    b. Click the Undo button on the Quick Access toolbar to remove the background. ***Note: The blue gradient background color will use a lot of ink. You may want to use the background color if your budget allows you to send the publication to a professional printer or if you are distributing the publication only electronically.***

c. Change the color scheme by clicking the More button in the Schemes group on the PAGE DESIGN tab and then clicking the *Meadow* option in the *Built-In (classic)* section.

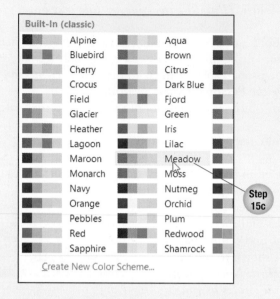

Step 15c

d. View the changes to the overall look of the publication.
e. Click the Undo button on the Quick Access toolbar to return to the original color scheme.
16. Run the Design Checker by clicking the FILE tab and then clicking the Run Design Checker button at the Info backstage area. At the Design Checker task pane, if necessary, click to add check marks in the *Run general design checks* check box and the *Run final publishing checks* check box. Review the items to fix in the *Select an item to fix* list box. **Hint: It is okay to ignore these particular suggestions.**
17. Click the Close Design Checker button located at the bottom of the task pane.
18. Save, print, and then close **C12-E02-EventPlanner.pub**.

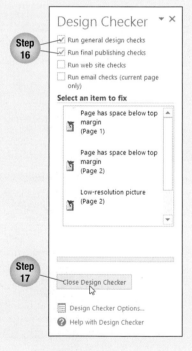

Step 16

Step 17

Figure 12.22 Brochure Created in Exercise 12.2B

Why pick Worldwide?

A key factor to the success of Worldwide Event Planning, Inc. is its thorough research of all its vendors and suppliers. Its dedicated research also involves reading up on issues of customs and etiquette in unfamiliar markets. Worldwide conducts research; creates an event design; finds a suitable site; arranges food, décor, and entertainment; and plans transportation to and from the event.

Corporate Events

Our team of event planners provides coordination, execution, and management of corporate events from start to finish. Worldwide offers services for the following corporate events:

Global Conferences
Networking Events
Fundraisers
Holiday Parties
Office Events
Marketing Events
Trade Shows

Personal Events

Our mission is to assist every client in creating memorable events with a personal touch.

Family Reunions
Birthdays
Bridal Showers & Engagements
Anniversaries
Weddings
Graduations
Travel Arrangements & Tours

Special Events

Coordinating and managing the details of a special event can be daunting. Our professional staff will plan, coordinate, and execute your special event to perfection.

We offer services for the following special events:

Theatre/Concert Events
Parades
Political Events
Fundraisers
Fashion Shows
Sporting Events
Cruises
Cultural Events

Inserting Building Blocks

Building blocks are reusable pieces of content such as business information, headings, calendars, borders, and advertisements that are stored in galleries. Publisher 2013 has a variety of built-in building blocks for you to choose from.

To insert a built-in building block, complete the following steps:

1. If your publication contains multiple pages, select the page where you want to insert the building block in the Page Navigation pane.
2. Click the INSERT tab and then click the desired building block button in the Building Blocks group.
3. Scroll to find a building block or click the *More <gallery name>* option to open the Building Block Library dialog box.
4. Click the desired building block. Figure 12.23 on page 554 illustrates the Page Parts building block gallery.

You can also access the Building Block Library by clicking the Building Blocks group dialog box launcher.

Page Parts

Calendars

Borders & Accents

Advertisements

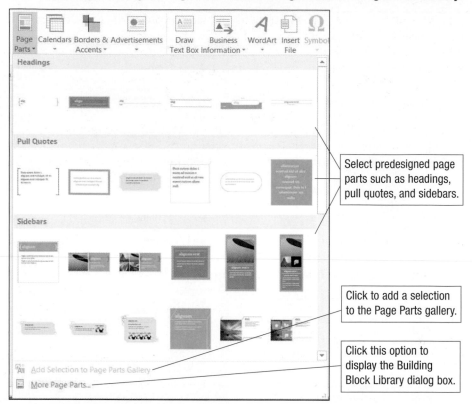

Select predesigned page parts such as headings, pull quotes, and sidebars.

Click to add a selection to the Page Parts gallery.

Click this option to display the Building Block Library dialog box.

Working with Pictures, Captions, and Shapes

With buttons on the INSERT tab, you can insert a picture placeholder, picture, clip art, or shape. You can then adjust the appearance of the picture or modify it with picture styles, effects, and captions. Using the drawing tools, you can create lines and basic shapes, as well as custom shapes that include balloons, arrows, stars, and many more elements that will add interest to your publication.

Inserting a Picture Placeholder

Picture Placeholder

Pictures

Online Pictures

To insert a picture placeholder, click the Picture Placeholder button in the Illustrations group on the INSERT tab. The picture placeholder is an empty picture frame that is used to reserve space for pictures you want to add later. You can insert a picture into the picture frame by selecting the picture placeholder and then clicking either the Pictures button or the Online Pictures button in the Illustrations group on the INSERT tab to search for and insert the desired image.

When you insert an image, the PICTURE TOOLS FORMAT tab displays with options to change the image brightness and contrast; recolor the image; apply a picture style; change the picture border, shape, caption, or shadow; crop the image and change the text wrapping; and more.

Inserting a Caption

Publisher includes a caption gallery with numerous picture caption designs. Insert an image, select the image, and then click the Caption button in the Picture Styles group on the PICTURE TOOLS FORMAT tab. Click the desired caption format from the drop-down gallery as shown in Figure 12.24.

Caption

Inserting a Shape

To insert a shape, click the Shapes button in the Illustrations group on the INSERT tab and then select the desired shape from the drop-down list. Click and drag to draw the shape, and then customize the shape with options on the DRAWING TOOLS FORMAT tab.

Shapes

Viewing the Graphics Manager

The Graphics Manager task pane helps you to efficiently manage all of the pictures that you have inserted into your publication, such as ***embedded pictures*** (pictures that are stored within a publication rather than being linked to a source file outside of the publication) or ***linked pictures*** (pictures that link to a high-resolution image file that is stored outside of the publication file). Display the Graphics Manager task pane by clicking the VIEW tab and then clicking the Graphics Manager check box in the Show group to insert a check mark.

embedded picture
A picture stored within a publication rather than in a file outside of the publication

linked picture
A picture that links to a high-resolution image file stored outside of the publication

Figure 12.24 Inserting a Caption

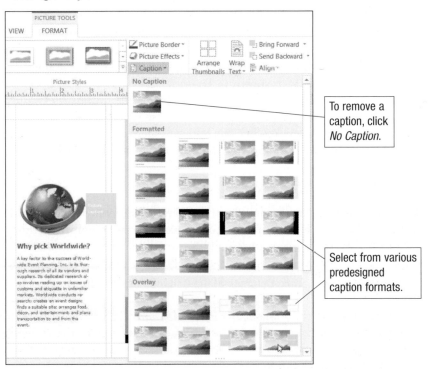

Formatting Text

Publisher has many features to help you format text in publications. Text boxes can be set in single or multiple columns and they can be connected so that text flows from one text box to the next. Good publication design helps guide the reader, and Publisher helps you create text elements like drop caps, continued notices, and page numbers. These features will be applied to the newsletter created in Exercise 12.3.

Inserting Columns

In Publisher, columns are created using text boxes. To create a text box, click the HOME tab, click the Draw Text Box button in the Objects group, and then drag in the publication to create the text box. Format the text box for columns by completing the following steps:

1. Right-click the text box that you want to change and then click *Format Text Box* at the shortcut menu.
2. At the Format Text Box dialog box, click the Text Box tab and then click the Columns button in the *Text autofitting* section.
3. At the Columns dialog box, shown in Figure 12.25, type the number of columns you want in the *Number* measurement box and then type the spacing value between the columns, which is known as the gutter, in the *Spacing* measurement box.
4. Click OK to close the Columns dialog box and then click OK to close the Format Text Box dialog box.

You can also insert columns in a text box by selecting the text box and then clicking the Columns button in the Alignment group on the TEXT BOX TOOLS FORMAT tab. If you want to add a line between the columns, complete the following steps:

Columns

1. Right-click the text box, click *Format Text Box* at the shortcut menu, and then click the Colors and Lines tab at the Format Text Box dialog box. The dialog box will display as shown in Figure 12.26.
2. Click the center vertical line option below the image area in the *Preview* section and make sure no other options are selected in the *Preview* section.
3. In the *Line* section, click the options (such as color, transparency, width, and type) you want to apply to the center line and then click OK.

Creating a Drop Cap

Recall from Chapter 6 that a drop cap is created by setting the first letter of the first word in a paragraph in a larger font size, dropped down into the paragraph or extended into the margin. Drop caps identify the beginning of major sections or parts of a document.

Figure 12.25 Formatting Columns at the Columns Dialog Box

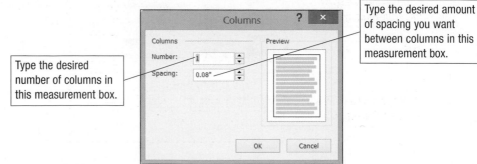

Type the desired number of columns in this measurement box.

Type the desired amount of spacing you want between columns in this measurement box.

Figure 12.26 Adding a Line between Columns at the Format Text Box

To create a drop cap in Publisher, complete the following steps:

1. Click anywhere in the paragraph in which you want to create a drop cap.
2. Click the Drop Cap button in the Typography group on the TEXT BOX TOOLS FORMAT tab, and then click the desired drop cap format. Figure 12.27 shows the Drop Cap gallery.

Drop Cap

Customize a drop cap by selecting it and then using buttons and options in the Font group on the HOME tab to change the font, font color, font style, position, and size. Alternatively, you can create a custom drop cap by selecting *Custom Drop Cap* at the Drop Cap button drop-down gallery, making changes at the Drop Cap dialog box, and then clicking OK. When you create a custom drop cap, the custom style is added to the available drop caps list, and you can use this style to create other drop caps in the current publication.

Figure 12.27 Inserting a Drop Cap from the Drop Cap Button Drop-down Gallery

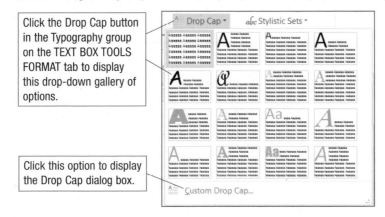

Using Linked Text Boxes

Text boxes are generally used in creating newsletters and many other publications in Publisher. Layout guides can be set up in a column format and then used to assist in sizing and positioning the text boxes for consistent-looking columns. For text to flow from one text box to the next, you must use the linked text box feature. As mentioned previously, Publisher refers to linked text boxes in a series as a *story*.

To create a story, complete the following steps:

1. Create as many text boxes as you think you may need.
2. Select the first text box in the series.
3. Click the Create Link button in the Linking group on the TEXT BOX TOOLS FORMAT tab. The pointer becomes an upright pitcher when you move it over the selected text box.
4. Position the pointer (pitcher) over the empty text box that will be the next one in the series and the pitcher tilts, as shown in Figure 12.28.
5. Click the empty text box to create the link to the original text box.
6. Repeat steps similar to Steps 2–4 to link all the text boxes in the story.

Text boxes that are linked will display a right-pointing arrow and a left-pointing arrow to help you advance from one box to the other.

Create Link

DTP POINTER

Linked text boxes make it easy to start a story on one page and continue it on another.

Adding a Jump Line

When you link text boxes, text that does not fit into the first text box flows into the next linked text box. A chain of linked text boxes can span numerous pages. When a story spans several pages, it is a good idea to include a jump line—a short note indicating the location where the article continues or is being continued from—to help the reader know where to go next. To add a jump line to a text box, complete the following steps:

1. Select the text box where you want to place the jump line and then click the TEXT BOX TOOLS FORMAT tab.
2. Click the Text group dialog box launcher.
3. At the Format Text Box dialog box, click the Text Box tab. In the *Text autofitting* section, click to add a check mark in the *Include "Continued on page…"* check box, or click the *Include "Continued from page…"* check box to add a check mark as shown in Figure 12.29, and then click OK.

Figure 12.28 "Pouring" Text into a Linked Text Box

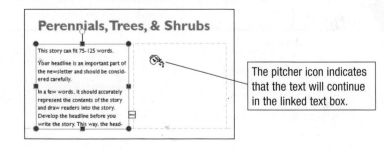

Figure 12.29 Adding a Jump Line

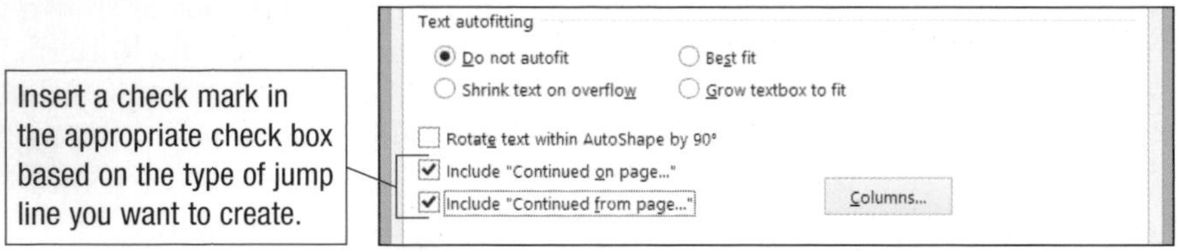

Insert a check mark in the appropriate check box based on the type of jump line you want to create.
Text autofitting
Do not autofit
Best fit
Shrink text on overflow
Grow textbox to fit
Rotate text within AutoShape by 90°
Include "Continued on page..."
Include "Continued from page..."
Columns...

Inserting Page Numbers

Page numbers can be added to a publication by clicking the Page Number button in the Header & Footer group on the INSERT tab. At the Page Number drop-down list, click an option to position the number at the top left, top center, top right, bottom left, bottom center, or bottom right of the page; to position the number in the current text box; to show or remove the page number on the first page; or to change the format of the numbers as shown in Figure 12.30. Page numbers are inserted in the master page of a publication.

In Exercise 12.3A, you will use a Publisher template to create the newsletter shown in Figure 12.31 on page 566 You will create linked text boxes, insert and format a picture, create a drop cap, and use building blocks to insert a pull quote and an advertisement.

Figure 12.30 Inserting Page Numbers

ookmark
Header
Footer
Page Number
Top Left
Top Center
Top Right
Bottom Left
Bottom Center
Bottom Right
Insert in Current Text Box
Format Page Numbers...
Show Page Number on First Page
Select a desired page number location.

Start

Exercise 12.3A Creating a Newsletter from a Publisher Template — Part 1 of 2

1. With Publisher open, click the *BUILT-IN* option at the New backstage area and then click the *Newsletters* category.
2. Scroll through the newsletter templates, click the *Summer* template in the *More Installed Templates* section, and then customize the template with options in the task pane at the right side of the screen by completing the following steps:
   a. Change the color scheme to *Field.*
   b. Change the font scheme to *Solstice (Gill Sans MT).*
   c. Click the down-pointing arrow at the right of the *Business information* option box and then click the *Create new* option.

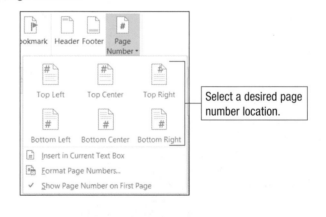

d. Type the information in the Create New Business Information Set dialog box as shown below. Type your first and last names in the *Individual name* text box. Add the Butterfield Gardens logo (**ButterfieldGardenLogo.png**) by clicking the Add Logo button, or if a logo already exists, clicking the Change button. The Butterfield Gardens logo is located in your Chapter12 folder. Type **Butterfield** in the *Business Information set name* text box and then click the Save button when you are finished typing the remaining text.

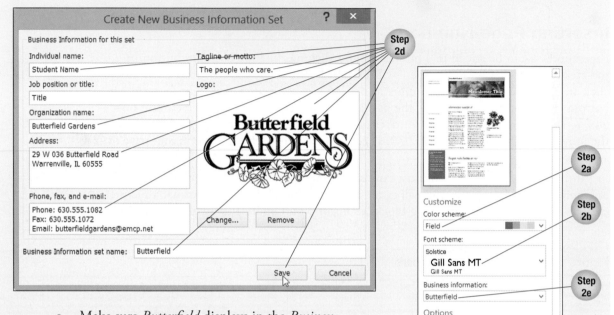

e. Make sure *Butterfield* displays in the *Business information* option box in the task pane.
f. Scroll down the task pane and then change the *Page size* option to *One-page spread*.
g. Click the CREATE button.
3. Save the newsletter with the name **C12-E03-Butterfield**.
4. At the Page Navigation pane, click the page 2 thumbnail, hold down the Shift key, and then click the page 3 thumbnail.
5. Click the PAGE DESIGN tab and then click the Delete button in the Pages group. At the Microsoft prompt asking if you want to delete the pages, click the Yes button.
6. Display the first page and then press F9.
7. Click the *Newsletter Date* placeholder and then type **August 2015**.
8. Click the *Volume 1, Issue 1* placeholder and then type **Volume 2, Issue 8**.
9. Click in the *Business Name* placeholder (contains *Butterfield Gardens*), click the Smart Tag button that displays at the left of the placeholder, and then click *Convert to Plain Text* at the drop-down list.
10. Select the text in *Butterfield Gardens* in the placeholder and then type **The people who care.**
11. Click the *Newsletter Title* placeholder and then type **Butterfield Gardens**.
12. Select *Butterfield Gardens,* click the HOME tab, and then click the Font group dialog box launcher.

13. At the Font dialog box, change the font to 48-point Gabriola, click the down-pointing arrow at the right of the *Stylistic Set* option box, click *6* at the drop-down list, and then click OK.

14. Click the *Lead Story Headline* placeholder and then type **Winterizing Your Yard**.

15. The article text that you will insert will not fit into the linked text boxes on page 1; therefore, you will need to continue your story on page 2. To do this, complete the following steps:

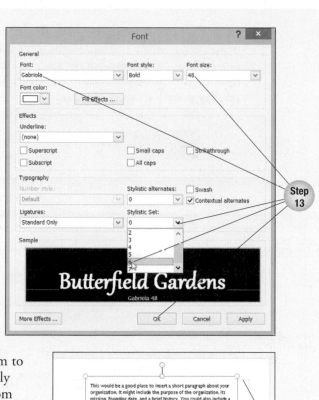

a. Click the page 2 thumbnail in the Page Navigation pane. *Hint: Notice that the text you added to the Business Information set automatically appears in the placeholders in the template.*

b. Select the text box at the top right side of page 2, change the zoom to a percentage that allows you to clearly see the text, and then drag the bottom center sizing handle downward to the horizontal line at the top of the *Back Page Story Headline* placeholder to increase the height of the text box. Drag the top middle sizing handle upward to the blue margin guide. *Hint: Once you release the mouse button after dragging the sizing handle to the desired location, the text box will expand below the green horizontal line and above the blue layout guide; however, the text within the text box is still aligned at the horizontal line and layout guide.*

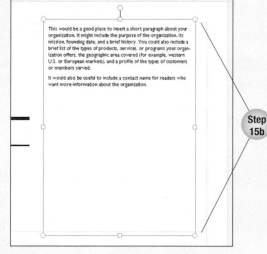

c. Click the page 1 thumbnail in the Page Navigation pane and then click to select the third connected text box (click below the flower graphic caption to select the text box, not the flower) under the heading *Winterizing Your Yard*. *Note: When you click to select a specific connected text box, you will see a Go To Previous Text Box button (displays as a left-pointing triangle) or Go To Next Text Box button (displays as a right-pointing triangle) near the top or bottom of the selected text box. Use these buttons to move between the connected text boxes.*

d. Click the TEXT BOX TOOLS FORMAT tab and then click the Create Link button in the Linking group. The mouse pointer will display as a pitcher when you point at the page.

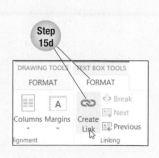

e. Click the page 2 thumbnail in the Page Navigation pane, position the mouse pointer (displays a pouring pitcher) in the text box at the top right side of the page (the one you just resized), and then click the left mouse button. The text box should now be linked to the text boxes on the first page. ***Hint: The Go to Previous Text Box button should display near the top of this box.***

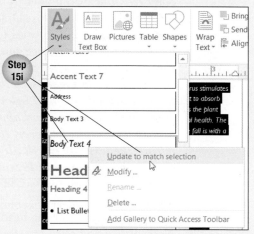

Step 15e

f. Click the page 1 thumbnail in the Page Navigation pane, click in the first connected text box under *Winterizing Your Yard*, and then insert **Winterizing.docx** from your Chapter12 folder.

g. With the insertion point positioned anywhere in the article, press Ctrl + A and then apply the Body Text 4 style.

h. If you look at the linked text box on page 2, you will see an overflow symbol near the bottom of the text box. This symbol indicates that all the text does not fit in the text box. To correct this situation, make sure all of the text is selected, verify that the font is Gill Sans MT, and then change the font size to 9 points.

i. Click the HOME tab, click the Styles button, right-click the *Body Text 4* option, and then click *Update to match selection* at the shortcut menu.

j. Display page 1 and then click two times on the flower graphic (do not double-click) in the *Winterizing Your Yard* article. (Sizing handles with small *Xs* should display.)

k. Click the Change Picture button in the Adjust group on the PICTURE TOOLS FORMAT tab and then click *Change Picture* at the drop-down list.

l. At the Insert Pictures window, click in the *Office.com Clip Art* text box, type **gardening**, and then press Enter. Double-click a gardening image that interests you.

m. Delete the original picture from the scratch area. (Make sure you do not delete the new image.)

n. Select the new image and then click the PICTURE TOOLS FORMAT tab if necessary to make it active.

o. Click the Caption button in the Picture Styles group and then click the *Box, Reversed - Layout 2* option (second column, second row in the *Overlay* section).

p. Select the caption placeholder text, *Picture caption*, and then type **Think spring!**

q. Select *Think spring!*, click the Character Spacing button in the Font group, and then click *Loose* at the drop-down list.

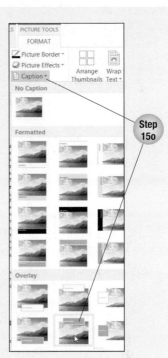

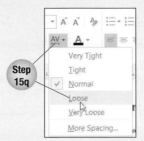

16. Add a jump line from the *Winterizing Your Yard* article on page 1 to the rest of the article on page 2 by completing the following steps:

a. Right-click the third connected text column on page 1 of the winterizing article and then click *Format Text Box* at the shortcut menu.

b. At the Format Text Box dialog box, click the Text Box tab.

c. Click the *Include "Continued on page..."* check box to insert a check mark and then click OK.

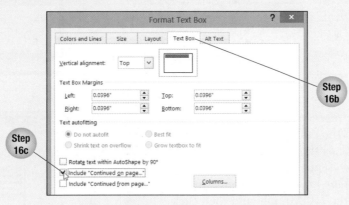

d. Click the Go to Next Text Box button in the third linked text box on page 1.

e. With the insertion point positioned in the text box containing the rest of the article on page 2, right-click in the text box and then click *Format Text Box* at the shortcut menu.

f. At the Format Text Box dialog box, click the Text Box tab.

g. Click the *Include "Continued from page..."* check box to insert a check mark and then click OK.

h. Click the Go to Previous Text Box button in the text box on page 2 and the Go to Next Text Box button in the last text box on page 1 to view the jump lines.

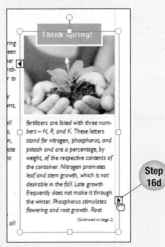

17. Click to position the insertion point in the first text box that contains the *Winterizing Your Yard* text on page 1, click the TEXT BOX TOOLS FORMAT tab, click the Drop Cap button in the Typography group, and then click the *Drop Cap Style 7* option at the drop-down gallery (fourth column, second row).

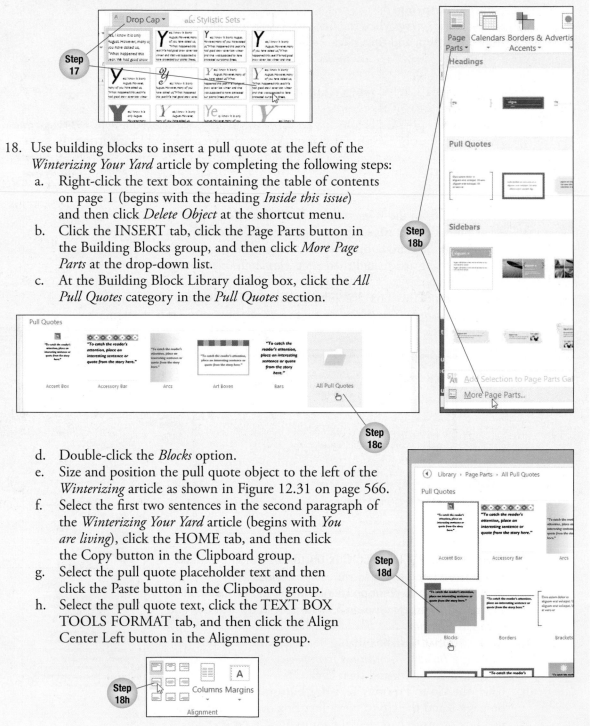

18. Use building blocks to insert a pull quote at the left of the *Winterizing Your Yard* article by completing the following steps:
    a. Right-click the text box containing the table of contents on page 1 (begins with the heading *Inside this issue*) and then click *Delete Object* at the shortcut menu.
    b. Click the INSERT tab, click the Page Parts button in the Building Blocks group, and then click *More Page Parts* at the drop-down list.
    c. At the Building Block Library dialog box, click the *All Pull Quotes* category in the *Pull Quotes* section.
    d. Double-click the *Blocks* option.
    e. Size and position the pull quote object to the left of the *Winterizing* article as shown in Figure 12.31 on page 566.
    f. Select the first two sentences in the second paragraph of the *Winterizing Your Yard* article (begins with *You are living*), click the HOME tab, and then click the Copy button in the Clipboard group.
    g. Select the pull quote placeholder text and then click the Paste button in the Clipboard group.
    h. Select the pull quote text, click the TEXT BOX TOOLS FORMAT tab, and then click the Align Center Left button in the Alignment group.
    i. With the pull quote text still selected, change the font to 8-point Gill Sans MT and then apply bold formatting.

j. Click at the end of the pull quote text and then press the Enter key to insert an extra blank line at the end of the text.

k. Insert quotation marks around the text. (Your text should appear as shown in Figure 12.31.)

19. Format the sidebar object located below the pull quote object by completing the following steps:

a. Select the bulleted text under the subhead *Special points of interest:*.

b. Type the following:

Winterizing includes good hydration, feeding, pruning, and disease control. [Press Enter.]

Perennials, trees, and shrubs on sale. [Press Enter.]

Taking care of birds.

c. Add 6 points of space before *Special points of interest:*, select *Special points of interest:* and change the font to 12.5-point Calisto MT, and then apply bold formatting.

20. Select the *Secondary Story Headline* placeholder and then type **Perennials, Trees, & Shrubs**.

21. Select the story placeholder text below the *Perennials* headline and then insert **Sale.docx** from your Chapter12 folder.

22. Press Ctrl + A to select the entire article, apply the Accent Text 7 style, and then change the font size to 10 points.

23. Use building blocks to insert an advertisement object by completing the following steps:

a. Click the INSERT tab.

b. Click the Advertisements button in the Building Blocks group.

c. Click the *Pointer* option in the *Attention Getters* section.

d. Drag the pointer object to the location shown in 12.31.

e. Select the placeholder text inside the pointer object and then type **50% Off**.

f. Click two separate times on the bottom edge of the black pointer object to display the black *X*s around the entire shape (not just the text within the shape).

g. Click the DRAWING TOOLS FORMAT tab.

h. Click the More button in the Shape Styles group and then click the *Horizontal Gradient - Accent 2* option at the drop-down gallery (third column, seventh row).

24. Save **C12-E03-Butterfield.pub**.

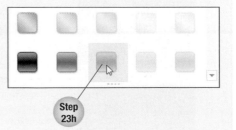

Figure 12.31 Newsletter Created in Exercise 12.3A

August 2015

Volume 2, Issue 8

The people who care.

Butterfield Gardens

Winterizing Your Yard

> "You are living in USDA Hardiness Zone 5. The average minimum temperature is minus 20 degrees Fahrenheit."

Yes, I know it is only August. However, many of you have asked us, "What happened this year. We had good snow cover last winter and that was supposed to have protected our plants (trees, shrubs, and perennials), but we lost some." Answering that question—and helping you avoid similar losses next year—is the reason for this article.

You are living in USDA Hardiness Zone 5. The average minimum temperature is minus 20 degrees Fahrenheit. We tend to have some miserable winds out of the north and west during the winter creating wind chills as low as minus 80 degrees. Winterizing issues include hydration, feeding, pruning, and disease control.

Hydration. We had a good spring for moisture. The summer has been extremely dry, as was last summer and fall. Lack of moisture was probably the largest single contributor to winter losses this past year. Two seasons of drought will be deadly for your plants, trees, shrubs, lawns, and perennials. Make sure that your plants go into the winter well watered. Many evergreen shrubs, including boxwood, rhododendron, holly, and bayberry, also appreciate some winter protection to prevent desiccation by our vicious winds. Wrap them loosely, with burlap and/or apply an anti-desiccant spray.

Feeding. After August 1, avoid feeding plants with high nitrogen fertilizers. As you will remember, all

Think spring!

fertilizers are listed with three numbers—N, P, and K. These letters stand for nitrogen, phosphorus, and potash and are a percentage, by weight, of the respective contents of the container. Nitrogen promotes leaf and stem growth, which is not desirable in the fall. Late growth frequently does not make it through the winter. Phosphorus stimulates flowering and root growth. Root

(Continued on page 2)

Special points of interest:

- Winterizing includes good hydration, feeding, pruning, and disease control.
- Perennials, trees, and shrubs on sale.
- Taking care of birds.

Perennials, Trees, & Shrubs

50% Off

Fall is an excellent time to plant. The hot weather has been replaced by cool temperatures and the plants no longer feel the urge to grow leaves. They can concentrate on roots and build a firm base for next year's growth spurt.

Cool weather also means that we do not need to be quite as careful with the watering schedule.
The perennials go on sale September 1. The trees and shrubs go on sale October 1. Take advantage of this oppor-

tunity to add to the value of your property and the overall enjoyment of your yard or garden. Your family will thank you for your efforts next spring!

Sharing a Publication

After your publication has been designed and created, you can print it, send it to a commercial printer, or send it as an email message.

Sending as an Email Message

You can send your newsletter as an email message or as an attachment to an email message to one or more recipients. If you want to send your newsletter to just a few recipients, you can simply send it as an email message. To send a newsletter as an email, click the FILE tab, click the *Share* option, click the *Email* option in the middle panel, and then click the *Send Current Page*, *Send as Attachment*, *Send as PDF*, or *Send as XPS* button as shown in Figure 12.32. If you click the *Email Preview* option in the middle panel and then click the Email Preview button, a preview of the newsletter will display in your web browser.

Using Mail Merge or Email Merge

If you want to send your newsletter to many recipients and you want to personalize it for each recipient, you can perform a mail merge or an email merge. To perform a mail merge, open the publication, click the MAILINGS tab, and then click the Mail Merge button arrow in the Start group. At the drop-down list either click *Mail Merge* and use the buttons on the MAILINGS tab or click *Step-by-Step Mail Merge Wizard* and use the Mail Merge task pane as shown in Figure 12.33 on page 568. You can use an existing list of contacts or type a new list.

Mail Merge

Just as when you perform a mail merge, when you perform an email merge, you must open the publication you wish to share. In this case, you click the E-mail Merge button arrow in the Start group on the MAILINGS tab. From the drop-down list click either *E-mail Merge* or *Step by Step E-mail Merge Wizard*.

E-mail Merge

Figure 12.32 Emailing a Publication with the Share Backstage Area

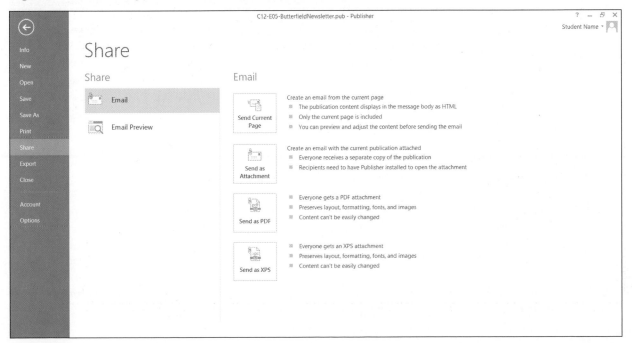

Figure 12.33 Emailing a Publication with the Mail Merge Task Pane

Mail Merge ▾ ✕

How Mail Merge works

Use Mail Merge to automatically add mailing addresses or personalized information to publications. Mail Merge is made up of three parts.

1 Recipient list	2 Publication with merge fields

First Name	Last Name	Dear
Tony	Allen	<<First Name>>
Adam	Barr	<<Last Name>>
Judy	Lew	

3 Merged publications	Dear Tony Allen	Dear Adam Barr	Dear Judy Lew

Create recipient list

Select the data source you want to use to create your recipient list. You can add more data to your list from other sources later.

◉ Use an existing list
  Select a file or database with recipient information

○ Select from Outlook Contacts
  Select names and addresses from an Outlook Contacts folder

○ Type a new list
  Type the names and addresses of recipients

Step 1 of 3

In Exercise 12.3B, you will create the second page of the newsletter you started in Exercise 12.3A. You will add article text and insert and format images. You will also add page numbers to the master page.

Exercise 12.3B Creating the Second Page of a Newsletter **Part 2 of 2** PORTFOLIO

1. With **C12-E03-Butterfield.pub** open, save it with the name **C12-E03-ButterfieldNewsletter**.
2. Click the page 2 thumbnail in the Page Navigation pane and make sure all the placeholder text is complete with the information that you entered into the Business Information set for Butterfield. If any of the information is missing, insert the text as shown in Figure 12.34 on page 570.
3. Select the placeholder text *The people who care.*, above the Butterfield logo, and change the font size to 18 points.
4. Increase the size of the Butterfield logo as shown in Figure 12.34.
5. Edit the text box containing the web address by selecting the *Web Address* placeholder text, typing **We're on the Web!**, pressing the Enter key, and then typing **www.emcp.net/butterfieldgardens**. Make sure the first *w* in *www* is lowercase.
6. Format the back story on page 2 by completing the following steps:
    a. Click to select the *Back Page Story Headline* placeholder text and then type **Fine Feathered Friends**.
    b. Click two times on the corn image (make sure only the corn image displays with black x's around it) in the lower left corner of the second page of the newsletter and then replace the image with the image shown in Figure 12.34. Use the search word *flycatcher* to find the image at Office.com. Delete the corn image from the scratch area. ***Hint: If the flycatcher image is no longer available, choose a similar bird image.***

c. Select the flycatcher image, click the PICTURE TOOLS FORMAT tab, click the Recolor button in the Adjust group, and then click the *RGB (204, 153, 51), Accent color 2 Dark* option at the drop-down list (second column, second row).

d. Click the Rotate Objects button in the Arrange group and then click *Flip Horizontal* at the drop-down gallery (second column, second row).

e. Select the caption placeholder for the flycatcher image and then type **Come see our selection of feeders, birdbaths, heaters, and quality bird food.**

f. With the insertion point positioned in the caption text box, add a fill color to the box by clicking the DRAWING TOOLS FORMAT tab, clicking the More button in the Shape Styles group, and then clicking the *Diagonal Gradient - Accent 2* option at the drop-down gallery (third column, sixth row).

7. Click in the placeholder text in the linked text boxes below *Fine Feathered Friends* and then insert **Birds.docx** from your Chapter12 folder.

8. Add a page number to page 2 by completing the following steps:

a. Click the INSERT tab and then click the Page Number button in the Header & Footer group.

b. Click *Show Page Number on First Page* at the drop-down list. (This will remove the check mark from the option).

c. Click the Page Number button again and then click the *Bottom Right* option in the drop-down list.

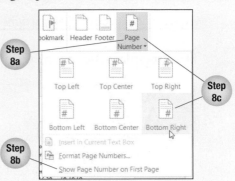

d. The page number exists in a footer in the Master Page view. Click the VIEW tab and then click the Master Page button in the Views group. Notice that *Master Page A* displays in the Page Navigation pane. With *Master Page A* selected in the Page Navigation pane, notice the page numbering code located in the footer. If additional pages are added to the newsletter, each page will be numbered consecutively.

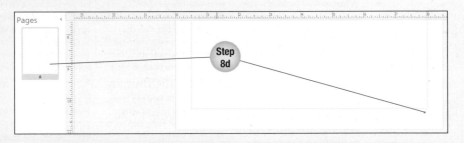

e. Click the Close Master Page button in the Close group.

f. Click the page 1 thumbnail in the Page Navigation pane and notice that no page number displays on page 1 in the newsletter. Click the page 2 thumbnail in the Page Navigation pane and notice that *2* displays in the lower right corner of the newsletter.

9. Save **C12-E03-ButterfieldNewsletter**.

10. Print both pages of the newsletter using one sheet of paper.

11. Close **C12-E03-ButterfieldNewsletter.pub**.

Figure 12.34 Newsletter Page Created in Exercise 12.3B

Butterfield Gardens

29 W 036 Butterfield Road
Warrenville, IL 60555

Phone: 630.555.1082
Fax: 630.555.1072
Email: butterfieldgardens@emcp.net

We're on the Web!

www.emcp.net/butterfieldgardens

The people who care.

(Continued from page 1)

growth enables the plant to absorb necessary water and nutrients from the soil. Potash helps the plant absorb micronutrients in the soil and promotes nutritional health. The most important feeding you can do for your plants in the fall is with a fertilizer in the 10-16-20 or 10-10-10 range.

Pruning. Pruning is stressful in the fall when the plant is still actively growing. If you feel the need to prune trees and scrubs, wait until they are completely dormant, usually in January or February. There are exceptions to this. Dormant pruning of flowering shrubs cuts off next year's flowers. Flowering shrubs should be pruned within a month of flowering. If you can, wait until next season. Lawn pruning should be reduced by raising the mowing deck to a much greater height.

Disease. Proper management of the preceding issues reduces stress that would otherwise weaken the plants, leaving them susceptible to diseases. Fungal problems can be treated at this time, as can insect infestations. A horticultural oil spray can be used to smother any insects that would like to overwinter on your trees and shrubs. This can be applied at any time from now through March. Fungal problems can be treated with lime sulfur spray.

Fine Feathered Friends

Come see our selection of feeders, birdbaths, heaters, and quality bird food.

When to feed birds. It is best to provide food all year long. February through August, when natural grasses and fruit bearing trees are not mature and birds are nesting and producing young, is very important. During the winter months, it is often difficult for birds and wildlife to find adequate food sources. The fall months are important because the feeding patterns are established for the winter.

What about water? Clean fresh water should be provided at all times. During winter months water sources are often frozen. A birdbath with a water heater will supply outdoor creatures with needed water. During the summer, drinking and bathing water is important. City (tap) water often contains chemicals that are not part of nature. Using a nutritionally fortified wild bird food is recommended.

How will birds find my feeders? Birds find food by sight. Place feeders in easily seen areas. Be patient and the birds will come. To have many birds on a frequent basis can take a year or two depending on your geographical area and the migration patterns of the birds. If you don't seem to be attracting birds, make sure you have the right food. If you purchase inexpensive mixes containing a lot of milo, millet, and corn, you may not attract the more desirable songbirds. If you have a good food available, try tying a piece of tin foil on top of the feeder. A little glint from this foil will catch their eye.

How much will the birds eat? Songbirds have a very high metabolic rate and a body temperature of 109 degrees. They need to eat constantly in order to store up energy for cold winter periods and need to eat frequently in summer months to burn off heat. Some birds will consume more than their body weight on a daily basis.

2

Preparing Publications for Commercial Printing

If you need printing options that you do not have on your desktop printer, you can send your publication to a commercial printer that can reproduce your work on an offset printing press or a high-quality digital printer. Publisher provides several tools to help prepare publications to allow for high-quality printing.

Using the Pack and Go Wizard

The Pack and Go Wizard is used to pack a publication and its linked files into a single file that you can send to a commercial printer to be printed. Pack and Go ensures that you have all the files necessary to hand off the publication to a commercial printer. Access the Pack and Go Wizard by clicking the FILE tab, clicking the Export option, and then clicking *Save for a Commercial Printer* or *Save for Another Computer* in the Pack and Go section, as shown in Figure 12.35.

Embedding Fonts

Embedding the fonts used in your publication is one of the best ways to ensure that a font is always available, even if you move the publication to a new computer or take it to a commercial printer. Publisher embeds TrueType fonts by default when you use the Pack and Go Wizard to prepare your publication for commercial printing.

In Exercise 12.4, you will create the real estate flyer shown in Figure 12.36 on page 575 from scratch. You will add text, images, design elements, and other features to the page, arrange them, and then prepare the publication for commercial printing.

◀DTP POINTER

Use a commercial printer if you want to print a publication in larger quantities; print on special paper such as card stock; or use binding, trimming, and finishing options.

◀DTP POINTER

Consult with your commercial printer before and during the design process to save time and money later.

◀DTP POINTER

Before you start your project, describe your project and goals and find out your commercial printer's requirements.

◀DTP POINTER

You can embed a font so that it will be included in your publication even if the printer doesn't have it.

Figure 12.35 Using the Pack and Go Wizard

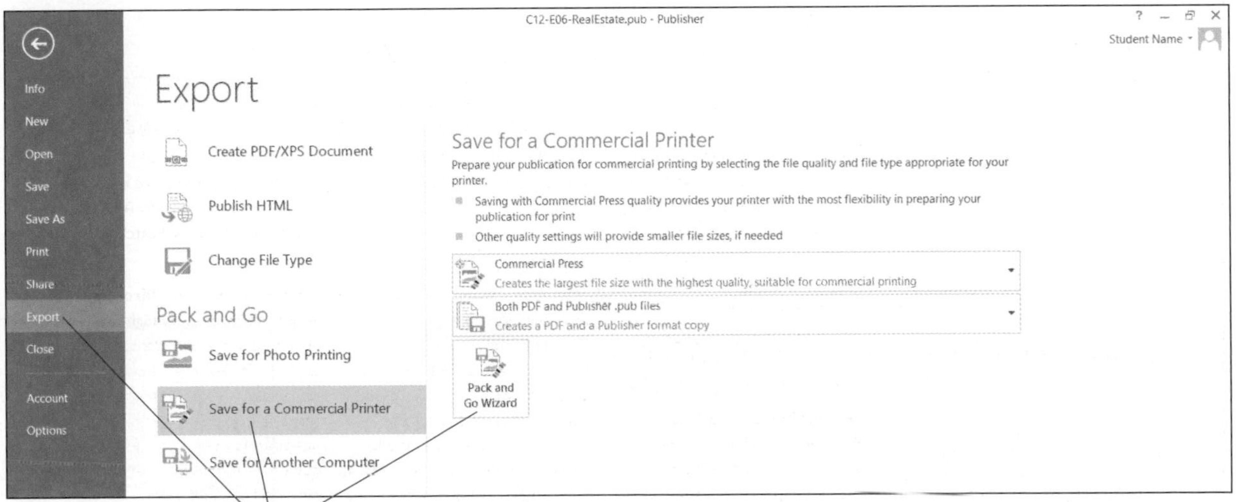

Click the *Export* option, click *Save for a Commercial Printer*, and then click the Pack and Go Wizard button.

1. At the New backstage area with the *FEATURED* option selected, click the *Blank 11 x 8.5"* option.

2. Click the PAGE DESIGN tab, click the More button in the Schemes group, and then click *Field* in the *Built-In (classic)* section of the color scheme palette.

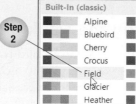

3. Click the INSERT tab, click the Borders & Accents button in the Building Blocks group, and then click *More Borders and Accents* at the bottom of the drop-down list.

4. At the Building Block Library dialog box, double-click the *Open Border* option in the *Frames* section.

5. With the open border frame selected, click the DRAWING TOOLS FORMAT tab, click the Rotate button in the Arrange group, and then click *Rotate Right 90°*.

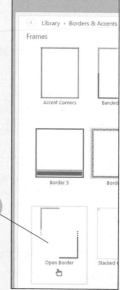

6. Drag the sizing handles on the frame to fit the frame inside the margin guides.

7. Click the PAGE DESIGN tab, click the Guides button in the Layout group, and then click the *2 Columns with Heading* option (first option in the *Built-In Ruler Guides* gallery). These guides will help you visualize where the design elements will be placed on the page.

8. Click the INSERT tab and then click the Online Pictures button in the Illustrations group. Type **house** in the *Office.com Clip Art* text box, press Enter, and then insert the house picture shown in Figure 12.36 on page 575 or a house picture of your own choosing.

9. Crop the image and then size and position the image similar to what is shown in Figure 12.36. ***Hint: Use the guides to help position the image. Align the top of the image with the green top guide line below the margin guide line.***

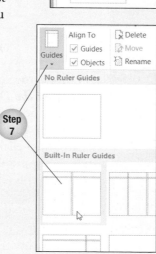

10. Click the INSERT tab, click the Advertisements button in the Building Blocks group, and then click *More Advertisements* at the bottom of the drop-down list. At the Building Block Library dialog box, double-click the *Explosion* option in the *Attention Getters* section.

11. Increase the size of the explosion shape and then position it in the upper left corner of your house image, as shown in Figure 12.36.
12. Select the placeholder text in the explosion shape and then type **New!**
13. Select the shape so that the sizing handles with the small *Xs* display, click the DRAWING TOOLS FORMAT tab, click the More button in the Shape Styles group, and then click the *Horizontal Gradient - Accent 1* option (second column, seventh row).

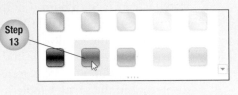

14. Click the INSERT tab, click the Borders & Accents button in the Building Blocks group, and then click the *Awning Stripes* option (second column, first row in the *Bars* section).
15. Size and position the awning stripes border as shown in Figure 12.36. ***Hint: Drag one of the corner sizing handles outward and down to increase the size of the border.***
16. Draw a text box below the awning stripe border to accommodate the two columns of text shown in Figure 12.36. The size of the text box should be approximately 3.2 inches in height by 4.4 inches in width. ***Hint: Change the size of the text box with options in the Size group on the DRAWING TOOLS FORMAT tab.***

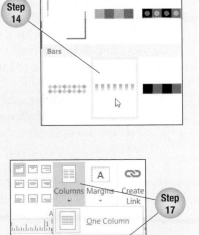

17. With the text box selected, click the TEXT BOX TOOLS FORMAT tab, click the Columns button in the Alignment group, and then click *Two Columns* at the drop-down list.
18. Change the font to Gill Sans MT, remove the spacing after paragraphs, and then type the text (without the bullets) in the columns as shown in Figure 12.36.
19. Press Ctrl + A to select all of the text you just typed, click the HOME tab if necessary to make it active, click the Bullets button in the Paragraph group, and then click the first bullet style (*Small Bullets*).
20. With the text still selected, click the Bullets button and then click *Bullets and Numbering* at the bottom of the drop-down gallery.

21. At the Bullets and Numbering dialog box with the Bullets tab selected, select the current measurement in the *Indent list by* measurement box, type **0.1**, and then click OK.

22. Insert four photographs of your choosing of rooms in a house and then size and position the images in the upper right section of the publication as shown in Figure 12.36.

23. Insert a professional-looking photograph of a woman or man who might be the real estate agent for this property.

24. Size and position the image you inserted in Step 23 as shown in Figure 12.36. Use the cropping tool, if necessary.

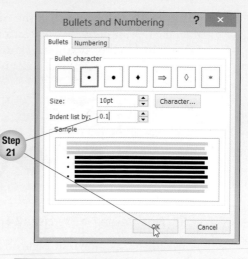

Step 21

25. With the image of the real estate agent selected, add the caption as shown in Figure 12.36 by clicking the Caption button in the Picture Styles group on the PICTURE TOOLS FORMAT tab and then clicking the *Box, Reversed - Layout 4* option (fourth column, second row in the *Overlay* section).

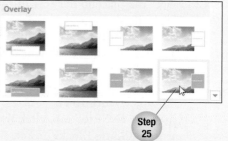

Step 25

26. With the caption text box selected (black *X*s displaying in the sizing handles), click the HOME tab if necessary to make it active and then click the Ungroup button in Arrange group to ungroup the caption from the photograph

27. Click in the caption text box, type **Call Simone**, press Enter, and then type **630.555.5674**. Center the text in the caption text box, change the font size of the phone number to 8 points, and make sure that *Call* and *Simone* display on separate lines and also that the phone number does not wrap onto two lines. If necessary, increase the size of the caption text box. Refer to Figure 12.36.

28. Insert **RealEstateLogo.jpg** from your Chapter12 folder. Size and position the logo as shown in Figure 12.36.

29. Save the publication with the name **C12-E06-RealEstate**.

30. Print **C12-E06-RealEstate.pub**.

31. Prepare the publication to be sent to a commercial printer by completing the following steps:

    a. Click the FILE tab and then click the *Export* option.

    b. Click the *Save for a Commercial Printer* option in the *Pack and Go* section in the middle panel.

    c. Click the Pack and Go Wizard button in the *Save for a Commercial Printer* section in the right panel.

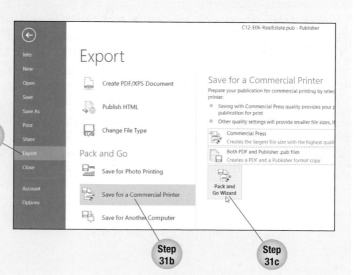

Step 31a

Step 31b

Step 31c

d. At the Pack and Go Wizard dialog box, click the *Other location* option, click the Browse button, browse to your Chapter12 folder, click the folder to select it, and then click the Select folder button in the dialog box.
e. Click the Next button in the Pack and Go Wizard dialog box.
f. At the Pack and Go Wizard dialog box, click OK to print a composite proof of the publication.
g. Close **C12-E04-RealEstate.pub**.
h. Locate the file **C12-E04-RealEstate.zip** in your Chapter12 folder and then double-click the file to unzip it. Open the file **publication.pub** and then click OK if the Load Fonts dialog box displays. View the publication and then close it.

Figure 12.36 Flyer Created in Exercise 12.4

Chapter Summary

➤ Microsoft Publisher 2013 is an easy-to-use desktop publishing program designed for small business users and individuals who want to create their own high-quality, professional-looking personal and business documents without the assistance of professional designers.

➤ Begin your publication at the Publisher opening screen where you will find options to select templates or choose blank page sizes and recent publications from which you can base your publication.

➤ Consistency can be reinforced by using design sets and styles for spacing, fonts, alignment, repetition, color, and decorative elements such as borders, drop caps, initial caps, and so on.

➤ In Publisher, unlike Word, all objects such as text, graphics, pictures, WordArt, and shapes must be placed inside a frame before you can use them in your publication.

➤ The Page Navigation pane displays each page of a publication and allows you to navigate from one to the other.

➤ The Text Fit feature includes options to automatically resize text so that it will fit into the allotted space. Choices include *Best Fit, Shrink Text On Overflow, Grow Text Box to Fit,* and *Do Not AutoFit.*

➤ A Business Information set inserts data stored on its page to placeholder text containing information about a company, including name, contact information, and logo.

➤ Font schemes make it quick and easy to pick fonts that look good together. To change all of the fonts in your publication, you can apply a new font scheme.

➤ Layout guides create a framework or grid for margins, text boxes, columns, graphics, headings, and other objects used in a publication.

➤ Baseline guides are guides to which lines of text can be aligned to provide a uniform appearance between columns of text.

➤ Ruler guides display as green dotted lines on the page and are useful when you want to align several objects or position an object at an exact location on the page.

➤ Every page in a publication has a foreground and background layer. The foreground is where you insert text and design objects. The background layer is known as the master page.

➤ Any objects placed on the master page, such as page numbers, will appear on every page.

➤ Use the Design Checker to review your publication for a variety of design and layout issues. The Design Checker will identify the potential problems and suggest options to fix them.

➤ Building blocks are predesigned objects you can insert in a publication to enhance the publication and include logos, headlines, calendars, pull quotes, and attention-getters.

➤ When text boxes are linked, text that does not fit into the first text box flows into the next linked text box. Publisher 2013 refers to linked text boxes in a series as a *story.*

➤ To help a reader follow a story that may begin on one page and continue to another page, a jump line can be added at the bottom of the text box to inform the reader where to find the rest of the story. Another jump line can be inserted at the top of the next text box.

➤ Share a publication with others with options at the Share backstage area, which contains options for sending a publication as an email message or using mail merge or email merge to send a publication to many recipients.

➤ Publisher includes a Pack and Go Wizard for packing a publication for a commercial printer. The wizard helps ensure that all the necessary files and fonts are delivered to the printer.

Commands *Review*

FEATURE	RIBBON TAB, GROUP/OPTION	BUTTON
advertisements	INSERT, Building Blocks	
borders and accents	INSERT, Building Blocks	
Business Information set	INSERT, Text	
calendars	INSERT, Building Blocks	
caption	PICTURE TOOLS FORMAT, Picture Styles	
color schemes	PAGE DESIGN, Schemes	
columns	TEXT BOX TOOLS FORMAT, Alignment	
create text box link	TEXT BOX TOOLS FORMAT, Linking	
Design Checker	FILE, *Info*	
drop cap	TEXT BOX TOOLS FORMAT, Typography	
font schemes	PAGE DESIGN, Schemes	
guides	PAGE DESIGN, Layout	
hyphenation	TEXT BOX TOOLS FORMAT, Text	
master page	PAGE DESIGN, Page Background	
Pack and Go Wizard	FILE, *Export, Save for a Commercial Printer*	
page parts	INSERT, Building Blocks	
picture placeholder	INSERT, Illustrations	
styles	HOME, Styles	
text direction	TEXT BOX TOOLS FORMAT, Text	
text fit	TEXT BOX TOOLS FORMAT, Text	

Key Points Review

A. Advertisements
B. Borders & Accents
C. Business Information set
D. Calendars
E. color scheme
F. Create Link

G. drop cap
H. font scheme
I. layout guides
J. master page
K. Pack and Go
L. Page Navigation pane

M. Page Parts
N. Pantone
O. picture placeholder
P. story
Q. Text Direction
R. Text Fit

Matching: In the space at the left, provide the correct letter from the above list that matches each definition.

_____J_____ 1. Another name for the background layer in a Publisher publication

_____C_____ 2. Publisher feature that stores information about a business and then automatically inserts that information into placeholder text

_A,D,M__ 3. Four categories of building blocks that are available in Publisher

_____I_____ 4. These create a framework or grid for aligning text boxes, columns, graphics, headings, and other objects used in a publication

_____H_____ 5. Feature that makes it quick and easy to pick fonts that look good together

_____R_____ 6. Button in the Text group on the TEXT BOX FORMAT tab used to specify how text will fit into an allotted space

_____F_____ 7. Button used to connect one text box to another

_____K_____ 8. Wizard used for packing a publication for reproduction by a commercial printer

_____P_____ 9. Publisher 2013 term for linked text boxes in a series

_____N_____ 10. A popular color matching system used by the printing industry

_____E_____ 11. Predesigned color combinations that you can apply to the design objects in your publication

_____O_____ 12. Feature that inserts an empty picture frame to reserve space for pictures you want to add later

_____G_____ 13. The first letter of the first word in a paragraph set in a larger font size and dropped into the paragraph or extended into the margin

_____L_____ 14. Area of the Publisher screen that displays each page as a thumbnail

Chapter *Assessments*

Assessment 12.1 Create a Real Estate Sale Advertisement

In this assessment, you will create a flyer in Publisher 2013 that advertises the sale of a condominium on Kiawah Island in South Carolina. Consider your target audience and the topic of the flyer in the layout and design of your publication. Use Figure 12.37 on page 580 as an example.

1. Using a template or starting at a blank publication, include the following features in the advertisement:
   a. Highlight the following amenities: 10-mile beach, tennis courts, swimming pools, golf courses, bicycle trails, and a natural environment. Consider these amenities in choosing images that will create focus in your flyer.
   b. Use colors that are bright and cheerful.
   c. Include an attention-getter building block.
   d. Include a tear-off design object as shown in Figure 12.37. Insert the tear-off object by clicking the Building Blocks group dialog box launcher on the INSERT tab, clicking the *Business Information* category, and then double-clicking the *Phone Tear-Off* option in the *Contact Information* section.
   e. Type the text in the tear-off section as shown in Figure 12.37.
2. Save the publication as **C12-A01-Kiawah**.
3. Print and then close **C12-A01-Kiawah.pub**.

Assessment 12.2 Create a Real Estate Postcard

As a Realtor in Columbus, Ohio, you are eager to inform neighbors, friends, and prospective clients of a new marketing approach where clients may view a panoramic video of a home by visiting your company website.

1. Use Publisher 2013 to create only the front side of a postcard that promotes a virtual home tour. Include the following specifications:
   * Use an appropriate postcard template or create the postcard from scratch.
   * Choose a color scheme and a font scheme.
   * Apply a ligature and stylistic set to the real estate company name and address. ***Hint: Change the font to Gabriola.***
   * Include a logo, graphic, or picture.
   * Use the Text Fit feature in at least one text box.
   * Include the following information:
        Virtual Home Tour
        Call me for information on having a customized 360-degree panoramic video of your
            home placed on the Internet for buyers to view.
     Pleasantville Realty
     One Northbrook Lane
     Columbus, OH 43204
     [your first and last names]
     Phone: 513.555.3489
     Fax: 513.555.3488
     Email: pleasantvl@emcp.net
     www.emcp.net/pleasantvl
2. Save your publication with the name **C12-A02-Virtual**.
3. Print and then close **C12-A02-Virtual.pub**.

Figure 12.37 Sample Solution for Assessment 12.1

Assessment 12.3   Create a Gift Certificate

In this assessment, you will create a gift certificate for Butterfield Gardens.

1. Start with a template or create the certificate from scratch, and include the following specifications:
   a. Refer to the Butterfield newsletter created in Exercises 12.3A and 12.3B for facts about Butterfield Gardens such as the address, phone number, fax number, and email address.
   b. Insert a certificate number, expiration date, and redemption value.
   c. Choose a color scheme that complements the newsletter created in Exercises 12.3A and 12.3B.
   d. Choose a font scheme that is interesting and appropriate for the publication.
   e. Include one graphic image, one picture, and/or the Butterfield logo. The Butterfield logo is located in your Chapter12 folder.
2. Save your publication with the name **C12-A03-GiftCertificate**.
3. Print and then close **C12-A03-GiftCertificate.pub**.

Assessment 12.4 Merge a Postcard with an Access Database

In this assessment, you will use the Publisher Mail Merge feature to merge data to the postcard. You will edit the Access database and use the filter feature to select only the addresses in Columbus, Ohio. Complete the following steps:

1. Open **RealEstate.pub** and save it with the name **C12-A04-MainDoc**.
2. Click the page 2 thumbnail in the Page Navigation pane.
3. Select and then delete the text *Type address here.* that displays in the placeholder text box in the middle of the page.
4. With the insertion point still positioned in the placeholder text box, click the MAILINGS tab, click the Mail Merge button arrow in the Start group, and then click *Mail Merge* at the drop-down list.
5. Click the Select Recipients button in the Start group on the MAILINGS tab and then click *Use an Existing List*.
6. At the Select Data Source dialog box, navigate to your Chapter12 folder and then double-click **OhioList.mdb**.
7. At the Mail Merge Recipients dialog box, click the down-pointing arrow in the *ZIP Code* column header and then click *43204* at the drop-down list. (This displays only the entries with a ZIP code of 43204). Click OK to close the Mail Merge Recipients dialog box.
8. With the insertion point still positioned in the recipient placeholder text box, click the Address Block button in the Write & Insert Fields group on the MAILINGS tab.
9. Click OK at the Insert Address Block dialog box.
10. Click the Finish & Merge button in the Finish group and then click *Merge to New Publication* at the drop-down list.
11. Save the merged publication as **C12-A04-Merge**.
12. Print **C12-A04-Merge.pub** using the Multiple pages per sheet setting and printing on both sides of the paper.
13. Close **C12-A04-Merge.pub**.
14. Save and then close **C12-A04-MainDoc**.

Assessment 12.5 Create a Poster

In this assessment, you will form a group and delegate tasks for each member of the group to help create a poster in Publisher 2013. The poster should advertise a business, workshop, class, or activity of your own choosing and be based on a template you download from Office.com. Add text to the poster. Consider using a digital camera or cell phone camera to take pictures of your college or classroom, your home or apartment, your community buildings and landscapes, or anything else you deem appropriate to use in your poster. Use interesting and attention-getting fonts. Demonstrate your knowledge of the design concepts discussed throughout this textbook. Save the publication with the name **C12-A05-GroupPosterProject**. Print and then close **C12-A05-GroupPosterProject.pub**. *Hint: You may need to trim the pages after printing.* Present the poster to the class and discuss how your group prepared the publication in Publisher 2013.

Chapter 13

Creating Presentations Using PowerPoint

Performance Objectives

Upon successful completion of Chapter 13, you will be able to:

- Plan, design, and create presentations
- Create slides and insert text, images, SmartArt, charts, and audio files
- Apply design themes and colors
- Insert and delete slides
- Print and run a presentation
- Apply transition and sound effects to slides
- Apply animations to objects in slides

Desktop Publishing Terms

MPEG-4	outline	PDF	XPS

PowerPoint Features Used

action buttons	importing and exporting	slide layouts	SmartArt
animations	Notes Master view	Slide Master view	templates
artistic effects	pictures	Slide Show view	themes
Handout Master view	rehearse timings	Slide Sorter view	transitions
hyperlinks	sections	slide thumbnails pane	

Note: Before completing computer exercises for this chapter, copy to your storage medium the Chapter13 folder from the CD that accompanies this textbook and then make Chapter13 the active folder. Remember to substitute for graphics that may no longer be available.

Getting Started with PowerPoint 2013

DTP POINTER

Learn about PowerPoint features at the PowerPoint Help window. Open this window by clicking the Microsoft PowerPoint Help button located in the upper right corner of the screen.

PowerPoint is a presentation graphics program you can use to organize and present information in the form of slides. In addition to text, PowerPoint slides can contain animations, pictures, illustrations, video, and audio. Presentation files can be saved in different formats that allow them to be easily shared. The PowerPoint interface is similar to that of other Office programs, such as Word and Publisher, but it also has some unique features. Figure 13.1 illustrates some of the major areas of the PowerPoint window.

Opening PowerPoint

The steps to open PowerPoint may vary depending on your system setup. Generally, to open PowerPoint, click the PowerPoint 2013 tile at the Windows 8 Start screen. At the PowerPoint opening screen, click the *Blank Presentation* template to open a blank presentation, click a design template to open a preformatted presentation, click a file name in the *Recent* section in the left pane to open a presentation that was previously opened on your computer, or click the <u>Open Other Presentations</u> hyperlink that displays in the lower left corner of the screen to display the Open backstage area where you can locate and open an existing presentation.

When you open a presentation, the PowerPoint window displays in Normal view. What displays on the screen will vary depending on the type of presentation you opened. If you click the *Blank Presentation* template at the PowerPoint opening screen, a blank presentation opens, and the screen will appear similar to the one shown in Figure 13.2.

Figure 13.1 Investigating the PowerPoint Window

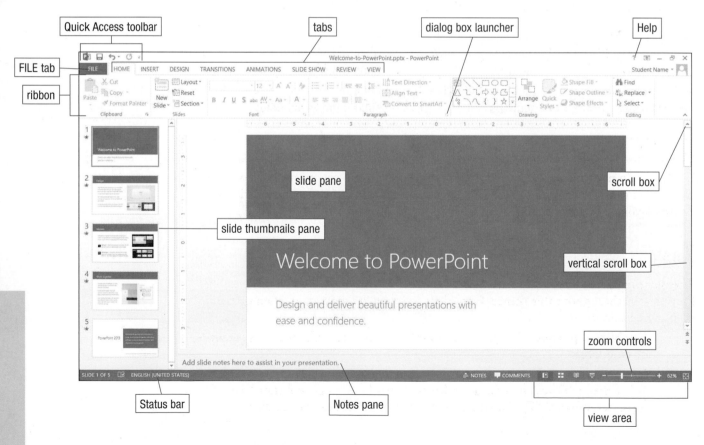

Figure 13.2 Reviewing a Blank Presentation in Normal View

Click the Layout button in the Slides group on the HOME tab to display slide layout options.

slide with Title Slide layout applied

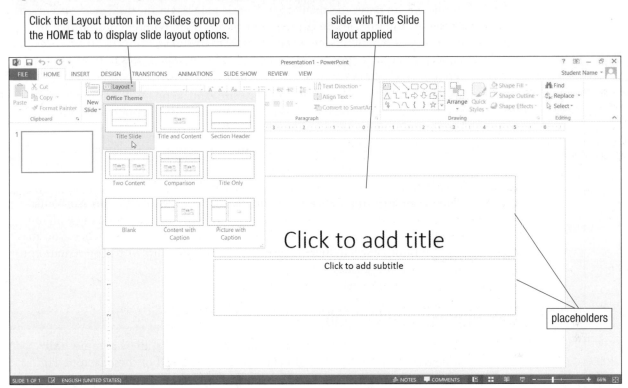

placeholders

Working with Layouts

When you open a blank presentation, the first slide will display with the slide layout named *Title Slide*. Slide layouts define positioning and formatting for the content that will appear on a slide. They contain placeholders for text such as titles, subtitles, and bulleted text, and for items such as tables, charts, SmartArt, images, and audio and video files. To select a slide layout, click the Layout button in the Slides group on the HOME tab and then select an option from the drop-down list, or right-click a slide thumbnail in the slide thumbnails pane, point to *Layout* at the shortcut menu, and then click an option at the side menu.

Layout

If you do not find a slide layout that suits your needs, you can create a custom layout. You can save your custom layouts for use later on, and you can also distribute custom layouts as part of a template.

Planning the Presentation

The planning process for a presentation is much the same as for other documents you have created throughout this course. Consider the following guidelines when planning your presentation:

- **Establish a purpose.** Do you want to inform, educate, sell, motivate, persuade, or entertain?
- **Evaluate your audience.** Who will listen to and watch your presentation? What are their ages and education levels? What knowledge will they have of the topic beforehand? What image do you want to project to your audience?

- **Decide on content.** Decide on the content and organization of your message. Do not try to cover too many topics—this may strain the audience's attention or cause confusion. Begin by identifying your main point, and keep that in mind as you determine other information to include.

- **Determine the medium to be used to convey your message.** To help decide the type of medium you will use, consider such items as topic, equipment availability, location, lighting, audience size, and so on. Will an Internet connection be available? Will there be adequate sound support for audio in the location where the presentation will be run?

- **Establish and maintain a consistent design.** Repeating design elements and sticking to a color scheme will create continuity and cohesiveness. Do not use too many colors, pictures, or other graphic elements.

- **Determine printing needs.** Will you provide your audience with handouts? If so, how do you want these handouts to be formatted? How many will you need? If your presentation is very long and you have a large audience, you may need to limit your handouts to the most important parts of the presentation to save on printing costs.

Designing the Presentation

When choosing a design for your presentation, consider your audience, topic, and method of delivery. The design should make sense based on all of these factors. For example, if you will be presenting to a group of young students, choose bright colors and interesting graphics. If the topic of your presentation is your company's financial outlook for the year, choose an uncluttered, professional design with subdued colors. If you plan to print your presentation, choose a design with lots of contrast and white space to make the pages look clear and keep printing costs low.

Designing the Structure and Layout

In addition to design, consider the following items when determining the structure, layout, and content of your presentation:

- **Ensure continuity.** Repeat specific design elements such as company logos, color, fonts, and bullets throughout your presentation. Consistent elements help to connect one slide to the next and help the audience know what to expect. Some of PowerPoint's design templates coordinate with Microsoft Publisher design sets and Word templates to provide a consistent design among various documents.

- **Maintain legibility.** Use only one or two sans serif typefaces, creating variation through the careful use of type styles such as bold and italics. Make sure to use a large enough font size—at least 24 points. You want everyone in the room to be able to read what you have taken the time to prepare. Choose a thicker font or apply bold when necessary to increase the readability of the text. Keep titles short if possible; long headings are harder to read. Kern and track if necessary.

- **Consider color.** Studies on the psychology of color suggest that certain colors elicit certain feelings in an audience. For example, blue backgrounds promote a conservative approach to the information presented and provide general feelings of calmness, loyalty, and security. Yellow or white text against a dark blue or indigo background is an appealing combination. Black backgrounds are effective in financial presentations. Black also seems to convey directness or forcefulness. Green backgrounds project an image of being direct, social,

DTP POINTER
Good presentation skills include attention to message, visuals, and delivery.

DTP POINTER
Consistency is important in maintaining a professional appearance.

DTP POINTER
Be consistent when using color to present facts in a presentation.

DTP POINTER
Avoid narrow fonts, such as Arial Narrow, and avoid fonts that include fancy serifs, such as Lucida Calligraphy or Harrington.

DTP POINTER
Remember that the audience must be able to read your slides from a distance. A font size smaller than 18 points might be too difficult for the audience to see.

or intelligent. Green also stimulates interaction and is a good choice for use in training and educational presentations. Purple or magenta is appropriate in presentations meant to entertain or represent less serious topics. No matter what colors you choose, use them sparingly and make sure they contribute to and emphasize your message.

- **Create an outline.** An *outline* is a list of content created in the chronological order of the presentation. When creating an outline, use the titles of your slides as the top-level headings, and remember that you should have at least two supporting points for each main point. You can create an outline in Word, format it with heading styles, and then import it into a PowerPoint presentation. You will learn how to do this later in the chapter.

- **Create a storyboard.** Recall from Chapter 11 that a storyboard is a series of sketches that outline the information you want to convey. In this case, the storyboard should be a visual version of the information in the outline. When creating a storyboard, your information should not exceed what will fit on a 5-by-7-inch index card. The goal is to limit the amount of information the audience must read so that they can focus on the speech of the presenter and the visual content of the presentation. Write in phrases instead of sentences so that you will be less inclined to read from your presentation.

◄DTP POINTER
Keep slide titles and headings short.

- **Present one idea per slide.** Each slide in a presentation should convey only one main idea. Too many ideas on a slide may confuse the audience and cause you to stray from the purpose of the slide.

◄DTP POINTER
Introduce one concept per slide.

- **Keep slides uncluttered.** Carefully edit the content of each slide. Keep each bullet point to one or two lines, and limit the number of bullet points to five or six. To create variety, consider using SmartArt and other visuals to graphically illustrate your points when possible.

- **Use graphics to illustrate your message.** Graphics break up text and stimulate interest. One graphic every two or three slides is sufficient. Graphics can include photos, illustrations, charts, graphs, and tables.

Designing with Themes

Like Word, PowerPoint provides a variety of design themes you can use when creating a presentation. Choose a design theme template at the New backstage area or with options in the Themes group on the DESIGN tab. Click a design theme thumbnail in the Themes group to apply it to the current presentation. Click the More button at the right side of the Themes gallery to display any additional themes, as shown in Figure 13.3. Click the up-pointing and down-pointing arrows at the right side of the theme thumbnails to scroll through the list. Hover your mouse pointer over a theme to see its name. The live preview feature will demonstrate how the theme formatting will look in the active slide in the presentation.

When you click a design theme, the theme formatting is applied to all slides in the presentation. If you want to apply a design theme to specific slides in a presentation, select the slides by clicking the desired slide in the slide thumbnails pane or holding down the Ctrl key and clicking the desired slides in the slide thumbnails pane and then click the desired theme in the Themes group on the DESIGN tab. You can also select the slides, right-click a theme thumbnail, and then click *Apply to Selected Slides* at the shortcut menu.

Figure 13.3 Choosing Design Themes on the DESIGN Tab

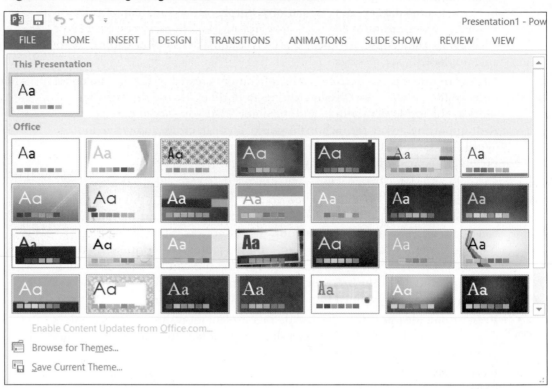

Each design theme contains color variations that display in the Variants group on the DESIGN tab. Click a color variant to apply the colors to the slides in the presentation. Additional theme colors are available by clicking the More button that displays at the right side of the Variants gallery and then pointing to *Colors* at the drop-down list. This displays a side gallery with color options. In addition to changing theme colors, you can change theme fonts, theme effects, and background styles with options at the same More button drop-down list.

Running a Presentation

While you are creating your presentation, you may want to stop from time to time and view the slides in a slide show as your audience will eventually see them. This will help you to ensure that your content is effective and that any animations or other effects you have applied are working properly.

From Beginning

Slide Show

To run a slide show from the beginning, click the Start From Beginning button on the Quick Access toolbar or click the Slide Show button in the view area on the Status bar. You can also run the presentation by clicking the SLIDE SHOW tab and then clicking the From Beginning button in the Start Slide Show group. Click the From Current Slide button in the Start Slide Show group to start the slide show from the slide that is currently active. To exit a slide show, press the Esc key; right-click on a slide and then click *End Show* at the shortcut menu; or hover the mouse over the Slide Show toolbar, click the More slide show options button, and then click *End Show* at the pop-up list. The More slide slide show options button and other buttons available on the Slide Show toolbar are shown in Figure 13.4.

Figure 13.4 Using the Slide Show Toolbar

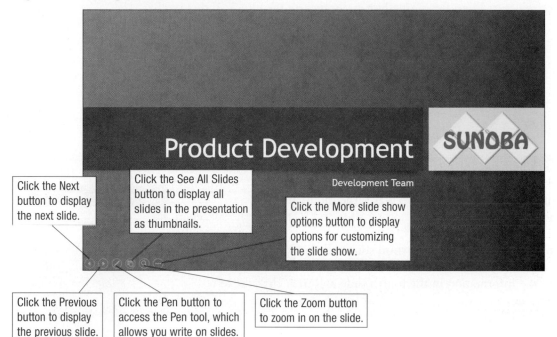

Click the Next button to display the next slide.

Click the See All Slides button to display all slides in the presentation as thumbnails.

Click the More slide show options button to display options for customizing the slide show.

Click the Previous button to display the previous slide.

Click the Pen button to access the Pen tool, which allows you write on slides.

Click the Zoom button to zoom in on the slide.

Several methods are available for moving through the slides in a slide show. Advance slides while running a slide show by clicking the left mouse button, pressing the spacebar, Right Arrow key, Down Arrow key, Page Down key, or Enter key on the keyboard, or by clicking the Next button on the Slide Show toolbar. Slides can also be set up to advance automatically or to run continuously. Display a previous slide when running a slide show by pressing the Left Arrow key, letter P, Backspace key, Up Arrow key, or Page Up key on the keyboard or by clicking the Previous button on the Slide Show toolbar.

In Exercise 13.1, you will open an existing presentation and then run the slide show. This presentation has a transition and sound applied to each slide. You will learn more about these features later in the chapter.

Exercise 13.1 Opening and Running a Presentation

1. Open PowerPoint.
2. At the PowerPoint opening screen, click the <u>Open Other Presentations</u> hyperlink that displays near the lower left corner of the screen. At the Open backstage area, navigate to your Chapter13 folder and then double-click *Welcome-to-PowerPoint.pptx*. (If PowerPoint is already open, display the Open backstage area by clicking the FILE tab and then clicking the *Open* option.)

Step 2

3. Click the Start From Beginning button located on the Quick Access toolbar.

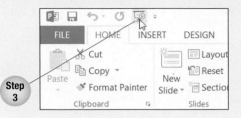

Step 3

4. When the first slide fills the screen, read the information and then click the left mouse button to advance to the next slide. (Notice the transition and sound when you click the mouse button.)
5. Read the information in the second slide and then press the spacebar to advance to the next slide.
6. Read the information in the third slide and then press the Enter key to advance to the next slide.
7. Read the information in the fourth slide and then click the left mouse button.
8. Read the information in the fifth slide and then click the left mouse button.
9. Click the left mouse button to return to the Normal view.
10. Close the presentation by clicking the FILE tab and then clicking the *Close* option.

Step 10

Creating and Editing a Presentation

Now that you have studied a professionally prepared presentation, you are ready to create your own presentation from scratch. Create a presentation from scratch by opening a blank presentation and then inserting and formatting slides.

Inserting a New Slide

New Slide

Create a new slide in a presentation by clicking the New Slide button in the Slides group on the HOME tab. This inserts in the presentation a new slide with the Title and Content layout. If you want to choose a different layout, click the New Slide button arrow and then click a layout option at the drop-down list, as shown in Figure 13.5. The new slide is added after the active slide. The New Slide button drop-down list also contains options to duplicate selected slides, create slides from an outline, and reuse slides.

Figure 13.5 Choosing a Slide Layout from the New Slide Button Drop-down List

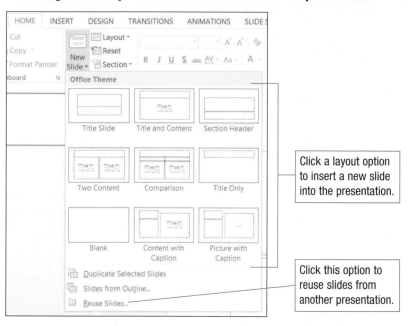

Click a layout option to insert a new slide into the presentation.

Click this option to reuse slides from another presentation.

The *Reuse Slides* option allows you to insert slides from other presentations. With the presentation to which you want to add slides open, click the New Slide button arrow on the HOME tab and then click *Reuse Slides* at the drop-down list. In the Reuse Slides task pane that displays at the right side of the screen, click the Browse button and then click *Browse File* at the drop-down list. At the Browse dialog box, navigate to the desired folder and then double-click the presentation file from which you want to reuse slides. Click the slides in the task pane that you want to insert in the presentation.

Inserting and Customizing Objects

After you create a slide and select a desired slide layout, any of the placeholders or objects on the slide layout can be modified or you can insert your own objects at a blank slide layout. The items in the following sections present suggestions for customizing objects.

Customizing Bullets

Most predesigned slide layouts contain at least one placeholder for a bulleted list. To add text to this placeholder, click in the placeholder and begin typing. If you are starting from a blank slide layout, add a bulleted list by clicking the Text Box button in the Text group on the INSERT tab, drawing a text box, clicking the Bullets button in the Paragraph group on the HOME tab to turn on bullet formatting, and then typing your content.

To change the style of bullets, click the Bullets button arrow and then click the desired style at the drop-down gallery. To use a picture as a bullet, select the bulleted text, click the Bullets button arrow, and then click *Bullets and Numbering* at the drop-down gallery. At the Bullets and Numbering dialog box with the Bulleted tab selected, click the Picture button, as shown in Figure 13.6 on page 592. At the Insert Pictures window, search for and download an image from Office.com or Bing Image Search, or click the Browse button and then insert a picture from a folder.

◀DTP POINTER

Increasing the size of the placeholder automatically increases the size of the text in the placeholder. This is a default AutoFit feature.

◀DTP POINTER

Make sure all of your bulleted lists are parallel, meaning they all begin with an active verb or a noun and end with a period or no period.

Figure 13.6 Using Options in the Bullets and Numbering Dialog Box

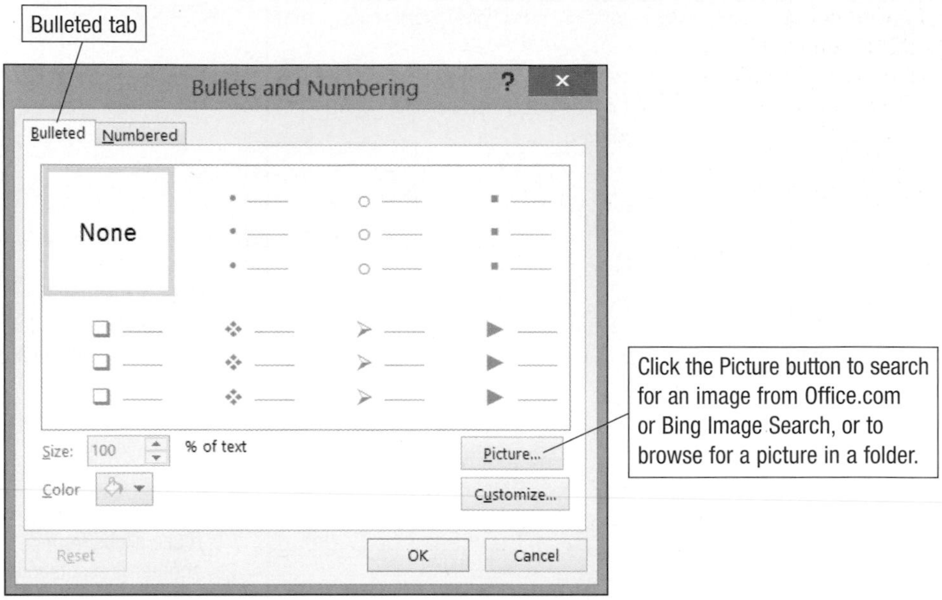

Bulleted tab

Bullets and Numbering

Bulleted | Numbered

None

Click the Picture button to search for an image from Office.com or Bing Image Search, or to browse for a picture in a folder.

Size: 100 | % of text | Picture...

Color: | | Customize...

Reset | OK | Cancel

Inserting Images

Pictures

Online Pictures

To insert an image from your computer's hard drive, click the Pictures button on the INSERT tab or click the Pictures button in the middle of the slide content placeholder. At the Insert Picture dialog box, navigate to the folder containing the picture file and then double-click the file. To insert an image from Office.com, click the Online Pictures button on the INSERT tab or click the Online Pictures button in the middle of the slide content placeholder. At the Insert Pictures window, search for and insert a clip art image or photograph.

Compressing a Picture

Compressing a picture reduces the size of the file so that it takes up less space, making the presentation easier to save, edit, and share. However, compressing a picture also changes the amount of detail retained in the source picture. This means that after compression, the picture can look different than before it was compressed. Because of this, you should compress a picture and save the file before applying any artistic effects. Compress a picture using the Compress Pictures button in the Adjust group on the PICTURE TOOLS FORMAT tab.

Compress Pictures

Applying Artistic Effects

Artistic Effects

Just as in Word, interesting artistic effects can be added to images in PowerPoint, as shown in Figure 13.7. To apply an artistic effect, select the image, click the Artistic Effects button in the Adjust group on the PICTURE TOOLS FORMAT tab, and then click an option at the drop-down gallery. To fine-tune the artistic effect, click *Artistic Effects Options* at the drop-down gallery and then makes changes with options at the Format Picture task pane.

Other picture enhancements include background removal, color, correction, picture styles, borders, effects, and layouts. All of these features are similar to the enhancements you applied to pictures in Word.

Figure 13.7 Applying Artistic Effects

Click the Artistic Effects button in the Adjust group on the PICTURE TOOLS FORMAT tab to display this list of options that can be applied to an image.

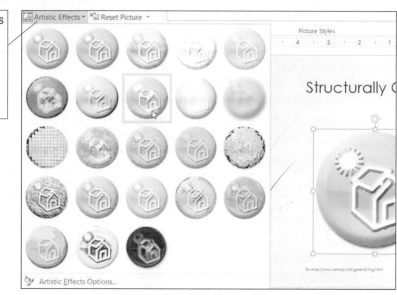

Inserting an Image as a Slide Background

To add an image as the background of an entire slide, as shown in Figure 13.8, click the slide thumbnail or select multiple slide thumbnails in the slide thumbnails pane, click the DESIGN tab, and then click the Format Background button in the Customize group. At the Format Background task pane that displays, click the *Picture or texture fill* option and then click the File button in the *Insert picture from* section. At the Insert Picture dialog box, navigate to the desired folder and then double-click the picture file. You can also click the Online button in the task pane and then search for and insert an image from Office.com.

Format Background

◀ DTP POINTER

Considering adding a background picture to a slide or slides to reinforce the message or to emphasize a point.

Figure 13.8 Inserting a Picture Background

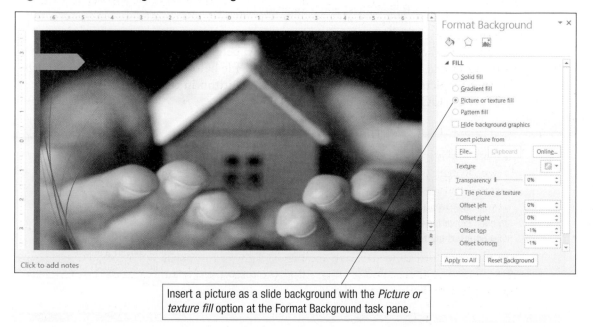

Insert a picture as a slide background with the *Picture or texture fill* option at the Format Background task pane.

Inserting SmartArt

PowerPoint presentations lend themselves well to visual representations of data. SmartArt presents simple text using attention-getting shapes and colors that enhance your message, as shown in Figure 13.9. You can create animated SmartArt graphics to provide additional emphasis or use multiple graphics to reveal your information in phases. You can animate your entire SmartArt graphic or an individual shape in the graphic. You will learn more about animation later in the chapter.

SmartArt

To convert an existing bulleted or numbered list into a SmartArt graphic, select the bulleted list, click the Convert to SmartArt button in the Paragraph group on the HOME tab, and then click the desired SmartArt option, as shown in Figure 13.10. Use the options on the SMARTART TOOLS DESIGN tab and the SMARTART TOOLS FORMAT tab to adjust and format the SmartArt graphic.

Adding a Header and Footer

Header & Footer

Headers and footers display information such as the title of the presentation, the slide numbers, and the date. Headers and footers can be inserted to display and print at the top or bottom of individual slides or all slides. To insert headers and footers, click the INSERT tab and then click the Header & Footer button in the Text group.

Figure 13.9 Using SmartArt Graphics in PowerPoint Slides

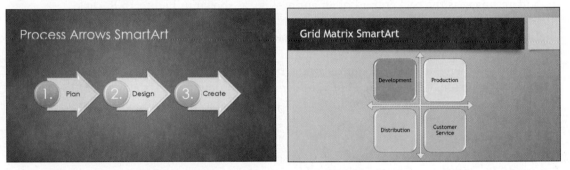

Figure 13.10 Converting a Bulleted List into a SmartArt Graphic

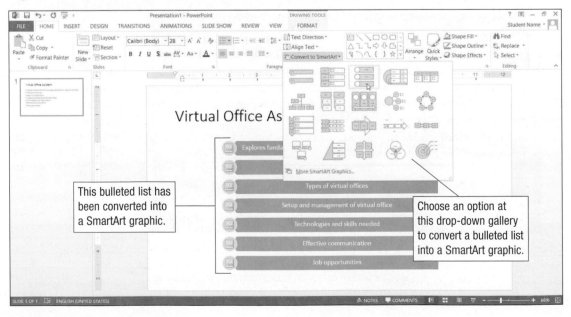

This bulleted list has been converted into a SmartArt graphic.

Choose an option at this drop-down gallery to convert a bulleted list into a SmartArt graphic.

Understanding Presentation Views

PowerPoint provides a variety of ways to view your presentation. Change the view with buttons in the view area on the Status bar or with options in the Presentation Views group on the VIEW tab. The viewing choices include Normal, Outline, Slide Sorter, Notes Page, Reading, and Slide Show view, and they are described in Table 13.1. The Presentation Views group on the VIEW tab contains buttons for changing to normal, outline, slide sorter, notes page, or reading view. The view area on the Status bar contains buttons for changing to Normal, Slide Sorter, Reading, or Slide Show view.

Table 13.1 Presentation Views

Normal view	This is the default view, and it includes two panes—the slide pane and the slide thumbnails pane. You can enter text in a slide in the slide pane and manage slides in the slide thumbnails pane.
Outline view	In this view, the slide thumbnails pane changes to an outline pane where you can type text for slides.
Slide Sorter view	In this view, all slides in the presentation are displayed as thumbnails, allowing you to easily add, move, rearrange, and delete slides.
Notes Page view	In this view, each individual slide displays on its own with any added notes displayed below it.
Reading view	In this view, the slide show displays in full screen like Slide Show view and includes some controls for navigating through slides. Use Reading view when running a slide show without a presenter.
Slide Show view	In this view, each slide fills the entire screen. Use Slide Show view to run a presentation.

Normal

Outline View

Slide Sorter

Notes Page

Reading View

Slide Show

Saving and Printing a Presentation

Once you have created a presentation design that you like, you may want to save it as a template for future use. You may also want to share the presentation you created with other people. When sharing a presentation, if you know the person or group with whom you are going to share it has PowerPoint 2013, then saving the presentation as a PowerPoint file with a .pptx extension will work just fine. However, you can also save your presentation as a template, as a PDF that can be viewed with Adobe Reader, or even as a video saved in *MPEG-4* format. In addition, you can also print a PowerPoint presentation in a variety of formats.

MPEG-4
An audio and video file format

Saving a Presentation as a Template

To save a presentation as a template that can be used over and over, display the Save As dialog box by pressing the F12 function key or by clicking the FILE tab, clicking the *Save As* option, click the *Computer* option, and then click the Browse button. At the Save As dialog box, click the *Save as type* option box and then click *PowerPoint Template (*.potx)* at the drop-down list. Navigate to the folder where you want to save the template, type a name for the template in the *File name* text box, and then click the Save button.

Saving a Presentations in PDF or XPS Format

PDF

A file format created by Adobe that preserves formatting to make file sharing easier

PowerPoint 2013 supports saving your presentations in **PDF** format to preserve file formatting and enable file sharing. The PDF file format ensures that when the file is printed or viewed online, it retains the format that you intended. It also ensures that data in the file cannot be easily changed. The PDF format is also useful for files that will be reproduced using commercial printing methods. **XPS** is a similar electronic file format that also preserves file formatting and enables file sharing.

XPS

A file format created by Microsoft that preserves formatting to make file sharing easier

Save a file in PDF or XPS format by clicking the FILE tab and then clicking the *Export* option. At the Export backstage area, make sure the *Create PDF/XPS Document* option is selected in the middle pane and then click the Create PDF/XPS button in the right pane. At the Publish as PDF or XPS dialog box, choose the PDF or XPS file type, specify a folder location, type a name in the *File name* text box, and then click the Publish button.

A PDF file will open in Adobe Reader, Internet Explorer, or Windows Reader, and an XPS file will open in Internet Explorer, Windows Reader, or XPS Viewer. One method for opening a PDF or XPS file is to open File Explorer, navigate to the folder containing the file, right-click the file, and then point to *Open with*. This displays a side menu with the programs you can choose from to open the file.

Saving a Presentation as a Video

You can save your presentation as a video file in the MPEG-4 file format and then share it with others on a website, DVD, or network. To save a presentation as a video, click the FILE tab and then click the *Export* option. At the Export backstage area, click the *Create a Video* option in the middle pane, as shown in Figure 13.11. In the *Create a Video* section of the Export backstage area, choose a viewing option (Computer & HD Displays, Internet & DVD, or Portable Devices), indicate whether or not you want recorded timings and narrations included, specify the number of seconds spent on each slide, and then click the Create Video button. A file saved in the MPEG-4 file format (*.mp4) can be opened with Windows Media Player, iTunes, VLC, and Quicktime.

Figure 13.11 Saving a Presentation as a Video

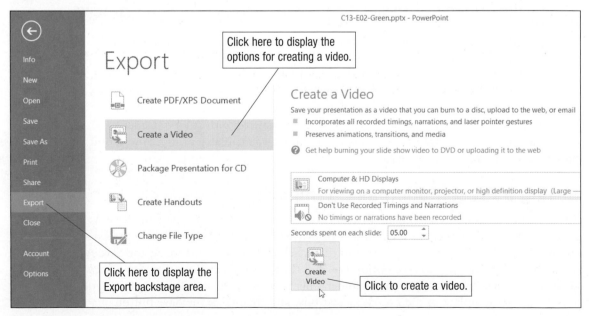

Printing a Presentation

A presentation can be printed in a variety of formats. You can print each slide on a separate piece of paper; print each slide at the top of a page, leaving the bottom of the page for notes; print all or a specific number of slides on a single piece of paper; or print the slide titles and topics in outline form. To print a presentation, click the FILE tab and then click the *Print* option. At the Print backstage area shown in Figure 13.12, click the second gallery in the *Settings* category and then click the desired format at the drop-down list. Print individual slides by typing the slide number in the *Slides* text box in the *Settings* category.

Figure 13.12 Printing a Presentation

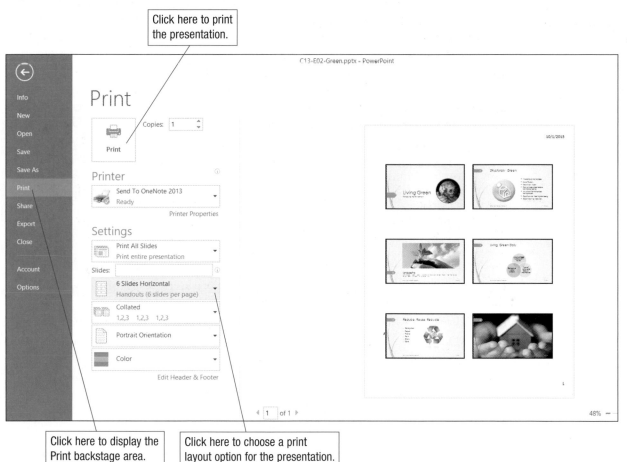

Click here to print the presentation.

Click here to display the Print backstage area.

Click here to choose a print layout option for the presentation.

Tips for Giving a Presentation

As the actual day for your presentation approaches, prepare fully. Be ready for the unexpected. You can feel at ease and remain poised and confident in front of an audience by being fully prepared and practicing the presentation. Review the following points to make sure you are ready:

- Arrive early to check the equipment and then view the screen from your audience's perspective.

- Be prepared for technical problems—carry extra hard copies of your presentation to use as handouts if the equipment is faulty. Have a backup plan for equipment failures or forgotten materials.

- Have your presentation ready—display the first slide with your name, topic name, and other pertinent information on the screen as your audience enters the room.

- Bring a pointing device, such as a laser pointer, or use your mouse as a laser pointer by running the presentation and then holding down the Ctrl key while pointing to objects on the slides. Change the color of the laser pointer by clicking the Set Up Slide Show button in the Set Up group on the SLIDE SHOW tab.

- Depending on the nature of your presentation, use your imagination to come up with a clever attention-getting device. For instance, if your presentation is on gardening, give each member of your audience an inexpensive package of seeds; if you are presenting information on taking a vacation to Belgium, pass out Belgian chocolates; if your presentation is on a new budget plan, mark one of your handouts with a star and offer a free lunch to the audience member holding that particular handout.

- Practice makes perfect—be sure you are proficient in using the equipment and the software.

- Use good volume and speak at a moderate speed.

- Clearly identify each of the points, but do not read them from your slides.

- Do not over-entertain your audience—sounds can get annoying, too many graphics are distracting, and too many slides are boring.

- If your presentation is of a serious nature, do not use unnecessary sound, graphics, or animations. Choose your visual theme and colors carefully.

- Summarize your presentation and ask for questions if appropriate.

- Provide your audience with a handout to take with them—it reinforces follow-up and continued interest. Make sure you have enough handouts for everyone in the audience.

In Exercise 13.2, you will practice creating and adding content to a presentation. You will then save the presentation, run it, and print it in two different ways.

Set Up Slide Show

DTP POINTER

You want your audience to listen to you present your information, rather than read the screen.

1. At a blank PowerPoint screen, click the FILE tab, click the *New* option, and then click the *Blank Presentation* template at the New backstage area. (This opens a blank presentation.)
2. Apply a design theme and change the theme colors by completing the following steps:
    a. Click the DESIGN tab.
    b. Click the More button at the right side of the design theme thumbnails in the Themes group and then click the *Wisp* option.
    c. Click the More button at the right side of the variant thumbnails in the Variants group, point to *Colors*, and then click the *Green* option at the drop-down gallery.

3. Change one of the colors in the Wisp theme by completing the following steps:
    a. Click the More button in the Variants group, point to *Colors*, and then click the *Customize Colors* option at the bottom of the drop-down gallery.
    b. At the Create New Theme Colors dialog box, type **XXX-LivingGreen** in the *Name* text box. (Use your initials in place of the *XXX*.)
    c. Click the color button that displays at the right side of the *Text/Background - Light 2* option and then click the *Lime, Accent 3, Lighter 80%* option (seventh column, second row in the *Theme Colors* section).
    d. Click the Save button.
4. At the slide, click anywhere in the text *Click to add title* and then type **Living Green**. Click anywhere in the text *Click to add subtitle* and then type **Protecting the Environment**.
5. Insert the earth image as shown in the first slide in Figure 13.13 on page 604 by completing the following steps:
    a. Click the INSERT tab and then click the Pictures button in the Images group.
    b. At the Insert Picture dialog box, navigate to your Chapter13 folder and then double-click ***earth.png***.

c. Click the More button in the Picture Styles group and then click the *Beveled Oval, Black* option (third column, second row).

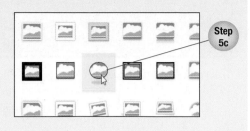

Step 5c

d. Drag the image so it is positioned in the slide as shown in Figure 13.13.

6. Save the presentation with the name **C13-E02-Green**.

7. Insert a new slide by completing the following steps:
   a. Click the HOME tab.
   b. Click the New Slide button arrow in the Slides group and then click the *Two Content* layout option (first column, second row).

8. Type text in the new slide by completing the following steps:
   a. Click anywhere in the text *Click to add title* and then type **Structurally Green**.
   b. Click anywhere in the text *Click to add text* that displays in the content placeholder at the right and then type the following text (press the Enter key at the end of each line except the last line):

   > **Wood-burning fireplace**
   > **Solar panels**
   > **2-by-6 wall studs**
   > **Reclaimed-wood floors or bamboo flooring**
   > **Insulation from recycled newspapers**
   > **Geo-thermal heating and cooling**
   > **Green roofing materials**

9. Insert a clip art image in the content placeholder at the left by completing the following steps:
   a. Click the Online Pictures icon in the content placeholder.
   b. At the Online Pictures window, type **green house** in the *Office.com Clip Art* text box and then press Enter.

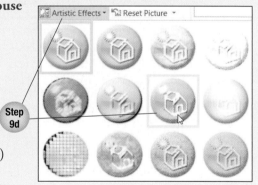

   c. Double-click the image shown in the second slide in Figure 13.13.
   d. Click the Artistic Effects button in the Adjust group on the PICTURE TOOLS FORMAT tab and then click the *Paint Brush* option (third column, second row).

   Step 9d

10. Insert another slide (the third slide in Figure 13.13) by completing the following steps:
   a. Click the HOME tab, click the New Slide button arrow, and then click the *Picture with Caption* layout option.
   b. Click the Pictures icon in the content placeholder.
   c. At the Insert Picture dialog box, navigate to your Chapter13 folder and then double-click *handsplant.png*.

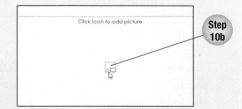

   Step 10b

   d. Click in the text *Click to add title* and then type **Landscaping**.
   e. Click in the text *Click to add text* and then type the following: **Green landscaping includes collecting storm water for irrigating lawns and plants, collecting food scraps and yard and plant clippings in a compost bin, and planting trees.**

11. Insert another slide (the fourth slide in Figure 13.13) by completing the following steps:
    a. Click the New Slide button arrow and then click the *Title and Content* layout option (second column, first row).
    b. Click in the text *Click to add title* and then type **Living Green Daily**.
    c. Click the Insert a SmartArt Graphic icon in the content placeholder.
    d. At the Choose a SmartArt Graphic dialog box, click *Relationship* in the left panel, scroll down the list box in the middle panel, and then double-click the *Basic Venn* option (second column, ninth row).
    e. Click the Change Colors button in the SmartArt Styles group on the SMARTART TOOLS DESIGN tab and then click the *Colorful - Accent Colors* option (first option in the *Colorful* section).
    f. Type the text inside each circular shape as shown in the fourth slide in Figure 13.13.

12. Insert another slide (the fifth slide in Figure 13.13) by completing the following steps:
    a. Click the HOME tab.
    b. Click the New Slide button arrow and then click the *Two Content* layout (first column, second row).
    c. Click in the text *Click to add title* and then type **Reduce, Reuse, Recycle**.
    d. Click in the text *Click to add text* that displays in the left content placeholder.
    e. Change the default bullets by clicking the Bullets button arrow and then clicking *Bullets and Numbering* at the drop-down list.
    f. At the Bullets and Numbering dialog box, click the Picture button.
    g. At the Insert Pictures window, click in the *Office.com Clip Art* text box, type **recycle globe**, and then press Enter.
    h. Double-click the recycle globe image shown below.

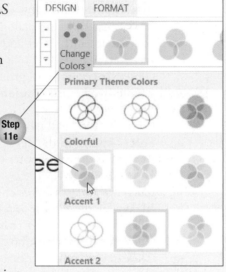

i. Type the bulleted text as shown in the fifth slide in Figure 13.13.
j. Click the Online Pictures icon in the right content placeholder.
k. At the Insert Pictures window, type **recycle globe** and then press Enter.
l. Double-click the same image used for the bullets.
m. Position the image as shown in the fifth slide in Figure 13.13.

13. Insert another slide (the sixth slide in Figure 13.13) by completing the following steps:
   a. Click the HOME tab, click the New Slide button arrow, and then click the *Blank* layout option (first column, third row).
   b. Click the DESIGN tab and then click the Format Background button in the Customize group.
   c. At the Format Background task pane, click the *Picture or texture fill* option.
   d. Click the File button in the *Insert picture from* section of the task pane.
   e. At the Insert Picture dialog box, navigate to your Chapter13 folder and then double-click **greenhouse.png**.
   f. Close the Format Background task pane.

14. Add a footer to the presentation by completing the following steps:
   a. Click the INSERT tab and then click the Header & Footer button in the Text group.
   b. At the Header and Footer dialog box, make sure the Slide tab is active.
   c. Click the *Date and time* check box to insert a check mark.
   d. Make sure the *Update automatically* option is selected.
   e. Click the *Slide number* check box to insert a check mark.
   f. Click the *Footer* check box to insert a check mark.
   g. Click in the *Footer* text box and then type **Source: http://www.emcp.net/greenliving.html**.
   h. Click the *Don't Show on title slide* check box to insert a check mark.
   i. Click the Apply to All button.

15. Insert a note in the Notes pane for Slide 1 by completing the following steps:
    a. Click the Slide 1 thumbnail in the slide thumbnails pane that displays at the left side of the PowerPoint window.
    b. Click the NOTES button that displays on the Status bar.
    c. Click the text *Click to add notes* in the Notes pane that displays below the slide and then type **Optional: Instructors, ask your students to add three more slides to this presentation. Choose appropriate slide layouts and add text and graphics that reinforce the overall theme of this presentation.**

Step 15c — Optional: Instructors, ask your students to add three more slides to this presentation. Choose appropriate slide layouts and add text and graphics that reinforce the overall theme of this presentation.

16. Save the presentation with the same name (**C13-E02-Green.pptx**).
17. Change views by completing the following steps:
    a. Click the VIEW tab and then click the Slide Sorter button in the Presentation Views group.
    b. Click the Notes Page button in the Presentation Views group.
    c. Click the Reading View button and then press the spacebar to advance through Slides 1 through 6 and exit the presentation.
    d. Click the Normal button on the Status bar.
18. Print all six slides on one page by completing the following steps:
    a. Click the FILE tab and then click the *Print* option.
    b. At the Print backstage area, click the second gallery in the *Settings* category (contains the text *Full Page Slides*) and then click *6 Slides Horizontal* in the *Handouts* section of the drop-down list.
    c. Click the Print button.

Step 18b

19. Print Slide 1 as a notes page by completing the following steps:
    a. Click the FILE tab and then click the *Print* option.
    b. At the Print backstage area, click in the *Slides* text box in the *Settings* category and then type **1**.
    c. Click the second gallery in the *Settings* category and then click *Notes Pages* in the *Print Layout* section of the drop-down list.
    d. Click the Print button.
20. Save the presentation as a video file by completing the following steps:
    a. Click the FILE tab and then click the *Export* option.
    b. At the Export backstage area, click the *Create a Video* option and then click the Create Video button.
    c. At the Save As dialog box, navigate to your Chapter13 folder and then click the Save button.
    d. Open the video file by clicking the File Explorer icon on the taskbar, navigating to your Chapter13 folder, and then double-clicking **C13-E02-Green.mp4**.
    e. After viewing the presentation video, close the video file.
21. Close **C13-E02-Green.pptx**.

Figure 13.13 Presentation Created in Exercise 13.2

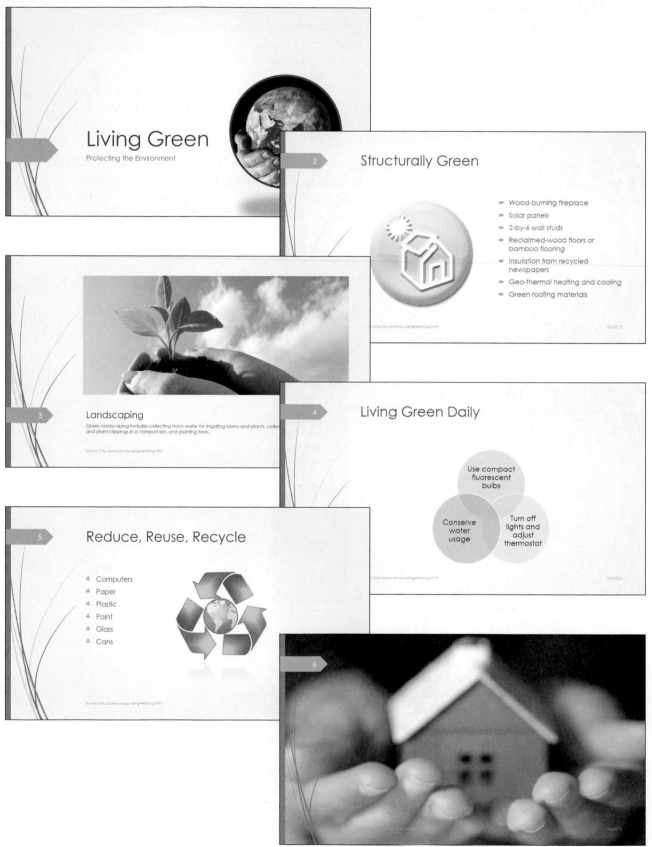

Using Masters to Maintain Consistency

Each PowerPoint presentation comes with a set of masters: slide, notes, and handout. These masters maintain consistency among the slides in a presentation. Figure 13.14 shows the slide master and slide master layouts for the presentation you created in Exercise 13.2.

Using the Slide Master

To view the slide masters for a presentation, click the VIEW tab and then click the Slide Master button in the Master Views group. When you first open a blank presentation, it will contain one blank slide master. In the slide thumbnails pane, the slide master thumbnail will appear at the very top of the pane and will be numbered 1. It will be followed by a series of smaller slide thumbnails showing the various layout options for that master.

Customize the slide master by changing the theme, theme colors, or theme fonts; inserting, deleting, or changing the location of placeholders; applying a background style; applying any graphics you want to appear on more than one slide in the presentation; and changing the page setup and slide orientation. These changes will be stored within the slide master and will be applied to any slide that uses the master.

A presentation can contain as many slide masters as you need, and each slide master can contain a variety of different layouts. Hover the mouse pointer over each slide master layout to see which slides use it. If you want to make a change to multiple slides in your presentation at once, use the slide master. The change you make there will be applied to all slides that use that master.

If you edit the formatting of text in a slide in Normal view, that slide's link to the slide master is broken. For this reason, make global formatting changes in Slide Master view before editing individual slides in a presentation.

Slide Master

◀ **DTP POINTER**

To display a logo on every slide in your presentation, add the logo to the slide master.

Figure 13.14 **Viewing a Presentation in Slide Master View**

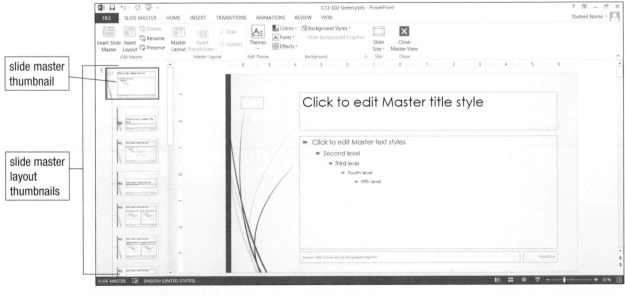

slide master thumbnail

slide master layout thumbnails

Using the Handout Master and the Notes Master

Depending on your presentation needs, you can customize your handouts or notes to accommodate your text, logo, graphics, charts, SmartArt, or other objects. Placing these objects within a master page reinforces consistency on each of the slides in the presentation and on all handouts and notes that you may use during your presentation.

Customize a handout with options in the Handout Master view. Display a presentation in this view by clicking the VIEW tab and then clicking the Handout Master button in the Master Views group.

Handout Master

Notes Master

You can insert notes in a presentation and then print the presentation as notes pages with the notes printed below the slides. If you want to insert or format text or other elements as notes on all slides in a presentation, make the changes in the Notes Master view. Display this view by clicking the VIEW tab and then clicking the Notes Master button in the Master Views group.

Working with Slides

Besides adding text to slides in Normal view, you can also enter text in the outline pane, or you can create an outline in Word and import it into a PowerPoint presentation. After your text is entered, you can apply transitions to the slides and then run the presentation automatically, if desired.

Adding Text to a Slide in Outline View

If your presentation is text heavy, consider using the outline pane, shown in Figure 13.15. Display the outline pane by clicking the VIEW tab and then clicking the Outline View button in the Presentation Views group.

Figure 13.15 Adding Text in Outline View

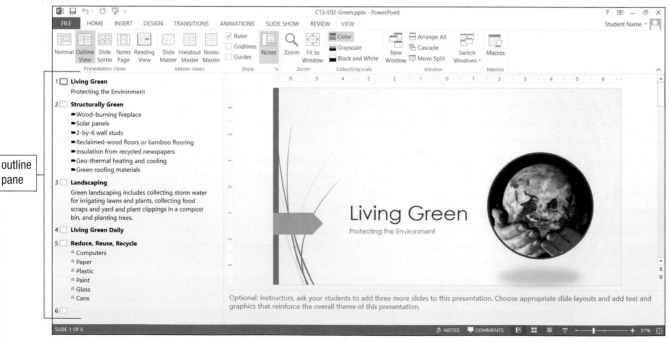

outline pane

The outline pane replaces the slide thumbnails pane at the left side of the screen. A slide number displays in the pane followed by a small slide icon. To create slides in the outline pane, display the outline pane, click immediately right of the slide icon in the outline pane, type the title for the first slide, and then press the Enter key. This creates a new slide in the presentation and another slide icon displays in the outline pane. If you want to continue typing text on the first slide, press the Tab key. This removes the second slide and slide icon and moves the insertion point below the title in the outline pane. Type a subtitle for the slide and then press the Enter key. This moves the insertion point below the subtitle. Press Shift + Tab to move the insertion point back to the previous tab stop, which is the left margin. This inserts a second slide and slide icon. Type the title of the second slide and then press the Enter key. Press the Tab key to remove the third slide. This moves the insertion point below the title of the second slide in the outline pane and also inserts a bullet. Type the text for the first bullet and then press the Enter key. Continue typing the bulleted text for the second slide. When you are finished typing the bulleted text, press Shift + Tab. This moves the insertion point back a tab stop (to the left margin) and inserts a third slide and slide icon. Continue in this manner until you have created all desired slides.

Importing a Word Outline into PowerPoint

An outline created in Word can be imported into PowerPoint to populate a presentation. PowerPoint will create new slides using the Title and Content slide layout based on the heading levels used in the outline. Note that for this to work, you must apply heading styles from the Styles gallery on the HOME tab in Word. Paragraphs formatted with the Heading 1 style become titles, the Heading 2 style becomes bulleted text, and so forth. If styles were not applied in the Word outline, PowerPoint uses tabs or indents to place the text on slides.

To import a Word outline into an open PowerPoint presentation, click the HOME tab, click the New Slide button arrow in the Slides group, and then click *Slides from Outline* at the drop-down list. At the Insert Outline dialog box, navigate to the folder containing the outline you want to import and then double-click the file.

Organizing Slides

As you edit a presentation, you may need to reorganize slides, insert new slides, or delete existing slides. Manage slides using the slide thumbnails pane or the Slide Sorter view. Switch to Slide Sorter view by clicking the Slide Sorter button in the view area on the Status bar or by clicking the VIEW tab and then clicking the Slide Sorter button in the Presentation Views group.

Slide Sorter

To move a slide, select the slide and then drag it to a new location. To delete a slide, select it and then press the Delete key. To insert a slide, position the insertion point (vertical line) at the location where you want to add the slide and then click the New Slide button on the HOME tab or press Ctrl + M.

You can also rearrange the content of your presentation in Outline view. Position the mouse pointer to the left of the slide icon or bullet in the outline pane until the pointer displays as a four-headed arrow. Hold down the left mouse button, drag the pointer (a thin horizontal line displays) to the desired location, and then release the mouse button.

Adding Slide Transitions

Slide transitions are the effects that occur when you move from one slide to the next in Slide Show view. You can control the speed of each slide transition effect, and you can also add sound. Transitions are available in the Transition to This Slide group on the TRANSITIONS tab. To view additional transitions, click the More button at the right side of the transition thumbnails in the Transition to This Slide group. This displays a drop-down gallery of transitions, as shown in Figure 13.16.

Click a transition in the drop-down gallery and then customize the transition with options in the Timings group. Each transition has a default duration. Increase or decrease this time using the *Duration* measurement box. Add a sound transition with the *Sound* option box. Transitions and sounds apply to the active slide. If you want transitions and sounds to affect all slides, click the Apply To All button. Click the Preview button located in the Preview group at the left side of the TRANSITIONS tab to view the transition before running the presentation.

Apply To All

Preview

Running a Slide Show Automatically

You can set the slides in a slide show to automatically advance after a specific number of seconds with options in the Timing group on the TRANSITIONS tab. To advance slides automatically, click in the *After* check box and then insert the desired number of seconds in the measurement box. Click the *On Mouse Click* check box to remove the check mark. If you want the transition time to affect all slides in the presentation, click the Apply To All button. In Slide Sorter view, the transition time displays below each affected slide. For further options, display the Set Up Show dialog box by clicking the SLIDE SHOW tab and then clicking the Set Up Slide Show button in the Set Up group.

Set Up Slide Show

In Exercise 13.3, you will import a Word outline into a presentation, format and reorganize the presentation, make changes using the slide master, and then set the presentation up to run automatically. The completed presentation for this exercise is shown in Figure 13.17 on page 612.

Figure 13.16 **Adding Transitions**

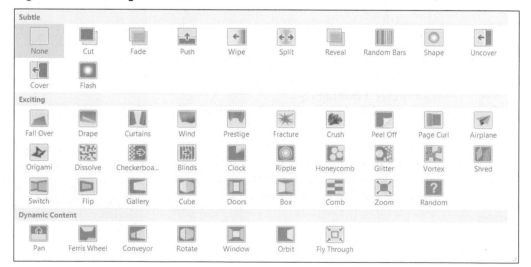

Exercise 13.3 Importing a Word Outline into a Presentation,
Formatting and Reorganizing the Presentation,
Making Changes Using the Slide Master, and
Running the Presentation Automatically

1. Open a blank presentation by clicking the FILE tab, clicking the *New* option, and then clicking the *Blank Presentation* template at the New backstage area.

2. Import a Word outline into the presentation by completing the following steps:

   a. Click the New Slide button arrow in the Slides group on the HOME tab and then click *Slides from Outline* at the drop-down list.

   b. At the Insert Outline dialog box, navigate to your Chapter13 folder and then double-click ***VCT-Training.docx***. Your presentation should now include a blank first (title) slide followed by five slides with titles and bulleted lists.

3. Apply a design theme and change theme colors by completing the following steps:

   a. Click the DESIGN tab.

   b. Click the *Facet* theme thumbnail in the Themes group.

   c. Click the More button in the Variants group, point to *Colors*, and then click the *Blue* option at the drop-down gallery.

4. Display the presentation in Outline view by clicking the VIEW tab and then clicking the Outline View button in the Presentation Views group.

5. Type text in the outline pane by completing the following steps:

   a. In the outline pane located at the left side of the PowerPoint window click immediately right of the Slide 1 icon.

   b. Type **Computer Training** and then press Enter.

   c. Press the Tab key and then type **Virtuosity Computer Training**.

6. Reorganize the slides by completing the following steps:

   a. Click the Normal button in the Presentation Views group on the VIEW tab.

   b. Click the Slide 6 thumbnail in the slide thumbnails pane. (This selects the slide thumbnail and inserts an orange border around the thumbnail.)

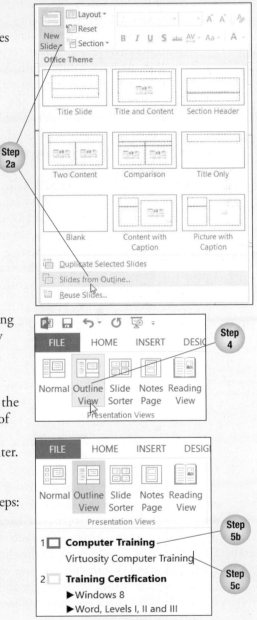

c. Position the mouse pointer on the Slide 6 thumbnail in the slide thumbnails pane, hold down the left mouse button, drag up until the slide thumbnail displays between Slides 2 and 3, and then release the mouse button.

7. Insert a logo in a slide master layout so the logo appears on all slides that use that layout (in this case, all but the first slide in the presentation) by completing the following steps:

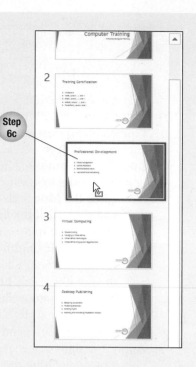

Step 6c

a. Click the Slide Master button in the Master Views group on the VIEW tab.

b. Make sure the last slide master layout thumbnail is selected in the slide thumbnails pane (the slide master layout named *Title and Text Layout*).

c. Click the INSERT tab and then click the Pictures button in the Images group.

d. At the Insert Picture dialog box, navigate to your Chapter13 folder and then double-click ***VCT-logo.png***.

e. Drag the logo so it is positioned in the lower right corner of the slide master layout as shown in Figure 13.17 on page 612.

f. Click the SLIDE MASTER tab.

g. Click the Close Master View button in the Close group.

8. Apply a slide transition to Slide 1 by completing the following steps:

a. Click the Slide 1 thumbnail in the slide thumbnails pane.

b. Click the TRANSITIONS tab.

c. Click the More button in the Transition to This Slide group.

d. Click the *Peel Off* option (eighth column, top row in the *Exciting* section).

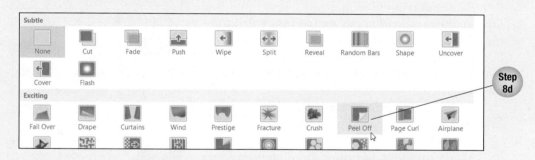

Step 8d

9. Click the Slide 2 thumbnail in the slide thumbnails pane and then apply the Origami transition effect (first column, second row in the *Exciting* section). ***Note: Applying a different transition to each slide is not recommended; however, to familiarize you with some of the different transitions available in PowerPoint 2013, you are being asked to apply different transitions for each slide in this presentation.***

10. Click the Slide 3 thumbnail in the slide thumbnails pane and then apply the Page Curl transition effect (ninth column, top row in the *Exciting* section).

11. Click the Slide 4 thumbnail in the slide thumbnails pane and then apply the Prestige transition effect (fifth column, top row in the *Exciting* section).

12. Click the Slide 5 thumbnail in the slide thumbnails pane and then apply the Flash transition effect (last option in the *Subtle* section).
13. Click the Slide 6 thumbnail in the slide thumbnails pane and then apply the Shape transition effect (ninth column, top row in the *Subtle* section).
14. Save the presentation with the name **C13-E03-VCT-Presentation**.
15. Run the presentation by clicking the Start From Beginning button on the Quick Access toolbar. Advance slides by clicking the left mouse button. Notice the slide transitions as you run the slide show. When the slide show is finished, click the left mouse button.
16. Apply one transition effect and sound effect to all slides in the presentation and specify that you want slides to advance after four seconds by completing the following steps:
    a. Click the More button in the Transition to This Slide group on the TRANSITIONS tab and then click the *Glitter* option (eighth column, second row in the *Exciting* section).
    b. Shorten the transition time for the Glitter transition by clicking the down-pointing arrow in the *Duration* measurement box in the Timing group until *01.50* displays in the measurement box.
    c. Click the *Sound* option box arrow and then click *Chime* at the drop-down list.
    d. Click the *On Mouse Click* check box in the Timing group to remove the check mark.
    e. Click the *After* check box to insert a check mark.
    f. Click the current time in the *After* measurement box (this should select the default time), type 4, and then press Enter.
    g. Click the Apply To All button.

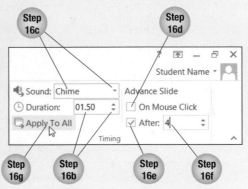

17. Run the presentation by clicking the Start From Beginning button on the Quick Access toolbar. (The slides will each automatically advance after four seconds.) When the slide show is finished, click the left mouse button.
18. Save the presentation with the same name (**C13-E03-VCT-Presentation**).
19. Print the presentation with six slides printed horizontally on the page and then close the presentation.

Figure 13.17 Presentation Created in Exercise 13.3

Inserting Sections in a Presentation

If you are working on a large presentation or collaborating on a presentation with others, you can organize your slides into sections that can make the process much easier. You can assign different sections to different people on your team and then consolidate them to create a complete presentation.

Section

To create sections in Normal view, click the Section button in the Slides group on the HOME tab and then click *Add Section* at the drop-down list, as shown in Figure 13.18. PowerPoint will create a new section titled *Untitled Section* from the currently selected slide to the last slide in the presentation. Any slides above the currently selected slide will be given the title *Default Section*. The section names will appear in the slide thumbnails pane, above the first slide in the sections.

Figure 13.18 **Inserting a Section in a Presentation**

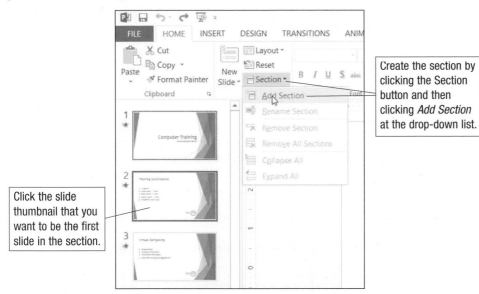

Click the slide thumbnail that you want to be the first slide in the section.

Create the section by clicking the Section button and then clicking *Add Section* at the drop-down list.

To rename a section, click the section name to select it, click the Section button in the Slides group on the HOME tab, click *Rename Section*, type a name, and then click the Rename button. To collapse or expand a section, click the Collapse or Expand arrow in the section name. To remove a section, click the section name, click the Section button, and then click *Remove Section* or *Remove All Sections*.

Customizing the Running of a Slide Show

In Exercise 13.3, you specified that when running the presentation, slides would automatically advance after four seconds. In addition to specifying times with the *After* measurement box in the Timing group on the TRANSITIONS tab, you can rehearse timings for each slide and run a presentation in a continuous loop.

Running a Slide Show in Rehearsed Time

To create rehearsed timings, click the SLIDE SHOW tab and then click the Rehearse Timings button in the Set Up group. As the slide show runs, rehearse your presentation by talking through the slides as though you were in front of your audience, clicking or pressing Enter to go to the next slide. Note the seconds as they display in the Recording toolbar as shown in Figure 13.19. When you are finished, note the total time for the slide show and then click Yes to accept the timings. To test the timings, start the slide show and note when the slides advance too quickly or too slowly. Review and edit the individual timings in Slide Sorter view.

Rehearse Timings

Figure 13.19 **Setting Rehearsed Timings for Slides**

Next Pause Repeat Close

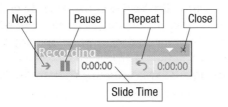

Slide Time

Figure 13.20 Setting Up a Presentation Using the Set Up Show Dialog Box

Insert a check mark in this check box to run a slide show repeatedly.

Click to select another pen color.

Click to select another laser pointer color.

The *All* option is the default setting, or you can specify certain slides to include in the slide show.

Click this option to manually advance the slides.

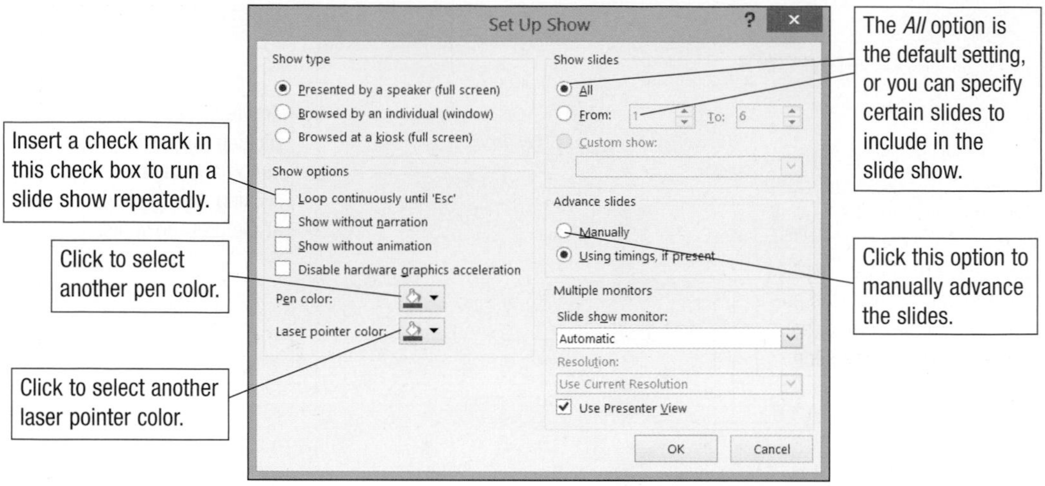

Running a Slide Show in a Continuous Loop

In a continuous-loop slide show, the presentation runs over and over again until you stop the show. This feature is especially effective when running an unattended presentation on a new product or service at a booth at a trade show or at a new store opening. To run a presentation in a continuous loop, click the SLIDE SHOW tab and then click the Set Up Slide Show button in the Set Up group. At the Set Up Show dialog box, click the *Loop continuously until 'Esc'* check box in the *Show options* section to insert a check mark, as shown in Figure 13.20, and then click OK.

Adding Animations to a Presentation

You can animate text or objects in a slide to add visual interest to a presentation. PowerPoint includes a number of animations you can apply to items in a slide, and these animations can be modified to fit your specific needs. For example, you can have your bullet points fly in from the left, one paragraph at a time, or specify a path for an object to follow as it enters a slide.

Try not to overwhelm your audience with too much animation. In general, you want them to remember the content of your presentation rather than the visual effects.

Applying and Removing Animation Effects

To animate an item, click the desired item, click the ANIMATIONS tab, click the More button at the right side of the animation thumbnails in the Animation group, and then click the desired animation at the drop-down list, as shown in Figure 13.21. Once you have applied an animation, you can specify the animation effects with options in the Effect Options button drop-down gallery. Some of the animation effect options may include the direction from which you want the item to appear and whether you want items such as bulleted text or SmartArt to appear as one object, all at once, or by paragraph. Having items such as bulleted text appear one at a time is called a build.

When you apply animation effects to items in a slide, an animation icon (a star shape) displays below the slide number in the slide thumbnails pane. If you want to see the animations in the active slide without running the presentation, click the Preview button on the ANIMATIONS tab.

DTP POINTER
Do not overuse the animation feature.

DTP POINTER
Add a build to bulleted items to focus attention on one item at a time.

Preview

Figure 13.21 Selecting Animations at the Animation Gallery

Click an option at this drop-down gallery to apply an animation effect to an item as it is entering the slide, as an emphasis to the item, or as the item is exiting the slide.

Click one of these options to display a dialog box of additional entrance, emphasis, exit, or motion path animation effects.

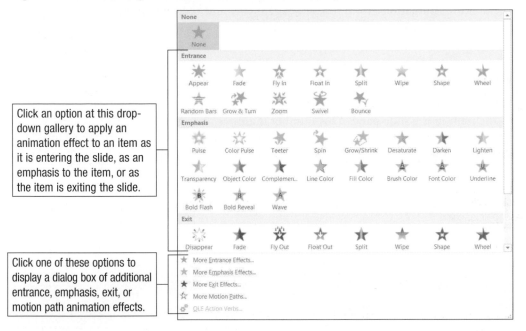

The Add Animation button in the Advanced Animation group on the ANIMATIONS tab provides four types of animation effects. You can apply an effect as an item enters the slide, as an item exits the slide, as emphasis to an item, and as a motion path that will cause an item to move in a specific pattern on, or even off, the slide.

Add Animation

If you want to remove an animation effect from an item, click the item in the slide in the slide pane, click the ANIMATIONS tab, and then click the *None* option in the Animation group. (You may need to click the More button in the Animation group to display the *None* option.) If you apply an animation effect to bulleted text, you can remove the animation effect from a specific bulleted item by selecting the bulleted text and then clicking the *None* option in the Animation group.

Modifying Animation Effects

When you apply an animation effect to an item, you can use options in the Timing group on the ANIMATIONS tab to modify the animation effect. With the item selected, use the *Start* option box drop-down list to specify when you want the item inserted in the slide. Generally, items display in a slide when you click the mouse button. Click the *Start* option box arrow and then click *With Previous* or *With Next* at the drop-down list to make the items appear on the slide with the previous or next item.

Use the *Duration* measurement box to specify the length of an animation. Click the up-pointing arrow in the measurement box to increase the time or click the down-pointing arrow to decrease the time. You can also select the current time in the *Duration* measurement box and then type the desired time.

The *Delay* measurement box allows you to specify that an animation play for a certain number of seconds after the previous animation plays. Click the up-pointing arrow to increase the amount of time and click the down-pointing arrow to decrease the time. You can also select the current time in the *Delay* measurement box and then type the desired time.

In addition to the options in the Timing group, animations can be modified by clicking the Animation group dialog box launcher and then making changes at the dialog box that displays. The name of the dialog box varies depending on the animation effect applied.

Reordering Animation Effects

When you apply an animation effect to an item, an animation number displays next to the item in the slide pane. This number indicates the order in which the item will appear in the slide. When more than one item displays in the slide, you can change the order with options in the Reorder Animation section of the Timing group on the ANIMATIONS tab. Click the Move Earlier button to move an item before another item or click the Move Later button to move an item after another item.

In Exercise 13.4A, you will create a new presentation, add content, and apply animations.

Exercise 13.4A Inserting Animation Effects in a PowerPoint Presentation   **Part 1 of 2**

---

1. In PowerPoint, open a presentation based on the Droplet design theme and then apply a variant color by completing the following steps:
   a. Click the FILE tab and then click the *New* option.
   b. At the New backstage area, double-click the *Droplet* template.
   c. At the presentation, click the DESIGN tab.
   d. Click the blue variant option (third thumbnail) in the Variants group.
2. Reuse slides from another presentation by completing the following steps:
   a. Click the HOME tab.
   b. Click the New Slide button arrow in the Slides group and then click *Reuse Slides* at the drop-down list.
   c. At the Reuse Slides task pane, click the <u>Open a PowerPoint File</u> hyperlink.

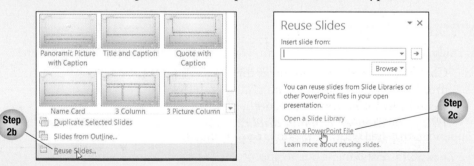

3. At the Browse dialog box, navigate to your Chapter13 folder and then double-click **KiawahPresentation.pptx**.
4. Right-click the first slide in the Reuse Slides task pane and then click *Insert All Slides*.
5. Delete the first slide by clicking the first slide thumbnail in the slide thumbnails pane and then pressing the Delete key
6. Save the presentation with the name **C13-E04-KiawahPresentation**.
7. Close the Reuse Slides task pane.

8. Add a section by completing the following steps:
   a. Click the Slide 2 thumbnail in the slide thumbnails pane.
   b. Click the Section button in the Slides group on the HOME tab.
   c. Click *Add Section* at the drop-down list. ***Hint: You are adding a new section to the presentation so that you can format Slide 1 differently from the remaining slides.***

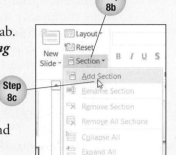

9. Click the Slide 1 thumbnail in the slide thumbnails pane to make it the active slide and then apply the following formatting:
   a. Click the DESIGN tab and then click the Format Background button in the Customize group.
   b. At the Format Background task pane, click the *Picture or texture fill* option.
   c. Click the Online button in the *Insert picture from* section.
   d. At the Insert Pictures window, type **beach chairs** in the *Office.com Clip Art* text box and then press Enter.
   e. Double-click the beach photograph shown below and in Figure 13.22 on page 620.

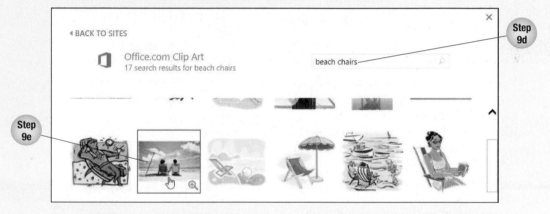

   f. Close the Format Background task pane.
10. Animate the objects in Slide 1 by completing the following steps:
    a. Click in the title, *Welcome to Kiawah Island, South Carolina*.
    b. Click the ANIMATIONS tab.
    c. Click the More button in the Animation group.
    d. Click the *Grow & Turn* option at the drop-down gallery (second column, second row in the *Entrance* section). ***Hint: The number 1 should display to the left of the* Welcome to Kiawah Island, South Carolina *text box.***
    e. Select the red crab image in the bottom left corner of Slide 1, click the More button in the Animation group, scroll down the drop-down gallery, and then click the *Custom Path* option (last effect in the *Motion Paths* section).
    f. Using the mouse, drag the crosshairs along the bottom of the slide from the crab image on the left to the bottom right edge of Slide 1. Double-click the mouse button to end the path.
    g. Click in the *Duration* text box, type **6**, and then press Enter.

11. Click the Slide 2 thumbnail in the slide thumbnails pane and then animate the objects in the slide by completing the following steps:
    a. Click in the title.
    b. Click the *Fly In* animation option in the Animation group.
    c. Click the Effect Options button in the Animation group and then click the *From Bottom-Left* effect at the drop-down list.
    d. Click in the *Duration* text box, type **2**, and then press Enter.
    e. Click in the bulleted text.
    f. Click the *Float In* animation option in the Animation group.

12. Click the Slide 3 thumbnail in the slide thumbnails pane and then animate objects by completing the following steps:
    a. Click in the title and then click the *Shape* animation option in the Animation group.

    b. Click in the bulleted text.
    c. Click the More button in the Animation group and then click the *Wave* effect (last option in the *Emphasis* section).
    d. Select the three photographs by holding down the Shift key and then clicking each photograph.
    e. Click the More button in the Animation group and then click the *Float Out* animation option (fourth effect in the *Exit* section).
13. Format Slide 4 as shown in Figure 13.22 by completing the following steps:
    a. Click Slide 4 in the slide thumbnails pane.
    b. Click in the title and then click the *Appear* animation option in the Animation group.
    c. Click the Animation group dialog box launcher.
    d. At the Appear dialog box that displays, click the down-pointing arrow at the right side of the *Animate text* option box and then click *By word* at the drop-down list.

e. Click OK to close the dialog box.

f. Click the Insert a SmartArt Graphic icon in the left content placeholder.

g. At the Choose a SmartArt Graphic dialog box, click *Picture* in the left panel and then click the *Circular Picture Callout* option in the middle panel (second column, first row).

h. Click OK.

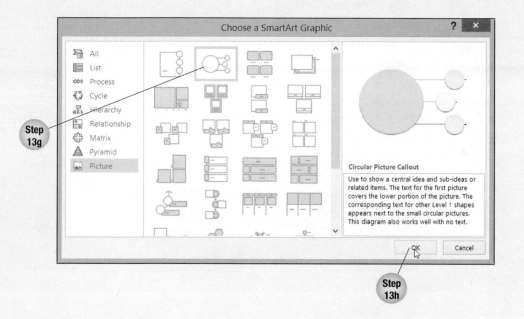

i. Click the border of the SmartArt, click the picture icon in the large circle picture, browse to your Chapter13 folder, and then insert **SC-home.png**.

j. Click the picture icon in each of the remaining smaller circle picture placeholders and insert the **aquarium.png**, **food.png**, and **park.png** images located in your Chapter13 folder.

k. Position the SmartArt graphic as shown in Figure 13.22.

l. Click in the bulleted text, click the More button in the Animation group on the ANIMATIONS tab, and then click the *Brush Color* animation option (sixth column, second row in the *Emphasis* section).

14. Run the presentation by clicking the Slide 1 thumbnail in the slide thumbnails pane and then clicking the Start From Beginning button on the Quick Access toolbar. Click the mouse to advance slides and animate items on slides. When Slide 4 displays (contains the title *THE CHARM OF CHARLESTON*), press the Esc key to end the presentation.

15. Save **C13-E04-KiawahPresentation.pptx**.

Figure 13.22 **Slides 1 through 4 Formatted in Exercise 13.4A**

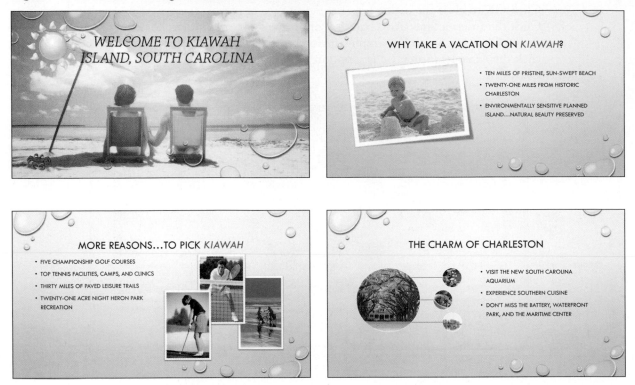

Enhancing a Presentation

You can enhance PowerPoint presentations with screenshots, action buttons that allow for better navigation, hyperlinks, and audio and visual files.

Using Screenshots

Screenshot

DTP POINTER

After you insert the screenshot, you can use the options on the PICTURE TOOLS FORMAT tab to edit and enhance it.

Screenshots, such as the one shown in Figure 13.23, are useful for capturing snapshots of information that might change or expire. Screenshots are also helpful for copying from web pages and other sources whose formatting might not successfully transfer into the file by any other method. When you take a screenshot of something (for example, a web page), and the information changes at the source, the screenshot is not updated.

Create a screenshot with the Screenshot button on the INSERT tab. When you click the Screenshot button, you can insert the whole application window or use the *Screen Clipping* option to select a portion of a window.

Adding Action Buttons

Action

Action buttons are drawn objects placed on a slide that, when clicked, will perform a specific action. For instance, an action button can advance to a specific slide, file, or location on the Web. To insert an action button, click the INSERT tab and then click the Action button in the Links group. At the Action Settings dialog box, select an option to create a hyperlink to the Next slide, Previous slide, or other location; to run a program, macro, or object action; or to play a sound.

Figure 13.23 Using a Screenshot in a PowerPoint Slide

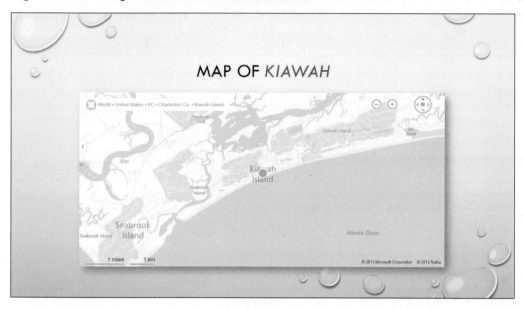

Using Hyperlinks

You can enrich your presentation by inserting hyperlinks. A hyperlink can take you to a location within the same presentation, a different file, or a location on the Web. You can even use hyperlinks to advance to multimedia files, such as sounds or videos. To add a hyperlink, click the INSERT tab and then click the Hyperlink button in the Links group.

Hyperlink

Inserting Audio and Video Files

Adding audio and/or video files to a presentation will turn a slide show into a true multimedia experience for your audience. Insert an audio file by clicking the INSERT tab, clicking the Audio button in the Media group, and then specifying whether you want to find an audio file online or in a folder on your computer, or record a new audio file.

Audio

Complete similar steps to insert a video file, except click the Video button in the Media group. (However, unlike the Audio button, the Video button does not offer the option of recording a new video.) You can also insert a video file by clicking the Insert Video icon in a content placeholder on a slide and then, at the Insert Video window, navigating to the desired folder. Customize audio files with options on the AUDIO TOOLS FORMAT tab and the AUDIO TOOLS PLAYBACK tab, and customize video files with options on the VIDEO TOOLS FORMAT tab and the VIDEO TOOLS PLAYBACK tab.

Video

In Exercise 13.4B, you will insert a screenshot, an Excel workbook, and an audio file into a presentation.

1. With **C13-E04-KiawahPresentation.pptx** open, save the presentation with the name **C13-E04-KiawahVacation**.
2. Click the Slide 5 thumbnail in the slide thumbnails pane and then insert a Word table in the slide by completing the following steps:
   a. Open Microsoft Word.
   b. Open **KiawahTemperatures.docx** from your Chapter13 folder.
   c. Select the table in the Word document and then click the Copy button on the HOME tab.
   d. Close the Word document and then close Word.
   e. If your PowerPoint presentation is not displayed, click the button on the Taskbar representing the PowerPoint presentation.
   f. Make sure Slide 5 displays in the slide pane.
   g. Click the Paste button arrow on the HOME tab and then click *Paste Special* at the drop-down list.
   h. At the Paste Special dialog box, click *Microsoft Word Document Object* in the *As* list box.
   i. Click OK to close the dialog box.
   j. Increase the size of the table and then position the table on the slide as shown in Figure 13.24 on page 625.

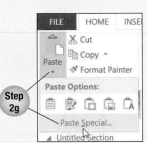

3. Click the Slide 6 thumbnail in the slide thumbnails pane and then insert a map in the slide by completing the following steps:
   a. Read the instructions in the slide.
   b. Access www.bing.com/maps and then search for a map of Kiawah Island, South Carolina.

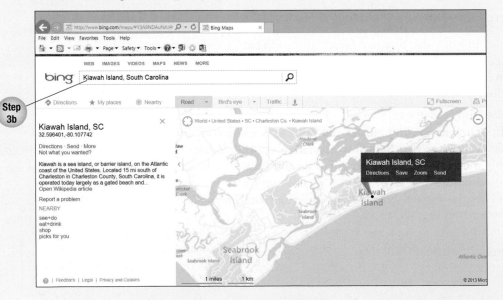

   c. When the map displays, adjust the zoom until it displays as shown in Figure 13.24. Click anywhere in the map to minimize the black pop-up box so that it displays as a blue dot.
   d. Click the PowerPoint button on the Taskbar to redisplay your PowerPoint presentation.

    e.   Click the INSERT tab, click the Screenshot button arrow in the Images group, and then click *Screen Clipping* at the drop-down list.

    f.   When the map website displays in a dimmed manner, drag the crosshairs to draw a box around the map showing Kiawah Island.

    g.   Click the Internet browser button on the Taskbar and then close the browser.

    h.   Click the *Drop Shadow Rectangle* option in the Picture Styles group (fourth option).

    i.   Size and position the map in Slide 6 as shown in Figure 13.24. ***Hint: Make sure you delete the direction text in the slide.***

4. Click Slide 7 in the slide thumbnails pane and then insert a map of the condo layout by completing the following steps:

    a.   Click the Pictures icon in the content placeholder at the right side of the screen.

    b.   At the Insert Picture dialog box, navigate to your Chapter13 folder and then double-click ***condolayout.png***.

    c.   Click the More button in the Picture Styles group and then click the *Bevel Rectangle* option (last column, third row).

    d.   Position the image in Slide 7 as shown in Figure 13.24.

    e.   With the image selected, apply the *Shrink & Turn* exit animation effect (second column, second row in the *Exit* section of the animation drop-down gallery).

5. Click Slide 8 in the slide thumbnails pane and then insert an Excel worksheet by completing the following steps:

    a.   Open Microsoft Excel.

    b.   Open the worksheet named **VillaRentalRates.xlsx** from your Chapter13 folder.

    c.   Select cells A1 through C8 and then click the Copy button in the Clipboard group on the HOME tab.

    d.   Click the button on the Taskbar representing your PowerPoint presentation.

    e.   Make sure that Slide 8 is selected in the slide thumbnails pane, click the Paste button arrow in the Clipboard group on the HOME tab, and then click *Paste Special* at the drop-down list.

    f.   At the Paste Special dialog box, make sure *Microsoft Excel Worksheet Object* is selected in the *As* list box and then click OK.

    g.   Size and position the worksheet in Slide 8 as shown in Figure 13.24.

    h.   With the worksheet selected in the slide pane, apply the *Wheel* exit animation effect (last column, first row in the *Exit* section of the animation drop-down gallery in the Animation group on the ANIMATIONS tab).

    i.   Click the button on the Taskbar representing Excel, close **VillaRentalRates.xlsx**, and then close Excel.

6. Click Slide 9 in the slide thumbnails pane, click in the title *Contact us today!*, and then apply the *Fade* entrance animation effect.

7. Assume that when running the presentation, you want the last slide to remain on the screen and music to play while you answer any questions from the audience. Complete the following steps to insert an audio file that will play continuously on the last slide:
   a. With Slide 9 active, click the INSERT tab.
   b. Click the Audio button in the Media group and then click *Audio on My PC* at the drop-down list.
   c. At the Insert Audio dialog box, navigate to your Chapter13 folder and then double-click ***AudioFile-01.mid***.
   d. Click the down-pointing arrow at the right of the *Start* option box in the Audio Options group on the AUDIO TOOLS PLAYBACK tab and then click *Automatically* at the drop-down list.
   e. Click the *Loop until Stopped* check box in the Audio Options group to insert a check mark.
   f. Click the *Hide During Show* check box to insert a check mark.

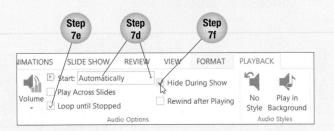

8. Apply a transition to all slides by completing the following steps:
   a. Click the TRANSITIONS tab.
   b. Click the *Fade* option in the Transition to This Slide group.
   c. Click the *Apply To All* button in the Timing group.
9. Click the Save button on the Quick Access toolbar to save the presentation with the same name.
10. Run the presentation by clicking the Start From Beginning button on the Quick Access toolbar. Click the left mouse button to advance slides, play animations, and play the audio file on the last slide. After listening to the audio file for a minute or two, press the Esc key to end the slide show.
11. Print the presentation with nine slides printed horizontally on the page.
12. Close **C13-E04-KiawahVacation.pptx**.

Figure 13.24 Presentation Formatted in Exercise 13.4

Chapter *Summary*

➤ A presentation communicates information using visual images to convey the message to an audience.

➤ Layouts can be used to arrange objects and text on a slide. Layouts contain placeholders, which hold text, such as titles and bulleted lists, and slide content, such as SmartArt graphics, tables, charts, images, and shapes.

➤ When choosing a presentation design for slides, consider the audience, topic, and method of delivery.

➤ Theme colors, theme fonts, and theme effects reinforce consistency in your presentation.

➤ Run a presentation by clicking the Start From Beginning button on the Quick Access toolbar, clicking the Slide Show button in the view area on the Status bar, or clicking the From Beginning button or From Current Slide button in the Start Slide Show group on the SLIDE SHOW tab.

➤ Insert a new slide in a presentation with the New Slide button in the Slides group on the HOME tab.

➤ Customize bullets with options at the Bullets and Numbering dialog box with the Bulleted tab selected.

➤ Use the Pictures button in the Images group on the INSERT tab to insert images from your computer and use the Insert Pictures button to insert images from Office.com.

➤ Use the Compress Pictures button on the PICTURES TOOLS FORMAT tab to compress a picture to reduce the size of the file.

➤ Apply formatting to an image, such as artistic effects, with options on the PICTURE TOOLS FORMAT tab.

➤ The background of a presentation should correlate to the visual medium that you are using. You can create a picture background that fills the entire slide with options in the Format Background task pane.

➤ SmartArt graphics help you illustrate processes, concepts, hierarchies, and relationships in a visual, dynamic way.

➤ PowerPoint provides a variety of presentation views including Normal, Outline, Slide Sorter, Reading, and Slide Show view.

➤ The PDF format ensures that when the file is viewed online or printed, it retains exactly the format that you intended and that data in the file cannot be easily changed.

➤ Presentations can be printed with each slide on a separate piece of paper; with each slide at the top of a page, leaving room for notes; with all or a specific number of slides on a single piece of paper; or with slide titles and topics in outline form. Specify printing options at the Print backstage area.

➤ The slide master stores information about the design template applied, including font styles, placeholder sizes and positions, background design, and color schemes.

➤ If you want changes made to a slide to affect all slides in a presentation, make the changes at the slide master.

➤ If you are creating a long presentation with many slides and text, use the outline pane to create slides. Display the outline pane by clicking the VIEW tab and then clicking the Outline View button in the Presentation Views group.

➤ Rearrange slides within a presentation in the slide thumbnails pane in Normal view or in Slide Sorter view.

➤ An outline can be created in PowerPoint or imported from another program, such as Microsoft Word.

➤ A transition is an action that takes place as one slide is removed from the screen during a presentation and the next slide is displayed.

➤ Slides in a slide show can be advanced manually or automatically at specific time intervals, or a slide show can be set up to run continuously.

➤ Animate text or objects in a slide to add visual interest to a presentation.

- A custom motion path can be created that lets you control where an object will move.
- Use the Screenshot button in the Images group on the INSERT tab to capture an entire screen or a portion of a screen.
- Action buttons are drawn objects placed on a slide that will perform a specific action. Insert an action button with the Action button in the Links group on the INSERT tab.
- Insert a hyperlink to navigate to a location within the same file, a different file, or a location on the Web. Insert a hyperlink with the Hyperlink button in the Links group on the INSERT tab.
- Audio and/or video files can be inserted in a presentation to play when running the presentation.

Commands *Review*

FEATURE	RIBBON TAB, GROUP/OPTION	BUTTON, OPTION
convert to SmartArt	HOME, Paragraph	
effect options	ANIMATIONS, Animation	
format background	DESIGN, Customize	
header and footer	INSERT, Text	
hyperlink	INSERT, Links	
new slide	HOME, Slides	
Normal view	VIEW, Presentation Views OR view area on Status bar	
Notes Page view	VIEW, Presentation Views OR view area on Status bar	
Online Pictures	INSERT, Images	
Outline view	VIEW, Presentation Views	
pictures	INSERT, Images	
Reading view	VIEW, Presentation Views OR view area on Status bar	
rehearse timings	SLIDE SHOW, Set Up	
screenshot	INSERT, Images	
section	HOME, Slides	
Set Up Show dialog box	SLIDE SHOW, Set Up	
slide layout	HOME, Slides	

FEATURE	RIBBON TAB, GROUP/OPTION	BUTTON, OPTION
Slide Master view	VIEW, Master Views	
Slide Sorter view	VIEW, Presentation Views OR view area on Status bar	
SmartArt	INSERT, Illustrations	
start from beginning	SLIDE SHOW, Start Slide Show	

Key Points *Review*

A. build
B. Ctrl
C. Esc
D. HOME
E. INSERT
F. Normal

G. Online Pictures
H. PDF
I. Pictures
J. Quick Access
K. Screenshot
L. slide master

M. Slide Show
N. Slide Sorter
O. SmartArt
P. storyboard
Q. Title Slide
R. transition

Matching: In the space at the left, provide the correct letter from the above list that matches each definition.

_____ 1. Tab containing buttons to insert a variety of objects in slides such as pictures, shapes, and SmartArt

_____ 2. Visual example of the headings in an outline

_____ 3. Toolbar containing Start From Beginning button to run a presentation

_____ 4. Key on the keyboard to end a presentation without running all of the slides

_____ 5. Button on the INSERT tab used to display the Insert Pictures window

_____ 6. Feature that converts simple text into attention-getting shapes and colors that enhance your message

_____ 7. Default view that displays two panes—the slide pane and the slide thumbnails pane

_____ 8. View used to run a presentation

_____ 9. Format used to save a presentation that preserves file formatting and enables file sharing

_____ 10. Stores information about the design theme applied, including font styles, placeholder sizes and positions, background design, and color schemes

_____ 11. View used to reorganize slides

_____ 12. How one slide is removed from the screen and replaced with the next slide when running a presentation

_____ 13. Having items such as bulleted text appear one at a time

_____ 14. Feature used to capture a snapshot of the current screen

Chapter *Assessments*

Assessment 13.1   Create a Product Development Presentation

1. In PowerPoint, create a presentation with the Berlin design theme.
2. Apply the Yellow theme colors.
3. Create the eight slides in the presentation as shown in Figure 13.25 on page 630 by completing the following steps:
    a. Insert and then size and position the logo in Slide 1 as shown in Figure 13.25. The logo is located in your Chapter13 folder and is named **SunobaLogo.png**.
    b. Create the SmartArt in Slide 2 by completing the following steps:
        1) Select the Continuous Cycle graphic.
        2) Type the following text in the boxes in the graphic, starting with the top graphic and moving clockwise around the circle, adding shapes as necessary:
            Idea Generation
            Business Analysis
            Technical Implementation
            Product Development
            Commercialization
            Product Review
        3) Change the colors to *Colorful - Accent Colors* and apply the Cartoon SmartArt style to the SmartArt.
        4) Size and position the SmartArt as shown in Figure 13.25.
    c. Insert the image in Slide 3 using the keyword *ideas* in the *Office.com Clip Art* text box at the Insert Pictures window. ***Hint: The same image is available in different color combinations. You might need to scroll to locate the image with the color combination shown in Figure 13.25.*** Size and position the image as shown in Figure 13.25.
    d. Locate the image shown in Slide 6 by typing **finances** into the *Office.com Clip Art* text box at the Insert Pictures window. Insert, size, and position the image as shown in Figure 13.25.
4. Apply a transition effect and sound effect of your choosing to all slides in the presentation.
5. Apply an animation effect to the SmartArt in Slide 2 and the images in Slide 3 and Slide 6.
6. Make Slide 4 the active slide, click the NOTES button on the Status bar to display the Notes pane, and then type the following text in the Notes pane: **Distribute a copy of the current year business analysis report to all participants.**
7. Save the presentation with the name **C13-A01-SunobaPresentation**.
8. Print the presentation with four slides printed horizontally on the page.
9. Print only Slide 4 as a notes page. ***Hint: Refer to Step 19 in Exercise 13.2 for steps on printing an individual slide as a notes page.*** Click the NOTES button on the Status bar to close the Notes pane.
10. Save the presentation as a video file to your Chapter13 folder. ***Hint: Refer to Step 20 of Exercise 13.2 for steps on saving a presentation as a video file.***
11. Open File Explorer, navigate to your Chapter13 folder, and then double-click **C13-A01-SunobaPresentation.mp4**. After viewing the video file, close the file.
12. Close **C13-A01-SunobaPresentation.pptx**.

Figure 13.25 Presentation Slides Created in Assessment 13.1

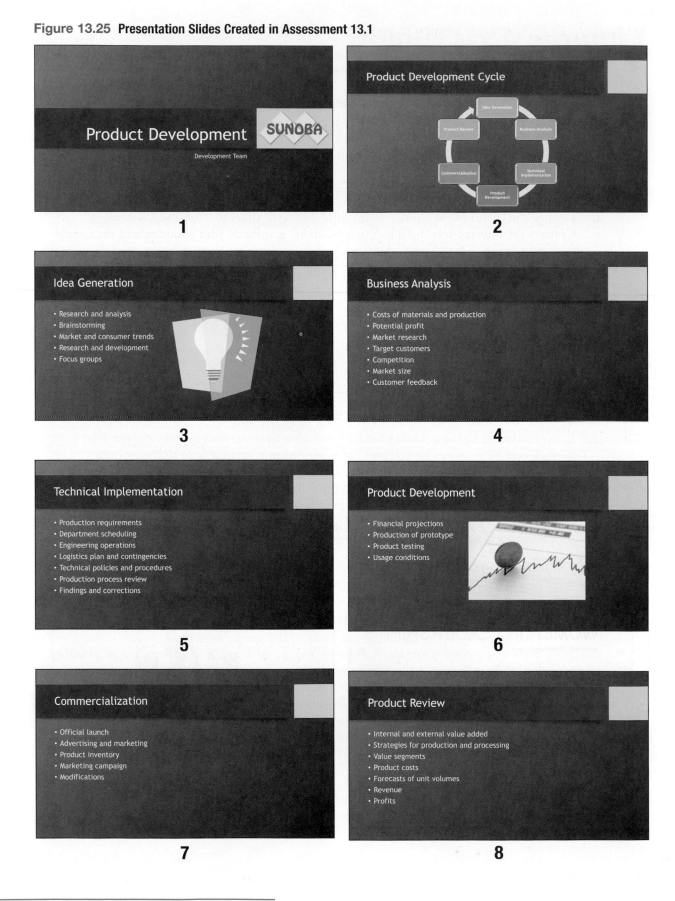

Assessment 13.2　Create a Women in Leadership Presentation

1. At a blank PowerPoint presentation, create a leadership presentation (Figure 13.26 displays the first two slides of the presentation) with the following specifications:
    a. Import the Word outline document *Leadership.docx* from your Chapter13 folder. ***Hint: Refer to Step 2 of Exercise 13.3 for steps on importing a Word outline.***
    b. Apply the Vapor Trail theme and then apply the third variant. (Refer to Figure 13.26.)
    c. Delete the first slide.
    d. Change the layout of the first slide to Title Slide.
    e. Change the layout of the second slide to Title Only. Format the text as shown in the second slide in Figure 13.26 and then insert and format an image similar to the one shown in the figure.
    f. Change the layout of the third, fourth, fifth, and sixth slides to Title and Content.
    g. Convert the bulleted text in Slide 5 to a SmartArt graphic of your choosing and then apply formatting to the SmartArt graphic.
    h. Display the presentation in Slide Master view, click the third slide master layout thumbnail in the slide thumbnails pane (the Title and Content Layout used by slides 3–6), and then insert **WLGLogo.png** from your Chapter13 folder. Change the height of the logo to 0.6 inch, position the logo in the lower left corner of the slide master layout, and then close Slide Master view.
    i. Add a transition and sound of your choosing to all slides.
    j. Add animations of your choosing to the items in Slides 3, 4, and 5.
    k. Insert slide numbers.
    l. Insert the audio file *AudioFile-02.mid* on Slide 6 that will play continuously. ***Hint: Refer to Step 7 of Exercise 13.4B for steps on inserting an audio file.***
2. Save the presentation and name it **C13-A02-Leadership**.
3. Run the presentation.
4. Print the presentation with six slides printed horizontally on the page.
5. Close **C13-A02-Leadership.pptx**.

Figure 13.26　Slides 1 and 2 Created in Assessment 13.2

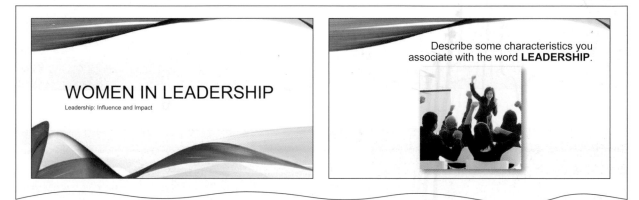

Assessment 13.3   Create a Virtual Office Presentation

Use the Internet to research the benefits of the virtual office work environment. Create a presentation from your findings. Figure 13.27 displays the first two slides from a sample presentation on this topic.

1. Include the following in your presentation:
   a. Create at least five slides.
   b. Use an appropriate design theme or template.
   c. Insert a least one clip art image or photograph to reinforce the message in the presentation.
   d. Use at least one SmartArt object to emphasize an important point.
   e. Add transitions and animations to the slides.
   f. Time the slides to change every five seconds.
2. Save your presentation with the name **C13-A03-Virtual**.
3. Run your presentation for your class and prepare handouts for all the students in the classroom. Critique each other's presentations along with the professionalism of the delivery using the **PresentationEvaluation.docx** form available in your Chapter13 folder.
4. Close **C13-A03-Virtual.pptx**.

Figure 13.27 Sample Solution for Assessment 13.3, Slides 1 and 2

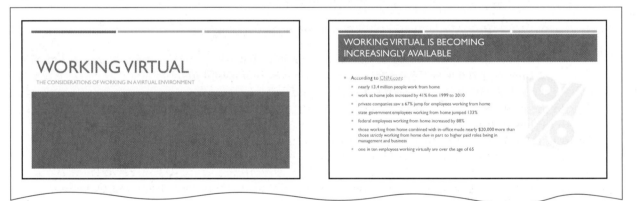

Assessment 13.4   Create a Personalized Presentation

Prepare a PowerPoint presentation of your own choosing. Some suggestions for presentation topics include outlining your medical plan at work, planning an international vacation, highlighting the advantages of attending a particular college or university, pursuing a career in real estate, highlighting your home town, or planning an event. Create a PowerPoint presentation according to the following specifications:

1. Use a design theme or a template from Office.com and customize it to complement your presentation. ***Hint: Photographs make dramatic backgrounds.***
2. Use the Internet and a search engine to research a topic of your own choosing.
3. Create at least five slides and use several slide layouts to vary the look of your presentation.
4. Add any appropriate images.
5. Use a build effect for the bulleted items. You decide on the bullet symbol to be used.
6. Apply transition effects to your slides.
7. Time the slides to change every five seconds.
8. Save the presentation with the name **C13-A04-MyPresentation**.
9. Run the presentation for your classmates.
10. Open and then print a copy of **PresentationEvaluation.docx**, located in your Chapter13 folder. Ask your audience to evaluate your presentation.
11. Print and then close **C13-A04-MyPresentation.pptx**.

Assessment 13.5   Add Visual Effects to PowerPoint Presentations

1. Open **SlideEffectsPresentation.pptx** located in your Chapter13 folder.
2. This is a PowerPoint 2010 presentation that provides information on how to create a variety of slide effects using PowerPoint 2010.

GROUP PROJECT

3. As a team, look through the slides and determine a slide effect that your team would like to learn how to create.
4. Read the directions on the first slide on how to print the instructions and then, following the instructions, print instructions for the slide effect that you chose in Step 3.
5. In a Word document, rewrite the instructions that you printed in Step 4 for PowerPoint 2013. Save the document with the name **C13-A05-SlideEffectsInstructions**. Print and then close **C13-A05-SlideEffectsInstructions.docx**.
6. In PowerPoint, create a slide effect following your directions. Save the presentation (one slide) with the name **C13-A05-SlideEffect**. Print and then close **C13-A05-SlideEffect.pptx**.
7. Exchange your instructions with another team and then create the slide effect following the other team's instructions.
8. Provide feedback to the other team on the written instructions and the slide effects outcome. Were you able to follow the instructions? Were the instructions clear and concise? Were you able to create the slide effect?

Performance Assessments

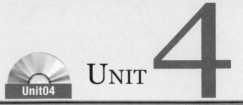

Producing Web Pages, Microsoft Publisher Publications, and PowerPoint Presentations

ASSESSING PROFICIENCIES

In Unit 4 you learned how to create web pages and fill-in forms in Word, were introduced to the basic features and functionalities of Publisher, and practiced creating dynamic presentations in PowerPoint. The following assessments will test your proficiency in each of these areas.

Note: Before beginning computer exercises for this section, copy to your storage medium the Unit04 folder from the CD that accompanies this textbook and then make Unit04 the active folder. Remember to substitute for graphics that may no longer be available.

Assessment U4.1 Create a Fill-in Form

In Word, create a tuition wavier dependency verification form similar to the one shown in Figure U4.1 on page 636 by completing the following steps:.

1. At a blank document, type the text as shown in Figure U4.1. Create tables as the underlying structure for the form. Apply appropriate styles, font, font sizes, and font color to the text in the form. Change the top and bottom margins to 0.5 inch to ensure everything fits on one page.
2. Create a logo for Midwest College.
3. Display the DEVELOPER tab and then insert legacy text form fields to the right of the bold labels in the form and insert check box form fields to the left of the labels in the *Choose One* section. (Make sure the check boxes are centered in the cells.) Insert a date picker content control next to the signature line at the bottom of the form.
4. Click the Restrict Editing button in the Protect group. Select the option to allow the user to fill in the form. A password is not necessary.
5. Save the form as a template in your Unit04 folder with the name **U4-PA01-TuitionForm**.
6. Close the form template.
7. Using File Explorer, open a document based on the template **U4-PA01-TuitionForm.dotx**.
8. Fill in the form with information of your choosing.
9. Save the filled-in form with the name **U4-PA01-CompletedTuitionForm**.
10. Print and then close **U4-PA01-CompletedTuitionForm.docx**.

TUITION WAIVER DEPENDENCY VERIFICATION

FORM FOR BENEFITED EMPLOYEES

Key all **highlighted** sections, print, sign/date hard copy, and return to Human Resources **OR** print blank form, print in all **highlighted** sections, sign/date, and return to Human Resources.

Employee Name: (type or print)	
Employee ID #:	

Choose One: (X)

☐	Administrator	☐	FT Faculty
☐	Benefited Classified	☐	Operating Engineer
☐	FOP	☐	Retiree

1. Spouse

Last Name:	
First Name:	
Spouse ID # OR Social Security Number:	

2. Dependent

Last Name:	
First Name:	
Relationship:	
Dependent ID # OR Social Security Number:	
Date of Birth (mm/dd/yyyy):	

3. Dependent

Last Name:	
First Name:	
Relationship:	
Dependent ID # OR Social Security Number:	
Date of Birth (mm/dd/yyyy):	

If you have additional eligible dependents, please complete and attach a second form.

I hereby certify that the above named dependent(s) are eligible to be a tax dependent on my United States Federal Tax Form 1040/1040A for the calendar year ended December 31, 2015.

Employee Signature

_____

Date   Click here to enter a date.

_____

Assessment U4.2   Create a Heart Scan Flyer Using Publisher

Use Publisher to create a flyer about a heart scan test similar to what is shown in Figure U4.2 by completing the following steps:

1. Open Publisher.
2. At a blank 8.5-by-11-inch publication, draw text boxes to hold the text. Type the text shown in Figure U4.2 and format the text similarly. Drag the text boxes to position them as shown in the figure.
3. Insert an image that supports the subject of the flyer and apply a shadow effect to the image.
4. Select a color scheme that complements the image. Add text color to add spot color to the document and reinforce the image.
5. Insert the **EdwardCardioBW.png** file located in your Unit04 folder.
6. Make any necessary adjustments in leading to make the text look similar to Figure U4.2.
7. Save the flyer with the name **U4-PA02-HeartScan**.
8. Print and then close **U4-PA02-HeartScan.pub**.

Figure U4.2 Sample Solution for Performance Assessment U4.2

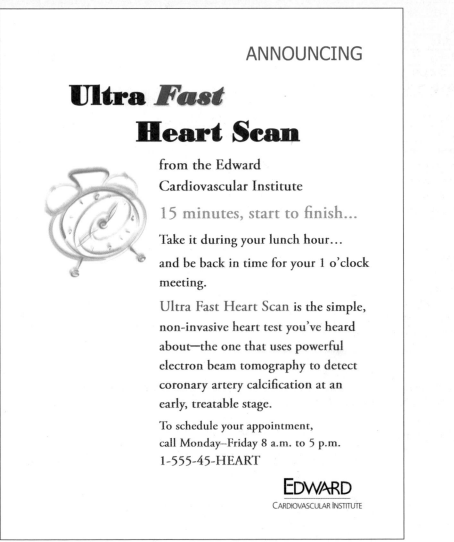

Use Publisher to create a flyer with tear-offs as shown in Figure U4.3 by completing the following steps:

1. Open Publisher.
2. Type the text shown in the top part of Figure U4.3. Use your own design ideas in creating the flyer. Figure U4.3 is a sample document.
3. Insert the tear-offs by clicking the Business Information button in the Text group on the INSERT tab and then clicking the *Phone Tear-Off* option in the *Contact Information* section of the drop-down list. Increase the amount of tear-offs and position the tear-offs where shown in the figure. ***Hint: You will need to change the paragraph spacing for the tear-off text.***
4. Type the following text in the tear-offs:

   Julia Hatcher, Steppin' Out
   Phone: 952.555.3234
   www.emcp.net/steppinout

Figure U4.3 **Sample Solution for Performance Assessment U4.3**

5. Insert image(s) of your own choosing.
6. Select a theme, fonts, and colors that complement the message and the image(s) you have chosen.
7. Insert an attention-getter by clicking the Advertisement button in the Building Blocks group and then clicking *More Advertisements* at the bottom of drop-down list. ***Hint: The theme you select will influence the fonts available and the colors that appear in the building block objects.***
8. Save your flyer with the name **U4-PA03-Dance**.
9. Print and then close **U4-PA03-Dance.pub**.

Assessment U4.4   Create a PowerPoint Presentation

At a blank PowerPoint presentation, create the presentation shown in Figure U4.4 on page 640 by completing the following steps:

1. Apply the Basis design theme, apply the third color variant, and then change the theme colors to Green.
2. Change the layout for the first slide to Blank, insert **NVC-Logo.png** from your Unit04 folder, and then size and position the logo as shown in Figure U4.4.
3. Change to Slide Master view, click the Title and Content Layout slide master layout, insert **NVC-Logo.png**, and then size and position the logo in the upper right corner of the slide as shown in Figure U4.4.
4. Insert Slide 2 using the Title and Content Layout, and type the title and text as shown in the figure.
5. Insert Slide 3 using the Title and Content Layout and type the title as shown in Figure U4.4. Create the SmartArt on Slide 3 using the Radial Cycle SmartArt.
6. Create Slides 4, 5, and 6, typing the titles and text as shown in the figure Insert images of your choosing similar to what is shown in these slides.
7. Apply a transition and sound effect to all slides.
8. Apply animation effects to some of the items in slides.
9. Save the completed presentation with the name **U4-PA04-NVCPresentation**.
10. Print the presentation as a handout with six slides printed horizontally on the page.
11. Close **U4-PA04-NVCPresentation.pptx**.

Assessment U4.5   Re-create a Document

1. Find a printed document and re-create the document using Publisher, Word, or PowerPoint.
   a. If the document needs improvement, re-create the document to enhance the appearance.
   b. Be sure to demonstrate the use of good design—review Chapter 1 if necessary.
2. Save the document as **U4-PA05-Recreate**.
3. Print **U4-PA05-Recreate.pptx** and then attach it to the original document.
4. Close **U4-PA05-Recreate.pptx**.
5. Write a short summary describing how you improved the document and how you went about re-creating it.

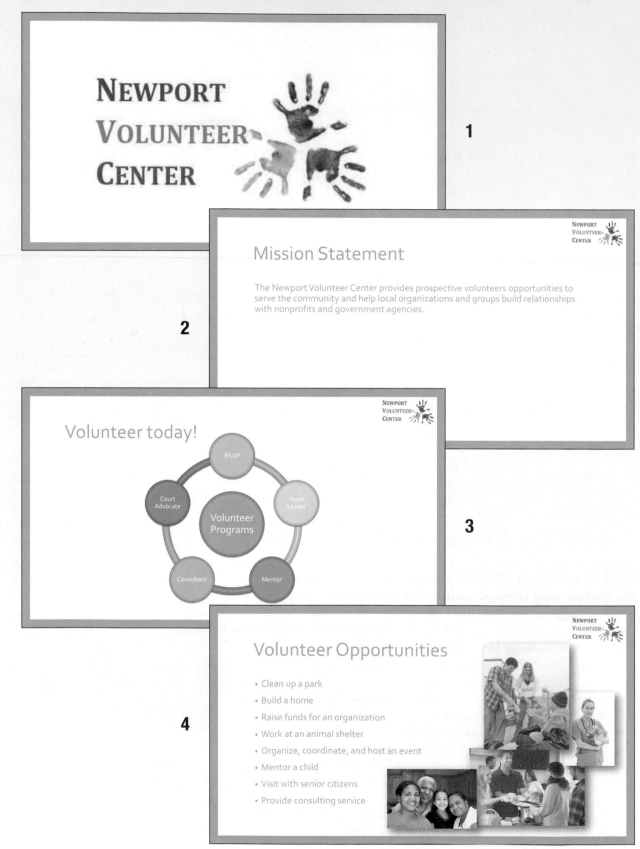

Figure U4.4 Presentation Created in Performance Assessment U4.4 (continued)

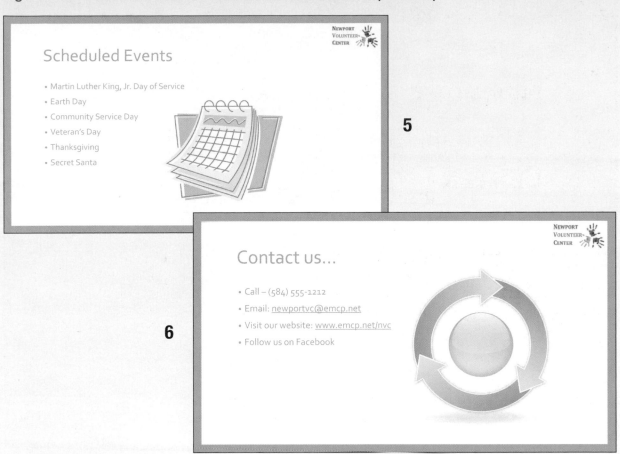

DTP CHALLENGE

Assessment U4.6   Create a Social Networking Presentation

Take your skills to the next level by completing this more challenging assessment. Research social and professional networking sites on the Internet using keywords such as *Facebook*, *LinkedIn*, *Instagram*, *Twitter*, *Blogging*, and *YouTube*. Create a PowerPoint presentation highlighting one social or professional networking site. Include information on membership requirements, costs, and pros and cons of the site.

1. Include the following in the presentation:
   a. Create at least five slides.
   b. Insert images or SmartArt to enhance your presentation.
   c. Vary your slide layouts.
   d. Apply slide transitions and animations.
2. Save your presentation as **U4-PA06-OnlineNetworking**.
3. Print your presentation with three slides per page. This allows for an area to take notes at the right of the printed slides. *Optional:* Print enough copies for your instructor and all the students in your class.
4. Run your presentation using appropriate timed durations.
5. Close **U4-PA06-OnlineNetworking.pptx**.

Index

A

Accordion fold, 387
Action button, 620
Action buttons: adding to presentations, 620
ActiveX controls, 504
Add Animation button, 615
Address labels: creating personal, 158
Adobe Illustrator, 4
Adobe InDesign, 4
Adobe Reader, 595, 596
Advertisements button, 553
Align button, 155, 438
Align Left button, 254
Alignment
  bullets and, 99
  changing paragraph, 254–255
  choosing, 27
  creating directional flow with, 23
  creating focus with, 8, 27
  creating with tables, 438
  of objects in Publisher, 543–545
  proportional typefaces and, 53
  Publisher, in, 530–531, 543–545
Align Right button, 254
Anchoring text boxes, 193–194
Animation effects
  adding to presentations, 614–615
  editing, 615–616
  removing from presentations, 615
  reordering, 616
Animation gallery, 615
Announcements
  adding fill, 349
  adding shape and picture effects, 356
  adding special effects, 349–350
  adjusting brightness, contrast, sharpness, and softness, 360–361
  adjusting pictures, 360–364

adjusting saturation, color tone, and recolor, 361, 362
applying artistic effects, 363
compressing pictures, 364
creating focus with text, 336–337
creating using tables, 334–335
creating with shapes and picture fill using drawing grid, 349–350
defined, 334
enhancing with color, 343–344
inserting images from scanner or digital camera, 342–343
making color transparent, 363
matching colors, 354–355
planning and designing, 334–338
printing, 344
using clip art, 337
using color, 343–344
using drawing gridlines, 349–350
using graphics for emphasis, 337–338
Application forms: creating, 436–438
Apply To All button, 608
Artistic effects
  applying in PowerPoint, 592–593
  applying to promotional documents, 363
Artistic Effects button, 363, 592
Ascenders, defined, 52
Asymmetrical balance
  creating, 14, 15, 16
  newsletters, in, 240–241
Asymmetrical design: defined, 14
Attachments, email, sending newsletters as, 314, 567
Audio button, 621
Audio files: inserting in presentations, 621
AutoFit default, 591
Automatic kerning, 217

B

Background layer, 95–96
Balance
  asymmetrical, 14, 15, 16
  creating, 14–16
  defined, 14, 343
  letterheads, in, 189
  newsletter columns, in, 241
  newsletters, in, 238
  rule of thirds, 8, 16–17, 336
  symmetrical, 14, 15, 16
Banners. *See* nameplates (of newsletters)
Baseline, defined, 52
Baseline guides: working with in Publisher, 544
Bevel effects: adding to promotional documents, 348
Binding and margins, 239–240
Bitmapped (BMP) graphics, 281, 342, 343
Blank Page button, 89
Bleed, 344
BMP (Bitmap Image), 281, 342, 343
Body text (of newsletter)
  defined, 236, 254
  example, 237
  formatting, 254–255
Bond paper, 433
Book fold
  using in booklets, 404
  using to create columns, 392
Booklets. *See also* brochures
  creating, 404
  creating using 2 pages per sheet, 411–412
  defined, 386
  planning, 386
Bookmark button, 498
Bookmark dialog box, 498

Bookmarks (in documents): creating, 498

Bookmarks (promotional): creating, 461–462

Book paper, 433

Borders
adding, to newsletters, 244
adding around text boxes, 244
adding to pages, 161–162
adding to paragraphs, 162
adding to promotional documents, 348
adding to table of contents, 290
adding to tables, 161
changing color of text box borders, 196
changing margins, 162
creating horizontal lines as, 200

Borders & Accents button, 553

Borders and Shading dialog box
Borders tab selected, 200
selecting artistic page border, 162

Borders button, 161, 200

Break Link button, 299

Breaks button, 89, 241, 394

Brightness
adjusting picture, 360
defined, 343

Bring Forward button, 96, 156

Brochures
creating using 2 pages per sheet, 411–412
customizing columns, 393–394
deciding on page layout, 388–389
defined, 386
deleting section breaks, 395
determining panel widths, 389–392
folding options, 387
formatting, 390
formatting with columns, 393–396
inserting column breaks, 395
page layout, 388–392
paper choices, 387–388
planning, 386
saving, 388, 396

setting margins, 389
varying column formatting, in same document, 392

Building blocks. *See also* quick parts
as content control, 507
inserting calendar, 149
inserting in Publisher, 553–554

Building Blocks Gallery button, 507

Building Blocks Organizer, 86

Bullets
adding to table of contents, 290
adding to web pages, 498
convert list to SmartArt graphic, 594
customizing for presentations, 591–592
inserting, 99–100
using pictures as, 591

Bullets and Numbering dialog box, 592

Bullets button, 99

Business cards
creating, 209–211
creating using online templates, 211
creating using Word's label feature, 210
online template resources, 211

Business documents. *See* presentations; *specific types*; *specific types* such as brochures

Business image: projecting, 183

Business Information button, 535

Business Information sets
about, 534
creating, 535
using in Publisher, 534–536

Bylines (of newsletters)
creating, 254
defined, 236, 254
example, 237

C

Calendars
adding shapes, 150
adjusting color, 150
creating, 148–150

editing pictures in, 149–150
examples, 148
inserting building blocks, 149

Calendars button, 553

Callouts
creating in newsletters, 294
defined, 294

Cap height, defined, 52

Caption button, 555

Caption dialog box, 304

Captions
creating, 303–304
customizing, 304
defined, 303
inserting, 304
inserting in Publisher, 555

CD labels/inserts
creating, 139–142
creating face from templates, 146
working with placeholders in templates, 140

Cell, defined, 107

Center button, 254

Character spacing
adjusting, 72, 217
automatic, 217
character pairs, 217, 218
defined, 72
manual, 217–218
subtitles and, 251
text boxes and, 530
using, 72

Check Box button, 507

Check Box Form Field button, 507

Clear All Formatting button, 62

Click and Type: using, 189

Clip art
creating focus with, 10, 11
inserting in PowerPoint, 592
Office.com, from, 40
using in promotional documents, 337
using Internet to obtain, 38

Close Header and Footer button, 279

CMYK: defined, 343

adding between columns, 244

creating and customizing, 199–200

using to separate web pages, 498

Video button, 621

Videos

inserting in PowerPoint presentations, 621

saving PowerPoint presentations as, 595, 596

Visual alignment and alignment, 27

W

Watermark button, 91

Watermarks

creating custom, 91–93

creating focus with, 10, 11

defined, 91

editing, 93

inserting, 91–92

removing, 92

troubleshooting, 94

Web Layout button, 493, 494

Web Page Preview button, 494

Web pages

accessing using Document Location text box, 491

ActiveX controls, 504

adding background color, 499

adding bullets, 498

adding lines, 498

adding Preview button to Quick Access toolbar, 315

address, 490–491

defined, 490

design tips, 492, 496

hyperlinks, 491, 496–497

planning, 493, 494

previewing, 494

printing background from browser, 499–500

saving documents as, 496

separating with ruled lines, 498

using Microsoft Office components, 494

using tables as framework, 493–494, 494–495

Websites

defined, 490

secured, 490

White space. *See also* kerning

in business cards, 211

defined, 8

desirable amount, 526

graphics and, 337

headings and, 10

legibility and, 336

newsletters, in, 238

using, 8–9

using to achieve balance, 14

using to achieve contrast, 22

using to achieve proportion, 19

Widows

defined, 255

preventing, 255

Windows 8

Snipping Tool, 44

using fonts, 57–58

Windows Fax and Scan: using for images, 258

Windows Paint: using for images, 258

Word 2013, 4, 5

creating personal documents with, 138

using in desktop publishing, 37

WordArt

creating focus with, 10

creating objects with, 216

formatting text, 216

formatting text box, 216

using, 216

using in Publisher, 530–531

WordArt button, 216

Word layers, using, 95–96

World Wide Web (www): defined, 490

Wrapping text around text boxes, 194–195

Wrap Text button, 95, 194

X

X-height, defined, 52

XML format, 494

XPS files, 596

Z

Z pattern, 26, 27